The Awakened Ones

Tissa Ranasinghe, *The Awakened One. Collection of the author*

The Awakened Ones

PHENOMENOLOGY

OF *Visionary*

EXPERIENCE

Gananath
Obeyesekere

COLUMBIA UNIVERSITY PRESS   NEW YORK

Columbia University Press
Publishers Since 1893
New York Chichester, West Sussex
Copyright © 2012 Columbia University Press

Library of Congress Cataloging-in-Publication Data

Obeyesekere, Gananath.
  The awakened ones: phenomenology of visionary experience /
Gananath Obeyesekere.
     p.   cm.
  Includes bibliographical references (p.) and index.
  ISBN 978-0-231-15362-1 (cloth: alk. paper)—
ISBN 978-0-231-52730-9 (e-book)   1. Visions—Comparative
studies.   I. Title.
  BL625.O24 2012
  204'.2—dc22

                                        2011015304

Casebound editions of Columbia University Press books
are printed on permanent and durable acid-free paper.

Printed in the United States of America

c 10 9 8 7 6 5 4 3 2 1

Designed by Lisa Hamm

IN MEMORY OF

Neelan Tiruchelvam

January 21, 1944–July 29, 1999

AND

for those who died
on both sides of the divide
caught in the cross-fire

CONTENTS

Book 1.

Book 2.

Book 3.

Book 4.

Book 5.

Book 6.

Book 7.

Book 8.

PREFACE

T HE AWAKENED ONES: *Phenomenology of Visionary Experience* had a very modest beginning. In the first manuscript version of my book *Imagining Karma: Ethical Transformation in Amerindian, Buddhist, and Greek Rebirth* (2002) I had included a brief account of the Buddha engaged in deep meditation that in effect outlined the "phenomenology" of visions documented in this essay. I subsequently deleted this discussion as irrelevant to the methodological thrust of *Imagining Karma.* However, recognizing its intrinsic importance, I subsequently revised that deleted section and used it as a base for lectures that I delivered at several universities, the most memorable being the William James lecture at the Harvard Divinity School in April 2004 entitled "The Buddhist Meditative Askesis: Probing the Visionary Experience." Over the years I have expanded that early essay beyond all decent bounds, and the result was a hugely overlong work completed in early 2008. During 2009, however, I have reduced it to roughly its present size, still somewhat long, I am afraid.

While *The Awakened Ones* involves a break from my earlier work, some of it continues and develops the theoretical thinking of my two books *Medusa's Hair* and *The Work of Culture,* revising and developing my ideas of deep motivation, the dark-night-of-the-soul experience and the idea of personal symbols that operate simultaneously on the level of both culture and psyche. My thinking on the visionary experience cannot be divorced from dreams that, as I shall demonstrate, entail the absence of the thinking-I or ego. In my discussions of dreams and visions I am deeply indebted to Wendy Doniger's pioneer work, *Dreams, Illusion, and Other Realities.* More immediately relevant is another pioneer work, Jeff Kripal's *Roads of Excess, Palaces of Wisdom* that is congruent with mine even though Kripal is primarily interested in contemporary "mystics." This is the place for me to mention two books that were guides to further reading and reflection: the indispensable and encyclopedic *Dream Reader* by Anthony Shafton and Wouter Hannegraaff's *New Age Religion and Western Culture,* the latter introducing me to the complex world of new age religion. I had to read a huge amount of material on medieval Christian religious ecstasy and here many people have helped me, too many for me to enumerate.

The spirit of William James's *The Varieties of Religious Experience* is present everywhere in the present essay, which I have organized into eight "books," with book 1 in effect a revised version of my William James lecture. That "book" is essential reading because it contains my theoretical thinking on the nature of the visionary experience and the interplay between visionary thought and reason. Thereafter, the reader put off by the length of this work can pick and chose the books or sections that interest her or him. Nevertheless, I think of my book as an *essay* because, like others of the same genre, this work can be read straight through as a long disquisition on ways of knowing that bypass the Cartesian cogito and the associated idea that Reason is the only legitimate access to knowledge.

The reader will notice some stylistic quirks, the gender issue being the most important. I know that it is considered offensive and sexist to use "he" when one should use the phrases "him or her" or "she or he." Some of us get a measure of relief from embarrassment by interspersing "she" and "he" in the body of the text without much rhyme or reason. My solution to this problem is simple. Because I am generally classified as a "male," for no doubt absurd reasons, I will for the most part use "he" as befits my official gender classification. When the context demands I will obviously use "she" and in some instances I will adopt the "she/he" usage when the context is not clear. I think embarrassment will cease if an author uses the personal pronoun appropriate to his or her public gender identity, even though privately he-she might not be sure of it.

In another methodological quirk I convert figures of history into "informants" but not "consultants" as is fashionable in ethnography today. "Consultants" for me has more negative connotations than "informants," having witnessed the work of so many of that species in UN organizations, among NGOs, and in the business community and having on occasion foolishly acted as one myself. My imaginary fieldwork areas are also circumscribed and restricted to the multiple forms of Buddhism and Christianity and those modern-day thinkers influenced by both. To complicate matters, *The Awakened Ones* ranges over long historical time periods and cultural traditions loosely contained in the vast expanses of thought that we label Buddhism or Christianity or for that matter Theosophy or psychoanalysis. Some of these traditions might not be familiar to the Western reader, and some to the Buddhist, but I have tried to render them in as intelligible a form as I can. I have the fantasy that this book will appeal to the intellectually curious, not just those of us in the human sciences. Consequently, even when I discuss difficult ideas, I try to write clearly, confining to endnotes theoretical details and historical and ethnographic information that might appeal to a more specialized reading public.

Several of my anthropological friends and critics have pointed out that my "informants" are dead and gone and appear only in hagiographical texts whereas in fieldwork one can interview living informants. This is of course true, but the voices of living informants and interpreters have their own limitations and dilemmas that we are now familiar with. I am aware of the difficulties involved in reading autobiographical, hagiographical, and other texts relating to visionaries long dead. I employ them judiciously I hope. I also find that autobiographical statements by female Christian penitents extremely helpful for the examination of "deep motivations" I sometimes engage in here. For example, they could unabashedly speak of their sexual and erotic experiences because their readership would know that such experiences are the work of the devil and not that of the personal motivations of the sufferer. In this sense these texts tell us more about the life of penitents than the life histories many ethnographers gather in the field. I would add that contemporary visionaries such as Patricia Garfield, whose work I discuss in some detail, can open up their sexual experiences for us in their texts for reasons quite different from medieval penitents, namely, the loosening of inhibitions after the sixties in the U.S. followed by the contemporary unabashed openness of eroticism.

Questions of eroticism bring me to a serious lacuna in my essay, and that is my inability to deal with the fascinating instances of the radical transformation of sexuality into the complex soteriological eroticism of Tibetan Buddhism. In earlier drafts of this essay I had a long appendix entitled "Tibetan erotic soteriology" which treated this topic, but I was not satisfied with my effort at dealing with what must surely be one of the most radical forms of sublimation on record. There are detailed scholarly accounts of the Tantric meditation that transforms sexuality into a kind of transcendental eroticism, especially in the movement of the winds and channels in the "subtle body" that is created in the mind of the meditator. And then the equally radical *karma mudra,* or "action seal," in which one has sexual intercourse with a select consort whereby orgasmic bliss is transformed into the bliss that promotes one's salvation quest. My difficulty is a simple one: I couldn't find a single autobiographical account of a monk or any interview with a current salvation seeker using the path of *karma mudra,* except for one study, *Sky Dancer: The Secret Life and Songs of the Lady Yeshe Tsogyel,* but that also, I shall show later, had its limitations. It was extremely difficult for me to extrapolate actual religious eroticism from idealized accounts. Until this lacuna is filled by scholars investigating the lives of current practitioners it is impossible for me to make any in-depth study of Tibetan soteriological eroticism from the standpoint of deep motivation. I had to drop my long speculative appendix, but the reader will find some suggestions in my discussion of Tibetan Buddhism and in my note 92, book 5, on "the subtle body."

Many of the technical terms in Buddhism might be unfamiliar to nonspecialist Western readers. I have tried to explain them in the body of this work, but the glossary might also provide a kind of guide to the reader, as indeed many of the notes. All unfamiliar technical terms from Indic and Tibetan religions will be italicized with the exception of popular terms like *nirvana* or *karma,* which will appear without diacritics. Other technical terms might be italicized in the first instance and then converted into roman script. As far as Tibetan Buddhism is concerned, I often use the Sanskrit rather than the Tibetan equivalent, but on occasion I employ both. In relation to Theravāda Buddhism (or Hinayāna, as it is sometimes labeled), I will use both Sanskrit and Pali terms, Pali being the language of its Scriptures. Sometimes the Sanskrit is preferable to the Pali, for example, the term *nirvana* rather than the Pali *nibbāna.*

The reader of this essay will notice an occasional definitional pitfall, terms that might invite confusion, even well-known ones. For example: everyone is familiar with the term *consciousness,* at least as ideas immediately accessible to our minds. However, the equivalent of consciousness is used in Buddhist texts in multiple ways that I mention in the course of this work. Others like William James include such things as *subconscious*, or what Freud would call *unconscious*, within the broad category of consciousness. I do too when I speak of visionary consciousness, overruling the ordinary sense of the term *consciousness* because I find a term like *visionary unconscious* or *visionary unconsciousness* too much of a barbarism. Visions when they first appear to the devotee or penitent in "trance" could emerge from outside consciousness, perhaps the unconscious in the psychoanalytic sense; but they can be recalled into consciousness later on. Another source of confusion might be the words *mystic* and *mysticism* that appear in this text. These words are rarely defined in the literature, with *mysticism* even used in a derogatory sense of "mysticism and nonsense" and a whole range of more positive meanings to designate any form of life that is "intuitive" or outside the realm of Reason and employed to designate such phenomena as séances, spirit possession, trances, states of absorption and that of identity with some spiritual being or cosmic principle and many more usages. This vague language use is peculiarly Western, and as far as I know is not found in Indic languages. There is no way that I can avoid using this term in its vague sense in this essay, especially in relation to Christian penitents, because the scholarly literature endows their experiences with that term. Although I have been somewhat liberal in my use of *mystic* and *mystical*, I am more cautious and sparing in my use of the term *mysticism*. The reader should note that all of these terms should appear in invisible quotation marks. However, as this essay progresses I will define *mysticism* in a more rigorous sense, appropriate to the themes I explore here. There are similar usages whose sense the reader will grasp as he proceeds in this book.

My book *Imagining Karma* appeared in 2002. While writing that book I was also working on *Cannibal Talk* (2005) and at the same time fully involved in fieldwork in the somewhat remote southeastern regions of Sri Lanka, a task I am still engaged in. Nevertheless, the subject of this essay continued to haunt me right through, giving me no peace. As with most of us, what stimulated my thinking were the lectures I delivered in various universities in the U.S., Europe, and India. These are too numerous to enumerate here. However, especially memorable were the graduate seminars on this very topic that I conducted in two universities. First, when I was Numata Visiting Professor of Buddhist Studies at the Harvard Divinity School in the fall term of 2005, and, second, as New York City Fellow at the Heyman Center, Columbia University in 2006 during the fall term. I am grateful to the students who participated in these seminars because we all know how much we learn from our students. Additionally, in both universities I gave several lectures on the some of the topics covered in this essay. I am extremely grateful for my friends at Harvard who conspired to have me there and make it so memorable, especially Janet Gyatso, Charlie Hallisey, and Don Swearer and my colleagues in the medical anthropology seminar at Harvard, especially Mary Jo Delviccio Good and Byron Good and the many student participants in that seminar series. At Columbia I thank Akeel Bilgrami and his colleagues at the Heyman Center for inviting me there and Eileen Gilloly for giving me a helping hand when I had to wander into bureaucratic mazes. Sarah H. Jacoby, a fellow fellow at the Heyman Center at that time, generously gave me several chapters of her Ph.D. dissertation on the rare case history of a female Tantric virtuoso, Sera Khandro (1892–1940). Unfortunately, given my interest in "deep motivation," I have not been able to use that wonderful account. During my stint at Columbia I delivered the Franz Boas lecture in the anthropology department on the deep motivation of Christian penitents, which I discuss in more detail in this essay. As always, I am deeply indebted to my friends there who asked provocative questions, in the seminar and outside of it, particularly Val Daniel and Laila Abu-Lughod. Perhaps one of the more memorable events in my long intellectual career was when I was invited to take up the Rajni Kothari Chair at the Center for the Study of Developing Societies in Delhi in October 2008, which effectively permitted me to do whatever I wanted in the way of research and writing. The major conspirator who was instrumental in inviting me there is my old friend

T. N. (Loki) Madan. I spent seven months at the center, and my wife Ranjini and I had the pleasure of renewing old friendships and making new ones both in the center and in Delhi itself: Ashis Nandy and Romila Thapar, among the old, and my newer friends Rajeev Bhargava, Shail Mayaram, and many new friends at the University of Delhi and JNU, all *kalyāna mitra*, true friends, a list too long to enumerate. And, of course, Jayasree Jayanthan, Rahul Govind, and the administrative staff at the center. It might well be a feature of the Indian intellectual scene that one could have warm relationships with academic spouses. But then I suspect that this must be due to the presence of my gracious wife who as always helped to push me out of my shell into the social world outside. It was in the inspirational setting of the center that I revised this essay to its near final form.

At Princeton my friends and colleagues in anthropology have been a continuing source of help and encouragement, and, as far as the writing of this essay is concerned, I am grateful to Joao Biehl, John Borneman, Mo Lin Yee, and Carol Zanca. Others who have helped me in my Buddhist and Hindu interests are my friends M. Maithrimurthi at Heidelberg and Heinz Muermel at Leipzig, Richard Gombrich at Oxford, Patrick Olivelle at Texas, Austin, and two scholars of Mahāyāna, Paul Williams and Paul Harrison. As far as my work on Christian penitents is concerned, I have benefited from the advice and help of Cathleen Medwick, Father Kieran Kavanaugh, Allison Weber, Barry Windeatt of Cambridge and Julia Frydman, a Princeton graduate. I must thank Stewart Sutherland for introducing me to Edwin Muir's important autobiography. My nephew Nalin Goonesekere was helpful for my work on the great chemist August Kekulé and for acquainting me with the work of Alan J. Rocke; Alan Rocke himself provided me with much information. The Theosophical Society library in New York was a good resource for me, as was its librarian Michael Gomes. The quotation from *Les Fleurs du mal* is from Roy Campbell, *The Poems of Baudelaire* (New York: Pantheon, 1959), and the long epigraph by Hegel in book 5 is, with minor changes, from Leo Rauch, trans., *Introduction to the Philosophy of History* (Hackett: Indianapolis, 1988). It is awfully hard nowadays to get an overlong book published, and I want to express my special thanks to Wendy Lochner, editor at Columbia, who not only read the much longer version, but wanted to publish it without too much cutting. I am also grateful to my manuscript editor Susan Pensak for a careful reading of my original text and for having saved me from many egregious blunders. My immediate editor, Christine Mortlock, and Alice Wade, who did considerable detective work in locating the photographs that appear here, deserve my warm thanks. The cost of production was defrayed by two generous grants, from

Princeton University and from the Hershey Family Foundation, and a donation from Ranjini Obeyesekere.

This preface will not complete unless I pay tribute to my dear friend Neelan Tiruchelvam, a Harvard-trained lawyer and human rights activist who, in his own quiet, self-effacing, and yet insistent way, tried to bring about a resolution of Sri Lanka's ethnic conflict. He was a founder and the spirit behind the International Center for Ethnic Studies, an organization engaged in research on issues of violence, human rights, and national integration. He was killed by one of his own ethnic group, a Tamil suicide bomber, a few days before he was planning to leave for Harvard Law School on a teaching assignment. Neelan represents to me the fate of the dozens of moderate Tamils and Sinhalas who have been systematically mowed down by the LTTE, leaving a nation almost empty of actual or potential leaders and opening up a space for criminal elements to have a say in the politics of governance. In a sense this book is dedicated to both Tamils and Sinhalas who laid their lives for the cause of moderation and the necessity to abdicate violence as a solution to the ills of a nation. Of them I only knew Neelan well. Violence can be an addiction and an infection, and in Sri Lanka it has poisoned the whole nation, such that state terror, human rights violations, and the intolerance of dissident opinions have become a regular feature of our moral landscape. The dread shadow of the long war is everywhere and will continue to smother us, even though, as I write this preface, the signs indicate that the long war will shortly end. Yet I find it troubling to hear some of my friends and relations reiterating the European myth of "just wars." Wars might be necessary, but they are too complicated to be labeled "just," when each side claims that it is their war that is "just." It is the Buddha who has insisted that there are no just wars, even though one can invent reasons for justifying them. Fear of political reprisal is everywhere, and concerned intellectuals sometimes have little choice but to remain silent, particularly if they are afraid for their families. But worse are intellectuals and former left-wing politicians who for gain's sake have abdicated their intellectual integrity and in effect condone violence and human rights abuses. Against this backdrop of omnipresent violence and social and political anomie, Neelan's work, his writing, his example, and his spirit will remain with us. He is one of those rare individuals who in life and in memory would not permit our conscience to go to sleep. May he sleep in peace and may his spirit be with us.

Center for the Study of Developing Societies
Delhi
April 2009

LIST OF ABBREVIATIONS

A	Boehme, *The Aurora*
AA	Muir, *An Autobiography*
AS	Gyatso, *Apparitions of the Self*
BJ	Bair, *Jung*
BGE	Nietzsche, *Beyond Good and Evil*
BR	Bentley, *Blake Records*
C	Cranston, *HPB*
CN	Gilman, *Conversations with Nietzsche*
CW	Blake, *Collected Writings*
Dial.	Rhys-Davids, *Dialogues of the Buddha*
E	Spinoza, *Complete Works*
EM	Bateson, *Steps to an Ecology of Mind*
Enn.	MacKenna, *The Enneads*
GM	Gibbons, *Gender in Mystical and Occult Thought*
HA	Bell, *Holy Anorexia*
HTS	Aris, *Hidden Treasures and Secret Lives*
HTT	Rinpoche, *Hidden Teachings of Tibet*
ID	Freud, *Interpretation of Dreams*
L	Teresa, *Book of Her Life*
LT	Julian of Norwich, *Long Text*
M	Schreber, *Memoirs of My Nervous Illness*
MB	Williams, *Mahāyāna Buddhism*
MK	Windeatt, *The Book of Margery Kempe*
MDR	Jung, *Memories, Dreams, Reflections*
ODL	Olcott, *Old Diary Leaves*
PA	Jung, *Psychology and Alchemy*
RB	Jung, *The Red Book*
SE	Freud, *Standard Edition*

The Awakened Ones

INTRODUCTION

So huge a burden to support
Your courage, Sisyphus, would ask;
Well though my heart attacks its task,
Yet Art is long and Time is short . . .
—Charles Baudelaire, "Ill Luck," *Les Fleurs du mal*

I N THIS INTRODUCTION I want to give the reader a glimpse of what I aim to
do in this work and a sense of the epistemological and psychological assumptions that underlie it. My "essay" is enormously long, in the old style, such
as that of John Locke's *An Essay on Human Understanding*. And I might say, albeit
with a shrug, mine also is a piece of "human understanding," but one that refuses
to be tied down to any epistemology of empiricism. The task that I attack here
is the "visionary experience," not in its metaphoric sense but literally referring
to those who actually see fantastic scenarios appearing before them. The essay's
subtitle also puns on G. W. F. Hegel's *Phenomenology of Spirit* (1807), ironically, of
course, because unlike Hegel's powerful philosophical and epistemological work,
mine is a modest venture where "spirit" is firmly grounded in practice. In that
sense my essay contains an oblique critique of Hegel's spirit (*Geist*), his notion of
the becoming of spirit with its permeation in varying degrees in man and nature,
its movement in world history and its ultimate source in the Absolute or God.
Nor is my book concerned with the work of Edmund Husserl, from which much
of modern phenomenology from Heidegger to Merleau-Ponty takes its bearings.
I find it hard to heed Husserl's advice, "to the things themselves," "things" being phenomena that appear to immediate or direct experience and reflected in,
or showing themselves to, consciousness. Given Husserl's primacy of consciousness, his work entails a double reification of the cogito, first in the Cartesian
sense of the certainty of the ego and second as a "transcendental ego," ideas that

are simply inapplicable to the subject of visions, dreams, and related phenomena wherein the "ego" in any of these senses simply does not appear. I am much more sympathetic to the later Husserl and his notion of the "life-world" (*Lebenswelt*), which can be related to the much more interesting Wittgensteinian idea of "forms of life." Visions are not the conventional stuff of "phenomenology," but they are the "things" or the phenomena that I am interested in. They also defy the Kantian distinction between phenomenon and noumenon, the former are things that are amenable to description and scientific investigation, and the latter outside of it, but can be reasoned on an a priori basis, as for example the idea of God and the soul or the numinous on the basis of faith and moral necessity. I want to blur such Kantian distinctions. Neither do I want to bracket my own "prejudices"—an impossible task anyway—but rather to employ them creatively. My strategy is to treat such intangibles as visions and dreams as phenomena worthy of investigation and description and unabashedly make general statements ("theorize") about them.

Not unrelated to these prejudices is the larger epistemological investigation that I undertake in this project and that is the critique of Reason and the idea of the certitude of knowledge derived from Reason. These ideas have had a long run in the West, as I demonstrate in this essay. However, I am primarily interested in the specific reification of Reason or rationality that finds its expression in Cartesian thought that had become normative during the early phase of the European Enlightenment, such that the criticisms of Reason in Europe's past seem to have lost their force and their relevance for the generation of knowledge. Criticisms of Reason are also true for the century before Descartes, the prime example being Michel de Montaigne (1533–1592), who, as others of his time, was profoundly influenced by the skeptical tradition of the Greek Sextus Empiricus (c. second century CE). That latter work, which doubted the possibility of any kind of true knowledge based on reason, came into prominence in Europe in the late fifteenth and the sixteenth centuries.[1] It was Descartes (1596–1650) whose work systematically criticized this tradition of skepticism in his famous formula of the cogito: *I think, therefore I am*, namely, that in this sea of methodological doubt true knowledge is possible through the indubitable certitude of the thinking-I, exemplifying Descartes's unshakable faith in the idea that *because I think, I know that I exist*. Yet Descartes has to justify how he can derive the cogito through Reason, that is, how could one deduce the cogito without postulating some other assumption, such as the existence of a first principle or a God who embodies Reason. He resolves this problem by saying that the cogito is apparent through *intuition,* by which he did not mean knowledge arrived at through a process of logical deduction but rather by something that ought to be obvious to everyone, namely, the notion of the thinking-I.[2] Hence intuitive knowledge of the cogito is not contrary to Reason; it "is the indubitable conception of a clear and attentive mind which proceeds solely from the light of reason."[3] This is what one might call the Cartesian paradox, a paradox that many a rationalist including Baruch de Spinoza (1632–1677) had to contend with, namely, that while the philosopher extols the value of Reason, the very basis for Reason lies in intuitive understanding, whether of the cogito in Descartes's sense or of Spinoza's God. Given the centrality of Reason in his work, Descartes had little choice but to link intuitive understanding with Reason, however farfetched such a connection may seem to us.[4] One might even designate the stratagems and ruses whereby intuition is brought within the discourses of a reified Reason as "Reason's cunning," if not the "cunning of Reason."[5]

The certainty of the thinking-I provides a foundation for the reasoning sciences Descartes constructed, which went into the development of Enlightenment science and rationality. But beyond this the Cartesian revolution led to the primacy of consciousness and the certitude of the self, the "I am" of the formula or of an ego distinctively and intrinsically separate from the body. The cogito, as I use it in this essay, is a shorthand way of dealing with two things: first, the critique of Reason as the path to true knowledge and then the critique of the ego/self or thinking itself as a product of a self-conscious I. These two ideas may be separate or conjoined, as in the Cartesian formula, but either way they have had a long run in European thought.

The Enlightenment we know is not a single movement. It had its own ups and downs, but, whether in its early mild or later moderate and radical forms, one thing is clear: the persistence of Reason as the pathway to knowledge, leading to what Peter Gay calls its "rationalistic myopia."[6] I am also not interested in what Descartes *really thought* but rather in the impact of his thought, imagined or not, on later European traditions and the human sciences of our time. Descartes is not the villain of my essay, but someone on whom I invest the mantle of Enlightenment rationality. Jonathan Israel tells us that there was a "collapse" of Cartesian thought owing to the "radical enlightenment," that is, the work of those philosophers following Spinoza who put greater emphasis on scientific and mathematical knowledge and the developing empiricism.[7] I am much more sympathetic to the idea that Spinoza, in spite of his criticism of Descartes, built his thinking on his rival and older contemporary.[8] The philosophers of the Radical Enlightenment might have successfully dismantled Descartes; nevertheless his mantle fell on European thought right down to our own times such that nowadays many of us in the human sciences continue to deal with the split between mind and matter, with scientific rationality, the importance of the cogito, and the reification of the self *as if* Descartes's thought is still with us. We cannot ignore the fact that Nietzsche, who is a prominent presence in my essay, criticized the cogito at length, as did others who appear here.

In my own self-definition, I consider myself a product of two Enlightenments, the European and the Buddhist. One cannot live *without* Reason and one cannot live *with* it either, at least in its exclusionary Enlightenment or Euro-rational sense. Rationality for me still remains a powerful means of knowing, but I criticize here the closure of our minds to modes of knowledge, especially visionary knowledge, that bypass the cogito. Hence the focus of this essay is on those who brought their visions and intuitive understandings within the frame of rational thinking. Visions *appear* before the dimmed consciousness of the seeker of truth. They are not *thought out* through the operation of Reason and the work of the cogito or the thinking-I. My ideal is the Buddha who discovered the foundations of his epistemology through meditative trance but then reworked these foundational ideas later in more rational and philosophically profound form in his discourses. In others the interplay between what I call the *It* and the *I* may not be all that clear, but, nevertheless, it does occur. For example: I deal with Catherine of Siena and Madame Blavatsky, both of whom claim to have discovered long texts through their dream visions, but vision is soon followed by revision.

The interplay of the two broad forms of knowing is what this book is about. When this interplay does not occur, the consequences could be tragic, as was the case with the Theosophist Damodar Mavalankar, whose sad death I record in some detail. Rarely did the virtuosos described in the following pages live exclusively under the aegis of nonrational knowledge. That would be as dangerous as rational exclusivity, leading the way to a kind of hallucinatory madhouse. Moreover, opening up one's mind to visionary knowledge is an uncommon phenomenon, even among those most receptive to it. But while quantitatively negligible, visionary knowledge is qualitatively significant for visionaries and for those of us who benefit from their insights. Or, for that matter, might even be troubled by them, because we know that absurdities can also emerge from visions, then and now, as much as absurdities can also emerge from rational discourse. Nonsense exists everywhere. And how can we neglect the impact of visionary knowledge on history? In that sense, mine is a restorative undertaking, bringing back forms of knowing that surely existed in elementary form from the time that *homo* became *sapiens*, if not before. One might even say that this work is an insurrection of suppressed knowledge, to use a Foucauldian phrase, in this case visionary knowledge that tends to be suppressed when hyperrationality holds sway over our lives. Unfortunately, Foucault was too much of a child of the European Enlightenment to appreciate the kind of "inner experience" that I document here and that some of his French predecessors like Georges Bataille unabashedly spoke about, although not quite in the way that I do in this essay. I will also exclude "closet visionaries," found everywhere in the very thick of Enlightenment rationality, who with the right hand consciously believe in reason and with the left consult séances and have visions with new age gurus in the privacy of their homes. They exemplify for me the vulnerability of the Enlightenment project and sadly illustrate my dictum on the dilemma of our modernity with its reification of rationality: one cannot live *without* Reason and one cannot live *with* it either. Closet visionaries have no impact on history and little on the world outside, and they do not engage in the dialectic that I am concerned with here, the interplay between visionary knowledge and rationality, between the "It" and the "I."

The question a critic might raise is this: can the visionary mode of knowledge, so unlike scientific experimentation that we all value, provide us with "truth"? This is not easy to answer, outside the obvious fact that even the history of science is riddled with errors of judgment, half truths, fouled and corrupt experiments, and out-and-out prejudices that have been at sometime or other touted as truth. The history of science contains an often understated history of falsehoods.[9] Philosophical discourse is different because its truths do not depend on verification but rather on intersubjective consensus among intellectual elites whose composition vary with time, place, and history. It is the richness and complexity of philosophical knowledge that attract us as is their relevance for understanding existence or the epistemological bases of science or other issues that stem from within an intellectual tradition. Recently, cross-philosophical knowledge has begun to make its appearance in a world where boundaries are being gradually effaced, but Western philosophical knowledge still dominates the world's intellectual scene. And, when it comes to visionary thought in the West, we are posed with an immediate roadblock owing to the entrenchment of rationality, which discourages it. The European visionaries that I mention here unfortunately constitute at best a minor or neglected philosophical tradition. In Buddhism there is no such problem: profound truths have always been intuitively grasped through visionary and other arational means and then expounded at length through secondary rational reworking. Implicit in this book is a plea to open our minds to forms of intuitive understanding rather than shut the door on them. If that were to happen, Western thought might not only be receptive to the epistemological thinking of Hindu and Buddhist philosophers, but they might also be able to enrich their own philosophical and scientific traditions by opening themselves to the varied forms of visionary and intuitive thinking that appear in this essay.

Let me now briefly state the assumptions that underlie my examination of the forms of life I treat here, such as visions, dream-visions, trances, and what I have called "aphoristic thinking." Visions arise when consciousness has dimmed, sometimes only for a moment, and in that instant one can experience a visionary "showing" of variable duration, characterized by the absence of the active thinking "I" or the ego of the rational consciousness. Thus dimmed consciousness and the absence of the ego are the minimum assumptions necessary to understand the genesis of showings, hearings, and aphoristic thoughts that are the phenomena or "texts" that I deal with. My strategy is to relate the text to the cultural tradition and the personal life of the experiencer whenever such information is available. While recognizing these minimal requirements, let me nevertheless develop my assumptions further.

In our ordinary lives, in such things as day dreaming, reveries, and daytime imaginings, we simply let our conscious thinking temporarily lapse as we let our minds stray into whatever realms of fantasy and loose thinking animate us. It is these imaginings during conditions of suspended awareness that led to the modern fictional "stream of consciousness" device. That is, even during the daytime we often drop ego-thinking and enter into a mental realm where visual fantasies and straying thoughts ("reveries") are given free range. These reveries rarely have an organizing plot. My own reveries are often association based, one association leading to another and on and on, such that my last set of reveries seem to have no connection with the initial instigating thought. Hence reveries are often enough disorganized, sporadic or vague; at other times they are more or less "coherent." Visualizations that occur when we shut our eyes during reveries can be shaken off anytime we want, or they simply disappear the moment our attention span is over.

There are other features of our daytime fantasies that are different from visions and dreams. They are rarely translated into something I *see* out there before me, as I would with visions and related phenomena. The processes whereby daytime fantasies are transformed into a *showing* or an *appearance* that emerges before us does occur occasionally, as the case of Emanuel Swedenborg demonstrates. He believed that the visionary might see apparitions "in a state of wakefulness as clearly as in daylight, but with closed eyes."[10]

In my thinking it is a mistake to assume that dreaming can be fully isolated from daytime reveries. The externalization and "pictorialization" of thoughts distinguish night dreams from daytime reveries, but it is likely that reveries continue to intervene at the interstices between dreams and influence the content of dreams. This means that "night residues" might be as significant, or perhaps more so, than day residues in dream formation. In reverie, as with the dream, the thinking "I" or ego does not appear, and it is as if my thoughts and fantasies seem to float in and around my mind without my conscious awareness. However, when consciousness is fully blocked out as at night, or when one is temporarily "out," pictorialization of thoughts appears with great clarity and with it a mode of experience different from reverie. These questions need further investigation, but one can, I think, affirm that our minds at night are rarely, if ever, a blank slate, even when consciousness has lapsed.

Daytime fantasies have yet another feature: for the most part they are treated by us as nothing but fantasies or imaginings and do not possess any truth value. Whereas the truth of what one sees is the salient characteristic of visions, dream-visions, and also of psychotic hallucinations, at least from the point of view of the sick person. With the suspension of the thinking-I and the dimming of consciousness, there occurs in such states a form of "thinking" that I label *passive cerebration* or *passive cognition* or, following John of the Cross, the work of the *passive intellect.* In this essay I will use these terms interchangeably. These terms imply that the unconscious *thinks,* but in a special way. Over a hundred years ago William James noted the passive nature of the mystical consciousness. "Although the oncoming of mystical states may be facilitated by preliminary voluntary operations, as by fixing the attention, or going through certain bodily performances, or in other ways which manuals of mysticism prescribe; yet when the characteristic sort of consciousness has once set in, the mystic feels as if his own will were in abeyance, and indeed sometimes as if he were grasped by superior powers."[11] James's "mystics" and my vision seekers overlap, but my focus is primarily on those who experience "visions" whether or not these visions lead to a so-called mystical state.

My term *passive cerebration* opens the way for a futuristic neurology that can link the phenomenology of visions with the workings of the brain without reducing the one to the other, something that Emile Durkheim noted ages ago when, arguing against the neurologists of his time, he insisted that individual and cultural representations cannot be reduced to the workings of the brain cells.[12] Given this prejudice of mine, I couldn't disagree with Francis Crick more when he presents us with an astonishingly naive hypothesis in the very first sentence of his book *The Astonishing Hypothesis*: "The Astonishing Hypothesis that 'You,' your joys and your sorrows, your memories and your ambitions, your sense of personal identity and free will, are in fact no more than the behavior of a vast assembly of nerve cells and their associated molecules. As Lewis Carroll's Alice might have phrased it: 'You're nothing but a pack of neurons.'"[13]

Unfortunately, at the other end, there are ethnographers and practitioners of the human sciences who adopt an equally obtuse stance when they deny the neurobiological roots of our being and their relevance for the phenomenological understanding of cultural forms or collective representations. For me an important study that attempts to bridge the gap between neurological science and a phenomenology such as mine is that of Mark Sohms and his colleagues on "neuro-psychoanalysis." Sohms, however, relies too much on Freud's second topography, the simplistic neo-Cartesian id-ego-superego model that I criticize in this essay and elsewhere in my writing.[14] And Antonio Damasio, a highly literate neurologist and stylist, whose work I greatly admire, is critical of the so-called Cartesian split between mind and matter, which to him is also a split between reason and emotion. Emotion is often tied to reasoning, and the interplay of both have to be understood in terms of the work of the brain, such that the classical distinction between mind and brain can be overcome without reducing the mental processes solely to the operation of neurological structures. This is true and can be reconciled with our phenomenological understandings, which show time and again the investment of emotion on Reason and the other way around (sometimes leading to ideological fanaticism and cruelty, exemplified in secular and religious political *isms*).[15] I deal with the larger issue of the Cartesian split between mind and matter, between *res cogitans* and *res extensa,* briefly in relation to thinkers like Boehme, Blake, and Jung. Many contemporary thinkers have tried to close this gap, among them, once again, Davasio in his recent book, *Looking for Spinoza.*[16] From the point of view of this essay, I have recently become interested in quantum physicists who have attempted to bridge the division between mind and matter by postulating another order of reality underlying the physical world as developed in relativity theory and quantum mechanics. They have paved a way to bring older notions of the Absolute back into the world picture. I do not have the expertise to deal with them at length but shall hesitantly bring into this essay the work of David Bohm, a physicist cum metaphysician and a major exponent of an "implicate order" that enfolds the "explicate order" of contemporary physics.

How do I connect the phenomenon of dreams with passive cerebral activity? It is in the process of dreaming, rather than in the dream itself, that one can infer its operation. When consciousness has been suspended in dreaming, the work of the passive intellect takes over, but, unlike daytime fantasizing and reverie, passive thinking in dreams is pictorialized or represented in images with varied levels of organization, from chaos to coherence. One can even say, following Jacob Boehme, that coherence is created out of chaos. I cannot speak of the neurology of pictorialization except to affirm that pictures appear as if they were projected outside the dreaming person. Hence my notion of the process of dreaming: the passive intellect produces the dream; the dream appears in the sleeping mind of the dreamer; it is perceived as true during the period of dreaming; the dreamer awakes and passive celebration ceases, and he might say, "this is just a dream."

On recollecting the dream, there inevitably occurs what Freud calls "secondary revision," a cognitive process that transforms the dream-as-dreamt to the dream-as-recalled, in which case the dreamer might say that the dream is plain nonsense or that it has *meaning.* After some delay, the dreamer or his amanuensis might give a further interpretation of the dream wherein secondary revision might develop into *secondary elaboration,* a much more thought-out process.[17] The emergent cognitive knowledge of the dream might affect our fantasy lives and influence further dreaming; it could influence culture if the dream has symbolic or parabolic or prognosticative value or if the dreamer is a spiritually sensitive and important person like a shaman; in which case the dream becomes a dream vision, an oneiromantic experience believed to be true. If the dream vision gets talked about, then the level of participation in the meaning of the dream expands to include others. This means that dream visions are inevitably affected by the culture and in turn might further affect the culture, perhaps even changing it. A dream *stricto sensu* never repeats itself because, I will show in this essay, dreams are characterized by a radical relativism such that no two dreams are fully alike.

It was a methodological error in early dream theorizing that dreams occur during rapid eye movements (REM) when the subject is asleep. We now know that dreaming occurs both during REM periods and non-REM periods, which render these two distinctions somewhat fuzzy. From my point of view, passive cerebration, which includes reverie, occurs throughout the night but might develop differently and perhaps at a much faster rate or with more pictorial clarity, elaboration, and tapping richer memories during REM periods when the body is "paralyzed" (muscle atonia) as sometimes occurs in the case of visionaries also. When we focus on the passive intellect rather than on one of its specific products, we can bring visions that often occur during the day into our analysis as well.

Thus, while I believe that these special thought processes occur outside the thinking-I or ego, I do not have a verifiable or falsifiable *theory* of such thinking, except for the *phenomenological inferences* I make based on case studies and the intuitive understanding of my own dreams. In European language games the term *passive* has negative connotations, itself a product of the idealization of the active thinking ego or "I." There is little I can do to remedy this prejudice. I will admit that the demonstration of "passive cerebration" must await developments in the neurological sciences. Unfortunately, most neurologists operate with implicit or explicit Cartesian or neo-Kantian models that emphasize the primacy of the ego and rational thought even though they should know that most of us, including scientists, hardly employ rationality in conducting our everyday lives. Life would be incomplete and deadly boring if we were to do so. And because the major part of our ordinary lives are given to day and night dreaming, reverie, fantasizing, and letting our visualizing minds wander, we can confidently assert that most of our thought processes occur outside the domain of rationality or a reified reason.

This essay is against the trend in much of ethnographic writing where the emphasis is on a detailed and specific study of a single society or culture rather than the comparative sweep that I embrace here, focusing on two traditions I know best, the Buddhist and the European, thereby transcending cultural and historical periods. I make no apologies for this stance. I studied anthropology at a time when comparative studies and large theoretical issues were popular, if not normative. These were the sort of issues that animated the work of the great social thinkers: Marx, Nietzsche, Freud, Durkheim, Weber, and Lévi-Strauss. Unhappily they have mostly gone out of fashion, swept away by poststructuralist and postmodern discourse. I am not immune to such thinking, but for me deconstruction without the restoration of meaning is an empty enterprise. I find the effect of postmodern discourse on much of contemporary scholarship baneful when it resorts to convoluted prose, often difficult and sometimes impossible to unscramble. Worse: the pall of such discourse has cast its long shadow over the minds of younger scholars. I will confess that I am rather tired of that sort of writing and I abjure it. And I will shamelessly admit that I can learn more about "spirit" from the visionaries in my essay than from Jacques Derrida's critique of Heidegger in *Of Spirit*.[18] At the same time I don't want to deride Derrida and my Derridean friends because of genuine insights that I, for one, have benefited from. Without closing my mind to poststructuralist insights, I want to return to the issues of life and existence that fired the imaginations of the great social thinkers I have mentioned. If Nietzsche is a kind of avatar of our postmodernity, as many think, he was also someone who dealt with such issues as Dionysian and Apollonian modes of thought, the origins of guilt, the critique of the Cartesian cogito, and many a problem of existential meaning and significance. In my view, he is closer to Weber and Freud than he is to Derrida and Foucault or, for that matter, Heidegger, even though the last three have, in their different ways, appropriated Nietzsche as part of their own varying charter myths.[19]

In spite of the reservations I have about contemporary writing in the human sciences, I remain an ethnographer in the sense that I place considerable emphasis on case studies of individual virtuosos, however imperfect the historical record. Wherever possible, I examine intensively the lives and visions of these special individuals because they illustrate my theoretical thinking. Consequently, there are large gaps in my narrative simply because it is not meant to illustrate historical continuity. These gaps I fill with three "hinge discourses" (in the ordinary sense of "hinge" and not to be confused with "hinge propositions" à la Wittgenstein). Hinge discourses fill some but not all lacunae in this essay, and they are not meant to be exhaustive. For example, I have a hinge discourse entitled "The Movement Toward Mahāyāna and the Rise of Theistic Mysticism." The discussion there might seem shallow to Buddhist scholars of Mahāyāna, but I think it necessary for my readership and for my own self-understanding. So is it with the other hinge discourses.

My choices of visionary thinkers developed as the argument in the book progressed, sometimes serendipitously. For example, I had not planned to include Blake, Jung, or lucid dreamers in this essay. They appeared before me as my reading progressed. Take the case of William Blake. I knew and loved Blake, but mostly from my reading of the *Songs of Innocence* and *Songs of Experience* and other poems written in conventional stanza form, until one day at dinner at a friend's house in Colombo, while discussing my hypotheses on visions, Michael Ondaatje asked me: What about Blake? And soon Blake the visionary, and his crazy prophetic books and surreal paintings, had me hooked! Blake walked into my book somewhat late in the day, and I am sure I've missed much of what has been written about him recently. In my earlier writing I had been somewhat short on Jung, even though I had read a fair amount of his work. But one day, on a Manhattan sidewalk, I picked up a copy of *Memories, Dreams, Reflections*, and there I suffered a conversion! I cannot escape the fact that given my ignorance of the vast critical and exegetical writing on figures like Blake, Blavatsky, and Jung, I might have on occasion been reinventing the wheel. I hope, however, that the point of view I adopt is sufficiently original, such that my trespass on the ideas of others is minimal and unintended. And may such trespasses be forgiven.

Moreover, owing to the huge information overload on the topics I deal with here, my reading has been extremely selective. Friends have asked me why I neglected Hindu visionaries, why I ignore Sufis, and so on and on. I have a simple response: constraints of length compel me to restrict my reading and focus on thinkers that interest me—and a not-so-simple sense of urgency, as time and the hour keep running inexorably toward my own short day. As a result of these constraints, my essay might seem a bit lopsided, without a proper balancing of beginning, middle, and end. Yet what holds the work together is a thematic unity. Alongside my central concern with visionary knowledge, I also deal with an important life experience of the "awakened ones," those religious virtuosos who have emerged from some deep spiritual crisis, a dark-night-of-the-soul type of experience, seen as a kind of death followed by a symbolic rebirth or awakening. Often enough the dark night is associated with a "trance illness." And everywhere in this essay I explicitly or implicitly share with the reader my personal existential preoccupation with problems of death, decay, and human finitude. Hence this essay can be read as a meditation on death, a preoccupation that also concerns the visionaries inhabiting these pages. These concerns pile up as my essay moves toward its end. The epigraphs found scattered in the body of this essay also mirror them, as indeed the quotations from some of my favorite poets, which have been, partially or wholly, stuck in my memory: Yeats, Hopkins, Blake, Marvell, Baudelaire, Eliot, Herbert, Shakespeare, and Donne and many more. Being a poetry fanatic, I take all sorts of liberties with them, echoing them oft-times without citation when they appear in the middle of my thoughts! Their spirit and the spirit of the many Buddhist thinkers appearing here will, I hope, light up these pages and also lighten the burden of an overlong and occasionally difficult text.

Let me now return to the term *spirit.* My readership will note that I use the terms *spirit* and *spiritual* quite unabashedly, a usage that some of my anthropological colleagues might find disconcerting because these terms, in popular discourse at least, are used to designate whole civilizations, as, for example, the cliché that India is a spiritual civilization whereas the West is materialistic. It is true that the term *spirit* and its derivatives come mostly from the Christian tradition, but then many of the terms and concepts we employ in the human sciences come from Western discourse anyway. As for *spirit*, it is not difficult to find its representatives in virtually every religion. Many of us use these terms metaphorically in such statements as "when the spirit moves me." That metaphor contains a truth that I explore in this work, especially in my notion of "secular spirituality." I deliberately ignore the debasement of spirituality in the global market place such that nirvana becomes a hedonistic paradise and known to many as a designation for an Indian restaurant in Manhattan, Bali, London, New Orleans, Geneva, Beverly Hills, and in the cosmopolitan Everywhere.

In general, the term *spirit* and its derivatives are difficult to define except ostensively, that is, to point out the thread that connects *spirit* with related ideas expressing continuity of life after death or an essence underlying existence: soul, spirit entity, mana, Self, "ghost," or the Vedic "breath of life" (*prāna vāyu*) or the Buddhist rebirth-linking-consciousness or the Christian or Hegelian notions of Spirit and their many antecedents, derivatives, and so on and on. I explore the manner in which they come into being. Divinities, one may add, are beings endowed with some animating force or "spirit" that gives them special powers of creativity, destruction, and the propensity to ameliorate human suffering. In Buddhist and Hindu thought, a statue of a deity is "dead" unless ritual techniques infuse it with spirit, generally through the fixing of the "eyes" on the statue. For me, spirit, self, soul, and so forth—even "no-self"—are human inventions designed to deal with problems of life, death, and existence in general.

Once rooted in the imagination of a people or culture, ideas like these take on a life of their own, such that some believe the self or soul actually exists within us and others do not, yet others such as Buddhists believe that they are at best changing phenomena without any stability or ontological reality. Whether these multiple manifestations of spirit prove or disprove the existence of Spirit is simply outside the purview of this essay.

Nevertheless, one cannot escape the debate that goes on everywhere in contemporary societies on the death of God, using that phrase broadly to refer to the decline of religious beliefs in a hereafter. The more scientists and philosophers assert the demise of such beliefs, or their irrelevance or delusional nature, the more vehement is the denial of the believer. This then brings atheist philosophers to further vindicate their positions, leading to a futile incremental dialectic with believers that can go on forever unless a bored or exasperated readership or audience puts an end to it. Spirit, in the sense I have defined it, cannot be proved or disproved on the basis of our contemporary scientific knowledge, quite unlike creation myths, traditional cosmological theories, or other culturally specific beliefs like sorcery or witchcraft. Moreover, even the most seemingly convincing evidence for the falsity or falsification of religious beliefs will not make the slightest dent on those who believe. They can only convince those who are already inclined to disbelieve. (See the following endnote for my discussion of the "god delusion.")[20] I would add that much of what anthropologists have labeled "culture," those webs of meaning that human beings construct to make sense of the worlds in which they live, are constituted of false beliefs, at least from the viewpoint of modern scientific knowledge. And where are the truths of yesteryear? The political and economic beliefs once fanatically held by progressive intellectuals are today's falsehoods. And today's truths? Most of what we write is, after all, writ on sand.

Consider a powerful cultural relativist position on the death of God in a literal sense. I would say that every single historical religion subscribing to a doctrine of salvation, now or in the past, will assert the following proposition: that their belief system is universally valid and carries with it the imprimatur of absolute truth. These two features—the universalism of belief and of absolute truth—mean that no two religions can be equally true and, furthermore, implies that among the hundreds of salvation religions of past and present only one could possibly be true. But that is surely a slim probability. This situation is further compounded when we consider the complex institutional frameworks of religions: churches, temples, popes and prelates, fraternities, courts, monks and nuns, priests, shamans and sorcerers, gurus, confessionals, and so on that conspire to make "truth" even more questionable. And then there is the remarkable issue raised by Baruch Spinoza in 1670: that even within a single religious tradition there are styles, forms of imagination, and variations in intellect and personality from one type of religious practitioner to another that make the certainty of religious knowledge even more problematic.[21] Although "problematic," the human imagination cannot be reined in or circumscribed, as we will demonstrate in this essay. And then there are religious innovators for whom these seeming "falsifications" of belief are themselves illusory, based on a version of the excluded middle. What about the gray areas, the favorite space for many nowadays? It is in this gray area that another kind of logic has to be discovered, and it is here that the "physics metaphysicians" try to carve out a domain of "mind" that refuses to accept the conventional formula of the opposition and separateness of mind and matter. Such thinkers are pioneers, but not the prophets of a new epistemology, and we have to seriously interrogate them, even if we disagree with them.

Most human beings will continue to believe or not to believe without bothering about such arguments, because ultimately the death of belief means that human death poses finality, a point of no return, something many would not want to accept. But the issue of the god delusion or illusion can scarcely be avoided for sensitive people living in today's world. One position is almost inevitable, given our knowledge explosion. And that is the gray area I spoke of earlier. At one time it was in these areas that new religions emerged, such as forms of Buddhism and Christianity or Sufi Islam. One can dip into that area and invent new forms of the religious life, often of a tentative and nonauthoritarian sort. The most powerful among these is the "perennial philosophy" first formulated in 1540 by Agostino Steuco in *De perenni Philosophia* and then by Leibniz, who used the term to designate the truths that underlie all religions.[22] It emerges in some form or other in later invented religions, especially Theosophy. It is given a modernist slant by Aldous Huxley in an anthology of writings from the world's great mystical virtuosos to justify the idea that "the divine Ground of all existence is a spiritual Absolute, ineffable in terms of discursive thought, but (in certain circumstances) susceptible of being directly experienced and realized by the human being."[23] The combination of the idea of an Absolute reachable through mystical apprehension is employed most prominently by new age religions and by intellectuals who might fall shy of embracing any form of religion, old or new age.

I know of colleagues in anthropology who are contemptuous of new age religion, even though they sympathize with invented forms of religious life among "native" populations that are much less interesting than new age inventions. Some of my nonacademic friends, whether Buddhist, Christian, or Hindu, might subscribe to an individually refined version of perennial philosophy; or a form of mystical religiosity; or a modified version of God as a principle underlying the cosmos or nature; or an ultimate reality posited by such thinkers as Spinoza, Einstein, Ananda Coomaraswamy, and many others, some of whom will appear in this work. One of my best friends, having heard of my project, told me, "I hope that your book will demonstrate the existence of metaphysical truths." Because I am incapable of such an enterprise, I must now make my shamefaced admission: my problem with European philosophers is that even when they affirm the primacy of human experience, as Hegel did, the reality is different, because for most of them human experience is founded on taken-for-granted metaphysical abstractions. To borrow a Plotinian kind of phrase: metaphysics is experience's prior. For my part, I cannot think *metaphysically* without first thinking *physically*, that is, grounding my thinking in the actual lives of human beings whose experiences are conditioned by their cultural traditions and the other way around.[24] Hence my sympathy for the visionaries who appear in this essay, almost all of them who think physically—by which I also mean psychically—prior to thinking metaphysically. Visions are metaphysics' prior.

However, I believe that it is ethically wrong for the scholar to denigrate the religious beliefs of people by denying the existence of god or spiritual beings or some other views of the afterlife such as rebirth and karma on the basis of empirical or scientific evidence. Or: attempt to prove the reality of metaphysical truths through science or pseudo-science. Science itself is so much open to debate, especially the problematic of verification or falsification and what I think is the very basis of "scientific truth," that is, its lack of finality. Scientific and scholarly truths are always in the making, and there lies their attractiveness for many of us. This is, of course, not to condone cruelty, injustice, and intolerance endemic to our own times whether they appear in a religious or in a secular nationalistic or patriotic mask or in any other guise. Sensitive believers and nonbelievers in our own day have condemned such practices.

Writing this final version while hovering between the U.S. and Sri Lanka and India, I am confronted with another dilemma. Buddhist and Hindu schoolchildren have few problems with Darwinism, and I think this is true of most Christians, some of whom will compartmentalize Darwinism and their Christian faith or reconcile them at some rational or fuzzy epistemological level. But in the United States I am confronted in the print media of evangelicals who steadfastly believe in the literal interpretation of Genesis. From my perspective, I am saddened by the thought that evangelical youth will find it hard to enter graduate school in the sciences and, for the most part, will continue to be steeped in poverty, not just economic but intellectual. Just as one can blame scientists for their attempts to disprove God, one can blame religious fundamentalists of all varieties for their willing discounting of science. But, as Gregory Bateson says, fighting the fundamentalists with the tools of science can lead us "into an empty headedness analogous to theirs."[25] These issues are to me inextricably tied to serious ethical, and even political, dilemmas for which there are no easy answers, least of all by denying the existence or nonexistence of spirit or Spirit in the name of another truth. As one believer in an *almost* traditional Catholic faith put it as he edged his way toward death:

> If there is no God,
> Not everything is permitted to man.
> He is still his brother's keeper
> And he is not permitted to sadden his brother
> By saying there is no God.[26]

The voice of the poet prompts me to deal with my own prejudices or preconceptions. Readers might note that a certain Buddhist "prejudice" animates my thinking. I was born and raised as a Buddhist, and this, in conjunction with my reading and experience of existence, has given my worldview a Buddhist slant. As Hans Georg Gadamer is at pains to say, no thinker can fully escape prejudice, but prejudice could be put to creative use.[27] In addition to being a Buddhist, I was also born and raised in the twilight of British colonialism and I believe my socialization and nurture and historical experience has given me creative insights wherever colonialism occurs. But the good side of prejudice coexists with blind spots, often terrible ones—areas that Gadamer underplayed. In my thinking, the terrible ones occur when a thinker appropriates another culture or worldview uncritically or unknowingly into his own biased world picture. Method then becomes a tool that covers up truth. I can only hope that my creative Buddhist prejudices take precedence over my prejudicial blind spots!

I have no answers in this work to the "existence of metaphysical truths," but I will confess that although I analytically dissect the visions and the voices of the virtuosos who appear in this work I am also sympathetic to what they stand for. I refuse to consider their voices and visionary experiences as pathological, abnormal, or paranormal. Normality to me is no ideal. In addition to recovering modes of thought gone out of vogue with the advent of Enlightenment rationality, I am very much interested in a few atheists and agnostics and those who do not believe in any kind of orthodox religiosity but give expression to some form of "secular spirituality" as Nietzsche and I think Spinoza, Jung, and Einstein did.

Theirs was the "heresy of the free spirit," and we can reinvent and then transfer that term, as Nietzsche did, from medieval heresy to our troubled modernity. In addition to these heretics are many more who can also believe in the spirit, at least in a metaphorical sense wherein we open up our minds to our dreams or dream visions and to aphoristic thinking, as I demonstrate in my discussion of Nietzsche, Wittgenstein, Jung, and Freud. But, beyond that, I must confess that I am naive enough to believe in the validity of some of the sensory gifts that visionaries possess. Others I am skeptical about, and some, I think, are spurious; yet of others I simply refrain from making judgment. Examples abound in the body of my essay, but for now let me point to an interesting episode from the life of William Blake that illustrates visionary hypersensitivity.

One day in September 1825 Samuel Palmer persuaded Blake and Mr. Edward Calvert and Mrs. Calvert to his grandfather's house in Shoreham, Kent. And then:

> The following evening William Blake was occupied at the table in the large room, or kitchen. Old Palmer was smoking his long pipe in the recess, and Calvert, as was his custom, sat with his back to the candles reading. Young Samuel Palmer had taken his departure more than an hour before for some engagement in London, this time in the coach. Presently Blake, putting his hand to his forehead, said quietly: "Palmer is coming; he is walking up the road." "Oh, Mr. Blake, he's gone to London; we saw him off in the coach." Then, after a while, "He is coming through the wicket—there!"—pointing to the closed door. And surely, in another minute, Samuel Palmer raised the latch and came in amongst them. It so turned out that the coach had broken down near to the gate of Lullingstone Park.[28]

Friends and colleagues who know of my interest in the visionary experience sometimes ask me whether I have experienced visions myself. Unfortunately, I have not been blessed with the profound visions of the informants that I record at length here. I personally believe in what I call aphoristic thinking, that is, ideas that occur when conscious thinking has been temporarily suspended. But of true visions, where one *sees* things, I have unfortunately not been gifted with. And yet, and yet: many years ago, when I was visiting a relation of mine who was the Sri Lankan ambassador in New Delhi, I was standing in his spacious garden under the shade of a large tree in which vultures were weirdly hanging. Suddenly I was transported to what I felt was Old Delhi, a place I had not visited previously, and yet everything I saw seemed very familiar: the Indian houses, lines of small shops, children, and cows. Because my vision or waking dream seemed "weird," I dismissed it simply as a case of déjà vu or neurons playing neurotic games. But now, as I write this introduction, it seems to me I was out only a few seconds and that I was in Old Delhi or the illusory place that, at the moment of the vision, seemed Old Delhi. After that brief moment, perhaps even a split second, I was back in the garden with the vultures weirdly hanging or flying overhead. What most affected me, however, was not so much the vision of Old Delhi but the vivid reality of the vultures that preceded or somehow provoked the "vision" and immediately reminded me of those black crows, harbingers of death, flying over the wheatfield in the convoluted strokes of Van Gogh's brush, one of his last paintings before he shot himself. The Delhi vultures reappeared in spectral form in a dream much later, and I use that dream to end my essay in the section entitled, "Envoi—Intimations of Mortality: The Ethnographer's Dream and the Return of the Vultures"

0.1 Vincent van Gogh, *Wheatfield with Crows* (1890). *Van Gogh Museum, Amsterdam*

Book 1

THE VISIONARY EXPERIENCE

Theoretical Understandings

THE AWAKENED BUDDHA AND THE BUDDHIST AWAKENING

> O the mind, mind has mountains; cliffs of fall,
> Frightful, sheer, no-man-fathomed. Hold them cheap
> May who ne'er hung there. Nor does long our small
> Durance deal with that steep or deep. Here! creep,
> Wretch, under a comfort serves in a whirlwind: all
> Life death does end and each day dies with sleep.
>
> —Gerard Manley Hopkins, "No Worst There Is None"

I HOPE MY READER will not be too surprised if I begin my discussion of the Buddha's spiritual awakening with an epigraph from a late-nineteenth-century Jesuit poet and priest. Here as elsewhere in this essay I blur the distinction between religions insofar as the visionary experience is concerned. Gerard Manley Hopkins, in his "terrible sonnets," powerfully evoked the dark night of the soul and the unfathomed depths of the mind that, even as he was writing, were being formulated by his scientific contemporaries, especially in Paris, as the "subconscious," in the more prosaic language of the psychological sciences of their time. Although products of different discourses, the rich metaphoric language of the poet and the scientific discourse of French psychologists like Jean Charcot and Pierre Janet dealt with those depths that lie outside our normal waking consciousness. A few years after Hopkins's death, William James gave expression to similar notions in his classic work *The Varieties of Religious Experience* in the chapter on "Mysticism." "One conclusion was forced upon my mind at that time, and my impression of its truth has ever since remained unshaken. It is that our normal waking consciousness, rational consciousness as we call it, is but one special type of consciousness, whilst all about it, parted from it by the flimsiest of screens, there lie potential forms of consciousness en-tirely different. . . . No account of the universe in its totality can be final which leaves these other forms of consciousness quite disregarded."[1] James was far too much of a rationalist to be able to get into a mystical trance state himself, but he did try to approximate that condition by experimenting with drugs, in his case with nitrous oxide (a noxious substance, though perhaps not as bad as ether, which he also recommended for this purpose). James believed, in this pre-LSD and pre-peyote era, that sometimes chloroform or even a large dose of alcohol would also suffice. Although an artificially induced state, his experiences did, he says, "converge towards a kind of insight to which I cannot help ascribing some metaphysical significance" and even a "genuine revelation." In that induced mystical experience the opposites of the world are reconciled. He admits this is a "dark saying," but adds, "I cannot wholly escape from its authority."[2] James was certainly aware that, whatever the religious tradition concerned, "mystical" experiences are often carefully cultivated and controlled and must therefore of necessity be qualitatively different from drug-induced hypnomantic states.[3]

Although in this essay I follow the footsteps of the master, I must confess that I have not experimented with hallucinogens; even a rare overdose of alcohol has not given me the kind of mystical insight that James was blessed with. More-over, James was only peripherally acquainted with Buddhism, whereas I come from a Buddhist background and, alongside my sympathy for both James and Buddhist thought, I also possess an intellectual affinity with thinkers like Nietz-sche and Freud who broke the barriers that separate our normal consciousness from other forms of consciousness (the subconscious for James and the uncon-scious for Freud). In this essay I will tentatively open up to critical reflection a specific variety of the so-called mystical experience that James dealt with more systematically.

Anthropology, the discipline I represent, has dealt extensively with alien "modes of thought" and made detailed sociological analyses of spirit possession, shamanic trances, and related states, but rarely as vehicles for ideas to germi-nate and emerge as modes of thinking. James believed that the pathologies from which mystics suffer did not disqualify their religious experience. Yet some mod-ern studies have implicitly and or explicitly tended to pathologize trance and vi-sionary states, and this is also true of such labels as "altered states of conscious-ness" or "out-of-body experiences" or the "paranormal." The moment you speak of altered states of consciousness you treat consciousness as the primary and indubitable desideratum and such things as trance, meditation, rapture, vision-ary experiences, and so forth are deviations of some sort from a norm of con-sciousness. So is it with the term paranormal. I would ask, are dreams paranormal?

Similarly with the body, which, in the West, is again a fixed point, an indubitable reality, and out-of-body experiences have implicit pathological connotations. That "indubitable reality" is something that virtually every dreamer and visionary in this book has explicitly or implicitly questioned. While there are multiple forms of trance in the cross-cultural record, every society outside the European Enlightenment held that, except for spirit attack, forms of trance were desirable experiences, even though difficult to achieve. It was almost everywhere believed that, while spurious trances did occur, genuine trances provided access to knowledge outside our rational cognitive faculties that operate during our waking consciousness. I want to begin this essay with a sympathetic phenomenological understanding of Buddhist meditative trance, a form of life that has lost its popularity in the West but nevertheless continues to exist in many contemporary societies, as it did in Europe's past, and its hidden present, and in the rest of the world as one of the most powerful ways of generating knowledge or "truth," which William James also clearly recognized.[4]

It was therefore not through William James that I initially came to understand trance but from my study of the Buddha's own "enlightenment," the process whereby he realized the soteriological goal of nirvana while yet living in the world. The term *Buddha* nowadays means one who is enlightened. And in both popular and Indological discourse the derivative term *Enlightenment* refers to the Buddha's spiritual experience as he lay seated under the "bodhi tree," the tree of enlightenment, in deep meditation. Though the term *Enlightenment* has come to mean the Buddha's own transformative spiritual ascesis, there are those who prefer the terms *awakened* and *awakening*—which to me is the better translation of the Pali word *bodhi* from which the word *Buddha* is derived. My guess is that late-nineteenth-century translators imagined Theravāda Buddhism not only as the original pristine Buddhism but also one that was consonant with the spirit of modernity and science, namely, rationality or Reason. I leave scholars better qualified than I am to explore the manner in which the European Enlightenment became fused with the Buddhist, but in this essay I will use the term *awakening* rather than the more popular term *enlightenment*.[5]

If, as I said, *bodhi* means awakening, one might ask: from what state did the Buddha awaken? To anticipate my later argument, the Buddha awoke from a physical and spiritual death into a new life very much in the way of an initiation ritual, imitating, in his own inimitable way, the lives of other heroes of myth. In order to understand this view of the Buddha's spiritual experience, one must take the Buddhist mythos seriously rather than relegate it to secondary importance, the strategy of many Indologists as well as that of contemporary intellectuals in Buddhist nations.

European scholarship, influenced by its own Enlightenment, has tried to read a history behind the myth of the Buddha, his birth, life, dispensation, and death. While this is an admirable exercise, the Buddha is nothing if not a figure of the imagination for Buddhists through the many centuries. The imagined Buddha is not all that different from other mythic beings who, in popular thought, lived and walked the world. Thus the Buddha was conceived in a miraculous manner when his mother Māyā was observing the precept on sexual abstinence. She could see him as a crystal in her womb. He emerged unsullied by blood, mucus, and other birth impurities. When he was born he took seven steps and then rose in the air and surveyed the eight quarters of the world, the locus of his universal and transcendental teaching. His mother Māyā (significantly meaning "illusion") died when he was seven days old because, as some texts put it, it was inconceivable for the pure womb of the Buddha's mother to be sullied by sexual and childbirth impurity. The Buddha's mother's sister and his father's cowife brought him up: she is Mahāprajāpati Gotamī, named after the Creator of Hindu mythology, perhaps because she was the creator of Gotama (Sanskrit, Gautama), the Buddha. The name of the father also takes on mythic significance: he is Suddhodana, *odana* meaning "pure boiled (milk) rice," which in the Indic context has considerable fertility significance, either as a ritual food (milk-rice) or, according to some Vedic texts, "as a substitute for the male seed."[6] If the latter interpretation holds, then Suddhodana is endowed with a pure and rich substance or perhaps even a pure seed.[7]

When the Buddha was born, sages predicted that he would either be a world-conquering monarch or a world-renouncing Buddha. Both are models of heroes or great men (*mahāpuruṣa*), but they were of radically different orientations: one totally involved in the world of wealth and power and the other totally removed from it. They possess thirty-two bodily signs, the details of which are spelled out in Buddhist texts.[8] Modern scholars who tell us that the father of the Bodhisattva (the Buddha to be) was a minor chief or *rāja* are not only missing the point but are guilty of extrapolating an empirical reality from a mythic or symbolic set of events. For all you know, the empirical Buddha might not have had a father at all or, more likely, he had plain ordinary parents like yours or mine. This is not to say that the Buddha was not a historical figure as, indeed, Jesus was. His speaking voice vividly appears in many of the doctrinal discourses of Theravāda Buddhism, if not of Mahāyāna, where he often appears as a surreal figure. Yet it is the case that the Buddha of the Buddhist imagination was born apposite to a world conqueror. The texts make this clear by the mythicization of his father, who is presented as a great king living in wealth, splendor, and power. The father wanted the Bodhisattva to be a world conqueror, as befits his heritage, and kept

him confined to the walls of the palace, tempting him with the seductions of hedonism. The mansion of the prince has everything to satisfy the senses: women,
music and dancing, luxury. Given this context, the birth of the Buddha makes
sense: he is cast in the heroic mold of the world conqueror, the conqueror over
the very things that embodied his other and more profound birthright—that of
Buddhahood.

The confrontation of the two ideal models—royalty and renunciation—occurs
in the famous myth of the four signs, which texts say were created by the gods.[9]
As I read this myth, the prince was a prisoner of hedonism, literally prevented
from knowing the outside world by his well-intentioned father. Yet, one day, the
prince goes for a drive into the city with Channa, his charioteer. There he meets
with the spectacle of a feeble old man, a sight from which he had been insulated.
In other visits to the city he sees the spectacle of sickness, then death, and finally the transcendence of all of these in the serene calm of the yellow-robed
renouncer. The hero is confronted with the skull beneath the skin, the true nature of the world from which he had been insulated—the world of transience and
decay. And he is also presented a model for overcoming them all in the sign of the
renouncer. Note the setting: the hero travels in his splendid chariot to the city;
what confronts him there is the very opposite of that which exists within the
prison walls of his palace. When he comes back from his final trip to the city, after witnessing the sign of the homeless renouncer, he is told that a son is born to
him, reminding him that he is trapped in a life of domesticity, that of the home,
which, in the Buddhist renouncer tradition is another kind of prison. The child is
named Rāhula, the "fetter," the chain that binds the Bodhisattva to the world and
imprisons him there. But he decides to break this fetter and, silently bidding his
wife and son farewell, he prepares to leave the palace.[10]

Prior to his departure, the Bodhisattva confronts the seamy spectral side of
his harem, the once-beautiful women in their resplendent attire. "He saw those
women who had lain aside their musical instruments and were sleeping, some
with saliva pouring out of their mouths, some with the bodies wet with saliva,
some grinding their teeth, some talking in their sleep, some groaning, some with
gaping mouths and some others with their clothes in disorder revealing plainly
those parts of the body which should be kept concealed for fear of shame. . . . The
large terrace of his mansion, magnificently decorated and resembling the abode
of Sakka [Indra, the king of the gods] appeared to him as a charnel ground full of
corpses scattered here and there."[11] The skull beneath the skin once again and
the images of disgust resurrected time and again in Buddhist meditative practices on "revulsion." This powerful myth is also known to practically everyone
attuned to the living Buddhist traditions. It is also a "myth model" for other sto-

ries and other lives in Buddhist literature. It is of someone who is a prisoner of hedonism and/or of domesticity, then, seeing their unsatisfactory nature, deciding to renounce the world that contains them and idealizes them, the worlds of the king and the Brahmin, the one representing power and the life of the senses, the other the life of domestic harmony.[12]

Satiated with hedonism and indifferent to political power, the Bodhisattva leaves his palace accompanied by his charioteer Channa and his horse, Kanthaka, the latter portrayed in heroic dimensions in the Buddhist imagination. The horse reached the river Anomā, which it cleared in one bound, landing on the other shore. There the Bodhisattva cut his hair and beard, shed his royal clothes, and then donned mendicant garb, a change of attire that is ritually enacted to this very day when novices are initiated as fully ordained monks. Crossing the river in this and in similar cases is also a symbolic act: a movement from one form of life to another, from the world of the world conqueror to that of the world renouncer. The cutting off of worldly ties is complete, but he has still not achieved his goal of Buddhahood. The Bodhisattva is still not a Buddha; he remains a liminal persona.[13] He has given up his royal status, but he has not yet "accomplished his aim," the meaning of his first name, Siddhārtha. Like neophytes in initiation rites and other heroes of myth, the Bodhisattva has many obstacles to overcome before he reaches his goal. These are not physical obstacles, however, but obstacles that have moral and spiritual meaning.

After he renounces the world, the Bodhisattva seeks the help of gurus, as is customary in the Indic traditions. Following such advice, he courts forms of extreme physical penance and deprivation—also common at the time—for six years. The pain, endurance, and suffering of the Bodhisattva are described in the first person in several texts, and his physical emaciation is vividly represented in memorable Buddhist sculptures and paintings. The Buddha himself says that at this time he lived on virtually nothing, "unclothed, flouting life's decencies, licking my hands (after meals)."[14] He describes the types of taboos pertaining to the acceptance of alms that perhaps was common practice among ascetic sects of the time and totally against the highly decorous practices formulated by the Buddha after the monk order was established. So with the kinds of cloths he wore: "I wore rags taken from the dust heap, and I wore tree-bark fiber . . . I wore a blanket of human hair, and I wore a blanket of animal hair, and I wore owl's feathers. I was one who plucked out the hair of his head and beard . . . I made my bed on covered thorns . . . Thus in many a way did I live intent on the practice of mortifying and tormenting my body."[15] And the effect of these practices? "Because I ate so little, all my limbs became like the knotted joints of withered creepers; because I ate so little, my buttocks became like a bullock's hoof; because I ate so little my

1.1 Tissa Ranasinghe,
Mortification: The Starving Buddha.
Collection of the artist

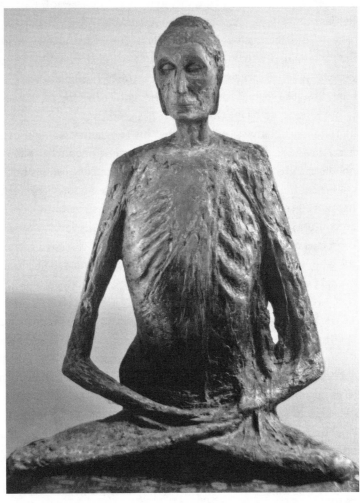

protruding backbone became like a string of balls; because I ate so little my gaunt ribs became like the crazy rafters of a tumble-down shed; because I ate so little, the pupils of my eyes appeared lying low and deep in their sockets as sparkles of water in a deep well appear lying low and deep; because I ate so little, my scalp became shriveled and shrunk as a bitter white gourd cut before it is ripe becomes shriveled and shrunk by a hot wind. If I, Sāriputta [addressing a chief disciple], thought: 'I will touch the skin of my belly,' it was my backbone that I took hold of. For because I ate so little, the skin on my belly, Sāriputta, came to be cleaving to my backbone. If I, Sāriputta, thought: 'I will obey the calls of nature' I fell down on my face then and there, because I ate so little."[16]

What then is happening here? On one level this is an experience with death, and some texts present it as a death. Thus the *Mahāsaccaka Sutta* of the *Majjhima Nikāya*: "Now when deities saw me, some said, 'the ascetic Gotama is dead.' Other deities said: 'The recluse Gotama is not dead, he is dying.' And other deities said: 'The recluse Gotama is not dead nor dying; he is an arahant, for such is the way arahants abide.'"[17] The popular *Jātaka Nidāna* puts it more bluntly: when the Buddha was practicing these austerities, the thirty-two bodily markers of the great man disappeared, and some deities thought he had died and announced to his father King Suddhodana that "your son is dead."[18]

Suddhodana knows, however, that his son cannot die without fulfilling his mission. And so does the anthropologist, because neophytes in initiation rites do not die in a physical sense either. On another level one can say that the Bodhisattva is now the prisoner of asceticism! In practicing asceticism, the Bodhisattva has moved from the indulgence of sensual pleasures to its very opposite—the mortification of the body. And yet there is a further level of personal, even unconscious meaning: by punishing his body, the Bodhisattva is trying to expiate the guilt he feels for violating powerful family values and ideals of filial and domestic piety by forsaking his wife, son, and parents. He must overcome this obstacle as well to achieve the "middle path."

The night he gave up asceticism the Bodhisattva dreamt five dreams prognosticating that he would be a Buddha. There are many versions of what happened when he decided to give up extreme asceticism, but let me give the version in the *Jātaka Nidāna*. His companions in asceticism left him when he went around in villages begging for alms and eating food once again. And soon enough the thirty-two signs of the great man reappeared in his body, indicating that the time was ripe to achieve his goal of Buddhahood. The first meal on this occasion is appropriately one consumed on auspicious occasions, namely milk-rice. It is given to him by a woman from the merchant class (*varṇa*) who had vowed to offer food to the deity of the banyan tree under which the Buddha was seated. She was the first human witness to the new birth or awakening, and this event determines her name, Sujātā, "happy birth."[19] After the Buddha consumes his meal, he wants to know whether he is going to achieve true knowledge or not. He makes a vow: if his begging bowl goes upstream when placed in the river Nerañjarā it would be a sign that he had achieved true knowledge. This happens, and the bowl is carried by the river's vortex into the realm of the *nāgas* (snake beings), generally devotees of the Buddha, and there it meets the bowls of three previous Buddhas. The symbolism here I think is clear: the Buddha, in practicing austerities, has experienced a kind of death. But this physical rebirth is not the crucial one; it is followed by a psychological and spiritual awakening to come later. The bowl that goes "against the current" symbolizes a teaching that goes counter to normal human drives.

The Buddha now moves from the banyan tree to the bodhi tree (*Ficus religiosa*) nearby, the tree under which he would achieve his spiritual awakening. Facing the East, again symbolizing a rising, he decided not to move till he had found out the truth of existence. The next mythic episode occurs when, meditating under the bodhi tree, he is assailed by Māra, or Death himself (who is also Eros of the Buddhist imagination), waging war against the Buddha. This final episode is described in graphic detail in the popular traditions, and I shall not deal with them here except to say that Māra attacked the Buddha with multiple weapons, but the sage remained untouched, such being the power of the perfections (*pāramitā*), the moral heroisms practiced in past births.

According to the *Bhayabherava Sutta* (The Discourse on Fear and Dread), the Buddha, during the first watch of the night, entered into the four states of meditative trance (Pali, *jhāna*; Sanskrit, *dhyāna*) leading to complete equanimity, which permitted him to recollect in all details his former existences. Thus: "I recollected all my manifold past lives, that is, one birth, two births, three births, forty births, fifty births, a hundred births, a thousand births, a hundred thousand births, many eons of world-contraction and expansion: 'There I was so named, of such a clan, with such an appearance, such was my nutriment, such my experience of pleasure and pain, such my life-term; and passing from there, I reappeared elsewhere; and there too I was so named, of such a clan, with such an appearance, such was my nutriment, such my experience of pleasure and pain, such my life-term; and passing away from there, I reappeared here.'"[20] Following this fantastic event, the text has the Buddha mention his own assessment of truth-realization through vision: "This was the first true knowledge attained by me in the first watch of the night. Ignorance was banished and true knowledge arose, darkness was banished and light arose, as happens in one who abides diligent, ardent, and resolute."[21] In the last part of this sentence, the Buddha is emphasizing another truth, as he does in other texts as well, that is, his experience of trance and knowledge arising from it is also available to other Buddhist virtuosos.[22]

During the second watch, the Buddha with his "divine eye" redirected his mind to the long panorama of the passing and rising of human beings such that he could see them "passing away and reappearing, inferior and superior, fair and ugly, fortunate and unfortunate" in this world and in heavens and hells and in subhuman existences through the operation of the universal action of karma and rebirth.[23] According to several sources, it was during the second watch that his divine eye was further purified:

> And then with that sight,
> spotless and divine,
> he saw the entire world,
> as if in a stainless looking glass.[24]

And in the last watch, which must surely be close to dawn and to a literal awakening, he discovered the nature of error and the Four Noble Truths of Buddhism and, according to some accounts, the critical theory of causal interconnectedness of things known as *paticcasamuppāda* (Sanskrit, *pratitya samutpāda*), translated as "dependent origination" or "conditioned genesis," that things have no reality on their own but are relative and dependent on one another and consequently lack inherent existence.[25] No form of essence underlies the changing world of existence.[26]

After this first awakening, according to popular accounts, the Buddha spent another seven weeks (some say seven days) in meditation where he met with further spiritual adventures in an entirely vivid imagistic medium. The most famous of these is where Māra's three daughters named Taṇhā (Desire or Greed), Aratī (Delusion), and Ragā (Sexual Passion) entice him with lustful pleasures. They tell their father Māra that some men desire virgins, others women in the prime of life, while yet others prefer middle-aged or old women, and that they would take all these guises to seduce the Bodhisattva. But the Buddha, still meditating on the moral perfections or heroisms (*pāramitā*), remained unmoved.[27] One can say that the daughters of Māra constitute the return of the women of the harem, but without their masks and marks of disgust. It is also the return of the repressed threatening to break through the controls imposed by asceticism. Yet eroticism cannot tempt the sage because his deep meditational trances (*jhānas*) have taken him beyond desire and he cannot succumb to temptation. To use Freudian language: with the extinction of sexual desire, the neurotic operation of the repetition compulsion ceases and the repressed cannot return to haunt the sage.[28]

After the seven weeks (or days) are over, the hero is reborn again, or, in Buddhist terminology, he is the Fully Awakened One (*sammā sambuddha*), a term that European scholars, influenced, I think, by their own Enlightenment, have generously sanctified as "the Enlightenment." The double entendre of *awakened* is very significant: first, the Buddha has passed the liminal stage and emerged into a new life form and the founding of a new order; second, his is a spiritual awakening, a discovery of a way of salvific knowledge.

While I have focused on the Buddha's spiritual awakening, I do not want to deny that other ascetics of the time did not have similar experiences. The initiatory model I have adopted helps us consider renouncers like the Jaina leader Mahāvīra who might have had similar experiences based on the following sequence: breaking away from the home to a life of homelessness; a liminal period of painful spiritual experiences (a form of the dark night of the soul), followed by the discovery of new knowledge; the symbolism of death and awakening and the initiate's reemergence into a new life form, that of a renouncer (and, for some, the formation of a new religious or monastic or ascetic order). *Awakened* then can be employed as a general term for those virtuosos who have achieved this state through the initiatory spiritual model based on a symbolic death and rebirth. So is it with Christ. Christianity's resurrection myth also begins with that of the founder, Jesus; his suffering on the cross; the abandonment by his father and his male disciples during his darkest hour; his ignominious death and empty tomb; and his glorious awakening. The Christ and Buddha mythos have radically different substantive and salvific meanings, but, on the structural level, they both conform to the model that I sketch here. The empirical or actual lives of the two founders have been retranslated into the symbolism of suffering, a death that is illusory or "empty," followed by an awakening that in their differing ways and historical trajectory led to the founding of a new religious order. I'd stretch the dictum of Tertullian of Carthage and say that, for believers, the Christ or the Buddha mythos and similar hero myths have to be "true" because they are "absurd."

The genealogy whereby the Buddha's spiritual awakening was fused with that of the European Enlightenment is outside the purview of this essay. The idea of Theravāda Buddhism as a "rational religion" was a popular nineteenth-century Eurocentric prejudice that soon filtered into the thinking of Buddhist intellectuals through such popular sources as Theosophy. It was the Theosophist cum rationalist Colonel H. S. Olcott who asserted that "Buddhism was, in a word, a philosophy, and not a creed."[29] This has become the standard view of later native intellectuals, some of whom even imagine the Buddha as an empiricist of the British sort. Yet, contrary to modern intellectuals, the Buddhist ratio is radically different from both the Greek and the European Enlightenments.[30] If the European Enlightenment with its reification of rationality ignored or condemned visionary experiences, not so with the Greek, it seems to me. Plato employed Reason to discover true knowledge, but neither he nor his Socrates condemned or ignored such things as the work of visionaries and prophets and he personally believed in the oracle at Delphi. By contrast, the Buddha denounced all sorts of popular "superstitions" as base or beastly arts in a famed discourse known as the *Brahmajāla Sutta* (the net of Brahma), but never visions and knowledge emerging through meditative trance (*jhāna*).[31] Other Buddhas had discovered the same truths before and, when the knowledge of the doctrine would have faded, yet other Buddhas would arise to rediscover it. The Platonic type of Reason or the rationality of the Enlightenment has second place in Buddhism, which involves the elaboration and discursive exposition of the intuitively discovered truths. Yet, like its European and Greek parallels, Buddhism's ratio is full of abstract terms ("conceptualism") to describe the nature of the world and the release from it, even though, at least in the Buddhist dialogues or *suttas*, they are embodied in a specific type of narrative framework (which is also true of their Platonic counterparts). Finally, relegation of the Buddhist ratio to secondary importance is once again apparent in Buddhism's soteriological stance. As in the case of the Buddha's own awakening, forms of discursive and rational thinking must be abandoned at a certain stage in the quest for salvation. I think one can even say that the Buddha's experience under the bodhi tree is the *mysterium tremendum* of Buddhism.

TIME AND SPACE IN VISIONARY EXPERIENCE

> Let the human organs be kept in their perfect Integrity,
> At will Contracting into Worms or Expanding into Gods,
> And then, behold! What are these Ulro Visions of Chastity?
> Then as the moss upon the tree, or dust upon the plow,
> Or as the sweat upon the labouring shoulder, or as the chaff
> Of the wheat-floor or as the dregs of the sweet wine-press,
> Such as these Ulro-Visions: for tho' we sit down within
> The plowed furrow, listening to the weeping clods till we
> Contract or Expand Space at will; or if we raise ourselves
> Upon the chariots of the morning, Contracting or Expanding Time,
> Everyone knows we are One Family, One Man blessed for ever.
> —William Blake, *Jerusalem* [32]

Let me get back to the Buddha's meditative trance during the second watch where, with his "divine eye," he sees human beings passing through *saṃsāra*, the realm of continuing existences, from their human lives to their fate in heavens and hells, all of which are dependent on their karma. The visuality of this experience mediated by his special sight or divine eye is what I want to consider.[33] During the first watch the text says that he recollected or remembered his past existences, including eons of world expansion and contraction, but whether this is "remembering" in our conventional usage is open to doubt. Here also I think his past life appears before him in visual form, as was his vision of the fate of others during the second watch. All of this occurs during the first two watches of the night, each watch being a period of four hours. In this kind of experience, empirical time, or time as we normally understand it in our waking lives, gets stretched in incredible ways. There is a disparity between normal time and dream time, or between time and visionary experience, such that we can dream of long episodes in a few short time-bound moments. In the first two watches of the night the Buddha's experiences of time embrace eons of world renewal and destruction. Yet these "timeless" experiences or experiences out of time are framed within four-hour time-bound periods ("watches"), culturally structured notions of time. I must emphasize, however, that the analytical distinction I have made between empirical and mythic time makes no sense to the visionary. The visionary has transcended empirical time and is attuned to another level of temporal reality, which is what is meaningful to him. Visionary time cannot be measured.

I like to make the case that in many ways the Buddha's experience with time has its parallel in the dream experience so brilliantly examined by Freud, who noted the compression-expansion of time as a feature of dreams, although outside the dream-work. He mentions the case of a "dramatic author" named Casimir Bonjour who wanted to sit with the audience during the first performance of one of his pieces. "But he was so fatigued that as he was sitting behind the scenes he dozed off just at the moment the curtain went up. During his sleep he went through the whole five acts of the play, and observed the various signs of emotion shown by the audience during the different scenes. At the end of the performance he was delighted to hear his name being shouted with the liveliest demonstrations of applause. Suddenly he woke up. He could not believe either his eyes or his ears for the performance had not gone beyond the first few lines of the first scene; he could not have been asleep for more than two minutes."[34] Although Freud did not think of the contrast between empirical and mythic or cosmic time as a function of the dream-work, every dreamer has surely experienced it.[35] And it needed a Hindu god to turn this notion of time on its head, such that empirical time is infinitesimally minute in comparison with the cosmic sense of time. Viṣṇu blinks his eyes and a billion years have passed, billion being a metaphor for the immeasurability of visionary time. As Śāntideva, the great Buddhist poet says: "In a dream one person enjoys one hundred years of happiness and then awakes, while another awakes after being happy for just a moment."[36]

The brilliant madman Daniel Paul Schreber, who will appear and reappear in the pages of my essay, also mentions a similar compression of time in his memoirs. "From the sum total of my recollections, the impression gained hold of me that the period in question, which, according to human calculation, stretched over only three to four months, had covered an immensely long period, it was as if single nights had the duration of centuries, so that within that time the most profound alterations in the whole of mankind, in the earth itself and the whole solar system could very well have taken place."[37] He recalls another experience when he was "sitting in a railway carriage or a lift driving into the depths of the earth and I recapitulated, as it were, the whole history of mankind on the earth in reverse order; in the upper regions there were still forests of leafy trees; in the nether regions it became progressively darker and blacker." Schreber left the vehicle temporarily and saw a cemetery with his wife's gravestone (in reality his wife was alive at that time). This is to be expected, because he is seeing mankind's "devolution" beginning in reverse from time future into time past, rather than the other way around (M, 78–79). This is an un-Darwinian dream, but it needed Darwin before one could dream it.

Schreber's vision of time expansion possessed a similar reality to the Buddha's vision of the arising and rebirth of countless existences. The difference is that the Buddha's is a vision of the past, not the reversed time of Schreber. Yet Schreber believes his expanded time was real time and that real devolutionary changes had taken place on earth.[38] One might add that in diving down into the depths of the earth Schreber was also delving (without being aware of it) into the depths of his psyche. To sum up: the compression-expansion of time then is found not only in the visionary experience but also in dreams and in the psychoses, although the one cannot be reduced to the other.

Later on in the dream book, Freud, in accordance with his view that there is no real creativity in dreams, asserted that dreams such as Casimir Bonjour's did not produce any fresh thoughts during sleep but rather "may have reproduced a piece of phantasy-activity . . . which has already been completed" (ID, 498–99). By "phantasy activity" he means a prepackaged fantasy, even a daytime fantasy or daydream that reappears at night and consequently there is no "distortion," that phenomenon crucial to the dream-work. "The dream-work is glad to make use of the ready-made phantasy instead of putting one together out of the material of the dream thoughts" (ID, 495). Here then is an interesting type of dream existing outside the dream thoughts even though dominated by unconscious fantasy and wish fulfillment. However, whether the Buddha's visionary knowledge is a fantasy activity in Freud's sense or one productive of original ideation is something I will deal with later.

What about space and how are visions related to space? This is a complicated question because in Buddhist visions space is virtually illimitable, and visionaries have space adventures of a fantastic nature surpassing that of shamanic visionaries in their cosmic travels. For now, following the preceding argument, I will present a few examples of the visionary expansion of empirical space into mythic space, once again, I believe, having its parallel in the dream life.

1. The first is a well-known story from the *Bhagavata Purāna*, the great text of devotional Hinduism. "One day, when Krishna was still a little baby, some boys saw him eating mud. When his foster mother, Yasoda, learned of it, she asked the baby to open his mouth. Krishna opened his tiny mouth, and, wonder of wonders! Yasoda saw the whole universe—the earth, the stars, the planets, the sun, and the moon and innumerable beings—within the mouth of Baby Krishna. For a moment Yasoda was bewildered thinking, 'Is this a dream or a hallucination? Or is it a real vision, the vision of my little baby as God himself?'"[39]

2. Consider now the extraordinary experience of an Indian sage who has a vision and a dream within the vision and a dream within the dream. "In the old days I lived alone in a hermitage. I studied magic. I entered someone else's body and saw all his organs; I entered his head and then I saw a universe, with a sun and an ocean and mountains, and gods and demons and human beings. This universe was his dream and I saw his dream. Inside his head, I saw his city and his wife and his servants and his son."[40]

3. Here is Julian of Norwich (c. 1342–1416): "And I was still awake, and then our Lord opened my spiritual eyes and showed me my soul in the middle of my heart. I saw my soul as large as it were a kingdom; and from the properties that I saw in it, it seemed to me to be a glorious city. In the centre of that city sits our Lord Jesu, true God and true man, glorious, highest Lord: and I saw him dressed imposingly in glory."[41] In Julian's *Revelations of Divine Love*, the vision of expanded space could be simultaneously literal and symbolic, at the very least a visualization of the idea that the kingdom of god is within oneself. As Julian says: "He sits in the soul, in the very centre, in peace and rest, and he rules and protects heaven and earth and all that is."[42]

The reverse process wherein a large space is telescoped into a small one also occurs but not as commonly. Here is the Tibetan space traveler and "treasure seeker" Pemalingpa (1450–1519) writing of this kind of experience: "I had a bamboo hut erected on the hill called Sershong above the monastery and while we, the lord and his disciples, were staying there I made the disciples attend to their training. While I was staying in retreat there for three months I had sight of the whole world like a myrobalan flower placed in the palm of one's hand, entirely clear and pure."[43] Reverse telescoping of space is also beautifully expressed in the Tibetan theory of meditation in the Kālacakra tradition wherein at a certain point during *sādhana* (Tantric practice) the meditator "can visualize the entire *maṇḍala* [the circle of deities] in a drop the size of a mustard seed at the tip of one's nose, with such clarity that one can see the whites of the eyes of all 722 deities—and can maintain this visualization with uninterrupted one-pointed concentration for four hours."[44]

Unsurprisingly, the expansion-contraction of space experienced by the visionary also appears in exaggerated form in the myths of Mahāyāna. I will quote a few accomplishments of awakened Bodhisattvas from the second- or third-century *Avatamsaka Sutra* (Flower Ornament Scripture), a Mahāyāna text later appropriated by the Chinese Hua Yan schools and Zen that also influenced Tibetan Buddhism. Bear in mind that these are authorial statements highlighting the powers of the idealized Bodhisattvas and not their actual voices. Nevertheless, I cannot imagine that these accomplishments could have been invented if they were experience-alien. "These enlightening beings [Bodhisattvas] have ten kinds of knowledge of skills in entry into great concentration: they make a billion-world universe a single lotus blossom and appear sitting cross-legged on this lotus blossom, covering it entirely, and in the body manifest another billion-world universe, wherein there are ten billion quadruplex earths, in each of which they manifest ten billion bodies, each body entering into one hundred sextillion billion-world universes."[45]

Soon the author of this text as a theoretician discusses, as I did, the distinction between visionary and empirical time and space. He attributes to the Bodhisattva the capacity to control his meditative trance to such a degree that visionary time and space can be coordinated with everyday temporal and spatial conceptions. It is not as if the Bodhisattva himself notes or cares about this issue. Rather the author qua theoretician informs us, his readership, about the Bodhisattva's power to frame the visionary experience in ordinary terms. Thus: "[In] the space of a moment he may manifest a day or a night, or he may make it appear to be seven days and nights, or a fortnight, a month, a year, a century, according to desire, he can manifest the appearance of cities, towns, villages, springs, streams, rivers, seas, sun, moon, clouds, rain, palaces, mansions, houses, all of this complete. Yet he does not destroy the original one day or one hour by making it appear that years have passed, and the brevity of the actual time does not destroy the appearance of the passage of days, months, or years."[46] The Bodhisattva, this text tells us, appears like a magician performing tricks at the crossroads. "So is it with the bodies of the buddhas: when they are seen as large, still there is no increase, and when they are seen as small, there is no decrease. Just as the moon is seen as small by people on earth, yet is not diminished, and is seen as large by beings on the moon, yet does not expand, so also do enlightening beings [Bodhisattvas] in this concentration see various transfigurations of the buddhas' bodies, according to their inclinations . . . there being all the while no increase or decrease in the body of the Enlightened [Awakened]."[47]

CRITIQUE OF THE COGITO: THE BUDDHA, NIETZSCHE, AND FREUD

Where got I that truth?
Out of a medium's mouth,
Out of nothing it came,
Out of the forest loam,
Out of dark night where lay
The crowns of Nineveh.
—W. B. Yeats, "Fragments"

I shall now present perhaps the more controversial part of my argument, namely, what I think is meant by the Buddha giving primacy to knowledge acquired through concentration, which requires the abandonment and the emptying of the mind of discursive knowledge and its readoption after the experience is over. In my view a special kind of thought operates in his meditative ascesis: the agency involved is not the "I" of the discursively reasoning and active consciousness; rather it is the "It," to use the Nietzschean term. Nietzsche says: "A thought comes when 'it' wishes and not when 'I' wish, so that it is a falsification of the facts of the case to say that the subject 'I' is the condition of the predicate 'think.' It thinks: but that this "it" is precisely the famous old "ego" is, to put it mildly, only a supposition, an assertion, and assuredly not an immediate certainty."[48] For Nietzsche, even "It-thinking" is tainted with agency, compelling one to think "according to grammatical habit."[49] It seems that Nietzsche is highlighting a form of thinking, seemingly without agency, and for purposes of convenience I will borrow his trope and call it "It-thinking."

Freud was indirectly influenced by Nietzsche when he borrowed the term "It" (*Es*) from the German physician Georg Groddeck. In *The Ego and the Id* (better translated as *The I and the It*), the seminal paper that gave conceptual rigor to the second topography, Freud wrote: "I am speaking of George Groddeck, who is never tired of insisting that what we call our ego behaves essentially passively in life, and that, as he expresses it, we are 'lived' by unknown and uncontrollable forces."[50] It was only in the later *New Introductory Lectures* that Freud recognized that his Id or It was a "verbal usage of Nietzsche" employed by Groddeck and reemployed by Freud as part of the tripartite division of the mind.[51] While Freud gave agentic significance to the It, he brought the term within the frame of his later neo-Cartesian framework of Ego-Id-Superego and thereby lost the prime place that Nietzsche gave to the passive It. I do not, however, believe "It-thinking" is the only way of knowing or that it is preferable to "I-thinking." Except that it is a way of thinking that has virtually gone out of vogue in mainline European intellectual life in the aftermath of the Cartesian "I think, I am" and its sense of "immediately certainty" that Nietzsche was critical of.

In similar Nietzschean fashion, William Butler Yeats speaks of the "frenzy" that possessed Timon or Lear or William Blake, those unusual people all of whom forced truth to obey the call of the seer, rather than the seer invoking the truth through the thinking-I.[52] So with the Buddha: it is certainly the case that meditation requires the Buddha to deliberately concentrate or focus his vision through an act of the will on key meditative devices that in later Buddhist thought were known as *kasina*s. But, once in full meditation, conscious discursive intellection or I-thinking or the will switches itself off as the meditator enters into states of trance or *jhāna* (*dhyāna*). It is then that knowledge appears before the Buddha, giving him the capacity for "divine vision." Not only can he see the coming into being and disappearance of people and worlds but also "thought comes" to him during the third watch of the night. While ordinary cognition and I-thinking makes sense in everyday life, not so in the meditative context, which is designed to explode the idea of a self as an enduring entity. Further, the meditator cultivates "awareness" or *sati*, but this Buddhist awareness is not a self-awareness or self-reflection as we conventionally understand those terms. For example, even in the simplest meditation on calming (*śamatha*), one is focused on breathing until everything else is cut off from consciousness and one becomes aware only of the movement of the breaths. In deeper meditative practices there is a passive opening of consciousness (using that term broadly) for thoughts to emerge or visions to appear. In fact the visions of the Buddha or those of the Buddhist seers

I discuss later have little to do with ordinary memory or the recollections of past events unless it is a recollection of past births or of a historical event. The latter are about memory inaccessible to normal or rational cognition but available to the visionary.

The Buddha's spiritual experience entails the furthermost development of the kind of "thinking" that Freud formulated in the dream-work. One must therefore go back once again to the dream book to reconsider Freud's insights about what I have labeled "It-thinking." Strictly speaking, one cannot say, as in accordance with European language use, "I had a dream." Most people would say, as Sri Lankans do, "I saw a dream." The significance of visuality in the dream thoughts was emphasized by Freud in several memorable phrases: "A thing that is pictorial is, from the point of view of a dream, a thing that is *capable of being represented*; it can be introduced into a situation in which abstract expressions offer the same kind of difficulties to representation in dreams as a political article in a newspaper would offer an illustrator" (ID, 340). Or: "A dream thought is unusable so long as it is expressed in an abstract form" but has to be "transformed into pictorial language." One might even say that dreams "dramatize an idea" (ID, 50). Again: "Dreams, then, think predominantly in visual images—but not exclusively. They make use of auditory images as well, and, to a lesser extent, of impressions belonging to other senses" (ID, 49). In dreams the causal, abstract, and logical thought processes that are associated with the waking consciousness cannot appear without being reformulated as indirect representations. When Blake says that "thought chang'd the infinite to a serpent," we find ourselves in the dream life where something abstract like the notion of the infinite could be changed into a concrete visual representation, a serpent.[53] Freud even asserts that "no" cannot be represented in dreams; and sequential logic is replaced by sequentially flowing images (ID, 312–19).

Aside from its visuality, the dream simply appears before one's dimmed and diminished consciousness. Even the dark "dream thoughts" that precipitated the manifest dream merely rise to the surface with the near suspension of the active consciousness during sleep. In dreams "we appear not to think but to experience; that is to say, we attach complete belief to the hallucinations" (ID, 50). When we are in the realm of the dream we believe what we see is real. It is governed by noesis (in James's sense of taken-for-granted truths), but of an ephemeral sort, unless the dream is also a vision and the dream-vision, like the visions we discuss in this essay, might persuade us about its truth value even after the visionary experience is over.[54] Freud adds that the hallucinatory features of dreams appear when "some kind of 'authoritative' activity of the self has ceased" (ID, 51). In other words, he is asserting that though dreams are "completely egotistical" the

"I" appears as a picture or is externalized into images that float before us in our state of sleep (ID, 358). Thus the German of "I had a dream" can be rephrased as "the dream came to me" (ID, 48). It is not surprising therefore that for Freud the dreaming mind functions like a "compound microscope or a photographic apparatus" (ID, 536). Hence in dreams the "everyday, sober method of expression is replaced by a pictorial one" (ID, 341). The "I" does not think out the dream during sleep; thinking in dreams is a passive occurrence. Even Freud's undefined "dream-ego" or "dreaming self" is not the ego of the waking consciousness (ID, 85). Freud, and later Jung, borrowed the idea of the dream-ego from K. A. Scherner, who actually used the term "fantasy-I."[55] I shall develop later my own notion of the dream-ego that takes the place of the waking "I" but, for the moment, affirm that dreams share the feature of visions as "appearances." They are "showings," as Julian of Norwich characterized her visions, perhaps recollecting the morality plays of her time. And a modern visionary mentions the folly of saying "'I imagined this'" when one should say "'the curtain was a little lifted that I might see'".[56]

We all know that for Freud the ego is not the master in his own house owing to the power of unconscious thought, thus, implicitly at least, dethroning the primacy of the Cartesian cogito. Nevertheless, though not explicitly stated, the dream book implies an even more radical position. The "I," or ego, does not appear in the formation of the dream in the first place. The physical person of course appears in the dream but pictorially, in a screen as it were, outside of the thinking "I." What is striking about the dream-work—the processes that transform thoughts into images—is that condensation and displacement can occur without the "I" being involved, though this is not how Freud himself formulated the issue. Even the "censor"—the dormant conscience of the dreamer that in vetting the dream distorts it—is a kind of mechanism that operates without the silently thinking "I" or the superego of Freud's later thought. It seems that the dream book introduces a radical model of the mind that eliminates the ego or self or reified "I" and yet, paradoxically, introduces a form of "agency" (if one may call it that) that is totally impersonal. Of course Freud uses the term *consciousness* and *preconscious* in his dream book to contrast with the unconscious, but there is no ego associated with consciousness in this early formulation. Thus the Freudian model (sometimes labeled as the "first topography") that I have extrapolated from the dream book is not the structuralist one that eliminates agency but rather one entailing a special form of agency.

The Interpretation of Dreams appeared for the first time in 1900, a reaction to Freud's earlier laboratory experiments in neurophysiology followed by his 1895 *Project for a Scientific Psychology*, later abandoned by him and published only posthumously. In that same year there also appeared the crucial work *Studies in Hysteria,* which he coauthored with Josef Breuer, whose detailed and sympathetic account of "Anna O." (Bertha Pappenheim) was creatively appropriated by Freud. In *Studies in Hysteria* Freud used what he called "cathartic techniques" or the "talking cure" (the latter term invented by Anna O.) along with hypnosis, though he was also beginning to realize the limitations of the latter in effecting a cure. Here, for the first time, appeared some important words in the Freudian lexicon in its purely psychological sense: *defense, repression, abreaction,* and, above all, the significance of unconscious motivation. And, though the term *ego* is rarely used in the dream book, it appears all the time in *Studies in Hysteria,* especially in Freud's own chapter, "The Psychotherapy of Hysteria." It also appears prominently in the *Project for a Scientific Psychology.* It reappears in virtually everything Freud wrote after the dream book. In other words, the dream book is sandwiched between texts that are full of references to the ego or the self. This means that it is the "first topography" expressed in *The Interpretation of Dreams,* rather than his later "second topography" of the tripartite Id-Ego-Superego that produced a model of the mind that fully rejects the Cartesian centrality of the ego. It is here one senses Freud's belatedly acknowledged debt to Nietzsche.

In his work on hysteria, Freud drew attention to a powerful visual mode of thought similar to that prevailing in dreams. He presents the case of a "very intelligent and apparently happy young married woman [who] had consulted me about an obstinate pain in her abdomen which was resistant to treatment" (SH, 276).[57] This originally muscular pain reemerged as a hysterical symptom later, and the lady herself recognized its "nervous" origin. At this time Freud had developed a somewhat bizarre therapeutic technique of putting pressure with his hand on the patient's forehead and, in somewhat of an authoritarian mode, insisting that she recollect her unconscious thoughts in the form of a picture or of an idea occurring to her. He then "pledges" the patient to communicate this picture or idea to him (SH, 270). Now, employing this technique, Freud asked his patient if she saw anything. Initially she reported visual pictures that Freud thought were "phosphenes" purely physiological in origin. But later the patient produced much more interesting images.

> She saw a large black cross, leaning over, which had round its edges the same shimmer of light with which all her other pictures had shone, and on whose cross-beam a small flame flickered. Clearly there could no longer be any question of a phosphene here. I now listened carefully. Quantities of pictures appeared bathed in the same light, curious signs looking rather like Sanskrit; figures like triangles, among them a large triangle; the cross once more. . . . This time I suspected an

allegorical meaning and asked what the cross could be. "It probably means pain," she replied. I objected that by "cross" one usually meant a moral burden. What lay concealed behind the pain? She could not say, and went on with her visions: a sun with golden rays. And this she was also able to interpret. "It's God, the primeval force." Then came a gigantic lizard which regarded her enquiringly but not alarmingly. Then a heap of snakes. Then once more a sun but with mild, silver rays; and in front of her, between her and this source of light, a grating which hid the centre of the sun from her. I had known for some time what I had to deal with were allegories and at once asked the meaning of this last picture. She answered without hesitation: "The sun is perfection, the ideal, and the grating represents my weaknesses and faults which stand between me and the ideal." "Are you reproaching yourself, then?"

(SH, 277–78)

She admitted this and said she was a member of the Theosophical Society and has been reading their literature, including some translations of Sanskrit texts. Freud concluded that the pictures were "symbols of trains of thought influenced by the occult and were perhaps actually emblems from the title-pages of books," that is, they represented what he would later label "phantasy activity" (SH, 278). He added that "hysterical patients, who are as a rule of a 'visual' type, do not make such difficulties for the analyst as those with obsessions." The pictures "emerge from the patient's memory," but as she proceeds to describe them the visual sequences become more and more fragmented. "The patient is, as it were, getting rid of it [the image] *by turning it into words*" (SH, 280; my emphasis). Freud seems to say that if discursive thought supervenes then hysterical imagery, just like the imagery of dreams, simply disappears "like a ghost that has been laid" (SH, 281).

Freud's discussion shows, among other things, how a particular culture, perhaps the Victorian middle class in general, suppresses a certain mode of "thought" that, in the terminology I have adopted, implies "It-thinking." Had Freud's talented female patients lived in Sri Lanka or ancient Greece, or almost anywhere else in the pre-Enlightenment world, they would have had at least the option of becoming prophetesses or priestesses or some type of respected religious specialist. Yet, in spite of his cultural belief regarding the "pathology" of such thought processes, Freud at least gave his patient the opportunity to formulate, even briefly, the allegorical significance of her visions. Further, as in dreams, visualization can be based on prior ratiocinative processes; that is, the patient had read theosophical articles on the occult, which perhaps also accentuated the significance of thinking in images. To put it differently: "I-thinking" can be converted into "It-thinking" during special conditions where "intention" has been suspended and, to switch to Breuer's late-nineteenth-century conceptual language, when the patient is in a kind of "somnolent" or "hypnoid" state.[58]

One must not assume that cerebral activity is suspended during this state. Hence my idea of passive cerebration as against the active I-dependent cerebral activity involved in our rational discursive thinking processes. Or, going back to Christianity's past, John of the Cross tells us that one hears God with the hearing of the soul and one sees God "with the eye of the passive intellect," that is, a kind of passive thinking that arises from the soul and not to be identified with ratio or Reason.[59] And, speaking of locutions, John perceptively adds that the "soul receives God's communication passively" and that the "reception of the light infused supernaturally into the soul is passive knowing."[60] And let us not forget Meister Eckhart, who posits the idea of man's active intellect, "but when the action at hand is undertaken by God, the mind must remain passive."[61] "If you forsake your own knowledge and will, then surely and gladly God will enter with his knowledge shining clearly;" and when "man's own efforts are suspended and all the soul's agents are at God's disposal" they "come flooding out of man from God."[62]

Breuer's famous patient Anna O., in a self-induced hypnoid state, had "frightening hallucinations of black snakes, which was how she saw her hair, ribbons and similar things" (SH, 24)—thereby showing the inner affinity between a Victorian fantasy and the cultural cum personal symbolic forms that I have recorded in *Medusa's Hair* for Sri Lankan priestesses who also saw their matted locks as snakes.[63] I am suggesting that a similar form of thinking characterizes the visions of shamans and spirit mediums. The vivid, hallucinatory knowledge appears before the individual in trance. The dream-work, as a seemingly impersonal and mechanistic, process led Freud to conclude that inventiveness and creativity do not appear in it, because he simply could not accept the idea of passive cerebral activity of the It, even though he was a pioneer formulating the irrational deep motivations or primary process or unconscious "thinking." The idea of the dream-work does not make sense if there is no "thinking" involved, as Freud recognized. Yet, it is hard to believe the absence of creativity when, through the dream-work, composite formations of rich visual panoramas, places, persons and events appear in the dream.[64] My own dreams are not unique when I often see places and people who are not known to me but must surely be constructed through the dream-work. Landscapes appeared in rich color and variety in my youthful dreams, but they were only peripherally connected with those familiar to me. They are invented or composed or put together in coherent form through the passive cerebral activity that occurs during the dream-work. Yet I believe that some such idea of creative inventiveness is implicit in Freud's notion of the products of the unconscious as "indirect representations."

So is it with surreal dreams of his patients in their manifest content. Freud could not think of his hysterics as creative people or that pathology might have a creative side to it. And, precisely because of their pathological nature, the patient's creative visual thinking cannot be permitted to remain in her mind. For Freud the patient's attempt to give allegorical meaning and significance to her visual images could not possibly have a therapeutic function. He and other Freudians think that creativity and innovation must entail the actively thinking "I," and this simply could not occur when consciousness is suspended.

Freud of course used the term *It* or *Id* in another sense in his second topography, to designate an area of the mind rather than a process of thought. I would like to retain the insights I have extrapolated from the dream book as a non-Cartesian model that deals with passive cerebral activity in the dream-work and the concomitant absence of the ego or the thinking-I.[65] In my view, the ideal goal of free association is to bring about a similar recollection of the past without the mediation of the "I," even though this ideal is rarely realized. Remember that the beginnings of this technique lay with Breuer's Anna O., whose "talking cure" (or "chimney sweeping" as she facetiously called it) occurred in a kind of hypnoid condition induced by the patient herself (SH, 30). In mature psychoanalysis, the analysand lies on the couch, a place of rest, and the analyst is the silent supportive being analogous to the *kalyāna mitra* (the "true friend") of Buddhist meditation who assists the truth seeker to overcome the terrors of the fantastic in the early stages of the meditative process. The *kalyāna mitra* acts as a stand-in for the rational consciousness of the meditator that has been temporarily suspended and whose terrifying visions threaten to overwhelm him. In this situation, the stand-in guide can further help the meditator to bring about a coexistence of the "I" and the "It" after awakening from his dark night of terror.[66]

Although not as radical as the Buddhist, in psychoanalysis also the analytic situation facilitates the suspension of discursive thought and sets the stage for free association (though Freud himself sometimes cavalierly disregarded his own rules). A space has been created for non-discursive thoughts to emerge, in spite of the fact that the couch itself is enveloped in the whole frame of Enlightenment rationality. Hilda Doolittle says of her experience of recall during her psychoanalysis by the master himself: "I wish to recall the impressions, or rather I wish the impressions to recall me." Again: "Let the impressions come in their own way, make their own sequence."[67] But these impressions that flow out of the analysand are quite different from dreams and hysteria because there is no transformation of thoughts into images. Hilda Doolittle's example suggests that other kinds of thoughts also can appear in the mind when discursive "I-thinking" has been partially suspended, as in free association and related conditions such as reveries and daydreams. The Buddhist meditative trances or *jhāna* by contrast are extreme developments of "It-thinking" and no wonder one must suspend discursive thought ("I-thinking") as a prerequisite and this in turn entails over-coming the false notion of "I," according to Buddhism. The crux of meditation is to develop "It-thinking" both in its visual and imagistic forms and what I might tentatively call its free-associational forms such that even philosophical ideas ("truths") appear into the field of the thinker's vision without the mediation of egoistic discursive thinking. James makes a similar point in relation to the "no-etic quality" of mystical knowledge: "Mystical states seem to those who experi-ence them to be also states of knowledge. They are states of insight into depths of truth unplumbed by the discursive intellect. They are illuminations, revela-tions, full of significance and importance, all inarticulate though they remain; and as a rule they carry with them a curious sense of authority for after-time."[68]

It seems appropriate to further consider Freud's notion of "phantasy activity" and ask ourselves whether knowledge emerging from meditative trance is itself based on prior "phantasy activity." Perhaps; but, even if the vision is influenced by phantasy activity or prior thoughts, it is not a reflex of such activity but trans-formed through the working of the "passive intellect." What we do know is that, once the truths have been discovered intuitively through the special passive agency of the "It," there is a later process, truly a process of "secondary elabo-ration," whereby the thinking "I" reappears and gives discursive meaning and significance to these intuitively discovered truths, including their formulation as abstract concepts. In other words, images are transformed back into thought when the Buddha expounds his visionary knowledge in his sermons or dis-courses to a congregation or a group of disciples, indicating that the discursive or rational reformulation of visionary thought occurs in a specific social and dia-logical context. And it is no accident that it is in the last watch of the night, prior to the arrival of dawn's bleak reality, that the sage intuited such abstract notions like the Four Noble Truths and "conditioned genesis" or "dependent origina-tion." It is in this sense—that of the later rational and abstract formulation of intuitively discovered truths—that one can speak of a "Buddhist Enlightenment" comparable with the European and the Greek. Nevertheless, the reemergence of the thinking "I" does not imply the certitude of the ego or the notion of a stable "self," a notion rejected in Buddhist doctrinal orthodoxy. Buddhism might posit the "I-think," but it is impossible for Buddhism to posit the conjoint "I-am."

Yet, the question remains whether the Buddha has become an enlightened thinker in the European mode after his awakening. The Buddha's spiritual awakening is never left behind; it constitutes the basis for forms of asceses that negate the view of the Buddha as a rationalist in the Enlightenment sense. Thus, alongside texts that seem to give a premium to conceptual rationality, there are others that seem to put the Buddha into a class with diviners, shamans, and spirit mediums, with an importance difference though: the Buddhist meditative ascesis entails a rigorous discipline and technology.

In the *Mahāpadāna Sutta,* monks are engaged in discussions about peoples' previous lives, and the Buddha, overhearing this conversation, mentions that he can, through meditative concentration, remember the lives of past Buddhas; furthermore, "gods also revealed these matters to him, enabling him to remember [all those things]."[69] This he actually does in the *Janavasabha Sutta* of the *Dīgha Nikāya* (The Long Discourses). Here the Buddha tells lay supporters what happened to their near and dear relatives after their deaths; consequently these people were "filled with joy and happiness at these solutions by the Exalted One of the problems that were put to him."[70] In this same text, his dead friend and patron King Bimbisāra, reborn in one of the heavens as Janavasabha, now appears before him and gives him a description of the heavenly hierarchy of gods and this information is then relayed to ordinary folk. On other occasions the Buddha talks of his capacity to get into meditative trances and perform actions reminiscent of shamanic virtuosity.

> From being one he becomes multiform, from being multiform he becomes one: from being visible he becomes invisible: he passes without hindrance to the further side of a wall or a battlement or a mountain, as if through air: he penetrates up and down through solid ground, as if through water: he walks on water without dividing it, as if on solid ground: he travels cross-legged through the sky, like the birds on wing: he touches and feels with the hand even the Moon and the Sun, beings of mystic power and potency though they be: he reaches, even in the body, up to the heaven of Brahma.[71]

When this experience is over, the Buddha, or his trained disciples, *arahants,* can switch back to normal life and to discursive I-thinking. And so back and forth from It-thinking to I-thinking without ever imagining that the existence of I-thinking implies the certitude of the ego and the primacy of Reason. Yet, once the mysterium tremendum of the Buddha's experience under the bodhi tree has become normalized, It-thinking begins to exist in a positive dialectical relationship with the thinking-I. But surely the one must influence the other in a kind of unwitting feedback process (but not a closed circuit), and this further implies that the original vision itself might be influenced by prior thoughts, if not fantasy activity in Freud's sense. If so, the visions concretize and give validation and profundity to prior knowledge, even knowledge taken for granted such as the common belief in rebirth. For example, before the Buddha's deep trance and his awakening, he studied under several gurus and he must already have had knowledge of rebirth, if not karma, and therefore, as Jung would say, these ideas would have been "incubating" in his mind for some time before the experience.[72] We can therefore say that ideally the dialectical interplay between the It and the I can be formulated thus: prior thoughts or fantasy activity with or without the mediation of the I > visions, dreams, and ideas mediated by the It > reformulation of the visionary knowledge through I-thinking > the process in reverse. This formula represents an ideal typical relationship and need not be empirically present because one can have a visionary experience and just leave it at that. And though I find it hard to believe that visions can be created de novo, out of a blank slate as it were, many visions probably gave clarity and noetic power to what existed in the mind as hazy thoughts or fantasy activity.[73] One must also remember that the Buddhist discourses, like its Greek counterparts, could exist as an independent discursive activity *without* a prior visionary experience. Thus Buddhism has many dialogues, such as those dealing with caste and human species equality that has nothing whatsoever to do with a prior visionary experience. So with the other side of the coin: many virtuosos perhaps were simply satisfied with the noetic knowledge imparted by the vision without bothering to reformulate it rationally.

DAYBREAK: THE SPACE OF SILENCE AND THE EMERGENCE OF APHORISTIC THINKING

Meanwhile the Mind, from pleasure less,
Withdraws into its happiness:
The Mind, that Ocean where each kind
Does streight its own resemblance find;
Yet it creates, transcending these,
Far other Worlds and other Seas;
Annihilating all that's made
To a green Thought in a Green shade.
—Andrew Marvell, "The Garden"

The first watch of the Buddha's night helps us understand problems of time and space that brings to the fore the idea of It-thinking. During the second watch, the Buddha's personal life histories are extended to include those of human beings in general, their births and rebirths in various realms of existence. Through the "pictorial representation" of births and rebirths, the Buddha can grasp the doctrine of karma, can *see* it operating. But what about the third or dawn watch: what is its paradigmatic significance? There the Buddha discovers the central doctrines of Buddhism, known as the Four Noble Truths. These are *dukkha*, suffering, the unsatisfactory nature of existence owing to the fact of impermanency; *samudaya*, how *dukkha* arises owing to *taṇhā*, thirst, attachment, greed, desire, or craving; *nirodha*, cessation of craving that will ultimately lead to nirvana; and *magga* or the path that might help us realize nirvana and also known as the "noble eightfold path:" right understanding, right thought, right speech, right action, right livelihood, right effort, right mindfulness, and right concentration. Right concentration is *samādhi*, the meditative disciplines leading to complexly graded states of trance (*jhāna*, *dhyāna*) that permitted the Buddha to intuit these very truths.[74] We do not know how the Four Noble Truths appeared to the sage in the dawn watch. But we do know that after he received this knowledge he delivered his first discourse in the Deer Park at Varanasi, titled, "Setting in Motion the Wheel of the Dhamma," in which the intuitively discovered truth is given rational reworking, although not in a very deep fashion in this early text.[75] More profound texts tell us that when an awakened being has arisen in the world there is a great light and radiance and then "there is the explaining, teaching, proclaiming, establishing, disclosing, analyzing, and elucidating the Four Noble Truths."[76]

We noted that some texts say that during the third watch the Buddha discovered the idea of conditioned genesis that highlights the interdependence of all actions, giving philosophical justification for the world of becoming, change, and instability. In the third watch, unlike the previous ones, thoughts are no longer represented in picture form. They appear as *ideas* entering the passive consciousness of the thinker when deep trance is thinning out into daybreak, a time of creativity that is not unfamiliar to some of us. *Daybreak* is the title of one of Nietzsche's aphoristic texts and I will try to understand the genesis of aphorisms by getting back to Nietzsche, his deconstruction of the ego, and his predilection for aphorisms.

I begin my inquiry by asking why Nietzsche made such a strong case for It-thinking when he surely should have known the obvious fact that there is no way one can escape from the thinking "I" in human discourse and writing, including his own. To resolve this issue let me consider in more detail Nietzsche's notion of It-thinking formulated in *Beyond Good and Evil* (1886).[77] There he lampoons those "harmless self-observers who believe there are 'immediate certainties,' for example, 'I think,' or as the superstition of Schopenhauer put it, 'I will'; as though knowledge here got hold of its object purely and nakedly as 'the thing in itself,' without any falsification on the part of either the subject or the object" (BGE, 21). This is Nietzsche's critique not only of Descartes derivation of the Ego on the basis of immediate certainty but also of much of Western metaphysics that held similar notions including an absolute a priori, unfalsifiable certainty (the Kantian "the thing in itself").

These ideas are hammered out in his late work *Twilight of the Idols* (1888) before his own reason was finally blotted out. During that twilight zone he makes the point that behind the reification of the ego is the idea of Reason (rationality), and this, in his horrendous sexist language of contempt, is what brings about "the horrendum pudendum of the metaphysicians."[78] Nietzsche's terrible wrath is focused on Descartes and Kant (Nietzsche's bête noires) who represents the folly of Western metaphysics. "It is this [reason] which sees everywhere deed and doer; this which believes in will as cause in general; this which believes in the 'ego,' in the ego as being, in the ego as substance [*res extensa*], and which projects its belief in the ego-substance on to all things. . . . Being is everywhere thought in, foisted on, as cause; it is only from the conception 'ego' that there follows, derivatively, the concept of 'being.'"[79] One cannot infer from our use of the "I" an entity known as the ego or self and beyond that to an entity known as the soul (and, of course, God), which was how Descartes reasoned in his third and fourth discourse on method.[80] For Nietzsche, the idea of the soul as an indestructible, eternal, and indivisible entity or "atomon" should be "expelled from science," though it could be retained as a trope, fruitfully redefined in such notions as "mortal soul," "soul as subjective multiplicity," or "soul as social structure of drives and affects" (BGE, 20).

When one analyses the phrase "I think," says Nietzsche, there are assumptions that are difficult, perhaps impossible, to prove: for example, that it is "I" who thinks; that there must be something that thinks; or "that thinking is an activity and operation of the part of a being who is thought of as a cause, that there is an 'ego,' and, finally, that it is already determined what is to be designated by thinking—that I know what thinking is" (BGE, 23). Reminiscent of the later Wittgenstein, Nietzsche calls these the "superstitions of logicians," and he would have none of it, even though, unhappily, Nietzsche himself could not escape from a notion of immediate certainty in his doctrine of the "will to power!"[81] To sum up: there are two sides to Nietzsche's deconstruction of the ego. First, a critique of the Cartesian cogito and the assumption in Western metaphysics of "substance," and the concomitant uncertainty regarding the nature of thinking itself, especially the notion that there is a reasoning "I" that thinks. (For substance, see my note 48, book 3, on "Spinoza's god.") Second, it seems to me that Nietzsche does not deny I-thinking in a purely nominal sense, but he downgrades it and resurrects the important notion of "It-thinking," albeit as a trope or a descriptive label rather than a theoretical term.

Let me develop the last idea further by asserting that there are several levels of It-thinking, beginning with our silent thinking, which occurs without reflexivity, such as reverie and daydreaming. It is therefore tautological to say that reflexivity or reflection is *self-reflection* appearing only with the "I" and hence the delusion that the existence of the "I" implies the existence of an ego, self, or soul. I-thinking requires the active consciousness, whereas the "It" operates for the most part in my silently emerging thoughts when, as with visions and dreams, ideas seem to float into my awareness. It is only when I speak or write down my thoughts that the thinking-I can reappear. And as there are different, though finite forms of It-thinking, so is it with the thinking-I. Thus all of us in our everyday living and decision making must necessarily employ I-thinking to function in the workaday world. This form of universal commonsensical I-thinking or practical rationality must surely be differentiated from the Cartesian cogito, the certitude of the ego, and the reification of reason. When dealing with theoretical issues, I will for the most part deal with this last.

At the other extreme from the passive ruminations I mentioned is the kind of meditative ascesis of the Buddhist, and, in between, there are gradations of It-thinking, depending on the degree of the active consciousness's suspension, as, for example, in Doolittle's experience with psychoanalysis. And so is it with our ordinary experience when creative ideas, including abstract thoughts or concepts, occasionally emerge into consciousness during states of "unawareness." These states can be fleeting ones, as for example when I am walking by myself in a cool morning outside my house in Kandy; or during greener years as I jogged or walked along the towpath by Lake Carnegie in Princeton; or when I am lazing around absentmindedly and thoughts simply come to the surface; or when I slip into a moment of unawareness; or when I shower; or (more rarely and ludicrously) when I sit on the commode letting silence invade me.[82]

"The gestation of all really great creation," Nietzsche mused sentimentally, "lies in loneliness" (CN, 128). By "loneliness" he did not mean hostility to human company but "solitude," which opens up the "inward eye" of European romantics such as Wordsworth. For both Wordsworth and Nietzsche, and others like them, solitude is something cultivated, like Marvell's garden, that "delicious solitude" into which the poet escapes and where he experienced his revelatory moment.[83] Our kinds of solitude seekers cultivate the space of silence that permits

It-thoughts to emerge into consciousness. Thousands seek solitude; and modern packaged tours tout them; but not the *cultivation* of solitude which, like the cultivation of meditation, is a disciplinary exercise. If in the nineties I could walk on the towpath of Princeton and let silence steal into my ear, not now as I walk at daybreak in Central Park. I am one of the very few who have not blocked out silence: most of the walkers and almost all joggers have plugged their ears with packaged music or cell phone conversations, as if silence is a noise that has to be eradicated. I am not suggesting that people should not listen to music, because we all do that during our normal lives. Only that, living in our increasingly turbulent world, we must be able to be in tune with the flow of the silence and tap its creative potential. We do know that, however difficult, one can sometimes block out noise that assails the ear and cultivate an area of silence within the stream of traffic, as I believe Wittgenstein did in World War 1 when he jotted his thoughts in his notebook, indifferent to the roar of cannons pounding away their message of death. But it is not easy nowadays to *elect* silence into one's life pattern as Buddhist monks did in times past and Hopkins did 142 years ago:

Elected Silence, sing to me
And beat into my whorlèd ear,
Pipe me to pastures still and be
The music that I care to hear.

Now let me consider Nietzsche's own visionary consciousness, which few have noted, and follow his aphoristic thinking for which he justly famous, those green thoughts that came to him in the green shades into which he meandered. Nietzschean visions were reported by Resa von Schirnhofer around mid-August 1884 in Sils-Maria, located about six thousand feet above sea level, where Nietzsche stayed at a hotel for several years after 1884, though not continuously. Here he ate alone, refusing the company of others. Here he told von Schirnhofer about "his bouts of raging headaches and the various medications he had tried against them," often deadly self-medications including chloral hydrate and potassium bromide, sometimes signing prescriptions for himself as Dr. Nietzsche![84] She also mentions that, after Nietzsche had remained invisible for one and a half days owing to his endemic illness, she and a friend visited him one morning.

As I stood waiting by the table, the door of the adjacent room on the right opened, and Nietzsche appeared. With a distraught expression on his pale face, he leaned wearily against the post of the half-opened door and immediately began to speak about the unbearableness of his ailment. He described to me how, when he closed his eyes, he saw an abundance of fantastic flowers, winding and intertwining, constantly growing and changing forms and colors in exotic luxuriance, sprouting one out of the other. "I never get any rest," he complained, words which were implanted in my mind. Then, with his large, dark eyes looking straight at me he asked in his weak voice with disquieting urgency: "Don't you believe this condition is a symptom of incipient madness? My father died of a brain disease."[85]

(CN, 164)

In spite of his Dionysian ideals, Nietzsche was in reality an Apollonian thinker searching for the stated ideal he could never realize, except in theory and in his fictionalized creation Zarathustra. It is not surprising therefore that he seemed unable to cultivate these visions (whether evoked spontaneously or provoked by his medications) and incorporate them into his being. Instead he related them in rational fashion to his inherited madness, thus pathologizing them as his middle-class contemporaries did, failing to accommodate these visions of burgeoning life into his intellectually formulated Dionysian scheme of things. Resa von Schirnhofer thought his condition at this time was one of "rampant anxiety." She adds that she could not find in the copious Nietzsche literature any reference to such a direct statement of his madness, fears that apparently attracted him to Strindberg, the dramatist who dealt with familial turmoil arising from inherited diseases (CN, 165). It is the case that in his later years Nietzsche was fearful of madness and, though he confessed it in his notebooks, he could not talk about it freely with others. Yet, the version he gave Schirnhofer was probably not fully symptomatic of his psychic state because this was the period he was working on book 3 of *Thus Spoke Zarathustra*. It is hard to believe that, although he was fearful of his mental health, Nietzsche was immune to the spirit of the prophet he had just created, his idealized alter (or "ego-ideal"). When he visited his old friends Franz and Ida Overbeck in Basel on June 15, 1884, the former wrote with rare insight: "It is now only in the world of his visions that he can sometimes feel happy, until it comes over him that he is, for the time being, alone in his understanding of them."[86] There was almost no one he could talk to freely, let alone find a congenial community to associate with. Ronald Hayman says that he could hardly speak of his philosophical work with his colleagues. "[Jakob] Burckhardt, embarrassed at having to comment on *Zarathustra*, asked whether he had ever thought of trying his hand at drama, and he [Nietzsche] failed to gather reassurance from his other ex-colleagues: 'It was like being surrounded by cows.'"[87] Surrounded, as he was, by cows, it was not surprising that Nietzsche kept his visions to himself, thereby closing the door on them as, unfortunately, he did with us as well.[88]

Nietzsche was an ascetic wanderer living under the shadow of chronic disease and dread of madness, never in one place for long, rarely in his German homeland. Many a friend or stranger noted Nietzsche's unending pain of mind *and* his creativity during his wandering life. As early as 1877, while still in the University of Basel, he was vacationing with a group of friends in Sorrento when one of them noted: "he walked with his head leaned back, like a Sorrento prophet, with half-closed eyes, through the long avenues of blossoming orange trees. . . . His manner of speaking was undramatic and matter of fact; in the simplest tone of voice he could pronounce sentences which were so seminal and significant that they seemed spoken *sub specie aeterni*" (CN, 92). Much later, Paul Lanzky, an older acquaintance, called him "the wandering philosopher" and "the former professor, now a fugitive" (CN, 174, 178). Victor Helling dubbed him the "great hermit of Sils-Maria" (CN, 21). Once, while walking with a stranger, Sebastian Hausmann, the latter reported: "He spouted his thoughts forth, more in the form of aphorisms, always leaping one to the other" (CN, 139). Another acquaintance reported in 1885 from Leipzig where he stayed on several occasions: "Every afternoon he strolled pensively, his hands behind his back . . . not far from the zoological garden" (CN, 141). Paul Lanzky thought that Nietzsche really valued human company; yet he also mentioned his "longing for stillness, indeed this temporary reveling in the idyllic" (CN, 171). The ambivalence toward his solitariness was intrinsic to his character, and, though he complained of his isolation and loneliness, he also seemed to enjoy it and could not do without it. That longing was probably best realized in Sils-Maria with its secluded forest paths tempting the wanderer to be alone with himself (CN, 182–83).

One reporter noted in September 1885 the philosopher wandering in a "heroic landscape." "The sight of the wanderer striding with a rapid step and upright head in the evening sun will always remain unforgettable to me" (CN, 188). It was in this kind of solitude that the aphorisms of *Daybreak*, *The Joyful Science,* and *Beyond Good and Evil* were written, according to Lanzky (CN, 161). But let us listen to Nietzsche himself praising the calm and silence of Sils-Maria in a beautiful poem composed sometime between 1882 and 1883 when parts 2 and 3 of *Zarathustra* were being written, inspired perhaps by the vision of the prophet himself:

I sat there waiting, waiting—not for anything.
Beyond good and evil, enjoying soon the light,

Soon the shade, now only play, now
The lake, now the noon, wholly time without end.

Then suddenly, friend, one became two
And Zarathustra passed by me.[89]

It is in such silent meditative contexts that aphoristic thinking emerges into consciousness without an intrusive I. I think these contexts led Nietzsche to downgrade the ego and reify the It. Visions were not Nietzsche's forte; but not so with his nondiscursive silent thoughts reexpressed by him through the literary genre of aphorisms. For Nietzsche, as for Wittgenstein, aphorisms became the vehicle for the expression of It-thoughts. Needless to say, they could also be expressed in other ways, for instance when aphoristic thinking can be reformulated in the highly discursive language of the thinking-I. Malwida von Meysenbug reports that it was Nietzsche's acquaintance with the French moralists that "led him to express his thoughts in aphorisms" (CN, 84). This observation was confirmed much later by Lou Salome: "For many years he [Nietzsche] had been walking around with a La Rochefoucauld or a La Bruyere in his pocket" (CN, 118). But it is a mistake to confuse the French *model* of aphorisms for Nietzsche's need or motivation to give aphoristic expression to his most profound nonreflexive thoughts. Thus what I call aphoristic thinking is not necessarily congruent with the literary genre of aphorisms; they can be expressed in other genres also, as in Blake's "proverbs of hell" and Laocoön;[90] and in the opening lines of Yeats's poem of my epigraph appropriately named "Fragments":

Locke sank into a swoon;
The Garden died;
God took the spinning-jenny
Out of his side.

Whether these aphorisms came from a medium's mouth as the poet claims or otherwise, one might appreciate the significance of his saying "out of nothing it came," if one takes that phrase to mean something indeterminate: a nothingness, an abyss, a void, a Buddhist store consciousness, an unconscious, or a state of unawareness. All these terms will appear in this essay. Similar "fragments" appear in the well-known enigmatic sayings of Zen masters. And consider this one line in Blake's "proverbs of hell" in his *Marriage of Heaven and Hell*: "The road of excess leads to the palace of wisdom." Blake's proverbs have a nice sound to them, but can one make sense of that one line without a full exegesis? Even if we reasonably take "palace of wisdom" to mean what it literally says, there is much we miss unless we can understand some of Blake's own ideas that can fill the semantic space left undetermined by the enigmatic statement. For example, we know that Blake felt that the "cleansing of the doors of perception" is a prerequisite to wisdom because "perception" is clouded by the physical senses extolled by rational science. Another aphorism makes the point that by yielding to sense perceptions man has "closed himself up, till he sees all things thro' the narrow chinks of his cavern" (CW, 154). We have to cleanse ourselves of bodily perception to reach spiritual knowledge or the "palace of wisdom." And we would miss the significance of "excess" unless we knew a little bit of Blake's own background knowledge, the impress of Luther's commentary on Psalm 115: "That is excessus when a man is elevated above himself . . . and illuminated sees that he is nothing. He looks down, as it were, from above into himself, into his own shadows and darkness. Nevertheless he is looking down from his position on a mountain."[91] Luther in turn borrowed the term from medieval theology, for example in Bonaventure for whom *excessus* refers to the adoration of God through prayer that leads the soul to ecstasy.[92] Thus it seems that while some aphorisms might have immediate intelligibility, others are often enigmatic, clouded in dense expressions requiring detailed exegeses.

I will borrow Lou Salome's phrase and label Nietzsche's silent thinking processes the "aphoristic mode of work" (CN, 118). The aphoristic mentality—the mentality that converts nonreflexive thought into aphorisms and other literary forms—does not necessarily require trance or somnolent states. It only requires moments when active egoistic thinking is in abeyance or, Wordsworth said, when one is "in vacant or in pensive mood." As in the case of dreams, one cannot capture such thoughts as they emerge into consciousness but, as with dreams, one has to be satisfied with the remembered text. I am not given to express my thoughts aphoristically, but when I used to walk into solitariness I sometimes carried pencil and paper to jot down thoughts floating into my ken. Why so? As with dreams, it is difficult to fully recollect ones It-thoughts, although one can be trained to do so, which clearly was the case with Nietzsche. In 1877, while still at the University of Basel, Reinhardt von Seydlitz reports that Nietzsche "kept next to his bed a slate tablet on which, in the dark, he jotted down the thoughts that came to him on sleepless nights" (CN, 91). Again much later, in 1884, in his favorite place, Sils-Maria, our prophet repeats the same marvelous advice to Resa von Schirnhofer: "keep paper and pencil in hand at night, as he himself did, since at night we are often visited by rare thoughts, which we should record immediately on awakening in the night, for by morning we usually do not find them again, they have fluttered away with the nocturnal darkness" (CN, 149). But these thoughts must also have arisen during his daytime walks into solitude, for it must be remembered that Nietzsche was near blind, so that he could hardly "recognize a person on the street" (CN, 33). Like the blind Tiresias, he also could see the truth with his powerful, penetrating near-blind eyes, noted by virtually everyone. For Nietzsche there was not that radical a distinction between night and day, between nocturnal and daytime creativity. In his early academic career, when he was lecturing at Basel, he could not tolerate sunlight, so that "even with moderate sunlight the window blinds had to be half-shut" (CN, 37).

If, in the case of shamans and similar visionaries, a drastic illness or a drastic asceticism, in the case of the Buddha myth, or a dark night of the soul (or combinations of these) was seen as a symbolic death heralding the visionary experience and the adoption of a religious vocation, not so with the Antichrist Nietzsche. The "nocturnal darkness" of approaching death and illness haunted his life, so that, I am sure, he would have sympathized with Alexander Pope who spoke of "this long disease, my life."[93] Nietzsche's was a prolonged but diffuse dark night of the soul at the end of which lay not a rebirth, or an awakening, but an unending silence and a blankness of mind and thought in which a great human being was metamorphosed, one might say, into the Idiot.[94] And Nietzsche seemed to have an intuitive grasp of that impending fate. Explaining to Arthur Egedi around 1882 about the practical necessity for his "aphoristic mode of expression," Nietzsche added: "I felt close to death and therefore pressed to say some things which I had been carrying around me for years. Illness compelled me to use the briefest of expression; the individual sentences were dictated directly to a friend; systematic realization was out of the question. That is how the book *Human, All Too Human* was written. Thus the choice of the aphorism will be understandable only from the accompanying circumstances" (CN, 129). This book contained the first mature expression of his aphoristic mode of thought and was written in 1878, a year before he retired from the University of Basel owing to unsupportable illness. It contained 638 aphorisms; in the next two years 758 were added.[95]

It would seem that Nietzsche's solitariness was conjoined to a prolonged, secular form of the dark night of the soul of those hermits, sages, shamans, penitents, and ascetics well known to us. No wonder the person who perhaps knew Nietzsche best, Lou Salome, found his thought and his solitary wandering life to be an expression of a "mystical" trait and that, at some level he was "a religious genius."[96] Nietzsche told Ida Overbeck that, though he had rejected the Christian god, he well might "perish from my passions, they will cast me back and forth; I am constantly falling apart, but I do not care" (CN, 145). Of his work style, Resa von Schirnhofer nicely noted it as "intensive work in brooding solitude" (CN, 146), and an acquaintance, Richard Reuter, described him as "a lonely man, seeking and loving loneliness, yet suffering deeply and painfully from it, lonelier of soul than any hermit ever was" (CN, 146, 82). Naturally, one might say, for here was a man suffering from painful illnesses, from the dread of impending death and oncoming madness. When he was abandoned in 1882 by Lou Salome, the one woman he truly loved (after his own fashion), Nietzsche could say that during the winter of his gloomy discontent he had become like Timon of Athens. And, owing to his sister's jealous hostility to Lou, he mournfully noted that "this internal conflict is pushing me step by step, closer to madness."[97] Yet I would like to stretch my metaphor to say that Nietzsche, even during his bleak nights of despair, remained *awakened* to thoughts, perhaps even to visions that reached him from the shadows encircling him until these shadows choked him into a permanent silence, a silence without redress.

It is now time to leave Nietzsche temporarily and get back to the Buddha's discovery of the highly complex doctrine of causal interconnections known as dependent origination (*paticcasamuppāda*). I noted that in the third, or dawn watch, thoughts are no longer represented in picture form but rather as ideas that enter into the passive consciousness of the thinker when deep trance is thinning out into daybreak. Unlike the discovery of the Four Noble Truths, which also occurred on the third watch, we can make an informed guess as to how conditioned genesis entered the mind of the Buddha. There are detailed discussions of this doctrine in Buddhist texts; yet one enigmatic formula repeats itself with only minor variations. For example, in *The Shorter Discourse to Sakuludāyin*, the Buddha tells Sakuludāyin "I shall teach you the Dhamma: when this exists, that comes to be; with the arising of this, that arises. When this does not exist, that does not come to be; with the cessation of this, that ceases."[98] In this discourse, at least, the Buddha equates conditioned genesis with the doctrine itself, anticipating similar formulations by later Mahāyāna thinkers. Here the formula exists by itself, whereas in the very next discourse it is incorporated in a larger context and then given a conceptual designation: *paticcasamuppāda*. Here one of the Buddha's favorite disciples, Ānanda, deliberately asks a question, "In what way can a bhikkhu [monk] be called skilled in dependent origination?" The Buddha responds:

When this exists, that comes to be;
With the arising of this, that arises.
When this does not arise, that does not come to be;
With the cessation of this, that ceases.

He then briefly *explains* the enigmatic formula thus: "That is, with ignorance as condition, formations [come to be]; with formations as condition, consciousness; with consciousness as condition, mentality-materiality; with mentality-materiality as condition, the six-fold base; with the six-fold base as condition, contact; with contact as condition, feeling; with feeling as condition, craving;

with craving as condition, clinging; with clinging as condition, being; with being as condition, birth; with birth as condition, ageing and death, sorrow, lamentation, pain, grief, and despair come to be. Such is the origin of this whole mass of suffering."[99]

The discursive strategy is reasonably clear. The formulaic four-line statement is elaborated in various degrees of complexity in the Buddha's discourses. In another example a simple elaboration of the formula is given in a discourse explicitly entitled "Dependent Origination," very much like the statement mentioned earlier. This brief exegesis is followed by a much longer and more detailed one in the next discourse, significantly named "*Analysis of Dependant Origination*."[100] According to a collection of short texts known as *Udāna* (Inspired Utterances), the Buddha is said to have uttered the same formula in the first watch in the order given above, and in the second watch in the reverse order and in the third watch in both forward and reverse order, but in effect repeating the formula uttered during the first watch!

> This being, that is; from the arising of this, that arises; this not being, that is not; from the cessation of this, that ceases.[101]

What is happening with the four-line formulation of dependent origination is that, as with the Four Noble Truths, ideas also reach the Buddha when everyday consciousness or I-thinking is suspended. Because conditioned genesis is a further theoretical understanding of the Four Noble Truths, it makes sense for us to assume that this knowledge also entered the consciousness of the Buddha during the third watch. Remember that in the Buddha's case he discusses conditioned genesis in soteriological terms—in terms of life's ills and their cessation. It was left to the great Buddhist philosophers, particularly Nāgārjuna and his disciples, to deal with conditioned genesis having applicability to all of existence. The present Dalai Lama explains the formula succinctly: "Everything is composed of dependently related events, of continuously interacting phenomena with no fixed, immutable essence, which are themselves in constantly changing dynamic relations. Things and events are 'empty' in that they do not possess any immutable essence, intrinsic reality, or absolute 'being' that affords independence."[102] As Buddhist texts put it, "this is the way things really are" (*yathā bhūta*). In the West it is David Hume who came close to the Buddhist position.[103]

I suggest that the Buddha's formula of conditioned genesis not only fits the third or dawn watch, or daybreak, but, as an expression of aphoristic thinking, it is not at all alien to us. While the Buddha is not given to aphorisms in general, Mahāyāna thinkers such as Nāgārjuna are masters in the aphoristic mode of expression. It is immaterial to me whether the empirical Buddha actually had this revealing experience during the third watch because often enough mythos represents in symbolic form the reality search of the truth seeker. The Buddha's dawn watch opens one's dimmed consciousness to aphoristic thinking wherein one can observe again the "passive intellect" at work. Aphoristic thinking condenses It-thoughts, just as dreams might be condensations of images. When I put my thoughts down as I walk lost in thoughtlessness, I, like the lonely Nietzsche, have had similar (admittedly less powerful) condensed insights that I then expand into discursive writing, although not as aphorisms. Even with Nietzsche or Wittgenstein, the written aphorism can be interspersed with I-thinking. Yet when written aphorisms are close to their original thought processes they exemplify the kind of enigmatic quality we noted in Blake's proverb on excess. They are not only thick with meaning but also frequently require exegeses, either by the author or by others, for them to be fully comprehended. The enigmatic, thick, often poetic nature of aphorisms defy translation and are amply demonstrated in Nietzsche's work and in the work of Wittgenstein, another wanderer with no fixed abode, and one who gave up his wealth and a comfortable existence for a life of ascetic simplicity.

Wittgenstein was familiar with Nietzsche's work, but it is not clear how much the latter influenced his own style of thinking, living, and writing. Some similarities are obvious. There is what I will call the "sensibility of the spirit," without giving the idea of "spirit" a narrow Christian doctrinal meaning. Nietzsche had killed the Christian god, but his biting denunciation of his father's religion in *The Anti-Christ* was tempered by his admiration for the sensibility of the spirit exemplified in Christ's own life and dispensation, without, however, the belief in God or in redemption through Jesus. His, I would say again, is a form of "secular spirituality." "Even today such a life is possible, for certain men even necessary: genuine, primitive Christianity will be possible at all times."[104] Wittgenstein, while rejecting the beliefs of his Catholic heritage or the trappings of the Church, was much more given to accepting the existence of God and redemption through him, even if the god was his own construction (inspired by Tolstoy's God) and was far removed from the abstract God of the philosophers of his time and of other times. Both were fascinated by Dostoyevsky: Nietzsche for Dostoyevsky's probing of the depths of the human psyche and Wittgenstein for his unique and unorthodox version of Christian mysticism. No wonder Wittgenstein also admired Blake, who rejected the "moral law" of the Christian churches for his own Dissenter's view of the Everlasting Gospel. Both Nietzsche and Wittgenstein eschewed the propositions of traditional logic, and both were sensitive to the power of music but ambivalent toward contemporary science, especially

Darwinism, to which they were hostile.[105] Perhaps both did not care to understand Darwin, although I think that Nietzsche was influenced by the evolutionary model when he sketched the prehistory of our ideas of punishment, guilt, and bad conscience in his *Genealogy of Morals*. Blake was the most radical of the three in flatly rejecting all propositions of science and logic and all forms of Enlightenment rationality. Wittgenstein and Nietzsche were also skeptical of the thinking of philosophers, with Wittgenstein brashly proclaiming that he had not read Aristotle, quite unlike Martin Heidegger who, in his lectures on Nietzsche, foolishly urged his students to "postpone reading Nietzsche for the time being, and first study Aristotle for ten to fifteen years."[106] Nietzsche did read Aristotle; but his resentment fell on his European predecessors, especially Kant, who, he felt, had no sense of the lived world, even as he formulated such notions as the categorical imperative and, especially, the idea of the noumenon ("the thing in itself"), owing to its vague and unverifiable nature.

If Nietzsche and Wittgenstein occasionally abjured Enlightenment rationality, it was because they felt, as Blake did, the expense of spirit that it fostered. Hence Blake and Nietzsche, if not Wittgenstein, idealized art in which they found spiritual solace for the ills of modernity. Our two philosophers were interested in psychology, but Wittgenstein, in spite of his avowed sympathy for Freud, was not interested in depth psychology, although he had brilliant discussions of perception, strongly influenced by the gestalt psychology of Wolfgang Köhler. He also, like Nietzsche, lived under the shadow of madness and impending death. And while Wittgenstein could often enough talk about "guilt," directly or indirectly, in respect of his own feelings, he could not probe the genesis or genealogy of guilt as Nietzsche did in his *Genealogy of Morals*.[107] Nietzsche, it seems to me, was the more profound thinker of the human psyche, while Wittgenstein was the more astute critic of philosophy and psychology. Yet, for me at least, Wittgenstein swam in the shallows of the psyche whereas Nietzsche plunged into its depths.

In both there lies a nobility of purpose in their intellectual honesty and passionate commitment to "truth," especially exposing intellectual obfuscation and "fishy" thinking. Nevertheless, the prejudice expressed in my earlier sentence compels me consider a few of the differences between them. To me the most appealing feature of Nietzsche's political views were his unpopular and no-nonsense criticism of German nationalism and his anti-anti-Semitism. Nevertheless he also succumbed to the prejudice of his times in asserting that blacks were an inferior race, quite unlike Blake, who had a more profound sense of species unity. By contrast, Wittgenstein was passionately German and fought for his nation in the First World War, proclaiming that he was "German through and through." He confessed that the "thought our race will be defeated depresses me tremendously," this in spite of his family or because his family, like that of Teresa's ages ago, were "conversos."[108] Wittgenstein's anti-Semitism, often unpleasantly virulent, was part of the self-hatred for his Jewish heritage, which he felt was a "tumor" in the body politic. He was insensitive to the tumor in the body politic of his beloved Austria, until its annexation by the Nazis.[109] And worse, notwithstanding the tragedy of Hiroshima, he seemed to have loved the bomb, foolishly believing that it might be a deterrent for future wars but also perhaps implicitly pitting himself in almost all his writing against the unrelenting pacifist Bertrand Russell, the father figure he both loved and hated.[110] And, while he expressed sympathy for what he considered mysticism, his imagination, nurtured by pulp detective stories rather than science fiction, found the thought of sending a person to the moon an "outlandish" one.

What then ties Wittgenstein to the paradigmatic third watch of the Buddha's meditative night? This lies as with Nietzsche in his search for solitude, that creative ground of aphoristic thinking. Fania Pascal, Wittgenstein's friend and teacher of Russian, mentions his craving for solitude: "When Wittgenstein wished to flee from civilization, no place was remote or lonely enough."[111] For the early Wittgenstein, this was Norway. In spite of the bitter cold, he loved it and had built his own house with the thought of Norway as a permanent home (a thought that never materialized or never could because he was by destiny a wanderer). Till the very end of his life, Wittgenstein idealized his sojourns in Norway, such that "Norway" had become a state of mind rather than just a place. And, when Norway was not there, there were many places in Ireland to retreat into. He loved walks into the countryside whether he was in Norway, Ireland, Cambridge, or admiring the coastal beauty of Wales around Swansea. At Red Cross in Ireland he carried his notebook with him. A neighbor who "often saw Wittgenstein out on his favorite walk, reports that he once passed him sitting in a ditch, writing furiously, oblivious of anything going on around him."[112] This is not surprising because, as early as 1931, he could say: "I really do think with my pen, because my head often knows nothing about what my hand is writing."[113] During the latter period of his life he also communed with himself aloud: "Nearly all of my writings are private conversations with myself. Things that I say to myself tête-á-tête."[114]

I have affirmed that solitude is something cultivated like Marvell's garden, and Marvell's garden in turn leads me to speculate on the role of gardens in meditative settings of different sorts and in different places and times. The Buddha initially isolated himself in the forest, and when monasteries were formed in the Buddha's own time there were spaces for meditative solitude. Indeed donors gifted their orchards and gardens to monks in the very earliest period of Buddhism. When Buddhism was introduced to Sri Lanka in the second century

BCE, the evidence is clearer: monasteries were associated with enclosed forests, gardens, or orchards. The myth of the arrival of the Buddhist missions into Sri Lanka gives us hints as to how this occurred. It says that the Buddhist saint (*arahant*) Mahinda flew through the air and arrived at a forest later known as Mihintale where the king Tissa, in accordance with the royal (*kṣatriya*) lifestyle was out hunting, which, according to Buddhist doctrine, was an archetypal wrong act. The monk converted the king, while the place of the hunt became the first monastic complex in Sri Lanka. The myth expresses a reality that went into later Buddhism where the forest is tamed and converted into a garden and a space for solitude. Buddhists believe that the meditating monk, then and now, has also tamed the forest animals through the emanation of his compassion and they can do him no harm. Compassion itself possesses power. The model of the forest monastery is not unique to Buddhism but is based on a long Indic tradition of the relation between the ashram and the forest, as Romila Thapar nicely points out.[115] Viewed in this light, the episode of the place of the hunt being converted into a meditational site is simply a Buddhist manifestation of this structural opposition in Indic thought.

Coming into more recent times, that is, sometime during the period of the last kingdom of Kandy (1469–1815), the Royal Palace was linked to a forest known as *uḍavatte kälē*, "the upper side forest garden," that still exists under the same name as a haunt for lovers, tourists, a few meditating monks, and lots more monkeys. What has happened here is that the forest has been tamed and incorporated as part of the royal gardens. We know that Sri Lankan queens had paths in their gardens for solitary meditative walks, and from very early times Buddhist texts mention walkways for monks to engage in meditation. Ashrams and gardens and similar places provided for meditation are also *retreats,* offering the monk or layperson a chance to opt out of life or more often temporarily retreat from the noise of political conflict and the less strident noise of everyday life. So is it with Zen and Japanese Buddhism in general where aesthetics, meditation, and silence fuse into a single conception. It is in gardens or in spaces of solitude like those provided by gardens that the enigmatic or aphoristic utterances of Zen monks happened. Unfortunately, for us South Asians living today, and for those who have outlived their yesterdays, we have become hopeless witnesses of ashrams sprouting everywhere and thrusting themselves into the political arena. So is it with Buddhist temples. Rarely are they spaces of silence and sanctuaries for ordinary people to retreat into. Worse: hideous statues of the Awakened One appear everywhere, even in choking intersections spewing smog, a sign that the Buddha has been transmuted into a figure of our hapless modernity. And Hindu and Buddhist spirituality, imitating its Western forms, can now be bought and sold in the market place. Hope withers on its stalk when *noise* invades the ashram.

Solitude is not the search for loneliness: the Buddha, Nietzsche, Wittgenstein, Zen monks, and others like them enjoyed congenial human company whenever it was available, and some of us know that such company is hard to find. Rarely did meditating monks live in total isolation from the world. Outside the cultivated spaces for solitude, they enjoyed the company of fellow meditators and lay folk without losing the capacity to be absorbed unto oneself, to live alone like the single horn of the rhinoceros.[116] Wittgenstein once put it, during his sojourn at Red Cross in Ireland where mental solitude was conjoined to the physical: "Sometimes my ideas come so quickly that I feel as if my pen was being guided," which, he well knew, simply could not occur in the stuffy academic world of Cambridge and its overwhelming preoccupation with Enlightenment rationality. Hence he could add, "I now see clearly that it was the right thing for me to give up the professorship."[117] The rejection of Enlightenment rationality could not be the sole reason for rejecting academia, but I suspect it was a major one.

I am also not sure whether Wittgenstein was aware of his spiritual affinity with some of the European visionaries who will appear later on in this book: Catherine of Siena, Teresa of Avila, William Blake, and Madame Blavatsky, all of whom claimed that large chunks of texts simply came to them through some divine or mysterious source, thoughts without a thinker as it were. It should be remembered that this was also a time when Wittgenstein came closest to orthodox Christianity: "I pray a good deal," but he is not sure "whether in the right spirit."[118] Nevertheless, I would say in relation to Nietzsche and Wittgenstein and to aphoristic thinkers in general that, in order to let oneself be hit by intuition, one does not have to *collapse* on the road to Damascus.

Unlike Nietzsche, Wittgenstein was not exclusively an aphoristic thinker. His *Tractatus Logico-Philosophicus* was written in aphoristic form, but not all of his work. Yet, aphorisms sparkle everywhere in his writing, and it is no accident that his views of Descartes seem to echo Nietzsche's, perhaps even borrowed from the latter, as when he says in the *Tractatus*:

> There is no such thing as the subject that thinks or entertains ideas (5:631)
> Where in the world is a metaphysical subject to be found (5:633)
> Here it can be seen that solipsism, when its implications are followed out strictly, coincides with pure realism. The self of solipsism shrinks to a point without extension, and there remains the reality co-ordinated with it (5:64)[119]

Bertrand Russell pointed out the significance of this mode of work in the *Tractatus* when in an admirable understatement he described some of its propositions as "obscure through brevity."[120] Wittgenstein's aphoristic density of expression eluded the brilliance of his two mentors, Russell and Gottlob Frege. When he was given a copy, Frege could barely begin to read it, and Wittgenstein thought that Russell did not understand a word of it. Neither could most philosophers until painful exegeses by Wittgenstein's disciples made his thoughts accessible to a larger audience of philosophers. Those enigmatic statements of the *Tractatus* are evident in its opening propositions, perhaps the very ones that baffled Frege and put him off:

1. The world is all that is the case.
1.1. The world is the totality of facts, not of things.
1.11. The world is determined by the facts, and by their being all the facts.
1.12. For the totality of facts determines what is the case, and also whatever is not the case.
1.13. The facts in logical space are the world.
1.2. The world divides into facts.
1.21. Each item can be the case or not the case while everything else remains the same.[121]

These propositions are expounded later in further aphorisms and therefore, in fairness to Wittgenstein, his aphoristic statements are less haphazard than Nietzsche's but ordered into a greater systemic totality through I-thinking without, however, losing their aphoristic quality. Nevertheless, whether it is Nietzsche or Wittgenstein, aphoristic thought is hostile to footnotes or bibliographical references. One could even say that it is meaningless to have such things in aphorisms. They would dilute, and distract from, the power of the aphoristic message.

SCHREBER AND THE PICTORIAL IMAGINATION

I cannot undertake to deny that madmen and dreamers believe what is false, when madmen imagine they are gods or dreamers think they have wings and are flying in their sleep.

—Plato, *Theaetetus*, 158b

Daniel Paul Schreber was surely the most famous madman in modern history. It was Freud who first used Schreber's *Memoirs* in his pioneer study of the psychodynamics of paranoia. Since then, Schreber has been "rehabilitated" such that he now appears to be a misunderstood genius, an avatar of modernity, a man haunted by his father's cruel ghost—to sample a few the bewildering ways in which he has been represented.[122] From my point of view he was all of the above—a madman who eludes all conventional classificatory labels, a "mystic" and "religious genius," and like Nietzsche a critic of the traditional philosophy of religion and of contemporary modernity while at the same time representing modernity as well in his critical stance. Perhaps the most sympathetic and insightful portrayal of him is found in Zvi Lothane's *In Defense of Schreber*. I however want to supplement the list of his virtues with my take on him as a penetrating and yet befuddled thinker about It-thinking.

Because so much has been written about the life of Schreber and his family from different viewpoints, I am only going to deal with a few of his visionary experiences and his attempts to theorize about them. (See the following note for a synoptic account of his life.)[123] Schreber's visions are not ones that were immediately experienced by him, but those recollected and written down later in his *Memoirs*. In this sense everything Schreber says is based on later reflection and is analogous to the distinction one makes between the dream as dreamt and the script of the dream as it is later put down in writing. Nevertheless, to depict the realm of what Schreber called "religion" or the mysticism of Wittgenstein and that of other virtuosos is a difficult if not impossible task, unless one takes the easy way out and asserts with the beautiful but unreasonable (even tautological) aphorism that concludes the *Tractatus*: "What we cannot speak about we must pass over in silence." Many recognize that the way out of tautology is to assert that that there are no words for expressing certain things, as for example the thing called "mysticism," a point we will take up later. One can nevertheless forgive Schreber if he sometimes finds it hard to express the "incomprehensible" in ordinary discourse without contradiction and ambiguity, even obfuscation and obtuseness. Yet at other times Schreber can employ his own visionary experiences for giving what he considers rational answers to "mystical" problems. Thus Christ's virgin birth could occur "only in a mystical sense" because "nobody would maintain that God, as a Being endowed with human sexual organs, had intercourse with the woman from whose womb Jesus Christ came forth" (M, 17). So is his explication of what he considers dubious points of Christian doctrine, such as the Ascension, which simply could not occur in reality. They were only visions seen by his disciples and must, according to the theories he developed, be a product of "nerve" force.[124] But I suspect that he is also making a case that, while his own visions were for the most part true, those of Christ's disciples were illusory.

However, when Schreber speaks of nonreligious matters such as the accounts of his stay in asylums or his plea for release to the high court, or when he is criticizing the psychiatry of the time, he is a model of clarity. I especially find his remarkable critique of the great psychiatrist Emil Kraepelin very appealing and in line with his views of the unspeakable nature of the "supernatural." Kraepelin, he says, may be partially right in his negative characterization of the "supernatural communication" of his sick patients, but "science would go very wrong to designate as 'hallucinations' all such phenomena that lack objective reality, and to throw them into the lumber room of things that do not exist." Kraepelin may be on the right track, however, when he is dealing with phenomena that cannot be characterized as "supernatural." "If psychiatry is not flatly to deny everything supernatural and thus tumble with both feet into the camp of naked material-ism, it will have to recognize the possibility that occasionally the phenomena under discussion may be connected with real happenings, which simply cannot be brushed aside with the catch-word 'hallucinations'" (M, 84).[125] It is these "real happenings" that Schreber describes in his maddening memoirs. Yet, in criticiz-ing naked materialism, he was close to many visionary thinkers such as Blake and to his near contemporaries the Theosophists and the many educated persons in Europe and in the U.S. influenced by evangelical and spiritualist movements.

Visions, in Schreber's own theory, are not based on ordinary human language but on the language of "nerves," which embraces both the ordinary meaning of *nerves* and an extended or extraordinary meaning of "spirit" or "soul stuff." Nerves don't speak, but they "vibrate in the way which corresponds to the use of the words concerned," as a kind of substitute for ordinary language (M, 54). Ordi-nary healthy individuals are incapable of understanding this "nerve-language." Schreber's God, who lives in the "forecourts of heaven," is literally a bundle of nerves, that is, he is constituted of soul material. Unhappily, that Being is some-what otiose; but if human beings act according to the "order of the world" no clash could occur between God and man.[126]

In his thinking, the rays emanating from God can "infuse dreams into a sleep-ing human being," thus causing either weal or woe (M, 55).[127] In Schreber's case, his psychiatrist Flechsig somehow used his (Flechsig's) nerves to cause woe to Schreber. He mentions that Flechsig has a dual persona; his hospital persona might be that of a humane person of "integrity and moral worth." But there is another Flechsig who, via his own nervous system, "maintained a hypnotic or similar contact with me in such a way that even when separated in space, you exerted an influence on my nervous system," that is, when he was in Pierson's or

Weber's lunatic asylum (M, 10). This means that Schreber has no mastery over his own nerves, a violation of his "natural right." Because he also experienced other voices of supernatural origin speaking to him, it may be that Flechsig wanted to investigate them out of "scientific" interest. It seems that Schreber's retrospective discourse reconciles the humane Flechsig with the Flechsig who runs the asylum. It is the latter Flechsig who causes "soul murder" by engaging in medical "malpractice."[128] The effect of his deleterious nerve contact on Schreber is "compulsive thinking," that is, being compelled "to think incessantly," although by "thinking" he does not mean rational discourse (M, 55).

Like other visionaries, Schreber also suffered the dark night of the soul from around the middle of March to the end of May 1894, which he characterizes as the "gruesome time" of his life but also "the holy time" because he was in constant touch with supernatural beings. He describes in graphic detail the cruel treatment he received from the outside, that is, the asylum; yet paradoxically this very situation facilitated "supernatural inspiration" when he was filled with the sublimity of God and Order of the World. He says that he was not a person given to passion; clearheaded and sober he was, implicitly imploring the reader to take him seriously. He had been a materialist and a believer in evolution, but all this changed during this "holy time," which was also a time of pain. He has to recollect the experiences of that time from memory because he lacked writing material. The last statement is a bit ambiguous because at this time he believed mankind had perished "so that there was no purpose in writing notes" (M, 71). Very likely he did have access to writing material, but the power of his religious experiences were such that perhaps he could not write, because writing entails a form of discursive activity that can only occur as "secondary elaboration" for those who experience visions. His later capacity for a more rational and reflective form of thought makes him skeptical about the empirical reality of some of his experiences. For example, he says "it is extremely difficult to distinguish mere dream-visions from experiences in a waking state, that is to say to be certain how far all that I thought I had experienced was in fact historical reality," a dilemma that also appears in others inhabiting this essay (M, 71). Then, in tune with his later reflective scribal spirit, Schreber draws a neat sketch of Flechsig's "nerve clinic" at Leipzig University, the premises where he lived, though occasionally in spirit form. "I was somewhere else for a time" existing in the other worlds or immersed in other states such as his downward descent and his reversed evolutionary fantasy that I have already mentioned.

I will describe a few more of Schreber's religious experiences. With the increasing sensitivity of his nerves, he is subject to increasing "attraction" by spiritual forces, especially of those souls who had known him when they were alive.

They originally had many nerves, but, when approaching his body, they lost all their nerves except one, and this one assumed the form of "little men," tiny figures in human form a few millimeters in height who occupied his head. "This was the final form of existence of these souls before they vanished completely." These little men occasionally acted as repositories of knowledge: "On these occasions I was frequently told the names of the stars or groups of stars from which they had emanated." Like shamans and other spiritual experts, Schreber is learning about the cosmos from these little men. "On some nights the souls finally dripped down on to my head, in a manner of speaking, in their hundreds if not thousands, as 'little men,'" though it is not clear whether these are the "fleeting improvised men" he mentions later (M, 75). It seems therefore that the little space of his head could accommodate these teeming hosts. In another sense, the little men and the fleeting improvised men are his own creation, through his androgynous self, as we shall soon see.

Because rays were emanations of God, they had names like "the Lord of Hosts," "the Almighty," etc., as if they were God's omnipotence itself, reminding us that for Schreber God is most often seen as otiose but sometimes as an all-powerful or dualistic being, depending on the context in which he is invoked. It is in conjunction with God's presence in the rays that Schreber experienced "in recurrent nightly visions the notion of the approaching *end of the world*, and the shattering of cosmic order, as a consequence of the indissoluble connection between God and myself" (M, 75). These "visions" were constituted of both voices and pictorial representations. "While I had these visions at night, in day-time I thought I could notice the sun following my movements; when I moved to and fro in the single-windowed room I inhabited at the time, I saw the sunlight now on the right, now on the left wall (as seen from the door) depending on my movements. . . . When later I regularly visited the garden again I saw—if my memory does not wholly deceive me—two suns in the sky at the same time, one which was our earthly sun, the other was said to be the Cassiopeia group of stars drawn together into a single sun" (M, 75–76). Schreber is addicted to binary oppositions and dualisms, so that the sun is split into two as indeed is Flechsig and God himself. He goes on to say that his "innumerable visions" of the end of the world were partly "gruesome" and "partly of an indescribable sublimity," a neat characterization of the dark night of the soul, as the following experiences indicate (M. 78).

First: reminding us of shamanic space travel, Schreber says that "I traversed the earth from Lake Ladoga to Brazil and, together with an attendant, I built there in a castle-like building a wall in protection of God's realms against an advancing yellow flood tide: I related this to the peril of a syphilitic epidemic," the latter a fin de siècle dread. Second: "At another time I felt as if I myself was raised up to Blessedness, it was as though from the heights of heaven the whole earth were resting under a blue vault below me, a picture of sublime splendor and beauty," a fantasy that reappears in lucid dreamers, including Jung, as we shall see (M, 79). In addition to these sublime ones there were others that were dreadful or possessing a combination of the sublime and gruesome. As for the latter, he was "doubtful whether they were only visions or at least in part real experiences"—again expressing doubts about some visions but little doubt of the sublime ones (M, 79). The horrible and gruesome ones were also known as "frightening miracles" and were occasionally pictured as "black bears" sitting around him with gleaming eyes; when "cats with glowing eyes appeared on the trees in the Asylum's garden" or in a "dense forest, a few meters only removed from the window" of his room, that he called a "holy forest" (M, 80). These beings were replacements for the demonic figures of medieval Christian penitents. At other times he was spiritually transformed when, for example, he possessed a halo like that of Christ, but "incomparably richer and brighter" and therefore, not surprisingly, he was endowed with a "crown of rays"(M, 80). "I lived for years in doubt as to whether I was really still on earth or whether on some other celestial body. Even in the year 1895 I still considered the possibility of my being in Phobos, a satellite of the planet Mars." In soul language he was called "the *seer of spirits*" or defined as a "man who sees, and is in communication with, spirits or departed souls," so much so that Flechsig's soul designated him as the "greatest seer of all millennia" (M, 81). To be a seer, he has to be "unmanned" and converted into a woman, reminding us of transvestite shamans familiar to us from the ethnographic record and, more generally, in the human imagination (M, 53).

How then does this great seer see the world? Through his doctrine of "picturing," a term which, says Zvi Lothane, "is a translation for Schreber's '*sogenannte Zeichen*' literally drawing pictures . . . and Schreber's term for thinking in images, or imagining."[129] But once he exercises control over the process of picturing, presumably through what he calls "obsessive thinking," pictorial images can be reproduced almost at will. "By vivid imagination [*lebhafte Vorstellung*, literally "vivid image"] I can produce pictures [*Bilder*] of all recollections of my life, of persons, animals and plants, of all sorts of objects in nature and objects in daily use, so that these images become visible either inside my head or if I wish outside, where I want them to be seen by my own nerves and by the rays."[130] But pictures cannot be put back into discursive thought. He has "to avoid becoming too discursive" because, he adds in a footnote, when it comes to describing the visions or "the *pictures* of which I have in my head," the task "is extremely difficult, in part impossible" (M. 98, n. 51).

Pictures came into play when he was moved from Flechsig's hospital to Pierson's private asylum for a few months in June 1894. He called it the "devil's kitchen," and his dread of being forsaken there was strong. This was a time of the wildest miracles, when "fleeting improvised men" began to appear in full force. He refers to the courtyard where patients were assembled as his "pen," for here he saw "only extraordinary figures, among them fellows in linen overalls covered with soot," and they were silent or uttered only fragmentary sounds. He knew some of these inmates. They entered the common room and, with the benefit of his "special eye," he "repeatedly witnessed that some of them changed heads . . . and suddenly ran about with a different head" (M, 105). The hospital attendant, who had accused him of masturbation, was magically converted into "my servant in the form of fleeting-improvised men," a form of magical revenge that we see in other visionaries as well, most commonly among sorcerers (M, 108).

Miracles animated lifeless forms. "I saw even articles of clothing on the bodies of human beings being transformed, as well as food on my plate during meals (for instance pork into veal or vice-versa) etc." What is interesting here is the infusion of life into inanimate things, as in some of the hysterical visions of Freud's and Breuer's patients, for example when Emmy von N saw "the legs and arms of the chairs were all turned into snakes" (SH, 62). Outside the window Schreber saw "a magnificent portico arise, just as if the whole building were going to be transformed into a fairy palace; later the image vanished, supposedly because the completion of the intended divine miracle was prevented by Flechsig's and von W.'s counter-miracles; the picture still stands out clearly in my memory" (M, 107). I shall later record similar fantasy creations in Tibetan visionaries and in Madame Blavatsky. Needless to say, such shifting images are very much in tune with the work of dreams.

Schreber was transferred to Sonnenstein in July or August 1894, and as always he wonders whether some of his experiences there are "objective events." He recollects the existence of a smaller sun first led by Fleschig's soul and later by that of Guido Weber, the director of Sonnenstein. Others might think this "sheer nonsense" because Weber is still alive. This Schreber knows is true, but "I must assume that some time in the past Dr. Weber departed from this life and ascended with his nerves to Blessedness, but then returned to life among mankind," a fact unfathomable for ordinary human beings without knowledge of supernatural power (M, 130). At this time he also saw God's omnipotence in its "complete purity," and "the radiant picture of his rays became visible to my inner eye" when lying in bed in a waking state, a phenomenon that will soon take us to the many ways in which the "eye" is represented in the visionary imaginations of the virtuosos who will appear in these pages (M. 131).

Following his preoccupation with dualisms, Schreber also splits God into a higher and lower deity, this time following the Zoroastrian model. He heard the voice of the lower god Ariman (Ahriman) in a loud bass directly in front of his windows. What was spoken wasn't friendly; Schreber was called "wretch" several times. But in spite of this he felt sublime because of the genuineness of the words spoken. On the following day, or perhaps a couple of days later, "I saw the upper God (Ormuzd) [Ahura Mazdā], this time not with my mind's eye but with my bodily eye." He appeared as the sun "surrounded by a silver sea of rays which covered a 6th or 8th part of the sky . . . a sight of overwhelming splendor and magnificence that I did not dare look at it continually" (M, 132). The bodily eye is one's physical sight, and seeing with it has special power because the vision is as real as those objects one sees with one's ordinary sight.

Others including his attendant did not see any of these or the "fleeting improvised men, who of course led a dream life." People would say he suffered from hallucinations, "but the certainty of my recollection makes this for me subjectively quite out of the question, the more so as the phenomenon was repeated on several consecutive days and lasted for several hours on each single day; nor do I believe that my memory fails me when I add that that more radiant sun spoke to me in the same way as the [other] sun [Ahriman] did before and still does without interruption" (M, 133). This, like other bodily visions, seem reasonable proof to him of their reality and is based on the commonsense adage that "seeing is believing."

Having sampled a few of Schreber's visions, let me now deal with the scattered references to what I have called "It-thinking." Schreber claims that he is possessed by a certain immobility, which "was not so much the actual lack of means of occupation but that I considered *absolute passivity almost a religious duty*" (M, 135, my emphasis; see also M, 159). But what is fascinating is his proclaiming "the natural right of man to think nothing" (M, 167). This is because the "soul language" and the voices that he hears are both external and internal. Like visions, voices also well forth from their celestial abode. Therefore cognition is passive, indicated by his marvelous phrases: "automatic-remembering thought" or "not thinking of anything thought" (M, 272, 273). Why passivity? He says that "*purposeful thought*, [is] essential for human beings, but apparently incomprehensible to the rays" (M, 275). Later on he repeats what he claims to have said several times that "rays are *essentially without thought* or that they lack thoughts. This idea did not arise in me spontaneously, but rests on statements I received and still receive from the voices themselves. . . . The rays' essential lack of thoughts is by no means to be taken in the sense that God Himself has lost His original wisdom or even that it has diminished" (M, 283).

In other words, Schreber is striving, with some difficulty, to express the idea of "thoughts without a thinker" or, better still, thoughts without a thinking-I. This entails passive cognition which, according to Schreber, has its own psychophysiology. "My *eyes* and the *muscles of the lids* which serve to open and close them were an almost uninterrupted target for miracles. The eyes were always of particular importance, because rays lose their destructive power with which they are equipped after a relatively short time as soon as they *see something*, and then enter my body without causing damage. The object seen can be either visual (eye) impressions, which are communicated to the rays when my eyes are open, or images which I can cause at will on my inner nervous system by imagination, so that they become visible to the rays." In soul language, Schreber reminds us, this is known as picturing. "Here I will only mention that attempts were made early on and kept up throughout the past years, to close my eyes against my will, so as to rob me of visual impressions and thus preserve the rays' destructive power. This phenomenon can be observed in me at almost every moment; whoever watches carefully will observe that my eyelids suddenly droop or close even while I am talking to other people; this never occurs in human beings under natural conditions. In order to keep my eyes open nevertheless, a great effort of will is needed; but as *I am not always particularly interested in keeping my eyes open I allow them to be closed temporarily at times*" (M, 148, my emphasis). I assume that when this happens, his inner eye or special eye takes over.

Schreber has a related theory of picture retention in memory and its recollection: "Perhaps nobody but myself, not even science, knows that man retains all recollections in his memory, by virtue of lasting impressions on his nerves, as pictures in his head. Because my inner nervous system is illuminated by rays, these pictures can be voluntarily reproduced; this in fact is the nature of picturing" (M, 209–10). Thus some of his visions appear involuntarily when he is in hospital; others appear voluntarily when he invokes the visions contained in the brain through "obsessive thinking," but even in this case presumably without the intervention of the "I" and most often with the eyes closed.

Schreber then refers to a quote of his from October 29, 1898: "To picture (in the sense of the soul language) is the conscious use of the human imagination for the purpose of producing pictures (predominantly pictures of recollections) in one's head, which can then be looked at by the rays" (M, 210). And then: "By vivid imagination I can produce pictures of all recollections from my life, of persons, animals and plants, of all sorts of objects in nature and objects of daily use, so that these images become visible either inside my head or if I wish, outside, where I want them to be seen by my own nerves and by the rays." I think the reference is to recollections stored in memory that can be brought forth through concentration or obsessive thinking. "I can do the same with weather phenomena and other events; I can for example let it rain or let lightning strike—this is particularly effective form of 'picturing,' because the weather and particularly lightning are considered by the rays manifestations of the divine gift of miracles; I can also let a house go up in smoke under the window of my flat, etc. All this naturally only in my imagination, but in a manner that the rays get the impression that these objects and phenomena really exist" (M, 210–11).

He can manifest himself as a double appearing in two places at the same time, a gift of bilocation that other religious virtuosos also possessed, without exactly embracing Schreber's unique fantasy. "I can also 'picture' myself at a different place, for instance while playing the piano I see myself at the same time standing in front of a mirror in the adjoining room in female attire; while I am lying in bed at night I can give myself and the rays the impression that my body has female breasts and a female sexual organ. . . . 'Picturing' in this sense may therefore be called a reversed miracle. In the same way as rays throw on to my nerves pictures they would like to see especially in dreams, I too can produce pictures for the rays which I want them to see" (M, 211). When in bed "it requires only a little exertion of my imagination to attain such sensuous pleasure as gives a pretty definite foretaste of female sexual enjoyment in intercourse" (M, 239; see also M, 211).

In this instance the rays are not sending visions. Rather Schreber has trained himself to evoke stored images in order to "conquer the otherwise often unbearable boredom," raising the question whether Schreber would have experienced much of his liberating visions if he were not forcibly confined to his imprisoning asylum or "pen" (M, 212). Perhaps this kind of picturing is associated with his "compulsive thinking," whereas the visions are pictures appearing before Schreber as a work of rays. The recollected pictures are a kind of challenge thrown down by Schreber to God/rays. He thinks that these objects conjured are in his imagination, but the rays think they actually exist. Is he being merely playful or is he playing dice with god? By contrast, he mentions in chapter 18 a different kind of vision, another frightening miracle or waking dream: "In early years there sometimes appeared when I was in bed—not sleeping but awake—all sorts of large, queer, almost dragon-like shapes, immediately next to my bed, and almost as big as my bed; they were so close that I could almost have touched them with my hands" (M, 223)

I have resisted giving psychiatric labels to Schreber because from my point of view the varying and sometimes contradictory diagnoses of his condition might provide insights into the causes of his illness but not our understanding of the man. His visions and explanations of them are not unlike those of other religious visionaries, but Schreber has no audience or congregation, unlike his contemporaries, the Theosophists, whose visions and discourses I will take up later. In Schreber's case the writing down of his experiences is expressly directed to a reading public that might at least recognize their validity and thereby help create a public discourse out of his private visions. If thoughts can be transformed into images in dreams, then visionary images could also be transformed into thought through writing. But beyond that writing has an important therapeutic function: through scribal reflection Schreber's copes with what he calls his mystical or supernatural experiences, giving them rational organization and existential meaning, analogous to, but philosophically different from, the Buddha rationally reformulating thoughts experienced during the night of his awakening. The actual visions as immediately experienced must have been real to Schreber; on later reflection, in his *Memoirs,* he thinks some are real, some maybe not.

So are his attempts to give coherence to his mystical thoughts because "the picture[s] which I have in my mind [are] extremely difficult to express in words" (M, 110). His is not a picture theory of language, but, as with dreams, pictures take the place of language, in a different epistemological space. Without trying to belittle Wittgenstein's genius, I can now ask whether Schreber was any the less intelligible than Wittgenstein of the *Tractatus,* which, as I said, only few could initially understand. But there was no way that a psychotic could ever hope to get such an audience, although I know of another thinker who could obtain her thoughts from masters living in the Himalayas and thereby sanctify them. Blavatsky's visions were no more coherent than Schreber's, but, when expressed in terms of her esoteric Buddhism, they created an ever-expanding audience of truth seekers and a reading public searching for another god to replace the one whom Nietzsche had killed.

Schreber was psychotic in one sense at least; his thoughts were way out of sync with Victorian reality and the reality of fin de siècle Germany. Freud in his masterly study labeled him a paranoid, though a "gifted" one. And some of his utterances do have the flavor of a "paranoid imagination," especially when he is talking about his "unmanning" (M, 61–68).[131] Freud also used Schreber to demonstrate that paranoia is often associated with homosexuality, when it could well be that homosexuals of his time harbored paranoid thoughts ("paranoid imagination") because of the hostility of the public and the sense of guilt they felt about the "unnaturalness" of their actual or suppressed or disguised sexual orientation. I would suffer from a paranoid imagination if I were in that situation.[132] But beyond this I want to make the assertion that Schreber's visions, as that of many a "psychotic," is very close to what one experiences in dreams, with the proviso that when we wake up reality tells us that "this is only a dream." Schreber's visions and dreams were real to him, although he occasionally recognizes that he might have mistaken dream for reality. His visions were psychically real but could not be easily communicated to others. He could not carry out a rational conversation about them with fellow Germans, being out of sync with their cultural reality. His attempt to express his thoughts in his *Memoirs* was a brave but futile attempt to convince a public of the depth and urgency of his experiences. But, without intersubjective dialogue and at least minimal consensus among thoughtful persons, no vindication of the truth of an unusual experience could ever succeed.

For Freud, the most flagrant expression of Schreber's paranoia was his androgynous sexual fantasies. "The picturing of female buttocks on my body—*honi soit qui mal y pense*—has become such a habit that I do it almost automatically when I bend down," implying that he is ready to be mounted (M, 211). Schreber sometimes dressed himself in female clothes and gazed in the mirror, both the real mirror and the inner eye that mirrored his innermost thoughts as pictures. He justified his androgynous fantasy through a myth in which a catastrophe destroyed the world but spared a single man to propagate the species, and that man could be symbolized as the Eternal Jew. But how could this single person bear children? "The Eternal Jew (in the sense described) had to be *unmanned* (transformed into a woman) to be able to bear children. This process of unmanning consisted in the (external) male genitals (scrotum and penis) being retracted into the body and the internal sexual organs being at the same time transformed into the corresponding female organs, a process which might have been completed in a sleep lasting hundreds of years, because the skeleton (pelvis, etc.) had also to be changed" (M, 60). I doubt if he knew Blake, whose Eternal Man is also the perfect androgynous being, uniting within him the sexual attributes of both sexes. More likely he knew Jacob Boehme, from whom Blake derived this idea, in which case Schreber endows the older image of androgyny with his own deep motivations, converting the older idea into a personal symbol.

In his case, the process of body change was accelerated thanks to the rays. His bodily fantasy permits Schreber to repeat the problem of the Eternal Jew in respect to himself, such that the sexual fantasy of the androgynous vision helped create or procreate his own creatures, the "fleeting-improvised-men" then inhabiting his head. A fleeting-improvised-man is "a soul temporarily given human shape by divine miracle," a kind of production of his own body fertilized by God or through androgynous copulation. "Twice at different times (while I was still in Flechsig's Asylum) I had a female genital organ, although a poorly developed one, and my body felt quickening like the first signs of life of a human embryo: by a divine miracle God's nerves corresponding to male seed had been *thrown* into my body, in other words fertilization had occurred" (M 18, n. 1, my emphasis; see also M, 28 and book 5, note 55 on "thrownness"). This fantasy could partly be related to his real-life disappointment in not having children, his wife having suffered several miscarriages. Schreber compensates for this loss with the mass production of illusory children from his own illusory androgynous body. But, beyond that personal need, Schreber is refantasizing a preoccupation of many cultures wherein the original being such as Adam or a perfect being like the Buddha or Christ becomes transformed in the human imagination into a composite of both male and female. And then there is the fabulous discussion of original androgyny by Aristophanes in Plato's *Symposium*, a text that maybe Schreber knew.[133] Had he lived in our time and in a place that tolerated such sexual transformations, he might have communicated some of his ideas to a sympathetic audience with similar beliefs or fantasies. Perhaps he might have managed through sympathetic dialogues and interaction with fellow "sufferers" to convert his more flagrant psychic realities into culturally acceptable ones or at least to ones acceptable to a small subculture.

MAHĀYĀNA

Salvific Emptiness, Fullness of Vision

HINGE DISCOURSE: THE MOVEMENT TOWARD MAHĀYĀNA AND THE EMERGENCE OF THEISTIC MYSTICISM

> May the regions of hell become glades of delight, with lakes scented by a profusion of lotuses, splendid and delightful with the chorus of song from grey geese, ducks, *cakravaka*s, swans, and other water-birds.
>
> Let the rain of burning coals, heated rocks, and daggers from this day forth be a shower of flowers; and let the warring with these weapons, one against the other, now be merely playful—a tussle of flowers.
>
> May the hungry ghosts be fed, may they be bathed, may they always be refreshed by the streams of milk flowing from the noble Avalokiteśvara.
>
> May the blind see forms, may the deaf always hear, and may expectant mothers give birth as did Māyādevī [the Buddha's mother], free from pain.
>
> May those who fall upon the wrong path in the wilderness meet with a merchant caravan and, free from weariness, may they proceed without fear of thieves, tigers, or other predators.
>
> May nuns receive support, be free of bickering and harassment, and may the ethical conduct of all those who enter the spiritual community remain unbroken.
>
> May the universe attain Buddhahood in a single, divine embodiment, without tasting the torment of hell, without the need for laborious effort.
>
> As long as space abides and as long as the world abides, so long may I abide, destroying the sufferings of the world.
>
> —Śāntideva, *Bodhicaryāvatāra*[1]

I N MY DISCUSSION of the Buddha's awakening, I dealt with one of the early traditions of Buddhism, the Theravāda or "the doctrine of the elders." The "elders" were among the first disciples of the Buddha who, it is said, committed the texts to memory. These texts were apparently first written down in the first century BCE in Sri Lanka, although the canon was not formalized until several centuries later.[2] The Theravāda Buddhist spiritual quest was a-theistic; not only was there no God in the doctrine, but its discourses were formulated against the immediate background of the Upaniṣads and prior to that of the Vedic tradition, the bedrock of what in more recent nationalist times has been designated as the "Hindu canon." The fundamental Theravāda doctrine of "no-self" or *anatta* (no-*ātman*) is a critique of the idea of a permanent entity such as "soul" or "self" and a divine Self that animates the universe. Thus, from the point of view of Western monotheism and all theistic religions, Theravāda Buddhism poses the fascinating problem of a form of spirituality in which neither God nor an enduring soul has a place. Beyond that, Buddhism poses a further challenge to Hindu and Western notions of the self or God or Good or Being by positing the idea that everything is in a condition of flux and there is no still point discernable in this perpetual change. Existence lacks essence. Thus in Theravāda Buddhism the human being, the container of the "self," is nothing but five aggregates or *skandhas* ("heaps"), broadly defined as the aggregates of matter, sensations, perceptions, mental formations, and consciousness, all of which have other components, discussed in great detail in all Buddhist traditions, as well.[3] That one possesses a permanent self is simply an illusion created by language and, in later Buddhist thought, only a conventional truth (*samvrti*) at best, not an ultimate truth (*paramārtha*). Nāgārjuna (c.150–200 CE) puts the idea of the two truths thus:

> The Buddha's teaching of the Dharma
> Is based on two truths:
> A truth of worldly convention
> And an ultimate truth
>
> Those who do not understand
> The distinction drawn between these two truths
> Do not understand
> The Buddha's profound truth.[4]

In early Buddhism that ultimate truth is the knowledge of nirvana, itself left undefined or at least without substantial discussion, a point I will take up in later discussions. *Saṃsāra,* or the cycle of existence in which we are caught, is an unstable place where everything is relative owing to "conditioned genesis." The idea of conditioning undermines the notion of any essence because essences are "unconditioned," as is God or the Upaniṣadic Self or the Theravāda nirvana. It is certainly true that early Buddhism did entertain the idea of gods, demons, and other supernatural beings, but they were also conditioned beings subject to the law of karma and hence devoid of essence.

The reaction against the Theravāda position came from Mahāyāna, or "the great vehicle," which downgraded the Theravāda and other early schools, with the former now labeled "Hīnayāna" or "lesser vehicle." The early Mahāyāna texts were written sometime between the first century BCE and the first century CE, about the time the Theravāda was put into writing. These Mahāyāna texts were collectively designated as the *Prajñāpāramitā sūtras*, *prajña* meaning "wisdom" and *pāramitā* being the perfections cultivated by the Buddha and mentioned by us earlier with respect to the "historical" Buddha, Gautama. They are six and sometimes ten exemplary deeds, namely, generosity, morality, patience, vigor, concentration (meditation), wisdom, truthfulness, resolution, loving-kindness, equanimity, all embodied in the past lives of the Buddha in his extraordinary acts of self-sacrifice.[5] The Mahāyāna texts do not deny the validity of the early schools but affirm their limitations, especially their doctrine of *arahant*s or saint-virtuosos who realize nirvana for their own (selfish) ends. They also rejected the associated idea of minor Buddhas, who, though awakened into full nirvana-realization, are only interested in their own salvation rather than the goal of true Buddhahood, which is the salvation of all beings. Thus the central feature of Prajñāpāramitā texts, and all of Mahāyāna, is the *bodhicitta*, the awakening mind, or the Bodhisattva aspiration, where the Buddha-to-be cultivates the perfections to become a Buddha himself with the altruistic motivation of saving all sentient beings (humans, animals, gods, and all kinds of spirits, even those confined in hell). Aside from this, Prajñāpāramitā texts reaffirm the Theravāda doctrine of no-self. They also assert, as against the Theravāda, that there is absence of inherent existence in all things especially the widely prevalent idea that there are unconditioned elements known as *dharma*s that constitute the building blocks of the universe. I will take up this theme later, but, for the moment, focus on Mahāyāna's greatest thinker, Nāgārjuna, who argued that not only were *dharma*s empty of essence but so was nirvana, which most Buddhist doctrines seem to have taken for granted as "unconditioned." This is, of course, the hole in the Theravāda tradition. If everything is conditioned, as conditioned genesis would have it, then what about nirvana? On the other hand, if existence is conditioned, it is not surprising that Theravāda Buddhists thought of nirvana as "unconditioned."

Further, in contrast with Theravāda, Mahāyāna postulates the radical idea that the altruistic motivation to be a Buddha is something that any human being can activate because the "seed" or "root" of that motivation is within us all. The bodhicitta or the awakening mind may take many unnumbered lifetimes, even eons, for realizing its goal of Buddhahood through the practice of the ethical perfections or *pāramitās*. Although based on early Theravāda and other foundational doctrines of the same period, Mahāyāna develops a more elaborate and powerfully metaphysical thinking in which visionary epistemology has a prime place. Yet, it must be remembered that the all-consuming compassion of the Bodhisattva that seeks the salvation of all sentient beings, exists in less radical form in Theravāda texts like the *Metta Sutta* of the *Sutta Nipāta*: "Let his thoughts of boundless love pervade the whole world: above, below and across, without any obstruction, without any hatred, without any enmity."[6] The idea that anyone can in principle aspire to be a Buddha is present in Theravāda also; and in popular rebirth aspirations in contemporary Theravāda societies, a person might wish parents or loved ones to eventually become Buddhas. Sometimes this becomes a personal aspiration realizable only in eons henceforth. Nevertheless, the goal of salvation remains nirvana, and each one aspires to seek it eventually after many lifetimes of striving.

The Bodhisattva motivation in Mahāyāna is followed by some profound epistemological thinking best represented by Nāgārjuna, who has been held is such awe that he is sometimes referred to as the second Buddha. Nāgārjuna's ideas are spelled out in his voluminous writings, the most important being the enigmatic and sometimes aphoristic *Mūlamadhyamakakārikā*, "the root wisdom of the middle way."[7] Basically, Nāgārjuna argues that there are no essences in the world, and everything is transient. To say that there are no essences is nothing new in early Buddhism, except a change seems to have occurred in the Abhidharma, the third of the three baskets (*tripiṭaka*) of the canon containing the great metaphysical and psychological treatises. The change began with the early schools both Theravāda and Sarvāstivāda (the latter at one time a very influential doctrine). Both these schools, but especially the Sarvāstivāda, believed that while everything was in a state of flux there were key elements, called *dharmas* (not to be confused with the meaning of "dharma" as doctrine), that were somehow or other "real" in the unreal world of becoming. All Buddhist schools had elaborate classifications of *dharmas*, Theravāda postulating eighty-one conditioned *dharmas* and one unconditioned, the latter being nirvana. As far as the conditioned *dharmas* were concerned, they were subject to change as every other phenomenon. But there was a catch: Theravāda also postulated the idea of a real entity, or *dravya*, and an inner nature, or *svabhāva*, while at the same time emphasizing the transitory nature of *dharmas*. This position inevitably led to debates and affirmations in the Abhidharma that the *dharmas* were "real" in the general unreality of existence. Although most Abhidharma schools formulated the idea that existence was based on *dharmas*, they also affirmed that *dharmas* have nothing to do with the soul or self. There is no "I" or "me" in the *dharmas*.[8]

Nāgārjuna contested this influential theory by suggesting that *dharmas*, or for that matter any theory of elements or atoms, are causally dependent on other *dharmas* and, as conditioned genesis would have it, cannot contain the idea of unchangeableness. However, it is not just the *dharmas* that he critiques. He pushes the idea of that absence to its logical conclusion such that there is no fundamental distinction between nirvana, the goal of Buddhist salvation, and *saṃsāra*, the world of becoming in which we live in our present existence and have lived through the multitudes of past lives and continue to live in future rebirths. This is a revolutionary formulation because most preceding Buddhist thought assumed that nirvana, though eluding description, remained (implicitly and sometimes explicitly according to Buddhist thinkers) "unconditioned." But how can the notion of "unconditioned" be reconciled with the lack of essence that characterizes everything? This is the issue that Nāgārjuna boldly confronted.

Nāgārjuna probably did not deny the obvious distinction between the world and its transcendence, but that nirvana which early doctrines thought was unconditioned is not so, thereby bringing the inexorable logic of conditioned genesis to bear on nirvana itself. Nāgārjuna was building on the space that the Buddha himself created when he did not fully deal with the question "what is nirvana?" and implied the fruitlessness of the inquiry. Nāgārjuna fills that space of silence or indeterminacy with *śūnyata* ("emptiness" or the "void") the key concept in all of Mahāyāna. If indeed nirvana is without essence, it is conditioned and hence Nāgārjuna's famed equation "nirvana is *saṃsāra*." The basic idea is not difficult to grasp: Nāgārjuna simply carries the idea of conditioned genesis to its logical conclusion, which then results in a world without any kind of essence, nirvana included. What is truly complex in his thought is his justification of that thesis and his enfolding all Buddhist thought within the notion of emptiness. However, to say with Nāgārjuna that nirvana and *saṃsāra* are both conditioned phenomena makes nonsense of the Theravāda claim that nirvana is *not* the world of becoming and change (*saṃsāra*). If nirvana is conditioned, as he claims, then what about emptiness? It is obviously not conditioned; were it conditioned then emptiness would be *saṃsāra*, in which case there is no difference between nirvana and emptiness. It is also obviously not unconditioned because the "philosophy" or thought of Nāgārjuna and his followers recognize that the Madyamaka means the "middle way," that between being and nonbeing or something in between eternalism (essentialism) and nihilism.[9] The middle way is of course conditioned genesis but it is also a response to critics for whom emptiness was a kind of nihilism. What Nāgārjuna is at pains to show is that emptiness is not a "thing," be it conditioned or unconditioned: hence his famed view on the "emptiness of emptiness." One can hardly blame his critics if they fail to grasp this elusive, even incomprehensible idea.

In what sense can we say that emptiness can become a salvific goal, taking the place of nirvana? This is a huge question, but one thing is clear: for Nāgārjuna, but not for Theravāda Buddhists, emptiness is logically justified by the doctrine of conditioned genesis, and therefore one could even say that conditioned genesis is in fact emptiness, as he states in a well-known verse in his *Mūlamadhyamakakārikā*:

> If you perceive the existence of all things
> In terms of their essence,
> Then this perception of all things
> Will be without the perception of causes and conditions.

> Whatever is dependently co-arisen
> That is explained to be emptiness.
> That, being a dependent designation,
> Is itself the middle way.[10]

The realization of emptiness has now become Mahāyāna's salvific goal. Although one can "understand" emptiness discursively or philosophically, such understanding remains conventional and not ultimate. Thus I might intellectually grasp the idea of emptiness, for example, by reading Nāgārjuna or other Mahāyāna texts, and this might even be necessary in a preliminary way. Yet one must let go of that form of understanding and replace it with a meditative understanding of its truth.

In Buddhism that meditative technology is of two kinds. There is *śamatha,* or calming meditation, which existed in the prior Hindu tradition and also exists under different names and guises in other traditions such as the Christian. And one can practice calming meditation without a guide or preceptor (guru). The uniquely Buddhist form of meditation is *vipassanā* (Sanskrit *vipaśyanā*) or "insight meditation," the idea behind which is to show the unreality that underlies our conventional conceptual understanding of the world, for example, that there is no self, that the world is in continuous and unrelenting change, that there are no essences of any sort underlying existence.[11] These meditational disciplines are multiple and extraordinarily detailed, complex, and dangerous, so that one should not engage in them without a guru, the "true friend" whom we have already met, unless they have been radically restructured as, for example, among middle-class meditators in virtually every part of our contemporary world.

Nevertheless, there are some meditation techniques that cut across the various schools of Buddhism. A good example is *asubha bhāvanā,* or meditation on the "foulness of the body," the goal of which is to show that neither the body nor the self exists in any conceptual or ontological sense. These techniques of foulness have been developed at length, and in deadly detail, in the classic manual of Theravāda meditation, *The Path of Purification,* by Buddhaghosa.[12] Let me quote a less obsessively detailed text on the revulsion of the body by our favorite saint-poet:

> Why, mind, do you protect this carcass, identifying with it? If it is really separate from you, then what loss is its decay to you?
>
> O Fool! You do not identify with a wooden doll even when it is pure. So why do you guard this festering contraption made of filth?
>
> First, just in your mind, pull apart this bag of skin. With the knife of wisdom loosen the flesh from the cage of bones.
>
> Cracking open the bones, too, look at the marrow within. Work out for yourself what essence is there.
>
> Searching hard like this, you have found no essence here. Now explain why it is that you still continue to guard the body.[13]

And so on: from the absence of essence to the absence of self, because when you break the body to its component parts or ever-changing aggregates the concept of the body vanishes as does the concept of the self. This idea in turn has an important ancestry in early Buddhism in its metaphor of the chariot. The chariot is nothing but a concept that we impose on the component parts of the vehicle designated for conventional usage as *chariot,* and this means that the label *chariot* is "empty." And each part of the chariot, when broken into its component parts, remains likewise empty, and these parts when broken into smaller atomic units are also empty. And so it goes on ad infinitum. One could therefore say that while the component parts of the chariot are interrelated via conditioned genesis, the chariot does not exist as a "whole" except in a purely nominal sense. All intellection and conceptual thought, and indeed all of language, belongs to the conventional, not to the ultimate truth which is conditioned genesis, absence of self/ Self, and the absence of inherent existence that then leads us to the knowledge of emptiness or the void, *śūnyatā.* But because the realization of the void is considered to be bliss, one might ask: What kind of bliss is emptiness?

The historical movement to Mahāyāna is of no concern to me except as an epistemological one: in what ways is emptiness invested with magical content or enchantment? To answer this we must get back to the question of how emptiness is apprehended in meditative asceses. In its conceptual purity Nāgārjuna's *Fundamental Wisdom* debates the prior Buddhist traditions, but he does not mention the Prajñāpāramitā texts that dealt with the career of the Buddha. As Mahāyāna develops in relation to political and historical forces in India, we see attempts to fuse emptiness with the salvific quest of the Bodhisattva ideal. Beyer puts this well with respect to Prajñāpāramitā texts and indeed to all Mahāyāna: "The metaphysics of the Prajñāpāramitā is in fact the metaphysics of the vision and the dream: a universe of glittering and quicksilver changes is precisely one that can only be described as empty. The vision and the dream become the tools to dismantle the hard categories we impose on reality, to reveal the eternal flowing possibility in which the Bodhisattva lives."[14]

This statement, while true, has to be qualified. It is the case that the unstable and changing vision is not real; the real is the truth behind the quicksilver vision and dream. The dream in turn is explicitly seen as a symbol or a metaphor for the illusory nature of all existence. Yet, within the space-time of that illusion, we already know from our previous discussions, the dreamer or visionary believes in the reality of what he sees. If the visionary has a glimpse of the Western paradise of Amitābha ("Illimitable Radiance"), he is transported to a magical world of unbelievable beauty, and this is the place where the meditator wants to be reborn in a long space-time, though not truly eternal, of bliss. Known as Sukhāvatī, its attraction lies in its "enormous jewel-lotuses, its absence of mountains, its fragrant rivers bearing jewel-flowers and making sweet sounds, its heavenly music whose soft and lovely sound produce happiness by suggesting 'impermanence, calm and no-soul.'" Those living here can, as we moderns, turn music on and off and control the temperature to suit their needs; they can listen to the chanting of the doctrine, including "the doctrine of emptiness, signlessness, uncommitedness, non-synthesising, not being born, non-occurrence, non-existence, cessation etc."[15] Now these are not all that far removed from the heavens of the prior Theravāda tradition, except that such realms were not identified with a Buddha presence; nor was it related to salvific goals. Sukhāvatī means "land of bliss" but it is vastly different from the undefined and indefinable bliss of emptiness. And when the Mahāyāna seeker of salvation sees the great Bodhisattva Avatilokeśvara in any of his apparitional forms, or he becomes Avatilokeśvara (or any other deity, male or female) through his meditative ascesis, there is a temporal reality to the illusion even while the illusion-creating dream is taking place.

This position is also well stated by Lambert Schmithausen in his study of a Mahāyāna text, the *Bhadrapālasūtra*. which anticipates the Yogācāra School of later Mahāyāna:

> Its main subject is a special kind of visionary meditation in which the Yogin sees himself face to face with any Buddha of the present time, especially with Amitābha or Amitāyus, the Buddha who resides in the western paradise Sukhāvatī.... These apparitions of the Buddha visualized in meditation are compared with dream visions, with reflected images, and with the decaying corpses and skeletons visualized in the "contemplation of the impure" (*asubha bhāvanā*). Just as these imaginary appearances, the Buddhas visualized in meditative concentration are also not really met by the meditating Bodhisattva but only projections of the Bodhisattva's mind; and what the Bodhisattva should realize is precisely this fact that the visualized Buddha is nothing but mind (*cittam eva*).[16]

Mind created or not, the meditator identifies with one or more of the Buddhas during the experienced vision. Beyer appropriately calls them "visionary theism," or, in my terminology, a form of theistic mysticism, even though in an *ultimate* sense visionary theism is illusory just as ordinary life is an illusion or *māyā*.[17] It would be hard to justify that the world of visions and visionary theism is the epistemological equivalent of the everyday illusory world in which we live because the object of the Mahāyāna vision quest is in fact to transcend the lived world. Moreover, in contrast to illusory everyday existence, the psychic reality of visions must surely have stunning emotional resonances to the meditator because, even though ultimately nominal, they express the powers that meditation provides. They constitute a vast repertoire of psychic powers possessed by advanced adepts on the Bodhisattva path. Many of these powers (*siddhi*) such as the capacity for levitation and retrocognition have been attributed to the historical Buddha and the arahants of Theravāda Buddhism, but they are described in mind-boggling detail in the Sanskrit literature on the Bodhisattvas.[18] And one must remember that, in spite of the ideals of compassion, the Tantric adept or *siddha* (the possessor of supernormal powers or *siddhi*s) can on occasion practice violence, especially to vanquish demons and enemies of Buddhism.

After Nāgārjuna, the next great thinker I want to consider is Asaṅga, the founder of Yogācāra ("the meditational way"), who composed his texts in what appears to have been a visionary experience. Consider the Tibetan historian Tāranātha's version of the myth of Asaṅga's ascension to the realm of Maitreya, the next Buddha. After his studies and his ordination, Asaṅga spent three years in a cave meditating on Maitreya. Because he had no luck, he decided to come out of the cave. There he was inspired by birds that went out in search of food and returned in the evening to their nests. Returning to his cave, he started to propitiate Maitreya for three more years; this too did not work and he reemerged from the cave. In this manner he propitiated Maitreya, meditating on him for three-year spells until he had reached the twelfth year, but still without success. Asaṅga then left the cave and went away. "In a city he came across a bitch, infested with worms on the lower half of her body, furiously scratching her wound. The sight made him full of compassion." Following the example of all Buddhas, he performed an exemplary act of selfless giving (*dāna pāramitā*) by cutting some flesh from his own body and placing the worms therein. He had shut his eyes while engaging in this act when, lo and behold, neither the worms nor the bitch did he see but instead Maitreya himself in his resplendent glory. Asaṅga apparently had failed to see Maitreya earlier owing to his previous bad karma. The Bodhisattva urged Asaṅga to carry him on his shoulder into the city, but there only two persons could catch even a meager glimpse of the Bodhisattva. When Asaṅga informed Maitreya of his wish to spread the Mahāyāna, the latter urged Asaṅga to "catch hold the corner of my robe," and then, clinging to the robe, he ascended into the Tusita heaven, the abode of the Bodhisattva. There "he listened to the Mahāyāna doctrine in its entirety from Ajitanātha [Maitreya]" and wrote it down for our salvific benefit.[19]

On the one hand, the myth of Asaṅga's ascension has a standard component. This is the Indian belief that the ancient Vedas and other key texts have been "heard" (*śruti*) or divinely revealed by inspired sages and hence infallible in contrast with texts that are *smriti*, given by tradition, a distinction that is often blurred. In this case Asaṅga meditates for a long period of time, but his bad karma inhibits his capacity to see Maitreya. Nevertheless, his exemplary act of giving saved him: he shuts his eyes and in a flash he is in the spirit and sees the resplendent Maitreya and then sees his own sojourn in the Tusita heaven. When we consider other visionaries, we find that there is nothing unusual in Asaṅga's cosmic adventures. Even his learning the Mahāyāna texts from Maitreya has its parallel in the visionary knowledge of other virtuosos, Christian, Buddhist, and Theosophist. Yet the case of Asaṅga hides an important reality, and that is the discovery of the truth in heaven must surely have accompanied the rational reformulation on earth. Another way of rephrasing that experience is to say that *śruti* must be followed by *smriti*, the "It" by the "I," although we do not know how the two occurred in the thinking of Asaṅga. The Asaṅga myth of ascension is important for yet another reason: it gives plausibility to the theory that some Mahāyāna texts might have been "discovered" during meditative visions, although we must recognize that such texts can be revised, even reformulated.[20]

The Mahāyāna visionary is a cosmic adventurer, surpassing the shamans of the non-Buddhist or pre-Buddhist world, as he traverses the cosmos, flies into different universes or Buddha worlds, comports with supernatural beings, dissolves his own nonself into that of a deity, and, above all, furthers the Buddhist cause by discovering texts hidden by previous Buddhas or Bodhisattvas, at least in the Tibetan forms of Mahāyāna. Even if salvation is emptiness, the meditative quest provides an enchanted cosmos that is psychically real to the adept. When we read a text like Nāgārjuna's *Mūlamadhyamakakārikā* or its commentaries, we are confronted with a profoundly abstract thinker; but such thought as his coexisted with the visualizations of the Mahāyāna adept engaged in deep salvific trance. So is it with the great gap between the Western philosopher dreaming of God in a purely intellectual sense and the Christian believer in God. The former has to be satisfied with the intellectual knowledge of God, which does not lead him to a salvific paradise of those who believe in the living, loving, omnipotent God of the monotheisms. Nevertheless, the fantastic worlds created by the Christian visionaries are nothing in comparison with the magical worlds and paradises opened up by the Mahāyāna meditator. We are now in a position to answer the question, how empty is emptiness? *Salvific emptiness coexists with the fullness of vision in almost all of Mahāyāna.*

But we cannot get rid of the problem of emptiness by postulating the copresence of its illusionary fantastic, because, in terms of ultimate truth, it is emptiness that the salvation quest demands in most schools of Mahāyāna. Underlying the absence of essence is a critique of the presence of Self or Being (Brahman) or God (Brahma and other gods and goddesses) of the Hindu tradition. Hence it is not surprising that two centuries after the Buddha the abstract doctrine of no-self was resisted by at least one school of Buddhism, the Personalists or Pudgalavādins, of whom unfortunately little is known except through the refutations of their opponents. Personalists believed that, while *dharmas* contain no self, there is no denying the idea of the person and a self of some sort transmigrating from one existence to another.[21] Thus the "debates," or contentious discourses, in the Buddhist tradition harp on the problem of whether one can avoid the notion of essence in dealing with soteriological issues. Even Nāgārjuna, that great deconstructionist of existence, is at pains to deny that emptiness is a form of nihilism. For example, the grammarian Panini used the same term *śūnya* to designate zero, a concept that had revolutionary impact on the development of mathematics. By itself *śūnya* represented in "0" or zero is empty, but when preceded by a numeral it no longer is empty.[22] In the same way, emptiness is meaningful only in relation to the illusory nature of existence and conditioned genesis. Yet Nāgārjuna, we noted, is categorical that even emptiness is empty or *śūnyatā-śūnyatā*, the "emptiness of emptiness," an idea further elaborated by his disciple Candrakīrti, which, if pushed to its logical conclusion, can only lead to an infinite and meaningless regress. If we say that emptiness deals with the absence of essence, it makes no sense to speak endlessly of the "absence of essence of the absence of essence," which proves that nonsense exists even in a profound philosophical tradition.

Where do we go from here? It seems to me inevitable that all the philosophical discourses and controversies of Mahāyāna revolve around the question of essence within existence. Further, while Buddhist thinkers view themselves as innovators, there are limits to innovational leeway, because philosophical and religious discourse occurs everywhere within the framework of ideas postulated by preceding traditions. In the Buddhist case, even the most radical or innovative thinkers are conducting debates on whether or not one can have Buddhism without some notion of essence when most surrounding Indic religions are committed to powerful essentialist doctrines. Hence the criticism of Nāgārjuna by his opponents that his nihilism leads us to a salvific no-where, whereas Nāgārjuna, as well as the philosophical schools that adopted his teachings, affirmed that the Madyamaka was in harmony with the idea of burning out defilements such that, when no discursive or conceptual thoughts arise, the subject-object dualisms characterizing ordinary thinking will be no more and the mind will be calmed. When that happens, emptiness also happens. But then the unanswered question: is emptiness bliss? That too brings us back to the earlier question: while emptiness might express a truth about the world, is emptiness in this abstract sense of knowledge of reality empty of attraction for seekers of salvation?

Let us therefore dip into history and begin with an early reaction to Nāgārjuna and his student Aryadeva within the Madyamaka itself by two powerful movements. First, the Prāsaṅgika or the *reductio ad absurdum* school founded by Candrakīrti (c. 700) on the basis of work by Buddhapālita (c. 470–550), who maintained the strict idea of the two truths.[23] The second was the Svātantrika ("independent school") by Bhāvaviveka (born c. 500) who also agreed with Nāgārjuna's idea of the lack of inherent existence except that inherent existence existed conventionally, but not absolutely or ultimately, drawing on the fundamental Buddhist distinction mentioned earlier. Thus, for example, I can believe that I possess a "self" or that God or the Self exists, but that is a purely nominal truth derived from ordinary experience. Because this is open to the criticism that inherent existence or essence is being brought through the back door, the great Candrakīrti denied the existence of self at any level, thus reaffirming a strict Madyamaka position. Influenced by the Buddhist logician Dignāga, Candrakīrti's technique was to "reduce one's opponent's position to absurdity, without taking a positive position oneself."[24] He took for granted that there is no stable entity, even on the conventional or nominal level, in effect maintaining that the self is simply a bundle of constantly changing or volatile "aggregates" without any *dharma*s or substrates, and this lack of inherent existence applies to everything in the universe. While these two groups did not deviate much from the Madyamaka, they could not resolve the deeper existential issue of the salvific attractiveness of a universe without essence formulated in the abstract ideal of emptiness.

To better grasp this problem let us reflect on the enduring Mahāyāna ideal of the "bodies" or *kāya* of the Buddha. The earliest formulation apparently posited a two-body theory, the form-body or *rūpakāya*, that is, the actual body of the Buddha, and the ultimate Buddha nature or the *dharmakāya*, the transcendent Buddha. Later the *rūpakāya* was further split into another two: *samboghakāya* ("body of bliss"), the celestial body of the Buddha and manifest as the many Buddhas and Bodhisattvas of the Mahāyāna pantheon, such as Avalokiteśvara, Tārā, Amitābha, and Mañjuśri, all living in paradisal realms; and the *nirmānakāya*, the existent or historic form of the Buddha exemplified in the Buddha Gautama and the previous "historical" Buddhas of the Theravāda tradition as well as the next Buddha, Maitreya. The *dharmakāya,* or the essence body of the Buddha, his true nature, was represented in general in Samantabhadra ("universal good") or his emanation Vajradhara. That Buddha essence is within us as a seed or "drop" of the *dharmakāya*, the final goal of the *bodhicitta* aspiration. That is, we want to "awaken" the Buddha nature within us and try to eventually realize the *dharmakāya* that exists unbeknown to us within ourselves. But then we are back to the idea of essence because, quite unlike *saṃsāra* and nirvana of Nāgārjuna's thinking, key Mahāyāna texts imply a Buddha essence within us all.

It will be a mistake to equate this conception with "self" or "soul" in the Upaniṣadic sense of *ātman* and Brahman, but it is hard to escape the idea of essence in oneself and the world. It is as if Mahāyāna Buddhists worked out a response to the Upaniṣads without succumbing to the idea of "soul" or self. Nevertheless, in Mahāyāna, as against Theravāda doctrine and one might even say against the spirit of Nāgārjuna, this notion of a Buddha nature or essence is intrinsically connected to salvation. One can put the Mahāyāna dilemmas differently: if one denies essence and at the same time denies nihilism by suggesting that things lacking essence may yet exist nominally, as it is possible to maintain in some forms of Mahāyāna, then a whole series of debates or contentious discourses are bound to arise, compounded further by the doctrines of the three bodies of the Buddha and the Bodhisattva aspiration that in turn is the attempt to realize these three bodies within oneself. These are the debates that circulate in the various doctrines of the Mahāyāna, including the Tibetan.

Let me now deal with a few of these Mahāyāna debates, beginning with Yogācāra, also known as Cittamātra, or the "mind-only" school, and founded by Asaṅga, whose visit to the Tusita heaven we are already familiar with. Asaṅga together with his brother Vasubandhu were the major figures of Yogācāra. Asaṅga inherited Nāgārjuna's idea of emptiness but tried to counter the imputed nihilism of the latter with a more positive view of it.[25] In Asaṅga's extreme form of the mind-construction of the world, everything is not only conditioned but the world also is simply the flow of mental representations that have no enduring quality whatever. According to this doctrine, life is an illusory dreamlike state and there is no subject or object (the absence of dualism is in the nature of things); suffering and pleasure are all illusory. Nevertheless, we can fall back on the standard solution by stating that we can still nominally experience pleasure and pain and other sensations, but not in a true epistemological sense.

Even in this extreme form of Mahāyāna "idealism," if one can call it that, Asaṅga affirmed that consciousness is divided into eight types, the most important being *ālayavijñāna* or "store-consciousness." Schmithausen defines *ālayavijñāna* as "the container or store-house of the latent residues or impressions of previous actions (*karman*) and mind processes;" or, in Tibetan thinking, "fundamental mind," which is the "basic layer of mind processes or even the very basic constituent of the whole living being." It is to be sought "in a (direct) *yogic* experience of the subliminal layer of the mind" and it perhaps taps what nowadays is designated as the "unconscious."[26] Vasubandhu thinks of store-consciousness as a "great torrent of water or river which is changing every moment but which nevertheless preserves a certain identity" (MB, 90–91). It is true that one cannot step into the same river twice. It is also the case that the rivering waters run on and yet, in a sense, the river remains the same. It has an identity, deep and meaningful, but lacks essence, unless we foolishly affirm that the essence of the river is its very changeability.

Although a very complex notion, the idea of a store-consciousness opened up criticism by opponents that it was a container surreptitiously bringing back the "self." Other thinkers were much more explicit and argued that store-consciousness "is the conventional self, the referent of the word 'I,' and is misapprehended by the tainted mind and taken as a real substantial Self, a permanent and stable 'I' or 'Me.'" That too is simply a restatement of the two truths, the nominal and the ultimate that then yielded further debates. Paramārtha (499–569 CE), a missionary to China, believed that when the store-consciousness ceases at liberation "there remains, shining in its own purity, a ninth consciousness, the 'immaculate consciousness' (*amalavijñāna*)" (MB, 92). And this in turn fosters arguments regarding the epistemological status of the immaculate consciousness viewed as a permanent and ultimate or true reality. But whether as store-consciousness or as immaculate consciousness, essence remains an abstraction still.

In the attempt to give a kind of concreteness to the abstract nature of essence we must consider the idea of the Buddha nature within us as the *tathāgatagarbha* or the Buddha womb or matrix, also affirmed by the Yogācāra thinkers. This is a development from earlier roots in Buddhist sects such as the Mahāsaṃghikas who postulated the idea that there was an intrinsically pure root consciousness (*mūlavijñāna*) or "substratum consciousness" that however is defiled in the course of our existence in *saṃsāra*.[27] Alex Wayman says that this theory was developed further in later texts "where it is taught that the Buddha's divine knowledge pervades sentient beings, and that its representation in an individual sentient being is the substratum consciousness." And, whether the term *tathāgatagarbha* was used or not, there emerged the idea that this pure consciousness contained the Buddha nature or *garbha* (womb), an idea that was systematized in the text with that title, the *Tathāgatagarbha Sūtra.* Other texts, such as *Lankāvatāra Sūtra,* simply identify the "womb" or matrix of the Buddha as the store-consciousness or *ālayavijñāna.*[28] But, while the equation of *tathāgatagarbha* with "store-consciousness" gives some concreteness to an abstract idea, the later *Tathāgatagarbha Sūtra* not only affirms that all living beings have within themselves the Buddha nature but adds that even those tainted with moral impurities "are possessed of the Matrix of the Tathāgata (*tathāgatagarbha*), endowed with virtues, always pure, hence not different from me" (MB, 97). If so, it would mean that all of us have the embryo of the Tathāgata, but, living as we do in *saṃsāra*, this pure nature is sullied. In principle it is possible for all human beings to achieve Buddhahood if they can be freed of the taints, and this goal is available even to those who have committed great sins. This is quite unlike most of Mahāyāna, which gives little hope to the latter class of beings.

The *tathāgatagarbha* idea does not necessarily imply the existence of that un-Buddhist doctrine of the self/Self, but it does postulate an essence behind existence. Further, even when the Buddha-womb doctrine is not present, there are texts that affirm similar ideas, such as "thusness" (*tathatā*). In some influential texts, *tathāgatagarbha* is not the pure essence mentioned earlier but an essence defiled by living in *saṃsāra,* whereas the undefiled condition is "thusness." And consider the beautiful text, written, perhaps, soon after the Prajñāpāramitā texts (that is, after the second century CE and before the third), that contains a woman's voice, *The Lion's Roar of Queen Śrīmālā* (*Śrīmālāsiṃhanāda Sūtra*). Queen Srimālā asserts that the Buddha embryo is intrinsically pure, but can be in a condition of defilement through ones existence in *saṃsāra*, or it can exist without defilement when it is nothing but the essence-body of the Buddha, the *dharmakāya*, which is emptiness, in theory at least.[29] She also does not think that there are two vehicles in Buddhism designated as Hīnayāna (Theravāda) and Mahāyāna; all vehicles make up the One Vehicle (*ekayāna*) through which one attains the "incomparable rightly completed enlightenment." "Lord," she lectures the Buddha who has appeared before her, "'incomparable rightly completed enlightenment' is an expression for the Nirvana-realm. 'Nirvana-realm' is an expression for the Dharmakāya of the Tathāgata. . . . Lord, the Tathāgata is not one thing, and the Dharmakāya something else, but the Tathāgata is himself the Dharmakāya."[30] Here is a text that links up both the idea of the *tathāgatagarbha* as essence and that of the *dharma*s, basic constituent elements of existence. Thus, *dharmakāya* is the *dharma* of *dharma*s, and it is the undefiled *tathāgatagarbha*, the Buddha or Tathāgata emanating himself in essence. It therefore should not surprise us that, in spite of formal adherence to the older idea of emptiness, the terms applied to the Buddha-womb in this and other texts express a different reality: "Lord, this Tathāgatagarbha is neither self, nor sentient being, nor soul, nor personality. . . . Lord, this Tathāgatagarbha is the embryo of the Illustrious Dharmadhātu, the embryo of the Dharmadhātu, the embryo of the supramundane *dharma*, the embryo of the intrinsically pure *dharma*," using *dharma* in the sense of the Buddhist doctrine.[31] It is no accident that *Śrīmālā* and related texts describe the *tathāgatagarbha* as permanent (*nitya*), steadfast (*dhruva*), calm (*śiva*), and eternal (*śāśvata*).[32] Even the heterodox idea of the self/Self emerges in texts such as the Mahāyāna *Mahāparinirvāṇa Sūtra*, influential in Chinese Buddhism, boldly affirming that the *tathāgatagarbha* is nothing but the Self, a piece of heterodoxy from the point of view of virtually all schools of Buddhism.

It seems that the old arguments cannot be suppressed; they seem to surface again and again as if there is no closure. But, then, is this not true of any complex system of thought? As far as Self is concerned, the absence of closure is not surprising because if one asserts a Buddha essence it is almost certain, given the power of Upaniṣadic thought, that the Self is going to reappear, even as a piece of heterodoxy. Thus the *Mahāparinirvāṇa Sūtra*: "I do not say that all sentient beings lack a Self. I always say that sentient beings have the Buddha-nature (*svabhāva*). Is not that very Buddha-nature a Self? So I do not teach a nihilistic doctrine" (MB, 99). According to this text, the Buddha teaches a doctrine of no-self or a nominal self in some contexts, and to some persons, but to others a true or essential Self, thus deploying the Buddha's "skill in means," or *upāya*, a discursive strategy geared to the salvific receptivity of a specific audience. This text gives another twist to the conventional opposition between nominal and ultimate truths. As Paul Williams says: "One thing anyway is clear. The *Mahāparinirvāna Sūtra* teaches a really existing, permanent element in sentient beings. It is this element which enables sentient beings to become Buddhas. It is beyond egoistic self-grasping—indeed it is the very opposite of self-grasping—but it otherwise fulfills several of the requirements of a Self in the Indian tradition" (MB, 99). But because this *sutra* as well as a few others use the word self or *ātman* for this entity, it is in effect a critique of the crucial no-self traditions in Buddhism.

There is no escaping the fact that all the preceding ideas revolve around the presence or absence of essence and the compensatory worlds of enchantment opened up by the Mahāyāna meditator. They are then further elaborated in the various schools of Tibetan Buddhism. Tibetan Buddhism or Vajrayāna incorporated into its scheme of things what is called Tantra, a form of salvation striving that some say developed in South India and then went into northern India, especially Kashmir, and later affected all Indian religions including Hinduism and Buddhism.[33] Buddhist and Hindu Tantric history has been well described by scholars, but we shall mention only the features that distinguished it from the dominant Mahāyāna traditions discussed thus far.

Vajrayāna also activated the awakening mind or *bodhicitta* in order to achieve Buddhahood *in one's present existence* and not eons hence, as Mahāyāna thinkers postulated. In attempting to compress the long duration of the salvific struggle to one lifetime, Tibetan Tantra had to develop its own meditational techniques, some of them borrowed from Hindu Tantra. Briefly stated, Tantric Buddhism reverses a key feature of previous forms of Buddhism that enjoined sexual abstinence (*brahmacariya*) as an ideal, imperative for monks, novices, and other salvation-seeking virtuosos. By contrast, eroticism is essential to the Tantric salvation quest and, however sublimated, is unthinkable without it. This produces a peculiar paradox unique to Tibetan Tantra: the high status and revered celibate monk cannot achieve the desired goal of Buddhahood in his current existence because he cannot engage in direct sexual intercourse with a consort. He can however achieve it after death or in another existence. Although sexual Tantra, or *karma mudrā* (action seal), as it is sometimes called, is taboo for monks, they can, through meditation, visualize deities locked in intercourse and identify with them.

The technology of Tantric salvation can be very complicated, even dangerous, and varies with the four dominant Tibetan schools, but everywhere the central figure is the guru who not only provides the empowerments or initiations of Tantra to the pupil but is also the key figure idealized in the Tibetan religious imagination.[34] "Initiation" in the context of these Tantric practices is not the classic rite-of-passage model employed earlier with respect to the Buddha's spiritual quest. Known in Sanskrit as *abhiṣeka,* or more traditionally as *dīkṣā,* these so-called initiations are better translated as "empowerments," generally four in number.[35] Sometimes the Sanskrit *adhiṣṭhāna* ("resolve") is used in the sense of empowerment. In general, during initiation or empowerment the guru imparts to his disciple knowledge and power along with an appropriate mantra, the magical formulaic utterance whispered into the right ear of the pupil.[36] The mantra is a secret formula that, according to one lama, is "the symbol word, the holy sound which, transmitted to the initiate by the preceptor, makes his personality vibrate in consonance and opens it up for higher experience."[37]

In Vajrayāna the disciple or pupil or adept identifies with the guru or with a deity who is represented in a circle or *maṇḍala.* "The basic structure of the *maṇḍala* assembly consists of the central deity surrounded by four or . . . eight other deities, who are conceived of as aspects of, or projections from, the central *yidam* [guardian deity]. Each deity may have a consort, and there may be several circles of such deities, with attendant figures, adding up to several hundred deities, all of whom need to be visualized precisely."[38] In general the central deity is the guru himself, who, more often than not, is an incarnation of the primordial Buddha Vajradhara or one of the Bodhisattvas. In most of Tibet this identification with the guru and the series of empowerments obtained from him through meditative ascesis or *sādhana* culminates in deep meditative trance, or *samādhi,* during which time the guru imparts to his pupil or disciple the secret knowledge, generally through the guru himself or through a deity who is simultaneously the devotee's guardian god or *iṣṭa devatā* (Tibetan, *yidam*).[39] The guru or deity or one of the former great lamas are visualized in front of the practitioner at the very start of the meditative session, though in a sense one might say that the guru can be the deity and simultaneously the old lamas reincarnated or identified with him. The meditator can then invoke any number of deities or his own parents or even the hell denizens who are visualized as taking refuge in the Buddha and hence eligible for salvation; and all these visualizations dissolve back into the guru at the center of the maṇḍala.

Sri Dharmakirti, a contemporary practitioner of Tibetan Buddhism, puts it well when he says that the guru, through his key initiations or empowerments and oral instructions, helps the disciple to apprehend the various maṇḍalas in which he appears. It is through the guru and only through him that the disciple can have access to the *sambhogakāya* and the *nirmāṇakāya* and ultimately realize the *dharmakāya,* or "essence body," of the Buddha. For this reason the disciple

"perceives the guru as a living embodiment of the Three Bodies of a fully Enlightened Buddha," at least according to the Gelukpa school of Vajrayāna to which the
Dalai Lamas belong. The ideal guru is thus a triple being "simultaneously existing
on three planes, of which only the physical one is evident to the senses of the disciple."[40] Thus, the meditator engaged in *sādhana* can eventually realize Buddhahood through the initial identification with the guru. When the Tibetan meditator identifies with the guru, he becomes the guru, who is, in effect, a Buddha.
When he identifies with a deity in his maṇḍala, he becomes that deity. Surely this
is a form of theistic mysticism, officially shunned by all, including the Tibetans of
the Gelukpa school, even though in an ultimate sense one can reconcile this with
the doctrine of emptiness. Although not "ultimate," the experience is not nominal either. Unfortunately, we don't have an intermediate term in either Buddhist
or Western thought. We have become, once again, prisoners of language.

We will bring up Tantrism again and again, but for the moment I want to sum
up our argument that Buddhist thought continues to circle around the fundamental idea that the religion postulated from its very inception, namely, the absence of any still point in the constantly changing world. As Mahāyāna developed
from this early base, two further ideas occurred: there is nothing called inherent
existence, and this means that the Buddhist salvific goal of nirvana itself has the
feature of changeability. But others say that this would be nihilism: not so, say
yet others, because there is indeed some kind of essence, even a changeable one,
as, for example, a substratum consciousness. Some argue there is a Buddha essence that is present within us, be it the *tathāgatagarbha* or its more purified representative known as the essence body of the Buddha, the *dharmakāya*. But most
thinkers assert that none of these constitute the horrendous idea of the Self/self
except, perhaps, in a nominal sense. But then a few texts insist that the elusive
essence is, in fact, the Self. It looks as if Buddhism has taken a radical turn with
that last affirmation. But perhaps not so radical, because that idea also circles
back to an early reactionary doctrine of the Pudgalavādins, who seem to have
asserted a self that moves through existences or *saṃsāra*. But then I noted that
the highly abstract salvific doctrine of Buddhism best exemplified in emptiness
is not unique in one respect at least, namely, in its very abstractness. It shares
that feature with the God of the philosophers and with much of Platonic and
neo-Platonic thought, all of which affirm an Absolute, although a un-Buddhist
one. But, unlike the empty God of the philosophers, Mahāyāna fills its emptiness
with visionary concreteness. And this is pushed to further heights in the form of
the Mahāyāna that took root in Tibet, the Vajrayāna, which boldly brought back
recalcitrant passion, eroticism, into the heart of the salvific enterprise. But more
of that as we proceed.

INTRODUCING TIBETAN TREASURE SEEKERS: VISIONARY KNOWLEDGE AND ITS TRANSMISSION

I saw Eternity the other night,
Like a great ring of pure and endless light,
All calm, as it was bright;
And round beneath it, Time in hours, days, years
Driv'n by the spheres
Like a vast shadow moved; in which the world
And all her train were hurl'd . . .

—Henry Vaughan, "The World"

It has been argued, I noted earlier, that some Mahāyāna texts might have been invented, formulated, and transmitted through the visionary experience. There is some truth to this assertion, but it is only a partial truth, because texts that have been acquired through visions are in the first place influenced by the prior tradition and the philosophical thinking of the visionary (or even "fantasy activity"). Moreover, often enough only fragments of texts are discovered, and then they have to be filled in and made whole through complicated processes that might entail more visions and rational revisions. Some of the discovered texts are so dense or enigmatic that they require commentaries written in mundane conditions. To elucidate these issues, let me begin with Tibetan treasure seekers briefly mentioned earlier and place their visionary experiences and their quest for knowledge in context, drawing largely on a contemporary exponent of that tradition, Tulku Thondup Rinpoche, whose book is based on a nineteenth-century work.[41] These treasure discoverers belong to the Nyingma ("the Old One" or "the old school") tradition of Tibetan Buddhism, and its adherents are collectively known as Nyingmapa (Tibetan, rNying-ma-pa). Their doctrines, according to Nyingma tradition, were originally taught by the Buddha Samantabhadra (Güntu Sangpo), the primordial Buddha, and through him to several other Buddhas. However, the most powerful figure associated with these treasures is Padmasambhava, who, in Tibetan thinking, helped to proselytize Tibetans into Buddhism during the reign of King Trisong Detsen (c. 755–797). The treasures are of course primarily Tantric texts; they sometimes contain sacred objects that have been sequestered originally by one of the Buddhas of the Mahāyāna tradition or by Padmasambhava himself.[42] Tradition has it that Padmasambhava controlled or subjugated the indigenous deities of the ancient Tibetan religions and cleansed the land, perhaps following the model of the Buddha Gautama himself as he cleansed the future Buddhist lands of demons and malign spirits in the noncanonical texts of the Theravāda traditions.[43]

Though not entirely confined to them, Nyingma visionaries or *tertons* are the primary discoverers of hidden Buddhist treasures or *terma*. Janet Gyatso says that the "respectability of the Nyingma lineages were enhanced after the brilliant synthetic and philosophical work of the fourteenth-century scholar Longchen Rabjampa" (or Longchenpa), a scholar who inspired the visions of both Pemalingpa and Jigme Lingpa whom we will meet again in the next section (AS, 127). Though the Nyingmapa virtuosos did not belong to the dominant Gelukpa tradition of the Dalai Lamas, they nevertheless influenced the latter, such that the great Fifth Dalai Lama, some of whose visions I shall present, had strong Nyingma sympathies, perhaps because he was born into a Nyingmapa family (AS, 127). However, the criticism from the more conservative Buddhist traditions gave the Nyingmapa "a less than fully orthodox image in Tibetan society" (AS, 130). In accordance with many religious traditions in Tibet, these virtuosos were considered reincarnations of previous masters, or *tulku,* and their dreams and visions confirm their reincarnation genealogies.

The discoverer, or *terton,* can be an incarnation of the king or an emanation of Padmasambhava himself. It is said that a disciple of Guru Padmasambhava, who received transmission from him in the ninth century, can transmit the empowerments and teachings to his disciples today (HTT, 64). Consequently, "the *tertons* already possess the transmission of the teachings even before their discovery. It is not the case that they receive the transmissions when they discover the yellow scrolls," which, in reality, could be of various colors (HTT, 103). The scrolls arouse in the *tertons* the recollection of entire teachings, some of which extend into several volumes, in which case the yellow scrolls are stand-ins for the more detailed teachings. Further, the discoverer's consort, indispensable in many forms of Tibetan Buddhism, has a similar function. She is someone who has made the right aspirations in the past and now engages with the *terton* as the key to his realization of the transmission through the bliss that she gives him in union. Most *tertons* are highly respected lamas, but rarely celibate. They remain in the household with consorts, children, and possessions, the consort helping the adept to attain the goal of bliss and emptiness in addition to the task of text discovery. Without the right consort, the task of gathering texts is difficult, if not impossible.

According to the Nyingma tradition, Padmasambhava is not only the recipient of textual knowledge from the primordial Buddha Samantabhadra or Vajradhara; he is also the one who has sequestered these texts waiting to be discovered by an appropriate awakened being. The *terton* destined to discover the *terma* might be a *bodhicitta* aspirant or a kind of *siddha* or perfected being, if not a Bodhisattva. The *termas* will appear to the *terton* "from the sky, mountains, lakes, trees and beings spontaneously according to their wishes and mental abilities." Or, those awakened ones who hid the original texts might have concealed them in books and other places entrusting "gods, nāgas and other powerful beings to protect and hand over to the right person at the proper time" and with the employment of the appropriate techniques (HTT, 57).

Tulku Thondup Rinpoche discusses two major types of concealment of Nyingma treasures among many others. First, there exists the "earth *terma*," where the concealment is through "symbolic scripts" and codes that then have to be decoded.[44] These symbolic scripts are written on scrolls of paper that have been concealed in rocks, lakes, and temples, places on the ground or earth, and hence the term "earth *terma*" (HTT, 61). Some scrolls were encased in caskets made of gemstones, metals, wood, clay, or stone and might contain other sacred objects in addition to texts. Often enough there is one teaching in a single casket, but occasionally a single teaching may be scattered in several caskets. They were originally stored in their lonely repositories by Padmasambhava who might have entrusted some of them to the *ḍākinīs* ("skyfarers") and sometimes to other guardians, even demonic ones. As the primary guardian of the *termas*, the *ḍākinīs* or other deities would hand them to the right treasure seeker, the *terton*. Second: in contrast to the earth *terma* is the "mind *terma*," where the symbolic script is found in the discoverer's own mind but originally transmitted from Guru Padmasambhava, who, in turn, obtained the teachings "through mind transmission" from the primordial Buddha and then fixed them in the minds of awakened disciples to be "discovered" or recovered later and brought back as the original text. The coded form is to "awaken the Terton's mind to the teachings concealed in ancient times [by Padmasambhava] in the disciple's vision of luminous vast expanse" (HTT, 125).

There are many ways of locating and recovering treasures, and I shall mention a few of them. Tulku Thondup Rinpoche mentions a "prophetic guide" who informs the *terton* in a vision as to where the *terma* is located. For example, one *terton* had a dream in which "a celestial *ḍākinī* came to him in the form of a youthful, beautiful, smiling lady attired in colorful silk with precious jewel ornaments. She began by showing him the expression and indications of great bliss. By having union with her he was liberated into the expanse of freedom from elaborations, the nature of the experiences of exquisite great bliss. . . . And she took off her precious ring and put it in his cup saying, 'Keep it as a sign of accomplishment.' Then she disappeared and he awoke" to find in his cup a scroll that gave him instructions for recovering a *terma* (HTT, 73–74). The scroll itself was in coded script "printed small in very thin letters as if written with a single hair" (HTT, 73).

In the case of earth *terma*s, the rock door sometimes opens spontaneously when a *terton* arrives, as one seeker noted: "I went to Ba ter rocky mountain, and just as I arrived a rock eight inches in diameter fell down from the mountain. In the place where the rock had been, I saw, in a heap of coal, an image of Tārā, a casket of sealing wax, and a beautiful old rosary. And I withdrew them" (HTT, 78). At other times it is a much more arduous task and involves considerable hardship and the use of hammers, chisels, and ladders to find the treasure. The guide may require preparatory exercises or the *terton* may himself decide to do so, for example by engaging in "the complete esoteric meditation and ritual performances of a deity" (HTT, 76).

Once a treasure is discovered, the *terton* places a substitute to take its place, generally religious objects or offerings to placate the protector deities. Although the *terma* is most often found in a casket, sometimes the yellow scripts are found without any case and at other times the symbolic scripts are written on the surface of some object. These symbolic scripts are of three kinds: a short one known as "just visible," consisting of a few syllables and sometimes without a noun. Second, "just an indication" script, one of medium length, that contains a fragment of a history, an outline, a text title, or a phrase that indicates a connection with the age of Guru Padmasambhava. The third is a "complete text," in which case there is no need for "awakening" the words of the text. Hence, strictly speaking, the third is not a symbolic script. But, like the others, it "helps to awaken the meaning and especially the Mind-mandate Transmission and concealment in the Terton" by Padmasambhava.

Some symbolic scripts are in the *ḍākinī* script or code and "as the discoverer reads the script, it changes frequently or appears unclear, or sometimes the meaning changes or is unclear. Sometimes both the script and the meaning change," but auspicious circumstances and preparatory practices help to make the reading stable and clear (HTT, 85). A symbolic script that behaves in this way is an "illusory miraculous script." In a nonillusory miraculous script, the words and meaning are clear from the very first and therefore need no exegesis or completion. Problems arise when the script is not in Tibetan and has to be decoded in the following ways. The casket and the symbolic script might be found with the decoding key, "a letter by letter equivalence between the symbolic script and the Tibetan alphabet" (HTT, 85–86). Or, the code might enter the mind of the *terton* through spiritual insight. Alternatively, the *terton* simply looks at the script and reads it off without effort owing to his *siddhi* or *yogic* powers. In yet other cases, "the power comes by looking at the script again and again," that is, through sheer concentration. If the *terton* cannot decode the script, then he might seek the aid of someone who "has the Mind-mandate Transmission of the same teachings from Guru Padmasambhava who may decode it for him" (HTT, 86).

The decoded script is often written down by professional calligraphers. In their normal writing, the speed of master calligraphers is the same as that of ordinary scribes. "But when they write Terma scripts, through their enlightened miraculous power they can write texts such as *La ma gong du* [in thirteen volumes] a hundred times in the snap of a finger" owing to their *yogic* powers (HTT, 111). I assume that such textual writing in a snap is either a metaphoric way of expressing the visionary transmission of texts or simply a myth of such text transmission. So it is when the treasure discoverer wants the original yellow scroll for himself (or his disciple) rather than in reconcealing them. In such a case he can ask a *ḍākinī* to make a copy, and she will do so in the blink of an eye (HTT, 142). It seems to me that these visionary transmissions of texts, imagined or real, hide the fact that revisions of the visions do take place, soon after transmission or, more likely, when the texts are written down by their authors and incorporated into the existing body of texts. Rational reworking of visionary texts takes place here as elsewhere.

Perhaps an example from the European tradition might help us to understand what occurs in remote Tibet! The case is that of Catherine of Siena (1347–1380), whose major work, *The Dialogue*, constitutes 332 pages in the modern translation but was dictated to her during a five-day ecstasy when the Lord replied to her queries by transmitting them into her soul. Yet this is but one phase of transmission. Another—a more complicated one—is mentioned by her contemporary, Thomas Antonii de Senis Caffarini:

> I say also that I have very often seen the virgin in Siena . . . rapt beyond her senses, except for speech, by which she dictated to various writers in succession sometimes letters and sometimes the book, in different times and in different places, as circumstances allowed. Sometimes she did this with her hands crossed on her breast as she walked about the room; sometimes she was on her knees or in other postures; but always her face was lifted toward heaven. . . . When emergencies would cause several days to pass in which she was kept from pursuing her dictation, as soon as she could take it up again she would begin at the point where she had left off as if there had been no interruption or space of time. . . . Sometimes after she had dictated several pages, she would summarize or recapitulate the main content as if the things she had dictated were (and in fact they were) actually present in her mind.[45]

In other words, there was another phase of visionary transmission: much more complicated than the one describing a five-day ecstasy wherein some revision of the text takes place—and a crucial third phase, when the *Dialogue* is written down in manuscript form and the thinking-I takes over the job of revision and craftsmanship.

PICTURING THE TIBETAN COSMOS

Buddhist Tibet is the playground of the visionary consciousness as it opens itself to the cosmos and pictures space with images from its unique Buddhist tradition, helping to reinvent that tradition or infuse it with new knowledge. In the following pages I shall continue my account of Tibetan *tertons* beginning with the treasure discoverer, Pemalingpa (1450–1521) from Bhutan. I follow this up with a brief discussion of a later treasure seeker, Jigme Lingpa (1730–98), and then of the Fifth Dalai Lama.[46]

The texts that Pemalingpa claimed to have discovered from their places of concealment in both Bhutan and Tibet fill twenty substantial volumes and "the sacred dances he and his relatives composed on the basis of the divine visions they experienced are performed in all the local and state festivals of Bhutan" to this day (HTS, 15). Thus treasure seekers not only discover texts, but they invent new cultural forms through their visions and these invented forms are congealed into traditions perpetuated through time.[47] Like other Tibetan virtuosos, Pemalingpa also wrote an autobiography, and this genre is close in spirit to premodern Western examples, according to Gyatso (AS, 101–2). As with many such autobiographies, Pemalingpa's is mostly narrated in the first person, beginning with his birth in 1450 down to 1519, three years before his death. Thereafter the story is taken up by a disciple and ends with Pemalingpa's funeral ceremonies. As far as his dream-visions and revelations are concerned, the wording of the autobiography suggests that he recorded them as soon as they came to him, as, for example, when he says that "after waking up I have written down just a brief account of this dream" (HTS, 18). This is true of other treasure seekers as much as it is true of many other visionaries who record dreams and dream-visions soon after they are experienced. Unlike dreams, visions tend to remain in one's memory, especially those experienced in meditative and related forms of asceses. The tradition of recording one's own dream-visions was well established in Tibetan Buddhism, but because writing is, everywhere, a preeminently discursive activity, it is the thinking-I that produces a written script alongside secondary elaboration.

Michael Aris says that "Pemalingpa may have lived his life in a world of dreams, fancies and visions, counterfeit or not, but almost the entire temporal, spatial and human setting of his autobiography can be confirmed and authenticated by what is independently known of the world he lived in" (HTS, 19–20). His work is generally free of learned allusions and references to other texts and has little literary polish. He used a form of "simple literary Tibetan intelligible to the whole range of disciples from every corner of the Lamaist world" (HTS, 20). I shall not deal with the details of Pemalingpa's life, but shall focus exclusively on his visionary experiences, although his "reincarnation genealogy" is relevant to us because it is derived and legitimated from his visionary trances.

Pemalingpa traces that genealogy from the very origin of the universe out of "the uncreated palace of the primordial Buddha, Samantabhadra" who appears in other traditions as Vajradhara. It is Padmasambhava, "Lotus-born," from whom Pemalingpa ("he of the lotus place") takes his name. In addition to converting Tibetans during the reign of King Trisong Detsen, Padmasambhava is credited with the construction of Tibet's first Buddhist monastery, Samye, c.779. And it is said that it was he who first promulgated the mystical and magical doctrines of the Tantras, the so-called esoteric Vajrayāna Buddhism of Tibet. He was a cult figure overshadowing the historical Buddha, Śakyamuni, and often enough a stand-in for the Buddha. In Pemalingpa's version of this myth, the king Trisong Detsen had a daughter Pemasel ("clear lotus") who suffered from a severe illness. Padmasambhava told her father that her illness was based on her bad karma where in a previous birth as a senior queen she had murdered the son of a junior queen. "Padmasambhava touches her head with a box containing all his scriptures and makes an aspiration that she should fulfill them in her future lives" (HTS, 26). These treasure texts were hidden by Padmasambhava and later discovered by Pemalingpa as the present reincarnation of Princess Pemasel.

Padmasambhava apparently made a prophecy that Pemasel will experience five impure lives and seven pure ones, the former to work out the bad karma that then permits her good karma to surface. At this point Pemalingpa reveals to us Pemasel's future lives, which are, in effect, his own past lives, beginning with three successive bad rebirths as a beggar woman in the valley of Yarlung, a white bitch in the village of Olka in Yarlung, a ewe in Lhasa. The good births are identifiable historic figures, beginning with two existences as nuns. Pemalingpa was also reincarnated as Longchenpa (1308–63), the famous philosopher-saint mentioned earlier.[48] At his birth which occurred two incarnations later, various marvels appeared such as the sun and moon shining simultaneously, which, reminiscent of European alchemy, represents the Tantric union of opposites. Trained by his maternal grandfather to be a blacksmith, Pemalingpa received no formal religious education. By his own admission he was a wayward, willful child, but this conforms "to the expected behavior of *yogins*, who are not bound by the ordinary conventions of human society" (HTS, 34). Aris adds: "The only authority he recognized was the divine sage Padmasambhava and what he learnt from that master came to him directly in dreams and visions" (HTS, 35). This, according to Gyatso, is true of others also, such as Jigme Lingpa, whose whole life "was predicted and engineered by the Precious Guru [Padmasambhava]" (AS, 128).

It was in 1475 that Pemalingpa had his first dream indicating the treasure of the Burning Lake, when, at his monastery, many girls came up to him and urged him to stay. This accorded with his own wishes, and while he was there he had a dream in which he found himself sitting on a pile of stones in a cemetery. "The place was full of dancers. He was offered nectar from a skull-cup and the dancers prostrated themselves before him and circumambulated him. He then proceeded to the summit of a mountain and from there he saw the four continents filled with light and they were laid out before him. The sun and moon were shining simultaneously . . . and when they descended towards him he picked one up and put it in the pouch of his robe and the other he placed on his lap" (HTS, 36). Aris says that "these dreams are to be taken as auguries pointing to the discovery of his first treasure," but they also show that he has already been initiated into Tantric mysteries, which empowered him to do so. The sun and moon, held in his hand, not only brings the famed opposites together but also heralds his power to control the "planets" and their courses.

In the monastery Pemalingpa was visited by a monk who wore a ragged robe and gave him a scroll and asked him to read it carefully. When he came to his family home with the scroll, he showed it to a nun (a relative), but his father said: "He's faking again. It's just a trick." But the nun wasn't sure, because of obvious traditional precedent. That very night Pemalingpa fell sick and lost consciousness, and in that state "many skyfarers [*ḍākinīs*] descended from Padmasambhava's palace in the sky and spoke many things" to him during that state of unconsciousness (HTS, 37). It seems as if Pemalingpa's brief "trance-illness" was a response to his family doubting the authenticity of the scroll. Nevertheless, public doubts whether Pemalingpa was faking or not seems to have dogged him through most of his career.

Because the family was now convinced of the authenticity of the trance, they did their best to persuade Pemalingpa to go search for the treasure text, but he refused, saying it was inconceivable that someone like him would be involved in a true hunt for spiritual treasures. Here is a complicated situation. The family initially discounted his scroll. Now Pemalingpa is telling them indirectly that if they are right then he surely could not be a genuine treasure seeker. He was also probably ambivalent about his quest, and his statement would be an expression of resistance like those you find in the shamanic quest and in most forms of psychotherapy. But his family decided to circumvent him and told him that they were joking and now had to go to a certain village to fetch a stolen yak cow. This was a ruse to get Pemalingpa to go past "the destined rock at the appointed time of the full moon." Pemalingpa was surely aware of his family's stratagem; and it is likely that he manipulated his family to do precisely something of this sort perhaps because, like many other prophets, he must have a recipe for failure.

But he did not fail. He set off with five members of his family (the number specified in the scroll) and tried "to give the impression of being quite ignorant of the ruse that was being played on him." When they neared the rock of Naring, it was raining heavily. The rock was on the opposite side of a river, and many people had already assembled there. Aris rightly says that the idea of the treasure hunt had spread, and people had assembled to satisfy their curiosity, which means that if the public was not fooled by the family ruse it is unlikely that Pemalingpa was either. Here Pemalingpa "fell down in a swoon and while still in a state of trance he removed his clothes and left them on the road. He plunged naked into the riverine lake and reached the rock on the opposite side. There he found an opening leading to a cave that could hold about a hundred people. It was called the 'Long Cave of Glory.' A throne stood there and upon it was found an image of the Buddha the size of a man. To the left of the image were many book chests. A girl with a single eye in her forehead picked up the chest containing the text of the *gSang-ba yan-bcud* ('The Quintessence of Secrets') gave it to him and said, 'Run!' He left and on hearing the roar of the river he regained consciousness." He was not sure how he was going to cross the river; yet he did "like a bird's feather blown by someone's breath" (HTS, 38). His five companions put his clothes back on and taking the book chest with them they reached home late at night.

It seems to me that the visit to the cave was in a state of trance, and therefore it is likely that Pemalingpa saw everything there in a vision; or that he wove a new fabric out of it ("fabrication") in retelling his experience. The fact remains, he did discover a chest, within which was a scroll that was kept for a few days in the family shrine with offerings. He eventually transcribed the text written in the "skyfarers' [*ḍākinī*] sign-script" into standard Tibetan with the aid of a conversion key provided in the original document. Treasures, we must insist, are often enough written in a symbolic script or in a *ḍākinī* code, the secret and secretive way in which Padmasambhava implanted them in the consciousnesses of future treasure seekers. All this is possible in terms of the doctrine of rebirth, and in Pemalingpa's case especially so because he is a reincarnation of Pemasel to whom Padmasambhava entrusted the treasure texts (AS, 173). "After further consultations and a prophetic dream he succeeded in finding the right scribe . . . to copy out the text. But since the man could not read it, Pemalingpa had to dictate it to him from the original scroll (presumably again using the conversion table as before). When the work was half finished the ink ran out and the light failed, but both were replenished miraculously" (HTS, 39). The latter incident indicates how easily hagiographical elements can enter into autobiography, then and now.

Note that it is only Pemalingpa who can read the text, but it is wrong to assume that he is cheating. I am convinced that he has a text before him and he sees and reads it, but with a "visionary eye," "inner eye," or "divine eye," which in turn reminds us of the "mental eyes" (oculis mentalibus) of medieval European alchemists. Pemalingpa's technique is not altogether different from Schreber translating his nerve communications into ordinary German through his "special eye." I know of a psychotic shaman in Sri Lanka who wrote letters to the gods and rulers in a script that he only could read. Then there is the case of the great Sri Lankan epigraphist, Senarat Paranavitana, who in his old age read whole texts written in flawless Sanskrit or ancient Sinhala found interleaved in old rock inscriptions. But while my shaman informant was psychotic, and people treated him as "mad," not so with Paranavitana, who was for all purposes a "normal" and moral man, a scrupulous scholar, though an intensely private person with an ascetic devotion to work. Yet, staring at nearly undecipherable inscriptions all his life in the glazed wall (known as the "mirror wall") of the sixth-century mountain fortress of Sigiriya, he began to see, with extreme clarity, "interlinear writing" mirrored on various rock slabs. Paranavitana was not a religious man and could not recognize the vision or waking dream for what it was. For the hallucinating epigrapher the writing on the mirror of rock slabs was no dream or vision, but plain literal grammatical Sanskrit. On the basis of his hallucinatory experiences, Paranavitana wrote several historical treatises with all the accoutrements of modern rational scholarship, which are cited to this day by lay intelligentsia and occasionally by professional historians.

To get back to our protagonist: once the text has been deciphered, Pemalingpa agreed to recite it in public with a lama as patron. He was in a bit of a quandary. Although he had discovered the text, he did not know the ritual procedures and the dances associated with such discoveries. While worrying about this, one night as he lay asleep at a hermitage he had a dream vision that the consort of Padmasambhava, Yeshe Tsogyel (a "skyfarer" or ḍākinī herself and also the polyandrous consort of the king Trisong Detsen) appeared before him and said: "Do the chants of the scripture like this" and sang the chants chapter by chapter. Then she told Pemalingpa how to perform the sacred dances of the five classes of ḍākinīs. "When I awoke everything remained clear in my mind and so I put it all into practice and showed it in stages to my disciple followers." The actual performance then took place and lasted for twenty-one days, and each day the skyfarers came down (presumably in his dream visions) to instruct him on how to expound the text for the following day.

> On the fifteenth day of the month, heralded by another dream of the sky-farers and by the arrival of another dirty looking Khampa [from Kham province, Eastern Tibet], he had a dream of the treasure revealer Ratnalingpa, who showed him great reverence and said that he, Ratnalingpa, had been his master during three of his former lives. He explained he was departing for the heaven of Padmasambhava and exhorted Pemalingpa to bring to full completion the welfare of the teachings and of living beings. Later this turned out to have happened on the day that Ratnalingpa died. We are meant to take the dream as a confirmation of Pemalingpa as the true successor of Ratnalingpa, the best and most accomplished of treasure finders.
>
> (HTS, 40)

After these momentous events, there occurred another one for which Pemalingpa is best remembered. He returned to Naring rock and a huge crowd assembled there for the next treasure hunt called "the extraction of a crowd-treasure." As Aris says, this was to convince people publicly of the truth of the first discovery. Pemalingpa climbed the rock with a lighted butter lamp and swore that "If I am the emanation of a demon, may I die in this river. If I am the heart-son of the Guru [Padmasambhava] may not even this lamp be extinguished and may I return after obtaining the required wealth." This statement was spurred by the standard public view that a treasure seeker might either be a fraud guided by a demon or a genuine one favored by the great guru himself. Pemalingpa jumped into the river and came up, presumably with the lamp still intact and in his hand a small image of the Buddha and a sealed skull containing miraculous substances. Apparently, in so doing, he fulfilled a prophecy found in another text discovered more than a century earlier by Ugyenlingpa:

> One called Ugyen Pemalingpa will come forth;
> And the treasure-trove hidden in the Burning Lake will be removed
> Having revealed the sign that it is not to be left but extracted.
>
> (HTS, 41)

Pemalingpa had to constantly prove the truth of his power, even though his autobiography records many other treasures he discovered. Thus "on the day of the new moon in the winter Bull month I recovered the text of the *Nor-bu lam-khyer* ("The Jewel Taken on the Path") from beneath a cliff shaped like a pile of nine skulls at the Bodyprint Rock (Kujédrak) in Bumthang. At that time people said, 'He's a fake!' and so there were very few who showed faith in me" (HTS, 43).

Consider now the power of the treasures and the consequences of recovering them. In theory the treasure that is recovered is based on a previous prophecy. Prophecy does not deter treasure seeking by the right kind of *terton* without prophetic authorization. Yet, when Pemalingpa recovered a treasure that was not prophetically foretold, his brother and another person succumbed during an outbreak of smallpox, though Pemalingpa was unscathed. Again in 1487 calamities befell those who came into contact with an unprophesized treasure recovered by Pemalingpa, such that even animals died, thus compelling him to perform animal sacrifices to placate the spirits or treasure masters, guardians empowered by Padmasambhava. Previously, in 1480, during a similar occurrence, his uncle fell seriously ill, and Padmasambhava appeared in a vision and scolded him for ignoring the instructions on the "entrance certificate," urging him to offer a large sheep to the treasure guardians.

Even when treasures are recovered as prophecy indicated, calamities occurred, owing to the intrinsic power of the treasures. In one instance three of Pemalingpa's companions were struck with illness, and one died. With these calamities, one would expect public accusation of fraud and forgery to surface, and such accusations are explicitly mentioned in the autobiography. Aris thinks that these accusations were mentioned by Pemalingpa because it gave him an opportunity to show his real power by countering them. In one instance a local official virtually challenged him to show his spiritual power for recovering a treasure that lay in a specific place according to an earlier prophecy. Pemalingpa recovered the treasure chest in front of a large crowd and bestowed the blessing of the chest by placing it against the foreheads of those assembled. Aris thinks this was fraud because there was no way he could have recovered the treasure. He must have placed the box ahead of time and then recovered it publicly. Moreover, the contents of the box were displayed much later, giving him chance to put various things in there. This is possible. But, if he did so, it was surely during a visionary experience, not a case of calculated fraud. Yet by the end of Pemalingpa's life he had become a powerful charismatic lama and the unchallenged master of the treasure hunt, which was enough to silence his critics.

Aris thinks that Pemalingpa combined the role of lama and shaman, or, better still, he remained a shaman under the guise of a lama. He had dream-visions and trances frequently, the dreams being of two types. First: visits of celestial spirits or *dākinīs* who helped him locate treasures and who indicated possible patrons and warned him against enemies. Second: the same celestial beings appeared before him and led him to the heavenly realms, "in particular to the divine palace of Padmasambhava where he is initiated and confirmed in his role as a treasure-revealer" (HTS, 53). These dream adventures were recorded by Pemalingpa after he "awakened" from his meditation. Aris says that both Pemalingpa and his readers or auditors regarded these adventures as having actually taken place, as the following example illustrates.

While staying in a monastery in southern Tibet, Pemalingpa had a dream-vision of an old man riding a white wolf with about forty attendants. The wolf rider prostrated before him and told him that he had been sent to summon him. Pemalingpa tried to fob him off with excuses, but the man insisted they leave immediately. The wolf rider laid a white silk cloth; then Pemalingpa lost consciousness, and he found himself being transported in the silk carpet to the mountain of Khari ("sky-mountain," on the Tibetan-Bhutan border). From there he flew to a beautiful green valley with herds of domestic animals; a rainbow shone across the central mountain where on its peak he saw a village of seven houses. "The inhabitants of the village had been planted as 'human seeds' for the future, and similar races descending from the mountain god Masang Yapangkye were to be found in Tibet" on two other peaks. In this piece of indigenous Tibetan science fiction, Pemalingpa could see the inhabitants of the village but they could not see him (HTS, 54–55).

From there, on his carpet of silk, he was taken to the home of the wolf rider, a palace surrounded by a wall (the wolf rider we later know is the eponymous mountain god Khari and a servitor of Padmasambhava). Escorted by a lady wearing a turban with peacock feathers and a necklace of little bells and mirrors, he was taken to the throne of the mountain god himself. The lady gave him food and drink, and Pemalingpa responded with a piece of Buddhist discourse on the *tathāgatagarbha*, "the Buddha matrix" that, as we noted in our discussion of Mahāyāna, is within us all, endowing us with the potentiality to be Buddhas:

> Faithful lady listen to me!
> The mind, the great self-begotten sky,
> Is the self-begotten site of the non-composite.
> The mind of all the Buddhas
> Is not different, not separate [from one's own mind].
> Put this into the meditations of your mind.

She gave him a present of a crystal vase; and once again he flew toward the west on his magic carpet until he reached a huge palace at the top of a peak.

There he was received in great glory with parasols, banners, and music. He entered the palace by first climbing a stone staircase, then a sapphire ladder, and finally a copper ladder till he was lead to a special throne prepared for him. "The old wolf-rider explained how the initiation of the *Bla-ma gsang-'dus* ('The Lama, the Collection of Secrets') had previously been bestowed upon him [the wolf man] by Padmasambhava himself and now he wanted to receive it again from Pemalingpa" (HTS, 55). A maṇḍala was drawn and a *pūja* prepared and the actual empowerment was given the next dawn, all pictured in the vision. When the names of the deities were recognized in the *pūja,* they actually appeared in the sky. (Pemalingpa claimed he made a drawing based on this vision and later got it repainted in a Tibetan temple wall hanging or *thangka*.) At this point the wolf rider introduced himself as the mountain god Khari and invited him to witness a spectacle arranged for him in the palace with a special throne. When Pemalingpa sat in the throne, a man dressed in a lotus hat and hair hanging in long braids (a *yogin*) appeared and scolded him for sitting on his master's (Padmasambhava's) throne and treasury, of which he was the guardian. But Pemalingpa replied that Padmasambhava was not interested in wealth, to which the guardian responded by showing him precious objects (destined for future revelation to other treasure hunters).

Then the god of Khari told Pemalingpa to climb to the roof of the palace where he was shown the Buddhist paradises. I shall not deal with the details here except to say that in an island in the center of an ocean was the "Glorious Copper Colored Mountain" of Padmasambhava. Thinking that the great guru might be in residence, Pemalingpa prostrated himself three times in that direction. He was then shown the palaces of the Bodhisattvas Mañjuśri and Avalokiteśvara, all described in the text. "After that Khari told him to look south and he saw a red and black triangular shaped land. Flames were issuing forth from the mountains, cliffs, water and trees. In the middle of this land was a lake from whose center there rose up a black mountain with a blue palace on its summit. The sun, moon and the stars appeared to be falling on it. It was explained to be Akavati," the heaven of Kuvera, the god of wealth and treasure. "Finally, Pemalingpa was instructed to look straight up in the sky and he saw there a palace made of rainbows. On its roof there stood a throne upon which he saw a blue Buddha seated with his right hand touching the ground and the other in the *mudrā* of meditation, surrounded by a great concourse of monks" (HTS, 57). This was the Buddha Vajradhara, the primordial Buddha, in his abode. Thereafter the god led him back to the throne he had been sitting on earlier and begged him to deliver a specific religious discourse. Then many people came in bearing gifts. The god of Khari himself gave him instructions on how to recover a skull full of gold in a specific location. "Pemalingpa was finally conducted on his way with music and he awoke" (HTS, 57).

Pemalingpa was not educated in Buddhism in any formal sense, but was a Buddhist autodidact. Aris says that he hardly meditated and that his visions are shamanic. But Tibetan meditation, we know, does produce the kind of visions that Pemalingpa experienced and that such visions were compounded of both Buddhism and shamanism and discussed at length by Geoffrey Samuel.[49] And, like other shamans and Buddhist *siddhas* (perfected ones), he dreams his world and traverses the cosmos. Aris adds that, in addition to dreams, Pemalingpa experienced trancelike states. "The vocabulary used to describe these states is obscure, difficult to translate and markedly un-Buddhist. The wording is suggestive of a swirling, darkening, burning, inebriated, uncontrollable condition. These states come upon Pemalingpa when fully awake, as he was approached by the spirits of the treasure or else on the point of finding one, also when he was about to dance or sing a song, and twice just before he left the imprints of his hands on stones" (HTS, 62). Unfortunately, Aris does not tell us how these trancelike states occurred when Pemalingpa was fully awake. Perhaps, like other visionaries, he slipped into a trance for a moment and then experienced his visions or he was engaged in waking dreams or, what we will later mention in greater detail, walking trances.

THE WAKING DREAM IN A BUDDHIST TEXT ON ILLUSION

> And the crack in the tea-cup opens
> A lane to the land of the dead.
> —W. H. Auden, "As I Walked Out One Evening"

On one occasion the Blessed One was dwelling at Rājagaha in the Bamboo Grove, the Squirrel Sanctuary.[50] There the Blessed One addressed the monks thus.

BUDDHA: Monks, once in the past a certain man set out from Rājagaha and went to the Sumagadha Lotus Pond, thinking: "I will reflect upon the world." He then sat down on the bank of the Sumagadha Lotus Pond reflecting about the world. Then, monks, the man saw a four-division army entering a lotus stalk on the bank of the pond. Having seen this, he thought: "I must be mad! I must be insane! I've seen something that doesn't exist in the world." The man returned to the city and informed a great crowd of people: "I must be mad, sirs! I must be insane! I've seen something that does not exist in the world."

PEOPLE: How is it, good man, that you are mad? How are you insane? And what have you seen that does not exist in the world?

THE MAN: Here, sirs, I left Rājagaha and approached the Sumagadha Lotus Pond ... I saw a four-division army entering a lotus stalk on the bank of the pond. That's why I am mad, that's why I am insane, and that's why I've seen what doesn't exist in the world.

PEOPLE: Surely you are mad, good man! Surely you are insane! And what you have seen doesn't exist in the world.

BUDDHA: Nevertheless, monks, what that man saw was actually real, not unreal. Once in the past the *devas* [gods] and *asuras* [titans] were arrayed for battle. In that battle the *devas* won and the *asuras* were defeated. In their defeat, the *asuras* were frightened and entered the *asura* city through the lotus stalk, to the bewilderment of the *devas*.

Therefore, monks, do not reflect about the world, thinking, "The world is eternal" or "The world is not eternal"; or "The world is finite" or "The world is infinite"; or "The soul and the body are the same" or "The soul is one thing, the body is another"; or "The Tathāgata [Buddha] exists after death," or "The Tathāgata does not exist after death," or "The Tathāgata both exists and does not exist after death," or "The Tathāgata neither exists nor does not exist after death." For what reason? Because, monks, this reflection is unbeneficial, irrelevant to the fundamentals of the holy life, and does not lead to revulsion, to dispassion, to cessation, to peace, to direct knowledge, to enlightenment [awakening], to Nibbāna [nirvana].

AMBIVALENCE, FAKERY, AND THE VALIDATION OF THE BUDDHIST VISION

In our Buddhist text, "Reflection About the World," people think the man is mad because he is seeing something that could not possibly exist empirically. The Buddha of the Theravāda tradition often enough denies that such visions express any reality or truth value unless it is a vision by an awakened one. Yet this text depicts an ordinary man who attempts to speculate intellectually on the nature of the world by gazing on the lotus pool. But pool gazing does not give him any idea of the origin of the world, which for the Buddha is a futile undertaking. Instead, like the archeologist Paranavitana's, the man's intense gaze changes the rational speculative quest into something else, namely, a waking dream when he has a vision of the four divisions of elephants, horses, chariots, and infantry of the Titan army who, because of their magical powers, can enter through the stalk of a lotus.[51] The text concludes with the Buddha showing the futility of speculating about the world, its origin and eternality, or the origin of the sun and moon. These are inquiries that do not befit the Buddhist quest. The "man" of this text cannot even begin to find answers to those questions but, like Plato's slave in *Meno,* finds himself instead seeing a past event that in fact seems to have occurred, providing for later virtuosos a hole in the Buddhist view that such visions must in fact be doubted. Our text also implies that visionaries are not necessarily mad. Neither are Tibetan visionaries mad, even if they are out of touch with empirical reality or the reality principle as a psychoanalyst understands it because, to borrow another term from psychoanalysis, they are not out of touch with the *psychic reality* of Tibetan Buddhism that permits them to make sense and even rationally explain the unreal visions.

The ambivalence regarding visions comes explicitly in the self-deprecatory words of the Fifth Dalai Lama: "What is the use of chattering discourse on delusive visions." Or: "As if the illusions of *saṃsāra* were not enough, this stupid mind of mine is further attracted to ultra-illusory visions."[52] As we have indicated earlier, a Buddhist vision is true and not true. It is true in a nominal sense, or true to the space-time of experiencing it, but without ultimate truth value that then produces the Buddhist virtuoso's ambivalence to visions. Ambivalence also appears in the idea that is found in all three virtuosos and part of the ideology of the Tibetan treasure-seeking tradition, that these visions are "secret." Though the visions were written down soon after they were experienced, the texts are not meant for public consumption, even though, strangely enough, the public was present during the visions! The word *secret* therefore must not be interpreted literally. The Sanskrit term *rahasyam,* secret, which has influenced Tibetan usage, refers to knowledge that has been unknown, and thus "secret," but left to be proclaimed by the guru to his set of disciples or to a "cult group" of believers from whom it reaches a larger public at a later point in time. *Secret* also has connotations of knowledge of something special, rich in meaning and power. Physicians in Sri Lanka have "secret" cures for illnesses, but, in fact, these secrets go to disciples and family members from where they ripple out into a larger domain. Similarly, it is the case that the visions of the three virtuosos discussed here are "secret" in this special sense. Texts have been hidden, hence "secreted," but eventually discovered and proclaimed. But by virtue of the fact that the charisma of the virtuosos is publicly known and their displays of virtuosity are also relatively open, the secrets do get published eventually. One exception perhaps is the case of the Fifth Dalai Lama whose secret visions were published only in recent times. But he wrote down his visions soon after he experienced them and had these painted on *thangka*s, as others also did. And his own words suggest quite clearly that he expected people to read his work:

> Let me now write the following pages,
> Though it will disappoint those who are led to believe that the desert-mirage is water,
> As well as those who are enchanted by folk tales,
> And those who delight in red clouds in summer.
>
> (SV, 15)

Ordinary Tibetans would not normally deny that treasures exist, but they would question the powers of the person claiming to seek them. Therefore let me reconsider Aris's idea that Pemalingpa must have been faking. I will admit this is possible and that Pemalingpa might have placed the treasures in the trove earlier so that he could retrieve them later. But often "fakery" is part of a virtuoso's expressive apparatus, just as Northwest coast shamans might "fake" their spirit journeys through ventriloquism before an awed audience of believers. I know of an exorcist in Sri Lanka who, in a ritual of countersorcery, will cut an "ash-melon" (*puhul*) in half with a sword, such that the melon will bleed, the blood simply being red dye neatly inserted into the fruit prior to the "melon-cutting ritual." Like a good physician's bedside manner or the "tricks" of a good university teacher at his podium, the exorcist's expressive act need not imply that his total performance is false or that he himself does not believe in the efficacy of his countersorcery. In the Tibetan case, as with Sai Baba or Blavatsky or the many gurus who have emerged to enchant our disillusioned world of modernity, the public acceptance of the authenticity of the visionary act depends to a great deal on the expressive efficacy of the impresario's performance, his displays of virtuosity (or genuine charlatanism).[53] This of course neither proves nor disproves the reality of "phenomena" and other psychokinetic powers.[54]

Beyond that, the visionary is like any other seeker of truth. He must establish some kind of intersubjective consensus regarding the authenticity of his vision, and this is no easy task. Most of us in the humanities do so through our rhetorical strategies, including such things as footnotes that are part of our expressive apparatus for convincing others. Even if someone were to contest what I write about, there is a culturally and academically constituted arena for such contestations. This is also true of the debates the treasure seekers engage in. Their visions cannot remain private but must be validated in public, and, because the public cannot see what the visionary sees, he is forced to create, much more than us academics, a convincing expressive apparatus that will foster public acceptance. The public must believe that the texts that he has discovered are genuine. Even the reluctant Fifth Dalai Lama often had his visionary experiences during "public ceremonies of long life" in a part of his apartment known as the "Joyful Reception Hall," implying that he practiced meditation, the sine qua non of his trances, before a small public group of disciples (SV, 5).

It is out of public talk and display that the successful visionary minimally creates the formation of a motley bunch of believers, and sometimes a more clearly defined "cult group" focused on the persona of the visionary himself, something vaguely familiar to us in academia when an exciting new thinker appears in our fold. Disciples are indispensable to this process, and the thinker or visionary actively solicits them. The latter in turn help form persons or groups that will give intersubjective validation or consensus to the visions. The credibility of the truth-seeking visionary is enhanced when he seeks believers or disciples among the power elite. Pemalingpa was born into a family of blacksmiths, and it was a hard journey for him to reach out to the powerful, as it was for him to create followers who would validate his visions. Thus spirits give information to him regarding useful political contacts and avoiding others. Not so with Jigme Lingpa: with his aristocratic family connections and his more orthodox and self-critical Buddhism, he could establish political contacts with the powerful of society, such as the queen of Derge [Dege], a virtually independent kingdom in East Tibet (AS, 124). Consequently, during his lifetime and after his death, his fame spread widely and so did his works. He was known as the "all knowing" and one "famed for his mastery of esoteric yogas and for his spectacular meditative experiences, especially a series of visions indicating his past life as the powerful Tibetan king Trisong Detsen, a principal actor in that numinous moment of national myth when Tibet became a Buddhist land" (AS, 3). He revived the Nyingma school of Tibetan Buddhism soon after it had suffered persecution and the destruction of its major centers. This must have been an added motivation for Jigme Lingpa to resurrect the Nyingmapa movement and renew it through his powerful visionary acts. His impact was so great that his followers continued his heritage until recent times. Even the great Fifth Dalai Lama, though belonging to the dominant Gelukpa school of Buddhism, was strongly influenced by the visionary tradition later revived by Jigme Lingpa.

It is a mistake however to imagine that the visionary creates charisma exclusively through his or her expressive acts. The Tibetan visionary is a guru, and in general most popular or successful gurus are idealized figures who by their very presence create a kind of "magnetism" or a special atmosphere sensed by those disciples or salvation seekers who come to visit him. The sighting of the guru is known as *darśana*, "seeing," the term used for the sight of the deity when the curtain leading to the inner sanctum of the god or goddess is dramatically opened and the worshiper experiences *darśana*. For Tibetans, the living guru is the counterpart of the divine guru Padmasambhava, partaking of his essence. Hindu gurus like Ramakrishna, Sri Aurobindo, or Sai Baba, or the many that have emerged in our times, emanate a feeling in the devotee of being in the presence of a special being, a feeling that is enhanced by stage management and mythmaking, for sure, but one that cannot be reduced to an expressive technology. This elusive sense of "presence" is beautifully described by Renée Weber, a philosophy professor and a sophisticated new age thinker, in respect to Jiddu Krishnamurti and other gurus, although we do not have to accept her new age religious idiom, according to which the guru is a channel for some form of cosmic energy. "[The] rare individual who functions as such a channel seems to those who come in contact with him to belong to a new species of man. (Krishnamurti, for anyone who has met him, clearly is a case in point.) Such a human being radiates clarity, intelligence, order and love by his mere presence. He seems capable of transmuting our chaotic interpersonal world into an ethical realm by his very *atmosphere*, which unmistakably is charged with energies for which we have neither names nor concepts. At best we can capture the presence and power of that atmosphere in metaphorical and approximate terms."[55] One should add that the virtuoso's charisma does not exist by itself but only in relation to the projective needs or fantasies of the devotee.

THE TIBETAN DREAM TIME AND
THE DISSOLUTION OF THE "SELF"

Monks, there are four kinds of knots. What four? The bodily knot of covetousness, the bodily knot of ill-will, the bodily knot of distorted grasp of rules and vows, the bodily knot of adherence to dogmatic assertion of truth.
—Buddha, "Knots"

If I be permitted to borrow a term invented by ethnographers to describe the culture of the ancient Australians, I would say that Tibetan virtuosos are steeped in the "dream time," and even ordinary folk whose thought and worlds are invented out of the dream time must perforce be influenced by it.[56] Dream time occurs in the space of real time, and the real world is *māyā*, which is the space of illusion. This does not imply that Tibetans, including their virtuosos, do not live, work, reproduce, and die in the everyday empirical world or that that world has no pragmatic saliency. After all, the Fifth Dalai Lama was a politician who formalized the Tibetan theocratic state, waged wars, and had astute diplomatic relations with Mongolia and China. Thus the dream time coexists with the pragmatic time of the everyday world, even though that world is an illusory one in Buddhist epistemology, as it is in certain forms of Western philosophy and the visionary wisdom of William Blake.

The dream time is of course where visions appear to the "inner-eye" or the "divine eye" or the "third eye" of the dreamer-visionary. I will now add that when the inner eye has to be represented in outer bodily form, it often appears in mythology as the eye in the middle of the forehead or, in the case of Jaina images of saints, as eyes that shine, enhanced by a gem-stone glittering in the middle of the forehead. In the Tibetan case, the physiology of "seeing" is derived from a Tibetan visionary tradition of the "supreme vision" (Tibetan, *thod-rgal*). While supreme vision practitioners might also recognize the illusory nature of the visions, that is, that they lack ultimate reality, it is also true that visions could be given salvific meaning or incorporated into the religious worldview of the visionary and in some instances assimilated into one's own being. Gyatso says that "a distinctive feature of its physiological theory is a focus on the sense organs, particularly the eyes and it posits subtle channels that are not commonly associated with Tantric fulfillment practice" (AS, 203). There are four such channels, and I refer the reader to Gyatso's detailed discussion of them. For my purpose the crucial one connects with the "inner field" in the heart and thence to the eyes and other sense organs. The heart's inner field is also known as the "crystal palace"; this site is also known as the "youthful vase body" and is a container of latent Buddhahood (AS, 204). "The effulgence of the youthful vase body/radiant light/subtle *tigle* emerges from the heart and travels to the eye along the 'crystal tube channel,'" opening doors "that make possible the dawning of the radiant light as a visual display of visions" (AS, 204–5).

The physiological significance of the heart is easy to explain because, in Indian medicine, the heart rather than the brain is the seat of thought and consciousness, and all Buddhist societies employ this notion. For me, however, the crucial feature of supreme vision is its physiology of passive perception, according to which supreme vision states can "*dawn naturally and effortlessly without any intentional construction*," thereby facilitating the emergence of visionary images without, I think, "I-thinking" (AS, 205, my emphasis). In his meditative trance, Jigme Lingpa himself notes the significance of the visionary eye and its exact location:

> That morning, while doing the waking-up yoga,
> I met on the luminous surface
>   of the ground's vision-producing radiant light
> The condensation of all refuges—
> Lake-Born Vajra,
> Inside a five-faceted rainbow tent-house,
>   straight ahead of where I was sitting
> in the space [in front of] the area between my eyebrows.
>
> (AS, 28)

In this scheme the visionary eye is the third eye invisibly located between the eyebrows like the forehead eye of Siva and other mythic beings we have mentioned. Very often in Jigma Lingpa's dream world, a difficult apprehension like the preceding one is followed by a more concrete vision.

> Then there appeared an object—
> the glorious ship Potala
> with an inconceivable [number of] doors and windows;
> and the sky above that;
> the body of Noble Lady [Tārā]
> the color of lapis,
> a body of light,
> not overly shiny.

But these visions haven't the straightforward character of mystical visions in medieval Christianity where the visionary has little doubt that she sees a divine reality, irrespective of the skepticism of others. For Jigme Lingpa, the vision implies an "attachment to dichotomized appearance," that is, a distinction between subject and object, something that violates the Buddhist orthodoxy he also must maintain.

> I am aware, therefore, of the fault
> in distinguishing *saṃsāra* and nirvana as separate

on the basis of the magical miracle
of awareness—or ignorance.

We are back to the double meaning of the visions. They do not provide a direct
access to salvific knowledge: they are "delusive" or dreamlike creations; though
delusive, they can provide "insight-awareness" in the sense that the world itself
is an illusion and yet can help the salvation seeker because salvation is possible
only by living in the world. Further, the attachment to visions is wrong because
attachment, *taṇhā* (Sanskrit *tṛṣṇā*), is a bodily knot of covetousness. It is the second noble truth of Buddhism and the cause of suffering, such that even attachment to meditation is wrong, according to Jigme Lingpa. Thus the dream world
and the empirical world both share the illusory or transient quality, the dream
world being a model, parable, or symbolic expression of the everyday world, as
is evident from the following text, which he quotes: "All phenomena are like a
dream, Subhūti. If there were to be some phenomenon beyond the phenomenon
of nirvana, even that would be like a dream, like an illusion. Thus have I taught,
Subhūti, all phenomena are imperfect, imputed. Although they don't exist, they
appear, like a dream, like an illusion." And he adds, in both prose and verse: "Everything in all of *saṃsāra*, nirvana, and on the path is but a category based on an
aspect that is only of one's own perception. Other than that, there's not even a
hair that is truly established in the ultimate sense. If this is so, then even more
delusive is the dream, whose apparitions, [the product of] residual properties,
are extremely hollow." As said,

Life is like a dream
If you examine it thoroughly
It's [hollow] like a plantain"

(AS, 16)

What then is there in the dream or vision that distinguishes it from "life" and
makes it such a powerful mode of searching for the salvific goal? The Supreme
Vision emanating from the heart through the crystal tube gives the meditator-
protagonist magical powers that can be seen both as illusory and as providing
a stimulus for accessing the Buddha-nature, for example, when Jigme Lingpa
meets the very founder of Tibetan Buddhism, Padmasambhava:

Propensities for meditative experiences and realizations
    have awoken from my inner depths.

I've met the own-face of Father Padma,
    the son of the conquerors [Buddhas].
I've attained the pith of the meaning,
    instruction deep to the nth degree.
I've not only attained it,
    it has dawned in my mind.

Padmasambhava seems real and appears with his "own face." Yet he is still an il-lusion of an illusion; and, if he appears in "proxy form" in the guise of some other apparitional being, he then is an illusion of an illusion of an illusion, an idea that seems outrageous from the point of view of European common sense but com-pletely acceptable in Tibetan Buddhism.

Whether one is a Tibetan or another kind of Buddhist, the fact is that only a Buddha or Bodhisattva can discover true knowledge, that is, salvific knowledge, and this knowledge is transmitted through generations of monks as the "long transmission." Hence, treasure seekers do not invent texts; texts are given by a Buddha or a Buddha figure and hidden in the memory of a guru like Padmasamb-hava or actually sequestered somewhere by Padmasambhava himself, who de-creed that they will be discovered by legitimate treasure seekers. The treasure seeker must then seek the sequestered treasure or access the original memory through his visions (AS, 147). Because the treasure texts have been hidden or are being guarded by ḍākinīs, it is not surprising that they often appear in ḍākinī code that cannot be deciphered by illegitimate aspirants.

A beautiful example of this comes from Jigme Lingpa's discovery of the col-lection of texts for which he is best known, that is, *Longchen Nyingtig* (The Heart Essence of Infinite Expanse).[57] In one of his visions, Jigme Lingpa mounts a lion-ess and reaches a place he identifies as the famous *stūpa*, the Bodhinath, in Nepal. He circumambulates the *stūpa* and there encounters the "*ḍākinī* of primordial consciousness" in front of him in actuality, "in the Dharma body," the nonbodily form of her own body.[58] She gives him a wooden casket in the shape of an amulet and then tells Jigme Lingpa that he is the great King Trisong Detsen and that the casket contains the text in the heart-mind of the Bodhisattva Samantabhadra, but coming to him via Padmasambhava and protected these long years by the ḍākinīs. Jigme Lingpa opens the casket but cannot decipher the text, written in scrambled ḍākinī writing inside a pictorial outline shape of a *stūpa*. "Since I could not read it, I began to roll it up, when just in that instant, like an optical illusion, the figure of the *stūpa* vanished, and all the symbolic characters inside turned at once into Tibetan" (AS, 57).

Padmasambhava is a Buddha-like being, and when he appears in visionary form he infuses Jigma Lingpa with his own spiritual "qualities," making it possible for the latter to discover those hidden treasures and also gain powers not available for ordinary mortals. The text then is a treasure (*terma*) transferred from the mind of the primordial Buddha Samantabhadra to the mind of Padmasambhava to that of Jigme Lingpa, himself an incarnation of the king, Trisong Detsen.

> In the center of the multicolored space,
>   covered by a rainbow canopy,
> Was Father-Awareness-Holder Padmasambhava,
> in the guise epitomizing the three types of bodies,
> seated in a field of air
> without support . . .
> With his retinue of heroes and *ḍākkis*,
> he was beautiful.

> In the center was a large stone throne,
> on top of which,
> without thinking,
> I myself arrived.
> At that moment memory was lost, uncontrollably,
> in veneration.
> My awareness,
> ejected like a shooting star,
> dissolved into the venerable Guru's heart.

(AS, 31)

Through this merging of hearts (or minds), the seat of the supreme visions, Jigme Lingpa is endowed with the Buddha-nature of Padmasambhava himself. In another instance, he sees an apparitional form of a former scholar-guru, Jampal Shenyen, whose body was "dark red, clear like quartz" (AS, 28).

> In his right hand
> he carried an especially excellent mace.
> His left, in the intimidating finger gesture,
> was pointed symbolically at my heart.
> At that moment, he gave me
> his hand accoutrement, a mace,

and then dissolved into me
indistinguishably.

(AS, 29)

By this merging, Jigme Lingpa becomes the guru or carries the being of the
guru in his own being. But more than that: by dissolving into the guru, the
subject-object distinction operative in everyday life is "dissolved" and presages
the salvific goal, owing to his intuitive understanding that dualistic thinking
does not operate in an ultimate sense. Thus, when one dissolves into the guru or
the God or the Bodhisattva, or if the reverse process occurs, the point is implicitly made that the dualistic separation of nirvana and *saṃsāra* is false and that
the equation holds: nirvana is *saṃsāra*. Yet, on another level, one could say that
by identifying with Padmasambhava, Jigme Lingpa is in effect engaged in theistic
mysticism, not only during the space-time of the experience but also because he
contains within himself the imprint of that experience.

Yet another question remains. How can we understand this dissolution of being and of the merging or fusion of the divine being with the visionary? Pemalingpa is neither a sophisticated thinker nor one given to deep meditative states,
quite unlike Jigme Lingpa and the Fifth Dalai Lama. One of the primary goals of
Buddhist meditation is to destroy the illusion of a stable soul or self as something
within the person or an entity such as the Upaniṣadic Self or even as an unknowable Kantian thing-in-itself. Through meditative experience, the imagined but
nevertheless nominally "real" self is dissolved in what can sometimes be a terrifying nightmare. Here the meditating Buddhist approximates the Christian idea
of the dark night of the soul, which then is overcome as one reaches the calm of
meditative equanimity. And, like the Christian, he has to have a spiritual mentor
or guide or mystagogue, the true friend I spoke of earlier, or an idealized guru or
lama to lead him back to everyday life and to a reintegration of the now nominal
"self" with an awareness of its fleeting and unstable nature. Ordinary Buddhists,
both monk and lay, might intellectually cognize the central doctrine of no-soul
or no-self, but it is the meditator who can give that idea experiential meaning
and salvific significance. It is the meditative experience then that makes the dissolution of the self and the merging of the virtuoso and his divinity possible during the visionary dream time, just as it might occur in our everyday dream life.
Dissolution and merging and fusion of the two selves, with its deep ontic meaning, can be beautifully seen, even through the bare summary available to us, in
the dream time of the Fifth Dalai Lama.

In 1652, at the age of thirty-six, "the Dalai Lama has a vision of all the divinities associated with the *Vajrakīla* or ritual dagger residing in its middle part

wherein the deities dance and the Dalai Lama himself joins in the dance. Eventually he comes up to a deity who holds a mirror and says to him: 'look into this!' The Dalai Lama sees India, China, Nepal, Oddiyana and Śambhala." The space further expands when he arrives at the paradise of Padmasambhava and in the ground floor of a three-story temple where the great guru gives him instructions for avoiding harmful spirits. Then in a white light, like that of a curtain, one of the two consorts of the guru appears in a white form and wearing bone ornaments. She "becomes the feminine partner in an empowerment initiation for the Dalai Lama who, in his union with her, experiences the non-duality of Bliss and Voidness," that is, the Mahāyāna idea of emptiness or śūnyatā (SV, 17).

Here is a beautiful instance in which emptiness becomes bliss owing to the act of sexual intercourse, even though eroticism has been transmuted and removed from the mundane sphere. And the sexual union where the two become one is proof for the Dalai Lama, as for others in the Vajrayāna traditions, of the meditational abolition of the subject-object distinction and with it the grasp of the absence of duality. I would add that the Dalai Lama's experience of fusion during cosmic erotic union, like that of others, integrates the female image into his own being, creating or enhancing his own bisexuality or androgyny. Also note the example of the contraction-expansion of space in the vision itself, based on a prior similar experience, now familiar to us, whereby a person peers into a small space that is then ballooned into a vast vision. In this example, the ritual diamond dagger is the vajrakīla; in the middle of that small space are divinities who dance with the Dalai Lama joining them. Then the fantastic vision of the geography of vast regions, which he sees through a small mirror held by a divinity; a space within a space, a vision within a vision within a vision. The mirror is the polished surface that many a visionary stares at; the crystal ball into which the Western magician peers; the tubes that link the crystal heart to the visionary eye of treasure seekers; the crystal through which Māyā sees her Buddha-child mirrored in her womb; the crystal and gold and pearl womb-cabinet from where Blake's little boy peers into the transformed world outside;[59] the mirrored stone wherein the archeologist Paranavitana read his interlinear writings; the water mirrored in the basin that opens up the crack in the teacup leading Auden into the upside-down land of the dead; the pool on whose mirrored surface the Buddhist visionary saw the return of a historic event where defeated Titans descend into their city through the hollow of a lotus stalk;[60] the mirroring stone through which the prophet Joseph Smith (1805–1844) saw the "golden plates" whose dictated contents constituted the Book of Mormon;[61] the stainless looking glass through which Aśvaghoṣa's Buddha sees the world during the second watch of the night. As the poet said, "mirror on mirror mirrored is all the show."[62]

Reverting back to mirrored reality, in another scenario the Dalai Lama has sexual intercourse with the wife of the guru, but this is also a projection on to the cosmic plane of the Tantric act of sexual union, sometimes with the actual guru's wife who is a mother to the disciple, thereby committing a doubly horrendous act. But while some Tantric virtuosos might perform orgasmic sex with the woman-mother, it is likely that both in his actual life and in his visionary life the Dalai Lama, being a celibate monk, can perform Tantric copulation only on the cosmic level. Thus he acts out his union with his consort (the consort of Padmasambhava, his own divine guru) while his head is in the clouds, as it were, withholding both semen ejaculation and orgasm, proving to himself and to the world the special kind of "sublimation" of an act that is normally an overwhelming one of passionate fusion. It is not clear whether the Dalai Lama is also an incarnation of Padmasambhava. If that is the case, then when he copulates with his guru's wife he is in fact copulating with his own wife in a previous incarnation. The Dalai Lama's detached act is also an initiation in the Tibetan sense, empowering him with the salvific realization of the nonduality of bliss and emptiness, given that emptiness is a kind of fullness that I mentioned earlier.

In another sequence a similar scenario is repeated: the Dalai Lama is transported to Sri Lanka, the classic abode of anthropologists and demons, and there he sees Karmaguru, a manifestation of Padmasambhava, as a composite or androgynous image of *yab* (father) and *yum* (mother); he is swallowed up by the *yab* and deposited in the womb of the *yum* where he is bathed in red and white *bodhicitta* (drops of transmuted or transubstantiated semen and uterine blood or "female emissions") and receives the four kinds of empowerment. "As he finally emerges from the womb, he feels pleasure mingled with the experience of the non-duality of Bliss and Voidness" (SV, 23). In this meditational sequence the Dalai Lama magically regresses into the primordial womb that I assume is also a transmuted version of a regression into his own mother's womb, a state of comfortable bliss that can, on yet another level, express the bliss of emptiness and nonduality because, once again, he is a merged composite sexual being. The symbolism is simultaneously a sublime womb-regression, imagined or real, and an understanding of salvific knowledge. Such simultaneous regression-progression-sublimation I think can only occur in states of deep meditative trance.

Now let us go back to the earlier vision: "After this, the Dalai Lama arrives in a citadel where a fearful woman with a dark brown complexion swallows him up; he becomes *rDo-rje gro-kid* in her womb, and comes out feeling the pride of being *rDo-rje gro-lod*, a wrathful aspect of Padmasambhava." The Dalai Lama awakens to a new status, endowed with the fierce aspect of the great deity and becomes that deity. A kind of "benevolent fierceness" is expressed in the dark brown color in contrast with the whiteness of the guru's consort and in further contrast to the red and the black of extreme fierceness and violence in Tibetan painting. Another white figure now approaches him. "The white *ḍākinī*, chief of the five kinds of *ḍākinī*s [the consort of Padmasambhava], appears before the Dalai Lama giving instructions as to how to avoid an undesirable situation. She then leads him through the sky and eventually arrives in a cave in the shape of a *vajra* on a rocky mountain whose summit seems to reach up to the heavens" (SV, 17). The guide is, once again, the divine counterpart of the "true friend" of the meditator; and the undesirable situation she talks about in this vision and in others refers, I presume, to bad visions, just as in actual meditative sessions. The diamond mountain cave is one of Padmasambhava's abodes, and it is here that the Dalai Lama meets the guru as an ordinary-looking *yogin*. This particular apparitional form of the deity I believe is very common in ecstatic or visionary religiosity. In the course of my own fieldwork, priests and priestesses have told me of meeting their favorite god in the guise of an old man or in some other ordinary apparitional form. In the Dalai Lama's case "Padmasambhava touches his head with a vase in a gesture of benediction. Then the *yogin* [Padmasambhava], dissolving into light, disappears into the Dalai Lama's heart" (SV, 17). The *yogin* or saint represents the good and benevolent side of Padmasambhava; it merges into the disciple's heart, the seat of both consciousness and visionary power.

The merging of consciousnesses expresses itself on the visionary level in a series of transformations. For example: Bodhisattva Avatilokeśvara transforms himself into a Tibetan king of times past; that king then dissolves into the heart of Lokeśvara ("Lord of the World"), who is another form of Avatilokeśvara; then the king infuses Lokeśvara with his power. It is as if the Bodhisattva can become the king, as indeed the Dalai Lama can become the Bodhisattva in some of his visions. Yet, this seems a circular process, because all three forms are that of Avatilokeśvara himself and, for that matter, so is the Dalai Lama![63] One can however suggest a political rationale for this text. Lokeśvara is a form of Avatilokeśvara as the divine guardian of the worldly realm and of the cosmos. Thus the infusion of power from the king as guardian of the secular order helps to reinforce Lokeśvara's protective role as a kind of divine king overseeing that very realm. And ultimately, because the Dalai Lama is both the chief of the worldly realm *and* an incarnation of Avatilokeśvara-Lokeśvara, it is he who benefits from this circular movement of power and sacredness (SV, 23).

In another instance of merging, the Dalai Lama's body "disperses into small pieces and then disappears altogether into lights. Padmasambhava then changes into *Guru drag-po* who in turn becomes the Dalai Lama himself" (SV, 22). *Guru drag-po,* who often merges with the Dalai Lama, is the embodiment of tranquillity, progress, subjugation, and violence, and these powers become in turn embodied in the Dalai Lama of the vision, which is as good as being embodied in the Dalai Lama of the flesh. The attributes of *Guru drag-po* once again nicely fits the needs of the Dalai Lama as king and monk, conqueror and renouncer combined. Here also the disintegration of the body is a refraction of similar processes occurring during deep meditation, especially in those sessions where one meditates on the body and through it into the recognition of "no-self." Minus the self as an entity, both the Dalai Lama and Padmasambhava and the Bodhisattva "dissolve" into other forms of the same divinity, thereby obtaining their power and attributes. The mind transmission of treasure can take place through these acts of merging; thus the Dalai Lama receives many texts that then become part of the Vajrayāna corpus. Texts are also given directly by Padmasambhava or one of his apparitional forms or from a previous guru. For example, in one vision, at age thirty-six, the Dalai Lama is on a visit to China and stops for a midday meal near a *stūpa.* There, in a vision, the great Indian scholar-monk Atiśa (982–1054), who lived in Tibet for twelve years, appears before the Dalai Lama and instructs him in the teachings of the *bKa'-gdams-pa* (Kadampa) order, a strongly ascetic, meditational, and ethical tradition of Buddhism associated with Atiśa and his disciples (SV, 32).[64]

I think it would be naive to give a simplistic psychoanalytic interpretation of the episodes of transformation, dissolution, and fragmentation of the body in the Tibetan tradition. I shall show later they have their parallels in dream life in the work of the dream-ego (see pp. 290–97). In the Dalai Lama's case, such transformations are products of the meditation experience, but projected into the cosmos through visions and dream-visions. These acts of merging and dissolving one into the other would be impossible in everyday reality. They occur in dreams but they are also familiar to us in the dissolution of personality that occurs in the psychoses. Interpretation of these meditational experiences in terms of deep motivation does not work here either. It would work, I think, only for the dark night of the early meditative sessions wherein childhood anxieties and forgotten memories begin to surface. But of these we have little documented evidence in the Tibetan tradition.[65] Nevertheless, on rare occasions the vision itself may provoke unconscious feelings of dejection and guilt, as is indicated in the following account of Jigme Lingpa's encounter with sorcery on the cosmological plane.

I saw, in a meditative experience
　　on the mirror surface of a lucid dream,

that another person had sicced
that harmer, the red rock fury, on me.

(AS, 25)

Let me render the incident of the harmer episode intelligible. An enemy has magically, perhaps also through a vision, sent a demon-harmer, a kind of being the virtuoso is normally trained to avoid. The magical act is to attack Jigme Lingpa in a battle occurring entirely in the realm of visionary reality and familiar to us ethnographers from shamanic battles with spirits.[66] Jigme Lingpa sees the harmer in a vision, but the harmer is a real being who is at the same time an invisible being, just as it is with other demons and deities. The sight of the harmer provokes Jigme Lingpa to respond in a not-quite-Buddhist fashion, illustrating his own vulnerability to the bodily knot of ill will:

I, in a state of anger
    within emptiness and compassion
turned his world completely around.
I plunged the point—
    the very weapon he had thrust,
        [now turned into] his own executioner—
into his heart.

(AS, 25)

The harmer sent by an unknown enemy tries to kill him, but Jigme Lingpa pierces the heart of the harmer with the same fateful weapon. It is a deadly unethical act that only sorcerers engage in, whereas in his meditative state Jigme Lingpa is encompassed within "emptiness and compassion." Why then the anger leashed against the harmer and why the act of violence against him? Let me postpone the answer and consider the next episode in the visionary sequence:

Two days later,
Samanta, my retreat assistant,
gave me in actuality,
a *pha-wong long-bu* stone
about [the size of] a fresh star [shaped berry].
I accepted it as a soul stone.

(AS, 25–26)

The *pha-wong long-bu* stone is a special kind of stone used for imprisoning an invisible spirit in magical rituals. I am familiar with a similar phenomenon in Sri Lanka where the exorcist entices a malignant ancestral spirit or *preta* to his magical knot, and, when he sees the frightening spirit enter the knot, he tightens it and imprisons it. Subsequently the knot is destroyed or dumped into the sea, nowadays after being encased in concrete. Similarly, the "dagger" that pierced the heart of the harmer did not kill him but helped to imprison him in the soul stone. The next fifteen lines tell us that Jigme Lingpa placed the stone under his bed with the threat to kill the harmer for having disobeyed the injunctions of Padmasambhava, the hero who had tamed the original Tibetan demons and forced them into the service of Buddhism. Although he does not consciously recognize it, Jigme Lingpa's violent practice while in Buddhist meditative trance is surely wrong for a lama given to compassion. But I suggest that he *unconsciously* recognizes his guilt feelings in the very next vision, which occurs immediately afterward.

> In that period,
> at the time of the vanishing of the moon of Kārttika
> during a vision of falling into a deep chasm,
> a voice was saying,
> "This is hell."

> (AS, 26)

Conventional Buddhist hells are actual places very much like the Christian ones, but Jigme Lingpa realizes that "hell is made by the mind," an idea that only rarely appears in Buddhism. Yet his violent acts, committed in the Buddhist meditative context, appear in his vision of hell as a place in the mind. Jigme Lingpa does not actually describe his visual experience of mental hell, leading us to believe that his guilt feelings are expressed in terms of felt mental pain that was not, or could not, be projected visually. However, his insight that hell is in the mind resulted in his being "discharged" from hell, and he says he "woke from sleep, absorbed in a state of sadness," an aftermath of his guilt feelings from harming the harmer (AS, 26).[67]

The preceding vision sequence can be speculatively reconstructed thus. In ordinary life sorcery is practiced against someone who has wronged another, and the original wrongdoer in this case must be Jigme Lingpa himself; the wronged person seeks retaliation by sending the harmer to hurt or kill Jigme Lingpa; the latter reacts by acting violently against the harmer and taming him in cruel fashion, the model being ordinary life where similar vengeful acts take place; yet all this is contrary to the Buddhist principles that Jigme Lingpa claims to profess, for he is trapped like the harmer in the bodily knot of a distorted grasp of rules and vows; not surprisingly, he feels guilty for his act; the next vision gives expression to unconscious guilt in the idea that hell is in the mind; that insight is enough to release Jigme Lingpa from his mental hell, but not totally because he awakes with a feeling of sadness.

Book 3

THE COSMIC "IT"

The Abstract Being of the Intellectuals

PLOTINUS: THE MYSTICAL REACH OF THE ABSOLUTE

God exists, but only philosophically.

—Attributed to Baruch de Spinoza

IN MY DISCUSSION of Mahāyāna Buddhism, I pointed out that the Buddhist doctrine of emptiness, in its very abstractness, shares that feature with many of the world's great religions and with forms of the Absolute participating in a form of "secular spirituality." That God exists "only philosophically," attributed to Spinoza, expresses a larger truth of the world in the religious and secular traditions, wherein philosophers posit an abstract entity or Absolute or Being that exist outside the phenomenal world of becoming. However, while the God of Spinoza's skeptical philosophy is based on the science and mathematics of his time, such a Being exists in other intellectual traditions as well. For me one of the fascinating features of the Absolute is that *It* can be reached from different routes or inferred logically from different cultural and epistemological premises or inferred existentially from some deep out-of-the-body or dreamlike experience. Thus Nāgārjuna's emptiness is an inference from conditioned genesis, but his followers in the Buddhist tradition can employ his model to justify or reinvent emptiness through meditation and the fullness of vision. Others, like Descartes, can logically infer God as Absolute based on the assumption of the cogito, whereas his younger contemporary Spinoza uses a different set of definitions and axioms from which he deduces formal propositions with relentless logic to prove the existence of his philosophical God ("an absolute infinite Entity").[1] It is this sense of an abstract deity that Blake criticizes in one of the aphorisms of *The Laocoön*: "The Gods of Greece and Egypt were Mathematical Diagrams—See Plato's Works."[2] As Blake said, these ideas had their counterparts in early Greek philosophers and later European thinkers who, consciously or not, used the Greek models in their own formulations of the Absolute, passionately seeking a dispassionate entity: Presence, Absolute, Good, Intellect, Unmoved Mover, Being, or whatever. Or you might call it God or divinity, but, once again, as an abstraction as in the deism of the Enlightenment. In India, Upaniṣadic seekers of salvation grasped the idea of Brahman intuitively and then used beautiful analogies to demonstrate its existence. That early idea of an abstract being or Brahman continued to appear in various guises throughout the history of Hindu philosophy.

Fleeting experiences can also give a person a sense of the Absolute in the post-Enlightenment West. In a vision that lasted only a few moments, one of James's informants experienced a state of "cosmic consciousness" that entailed "passive enjoyment, not actually thinking, but letting ideas, images and emotions flow of themselves, as it were, through my mind." And, like modern-day lucid dreamers, this person sensed that the "universe is not composed of dead matter, but is, on the contrary, a living Presence [and] I became conscious in myself of eternal life."[3] Another scientist friend of William James (perhaps a stand-in for James himself) formulated the issue thus: "Between twenty and thirty I gradually became more and more agnostic and irreligious, yet I cannot say that I ever lost that 'indefinite consciousness' which Herbert Spencer describes so well, of an Absolute Reality behind phenomena. For me this Reality was not the pure Unknowable of Spencer's philosophy, for although I had ceased my childish prayers to God, and never prayed to It in a formal manner, yet my more recent experience shows me to have been in a relation to It which practically was the same thing as prayer."[4] Most often, when a person has had an "out-of-the-body experience," he or she gives it simultaneous cultural and personal meaning. These are the issues that I shall explore in more detail, bearing in mind that in rare cases one can *identify* with the Absolute and in so doing experience a form of mysticism.

I will begin with Plotinus (204–76 CE), whose soteriology I am familiar with and whose thinking provides a bridge linking the two traditions I am primarily interested in, Buddhism and Christianity. Few are aware that Plotinus has a theory of rebirth and ethical reward that resonates with Indic religions, although not as systematically developed. Reincarnation did not have official sanction in the Christian Church, although Plotinus's mysticism did owing to the impact of Neoplatonic thought on Christianity (as well as Islam). I will also use Plotinus to counter the ethnocentrism of one of the leading scholars of Plotinian mysticism, Pierre Hadot, who says that although "this [mystical] phenomenon attains its plenitude only with Christianity it nevertheless exists, in a highly authentic way throughout human history."[5] Hadot's ethnocentrism coexists with the common scholarly denial or downplaying of reincarnation doctrines in both Plato and Plotinus and Greek thought in general.[6]

As with Plato and many Pythagoreans, Plotinus took for granted rebirth in the world of humans and animals literally, even though he took considerable liberties with Platonic cosmology and soteriology. While he thought of himself as Plato's heir, there is as much an epistemic break between Plato and Plotinus as between the Upaniṣads and early Buddhism, at least as far as his soteriology and doctrine of rebirth is concerned. Let me present Plotinus's philosophical thought, beginning with his lesser-known rebirth eschatology and soteriology, to draw attention to his karmalike doctrine of ethical compensation and his doctrine of salvation.

References to rebirth are scattered in Plotinus's masterwork, *The Enneads*, almost always in discussions of the soul and as part of an ineluctable cosmic law. These concepts of the soul in turn make sense only in relation to his highly innovative cosmology that he developed not only in relation to Plato but also in debates with Aristotle, with the Stoics, with contemporary Gnostic doctrines, and perhaps even with the Christians.[7] Briefly stated, Plotinus believed that all reality is united in the One that is beyond knowing. The One, also known as the Good, is derived (historically at least) from Plato's brief references to such an entity in *The Republic* and the more detailed discussion in *Parmenides*, along with the work of middle Platonists, like Plotinus's precursor, Numenius of Apamea.[8] In the Plotinian conception, the One is beyond Being, but it emanates other forms of Being that Plotinus labels the first principles or hypostases. While the One is unknowable, the derivative hypostases are knowable forms of Being spelled out in some detail in the fifth and sixth Enneads.

In this conception the One radiates the other realms of Being beginning with the second hypostasis, Nous or the Intellect (variously translated through other abstractions as Divine Intellect, Intelligence, Intellectual Principle, or the Divine Mind). The problematic relation between the first hypostasis, the One or Good, and the second derivative hypostasis can be put thus: if the One is immobile and cannot produce anything, how can one say that the second hypostasis derives from the first? Plotinus resolves this with his well-known trope. "It must be a circumradiation—produced from the Supreme but from the Supreme unaltering—and may be compared to the brilliant light encircling the sun and ceaselessly generated from that unchanging substance."[9] All "existences" have this character: they are emanations of a superior principle and share the nature of that principle, whereas the superior does not share the features of the lower principle. Nous, Intellect, or Intellectual Principle contains the intelligible universe and in it are Plato's ideal forms, those universals that have a role in generating the particularities and the multiplicities of our known world. Thus the multiple realities of lived existence are reflections of the archetypes of forms that radiate from the Intellect and ultimately unite in it. The relation between Intellect and forms has been a controversial one in Neoplatonism. Dominic O'Meara makes the reasonable proposition that for Plotinus "the Forms are the thoughts, the thinking activity, of the divine intellect."[10]

The Intellectual Principle or Nous in turn irradiates the soul such that the whole world is "ensouled." Soul "envelops the heavenly system and guides all to its purposes: for it has bestowed itself upon all that huge expanse so that every interval, small and great alike, all has been ensouled." Again: "By the power of the Soul the manifold and diverse heavenly system is a unit: through soul this universe is a God: and the sun is a God, because it is ensouled; so too the stars: and whatsoever we ourselves may be" (*Enn.*, 5:1.349). The Good or the One or even the Nous of Plotinus is no personal deity. True, Plato and probably Plotinus also believed in the Greek gods of their time and that included the sun and the stars. But these Greek gods cannot be credited with creation, and hence Plotinian theory has to "explain" the generation of life in the world. This is left for soul, which generates and accounts for multiple life in the world, which then becomes "ensouled." Thus Plotinus follows the Greek tradition of the world permeated with soul (*empsychon*), though the immediate precursor of his view is perhaps the Stoic conception of the universe filled with spirit, which he transforms in his own highly idealistic way.[11]

As with Plato, the beings inhabiting our world are not ensouled in the same degree: animals are not ensouled in the same manner as human beings; plants are even worse off because, unlike animals, they have no capacity for feeling. The universal soul is therefore compounded into diversity or subject to "engroupment," as was the case with the Nous. "Thus we have often in the Enneads a verbal partition of the All-Soul; we hear of the Leading-Principle of the Soul or the Celestial Soul, concentrated in contemplation of its superior, and the Lower Soul, called also the Nature-Looking and Generative Soul, whose operation it is to generate or fashion the lower, the material Universe upon the model of the Divine Thoughts, the 'Ideas' laid up within the Divine Mind [Nous]: this lower principle in the Soul is sometimes called the Logos of the Universe, or the 'Reason-Principle' of the Universe."[12] If the reasoning-soul (or the "rational soul" of other translators) is what makes us human as we aspire to reach Being and beyond Being into the originary One, the unreasoning aspect of soul is characteristic of animal life.

Plotinus has a knack of formulating each issue in different ways. Thus in a complicated discussion he shows how soul further diversifies into another engroupment, sense and nature, once again to account for the multiple forms of life in the world. For present purposes let me focus on the latter: "In the case of a soul entering some vegetal form, what is there is one phase, the more rebellious and less intellectual, outgone to that extreme; in a soul entering an animal, the faculty of sensation has been dominant and brought it there; in soul entering man, the movement outward has either been wholly of its reasoning part or has come from the Intellectual Principle [Nous] in the sense that the soul, possessing that principle as immanent to its being, has an inborn desire for intellectual activity and of movement in general" (*Enn.*, 5:2.362). In other words, there is no radical gap between the divine intellect and "our habitual and discursive form of thought." For, "since divine intellect constitutes soul it is always present to soul and thus to our souls; we always remain in contact with it and we can reach it through the deepening of our insight."[13] Thus, although soul is an emanation of the Intellect, its particular refractions in the phenomenal world will be diverse. "The depth of the descent [of the soul], also, will differ—sometimes lower, sometimes less low—and this even in its entry into any given Kind: all that is fixed is that each several soul descends to a recipient indicated by affinity of condition; it moves towards the thing which it There resembled, and enters, accordingly, into the body of man or animal" (*Enn.*, 4:3.266).

This Plotinian reformulation of Platonic rebirth is spelled out in detail in Ennead III:4, in a discussion of the guardian spirit. According to this conception, humans share the characteristics of other living beings, including plants, insofar as their lives are governed by sense perception. But, because of the rational soul that characterizes our very being, humans do not live by sense perception alone. Nevertheless, humans do have sense organs and "in many ways we live like plants, for we have a body which grows and reproduces." Consequently one's soul must not be tied down by our senses in such things as reproductive sexuality and gluttony. Instead a human being must "escape" from such activities and rise to the Intellect and the Good, which is the natural movement of the soul. Human beings then have a choice to follow the daimon or guardian spirit in this upward movement of the soul or let soul be dragged down by the dross of wrong and materiality. At death those special people or sages possessed of the purified higher soul (the celestial soul) will follow the upward movement toward Intellect and beyond that to the Good; whereas ordinary humans, possessors of the lower or rational soul, will be caught in the rebirth process or *metensomatosis* ("changing from body to body").[14] Plotinus says about the latter:

Those, then, that guarded the man in them, become men again. Those who lived by sense alone become animals; but if their sense-perceptions have been accompanied by passionate temper they become wild animals. . . . But if they did not even live by sense along with their desires but coupled them with dullness of perception, they even turn to plants. . . . Those who loved music but were in other ways respectable turn into song-birds; kings who ruled stupidly into eagles, if they had no other vices; astronomers who were always raising themselves to the sky without philosophical reflection turn into birds which fly high. The man who practiced community virtue becomes a man again; but one who has a lesser share of it a creature that lives in community, a bee or something of the sort.[15]

As in Plato, this account emphasizes the correspondence of the present life with the former one and the importance of "choice." In the passage I have quoted, all animal rebirths imply punishment for wrong choice, though some births, such as that of eagles and bees, are less degraded than others and songbirds perhaps are not so badly off. Rooted as he is in the Platonic idea of the correspondence between the past and present, Plotinus does not wholly deal with ethics. Soon, however, he moves in the direction of ethical choice in his discussion of the guardian spirit as the spiritual principle in oneself, thus giving ethical significance to the Platonic notion of daimon. We must choose the rational principle in our present life; otherwise when we die the soul weighted by the dross of unethical behavior must pay the penalty in another rebirth. Hence Plotinus's qualification of the previous account: "The wicked man, since the principle which worked in him during his life has pressed him down to the worse, towards what is like itself, enters into the life of a beast."[16] Then in a further ethical development, the guardian spirit or daimon operating as the spiritual agency within us will punish us for our wrongdoings, very much like the Freudian conscience.[17] "For the faults committed here, the lesser penalty is to enter body after body—and soon to return—by judgment according to desert, the word judgment indicating a divine ordinance; but any outrageous form of ill-doing incurs a proportionately greater punishment administered by the *surveillance of chastising daimons*" (*Enn.*, 4:8.340; my emphasis).

These ideas are given a different ethical turn in the third Ennead on "Providence: First Treatise" in relation to problems of theodicy (*Enn.*, 3:2.135–65). The basic argument is that everything in the universe flows according to a rational plan centering on the One or the Good. As far as ensoulment is concerned, this rational plan implies that "in the heavens of our universe, while the whole has life eternally, the souls pass from body to body entering into varied forms," and in some cases "a soul will arise outside of the realm of birth and dwell with the one Soul of all"—that in effect surely implies the abolition of rebirth or metenso-matosis (*Enn.*, 3:2.139–40). Plotinus seems to say that the soul—the world soul—is eternal but when a soul gets embodied in the rebirth process it drops its immortal nature unless it returns to the world soul and from there back to Nous and then to the One. This means that if there is an ineluctable law of descent from the One, there is also one of ascent in the reverse direction from the third principle to the first. Yet, if everything emanates from the Good and flows backward towards the Good, why is there wrongdoing and bad in the world?

We are back in the Platonic world of the soul dragged down by the body's dross and further developed in the Plotinian doctrine of matter, according to which the body is the container of soul and of nature, a composite of the physical and spiritual. Man's wrongdoing does not mean that he cannot aspire toward the Good, but human beings "foiled, in their weakness, of their true desire, they turn against each other: still, when they do wrong they pay the penalty—that of having hurt their souls by their evil conduct and of degradation to a lower place—for nothing can ever escape what stands decreed in the law of the Universe" (*Enn.*, 3:2.140). Thus punishment and reward are automatic processes, part of the law of the universe. "Punishment naturally follows: there is no injustice in a man suffering what belongs to the condition in which he is; nor can we ask to be happy when our actions have not earned us happiness; the good, only, are happy; divine beings are happy only because they are good" (*Enn.*, 3:2.140–41).

It seems that for Plotinus a nagging problem remains: how could the horrendous things that people do be reconciled with the Good and with his philosophical scheme in general? Fortunately, Plotinus does not have to deal with the idea of an omnipotent deity where theodicy becomes a problem. The One is not a living God in any theistic sense, and, like Plato's demiurge, it cannot be held accountable for the world's ills. Evildoers, however, "will not get off by death" but will be punished in another life (*Enn.*, 3:2.144). This is the "ordinance of the cosmos [and] is in keeping with the Intellectual Principle [Nous]" (*Enn.*, 3:2.149). This ordinance is a karmalike automatic process.

> Thus a man, once a ruler, will be made a slave because he abused his power and because the fall is to his future good. Those that have misused money will be made poor—and to the good poverty is no hindrance. Those that have unjustly killed, are killed in turn, unjustly as regards the murderer but justly as regards the victim, and those that are to suffer are thrown into the path of those that administer the merited treatment.
>
> It is not an accident that makes a man a slave; no one is prisoner by chance; every bodily outrage has its due cause. The man once did what he now suffers.

A man that murders his mother will become a woman and be murdered by a son; a man that wrongs [rapes] a woman will become a woman, to be wronged.[18]

Hence that "awesome word Adrasteia (the Inevadable Retribution)," which is similar to what Buddhists conceptualized as *karma vipāka*, the consequences of karma.[19] The awesome way in which the world is "enlinked" in a scheme of cosmic harmony is stated in a magnificent passage.

> No one can ever escape the suffering entailed by ill deeds done: the divine law is ineluctable, carrying bound up, as one with it, the foreordained execution of its doom. The sufferer, all unaware, is swept onward towards his due, hurried always by the restless driving of his errors, until, at last wearied out by that against which he struggled, he falls into his fit place and, by self-chosen movement, is brought to the lot he never chose. And the law decrees, also, the intensity and duration of the suffering, while it carries with it, too, the lifting of chastisement and the faculty of rising from those places of pain—all by the power of the harmony that maintains the universal scheme.
>
> (*Enn.*, 4:3.277)

Adrasteia is not the Greek goddess of the mystery religions exacting punishment but a metaphor for the automatism of punishment for wrongs done. Yet, on the formal level, this strand of compensatory ethics in Plotinus is quite unlike that of Plato and the Buddha. Though Plotinus pays lip service to Plato's ideas of heaven and hell when he is commenting on Platonic texts, in reality he ignores or downplays these realms. They are effectively bypassed as the soul gets reincarnated as man, woman, and animal (and also as plants) depending on the ethical actions of the motivating individual. Plotinus in effect reverses Plato's scheme of rewards and punishments administered in a heaven and a hell, and this also means that the role of Plato's guardian spirit becomes restricted because it does not accompany the dead person in its underworld journey, a theme that Plato fully developed in the last book of *The Republic*.[20]

What is the way of escape from the continual ensoulment in man and beast as part of the cosmic scheme of reincarnation? This answer is also found in Plotinus's doctrine of the irradiation process in reverse, the law of sympathy that ties the universe together: the soul's ascent to the world soul and then to Nous and then beyond all Being into the One. This is discussed in convoluted detail, but I shall give the gist of his thesis beginning with what happens to the soul upon leaving the body at death.

The soul at death cannot remain in the mundane world of becoming, which is an element alien to it, but must seek upward movement toward the sphere to which it naturally belongs, "wayfaring towards the Intellectual Realm [Nous]" (*Enn.*, 4:8.335). Those souls that are "body bound" (tied to the senses) by ill deeds are apt to "body punishment" through metensomatosis; whereas "clear souls" (celestial or higher souls) possessing no vestige of body, move upward, drawn to where there is Essence and Being. Thus the importance of the two kinds of soul: the rational soul at death seeking another body might give that body a divine quality by its mere presence while the higher or clear soul freed of body and of ill deeds moves upward. Following Platonic tradition, the latter ideal typically is the soul of the sage or philosopher.

What memory of the past do these respective souls retain? Basically the Plotonian thesis is that memory belongs to soul, not body, which by its materiality cannot be the vehicle for the Nous, the sphere to which the soul is naturally drawn. Soul uses the body and its organs, but body, owing to its shifting and fleeting nature, can only be an impediment to memory (*Enn.*, 4:3.280–82). Both kinds of souls have memories. After death, as time passes, the higher soul will remember the memories of past lives, and, dismissing some of the events of the immediately past life as trivial, it will revive things forgotten in the corporeal state owing to embodiment. It will begin to remember its originary condition. But what of the lower soul that seeks one body after another in the rebirth process? "It will tell over the events of the discarded life, it will treat as present that which it has just left, and it will remember much from the former existence" (*Enn.*, 4:3.281–82).

If the lower (rational) soul in Man seeks continual embodiment, the higher soul moves in the direction of the Supreme and into Nous, the sphere immediately above it, and as it does it forgets the past. In that sense, "the good soul is the forgetful." But what is most important is that "even in this world the soul which has the desire of the other is putting away, amid its actual life, all that is foreign to that order" (*Enn.*, 4:3.285). That is, even the embodied soul tries to put away dross and move upward, quite unlike the unreasoning animal soul, which, owing to its degradation, cannot make the upward movement. Both kinds of souls in us humans move up, but the embodied soul cannot ascend easily, weighted as it is by ill deeds done, which is ultimately translatable as materiality and dross. The soul that is freed of body—the clear soul—moving upward to its source in the Nous, the intellectual realm, would eventually find its way to that essence. It will have no memory whatever because the essence or Being is memoryless, even of the profoundest of thoughts and experiences. In this realm of Nous there is "no discursive thought, no passing from one point to another," and "all is presence" (*Enn.*, 4:4.286).

Plotinus then attempts the difficult task of describing the mystical identity of the soul with the Nous.

> Once pure in the Intellectual, it [soul] too possesses the same unchangeableness: for it possesses identity of essence; when it is in that region it must of necessity enter into oneness with the Intellectual-Principle [Nous] by the sheer fact of its self-orientation, for by that intention all interval disappears; the Soul advances and is taken into unison, and in that association becomes one with the Intellectual Principle—but not to its own destruction: the two are one, and two. In such a state there is no question of stage and change: the Soul, without motion (but by right of its essential being) would be intent upon its intellectual act, and in possession, simultaneously of its self-awareness; for it has become one simultaneous existence with the Supreme.
>
> (*Enn.*, 4:4.288)

Perhaps one can better understand what Plotinus meant by "simultaneous existence with the Supreme" if one looks at his own mystical experience.

> Many times this has happened: lifted out of the body into myself: becoming external to all other things and self-encentered; beholding a marvelous beauty; then, more-than ever, assured of community with the loftiest order; enacting the noblest life, acquiring identity with the divine; stationing within It by having attained that activity; poised above whatsoever within the Intellectual is less than the Supreme: yet, there comes the moment of descent from intellection to reasoning, and after that sojourn in the divine, I ask myself how it happens that I can now be descending, and how did the Soul ever enter into my body, the Soul which, even within the body, is the high thing it has shown itself to be.[21]

What is fascinating about Plotinus's oft-repeated experience of his own soul's ascent and descent is that it provides us with a concrete description of what the salvific condition might be, even though his experience of it was temporary and occasional. The soul, released from the body during a state of concentration, experiences the ecstasy of a sojourn with the divine. It is not clear whether this condition is identity with the One (the Plotinian Absolute or Good) or an experience that describes the soul going into the proper sphere of the Nous or Intellect, also a key Plotinian idea. The latter is the likely one. Nous is "intellection," not reasoning or discursive thought. For Plotinus, as for the Buddha and for all mystical virtuosos, the latter has been downgraded. But in my interpretation, admittedly tentative, the realm of the Intellect is where a passive cerebration still operates, a realm of It-thinking. Otherwise it makes no sense to say that Nous generates the realm of forms. Thus, when John of the Cross talks of the "passive intellect," the idea is not only derived from Plotinus originally but also helps us understand Plotinus's own idea of Nous more clearly. Identity with Nous means a duality still: the two are one and two, but duality is not the ultimate goal of the soteriological experience. The soul must ascend still further, beyond Nous and beyond Being, into the One. This movement toward the One by the human soul bereft of dross and materiality is beautifully described in the mystical language of "On the Good, or the One" (*Enn.*, 6:9.535–49).

Here Plotinus makes a philosophical case for the One as Unity, but, more important, he raises the issue of how we, our souls, "reach toward the Supreme" (*Enn.*, 6:9.545). To achieve this state we withdraw from external stimuli and, immersing inward, engage in the contemplation of the Supreme. Yet here as elsewhere he does not provide a technology or tell us in any detail how the withdrawal should take place. Plotinus even says that one might be able to report to others about that communion. But how is this possible, one might ask, if in the next breath he can say that communion with the One is beyond reason; it is reason's prior? And it does not make sense, given Plotinus's assumptions that once sunk into the Supreme he can engage in discursive I-thinking, describing the indescribable.

I do not think he can, and that is why his personal experience mentioned earlier pertains to the realm of the Nous and not to union with the One. He can describe the former because in Nous his soul or spirit are both one and two, whereas the ineffable condition of mystical identity with the One cannot be described in the discursive language of reason. Unhappily, even Nous is without memory. Therefore Plotinus has a problem that we will later consider: namely, how does he describe a movement into Nous and then describe Nous itself? For the moment, one can say that once in the Good or One all dualities are abolished and the soul of the sage fully merges with It, very much like that of ātman with Brahman of the Upaniṣadic guru.

In this seeing, we neither hold an object nor trace distinction; there is no two. The man is changed, no longer himself nor self-belonging; he is merged with the Supreme, sunken into it, one with it: centre coincides with centre, for centres of circles, even here below, are one when they unite, and two when they separate; and it is in this sense that we now (after the vision) speak of the Supreme as separate. This is why the *vision baffles telling*; we cannot detach the Supreme to state it;

if we have seen something thus detached we have failed of the Supreme which is
known only as one with ourselves.

(Enn., 6:9.547; my emphasis)

This text is very much in the Indian style. The soteriological vision "baffles
telling." Once filled with the Plotinian One, a person has even passed the "choir
of the virtues," that is, he is beyond good and evil. And what is most impressive
is that Reason, that great Platonic virtue, is nonexistent: "no movement now, no
passion, no outlooking desire, once this ascent is achieved . . . utterly resting he
has become the very rest" (*Enn.*, 6:9.548). This final rest in the One pertains to the
life of the gods or of those who are godlike among mortals; it is "liberation from
the alien that besets us here, *a life taking no pleasure in the things of earth*, the passing of solitary to solitary" (*Enn.*, 6:9.549; my emphasis). It seems to be a passion-
less, still, and desireless state.

It is not clear whether this union with the One can be achieved by human
beings in this very existence, and there is no indication that Plotinus himself
reached it. Once he is "sunken" in it there is no way that he can experience it
"many times." Hadot tries to solve this problem by saying that Plotinus realized genuine life up there in the One "in a fleeting flash" or in a "flash of an instant," but I doubt there is a warrant for this assumption in Plotinus's writing.[22]
Whether "sunken into it" refers to Plotinus's mystical identity with Nous or with
the One, there is no doubt in my mind of the power of the spirit that animates
that experience.

PLOTINUS AND THE BUDDHA: THE DISCOURSE ON
THE INEFFABLE

There are, indeed, things that cannot be put into words. They make themselves
manifest. They are what is mystical.

—Ludwig Wittgenstein, *Tractatus Logico-Philosophicus*

In the preceding pages I have dealt with Plotinus as a philosopher who believed
in a doctrine of rebirth (and practiced a vegetarian diet), thereby showing an
inner affinity with the preceding Pythagorean tradition and also bridging Greek
thought with the Indic traditions of Buddhism and the Upaniṣads.[23] I now want to
juxtapose Plotinus and the Buddha and the experience of the furthermost reach
of what some would call the mystical experience, though quite remote from the

passionate identity of the soul with Christ. It is a difficult path with an abstract salvific goal that could be grasped by only a few.

Let me defer my reaction to the term *mystic* or *mysticism* and begin with Plotinus's description of the ascent to Nous and beyond that to the reach of the One, which he hopes gives us a feel for the salvific condition. He describes the ascent to the One in the rational discourse of the *Enneads*. Yet the experience cannot be described. It is ineffable. While Plotinus admits that the experience is beyond "reason," and beyond language, he has no choice but to express himself in the very rational discourse that must be shed in order to enter the state of mystical union with either Nous or the Good. If the virtuoso is to persuade us, his disciples, he has no choice but to use language and discursive thought. He does not adopt what the Buddhist texts do and simply use exhortations or single terms or phrases such as *freedom* that are not even minimally discursive. He does have another choice, and that is not to worry about us but simply worry about his own salvation. There must surely have been many in the great historical traditions who have taken that path, ignoring a public proclamation of the mystical reach. One must remember that Plotinus, like the Buddha, was a thinker, formulating a worldview, a philosophy, and a way of salvation. The salvific condition of union is part of that larger project. Therefore, while one must respect Plotinus's idea of Nous as reason's prior, one must accept the fact that, given his Greek background, he has no choice but to express that condition through the language of discursive reasoning.

But can the mystical experience of identity with Nous or the One be expressed in another "language," the nondiscursive language of visions? Visions also cannot express the ineffable as "showings," though occasionally the mystical reach might be visually associated with a flood of light, a brightness that appears before the gaze of the person in trance, and on rare occasions as the sun itself. This is the furthest outreach that symbolic formation can take place in respect of the mystical or salvific experience of union with the One or the Absolute. It cannot tell us anything about the experience itself except to indicate its grandeur through a visual symbol. Further, the visual symbolism of brightness is not exclusively associated with the mystical experience of union; it also appears in other contexts as for example in Schreber's visionary experiences, in visions of Jesus, or during near-death experiences.[24] However, both visions and the mystical ineffable have one thing in common; they share, as it were, the absence of ego or I. Mystical states, to repeat Wittgenstein's phrase, "make themselves manifest." They cannot be put into words, no speech can describe them, and, as we have said, it is this position that Wittgenstein affirms in the famous conclusion of the *Tractatus*: "What we cannot speak about we must pass over in silence."

Let us now go back to the Buddha's salvific experience under the tree of awakening to see if it can throw further light on the condition that is given the label *nirvana* in Buddhism. Consider the first awakening, where at dawn the Buddha discovered the Four Noble Truths of Buddhism and also, by some accounts, the doctrine of conditioned genesis, both of which are intertwined in complex ways in Buddhist thought. The doctrine that ties both is that of the second noble truth of *taṇhā* (*tṛṣṇā*), desire, greed, or attachment that is the root cause of suffering, the first noble truth. Until one abolishes greed, there is no way to be saved. We noted that after the first awakening the Buddha continued to meditate and was attacked by Māra and his daughters. The daughters of Māra represent simultaneously the return of the women of the harem and the return of the repressed. But the Buddha has overcome these symptoms of desire. He remains indifferent to them, lost in trance. He is now the Fully Awakened One.

Richard Gombrich makes the fascinating and persuasive argument that the famous fire sermon of the Buddha is not only part of a long and continuing dialectic with Upaniṣadic and Vedic thought but also more specifically represents the idea of fire as the central symbol of desire or greed, *taṇhā*. In Vedic belief, fire is represented by the god Agni and the rituals for Agni, especially the domestic rituals, embody the idealization of the household life that Buddhism devalues in its salvific quest. The Buddha instead idealizes the homeless person (*anagārika*), developing earlier models of wandering mendicants.

The fire sermon describes the body on fire with *taṇhā*, and the goal of Buddhism is to extinguish this fire and with it the fires of hatred and delusion. Hence nirvana has one clear meaning, namely, the literal one of "extinction" or "blowing out," and that must necessarily be the blowing out of *taṇhā*. When that occurs there is a simultaneous calming of the body and mind.[25] Yet, blowing out the three fires tells us nothing about what it means to realize nirvana or to understand nirvana as salvation. Though mostly stated in negative terms, there is little discussion by the Buddha in the early texts *about* nirvana. Nevertheless, some of the words used to describe nirvana's realization are extremely instructive. These are *taṇhakkhaya*, "extinction of thirst"; *virāga*, "absence of desire"; and of course *nibbāna* (nirvana) "blowing out" or "extinction." Balanced against these negatives is the most common positive term, *vimutti*, "freedom."[26] What we have here is the idea that "freedom" is achieved when the conditions that propel human existence—the first and second noble truths of suffering (*dukkha*) and thirst (*taṇhā*)—are extinguished in the third noble truth, or *nirodha*, and, when that "happens," one realizes nirvana. But that requires entering the path or *magga* (*mārga*), which is the fourth noble truth. This last is only a path, not a guarantee of salvation. When nirvana happens, one realizes freedom from the entanglements of the otherwise endless worlds of becoming (*saṃsāra*). One cannot *explain* nirvana. One cannot speak about it, except analogically and indirectly; hence one must pass over it into the space of silence. In the aftermath of his awakening, we noted that the Buddha explains to his disciples in rational terms much of Buddhist epistemology, but not nirvana. One can explain karma as that which keeps existence or *saṃsāra* going in endless cycles, and can even explain the cessation of *saṃsāra* in nirvana, but not nirvana itself. If everything else is compounded or conditioned, it is not surprising that the Buddha spoke of nirvana in opposition to conditioned things, namely, that which is "unconditioned" (*asaṃkahata*). The implication is that nirvana cannot be a "condition," and it is conditioned states that can be described. Buddhist texts have terms to characterize nirvana, but no description of what nirvana *is*.[27]

One, of course, can explain why an explanation is not possible, and this we find in a fine dialogue, "The Shorter Discourse to Malunkyaputta." Malunkya was not satisfied by the Buddha's persistent refusal to ask certain kinds of metaphysical questions, one such being whether or not the Buddha continues to exist after death, which is really a question about nirvana. The Buddha insists that he will not budge from his refusal to deal with what he called "undeclared" issues. This, he said, is akin to a man wounded by a poisoned arrow saying "I will not let the surgeon pull out this arrow until I know whether the man who wounded me was a noble or a brahmin or a merchant or a worker." Or when he wants to know whether the man was tall or short or dark brown or golden skinned or whether he was born in such and such a place.[28] There is a kind of silence about metaphysical issues in early Buddhism, a silence that to me captures the calm—all passion spent—of the sage who has blown out or extinguished desire. What *is* nirvana is irrelevant to salvation, and one must experience it to grasp it. And, quite unlike Plotinus, nirvana happens to those who cultivate the meditative technology of Buddhism available in principle to anyone willing to undergo its difficult discipline.

The idea that to understand the mystical experience one must experience it oneself is only too common in mystical traditions. Experientially speaking, the mystical reach is "ineffable," although even to use that term would obliquely define it. Hence the Buddha's reluctance to speak about it except indirectly. For him even defining nirvana would be a "declaration." To speak about nirvana would open a Buddhist can of worms, because it might lead to a definition of nirvana and its essentialization or its conditionality. Because Buddhists believed that all structures of existence are unstable, they would be faced with the question whether or not nirvana is an essence or some permanent and unchanging state of bliss or, by contrast, whether nirvana is itself a conditioned phenomenon and subject to continual change like everything else. We have seen that the latter alternative has opened the way for the bold speculative thinking of Nāgārjuna and later Mahāyāna.

I assume that in Plotinus and the Buddha the mystical experience is prior to labeling and to philosophical formulation, both being inimical to an experience that entails emptying the mind of discursive thought. Yet the first step in communicating the experience is labeling: Brahman, nirvana, One. The Buddha employs the term *nirvana,* which comes from the prior Indic tradition; Plotinus employs the label *One* or the *Good* (and other terms), also coming from his Greek heritage. In both cases the thinking-I invests the term with fresh meanings. In the Buddhist case, the blowing out of desire; then silence. Obviously there is no need for language when one adopts the posture of silence or of not-speaking. Instead, the Buddha provides a technology for letting the experience *happen*; and it is this original idea of nirvana as happening that opens another can of worms in Buddhism leading the way to forms of instant awakening in Chan Buddhism or Zen and the realization of Buddhahood in one's present existence in Tibetan Buddhism, albeit through meditation's stony path.[29] In Theravāda Buddhism, those of the Buddha's disciples who made the nirvana experience happen gave it further labeling as "freedom," "bliss," "deathlessness," and so on. There were yet others known as Minor or Pacceka Buddhas to whom nirvana also happened, but they simply left it at that, implicitly recognizing the fact that "mystical" experience can remain "private."

Can the mystical experience be described in apophatic language, that of negative theology? It seems that one might express the mystical experience in apophatic language, but such a language is not about describing the experience but in fact showing its impossibility! Let me give one early Buddhist example that comes close from a poetic text, the *Udāna,* or the "inspired utterances of the Buddha":

> Where neither water nor yet earth
> Nor fire nor air gain a foothold,
> There gleam no stars, no sun sheds light.
> There shines no moon, yet there no darkness reigns.[30]

Beautiful lines, but we learn virtually nothing *about* nirvana from them. Apophatic language was fully developed in Christianity in the negative theology of the late-fifth-century thinker Pseudo-Dionysius (Dionysius the Areopagite) who believed that because God is unknowable he must be described in terms of what he is not (the *via negativa*). It goes without saying that if God is unknowable then any kind of mystical identity with God will also be unknowable or ineffable. In more general terms, Dionysius and his "negative theology" provide a platform to discuss the nature of experiences that defy discursive or rational formulation.

When mystical identity is associated with God as a gendered male figure, there is also no need for apophatic language. God as a being, not Being in the abstract, has human and transhuman qualities that can be described in gendered language. So is it with the Buddhas and Bodhisattvas of Mahāyāna traditions. They are also mostly identifiable beings, based on the human and often on the familial model. Hence to say that God or the Buddha is "not this—not this" is just nonsense and like saying my father is not this, not this. God has to be neutered before he could be described in apophatic terms, and this is true also of Plotinus, whose God is in effect the Good or the One, a neutered term, an "It". Once one has labeled the God or Being in the abstract, then problems of description arise. How does one come to *know* an entity such as Spencer's Unknowable? How does one describe the One or the Good or Absolute Reality or, for that matter, the God-head, with its peculiar notion of the Holy Spirit? Here also apophatic language might apply as part of a larger rhetorical strategy that also employs other techniques of persuasion. Let me examine some of these techniques by moving to the Upaniṣads in its relation to Buddhism.

The Upaniṣadic salvation quest we know contains the idea that *ātman*, the individual self or soul, is Brahman, the universal Self, if "Self" is defined as the abstract cosmic principle. Brahman is neuter (unlike its masculine form *Brahma*, "God"), and the salvific goal is to make one recognize the unity of *ātman* with Brahman and bring about that realization. Yet in the Indic scheme it is possible to move easily from neuter to masculine. So it is with James's scientist, who says that whenever he was depressed or had business or personal troubles he felt himself "in to this fundamental cosmical *It*." And then adds that his *It* is not Spencer's Unknowable but "just my own instinctive and individual God, on whom I relied for higher sympathy, but whom somehow I have lost."[31] Similarly, the Christian can move from God the father and God the son to the more abstract idea of the Godhead (and the other way around) without cognitive disarray.

In the case of the Upaniṣads, the guru tries to communicate to his disciple the salvific state of identity with Brahman. The technique through analogy dispenses with the Plotinian need to describe that state. Take this dialogue between the pupil Śvetaketu and his guru Uddālaka from the *Chāndogya Upaniṣad*:

"Put this salt into the water, and see me tomorrow morning," said Uddalaka.

Shwetaketu did as he was told.

Uddalaka said, "Bring me the salt you put into the water last night."

Shwetaketu looked, but could not find it. The salt had dissolved.

Uddalaka asked his son how the top of the water tasted. Shwetaketu said: "It is
    salt."

Uddalaka asked how the middle of the salt tasted.

Shwetaketu said: "It is salt."

Uddalaka asked how the bottom of the water tasted.

Shwetaketu said, "It is salt."

Uddalaka said: "Throw away the water; come to me."

Shwetaketu did as he was told and said: "The salt will always remain in the water."

Uddalaka said: "My son! Though you do not find that Being in the world, He is
    there.

That Being is the seed; all else but His expression. He is truth. He is Self. Shweta-
    ketu! You are That."[32]

The last phrase sums up beautifully the Upaniṣadic idea that the self ("You")
is Brahman ("That"). But if identity of the self with God/Self as neuter is the
goal of the salvific quest, then what is the nature of that identity and of the God
to which one yokes (*yoga*) oneself? It is here that apophatic language comes in,
neatly summarized in the phrase *neti, neti*: not this, not this. The early Upaniṣads
composed before the seventh century BCE might well be the earliest known example in the history of religions to use apophatic language to describe the indescribable nature of Being. However, it might well have been that the indescribable nature of Being was realized through a mystical identity with the Absolute
or through an undefined ineffable experience, such as that of Plotinus or James's
scientist and the many lucid dreamers that will appear later in this text, rather
than the other way around.

Now let me come back to the idea of mysticism to which I will now give technical specificity or definitional meaning, not to describe its ineffability or whatever else it might be, but to adopt an ostensive strategy, to point out the differences in the three forms of the mystical experience in the religious traditions I
investigate here. First, a person might identify or unite with a named female or
male deity, in which case one might label that union as *theistic mysticism*. Second,
one might identify with an abstract principle underlying the phenomenal world
of becoming such as Brahman, the Good, the Transcendent, the Supreme, Being,
and so on in what we might label *nontheistic* or *absolutist mysticism*. Often, but
not always, absolutist mysticism neuters a preexisting deity such as Brahma or
God and eliminates the theodicy. The identification and labeling of a principle
underlying the phenomenal world is not exclusively an invention of the mystics
themselves, because nonmystics also have speculated about it and continue to do

so in such notions as Being and other abstractions of the sort that attracted the attention of William James, Herbert Spencer, and other European philosophers. The "It" that James employs to characterize his friend's idea of a transcendent deity is also the god of many intellectuals and scientists. It is the god of the more abstract and intellectualized versions of intelligent design. As an intellectual tradition, absolutist thinking in the West can be atheistic, or it might come close to a theistic model, if, for example, the Absolute is identified with a version of the Christian God or Providence. Third, there is the *a-theistic mysticism,* exemplified clearly in only one religion, Theravāda Buddhism, where the question of union or identity does not arise. Hence my reluctance to use the term *mysticism* in its strictly technical sense of identity either with a Being or with an abstract principle. Instead, techniques are provided for achieving the various trance states or states of absorption that lead the meditator to extinguish desire, abolish discursive thinking, and deny the existence of a stable soul or self. My usage of the term a-theistic simply means "against theism" or "indifference to theism" rather than the modern-day "atheism" of nonbelievers. In theory all forms of Buddhism are a-theistic, but we have already shown that Mahāyāna occasionally takes on the form of a nontheistic (absolutist) mysticism and at other times a theistic one.

It should be noted that the earliest versions of the *Tractatus* do not contain references to mystical thought, but much of Wittgenstein's later work seems to hover around them, even when the term is not explicitly used. It is not likely that Wittgenstein literally meant that mysticism "cannot be put into words," but rather, even if one were to do so, it would remain a senseless act. Mystics, especially in Christianity, have tried to "express the inexpressible" (a logical impossibility), but it is awfully difficult to find a description of nirvana that is not simplistic and nondescriptive. Nirvana simply "cannot be put into words." Nirvana or any similar mystical condition is something that *happens* during the quest for salvation. To express it differently: one is *thrown* into nirvana at some indeterminate point during deep meditation (for a discussion of "thrownness," see book 5, note 55). Following prior Indic traditions, the person to whom nirvana "happens" continues to live in the world. In which case nirvana is a happening making itself manifest within oneself. What happens at death in the "final nirvana" is once again left undetermined and undefined.

The idea of nirvana as a happening compels me to consider a problem I have with Nāgārjuna's argument where he presents emptiness in its conceptual purity, refusing to invest that term with the fullness of visionary meaning. Emptiness is obviously not conditioned; yet it would be hard for Nāgārjuna to say that it is "unconditioned," a term Theravāda Buddha left undefined, just like the other labels attached to nirvana. Hence he opts for the middle position: conditioned genesis. But, insofar as conditioned genesis leads to a realization of emptiness, Nāgārjuna has to affirm the obvious, that emptiness is itself empty. "Obvious" because recognition of conditioned genesis is simply a recognition of emptiness. But if emptiness is empty, then it would be in the same category as Nāgārjuna's nirvana: thus one could say "nirvana is *saṃsāra* is emptiness." But would that not that bring us back to the idea of emptiness as conditioned as is nirvana in his thinking, thus leading us to a circular argument from which there is no escape? I would say therefore that there is no real salvific difference between nirvana and emptiness in his formulation, and, further, like nirvana, emptiness is also indefinable and ineffable. Whether we agree with Nāgārjuna or not, as far as salvific realization is concerned, emptiness is like nirvana in one respect at least: *emptiness is something that happens during the arduous salvation quest*. When the term is invested with the fullness of visionary meaning, it ceases to be Nāgārjuna's.

Once the processes of labeling begin, we are brought face to face with language and, with it, the possible use of apophatic terms to define that which normally eludes language. The Buddha himself refused to take this path, perhaps aware that when one begins to translate nirvana in discursive terms, one becomes a prisoner of language, a theme that I will now explore in relation to the neutering of God or the recognition of an abstract principle or an essence underlying the world of becoming and change.

Let me start with the proposition that when one speaks of an abstract essence underlying the phenomenal world and labels it Good or Being or Absolute or Spirit or whatever, then a whole host of problems arises. As the great Buddhist poet says: "If the Self is eternal and without thought processes, then it is evidently inactive, like space. Even in contact with other conditioning factors, what activity can there be of something which is unchanging?"[33] More immediately, and from a less exalted position: one cannot fall in love with the Good nor have an erotic relationship with It, quite unlike the situation in theistic mysticism or wherever the idea of a personal deity arises. I can love Brahma, the male God, erotically; I cannot love his neuter except in a highly idealized or sublimated sense. So is it with the Good or One or any such abstraction where love must necessarily be nonerotic. I think it a mistake to assume with Pierre Hadot that because the soul is often feminine in Plotinus it unites in the One in an erotic relationship reminiscent of the Song of Songs. There is very little in Plotinus reminiscent of erotic passion, but much to suggest a kind of "Platonic" or nonerotic love.[34]

It is Buddhism once again that recognizes the nonerotic nature of the salvation quest. During the period that heralded the second awakening, the Buddha has conquered desire. Indeed, the whole technology of meditation in Theravāda

Buddhism follows the Buddha's own model. It overcomes erotic desire and instead substitutes it with the four great Buddhist virtues of kindness, tenderness, compassion, and equanimity, something that the Absolutes are for the most part incapable of doing. None of the early Buddhist poems by monks and nuns who have realized nirvana deal with eroticism or for that matter any other form of passion. Passion, especially erotic desire, is perhaps the most potent form of *tanha*, that which has to be eradicated in the salvation quest. Early Buddhist poetry expresses the personal sense of peace and calm combined with compassion toward all living beings under the sun and the wish for them to be released from suffering. Compassion takes the place of passion. It is with the Tantric forms of Buddhism, such as the Vajrayāna of Tibet, that eroticism and compassion are conjoined.[35] In this sense Tantrism is a revolutionary movement within Buddhism.

The problem with current writing on apophasis relates to the scholarly belief that the mystic's view of the ineffability of the experience cannot be sustained because there is no way that one can escape language, and it is through language that the mystical experience is apprehended by the mystic and communicated to us. I have already argued that the apprehension of the mystical experience would occur prior to its writing down or speaking of it, and therefore one can make a case for what is known as its ineffability. Once the experience is spoken about, one is in the realm of language, but it is a mistake to say that because I use the label *ineffable* the mystical experience cannot be understood outside language. There are plenty of experiences in my repertoire, such as sexual climax, that I simply experience without bothering to discourse about it. If I do, I might use terms like *bliss, ecstasy,* and so forth, terms also used to describe the salvific happening. It would be foolish on our part to imagine that, because the descriptive terms used to describe orgasm are also used to describe nirvana, the two are the same!

Apophatic discourse or similar language games cannot be divorced from the philosophical tradition in which it is embedded. Thus Plotinus not only describes the Good, and the mystical experience of being sunken in It, but also encapsulates that description within the larger discourses inherited from his immediate predecessors and going back to Plato and the pre-Socratics and into Pythagorean thought. This inherited philosophical tradition is given to extreme "conceptualism," that is, the attempt to understand life and the world through abstract concepts.[36] One might argue therefore that insofar as apophatic language is part of that larger conceptual apparatus, it not only describes the mystical experience but also might *fail* to do so. Here I am sympathetic to Wittgenstein's idea of the ineffability of the mystical experience. That is, in attempting to describe the indescribable, the thinker might be a victim of obfuscating language and join the many thinkers who have failed to adequately communicate their thoughts through the abstractions of conceptualism. I can apply this criticism to much of contemporary postmodern and postcolonial writing when my students and colleagues feel obliged to use rhetorical models from contemporary thinkers but lack their capacity for clever if somewhat convoluted argumentation and seductive circumlocution. Either way, it is easy to get lost in obscurantist discourse.

I have shown in *Imagining Karma* that the Buddha himself made a critique of such discourse. He spoke ironically of "eel-wrigglers" and "hair-splitters," the latter familiar to us in academia who "go about, methinks, breaking to pieces by their wisdom the speculations of others."[37] Here is an example of thinking the Buddha lampoons that combines both apophatic language and "oppositional dialectics," namely, the rhetorical balancing of opposites. "There is not another-world. There both is, and is not, another-world. There neither is, nor is not, another-world. There are Chance Beings (so called because they spring into existence, either here or in another-world, without the intervention of parents, and seem therefore to come without a cause). There are no such beings. There both are and are not, such beings. There neither are or are not, such beings. There is fruit, result, of good and bad actions. There is not. There both is, and is not. There neither is, nor is not."[38] Nevertheless, similar oppositional dialectics are used by the Buddha himself, and Buddhists in general, when dealing with ideas that cannot be expressed in ordinary discursive language or when they deliberately reject the excluded middle of Western logic.[39] But note that this Buddhist critique does not pertain to the mystic experience per se but is directed to those who try to *explain* the essence of things. This language is then carried to extremes in Christian apophatic discourse, not so much in Pseudo-Dionysius as in his emulators, as, for example, from Scottus Eriugena (c. 810–877), a profound thinker who can occasionally descend to not-so-profound language, which strikes me as a futile straining of words to describe the indescribable:

> For everything that is understood or sensed is nothing other than the apparition of the non-apparent, the manifestation of the hidden, the affirmation of the negated, the comprehension of the incomprehensible, the utterance of the unutterable, the access to the inaccessible, the intellection of the unintelligible, the body of the bodiless, the essence of the beyond-essence, the form of the formless, the measure of the immeasurable, the number of the unnumbered, the weight of the weightless, the materialization of the spiritual, the visibility of the invisible, the place of the placeless, the time of the timeless, the definition of the infinite, the circumscription of the uncircumscribed, and the other things which

are both conceived and perceived by the intellect alone and cannot be retained within the recesses of memory and which escape the blade of the mind.[40]

Though parodied by the Buddha because of the extremes to which it is carried, these kinds of dialectics are intrinsic to conceptualism and exemplify a thoroughgoing operation of Reason in Western, Buddhist, Judaic, and Islamic philosophical thought. Thus one might make the case that apophatic language is part of oppositional dialectics and does not necessarily deal with the mystical experience per se. It might have originated in the mystical experience, but it is no description of it. It is an attempt to grasp the essence of things, the philosopher's neutered God. A concept or abstract term is hopelessly inadequate to describe the cosmic It because such a concept simply becomes an abstraction of an abstraction.

I suggest that while the ineffable might not be described, it also represents the most extreme example of experiences that elude description. Thus Elaine Scarry thinks that the experience of extreme pain cannot be expressed in language, though of course we know that even those who suffer tortures might use language to tell a story about that experience.[41] Most, however, find it hard; and so is it with other heightened experiences such as the already-mentioned orgasm. But I would go further than this: I might suffer a bellyache and express this through a nonverbal sign, such as a cry of pain. Or my doctor might tell me that the bellyache is caused by such and such a bacillus or virus. Or I might try to express the inexpressible nature of my pain though words. That is, I might employ a label to designate it or I will use the research of neuroscientists and note with some degree of precision the mechanisms generating pain or I will describe it in adjectives or sentences, but this will not even remotely approximate my experience. *There is always a breach or gap between saying and experiencing,* and the more complex or intense the experience the more difficult to find words to say it. So it is with orgasm or torture. Yet, though difficult to express in ordinary or extraordinary language, the experience does not simply happen or make itself manifest. Someone has to actively bring about the act of torture or orgiastic ecstasy.

Nevertheless, a counterargument could be made that one actively brings about the happening of mystical experience through a technology, as for example, Buddhist meditation. However, in torture the activity can be easily predicted: the inquisitor knows he can inflict pain, and the sufferer experiences it quite tangibly. I know that I can achieve orgasm through intercourse, but I don't know whether any kind of awakening can be realized by the mere fact of practicing meditation. Buddhist meditation of whatever variety can only point out the path for the happening to occur; it cannot predict the happening or make the happening happen. Meditation may make one feel good, as it does for many bourgeois meditators in the West and in modern Buddhist societies. It may even give us insights on the nature of the world, "things as they really are." But the practice of its technology rarely results in the happening of nirvana. This idea is put much better by my favorite psychotic than it has been by those who have written about language and ineffability:

> To make myself at least comprehensible I shall have to speak much in images and similes, which may at times be only approximately correct, for the only way a human being can make supernatural matters, which in their essence must always remain incomprehensible, understandable to a certain degree is by comparing them with known facts of human experience. Where intellectual understanding ends, the domain of belief begins; man must reconcile himself to the fact that things exist which are true although he cannot understand them.

(M, 18)

We can expand Schreber's argument to include nonsupernatural experiences like torture and sexual ecstasy and reaffirm that they can be told indirectly through analogies, metaphors, stories, and so forth. And, if many instances of the body in pain cannot be expressed in language, they can be represented in dreams, nightmares, and even visions that can be seen as another form of the dark-night-of-the-soul experience, but without bringing eventual relief to the sufferer. It is now time to make the point that visions are *not* a kind of language, nor are they structured like a language, as Lacan would say of the unconscious. Visions have one thing in common with language, and that is a capacity for complex symbolization, but they do not contain a grammar or syntax as language does.[42] Rather, they are a substitute for language trying to state difficult and sometimes inexpressible thoughts in an intelligible or immediately comprehensible visual medium.

Let me conclude this discussion by going back to the philosophical conception of an abstract divinity or principle or mind or being or whatever that animates the universe and, at least in the case of Plotinus and the Upaniṣads, an "It" that is possible to identify with. Although I pointed out that the abstract deity is the god of the intellectuals, there are important differences between nineteenth-century European philosophical conceptions and their older counterparts both in the West and in the Indic tradition. Consider the Upaniṣads where the Absolute or Brahman is a neuter, a principle of the universe with whom one can identify in mystical communion. I mentioned that it is impossible to relate to the Absolute erotically: I will add that it is hardly possible to *worship* Brahman or pray to It without converting Brahman into the personal male god Brahma. That personal god Brahma existed before the abstract deity Brahman, and there were other personal gods in the Vedic pantheon long before the idea of Brahman was discovered. Brahma or any one of his counterparts constituted the lords of creation whom one could propitiate and worship. This phenomenon has its parallel elsewhere. The very powerful and personal creator god of the Old Testament can coexist with his parallel abstract form as the Godhead or as a divinity of the apophatic thinkers, even though the Godhead is not as neutered a conception as Brahman. The feature of both these traditions is that the mystic has an option: one can identify with the It, the abstract principle of the universe, or one can identify with a living God in theistic mystical communion. Moreover, the person who believes in the Absolute, whether he or she identifies with it or not, can simultaneously believe in a personal god or goddess and indeed propitiate that living being. In Plotinian mysticism, there is no option: the Good *is* the Supreme and that alone. Yet the Plotinian spirit can soar into It, impossible to envisage in the deism of the Enlightenment or in later forms of the Absolute. It seems that Enlightenment thinkers, owing to their exclusive commitment to Reason, have forfeited the profound mysticism of Plotinus and others like him. So it is with Hegel's Absolute. While most philosophers agree that Hegel's Absolute or Spirit is *not* the Christian deity, there are the religiously musical who affirm that identity. The resultant dilemma is nicely expressed by the Jesuit scholar Quentin Lauer who says, "There has been and continues to be dispute as to whether the God of whom he [Hegel] speaks can legitimately be identified with the God of Christianity." But Lauer then adds, "If we take Hegel at his word, he quite clearly says that since there is only one God, then the God of philosophy and the God of (Christian) religion are one and the same—if not, then the God of philosophy would be but an abstract God, that is, no God at all."[43] Exactly. The problem with the abstract God of the Western metaphysicians and scientists is that they have a hard time relating the abstract It with a personal God to whom one could relate emotionally, nor can they invest the Absolute with deep emotional salience, and they have problems identifying with that abstract being in mystical communion.

We can only guess the intellectual processes that paved the way from Brahma to Brahman, from God to abstract divinity, except to say that these ideas could not have been invented and argued without a powerful intellectual or rationalizing imperative behind it. While recognizing the importance of metaphysical speculations that fueled this development, I will mention one possible strand that we can extricate from what would have been complex and varied debates on the nature of reality or the Absolute. That strand is the theodicy that is invariably built into the nature of an all-powerful God, the accountability of that god in respect of the world's ills, and the patently antiprovidential ways of Providence. Job's answer won't satisfy intellectual curiosity and a sense of justice, nor will it still existential perplexity. Hence the early Buddhist critique of the personal deity: why does the powerful creator god Brahma not put his creatures right? It must be Brahma who is unjust and under whose aegis the world's wrongs take place.[44] The Buddhist karma theory eliminates the theodicy, but the elimination of the theodicy is not the motivation for the invention of the karma theory. Nevertheless, the debates on theodicy would be central to the perpetuation, continuity, and justification of the karma theory. So with the Upaniṣadic Brahman or the absolutes that developed in the West: the problem of the theodicy simply does not apply to them.

Now let me get back to William James's scientific friend who had lost faith in a personal god but could accept the idea of an absolute reality underlying the phenomenal world. Here is a movement from a personal deity to an impersonal one, repeating in the life career of the scientist the historical trajectory I noted earlier. The path of return to God is also clear and available, and James' informant or alter ego can get back to his personal god, if he so wishes. Yet, unlike the mysticism of a Plotinus, the abstract deity of Spencer and similar versions have one feature about it, namely, its lack of emotional power. To complicate matters even further, the nineteenth-century discourse on the Absolute, while participating in the past history of that conception, occurs more than ever before in a *weltanschauung* of science. It is true that the arahant needs no god, but the Buddha himself believed such beings existed even though they, like humans, were karma bound. With the development of the intellectualist or absolutist view of god, there is no such need or recognition: the Absolute can be indifferent, and often is indifferent, to the existence of the personal creator god of Western monotheism or any form of a personal deity. Additionally, with the development of skepticism and the form of the Absolute that emerged and realized its peak in the nineteenth century, there was a concomitant decline in the belief in an immortal soul. Instead there developed an inflated cogito or a rarefied ego, a kind of homunculus within our bodies or minds usurping the place of the soul or coexisting with a soulless version of soul. Or better still: with the soul losing its hold over Europeans, Self comes into the fullness of being. Self then can become a replacement for soul, and this in turn further expands the space of secular spirituality. And with it emerge questions that affected the existential quest of the next century: is there a true self? What is selfhood? How does one realize the higher self or its highest reach? And a whole host of questions on self-realization and authenticity. Jung is the high priest of the new cult of the self.

It is rarely that intellectuals in the nineteenth century and after apprehended the Absolute in the mystical way of Plotinus, but some came close to it, the prime example being Einstein in his version of God. Max Jammer rightly says that Spinoza was a close European precursor of Einstein. "Though he employed the notion of 'God,' Spinoza applied it only to the structure of the impersonal cosmic order and declared that 'neither intellect nor will appertain to God's nature.' He therefore denied the Judeo-Christian conception of a personal God" or, one might add, any kind of a living God anywhere.[45] Jammer adds that Einstein, like Spinoza, did not believe in a personal god, but was not hostile to the idea of "a superior intelligence that reveals itself in the harmony and beauty of nature."[46] More to the point, Jonathan Israel says: "The claim that Nature is self-moving, and creates itself, became indeed the very trademark of the *Spinosistes*," and this "evolutionary thesis seemingly reinforce[s] Einstein's proposition that the modern scientist who rejects divine Providence and a God that governs the destinies of man, while accepting 'the orderly harmony of what exists,' the intelligibility of an immanent universe based on principles of mathematical rationality, in effect believes in Spinoza's God."[47] However, I doubt whether Spinoza's abstract deity, whose epistemological reality he took for granted, is reconcilable with Einstein's profounder conception (note 48 discusses Spinoza's god in detail).[48]

In what sense is Einstein's more profound? Einstein was concerned with "the knowledge of the existence of something we cannot penetrate, our perceptions of the profoundest reason and the most radiant beauty, which only in their most primitive forms are accessible to our minds—it is this knowledge and this emotion that constitute true religiosity; in this sense, and in this alone, I am a deeply religious man."[49] It is a deep intuitive awareness or apprehension of the harmony of the universe with its "profoundest reason and most radiant beauty," an emotional understanding based on his knowledge of laws of physics without being a *logical* inference from those laws. Yet, Einstein's awareness of the Absolute could not have existed without his sophisticated understanding of physics. Moreover, contra Max Jammer, I doubt one can force Einstein's beliefs into any form of the God of the Old Testament, although it is likely that Einstein had read much of Jewish mystical literature, which influenced his own conception of the Absolute. Yet Einstein had also read Spinoza, and it is Spinoza who completely rejected prophecy, revelation, and miracle in both the Old Testament and the New and indeed all other kinds of popular religion in his *Tractatus Theologico-Politicus* (1670). I have already stated that such an experience of harmony in nature was something that was anticipated very early in Greek thought in the Pythagorean music or harmony of the spheres and achieved its full mystical realization in Plotinus.

Yet Einstein is unlikely to have experienced an *identity* with the Supreme as Plotinus did, and for this reason I wouldn't label his experience "mysticism" in the ways I have defined it.

I would now give a thumbnail summary of the absolutes we have just discussed. When the idea of the Absolute is based on a complex intellectual argument, I will call it a *strong* version. Whether we agree with a particular version or not, many Enlightenment philosophical conceptions, be it Descartes or Spinoza or Hegel or their many Greek precursors, posited strong versions of the Absolute, whereas the versions that developed during and after the nineteenth century were *weak* versions, and these include James's informant or Spencer's Unknowable. When Spinoza says God exists only philosophically, one could add that he exists in the strong and in the weak. Getting back to Buddhism, I would say that Nāgārjuna's emptiness is of the strong variety, owing to the sophisticated intellectual reasoning behind it. So is the Buddha's nirvana. It is true that Buddha, and early Buddhists, did not describe nirvana, opting for silence, but the path to its realization is strongly presented. Further: Plotinus, Nāgārjuna, and the Buddha posited a doctrine of salvation and a theistic or a-theistic mysticism that carried with it a sense of emotional or salvific fulfillment, even though ill defined owing to the ineffability of the experience. Theirs was a *thick* experience of the salvific absolute. In terms of my own language game, I say that one can *comprehend* the Absolute in the strong or the weak, but its *apprehension* can be in the *thick* or the *thin* and in varying degrees in between.

To be fair to James and his informants, they also attempt to give expression to a thick sense of discovering something profound, a feel that the Absolute has cosmic meaning but weakly *comprehended*. Nevertheless, the emotional feel or apprehension for the Absolute can indeed occur in rare instances, even in the midst of such a boring conception as the deism of the Enlightenment, witness its poetic evocation in Pope's epistle to Bathurst, written soon after the not-so-inspired "Essay on Man":

> Ask we what makes one keep, and one bestow?
> That power who bids the ocean ebb and flow,
> Bids seed-time, harvest, equal course maintain,
> Through reconciled extremes of drought and rain,
> Builds life on death, on change duration founds,
> And gives the eternal wheels to know their rounds.[50]

So is it with the modern-day new age thinkers and lucid dreamers we will discuss later in this work. Einstein's is a rare instance in which strong comprehension of the Absolute can coexist with a thick apprehension of a harmony in the universe *without* being geared to any explicit salvific goal. It is a very modernist feel for the Absolute, and many more will emerge in the context of the death of God or of his slow asphyxiation in the intellectual traditions of the West. Nietzsche's secular spirituality and the conceptions of the absolute, which followed in the wake of Spinoza's thought, can be expressly atheistic, showing that atheism can have spiritual meaning, be it in the thick or the thin.

Let me end this discussion with a *strong* version of secular spirituality in Heidegger's notion of Being, which, for me but not for Heideggerians, is an attempt to forge (in the double sense of that term) a kind of secular spirituality for our own times. I have some sympathy for Heidegger's notion of man as a being toward death, but not the huge intellectual scaffolding within which Being exists. Heidegger's *Being* becomes another secular replacement for God and the soul, a spiritual presence, even an essence, sometimes implicit and sometimes explicit in the tradition of Greek (and more generally Western) metaphysics. It puts the resurgent self to shame. Nevertheless, the *sense* of Being, or its feel or apprehension, that Heidegger rescues for modern-day intellectuals comes perilously close to Christian mysticism but empty of God, and that of necessity must be an empty or thin kind of mysticism. It is one that remains obscure by its very nature and yet becomes a rarefied remedy for the spiritual emptiness of our times, such that intellectuals can *talk* about the nature of Being without having to *practice* mystical identity with Being in the now anachronistic Plotinian manner or in the thick Einsteinian manner. It is no accident that the thinking of Heidegger, in spite of his Nazi past, has gone into forms of existential psychotherapy and dream theory in competition with Freudian and Jungian ones, and these forms can also exist in the weak and strong versions and in the thick and the thin in the experiences of modern-day practitioners.[51]

The preceding discussion of the Absolute poses interesting differences and similarities between European and Indian notions. I described the Buddhist nirvana as a-theistic, but the related term *atheistic,* insofar as it denies the existence of a creator god, makes no sense, for the obvious reason that there is no such being in Buddhism. Yet the Buddha, and all believing Buddhists until recent times, recognized the existence of various gods and goddesses and malignant spirits, something the skeptical tradition in Europe following Spinoza helped dismantle. During the time of the Buddha, there were materialists and those who did not believe in any afterlife destiny, and they undoubtedly existed afterward, but their voices had little impact on the public consciousness, then and now, quite unlike the European situation. Nowadays, there are many skeptical Buddhists, not so much following a European philosophical tradition but rather influenced by contemporary science, which was, of course, also the case in Europe. The impact of these ideas is not so much to deny rebirth but to deny rebirth as a nonhuman being, especially as an animal, thereby dismantling the early Buddhist notion of "species unity," that is, the idea that humans as well as animals form part of a karmically regulated order. Some contemporary Buddhist intellectuals would publicly deny the existence of supernatural beings, which is not difficult to justify in Buddhism because these beings, whether they exist or not, have little to do with Buddhist soteriology or ethics. One can be a skeptic in the Buddhist tradition, for all that is required to be considered a Buddhist, at least in relation to one's public posture, is the simple taking of the Five Precepts prefaced by the formula, "I take refuge in the Buddha, the Dhamma, and the Sangha." Since the Five Precepts are a code of ethical conduct for layfolk, it is easy to be a Buddhist skeptic or a secularist, something much more difficult to do in Hinduism, which in general contains some notion of a deity associated with one's salvation. Nowadays there probably exist a few who do not believe in karma and rebirth but would consider the Buddha a great philosopher or teacher. That, in my view, would be a real break in the Buddhist tradition, a kind of radical skepticism, because the doctrine of karma and rebirth is intrinsic to Buddhism. So it is in the European skeptical tradition after Spinoza where the Absolute could coexist with a weak or strong version of providence, as Charles Taylor nicely points out.[52] We have seen that, in the nineteenth century, even this linkage was for the most part disrupted in a manner difficult to envisage in Buddhism as far as its theory of karma is concerned. Yet the epistemological need to posit some cosmic principle to take the place of the death of God cannot be stilled. A new reign of the Absolute had begun in European thought.

SECULAR SPIRITUALITY IN THE METAPHYSICS OF PHYSICISTS

> God in the beginning formed matter in solid, massy, hard, impenetrable moving particles, of such sizes and figures, and with such properties, and in such proportion to space, as most conduced to the end for which he formed them.
> —Newton, *Opticks*

The play with the Absolute can be seen in the very heart of the scientific establishment in the "secular spirituality" developed by a few physicists of our own times, strongly influenced by both quantum mechanics and what they perceive to be Eastern spirituality. Because I have neither training nor extensive knowledge of physics, I will limit myself to the work of David Bohm (1917–1992), who formulated much of his argument in abstract mathematical terms, but, for our benefit, also wrote clear and reasonably intelligible prose. Bohm's theory or metaphysics of mind is extremely speculative, and he attempts to do what Einstein in his appealing modesty refused to engage in, namely, give epistemological meaning to the idea of another order of reality that underlies the physical structure of the phenomenal world we live in, daring to make sense of the very constitution of the noumenon as it were. His is an attempt to found a new metaphysics, grounding the intellectualist view of the Absolute on relativity theory and quantum mechanics, but moving away from both. Let me present Bohm's thesis as simply as I can, without, hopefully, distorting his message.

Bohm initially points out that traditional Newtonian physics postulated an orderly world of matter wherein elementary particles constituted the building blocks of the universe. But unfortunately Newtonian particles were units in themselves, and scientists till recent times ignored their interrelationships, which led, Bohm thought, to a fragmented vision of the universe. As Vic Mansfield, a physicist cum Jungian, clarifies for us: "Newton envisioned the universe as being built from elementary or inherently existent point particles, entities existing in their own right that secondarily come together to build more complex structures from galaxies to people." These particles are localized in "well defined regions of space and time," an idea questioned by relativity theory and more radically by quantum mechanics.[53]

The Newtonian conception of physics was initially upset by Einstein's relativity theory, which "introduces new notions concerning the order and measure of time. These are no longer absolute, as was the case in Newtonian theory. Rather, they are now relative to the speed of a coordinate frame. This relativity of time is one of the radically new features of Einstein's theory."[54] Yet Bohm argues that, while relativity theory no longer postulates unchanging particles constituting matter, it leaves the whole question of ultimate irrefutable knowledge of the constituent elements of matter as a future possibility when our knowledge increases through experimental work based on the traditional logic of causality.[55] By contrast, in the new quantum physics there is no agreement or consistent notion of what kind of reality "underlies the universal constitution and structure of matter. Thus, if we try to use the prevailing worldview based on the notion of particles, we discover that the 'particles' (such as electrons) can also manifest as waves, that they can move discontinuously, that there are no laws at all that apply in detail to the actual movements of individual particles and that only statistical predictions can be made about large aggregates of such particles" (WIO, xv).

The existence of the object depends on its relations to other objects rather than the idea of isolated and localized objects. Einstein's opposition to this quantum view is that it is an incomplete one and that further research would confirm a more integrated view of nature. Hence his famed aphorism "One does not play dice with God."

It seems that with quantum theory there emerges a "new order in physics" where "events that are separated in space and time and that are without possibility of connection through interaction are correlated, in a way that can be shown to be incapable of a detailed causal explanation" (WIO, 164).[56] Thus quantum mechanics began a radical questioning of the prequantum order, including Einstein's view of the lawfulness of physics. Heisenberg's indeterminacy or uncertainty principle helps one to understand this aspect of quantum mechanics, namely, his famous microscope experiment that shows the interrelationship between the observer, the instruments and the indeterminate result of the experiment (WIO, 164). "Heisenberg's novel step was to consider the implications of the 'quantum' character of the electron that provides the 'link' between the *experimental results* and *what is to be inferred from these results*" (WIO, 165). Quantum theory therefore does not separate the "observed object" and the "observing instrument," or, to put it in more popular terms, the indeterminacy principle questions the notion of strict scientific objectivity and the subject-object separation.

Employing Heisenberg's indeterminacy principle, Bohm makes the inference that the experimental situation consists of a whole wherein autonomous and separable existent elements or particles do not enter into the picture (WIO, 169). "Relativity theory calls for this sort of way of looking at the atomic particles, which constitute all matter, including of course human beings, with their brains, nervous systems, and the observing instruments that they have built and that they use in their laboratories. So, approaching the question in different ways, relativity and quantum theory agree, in that they both implies the need to look on the world as an undivided whole, in which all parts of the universe, including the observer and his instruments, merge and unite in one totality. In this totality, the atomistic form of insight is a simplification and an abstraction valid only in some limited context" (WIO, 13–14). But with a difference: if relativity frames its experimental knowledge in terms of causal laws, quantum theory is characterized by "irreducible lawlessness" as it frames its conclusions in terms of statistical probability statements (WIO, 89). Further, in more radical fashion, Niels Bohr criticizes the Heisenberg principle with his insistence that nothing in the quantum domain is measurable; indeed there is nothing to measure there. Hence there can be no "disturbance" owing to the Heisenberg principle, which implies there is something out there to measure in the first place (WIO, 96). This is not to deny that the whole experimental situation is not relevant for our understanding of quantum mechanics simply because the latter postulates the interconnectedness of things.

Bohm says that his insight into physical reality can be called undivided wholeness in flowing movement. Flow implies a level of physical reality that is epistemologically prior to our dividing the world. Mind and matter are not separate entities in the Cartesian sense but rather different aspects of a whole unbroken movement. Because both are enfolded in a single unbroken flow, the distinction between mind and matter disappears. Bohm illustrates what he means by "whole" when he uses the metaphor of a pattern in a carpet. It is meaningless to say that parts of the pattern are separable from the whole; the pattern is the whole. "Similarly, in the quantum context, one can regard terms like 'observed object,' 'observing instruments,' 'link electron,' 'experimental results,' etc., as aspects of a single overall 'pattern' that are in effect abstracted or 'pointed out' by our mode of description. Thus, to speak of the interaction of 'observing instrument' and 'observed object' has no meaning" because they all constitute a pattern, a flow (WIO, 169). This flow is what he means by "whole" or an "undivided wholeness." Yet it seems that the distinction between the wholeness of relativity theory and Bohm's imputation of wholeness to quantum physics seems to be a definitional problem, or one of language use, because both Einstein's physics and quantum mechanics can be used to justify the idea of the whole. It is because the world of reality expresses a kind of unity, or the dream of a future discovery of a unified theory, that Einstein can speak of God as an expression of cosmic harmony. If that is not whole, I am not sure what is. It is however a whole without flow. Moreover, Bohm's critics might argue that flow or flux can hardly be considered "whole," a point that we will take up later.

"My main concern has been with understanding the nature of reality in general and of consciousness in particular as a coherent whole, which is never static or complete, but which is in an unending process of movement and unfoldment" (WIO, x). Bohm's argument extends into the domain of consciousness, where most physicists dare not venture. He says that we apprehend the experienced world as static or a series of static images when in reality it is a flow. Hence the inference from quantum physics applies to thought also. "In the actual experience of movement, one senses an unbroken, undivided process of flow, to which the series of static images in thought is related as a series of 'still' photographs might be related to the actuality of a speeding car. . . . That is to say, one can feel a sense of flow in the 'stream of consciousness' not dissimilar to the sense of flow in the movement of matter in general. May not thought itself thus be a part of reality as a whole?" (WIO, x–xi).

In his critique of the Cartesian cogito, Bohm points out that the idea of a separate self or ego that thinks independently of the larger reality is rooted in Western culture. By contrast, everything in the universe constitutes a "single, unbroken flowing actuality of existence as a whole, containing both thought (consciousness) and external reality as we experience it" and in that sense the ego or self, if such an entity exists, must be part of a flow, but definitely not something fragmented (WIO, xi).[57] The ego or I simply cannot exist as an immediate certainty or a separately knowable entity independent of the larger processes of thought. Bohm is strongly opposed to any notion of fragmentation of physical reality or consciousness, both being part of a totality of becoming or flow. But more than this. The sense of flow and the holistic unity underlying flow extend to everything: emotions, physical actions, social organizations, etc. Consequently, he feels that a new language, which he calls the "rheomode," or the flowing mode, will break the rigidity of conventional language and give expression to the unbroken and holistic flow of movement of existence (WIO, xiv).[58] In everyday life we fail to understand or apprehend this flow.

While recognizing the importance of relativity and quantum theory in its radical movement away from Newtonian physics, Bohm remains highly critical of both, although of quantum mechanics to a lesser degree. He does admit that both theories postulate order to the universe rather than the analysis of independent particles. Unfortunately, both are committed to a static and fragmentary mode of existence, "relativity to that of separate events, connectable by signals, and quantum mechanics to a well-defined quantum state." Hence a new theory is required that drops these ideas but "recovers some essential features of the older theories as abstract forms derived from a deeper reality in which what prevails is unbroken wholeness" (WIO, xviii).

The idea of a new order appropriate to a universe of unbroken wholeness is fully developed in Bohm's notion of the implicate or enfolded order. Ordinary notions of space, time, and dependent or independent particles or elements belong to the explicate or unfolded order, which has no independent reality because it is contained within the implicate order. Given Bohm's preoccupation with wholeness, he is especially critical of the "fragmentation" of the world, which he thinks is not only the product of the analytical strategy of those physicists concerned with the explicate order but also our ordinary thought processes and our disciplinary orientations where we cut up the world of knowledge into different specialties. Here he reiterates the idea that "wholeness is what is real, and that fragmentation is the response of this whole to man's action, guided by illusory perception, which is shaped by fragmentary thought" (WIO, 9). Bohm's existential quest is also clear: one must be aware of fragmentary thought in order to bring it to an end, and in one of his works he has almost a messianic wish to change disruptive thought such as the nationalisms of our times and the general depressing state of our contemporary world.[59] Then only will one's approach to reality be whole, as would one's responses.

In our academic disciplines, we foolishly look at a segment of reality, but without a vision of the whole of that reality. Consequently, we harbor the illusion that we can directly apprehend reality, when all we do is treat the explicate order as real. Yet, in spite of his criticism of contemporary physics, he realizes that, in order to understand the wholeness of things, physics is basic because theories here "are regarded as dealing with the universal nature of the matter out of which all is constituted, and the space and time in terms of which all material movement is described" (WIO, 10). Unfortunately, Bohm everywhere insists that relativity cannot get rid of the idea that the universe is made of basic objects or building blocks, rather than the implicate order that deals with "the universal flux of events and processes" (WIO, 12).

Here is a problem: for Bohm physics postulates a fragmented order, but there is another order, an implicit order, whose hidden variables is his task to elucidate. The empirical world that we experience and physicists also describe and analyze enfolds a deeper implicate order. He thinks that most physicists, whether quantum or relativity theorists (and biologists) still believe that life and mind can be ultimately understood in more or less mechanical terms. Hence, in the appendix to chapter 1, Bohm urges us to look at Eastern insights into wholeness: "Why, then, do we not drop our fragmentary Western approach and adopt these Eastern notions which include not only a self world view that denies division and fragmentation but also techniques of meditation that lead the whole process of mental operation non-verbally to the sort of quiet orderly and smooth flow needed to end fragmentation both in the actual process of thought and its content?" (WIO, 25) In Bohm's own thought, and in his version of Eastern religion, time simply does not exist. Hence the book dealing with his dialogue with Jiddu Krishnamurti is entitled *The Ending of Time*.[60]

In this context, Bohm makes the interesting point that in the West measure is the very essence of reality or at least the key to that essence. But not in his so-called East, or Orient, where the immeasurable, which cannot be named, described, or understood, is the primary reality. Measure is an illusion or *māyā* (WIO, 29). Gregory Bateson, another thinker searching for a new order of reality, makes a similar point, but from different theoretical stance: "Like other people, I normally experience much that does not happen. When I aim my eyes at what I think is a tree, I receive an image of something green. But that image is not 'out there.' To believe that is itself a form of superstition, for the image is a creation of my own, shaped and colored by many circumstances, including my preconceptions."[61] Bateson's world of everyday living is also one constituted of *māyā*. Measure or quantification per se has no place in it. (See book 3, note 75 for a summary of Bateson's thought.)

Bohm says there is no sense in going to a time prior to the splitting of Western and Eastern thought, implying that originally they constituted a single mode of thought. There is no doubt of Bohm's favorable impression of "Eastern thought," especially meditation, as it led him to his famed friendship with the philosopher-guru Krishnamurti. "In a way, techniques of meditation can be looked on as measures (actions ordered by knowledge and reason) which are taken by man to try to reach the immeasurable, i.e., a state of mind in which he ceases to sense a separation between himself and the whole of reality." Note that we are back to the familiar language of the Absolute in his notion of the "immeasurable." Unlike many others, Bohm recognizes the difficulties involved in the use of awesomely vague language. "But clearly there is a contradiction in such a notion, for the immeasurable is, if anything, just that which cannot be brought within limits determined by man's knowledge and reason" (WIO, 31). But then, how can he, Bohm, understand the wholeness, the unmeasurableness of reality, through his reasoning, which is what his book is about, a reasoned attempt to understand the implicate reality of the world? Bohm's is a familiar dilemma: can one understand the noumenon in terms of the phenomenon? How does one understand that which is outside reason, "reason's prior," through the language and logic of reason? Bohm recognizes that one cannot. But then one might question the enterprise that infers wholeness and the implicate order through Bohm's knowledge of contemporary physics. One could, of course, say that his is an intuitive understanding of the nature of reality, but can that have epistemological validity in the times in which we live unless it conforms to the operations of reason?

What then is his view of flow that he intuitively grasps? Naturally, he sees in Heraclitus a charter for his own beliefs; and in more recent times in Whitehead who gave the idea of flow "systematic and extensive development" (WIO, 61). Yet, given Bohm's interest in "Oriental thought," it is strange that Buddhism, which depicts all reality as a flow or as becoming, is never mentioned, except perhaps implied as "Eastern religion." Nor does he mention the central theory of dependent origination, at least as formulated by the Buddhist philosopher Nāgārjuna, especially as Bohm makes the statement that follows the previous one: "I regard the essence of the notion of process as given by the statement: Not only is everything changing, but all is flux. That is to say, *what is* is the process becoming itself, while all objects, events, entities, conditions, structures, etc., are forms that can be abstracted from this process" (WIO, 61). Heraclitus's river is his best trope: the river keeps flowing, and the ripples, vortices, splashes, etc., are abstractions from the flow and have no reality outside it. They are *māyā*. Bohm admits that in modern physics the river is not all flow because it is constituted of elementary particles, atoms. But then these atoms are not ultimate substances either, and they can be "created, annihilated and transformed, and this indicates that not even these can be ultimate substances but rather, that they too are relatively constant forms, abstracted from some deeper level of movement" (WIO, 62). He recognizes physicists might claim that these particles can be further broken down into other particles and these elementary particles may be the ones that possess ultimate reality (like the Buddhist *dharmas*). Bohm reasonably argues that the notion of flux he proposes denies such a reality. But here's the rub: the idea of flux as ultimate reality is still a supposition and not a demonstrable truth. Hence by the same logic it is indeed possible that subatomic particles might eventually constitute a demonstrable "truth" of an ultimate reality. Bohm's response to such an eventuality is simply to assert the idea of flux as the true but undemonstrable reality. He thinks that if physicists go on discovering ultimate particles as final reality they will be empty of significance because that "ultimate ground is to be regarded as the unknown totality of the universal flux" (WIO, 63).

Here Bohm is very close to Buddhist thought, especially Nāgārjuna. But, while Nāgārjuna and other Buddhists might be sympathetic to the idea of an implicate order, their philosophy of conditioned genesis does not entail any notion of wholeness. Indeed, most Buddhists thinkers would question the reality of such a doctrine, dependent as it is on universal flux, because flux, the Buddhist world of becoming, almost by definition does not imply wholeness. So with the body: it is nothing but a series of changing aggregates, never still for even a moment and, consequently, lacking wholeness, except nominally. But not for Bohm, who boldly brings "thought" within the implicate order as well. "Thought is, in essence, the active response of memory in every phase of life. We include in thought the intellectual, emotional, sensuous, muscular and physical responses of memory. They are all aspects of one indissoluble process. To treat them separately makes for fragmentation and confusion" (WIO, 64). I believe there is a language problem here: why should fragmentation lead to confusion? For example, I might think, as many postmodern thinkers do, that the world is fragmented, but why should my presupposition lead to confusion? If the explicate order, if not the implicate order, is characterized by fragmentation, then when I think the world is fragmented I apprehend a "truth" about that order. That truth might be limited, but surely it should not lead to confusion.

Bohm then goes on to assert that intelligence is part of the unknown flux and hence joins hands, one might say, with the physicist's notion of matter. "Intelligence is thus not deducible or explainable on the basis of any branch of knowledge (e.g., physics or biology). Its origin is deeper and more inward than any knowable order that could describe it" (WIO, 67). In his sensible critique of the correspondence theory of thought (or truth), he says the idea that "thought is in reflective correspondence with the thing has no meaning" and that "both thought and thing are forms abstracted from the total process" (WIO, 70). What is problematic is his search for the ground of that process in the reality that neither he nor anyone else can identify as an existent reality. To say that the reality is undefinable and unidentifiable is something that one has to take on faith, just as one takes religion on faith. It not surprising that Bohm's thinking would soon embrace existence itself, such that lived existence is an undivided flowing movement without borders (WIO, 218).[62]

Let me get back to the metaphor of the ever-flowing river. Where in it lies its wholeness? Is the flow of the river an example of wholeness? Or is Bohm dangerously hovering around some notion of an unverifiable or unproven essence of the river? Bohm's way out of his analytical dilemma is through a sensible distinction between explanation and understanding. "What is required here, then, is not an explanation that would give us some knowledge of the relationship of thought and thing, or of thought and 'reality as a whole.' Rather, what is needed is an act of understanding, in which we see the totality as an actual process that, when carried out properly, tends to bring about an harmonious and orderly overall action, incorporating both thought and what is thought about in a single movement, in which analysis into separate parts (e.g., thought and thing) has no meaning" (WIO, 71). Yet, surely understanding or *verstehen* has a logic of its own (or multiple logics) as hermeneutical philosophers have consistently maintained and simply cannot be a catch-all for an intuitive grasp of an important epistemological foundation of reality such as the implicate order that, if Bohm is correct, would have deep existential significance.

Toward the end of his book, Bohm links up his notion of flow and the implicate order with another powerful and well-established idea, that of the holographic paradigm based on the work of the Nobel laureate Denis Gabor in 1947. What is relevant for us is the later application of this model to the brain by the neuroscientist Karl H. Pribram. According to Pribram, "Gabor named the wave pattern store a hologram because one of the most interesting characteristics is that information from the object becomes distributed over the surface of the photographic film"[63] The picture appears as a blur, though it is not haphazard but rather like a pebble that, when thrown into the water, forms ripples over the surface of the pond. One can cut a piece of the hologram and this part will represent the whole. In slightly more technical terminology, Ken Wilber puts it thus: "Holography is a method of lensless photography in which the wave field of light scattered by an object is recorded on a plate as an interference pattern. When the photographic record—the hologram—is placed in a coherent light beam like a laser, the original wave pattern in regenerated. A three-dimensional image appears. Because there is no focusing lens, the plate appears as a meaningless pattern of swirls. Any piece of the hologram will reconstruct the entire image."[64] Literally hundreds of million bits of information can be stored in a small space.

Pribram's thesis is that the brain also functions like a hologram, such that any part of the brain codifies information that is found in the whole. In the same way that images can be reconstituted from small fragments of the hologram, so with the brain. The brain stores information in such a way that a part of the brain will provide access to the whole, which means, at least according to Pribram, "specific memory traces are resistant to brain damage."[65] Or again: "Removing a hunk of brain tissue or injuring one or another portion of the brain does not excise a particular memory or set of memories" although the process of remembering might be disturbed in a "general way." This means that the input from the senses "becomes spread over a sufficient expanse of brain to make the memory of that experience resistant to brain damage."[66] Insofar as the hologram is not an actual photograph, it taps a "frequency domain," that is, prior to the world perceived by our senses and recorded through our perceptual apparatus, the eyes and the brain. The brain's mathematics transforms the holographic blurs into perceptual images, such as sights, sounds, colors, and so forth that constitute the explicate world. Unlike a regular photograph, there is no one-to-one correspondence between the hologram and reality. "The hologram of a flower, no matter how lovely, will appear as a tangle of interfering wave fronts, because reality is presented to us in a different order."[67] The mathematics of the brain then converts the blurs or wave fronts to actual images as in photographs.

While working on these issues, Pribram was introduced to the work of Bohm, and they came to the realization that both the brain and the universe operated on the holographic model, the "holomovement." Pribram says that "this domain is characteristic not only of brain processing, as we have seen, but of physical reality as well," as Bohm also recognizes. The holographic model, especially as it applies to the brain, gives the much needed scientific grounding, if not validation, to Bohm's implicate order. What is fascinating is that the image that appears in the hologram has no space-time dimension, which is also characteristic of the implicate order, whereas space and time as entities appear in the explicate order. Thus one could legitimately say that the explicate order is not the true reality but rather *māyā*, illusion. Further, because space and time are collapsed in the frequency-implicate-holographic domain, the normal causal operations of science do not apply there. Hence, for Pribram, "complementarities, synchronicities, symmetries, and dualities must be called upon as explanatory principles."[68] I assume that "dualities" must be reconciled at some level and converted into holism, if Pribram wants to defend Bohm's position. In a further move, Pribram would say that mystics, psychics, and others dealing with paranormal phenomena might have the capacity to "tune in" on this domain. According to both Pribram and Bohm, this conception of the universe shows an affinity but not an identity with "Eastern religion."[69] Because they are also sympathetic to Tibetan Buddhism, new age intellectuals might find the Pribram-Bohm view of the universe appealing, especially the idea that Buddhist meditative asceses might be tapping the same domain as that of physics and that there is a homology between the holographic-implicate domain and the transcendental. Wilber, in spite of his serious qualifications of the work of Bohm and Pribram, could nevertheless triumphantly affirm that "modern science is no longer denying spirit. And that, that is epochal."[70]

In addition to the criticisms I have made, I find it puzzling that psi, synchronicity, mediumship, and the paranormal could all be explained or understood holographically. How does one eliminate fraud, charlatanism, or, for that matter, genuine prophecy or meditative asceses and find out whether they can be justified in terms of the model? In other words, there is no way one can say that x-experience is explained by the model (or understood in terms of it) but not y-experience. Another complication: not only synchronicity but almost everything else can be similarly understood. Thus *The Holographic Paradigm* asserts the holographic model touches "all aspects of human life," and that includes, for new age thinkers at least, learning, health, psychotherapy and religion, personal transformation, attention, philosophy and evolution, the arts, and so on.[71] Are we getting another replacement for God?

Finally, with respect to mystical identity with the frequency domain, one might ask: what about Tibetan meditators who dissolve themselves into a deity such as a Bodhisattva? Are we to say that they are wrong and in reality identified with the frequency domain, as Wouter Hanegraaff nicely points out?[72] Further, as we have seen, Pribram, if not Bohm, asserts that scientists have barely begun to explore the implicate order, quite unlike mystics, psychics, and other practitioners of the occult. It seems to me that, contrary to Bohm and Pribram, the holograph theory attempts to *explain* mystical and related phenomena, not to *understand* them. A genuine understanding must account for the multiple varieties of the so-called mystical experience that different cultures have formulated. I think it must account for the substance of visionary experiences, for example, when Buddhists speak of the paradise of Amitābha or when the rich content of the "mystics" of the Christian tradition defy incorporation into a single experience or even when the Buddha refuses to attach substance to the nirvanic ideal. It is a mistake to define mysticism in an essentialist manner and then bring the varieties of "mystical experiences" within the arbitrary definition, as is implicit in Bohm and Pribram and is explicitly formulated by Ken Wilber in his revamped notion of the perennial philosophy.[73]

A final critique: Hanegraaff has noted that Bohm in his later work has obscured the insights of his early notion of the implicate order. He now has other orders that unfold from within it, so that he can speak of superimplicate and super-superimplicate order, and so on. It reminds me of the logical casuistry of Mahāyāna's "emptiness of emptiness," which has the potential to develop into an infinite and meaningless regress. Yet, apparently, there is a final kind of enfoldment that brings Bohm close to the whole intellectualist tradition of the Absolute. "When I see the immense order of the universe (and especially the brain of man), I cannot escape the feeling that this ground unfolds a supreme intelligence. Although it is not quite so evident, I would say also that this 'intelligence' is permeated with compassion and love."[74] We seem to have come through another route to the intellectual's version of the Absolute. Gregory Bateson arrives at a similar version of God as an Absolute, but via cybernetics and systems theory, without any reference to quantum physics or an implicate order or a holomovement. (See the following note for a discussion of Bateson's thought.)[75] Surely we have the right to ask which version of the Absolute is the true or reasonable one, because Bateson and the physics metaphysicians come from such irreconcilable epistemological and philosophical positions they almost force us to ignore the gray area.

Because we have brought in Bateson in conjunction with Bohm and Pribram, we can continue with the following criticisms. Although these three metaphysicians come from different backgrounds, their theories of God are not all that different from their bête noire, Descartes. Indeed, one might say that all these metaphysicians, new and old, have little choice but to ground their thinking in some form of the Absolute. The fact is that the physics metaphysicians, like the systems theorist Bateson, are themselves trapped in a discourse of their own European heritage, the idea of the Good or the One or the Absolute or the immanent or the immeasurable on which they build their own physical edifice, which, they imagine, constitutes a much more solid ground than that of their predecessors. But one wonders whether the belief, or the need to believe, in some such entity, itself an argument with the prior tradition of Western metaphysics, is a new paradigm or simply the old Absolute dressed up anew with so-called Eastern religion added on? If, indeed, substantial evidence could be adduced to justify the idea of flow, of holomovement, of an implicate order that can be legitimately inferred from the data of physics and holography, then Bohm and Pribram have formulated an epistemology with epochal significance. But I remain one of the unpersuaded. While I am sympathetic to their criticism of the Cartesian paradigm, I find it hard to accept that, beneath the phenomenal physical world, however one describes it, there is another dimension of reality that can be identified as implicate order or holomovement or flow. I find it hard to accept these ideas on the basis of intuition, unless that intuition is justified by reasoning, as was the case with the Buddha. But we are not living in the time of the Buddha. It is certainly true that Bateson, Bohm, and Pribram and others like them employ reasoning to explicate the implicate order, but living in our times, when science has made such tremendous advances, one must, it seems to me, adduce reasonable evidential support for the existence of such an order and beyond that to justify the presence of an insubstantial compassionate intelligence about which little has been said by any of the aforementioned thinkers. I suspect that many believers nurtured on a personal God would find the scientists' compassionate intelligence or reified absolute not *absurd enough* to nurture their faith. And experimental scientists might find that same intelligence *absolutely absurd* in the ordinary sense of the term. For myself, I have much greater sympathy and feeling for the richness and variety of the mystical and visionary experiences of some of the virtuosos who appear in this essay, but who, in the thinking of the "physics-metaphysicians," were deluded into believing that when they were absorbed in mystical identity, theistic or otherwise, they were in error, in fact identifying with an implicate or holomovement or some other order of hollow reality.[76] Can I be blamed if I have some special feeling for those visionaries who fill that reality with the fullness of vision in Buddhism as well as for those in the Christian tradition whose visionary and ecstatic trances I will now describe at some length?

Book 4

PENITENTIAL ECSTASY

The Dark Night of the Soul

SHOWINGS: THE CHRISTIAN VISIONS OF JULIAN OF NORWICH

> A deeper enlightenment and wider experience than mine is necessary to explain the dark night through which a soul journeys toward that divine light of perfect union with God that is achieved, insofar as possible in this life, through love. The darkness and trials, spiritual and temporal, that fortunate souls ordinarily undergo on their way to the high state of perfection are so numerous and profound that human science cannot understand them adequately. Those who suffer them will know what this experience is like, but they will find themselves unable to describe it.
>
> —John of the Cross, *The Ascent of Mount Carmel*

ONE OF THE ISSUES I raised in my discussions of Tibetan treasure seekers is that, while their visionary trajectories were constrained by their complex cosmological presuppositions, their form of Buddhism did provide scope for innovative knowledge. Although framed in terms of recovery of lost Buddha words rather than new knowledge, in reality treasure discoverers were inventing new texts, though based on existing ones. Further, the flexibility of their Mahāyāna Buddhism was such that they could journey into unfamiliar cosmic realms, and to known or little-known geographic regions, to interpret in retrospect unusual visions, like that of the wolf rider and flying carpets, that could be incorporated into their traditional scheme of things. Thus, though constrained within the frames of their own thought, as all visions must be, there are openings in the frames or an expansion or blurring of them that permits the entry of innovative thoughts and images, a phenomenon more difficult in a monotheistic cosmology. A Christian visionary riding on a wolf or a flying carpet to view Jesus or reach the Christian heavens is inconceivable outside of out-and-out pathology or unless interpreted as Satan's work. Whereas, even though there is no explicit precedent for these images in Tibetan Buddhism, the treasure seeker can incorporate them into his more open epistemology. And we know from the history of Western science that, when Christian cosmology superseded the Greek, there was little room for envisaging a multiplicity of universes outside of our own small world until, perhaps, the first systematic epistemological accounting of the cosmos took place in Kant's early work, the 1755 *General History of Nature and the Theory of the Heavens,* such that "from now on, men had to reckon with an unlimited number of galaxies, scattered throughout Space, and even more remote from one another than the stars within our own galaxy."[1] For anyone socialized in a Christian worldview, it would be impossible to emulate the cosmic freedoms of our Tibetan visionaries. Christian mystics levitated, as did Teresa of Avila or Catherine of Siena or Jane Mary of Maillé, owing to the power of their devotion, it is said. But levitation was only a few feet up ("two cubits"), nothing like the cosmic travels of our Buddhists.[2] But, in fairness to our Christian mystics, they claimed to levitate in the body, defying gravity as it were, whereas the Buddhist treasure seekers, in their visionary trances, levitated in the "spirit" where the body is left behind.

Christian visions, if they were to be approved by the Church or one's conscience, had to be framed in terms of critical parameters: the Trinity, the devil and his disciples, the angels and the heavens and hells ordained by the Church and perhaps a few others that might have a revelatory or apocalyptic character. The Church and papal authority and its arm in the Inquisition acted as a further brake to departures from the orthodoxy of the times; witness the burning of the visionary Marguerite Porete at the stake in June 1, 1310, for her commitment to the medieval "heresy of the free spirit." Such fears led to recantations of unorthodox views. More pervasive than recantations was the dread of condemnation by the papal authorities that even thinkers like Meister Eckhart were threatened with. In general, in medieval times at least, one had to be a psychotic or a heretic or a devil worshipper to be emancipated from a Christian upbringing or question its fundamental premises. Madness, like heresy, had its benefits, in spite of the threat of being burned at the stake in times past or, closer to our own times, of being shoved into an asylum.

I am not suggesting that it is Christianity alone that restricts the visionary quest. Theravāda Buddhism, in spite of the Buddha's own precedence, is much less open than Mahāyāna to space travelers because of its relative lack of interest in metaphysics and cosmology. I will, nevertheless, now move to Christian visionaries to illustrate both the restrictions imposed by their religious presuppositions and also to consider sympathetically the more open and less culturally bound psychic realities that propel their visions, their attempts to free themselves from the straitjacket of their cultural framework. One can demonstrate the latter from the lives of fourteenth-century saints, a period that saw the flowering of female saints and visionaries. Take Christina Ebner (1277–1356), whose beautiful visions are almost heretical because they spill over the official bounds of Christian thought. During one of her trance-raptures, which she entered after communion, she "saw the luminous streets of heaven, strewn with pure gold, lilies and roses. She also saw that Christ was preparing a special celebration, and was inviting all his saints to it. She beheld a dance in heaven, in which God and Mary took part along with the saints."[3] Unlike the dancing Mary and Jesus, parades of saints and angels are also fairly well known, and visions of them are elaborations of paintings and stories known to the public.

Julian is of course a woman who derives her name from St. Julian's Church in Norwich, where she was an anchoress, one of the many anchorites who lived in tiny cells in churches all over Europe. Norwich apparently was one of the most popular places for them in the Europe of the fourteenth century. A contemporary of Chaucer, Julian was the first known female author in England and a writer of simple, elegant prose. We do not know much of her life—much less than of other female penitents of the medieval period—but this is not all that significant for understanding her visions, though not of the deep motivations precipitating them. These visions are recorded in two texts, now known as the "short text" and the "long text," the first containing twenty-five chapters and the second eighty-six.[4] Both texts were written by Julian and not by a mediator-guide, itself a remarkable feature in a historical context where female literacy was rare. The scholarly opinion is that the short text was the earlier version, whereas the long text was a more edited one. Both texts begin with Julian's wish for three things: "the first was vivid perception of Christ's Passion, the second was bodily sickness and the third was for God to give me three wounds" (LT, 3). The last is meant to be entirely metaphoric because the long text tells us that they are "the wound of true contrition, the wound of kind compassion and the wound of an earnest longing for God." It is impossible for us to determine when these wishes were made and in what context (LT, 2:43).

For the moment, let me deal with Julian's wish for bodily sickness and the courting of pain (both forms of simulated dying), which aligns her not only with others before and after her in the Christian tradition but also with visionary virtuosos everywhere. "I wanted this bodily sickness to be to the death, so that I might in that sickness receive all the rites of the Holy Church, that I might myself believe I was dying and that everyone who saw me might believe the same"

(LT, 2:43). She says that her wishes were fulfilled in the year 1373, when "God sent me a bodily sickness in which I lay for three days and three nights" receiving on the fourth the rites of absolution because she did not believe that she would live till morning (ST, 2:5). Yet she did not want to die because by living longer she could love God longer and better. Although alive, she was "dead to all sensation from the waist down." That is, her lower body was insensate, implying that her sexual feelings were extinguished. People sent for her parish priest to be present at her death; he placed a cross before her because her eyes "were looking fixedly upwards into heaven" where she felt she was going. "After this my sight began to fail and the room was dim all around me, as dark as if it had been night," fully expecting to die because the upper part of her body also began to fail and she was short of breath. Her whole body was now "dead," but the text clearly tells us that the darkness in which she lived during that period was set in the daytime (ST, 2:5–6).

She wanted God to fulfill her other two wishes: his Passion, so that his pains that would be her pains, and his wounds her "wounds." At this point she did not wish for "a bodily sight or any showing of God," but simply wanted to suffer with him. But then it just happened as the first showing: "I suddenly saw the red blood trickling down from under the crown of thorns, all hot, freshly, plentifully and vividly, just as I imagined it was at the moment when the crown of thorns was thrust upon his blessed head" (ST, 3:6). Note that, like many other devout Christians such as Ebner, her imagining of the bleeding Christ was fostered by church frescoes, paintings, and statuary. The vision brings forth the imagined Christ in vivid, hallucinatory reality as a "showing." "I strongly believed it was himself who showed me this, without any intermediary," that is, she saw the bleeding Christ with her own "bodily" or physical eyes. Each showing is like an act in a play: within each are several visions and divine understandings from God, like scenes within an act, and they appear before her without her volition.

In her language, this first act was a "bodily vision," that is, Christ as he actually suffered in Calvary (ST, 4:7). She sees that historic scene with her own "bodily eyes," a phenomenon not unusual among other female penitents and reminding us of Schreber's use of the same term. Both Schreber's and Julian's notion of the bodily eye, or the actual physical eye that can nevertheless see something from the past, comes from Augustine of Hippo, who in turn derives it from Paul. But for Augustine the bodily eye is the simple act of seeing (*corporis visio*); it cannot experience visions, whereas for Julian the bodily eye gives the vision an exceptional power because one sees something from the past as it occurred in reality.[5] The image of Jesus's bleeding head is beautifully described in the long text as part of the first showing: "The great drops fell down from under the crown of thorns like pills [pellets], as though they had come out of the veins; and as they came out they were dark red, for the blood was very thick; and as it spread it was bright red; and when it reached the brows it vanished, and yet the bleeding continued until many things were seen and understood. . . . It is as plentiful as the drops of water which fall so thickly that no human mind can number them. As for the roundness of the drops, they were like herring scales as they spread on the forehead. . . . This showing was alive and vivid, horrifying and awe-inspiring, sweet and lovely" (LT, 7:50–51). The foregoing adjectives indicate that the showings are thick with emotional meaning for this seer as well as for others who witnesses the Passion when the historic past is brought into the field of the vision.

During this first act of revelatory showing, God "showed me a little thing, the size of a hazel nut, lying in the palm of my hand" and round as a ball (ST, 4:7; LT, 4:47). When she thought what it could be, the answer came in the spiritual vision and not through her bodily sight: "It is all that is made" (ST, 4:7). God did not provide the answer directly; it simply entered her understanding; or as she later put it in another context, God "without any voice or opening of his lips, formed these words in my soul" (LT, 13:61). Unlike the bodily form of Christ, this object could in principle mean anything and makes sense only in terms of an interpretation that also enters her passive consciousness or understanding. Because it rests on the palm of her hand, she has no choice but to give it meaning. Another visionary might give this same object a different interpretation, for example, as a maṇḍala by our Tibetan virtuosos. Julian, however, must invest the object with her own private Christian meanings, either during the dream itself or recollected in tranquility or through scribal reflection while writing her book. "In this little thing I saw three attributes: the first is that God made it, the second that he loves it, the third is that God cares for it" (ST, 4:7). Or, as she later put it, everything that God makes is "wide, fair and good, but it looked so small to me because I saw it in the presence of him that is Maker of all things; to a soul that sees the Maker of all, all that is made seems very small" (ST, 5:9).

In interpreting this object Julian can express a certain degree of freedom as long as her exposition can be contained within the frame of her Christian tradition. We see this with respect to the visions of the devil in other female virtuosos in the Christian Middle Ages, such that for some the devil will appear in dreams as a cat, a dog, a snake, monstrous forms and shapes of lustful men, and all sorts of other guises. For an ordinary person such dreams might have meant nothing or anything, whereas the religious dreamer has no choice but to interpret such dreams and virtually all erotic dreams as the work of the devil. Thus Domenica dal Paradiso had a vision in the garden of "the devil approaching in the shape of a bear with long arms and hands, yellow feet, his tongue sticking out, eyes on fire and a hideous human head."[6] The garden with all of its associations carries a symbolic overload, and the frightening form that approaches her must compel her to interpret the vision as that of Satan.

In Julian's next vision, "God brought our Lady into my mind. I saw her spiritually in bodily likeness, a meek and simple maid, young of age, in the same bodily form as when she conceived" (ST, 4:8). Here is an important distinction that constantly appears in Christian visionary texts. In this instance, Julian did not see the Virgin with her "bodily eyes" but with her spiritual eye, that is, as it appears in the mystic's soul and projected outward. Julian clarifies this for us when she says that God's teaching was shown to her in three ways: "by bodily sight, and by words formed in my understanding, and by spiritual sight" (ST, 7:11). All these are "showings" of different sorts. Not just the visions but also the words delivered by Christ that enter into her spiritual "understanding" by being communicated to her soul. The vision of the Virgin through spiritual sight is not as powerful as that of Julian's sight of Christ through her bodily eyes, because the former is not Mary as she actually lived but an image appearing in her soul and analogous to the "proxy form" of the Tibetan seer. Yet we noted that it is likely her visions are also based on paintings and other representations, as St Teresa much later explicitly pointed out.[7] The imagined form reappears in the vision, transformed, as always, in more elaborate picturing.

In the vision of the Virgin we are still in the first showing. While God was showing the Virgin to Julian through her awakened spiritual sight, "the bodily sight of the plentiful bleeding from Christ's head remained" (LT, 7: 50). This compels us to change our metaphor from drama before it gets hopelessly muddled: both visions—her bodily vision of Christ and her spiritual one of Mary—are now contained within the same frame. However, when the form of the Virgin and Christ disappeared from her consciousness, the "spiritual vision remained in my understanding," that is, she can now conjure both through her spiritual eyes and endow the original images with all sorts of emotional and devotional meanings, public and private or both. Spiritual imaginings permit a certain leeway in interpretation precisely because it is not an actually witnessed historic occurrence.

While this relative freedom is found in her spiritual visions, not so with the bodily visions of Christ, which must of necessity be absolutely definitive, requiring no interpretation. Its meanings are already built into the vision. Julian can only reiterate them or elaborate them with vivid detail, as she does with the second showing or revelation: "I saw with my bodily sight in the face of Christ on the crucifix which hung before me, which I was looking at continuously, a part of his Passion: contempt and spitting, which soiled his body, and blows on his blessed face, and many lingering pains, more than I can tell, and frequent changes of color, and all his blessed face covered at one time in dry blood" (ST, 8:12). Continuous staring at the mirror of her crucifix opens up this vision, described in great detail in both texts.

The third revelation or showing is very brief. Once the previous experience was over, she saw "God in an instant." In a flash, she understood that God is in everything and that "nothing happens by accident or luck, but everything is by God's wise providence" (LT, 11:58). The instant vision produces an instant interpretation, a refusal to accept accident, coincidence, luck, and chance, which is, we have seen, true of all sorts of virtuosos inhabiting a religious landscape. The third revelation ends once again with her vision of the discoloration of Christ's face, consequent to the beatings he received and the violation of his body.

The obsessive themes of oozing blood, violence, and body mutilation continue to appear. "And after this I saw, as I watched, the body of Christ bleeding abundantly, in weals from the scourging. It looked like this: the fair skin was very deeply broken, down into the tender flesh, sharply slashed all over the dear body; the hot blood ran out so abundantly that no skin or wound could be seen, it seemed to be all blood. And when it reached the point where it should have overflowed, it vanished: nevertheless, the bleeding continued for a while so that it could be observed attentively" (LT, 12: 59–60).

Julian says that as far as "the spiritual sight is concerned, I have said something about it, but I could never recount it all" (LT, 73: 161). This is not surprising because, unlike spiritual visions, the power of the bodily vision is its horrifying immediacy. By contrast, what is seen through the spiritual sight has deeper symbolic meanings of God's love and grace, those public meanings that deal with such things as caritas, sin, redemption, and, in Julian's case, the radiation of her love for Christ and the Virgin to embrace all Christians in common fellowship. "In all this I was much moved with love for my fellow Christians, wishing that they might see and know what I was seeing; I wanted to comfort them, for the vision was shown for everyone," not literally, of course. "Then I said to those who were around me, 'For me, today is the Day of Judgment.' And I said this because I thought I was dying; for on that day that a man dies, he receives his eternal judgment, as I understand it" (LT, 8:53).

Here I find a lacuna in the text that I must now fill. In her time of "dying," she suffers bodily pains and then loses the capacity for sensation, owing to the "paralysis" of the lower part of her body followed by the upper. I must assume that she makes this speech after she awakens from the experience of dying, because during that dark night she would be incapable of rational discourse. Further, she is surrounded by people anxious about her condition and ready to serve her, and it is these people she addresses. They become by extension the universal

Christian community. "I said this because I wanted them to love God better, to remind them that life is short, as they might see by my example; for all this time I thought I was dying. . . . I beg of you all for God's sake and advise you for your own advantage that you stop paying attention to the poor being to whom this vision was shown, and eagerly, attentively and humbly contemplate God, who in his gracious love and eternal goodness wanted the vision to be generally known to comfort us all; for it is God's will that you should receive it with joy and pleasure as great as if Jesus had shown it to you all" (LT, 9: 53).

If this rational exhortation was given when she awoke from dying, can we then hazard a guess as to its timing? The answer is given in the long text. "Now I have told you of fifteen revelations as God deigned to offer them to my understanding, renewing them with flashes of illumination and touches, I hope, of the same spirit which was shown in them all. The first of these fifteen showings began early in the morning, at about four o'clock, and they lasted, appearing in due order most beautifully and surely, one after the other, until it was well past the middle of the day" (LT, 65: 151). In the long text she says that these visions were shown to her "in the year of our Lord 1373, on the eight day of May," when she was thirty and a half years old (LT, 2: 42). She was sick for three days and three nights, and all fifteen showings would have occurred during a six-hour period on the last day, during what seems a brief "trance illness." Her rational discourse to the faithful around her would surely have been much later, perhaps in the afternoon.

There was, it seems, a sixteenth and final showing, which proves that the preceding showings occurred on the fourth day, preparatory to her awakening following the period of dying. She had already felt better, but then the sickness returned "first in my head, with a noise and a din, and suddenly my whole body was full of sickness as it had been before, and I was as barren and dry as if I had received little comfort. And like a wretch I tossed and moaned with the feeling of bodily pain and a failing of spiritual and bodily comfort" (LT, 66: 151–52). While in this condition, the parish priest asked her how she felt, and she responded by saying that "'I had been delirious today.'" This provoked the priest to laugh aloud, but she then continued: "The cross which was before my face, I thought it was bleeding hard." Julian's parish priest was now impressed and marveled at what she had seen. In other words, she managed to convince a crucial person in her community of the authenticity of her vision. "And when I saw that he took it so seriously and so reverently, I wept, feeling very ashamed, and wanted to be given absolution; but at this time I did not feel I could tell any priest about it, for I thought, 'How could a priest believe me? I do not believe our Lord God.' I had truly believed while I was seeing him, and had then wanted and intended to do so for ever, but, like a fool, I let it pass from my mind." The reference is to her waking up and telling the priest that her vision was a delirium, not a genuine one, but, ironically, the priest actually believing in its authenticity. No wonder she felt like a sinner, and no wonder the next episode gives expression to these feelings of sin and guilt in the form of the devil attacking her when she fell asleep at night. "As soon as I fell asleep it seemed the Fiend was at my throat, thrusting a visage like a young man's close to my face; and it was long and extraordinarily thin, I never saw one like it. . . . He grinned at me with a wicked expression, showing white teeth, so that I thought him even more horrible. His body and hands were not properly shaped, but his paws gripped me by the throat and he tried to strangle me, but he could not. I was asleep during this horrible showing, but not during the others" (LT, 66:152). She had for a moment abandoned her lover, her God, and the result is the dream episode of violence and attempted rape by the devil as a grotesque incubus. She woke up, and the assembled faithful comforted her. Around her was the foul stench that she alone could smell, the stench one might say not only of the rapist's sexuality but also perhaps of her own guilty desires. This phenomenon of olfactory distortion will reappear in other cases. In Julian's case, she had recourse to what God had shown previously, his love and his embracive Church, and the smell vanished immediately. "I was brought to a state of great rest and peace without sickness of the body or terrors of the mind" (LT, 66:153).

And with this comes the wonderful vision I quoted in my discussion of the expansion of space: "And then our Lord opened my spiritual eyes and showed me my soul in the middle of my heart. I saw the soul as large as if it were an endless world and as if it were a holy kingdom; and from the properties I saw in it I understood that it is a glorious city. In the centre of the city sits our Lord Jesus, God and man, a handsome person and of great stature, the highest bishop, the most imposing king, the most glorious Lord; and I saw him dressed imposingly and gloriously. He sits in the soul, in the very center, in peace and rest" (LT, 67:153). This is the reward for love and faith in the Lord.

We are now told that, while everyone possesses spiritual eyes, we humans "are so blind, and we are so weighted down by our mortal flesh and the darkness of sin that we cannot see our Lord God's fair, blessed face clearly" (LT, 72:160). We can therefore say that it is God himself who opens her spiritual eyes to view the city of God within her own soul, a reward for Julian as the bride of Christ. God cares for her as her lover and maker, for "until I become one substance with him, I can never have love, rest or true bliss" (ST, 5:7). This trust, this love is rewarded in the culminating sixteenth showing, when God "gave me certain knowledge that it was he who had shown me all that went before." In other words, she receives final confirmation that the showings that appeared before her during her dark night of the soul was something created by God. Hence this assurance from God was "a ravishing sight and a restful showing," in contrast to the cruel ravishing of the devil, one might add. And God further speaks to her, assuring her of the power of his blessed Passion: "By this," says he, "the Fiend is overcome" (LT, 68:155). God added several times, "You shall not be overcome," referring to the machinations of Satan.

Yet is seems that the devil cannot be easily appeased, as he makes one final smelly descent, but no longer as the rapist-incubus. He now tests her will, her fortitude, and her faith. He no longer appears in physical form, but Julian felt his presence from the heat and stench he emanated and the jabbering and unintelligible noises he made, as if there were two people talking at the same time. It seemed to her that these voices were parodying Christian prayers, a piece of blasphemy expectable in her adversary. The devil's game was to drive her to despair, but with the now-renewed trust in God she could "overcome" the devil. "I set my bodily eyes on the same cross [crucifix] which had comforted me before, and my tongue to speaking of Christ's Passion and reciting the faith of Holy Church, and my heart clinging to God with all my trust and with all my strength." The fiend can now do her no harm with his smells and noises. "And thus I was delivered from them by the power of Christ's Passion, for that is how the Fiend is overcome, as our Lord Jesus Christ said before" (LT, 69:156). The overcoming of the devil is also the awakening from the dark night of dying into a tranquil faith in God.

DRYNESS: PSYCHIC REALITIES AND CULTURAL FORMATIONS IN FEMALE VISIONARY RELIGIOSITY

> Moyst, with one drop of thy blood, my dry soule.
> —John Donne, "Crucifying"

I noted earlier Julian's lament that during her spiritual crisis she was "barren and dry." "Dryness" is an image often used in mystical religiosity, for some simply as a convention. But for our penitents the conventional image is transformed into a personal symbol that has an overflow of meanings. In order to understand the symbolic meanings of dryness, I will interrogate the important study by Rudolph Bell on the parallelism between the "holy anorexia" of Christian female religious virtuosos and anorexia nervosa, the widespread neurotic condition of modern-day females. Contemporary anorectics are often well educated and by no means given to excessive religiosity, although they have strongly introjected the current cultural idealizations of slimness as a sign of beauty and self-worth and dieting as a way to achieving them. There is no doubt of the striking nature of the parallelism in terms of symptoms. Bell's sample consisted of 261 holy women who lived in the Italian peninsula in the Middle Ages, and of them 170 "displayed clear signs of anorexia" (HA, x). The symptoms of anorexia nervosa are well known and I shall mention a few significant ones: onset prior to age twenty-five; lack of appetite leading to a loss of about 25 percent of body weight; the compulsive wish to avoid food despite all forms of persuasion; an insistence that no illness is involved; the cultural background of idealization of thinness; and, from our point of view, with several crucial symptomatic formations, such as amenorrhea, periods of hyperactivity, bulimia or binge eating and vomiting that is often self-induced. Along with these symptoms are signs that are also found in trans-symptomatic cultural values among both normal and neurotic persons in a population: hyperactivity, a high level of intelligence and perfectionism, and the detestation of bodily desires, both food and sex (HA, 2–3).

William N. Davis, an authority on anorexia, tells us that, while these signs are found in holy anorexia, "the holy women described by Bell did not suffer from the eating disorder known today as anorexia nervosa. No doubt the saints starved themselves . . . and experienced all the physical symptoms that accompany extreme malnourishment. Just as certainly, they purged themselves, denied their nutritional needs, and strongly resisted external efforts to get them to eat. But missing from Bell's account of holy anorectic behavior is a dread of fatness, and a self-conscious, unremitting pursuit of thinness. This is the hallmark of anorexia nervosa, its single most telling diagnostic sign" (HA, 181). Unfortunately, Davis annuls the significance of his qualifying remarks by saying that the distinction between the two forms of anorexia are "more illusory than real" and that there is a "fundamental parallel when holiness for a holy anorectic is understood to be similar to thinness for a present-day anorectic" (HA, 181).

I couldn't disagree more. Davis's earlier qualifications perhaps provide us with a way out of the pathological model of sainthood that Bell, in spite of his sympathy for female virtuosos of his sample, is forced to adopt. Anorexia remains the defining symptomatology in Bell's notion of "holy anorexia," which I think might better be labeled *penitential fasting.* He is critical of the earlier diagnoses of these women as *hysterics,* but it seems to me that both terms carry a pathological load. And while it is necessary, I think, to recognize the troubled psyches of these women and empathize with their social and childhood deprivations, I want to adopt the strategy of *Medusa's Hair,* which highlights the transformation of symptom into symbol in the spiritual lives of religious ecstatics, be they Christian or Buddhist.[8]

Remember that anorexia nervosa is not recognized by the modern woman as an illness; it is diagnosed as such by her society—by her parents and significant others. So it is with penitential fasting or "holy anorexia." People might well recognize it as an illness or the work of the devil, but, once a woman's aspiration to saintliness is acknowledged, her voluntary starvation becomes an expression of her fortitude and single-minded devotion to God, a point that Bell does not miss. Saintly women's fame spread widely, and in some instances extraordinary fasting was seen as a miracle, a situation impossible to envisage in anorexia nervosa (HA, 126). I have not seen Christian paintings in which the women are represented in their anorectic personae. On the contrary, they appear of full figure, though sometimes the paintings do capture their melancholy expressions in addition to their more popular expressions of beatitude. The starving Catherine of Siena appears in a sixteenth-century painting of her marriage to Christ in full glory with a halo behind her, her full face painted in what seems to be an expression of spiritual love, surprising in someone whom everybody knew died of deliberately withholding food and water. Others show her as a beautiful woman, the very opposite of a starving penitent.

One is tempted to contrast these representations with the ascetic suffering of the Buddha prior to his Awakening. Buddhist iconography I noted depicts it in graphic detail. If the self-mortification of the Buddha is intrinsic to his mythic persona, this is not so with the starving Christian penitent. Bell is right to assume that fasting was not encouraged by the New Testament and the ideals of the Catholic Church (HA, 118–21). Nevertheless, not only were there models of penitential fasting in early Christianity, especially by the desert fathers, but we also know that penitents like Catherine of Siena explicitly followed their example, as perhaps did Henry Suso, a male virtuoso given to extreme penance.[9] If the desert fathers did practice extreme penances and a starvation regime, why does Bell ignore *their* "holy anorexia"? Further, female fasting, occasionally unto death, was also accepted by ordinary people as a sign of grace and was at least tacitly encouraged by the Catholic orders to which the saintly women were affiliated, especially among the Dominicans, who produced the largest number of cases of "holy anorexia."

Medieval penitents were not fasting for its own sake but for the purification of their bodies and the control of bodily urges in order to prepare themselves for eventual union, in the double sense of marriage and merging, with Jesus. This is the perfection they sought, and it has no connection whatever with the search for bodily perfection of anorectics. One sign of their search for perfection

4.1. *St. Catherine with Lily. Art Resource*

is the preservation of virginity, as far as unmarried women were concerned, and abstinence from marital sex for married women.[10] Caroline Walker Bynum says that virginity was a source of spiritual power and "a compelling religious ideal in its own right, not merely a second-best substitute for marriage."[11] This was so in Hinduism also, and in both religions abstinence from marital sex was the second-best substitute for virginity. I would add that Bell's analogy or model for comparison is flawed for another reason, namely, the modern woman's anorectic symptoms have their antecedents in the medieval past of European culture and its continuing tradition of fasting. Hence a more satisfactory model ought to envisage the continuity between that past and the present, rather than the present in the past. It would have meant more methodological sense to use holy anorexia to understand modern anorexia nervosa rather than the other way round.

Now consider Davis's assertion that modern anorectics are "unable to make connections with other people" and there "are no intermediaries" they resorted to; only their diet mattered (HA, 183). This is not so with saintly women. For example, Teresa of Avila, who was "anorectic" at times, established networks of relationships with politically important figures. She founded a new order of discalced or "barefoot" monks and nuns of the Carmelite order and established seventeen convents, maintaining steadfast loyalty to fellow sisters. She was no exception. Others also established connections with their sisters, and all related to their favorite confessors. Even the ideal typical holy anorectic, Catherine of Siena, traveled quite a lot and conversed with major figures in the Catholic hierarchy, including Pope Gregory XI. And, as a community, fasting Cistercians were especially sensitive to the needs of their sisters in cloister, and so with Benedictines.[12] One could make a further generalization regarding the relationship of the penitent or visionary irrespective of the religious tradition in which she was located. All of them can relate to a spirit community outside of their mundane social world. Thus all visionaries must relate to a divine hierarchy up above, which in Christianity is the family of God and all those associated with it. Catherine of Siena not only has intimate relations with the divine family and the apostles, but she also has intimate conversations with Mary Magdalene during her visionary states. She also relates to saints, especially Paul the Apostle, John the Evangelist, and sometimes St. Dominic, often St. Thomas Aquinas.[13] And, when Marie D'Oignies was dying, "some of her friends who had already died were sent to console her: John of Dinant who was then reigning with Christ, and Brother Richard of Menehen-Capella, a good man and holy but still in purgatory."[14] These examples could easily be multiplied in every religious tradition. The extended community of spirit companions is for the most part more real to all visionaries than the actual human companions of one's everyday existence. And demonic figures are more feared and hated than any imaginable human counterpart; consequently they have to be controlled, bound, defied, or extirpated.

It seems that disaggregating symptoms from their cultural and symbolic embodiment makes only limited sense. It is this larger issue that I must pose now and seek to answer. Let me start with a phenomenon that Bell does not deal with, namely, that the medieval European world was peopled by women who were afflicted with demonic possession and inhabited the same religious landscape as that of Christian penitents. One might even say that, unlike the wealthy who could afford to channel their dowries to the religious institutions to which they were affiliated, not so with the poor who were possessed by demons and incubi.

They would also have to undergo flagellation and other treatments to banish their demons, and it is likely that their afflictions also resulted in bodily emaciation. If our guess is correct, then there would be a larger number of females suffering from what one might label, facetiously to be sure, "unholy anorexia." Given the fact that forms of demonic possession are found the world over, one must surely expect them to have flourished in Europe prior to and contemporary with the development of Christian ecstatic religiosity among females. Their cures were brought about by Church exorcists and a variety of local curers from herbalists to shamanic specialists. Indeed, as late at the mid-sixteenth century, Teresa of Avila complained of "those *mujercillas* who seemed to be collapsing with religious fervor on every street corner."[15] Very little information on nonmonk curers and exorcists are found in the popular religious literature, but Barbara Newman has documented in great detail the ways in which demons were expelled from the female body by monk-exorcists, male exorcism of possessed females being nothing unusual from a cross-cultural perspective.[16] If so, one has to admire the earliest Christian penitents, who could cure themselves through their own psychic efforts, unmediated or only partially helped by exorcist monks.

Bynum says that thirteenth-century women created a new religious role, the beguine, an intermediate status between laity and clergy, and they also flocked "into the traditional monastic role (especially Cistercian and Dominican convents) at a time when it was losing some of its appeal for men."[17] Additionally there were many female followers of wandering preachers, both heterodox and orthodox.[18] The first well-known "new woman" was Clare of Assisi, a follower of St. Francis and the founder of the Poor Clare's, an order that continues into our own times. Clare literally attempted to escape patriarchal authority by fleeing away from home on Palm Sunday 1212 seeking refuge in a Benedictine shelter. She also fasted and become thin and emaciated, but sensibly followed Saint Francis's advice and began to eat. As Bell puts it: "What it does show is the emergence of a clear, attractive, fascinating model for female piety, one actively encouraged by Franciscan preachers" that, unlike later Dominicans, emphasized "sisterhood, obedience, quiet and retiring penance, and a steady regimen to tame bodily desires" (HA, 127, 130). Saint Clare (and perhaps unknown predecessors) heralded an emancipatory movement for female Christian virtuosos from the straitjacket of patriarchal authority, although this was not their conscious motivation. Many asserted a form of autonomy for females, though still under the law of the father and of the Father.

We might now add a footnote to Bell's observations. It makes sense that many of these pioneer women came from relatively well-off families, and, in an age of mass illiteracy, many were literate or, like Catherine of Siena, were willing to learn to read and write. Some of the torments suffered by them were continuations of fantasies associated with demonic possession. But once a penitential model, such as Clare's, has been created, it would provide an avenue for emulation, such that other women, not necessarily well-off ones, could now channel their frustrations and needs for spiritual fulfillment into saintly or holy aspirations. And women could also channel a demonic affliction, wherever it existed, into a divine one, into a salvific idiom consonant with their Christian heritage just like my Buddhist priestesses and just like the women in early Buddhism who flocked to the new nuns' order created in the time of the Buddha.

One of the earliest of Dominican virtuosos was Benvenuta Bojani (born 1255) who around the age of twelve flagellated herself with a chain and suffered from incubi and demonic attacks, as were her sisters possessed exclusively by demons in the Italy of her time (HA, 128). But other practices suggest that her asceticism, like Catherine of Siena's, was modeled on that of the desert fathers. She lived at home and had a loving father to whom she was devoted. Nevertheless, at age twelve she wore a hair shirt, which she kept on for six years continually, sleeping on the bare ground with a rock as a pillow and engaging in forty-day fasts, living mostly on bread and water. At age twelve many in her society would marry or prepare for marriage. Tying her ribs with an iron chain (also used for flagellation) and wrapping her hips with cords suggest not only ascetic practices but also simultaneous attempts to suppress her sexual desires, which nevertheless begin to resurface in incubus fantasies. Even in Benvenuta's time, as in ours, there were plenty of ordinary people, I am sure, who had erotic dreams and did not give them incubus interpretations. But, if you were a nun or a religiously devoted woman, the very moment a personal fantasy is expressed in a dream it is given a demonic or incubus interpretation; once that initial interpretation is made, other demonic or incubus infestations follow. Although it is impossible to assess the psychodynamics underlying Benvenuta's torments, Bell rightfully diagnoses some crucial dates, one of them being the death of her father, in 1275, when she was twenty-five and practicing a starvation diet during a five-year period. A remarkable thing happened then: Saint Dominic appeared before her, a substitute father figure, and urged her to get up. She was cured of all her ailments, and when her relatives offered her a heaping bowl of rice in a rich almond sauce, she ate it happily and did not regurgitate (HA, 128–29). But, after a promised pilgrimage to Dominic's tomb in Bologna, she joined a Dominican convent, and, under its harsh regime and patripotestal authority she reverted to her ascetic practices and died of willful starvation.

Even in this early example anorexia is but one strand in a larger complex of ascetic practices, and as the times progressed these features increased, both the

negative ones pertaining to self-punishment and the positive practices that ultimately led to love of Jesus, marriage, and final union with him after death, when
the unquiet spirit finally finds rest in him. One might say that anorectic symptoms have nothing whatsoever to do with the woman's search for autonomy in
the face of patriarchal authority. Rather it is her religious vocation, the path to
salvation through Christ's love that releases her from those bonds. It is a path
strewn with multiple practices and fantastic imaginings that one has to consider
as a symbolic totality: starvation, flagellation, and other forms of bodily mortification, visions and dream-visions, especially of the Passion, devil afflictions,
stigmata, a hyperevaluation of the Eucharist, seeking Christ's love and striving
toward divine marriage, and, for many, ecstatic rapture, without which visions
had little public appeal. Except for starvation, none of these symbolic formations
even remotely connect with contemporary anorexia nervosa, though obviously
there are family resemblances on the symptomatic level, which we have already
mentioned. It is true that in both the sufferer becomes skin and bone, but in the
case of religious women it is not weight loss but drying up of the body owing to
lack of nourishment that is both a physical reality and a symbolic one, a dryness
of the spirit or soul.

The dry spirit might well become moist with a drop of Christ's blood, but I am
interested primarily in the interplay between the dry body and the dry spirit
clearly seen in our female penitents. Physically speaking, in both anorectics and
religious women the menstrual flow has dried up; and in the conscious or unconscious imaginings of the latter there is a drying up of the sexual drive and reproductive capacity. I believe that among male virtuosos there is a similar drying
up of the sexual drive and a sense of being symbolically castrated, a deadness of
spirit and a loss of creativity, bringing with it a cry of pain beautifully illustrated
in Gerard Manley Hopkins's plea to God to send forth rain, a cry that God answers
by replenishing Hopkins's creative urge through the very act of writing a poem
deploring its loss.

> See, banks and brakes
> Now, leavèd how thick! lacèd they are again
> With fretty chervil, look, and fresh wind shakes
> Them; birds build—but not I build; no, but strain,
> Time's eunuch, and not breed one work that wakes.
> Mine, O thou lord of life, send my roots rain.[19]

Dryness, aridity, and deadness, however, are not confined to women who have
courted ascetic starvation, but it is found in many female aspirants, like Julian

of Norwich, who are not in any sense anorectic. Whether suffering from mal-nourishment or not, the visionary seeks "wetness" and nourishment, not from human source but from a divine one.

REPLENISHMENT AND RAPTURE:
THE CASE OF TERESA OF AVILA

> Once drinking deep of that divinest anguish,
> How could I seek the empty world again?
> —Emily Brontë, "Remembrance"

The ideal type of a fasting female penitent is not that of Catherine of Siena and those like her who deliberately starved themselves to death. More common are the large number who might have starved for short or long periods and then overcame this tribulation and reverted to the normal Spartan meals enjoined by the Church.[20] I will therefore examine the latter type and the spiritual nour-ishment that sustained them through a saint familiar to most Western readers, Teresa of Avila (1515–1582), who lived at a time when Christian ecstatic religios-ity and rapture was already beginning to wane. To keep the discussion short I shall use extensive notes and refer the reader to easily available accounts of her spiritual progress.[21] I will also omit Teresa's political and religious activity as she successfully institutes the discalced monks and nuns of the Carmelite order, her support groups of influential confessors and wealthy layfolk, and her enlistment of the young John of the Cross into her order. My primary source is the *Book of Her Life,* which expresses in her own words her progress from childhood to her final union with God at her deathbed. Unfortunately, *Life* records her visionary experiences and raptures as recollections with little chronological or sequential continuity. I will only present a few vignettes in order to highlight the theme of dryness and replenishment, visions and rapture, as a preliminary to my later dis-cussions of the relation between these phenomena and "deep motivation."

Teresa was born March 28, 1515, in a well-to-do family of former Jews, or *con-versos,* compelled after 1485 to embrace Christianity by the Inquisition. Teresa's father's first wife died in 1507; two years later her father married a fourteen-year-old woman. Teresa had two siblings from the first marriage and ten from the second, born during a nineteen-year period. A woman's continual produc-tion of children was a common feature of the times, an extreme example being the mother of St. Catherine of Siena who produced twenty-five. Teresa claimed she was "the most loved of my father," and there was no doubt that her father was constantly concerned about her welfare (L, 55). Teresa was close to fourteen when her mother died, almost the age when her mother herself married.[22] She said, "When I began to understand what I had lost, I went afflicted before an image of our Lady and besought her with many tears to be my mother" (L, 56). I am familiar with similar reactions to bereavement from my field notes when the loss of the earthly mother is immediately followed by the gain of a divine surrogate. Teresa's case also poses an existential dilemma that sensitive young women of the time had to face: the model of motherhood with its relentless production of children combined with the prospect of a strategically arranged marriage of a sexually inexperienced girl between the ages of twelve and fifteen, often enough to a much older male.[23] Given these facts, no wonder Teresa, as many others of her time, felt that motherhood was not for her and was drawn to the religious life. "Having parents seemed to us the greatest obstacle" for realizing that goal.

Teresa was sent by her father to study in a convent school of Santa Maria de Gracia, where she gave up "bad company," the fine clothes and romantic literature she was used to, and developed a "desire for eternal things," even though she did feel an "antagonism . . . strongly within myself toward becoming a nun" (L, 61). This is not an untypical reaction because taking the veil entailed the renunciation of sex, an existential issue that every woman had to contend with. After eighteen months in the convent school, she said prayers asking God to "show me the state in which I was to serve him." Yet she still "had no desire to be a nun, and I asked God not to give me this vocation; although I also feared marriage" (L, 61). Sometimes the thought of being a nun came to her but would then go away, and she could not be persuaded to become one.

As these conflict-ridden thoughts were going on, God sent her the first illness in 1533 to "prepare me for the state that was better for me" (L, 62). The nature of the illness is not given, but she had to return to her father's house. When she was better, she was sent to her sister's and, on the way, stayed with her uncle, a virtuous person, and there she read religious books, including the letters of St. Jerome. She stayed at her uncle's for a few days, followed by two weeks at her sister's. She then began to debate within herself about her vocation, the fear of hell if she were to die, the truths she knew from childhood, such as "the nothingness of all things, the vanity of the world, and how it would soon come to an end." But she was still not "completely" inclined to be a nun, although the "religious life was the best and safest state, and so little by little I decided to force myself to accept it" (L, 63). But this wasn't easy: "I was engaged in this battle within myself for three months," reasoning further that the hardships of being a nun was not as bad as being consigned to hell. Hence it would be a good idea to live a nun's life even if it felt like purgatory because thereafter she could fulfill her heart's desire and go to heaven. She had to resist the devil and his temptations to work this out, although we are not told what these temptations were. She does mention suffering from "high fever, great fainting spells," perhaps the first intimation of a "trance-illness" (L, 63).

On her seeking her father's permission to take the habit, he replied that she could do whatever she liked after his death. Nevertheless, at age twenty-one, accompanied by one of her brothers, she entered the Convent of the Incarnation, where she had a friend, initially as a postulant. A year after, on November 2, 1536, she took the habit, ignoring her father's wish. It is not surprising that she "felt that separation so keenly that the feeling will not be greater, I think, when I die," as if "every bone in my body was being sundered."

She now used the important metaphor of "dryness" for the first time: "God changed the dryness my soul experienced into the greatest happiness" (L, 64). Here also emerges the constant invocation of the Lord for the benefit of those who (in the Inquisition) would read the text. In fact her *Life* was written with that end in view—hence the deletion of her sexual fantasies. But she also speaks of "the espousal that I entered into with you, [Jesus]," who, she says, is "my Spouse" and of whom she cannot speak without tears (L. 65). Though the formal marriage to Christ upon taking the habit was a conventional one, for those like Teresa the spousal relationship with Christ was emotionally charged and expressed intense passion and a burning love.

Teresa's change in lifestyle affected her health. "My fainting spells began to increase, and I experienced such heart pains that this frightened any who witnessed them" (L, 66). Sometimes she lost consciousness completely. Her father consulted many doctors, but when they failed he took her to a famous *curandera* in Becedas, though the purgations and "harsh cures" only tormented her for three months without curing her. She went back to her sister's, and her uncle gave her a book, *The Third Spiritual Alphabet*. "I began to take time out for solitude, and confess frequently, and to follow the path, taking the book as my master" (L, 67). She spent nine months "in this solitude" and she refrained from committing mortal sins, that is, sins that alienate one from Christ. In Teresa's time they were listed in the broad category of the seven deadly sins, but harmless sexual fantasies were probably venial sins.[24] In retrospect she says that monastic quietude permitted her to arrive at union with God, "although I did not understand what the one was or the other," a puzzling statement that attempts to link the later experience with the present (L, 67). The union was fleeting, only "the space of a Hail Mary," yet powerful enough for her to imagine it retrospectively as a time when she "trampled the world under foot." But at that time she could not find a knowledgeable confessor who would help her give meaning to her experience; and so she lived and suffered for eighteen years "in that great dryness" (L, 68). Because the books were her master, she never could begin a prayer after communion without a book. Without a book she felt the familiar "dryness"; she was full of confusion, her "thoughts ran wild," but with a book "my soul was drawn to recollection [contemplation]" and to solitude (L, 69).

The period of dryness and "blindness" while in her father's house was relieved when she found a congenial confessor, a learned theologian, Father Vincente Barron. But before this she had found another confessor who became "extremely fond" of her and felt "a strong love" for her.[25] This cleric actually confessed, informally I presume, about his fallen condition, owing to his "dealings with a woman in that same place" during a seven-year period, and yet continued with his priestly duties (L, 72). The affair was public knowledge; and Teresa "loved him deeply," although one wonders whether her love was entirely spiritual. She therefore decided to rescue her friend from the bad woman. "The unfortunate woman had put some charms in a little copper idol she asked him to wear around his neck out of love for her, and no one was influential enough to be able to take this away from him" (L, 72). She is not sure that charms have this power but nevertheless advises men to be on guard against women who "have lost their shame before God." They "can be trusted in nothing; for they will stop at nothing so as to hold on to this friendship and passion the devil has placed in them." In Teresa's case, she would not "force anyone to love me," and, although she was tempted, "the Lord has protected me from this." "But if He should have let me, I would have done the evil that in everything else I did, for there is nothing trustworthy in me" (L, 73).

Teresa now set about reforming her errant priest. She persuaded him to give her the little idol which she threw into a river. The man then awoke from his deluded slumber and "began to abhor the woman," assisted by the Virgin herself, thought Teresa. "Finally, he stopped seeing this woman entirely," which surely meant that even when he had abhorred her he did go to see her! "Exactly one year from the first day I met him, he died." She then reports some important stuff: "He was very devoted to the service of God, for I never thought that the great affection he bore me was wrong, although it could have been more pure." This is a wonderful understatement, implicitly clarified in the next sentence: "But there were also occasions on which, if we had not remaind [sic] very much in God's presence, there would have been more serious offenses" (L, 73). The possibility that her sin could have been a mortal one meant that Teresa must learn to avoid such a calamity.

The *Life* is a public document written under the shadow of the Inquisition and several autos-da-fé. She is careful not to publicize her hidden thoughts, but it seems that Teresa's feeling around age twenty-four for the errant cleric had a strong erotic component. I have already pointed out that religious virtuosos do not accept accident, coincidence, and chance. Therefore it is hard to believe that she did not see the connection between her throwing the bad woman's magic idol into the river and the death of her loved cleric soon after, given the popular beliefs of her time regarding the deadly nature of magic charms. She probably held herself responsible for his death.

The starvation regime and the dejection that follows makes sense in terms of her guilt feelings in relation to leaving her father, whom she loved and who loved her in turn, and, alongside this, the priest's death and her conscious or unconscious recognition of sinful longings. "After two months, because of the potent medicines, my life was almost at an end. The severity of the heart pains, which I went to have cured, was more acute. For sometimes it seemed that sharp teeth were biting into me, so much so it was feared I had rabies. With the continuous fever and the great lack of strength (for because of nausea I wasn't able to eat anything, only drink), I was so shriveled and wasted away (because for almost a month they gave me a daily purge) that my nerves began to shrink causing such unbearable pains that I found no rest either by day or by night—a very deep sadness" (L, 74). Heart pains have an obvious double significance, and the sharp teeth biting into her is self-punishment for her guilt feelings. The vomiting and the starvation that followed is not a voluntary thing, at this point at least, but a form of self-punishment and a literal and psychic catharsis. Further, her body emaciation and dryness was intensified by the medical treatment of daily purges that, I take it, was a way of getting rid of bodily, if not psychic impurities. Thanks to the Lord, she patiently bore these "excruciating pains" for three months, especially by recollecting Job's plight. She wanted to go to confession, but her father forbade it, feeling that the strain of it would be too much. Confession surely would have alleviated her guilt. Hence it is not surprising that very "night I suffered a paroxysm in which I remained for four days, or a little less, without any feeling" that is, one might say, in a state of dryness of body and soul (L, 75).

This was August 15–19, 1539, when she was still young, twenty-four. Those around her sensed her impending death; the priests gave her the sacrament of anointing the sick; others recited the Creed and placed wax on her lids, a local custom of closing the eyes of someone dead or dying. And the grave was all ready in her convent for receiving her body. But the Lord allowed her to regain consciousness, to awaken from the seeming death. Now there was no way her father was going to refuse permission to confess. During the previous paroxysm, she said, "I suffered within myself: my tongue, bitten to pieces; my throat unable to let even water pass down . . . ; everything seeming to be disjointed; the greatest confusion in my head; all shriveled and drawn together in a ball." She could not stir during this period and was "unable to move as though I was dead; only one finger on my right hand it seems I was able to move. Since there was no way of touching me, because I was so bruised that I couldn't endure it, they moved me about in a sheet, one of the nuns at one end and another at the other" (L, 76). Remember, she was only dimly aware of these events, which were probably reported to her by others. Teresa being carried in sheets is another expression of the image of dying, that is, she is being wrapped in winding sheets. But her father, sorrowful of his daughter's condition, now relented, and she confessed her sins with tears, and soon enough his majesty brought her back to life.

I think Teresa addressing Jesus as "his majesty" is significant because at this time she sees him primarily in his divine persona as the son of God and not as the son of man, though, in fact, Jesus intrinsically possesses two natures as both god and man. Teresa got the faithful to bring her back into the convent at the end of August 1539. "The one they expected to be brought back dead they received alive; but the body worse than dead was a pity to behold" because she was "only bones" (L, 77). She was past danger of death but she was still not awakened because, though restored to life by God, her aches, chills, fevers continued. Although her bodily paralysis gradually got better, it lasted almost three years (from the mid-1539 till about April 1542). At this time apparently she regressed into childhood: "When I began to go about on hands and knees, I praised God" (L, 77). This is both an act of abnegation and an act of rebirth as God's child.

Because the doctors of earth could not cure her, she went to the doctors of heaven, she says (L, 79). And in this dire time she asked the help of St. Joseph, to whom Jesus himself was subject while he lived on earth. "It is an amazing thing the great many favors God has granted me through the mediation of this blessed saint, the dangers I was freed from both body and soul" (L, 79). Yet her physical troubles continued as did her obsession with sins, though they were, as always, never specified. She speaks of her going from "pastime to pastime, from vanity to vanity . . . to place myself in very serious occasions, and to allow my soul to become spoiled by many vanities [and because] the sins increased I began to lose joy in virtuous things and my taste for them. I saw very clearly, my Lord, that these were failing me because I was failing You" (L, 82).

These failings were the work of the devil, a standard attempt to foist blame on this demonic other for one's own feelings of guilt. Teresa even began to fear the practice of prayer. Her actions indicate a lot of the self-blame one associates with guilt, and, like virtually all Christian visionary texts, hers are peppered with self-recrimination. She says she was "wicked" and "among the worst" and that she merited being with the devils. She felt she was deceiving people, though "exteriorly I kept up such good appearances." Hence others thought she was good because she spent time in solitude to pray and read, speaking much about God and giving "the appearance of virtue" (L, 83). As a result she was given a lot of freedom in the monastery. Although others gave messages through holes in the wall or acted without permission, Teresa did not because "the Lord held me by His hand." She felt that this monastery was too open and "it did me great harm not to be in an enclosed monastery" (which was her aim in later founding the discalced order of the Carmelites). And she generalizes: "the monastery of women that allows freedom is a tremendous danger" (L, 83). It is dangerous for parents to put girls in monasteries of this sort (obliquely she means the Incarnation) because if she had bad desires she would not be able to conceal them for long at home but she could do so in the monastery. Why? "For youthfulness, sensuality, and the devil incite them and make them prone to follow after things that are of the very world." Again she is obliquely speaking of herself (L, 84).

Now we have a clue about her hidden guilt. "While I was once with a person, the Lord at the outset of our acquaintance desired to make me understand that those friendships were not proper for me and to counsel me and give me advice in the midst of such thorough blindness. With great severity, Christ appeared before me, making me understand what He regretted about the friendship. I saw Him with the eyes of my soul more clearly than I could have with the eyes of my body. And this vision left such an impression on me that, though more than twenty-six years have gone by, it seems to me it is still present. I was left very frightened and disturbed, and didn't want to see that person any more" (L, 85–86). Teresa did not identity this person, but the devil presumably knew and began to cause her more trouble, especially because he was a "married gentleman."[26] Satan urged her to continue with her temptations by "assuring me that it was not wrong to see such a person and that I was not losing my honor but rather it was increasing" (L, 86). This conversation with the devil can be seen as an on-and-off inner conversation with her own self. Teresa confesses to us that the experience with the devil felt like a "copy of hell" (L, 259).[27] About her "friend," Teresa says in retrospect that she engaged in this "noxious form of recreation," and it did not seem bad to her, "although sometimes I saw that clearly it was not good. But no other friendship was as much a distraction to me as this one of which I am speaking, for I was extremely fond of it" (L, 86). Her unconscious fears and dread are manifest in the next few lines. "Once at another time, when with this same person, we saw coming toward us—and others who were there saw it—something that looked like a large toad, moving much more quickly than toads do. In that part where it came from I cannot understand how there could have been a nasty little creature like that in the middle of the day, nor had there ever been one there before." While the effect of this apparition was not without mystery, she says, she missed its significance at that time, namely, that God "was warning me in every way, and how little it benefited me" (L, 86). The incident of the toad surely illustrates the tendency of religious virtuosos everywhere to give ordinary events extraordinary significance. In this case an ordinary creature becomes the devil in disguise or someone sent by him. In addition to the toady creature, she was also warned about this relationship by an older nun, a relative of hers, but this too had little effect.

Unlike her former relationship, this one endured; and she endured the guilt that sprang from it. Teresa does not give a continuous narrative of this relationship, and we have to put it together from her *Life*. She says that she voyaged in this "tempestuous sea" for twenty years but couldn't achieve the perfection she sought because she did not pay attention to venial sins. As for mortal sins, "though I feared them, I did not fear them as I should have since I did not turn away from the dangers" (L, 94). Her attachment to the world disturbed her; and she sees her conflicts as a troublesome war. "So, save for the year I mentioned [the one year which she avoided offending the Lord], for more than eighteen of the twenty-eight years since I began prayer, I suffered this battle and conflict between friendship with God and friendship with the world" (L, 95). Thus, it should not surprise us when she says: "for twenty years I had vomiting spells every morning so that I could not eat anything until after noon; sometimes I had to wait longer. From the time I began to receive Communion more frequently, I have had to vomit at night before going to bed. And it is the more painful because I have to induce it with a feather or some other thing, for if I let this go the sickness I have becomes very bad. I am almost never, in my opinion, without many pains, and sometimes very severe ones, especially in the heart, although the sickness that gripped me almost continually occurs very seldom" (L, 88).

This is a difficult text. First, the vomiting every morning might reflect "holy anorexia," but it might also be an unconscious wish to simulate pregnancy and morning sickness, probably based on the wish to be impregnated by the "lover" to whom she was attracted for nearly twenty years, the very period of the vomiting. It is not entirely clear why she should induce vomiting after she receives communion; but it is likely her resistance is at work because she is throwing out the blood and body of Christ, the one medicine that could cure her "dryness" by infusing her body with divine grace and helping her get over her erotic desire for the married friend. Or it could be purely cathartic in a psychological sense, a continual purgation of guilt feelings that would not go away.

In this situation it is not surprising that the Lord himself lends a hand, as she describes in chapter 9. One day she saw a statue of the wounded Christ, and she was keenly aware of his wounds and suffering. "My heart broke." She threw herself before Christ and "said I would not rise from there until He granted what I was begging Him for." And from that time her illness improved. Her method of prayer was not to think discursively with the intellect but to represent Christ within herself. Her "simple thoughts" were that she was alone and afflicted and Jesus had to accept her (L, 101). She now rationalizes her own situation by saying that "this torment is a characteristic of the method in which you proceed without discursive reflection on the part of the intellect. . . . Those who follow this path of no discursive reflection will find that a book can be a help for recollecting oneself quickly. It helped me also to look at fields, or water, or flowers. In these things I found a remembrance of the Creator" (L, 102). These are the symbols of generation that I think are opposed to the "great dryness" she feels within her (L, 104).[28]

The real cure of her sick body and soul came with the raptures she experiences, the very first one transporting her to a state of bliss. This occurred sometime during 1556, when she was around forty-one (or 1558 at age forty-three). "One day, having spent a long time in prayer and begging the Lord to help me please Him in all things, I began the hymn [*Veni Creator*]; while saying it, a rapture came upon me so suddenly that it almost carried me out of myself. It was something I could not doubt, because it was very obvious. It was the first time the Lord granted me this favor of rapture. I heard these words: 'No longer do I want you to converse with men but with angels,'" implicitly informing her to give up for good her attachment to the "gentleman" she had favored and to suggest further that her confessors (most of whom she did not like) no longer mattered. "This experience terrified me because the movement of the soul was powerful and these words were spoken to me deep within the spirit; so it frightened me— although on the other hand I felt a great consolation when the fear that, I think, was caused by the novelty of the experience left me" (L, 211). She says that she resisted these raptures from emerging for two years, until God communicated his wish that she accept them, not through her bodily ears that permitted her to hear his actual voice but to her soul, silently. It is perhaps during this period of resistance that the devil once again appeared to her, although it is not possible to fix dates accurately in Teresa's retrospective *Life*.[29] While she sometimes continued to resist the call to rapture, she had to finally accept the terrifying reality of that experience. She is giving up one form of love (a guilt-ridden one) for another, an obviously more satisfying experience for a nun. "These words have been fulfilled, for I have never again been able to tie myself to any friendship or to find consolation in or bear particular love for any other persons than those I understand love Him and strive to serve Him; nor is it in my power to do so, nor does it matter whether they are friends or relatives. If I am not aware that the persons seek to love and serve God or to speak about prayer, it is a painful cross for me to deal with them" (L, 212). God gave her in an instant what she had been struggling to attain for many years.[30]

Then, at age forty-three, the haunting by the married gentleman or by his memories are finally annulled by the fascinating account where she is transfixed by Christ himself, very much in the guise of the pagan god of love. It seemed at times "an arrow is thrust into the deepest and most living recesses of the heart in such a way that the soul doesn't know what has happened or what it wants. It well understands that it wants God and that the arrow seems to have been dipped in a poisonous herb so that for the love of this Lord it might despise itself; and it would gladly lose its life for Him." This is the combination of "pain and glory" of the wounded soul or the "pain of love" as she calls it (L, 251). The whole body is paralyzed, but instead of the old paralysis of illness there emerges the new paralysis of ecstasy. "Rather, if one is standing, one sits down, like a person being carried from one place to another, unable even to breathe. The soul lets out some sighs—not great ones—because it can do no more; they are felt within." In these states, God sends a cherubim in actual "bodily form" to appear on her left, his face all aflame.[31] This is especially striking because she claims to follow the orthodox Augustinian position that bodily visions are heterodox and consequently she mostly experiences spiritual or "intellectual vision." "I saw in his hands a large golden dart and at the end of the iron tip there appeared to be a little fire. It seems to me this angel plunged the dart several times into my heart and that it reached deep within me. When he drew it out, I thought he was carrying off with him the deepest part of me; and he left me all on fire with great love of God. The pain was so great that it made me moan, and the sweetness this greatest pain caused me was so superabundant that there is no desire capable of taking it away; nor is the soul content with less than God." She adds that "the pain is not bodily but spiritual," even though the vision of the cherub was a bodily one (L, 252). That the pain itself was a spiritual one is reaffirmed in tranquility in her "spiritual testimonies" when she says that the "arrow is thrust into the heart, or into the soul itself" (L, 430). There she also insists that, as far as "the wounds of love" are concerned, the "pain is not in the senses, nor is the sore a physical one," but rather "it lies in the interior depths of the soul without resemblance to physical pain" (L, 430). (See the following note for a further discussion of Teresa's wounds of love.)[32]

It is not surprising then that God seals the relationship by giving her a gift as an expression of his love. "Once while I was holding the cross in my hand, for I had it on a rosary, He took it from me with His own hands; when he gave it back to me, it was made of four large stones incomparably more precious than diamonds—there is no appropriate comparison for supernatural things. . . . He told me that from then on I would see the cross in that way; and so it happened, for I didn't see the wood from which it was made but these stones. No one, however, saw this except me" (L, 249).[33]

While for Teresa, Jesus was an experienced reality, the analyst can see that Jesus is also a symbolic figure and a highly overdetermined one. The oedipal father of childhood and the older married person she loved (in fantasy at least as an oedipal father figure) could now be transferred to Jesus who is both father and lover as well as God and king, these last also at some level isomorphic with "father." But transference or displacement occurs in the context of religious rapture. Hence one might say that there is a transformation of the oedipal father—a transfiguration even—that occurs in the sublime experience of rapture, such that Jesus is not just the oedipal father but a figure invested with both feelings of physical and spiritual love, Eros and Agape, at the same time. Sublimation is something that Freud dealt with but imperfectly understood. For ecstatic nuns rapture is the crucible in which sublimation occurs and the anvil in which it is forged. To put it more literally: the rapture of the female penitent is the one realm of experience that *sublimates* the sexual drive and transfigures the original secular emotions into divine love.

In Teresa's state of intense rapture the faculties are absorbed in the soul "as though stupefied," and that state continues for up to two or three days (L, 181). This is perhaps a reference to her first rapture and to her wandering about, lost in it. As she points out in her theoretical discussions, that wandering can last a long time—days on end—quite unlike the sexual rapture of orgasm, one would think. "For most of the time the eyes are closed even though we may not desire to close them; and if they are sometimes open . . . the soul doesn't notice or advert to what it sees" (L, 180). Again: "Now when the body is in rapture it is as though dead, frequently being unable to do anything of itself. It remains in the position it was when seized by the rapture, whether standing or sitting, or whether with the hands open or closed" (L, 181). Sometimes these raptures were so great that "even though I was among people I couldn't resist them." They became openly public and a model for other aspirants. "But when this pain I'm now speaking of begins, it seems the Lord carries the soul away and places it in ecstasy; thus there is no room for pain or suffering, because joy soon enters in" (L, 251). Rapture is like the meditative trances of Buddhists in one respect at least: the very powerful experience can be normalized so that rapture can be recreated, perhaps in modulated form, during moments of prayer or contemplation. In her discussions of rapture, Teresa is trying to describe the indescribable, the numinous, as she admits herself several times, taking refuge in the standard discourse of "mystical theology." In reality the classic theorists of mystical theology did not deal with the indescribable nature of rapture but rather the indescribable nature of God. But it may be that Teresa's experience suggests that it is through rapture, or similar conditions, that one comes to believe that God himself cannot be described except in apophatic terms.[34]

After the first definitive rapture, Teresa's life was punctuated with others even unto the point of death. Sometimes she resists rapture because of the fear that she might be deceived. She describes the expense of spirit in resistance; it was like fighting with a "giant," leaving one "afterward worn out." At other times rapture was impossible to resist; she says that "it carried off my soul and usually, too, my head along with it, without my being able to hold back—and sometimes the whole body until it was raised from the ground" (L, 173–74). Her popular fame to a large extent rested on her raptures and the seemingly impossible acts of levitation, twice before witnesses.[35] On the personal level, God had taken charge of her soul, "favoring it and awakening it to His service" (L, 189). When the soul is thus awakened "evil in me disappeared, and the Lord gave me strength to break away from it" (L, 189). And more: the devil ceases to have power over her. Devils appear before her in visions or uttering obscenities, but she could throw holy water at them and control them, though not completely (L, 265). Once she saw "a large multitude of devils around me and it seemed that a great brightness encircled me, and this prevented them from reaching me" (L, 268).

The encircling brightness is a kind of maṇḍala—a very Christian form of it. She is protected by God through the magic circle and she knows that the devil has only a "little power" and "the powers of devils are nothing if these devils do not find souls cowardly and surrendered to them." Further, on the Feast of the Assumption the family of God is installed in her heart during a powerful rapture, giving her extra protection from the devil (L, 291). "It seemed to me while in this state that I saw myself vested in a white robe of shining brightness, but at first I didn't see who was clothing me in it. Afterward I saw our Lady at my right and my father St. Joseph at the left, for they were putting that robe on me," recognizing her purity and virginity by her white vestment (L, 291). Yet, she honestly recognizes that the past cannot be wholly exorcised because, on occasion, "all the vanities and weaknesses of the past were again awakening within me," and she must commend herself to God. And then there is always the confessor who can put her at peace because in her life and that of other penitents the crucial figure that guides her and validates her visions or encourages them is a male confessor, sometimes friendly, sometimes decidedly hostile.

Rapture is Teresa's forte; nothing else compares with it. Through her rapture, and those of others like her, an anguished beauty seems to bloom within her. Locutions, when they occur in rapture, have a power they ordinarily do not possess. Yet what about union with Christ, the great goal of mystical religiosity? She discusses the difference between union and rapture, both of which consists of the "elevation or flight of the spirit, or transport, which are all the same" (L, 172). "The advantage that rapture has over union is great. The rapture produces much stronger effects and causes many other phenomena. Union seems the same at the beginning, in the middle, and at the end; and it takes place in the interior of the soul. But since these other phenomena [raptures] are of a higher degree, they produce their effect both interiorly and exteriorly" (L, 172). Thus she favors rapture, owing to its intensity. "In the union, since we are upon our earth there is a remedy; though it may take pain and effort one can almost always resist" the union from occurring, but not rapture for which there is no "remedy," coming as it does with "a force so swift and powerful that one sees and feels this cloud or mighty eagle raise it up and carry it aloft on its wings" (L, 173).[36]

In Teresa's opinion, not necessarily shared by others, union takes place on earth, unless it is combined with rapture, wherein the spirit ascends toward God in a transcendental plane. Union typically occurs at communion, that key sacrament for virtually all visionaries. In communion one sees Christ or one might "know that He is present." In this condition the "soul is completely dissolved and it sees itself consumed in Christ," and this fusion of souls is the commonest form of union. And often enough for Teresa as well as other mystics Christ appears before her visual field during communion. "The Lord almost always showed Himself to me as risen, also when he appeared in the Host—except at times when He showed me His wounds in order to encourage me when I was suffering tribulation. Sometimes He appeared on the cross or in the garden, and a few times with the crown of thorns; sometimes He also appeared carrying the cross on account, as I say, of my needs and those of others. But His body was always glorified" (L, 247). Teresa's visions, whether at Mass or during raptures, seem to be almost exclusively of Jesus, not surprising given her single-minded devotion to him.

While at Mass on the feast day of St. Paul she saw Christ in his risen form "as it is in paintings, with such wonderful beauty and majesty." But, she adds, she cannot easily describe the vision "without ruining it" (L, 237–38). Even if she took years to describe it she would not be able to do so: "it surpasses everything imaginable here on earth, even just in its whiteness and splendor," so that the sun itself appears diminished (L, 239). It seems that this particular vision appeared to her in a flash as an illumination and whiteness. "God gives it so suddenly that there wouldn't even be time to open your eyes, if it were necessary to open them. For when the Lord desires to give the vision, it makes no more difference if they are opened than if they are closed; even if we do not desire to see the vision, *it is seen*" (L, 239; my emphasis).

We are back to the theme that an individual cannot consciously evoke a vision, but instead "we must look at what the Lord desires to show us, when He desires, and as He desires," suggesting that once again we are in the realm of It-thinking (L, 246). And so are God's utterances. Vision and speech come together in the best epiphanies: "And in being aware that He was speaking to me and that I was beholding that great beauty and gentleness with which He spoke those words with His most beautiful and divine mouth—and at other times beholding His severity—and strongly desiring to know the color of His eyes, or how tall He was, so that I could be able to describe these things, I never merited to see them" (L, 246–470). It is apparent that visions cannot be cognitively conjured through the conscious will or I-thinking. "Nor was I able to obtain this knowledge; rather, by trying to do so, I would lose the vision entirely" (L, 247). Again: "If we want to look at some particular thing, the vision of Christ ceases" (L, 246).

So is it with locutions, even though they don't have the power of visions. Apparently, there are two types of locution: in both God directs the locution to her passive consciousness. In the first, God makes the "intellect" become aware and understand what is said, and he makes the soul listen without distraction. But the second type of locution is more mysterious. "Even this little thing of only listening, which the soul did in the previous locution, is taken away" (L, 231). The soul simply can sit back and enjoy God's gift. Thus "the mystery of the Blessed Trinity and other sublime things are so explained that there is no theologian with whom it would not dispute in favor of the truth of these grandeurs," permitting her to bring in the unorthodox viewpoints of women at which the Church normally looked askance (L, 231).[37] In this second locution the Lord makes things known "without image or explicit words" and one does not act or do anything because "all seems to be the work of the Lord" (L, 230). Sometimes God explicates to Teresa through locutions what she sees in her visions. In both forms of locution the discursive intellect does not operate. In intellectual discourse the "words are composed" but "they are listened to" in locutions (L, 214). It should be remembered that Teresa, like other penitents, uses "intellect" both in its ordinary meaning of conscious "thinking" or the work of the active intellect and its spiritual meaning of passive receptivity of the soul.

Teresa's writings, like her locutions and visions, can come with astonishing suddenness. Thus her biographer and contemporary Diego de Yepes testifies that Teresa told him on the eve of Trinity 1577 that "God showed her in a flash the whole book" of *The Interior Castle*, Teresa's spiritual injunctions to her Carmelite nuns. The book actually was written on the suggestion of her superiors, especially Father Gracian, her confessor and supporter, as an attempt to disarm the Inquisition. Nevertheless, the idea of the book appeared in picture form before her visionary consciousness through the mirroring crystal of an interior castle. There appeared before her "a most beautiful crystal globe like a castle in which she saw seven dwelling places, and in the seventh, which was in the center, the King of Glory dwelt in the greatest splendor. From there he beautified and illumined all those dwelling places to the outer wall. The inhabitants received more light the nearer they were to the center. Outside of the castle all was darkness, with toads, vipers, and other poisonous vermin."[38] Yepes adds that this vision is also described in her *Life*, written in the 1560s, though not as specifically as she related to him. It is entirely possible that the vision of the interior castle appeared twice to her, or the interpretation I favor, namely, that the latter vision is a pictorial representation of an idea formed much earlier, another expression of what Freud called "phantasy activity," wherein prior thoughts and daytime visualizations reappear in the dream.

Fully convinced that the ideas that fill her writings come as locutions or visions, Teresa is surprised by what she writes: "I am not the one who is putting all this down." One might say that she is the passive receptacle letting herself open to visions, locutions, and auditions of God's discursive intellect.[39] Thus, in respect of Christian visions, one might say with John of the Cross that "the powers of the soul should be at rest, keeping passive, if it is to receive what God infuses," and the body, like the inmates of a house at night, must be "lulled to sleep," or, to use Breuer's term, it must be in a state of "somnolence."[40] And "nuns who worked with Teresa, some of whom appeared as witnesses at her canonization hearings, remembered that she often wrote with her eyes lifted and her pen skimming along the page, as if moved by a supernatural power."[41] Clearly knowledge obtained through visions, inspired writings, and locutions contain both accepted theological truths and newer female viewpoints that are given with a directness and vividness vastly different from conventional scholastic understanding (L 231–32). In true visions and locutions the soul "understands that the intellect is talking nonsense; it pays no attention to it, almost as it wouldn't pay any attention to a person it knows is in a frenzy," (L, 215). In this one statement Teresa destroys the voice of the active intellect in locutions and also what to her are the pseudo raptures of the frenzied female ecstatics of her time shaking their bodies outside the doors of the monasteries and in the streets of Avila.[42] The idea that locution or vision is lost through the activity of the discursive intellect brings the visionary close to Freud's hysterics who, when they rationally describe the vision, finds that it disappears "like a ghost that has been laid." Locutions and auditions also help us to understand the voices that psychotics keep on hearing, sometimes endlessly. Those also occur without the intervention of the thinking-I, but they lack public meaning and cultural intelligibility. Yet, nowadays, owing to the power of the psychiatric establishment, even culturally structured visions or auditions, for example, of demonic attack in whatever part of the world, are considered on a par with psychotic hallucinations.

ANALYSIS: DEEP MOTIVATION AND THE WORK OF CULTURE IN CHRISTIAN PENITENTIAL ECSTASY

I met the bishop on the road
And much said he and I.
'Those breasts are flat and fallen now,
Those veins must soon be dry;
Live in a heavenly mansion,
Not in some foul sty . . .'

'A woman can be proud and stiff
When on love intent;
But Love has pitched his mansion in
The place of excrement;
For nothing can be sole or whole
That has not been rent.'
—W. B. Yeats, "Crazy Jane Talks with the Bishop"

Earlier in my discussion I was critical of Rudolph Bell's diagnosis of female virtuosos of medieval Christianity suffering from holy anorexia, as much as I was critical of seeing in them the model of latter-day hysterics or any attempt to reduce the nun's rapture to the psychic infrastructure.[43] Nevertheless I am sympathetic to psychoanalysis for the insights it might provide. I, like others who employ a psychodynamic framework, cannot accept the visionaries' view of themselves as having a "true" experience. This last is the position taken by modern-day Christian thinkers in respect to Christian visions in general and of such phenomena as near-death experiences.[44] While I can empathize with the spiritual quest of visionaries of whatever religious persuasion, I am also interested in the larger issue of the role of intuitive It-thinking in a wide realm of human experience, including science and art. One cannot avoid the inescapable methodological and epistemological reality that, whether one is speaking of Buddhists and Christians (or any other expressions of the religious life), visions are for the most part culturally patterned. There is no way that a Tibetan lama can envision Christ, the Virgin Mary, and the Christian pantheon, just as there is no way that a Christian ecstatic can fly into the realms of the Tibetan treasure seekers and talk of such things as the absence of an enduring soul and of God! However, both Tibetans and Christians might see a young maiden in a dream or in a vision; the one might project into it a ḍākinī image and the other into that of the Virgin, just as the sexual tempter in a person's dream might become an incubus in both Christian and Buddhist religiosity and the devil in disguise in both. To complicate matters, visions are also historically relative: thus Jesus appears to all Christian visionaries, then and now, but then he appeared as depicted in the paintings of medieval art, whereas now he often appears as he is depicted in children's calendars and popular iconography, sometimes with blue Anglo eyes, occasionally even transparent, perhaps influenced by films, both X-Ray and cinematic.[45] To believe in the empirical reality of these visions, one would have to say, for example, that Jesus opted to appear in the manner in which he is depicted in pop art to make things simple for believers, or that Christ does not appear in his bodily form but in what Tibetan virtuosos call his "proxy form," something perfectly acceptable in Christian theology, but entailing a revision or reformulation of the Augustinian theory of imaginative, spiritual, and intellectual visions. (See book 4, note 5, for a discussion of Augustine's theories of visions.)[46] In spite of the historical and cross-cultural relativity of visions, I nevertheless believe that structural and substantive resemblances do exist and are hence amenable to nomological understanding. This is especially so when one deals with psychic realities that transcend relativism, when one is theorizing It-thinking, or when one is dealing with discourses that spill over the boundaries that religions have erected for themselves.[47]

Reading Bell, I was struck by his insightful statement in respect to his sample of holy anorectics: "Often a death in a family seems to have been crucial. The pious and trusting little girl loses someone she loves deeply; her dependency is shattered and her faith is tested. Ultimately she passes the test and visualizes her dead mother, father, brother, or sister in heaven, or in purgatory and in need of human sacrifice and prayer." She feels that it is her body that brings death and that which caused the death of a beloved. Hence she punishes her body. "It is not any single zone—oral, anal, or genital—that she becomes fixated upon, but her entire body, all of which is hopelessly corrupt and impedes not only her own salvation but that of the people she loves" (HA, 115). I can appreciate this form of analysis, though not necessarily the specifics mentioned by Bell, because my Hindu-Buddhist priestesses in *Medusa's Hair* were also faced with a terrifying reality from childhood—the betrayal of a loved one, who then dies, and takes the form of an avenging deity that eventually possesses the woman. She suffers deep pain and experiences a version of the dark night of the soul. Finally, she expiates her past, and the erstwhile kinsperson now becomes a spirit medium that helps the woman to overcome her guilt and leads her to a joyous comportment with the gods and goddesses of the pantheon. The former patient becomes a priestess and prophetess helping others to cure their psychic travail through the aid of the gods, with whom she is now in close contact. The context of the Hindu-Buddhist priestesses is different from the Christian, but not the psychic pain they suffer, which they finally overcome through a culturally specified path. I want to creatively transfer the model I employed in *Medusa's Hair* to the entirely different cultural and soteriological world of medieval Christianity and hope some insights may emerge, even if they might disturb those who believe in the literal truth value of visions rather than in their symbolic provenance.

Troubled childhoods are important for the empathetic understanding of the lives of the visionaries who appear in this essay, as Wittgenstein recognized in 1929, with uncanny insight, long before he developed his famed ambivalence to psychoanalysis: "Anyone who listens to a child's crying and understands what he hears will know that it harbors dormant psychic forces, different from anything commonly assumed. Profound rage, pain and lust for destruction."[48] Unfortunately, I do not believe there is enough data to adequately consider the childhoods of medieval Christian nuns or anyone else who appears here. Instead I want to examine the significance of the dryness of body and spirit (or deadness and barrenness for Julian of Norwich) felt by them, beginning with that which is crucially important to their spiritual welfare, the Eucharist. Consider its powerfully overdetermined meanings. There is the sociological meaning of communion as an expression of fellowship of the Christian community, and this is explicitly recognized in the communal act of consuming the flesh and blood of Christ, who was sacrificed or sacrificed himself to redeem human kind. Nevertheless, an anthropologist like me cannot resist the comparative perspective: if in some small-scale societies human sacrifice involves a select group of devotees consuming consecrated flesh infused with the spirit of a deity, this model cannot be applied to a universal religion like Christianity. It is quite impossible to transfer the model of human sacrifice or an animal stand-in for a human sacrifice, both for pragmatic and moral reasons, to the hugely expanded community of Christian worshipers that knows no tribal or national bounds. It is the god that is consumed, and the dispersal of his flesh and blood to the expanded community must of necessity be both symbolic (bread and wine) and real (the flesh and blood of the sacrificed god).[49] Further, many Christians would agree with Jacob Boehme that Christ descended from heaven to earth and that "He now poured heavenly blood into our external human blood and tinctured it with love."[50] This means that the flesh and blood of Christ carries with it the "infusion of divine grace," to use Meister Eckhart's phrase. "The bread of the sacrament is changed into the body of our Lord and, however much it many still seem like bread, it is nevertheless the body of Christ. . . . If, therefore I am changed into God and he makes me one with himself, then, by the living God, there is no distinction between us."[51] Thus there is nothing unusual in Teresa dissolving into Christ during communion or when other mystics express a union with him through the consumption of his blood and body. The only difference is that for many, communion might not have the same profound personal meaning as for our mystics, that is, their visceral sense of union with Christ. Let me now hesitantly respond to the following question: does the consumption of the blood and body of Christ have other unconscious and unstated meanings that are related to the dryness of body and soul?

The body of the penitent is dry, parched, or arid because it is starved of nutrition and the soul is dry because the "sick soul," to use William James's term, seems abandoned by God. In communion however another source of nutritive replenishment is provided by the consumption of Christ's body. The bread is transubstantiated into flesh and the starved body consumes it, physically in minute quantities but psychically not so because the bread, even though a "spiritual food," is also a life-sustaining substance.[52] Angela of Foligno (c. 1248–1309) tells us that there were occasions when the host does not taste like bread but possesses "a meat taste." "It goes down so smoothly that if I had not been told that one must swallow it right away, I would willingly hold it in my mouth for a great while. . . . As I do so [swallow it], the body of Christ goes down with this unknown taste of meat" and it creates a pleasant sensation making her shake inwardly with delight.[53] And consider Dorothy of Montau, another fasting and flagellating penitent who says that when in communion Christ "held a great banquet" in her soul or "killed a fatted calf" within her.[54] It should be remembered that our penitents are eager, even compulsive consumers of the Eucharist. True, that this form of sustenance in itself will not keep the body alive for a long time, as we know for Catherine of Siena and others who die from emaciation and loss of nutrition during a deliberately cultivated yearlong fast, even abstaining from water. But, in their cases also, it is not as if they are committing suicide, but rather hastening their final union with Christ, a fact that some can explicitly formulate, as Angela of Foligno does: "I felt so peaceful and was so filled with divine sweetness that I find no words to express my experiences; and there was also in me a desire to die. The thought that I had to go on living was a great burden because of that inexpressible sweetness, quiet, peace, and delight which I felt; and because I wanted to attain the source of this experience and not lose it—that is why I wanted to leave this world."[55]

As far as most fasting penitents are concerned, there is no evidence to suggest that, before this decision to die, they were skin and bone, even though they practiced fasting and penitence. For women like Julian, Angela of Foligno, and Teresa, the incorporation of Christ's body into one's own sustains the body, spiritually and physically, particularly if, alongside communion, a minimal consumption of ordinary food takes place or, periodically or even sporadically, a reasonable food intake. Unfortunately, the life histories can only give us rare glimpses of how this happens. Thus Marie d'Oignies (c. 1177–1213) admitted that she ate a little bread and water during her periods of food abstinence, just as the Church had ordained. But her statements often hide the fact that supplementary food intake also occurred routinely. "Eating nothing, she abstained from all food and only interrupted her fast two or three times a week so that she might refresh herself."[56] Like virtually every other fasting penitent, her physical strength too remained intact and she did not even suffer from headaches.

Hence, as I said earlier, it is owing to this spiritual nourishment that these female virtuosos are represented in paintings and by witnesses not in their anorectic persona (if I might use that term) but in their fullness of face and body or in their expression of beatitude. Consider a later penitent from Peru, Rose of Lima (born c. 1586) whose "rosy healthy-looking face was explained in testimony and hagiography as miraculous, as defying and hiding the consequences of severe mortification and fasting."[57] It is certainly true that this fullness of face was taken by hostile critics to mean surreptitious food eating. But, unlike in modern anorexia, breaking a prolonged fast or a starvation diet was not only permitted but also encouraged by the Church. One need not feel guilty for such an act. Further, whether or not some food eating has taken place surreptitiously, the body of the suffering penitent is replenished by the host, giving her face the beatific expression captured in pictorial representations and accounts by witnesses. Even pain from starvation and penance need not result in anorexia, as is evident in Marie d'Oignies, according to her hagiographer Cardinal Jacques de Vitry: "the holy Body [bread] made her fat and the life-giving blood washed and purified her."[58] Sometimes the pain and suffering of the penitent gives the soul strength, and this in turn can feed into the strength of the body. Thus Catherine of Siena noted in her profound work, *The Dialogue*, that God himself told her that it is not "pain that troubles or shrivels up the soul. On the contrary, it makes her grow fat."[59]

Bread that is transubstantiated is then a personal symbol for our mystics, a symbol that operates simultaneously on both the cultural and psychic levels and is therefore hugely overdetermined in terms of meaning and motivation. Like other profound symbols, personal symbols contain a "surplus of meaning," as Paul Ricoeur points out in respect of highly charged symbolic forms.[60] If the bread-body of Christ sustains both body and spirit, then the blood of Christ is an even more powerful personal symbol for our penitents because it sustains and replenishes both body and soul—more so than bread. It is in respect to the blood of Christ that the experiences of medieval female penitents go way outside the experience of the Eucharist by ordinary Christians. For most penitents, the Eucharist is the trigger that releases their visions, particularly the initial vision, though obviously visions occur outside this context also.[61] These "showings" are, often enough, of the Passion or the wounded body of Christ, whether seen as a powerful bodily vision or as an imaginative or spiritual vision reflected in the soul. These "symbolic wounds" also become orifices that spout blood. Thus the not unusual experience of Catherine of Siena: "As so often, the Lord Himself appeared to her, determined to satisfy her, and, drawing her mouth towards the wound at His side, made a sign to her to sate herself to her heart's content on His body and blood. She did not need to be invited twice, and drank long from the rivers of life at their source in the holy side; and such sweetness ascended into her soul that she thought she must die of love."[62] As with others, she "did not know how to describe it."[63] The enraptured Angela of Foligno saw Christ on the cross and noted the purifying quality of Christ's blood, as Marie d'Oignies did before her. "He then called me to place my mouth to the wound at his side. It seemed to me that I saw and drank the blood, which was freshly flowing from his side. His intention was to make me understand that *by this blood he would cleanse me.*"[64]

Additionally there is another orifice that oozes blood, and that is Christ's sacred heart, wounded in a double sense, in the Passion and in the passion of love for the devotee, as when her confessor notes of Angela of Foligno: "Unexpectedly, the wound in the side of her beloved Jesus opened itself and in that opening she saw the heart of the Savior. In this ecstatic state she embraced the crucified Lord and felt transported on high towards heaven."[65] In one instance Jesus himself as the "Divine Doctor" informs Angela of the medicinal value of his blood: "My soul then understood that the medicine was his [Jesus's] blood and he himself was the one who administers this medicine to the sick," a reification of the medieval idea of the medical value of blood in general.[66] In Angela's case the medicine surely was effective because, during a two-year period of the dark night of the soul, when "she was always very ill and could eat very little, she was quite plump and rosy-cheeked."[67]

It is Christ's blood therefore that truly replenishes body and soul as a physically and spiritually nurturing substance—a substance, one might even say at the risk of parody, that provides a transfusion of blood through its transubstantiation. Let me present a few examples before I continue my unconventional exhumation of the symbolic meanings of the blood and wounds of Christ. Consider Julian's bodily vision, after she sensed that she was going to die before morning and that her body was "dead to all sensation from the waist down." Soon the upper part of her body also felt dead, but suddenly her shortness of breath and the failing of life ceased and she felt well, "especially in the upper part of my body" where the centers of consciousness existed. Then it occurred to her "suddenly" that she wanted Jesus to give her a second wound, so that his pain should be hers. But in reality she received from Jesus the life-sustaining blood, when, as I mentioned earlier, she saw suddenly "the red blood trickling down from under the crown of thorns, all hot, freshly, plentifully and vividly" (ST, 3:6). She describes the experience of his dying more fully a little later when she saw "God in an instant" followed by a detailed description of Christ "bleeding abundantly, hot and freshly and vividly" from the scrounging he received. "In my vision it [Christ's blood] ran so abundantly that it seemed to me that if at the moment it had been natural blood, the whole bed would have been blood-soaked and even the floor around" (ST, 8:12). And then we get some insight regarding the meaning of blood for the parched body of the woman: "God has provided us on earth with abundant water for our use and bodily refreshment, because of the tender love he has for us, yet it pleases him better that we should freely take his holy blood to wash away our sins; for there is no liquid created which he likes to give us so much, for it is so plentiful and it shares our nature" (ST, 8:12–13).[68]

Blood does what bread can never do: one cannot imagine the pieces of the broken flesh of Christ in the depiction of the Passion because, though wounded and bleeding, he must retain wholeness of the body according to popular thought and in some theological imaginings. However, imagining his flowing blood is fully consonant with the Christ mythos. Consuming that blood via the transformed wine is a much more powerful symbolic act than eating the flesh, especially for our fasting penitents. In other words, in drinking the tiny portion of wine, time and again, one is drinking the blood that drips from Christ's wounds or gushes from his bleeding heart according to the penitent's fantastically real imaginings. But can one push overdetermination even further?

Caroline Bynum, in *Jesus as Mother,* makes the important point that, for many Catholics, Christ is a mother figure, and this is part of his nontheological persona. I would say the same of the Buddha of popular imagination who can appear as Buddha the king or as Buddha the father or as Buddha the monk or as Buddha the mother. Like Christ, he also possesses a "feminine" persona. For Bynum the blood that the visionary drinks is Jesus's milk because blood in the medical literature of Europe (as it is in South Asia, I might add) is part of the process whereby the food that is ingested is converted into several substances, milk and blood among them. While this is true, the fact remains that Christ, in addition to his erotic persona, is also a nurturing figure for many, but only a few female mystics like Julian of Norwich and Catherine of Siena think of Christ explicitly as mother. And Julian herself makes the point that it is Christ's flesh and blood that nourishes her, not his milk. "The mother can give her child milk to suck, but our dear mother Jesus can feed us with himself, and he does so most generously and most tenderly with the holy sacrament which is the precious food of life itself" (LT, 60, 141). Christ has multiple human facets that constitute his several imagos. He does appear as nurturing, but the dominant image of Christ, for those engaging with him in erotic rapture, is as king and bridegroom or "his majesty" as Teresa constantly addresses him.

Jesus and the Buddha, like Padmasambhava in our earlier discussion, are male figures, but not authoritarian ones. In much of Europe, as in many patriarchal societies, the male role is generally thought of as an authoritarian one, and it is difficult to shake this image even in the contemporary West when males have taken over some nurturing roles. But, in many parts of South and Southeast Asia, and, I suspect, in places like Tibet, another nurturing model of the male prevails alongside a more authoritarian patriarchal one. When feminist scholars reify the imago of Jesus as mother, they are perhaps unwittingly perpetuating a larger patriarchal model in which the male and female roles are split and opposed to each other whereas an in-between model of nurture also prevails. It is embodied, for example, in the androgynous figures of the Buddha and the sons of the Buddha, the monks; and the many Hindu gurus idealized by the devotee.[69] These fantasized imagos feed back into the public consciousness.

It is not so much Christ's milk but the consumption of blood, directly or indirectly, through the orifices of the Lord that gives the penitent or nun courage to drink the pus of lepers or the water in which their sores are washed that converts the foul substance into a sweet-smelling one. Again, it is Angela of Foligno who expresses this beautifully when, following the example of her human ideal

St. Francis, she goes into a hospital with a convent servant and says: "We washed the feet of the women and the hands of the men, and especially those of one of the lepers which were festering and in an advanced stage of decomposition. Then we drank the very water with which we had washed him. And the drink was so sweet that, all the way home, we tasted its sweetness and it was as if we received Holy Communion."[70] When the leprous scab gets stuck in her throat, she says that "my conscience would not let me spit it out, just as I had received Holy Communion."[71] Similarly, the devil wanted to tempt Catherine of Siena's fortitude by upsetting her stomach, according to Raymond of Capua. When she was removing the bandages from a sore of a penitent, she was assailed by a stench so foul that "her inside turned over and a great sensation of nausea convulsed her stomach."[72] But this work of the devil failed because Catherine invoked the "bridegroom of her soul" and drank a bowlful of the fetid stuff, and she could say, "Never in my life have I tasted any food and drink sweeter or more exquisite."[73]

These transubstantiations of foul substances into desirable ones have to be taken seriously, and they are found in other religious traditions. In forms of Tantra the virtuoso ingests certain kinds of bodily effusions considered foul in mainline Hindu thought, such as the menstrual and sexual emissions of women. Just like the sores of lepers, these substances get converted into rich, sweet-smelling ones, into nectar in Tantra. In another instance, the five repulsive substances or acts abhorred in orthodox Hindu thought, namely, liquor, flesh, fish, parched grain (supposed to stimulate sexual desire), and sexual intercourse with a tabooed woman can be transformed through a *mantra* into nectar, and the substances are then consumed by the Tantric devotee in a conch shell along with "female discharge, and a drop of the menstrual blood of a girl in her first menses."[74]

To get back to our penitents drinking foul substances which are converted into tasty and sweet-smelling ones on the model of the Eucharist. Christ rewards Catherine of Siena for her heroic action with a plentiful supply of his own blood from *his* open wound, replenishing both her body and her soul. "And putting His right hand on her virginal neck and drawing toward the wound in His own side, He whispered to her, 'Drink, daughter, the liquid from my side, and it will fill your soul with such sweetness that its wonderful effects will be felt *even by the body* which for my sake you despised.' And she, finding herself thus near to the source of the fountain of life, put the lips of her body, but much more those of the soul, over the most holy wound, and long and eagerly and abundantly drank that indescribable and unfathomable liquid."[75] Not only is the impure substance transubstantiated, but it is cleansed by the transfusion of Christ's pure blood, converting the taste and bad smell of the former into the sweetness of the latter.

These examples remind us of an oppositional dialectic of smells that animate the olfactory senses of both Christian penitents and my Sri Lankan priestesses: the bad smells come from the devil and his disciples, from the husband or from the muck and ooze of intercourse (as Margery Kempe, the fourteenth-century English penitent puts it) and the place of excrement, whereas the sweet and fragrant scents are from the divine lover or his surrogates.[76]

The starvation diet that expresses the penitents' scorn for food also has multiple meanings. In the first place, food is a "natural symbol" that expresses a fundamental psychic reality that can be expressed in the equation food = love. Mother's milk is its primordial meaning, and food rejection by children is a well-known expression of protest against an actual or imagined deprivation of love by a parent. The young female who leaves home for the convent or cloister expresses rejection of the family and engages in a rite of passage in which she moves to a new form of life, whether veiled or not. The rejection of the family is expressed through food, the primordial symbol of parental love. And, in the Sri Lankan case I have discussed, the afflicted woman might drink "bitter milk," that is, milk mixed with a bitter medicinal leaf that is also applied on the nipple to wean children.[77] I find it fascinating to discover a similar example with Catherine of Siena, when, during her penitential fasting, she "chewed on bitter herbs while spitting out the substance" (cited in HA, 26). The significance of the bitter herb comes out indirectly in one of her letters, when she speaks of a mother who "puts something bitter on her breast so that he tastes the bitterness before the milk, so that for fear of the bitter he abandons the sweet" (HA, 33). Here again is an action that is hugely overdetermined by multiple motivations and meanings.

Food deprivation leads to dryness and, as with contemporary anorectics, with amenorrhea, which, in turn, would pose all sorts of dilemmas or psychic aporias for young nuns owing to the inability to reproduce and to menstruate, both normal female functions. It is doubtful whether this dilemma occurs for anorectics in our own times. In the Middle Ages the closed orifice is reopened in the fantasy life of mystics through a visual identification with Christ's wounded orifices and the orifice of his heart as blood flows freely from them, no longer impure menstrual blood but a pure life-giving substance, assuaging the dryness of body and soul.

I think one can extend this level of analysis to the phenomenon of rapture where, in deep trance, the penitent's soul is united with Jesus in divine marriage whose sensuousness and sensuality is captured in Bernini's famous sculpture. In spite of feminist critiques of Bernini, I think he beautifully rendered the spirit of rapture, its double meaning, which is analogous to the multiple meanings of *passion* and *union*. As scholars have noted time and again, there is only a thin line between eroticism and divine rapture, though naturally the ecstatics do not per-

4.2 Gian Lorenzo Bernini, *St. Teresa in Ecstasy* (1652). *Art Resource*

ceive rapture in quite that fashion. In my study of similar raptures among Sri Lankan priestesses, I pointed out the orgasmic nature of rapture and added that we must bridge the familiar distinction between Eros and Agape and posit that Eros *is* Agape and that Agape is Eros.[78] Can we transpose this notion into the context of medieval rapture of Christian nuns?

In dealing with the relationship between Eros and Agape, between eroticism and spirituality in rapture, it is necessary to abandon our contemporary ideas of love in the Western world, wherein lovemaking is having intercourse culminating in orgasm, along with the technologies employed to bring about mutual satisfaction in the post-Kinsey era. These ideas are remote for most of European history. Even in the last century, prior to Kinsey, "making love" mostly meant kissing or petting, not necessarily sexual intercourse, orgasmic or otherwise. In medieval Europe even romantic lovemaking was alien to the public consciousness. The European courts of love and their ideal of the unapproachable mistress was part of a man's world, removed from the realities of sexual intercourse or, perhaps, owing to the realities of sexual intercourse. It is certainly the case that some educated nuns and beguines were familiar with the romantic literature of their times. I noted that Teresa read them avidly during her adolescence, and Marguerite Porete, one of the most interesting female beguines, radically reformulated and eroticized the conventions of courtly love in her work, *The Mirror of Simple Souls,* to describe the Christ's ravishing of the soul, ending in "a state of utter selflessness, of annihilation of the will and reason."[79] Yet most female penitents were virgins who had left home for the religious life, and even those who were married in effect refrained from conjugal sexuality or were disgusted by it. An extreme case was the lay penitent Angela of Foligno. Once she gave herself to Christ, she prayed for the death of husband, mother, and children and was consoled when this happened, apparently following in deadly literalness the injunction in Luke 14:26, rather than the more humane version in Matthew 10:37–39: "If any *man* come to me, and hate not his father, and mother, and wife and children, and brethren, and sisters, yea, and his own life also, he cannot be my disciple."[80]

Given the unsatisfactory nature of the marital relationships, one wonders whether these women ever achieved orgasm or even knew what it meant or, for that matter, gave it thought or gave it a damn. Take the case of Teresa. She entered the convent a virgin and if, in her raptures, she achieved what *we* might call climax or orgasm, this would be totally incomprehensible to her as a purely sexual experience, not knowing what that experience meant in secular life. The so-called biological orgasm would be incomprehensible to her outside "rapture." The experience of the convolutions of the body in pleasure-pain or "delightful pain," as Teresa calls it, is integral to rapture and not to sexual orgasm, even if those of us living in a cynical age might believe that, biologically speaking, orgasm is an integral component of rapture.[81] Eros and Agape (our usage, admittedly) are fused in a single profound experience of marriage with Jesus, and that is what is meant by rapture. Moreover, rapture often enough entails the temporary "paralysis" of the body, and, however much it might resemble a hysterical conversion reaction, such a symbolic formation cannot be isolated from the totality of the penitent's experience. I would say that both hysteria and mystical ecstasy have family resemblances, but one cannot be subsumed to the other, although sexual inhibitions might underlie both expressive forms. In rapture not only is the body insensate but it is also, in extreme cases such as that of Catherine of Siena and Teresa of Avila, often associated with levitation, imagined or real. Either way the experience of levitation is surely much more powerful than the erotic dreams of flying highlighted by Freud because passion in levitation-rapture is "charged with the grandeur of God."[82] Further, as Kieckhefer says, "rapture was integrally linked with revelation."[83] While "revelatory messages" are found in both psychotics and in the hysterics discussed by us earlier, they lack cultural approval or an intersubjective consensus, that touchstone of reality by which unconventional experiences ought to be judged. And that is perhaps why Schreber and those psychotic visionaries less talented than he must in a sense remain psychotic, unable to get out of the hospital or be relabeled in more positive terms.[84]

To reiterate: the nun is Jesus's virgin bride, and this means that rapture can never be the result of sexual intercourse in any of our Christian nuns. The loss of Teresa's virginity comes a few days before her unusual death at age sixty-seven. "On the feast of St. Michael, 29 September, immediately after communion, she collapsed in bed and began to hemorrhage vaginally."[85] She was enraptured for a fourteen-hour period before dying.[86] "Earthly witnesses said that she died in ecstasy, her soul ripped away from her body by the force of God's love. The blood on her sheets, her biographer Yepes wrote, was proof of that holy consummation— and his opinion was borne out years later, when her coffin was reopened and some drops of blood on a cloth that had been buried with her were still fresh."[87] Teresa's vaginal hemorrhaging is the final consummation of a union with Jesus devoutly wished for by her and devoutly noted by her biographer and the doctors who attended on her.[88] And it is the final reopening of her dried up orifice.

The case of Teresa's final rapture or ecstatic moment forces us to consider the back-and-forth movement of sexuality and eroticism and its transformation or sublimation in our sample of Christian mystics. Borrowing terms from Paul Ricoeur, one might say that, unlike sexual ecstasy or orgasm, there is a progressive transformation or sublimation of an original sexual drive to an erotic relation with God, and there are degrees of symbolic remove from the original drive to a sublime relation with him where the erotic charge is *progressively* converted into a religious charge.[89] Thus Angela of Foligno echoes what many other female visionaries felt: "At times it seems to my soul that it enters Christ's side, as this is a source of great joy and delight; it is indeed such a joyful experience to move into Christ's side that in *no way can I express it and put words to it*." When she saw the suffering of Christ, depicted in a Passion play, "I was miraculously drawn into a state of such delight that when I began to feel the impact of this indescribable experience of God, I lost the power of speech and fell on the ground. . . . I lay there on the ground; my power of speech and use of my members was gone. It seemed to me that I had indeed entered at that moment within the side of Christ. All sadness was gone and my joy was so great that *nothing can be said about it*" owing to the ineffable nature of that experience.[90] During the dark night of the soul, the devil will tempt the saint with sexual desires and seductive pantomimes, in which case there could be a reversal or a regression to sexual desire or a threat that it might happen. The penitent then tries to bring the demonic temptations under control and with it to a progressive movement of sublimation once again. Failure of the work of sublimation must surely have occurred time and again in the lives of many nuns whose biographies do not appear in this essay.

Let me now come back to the symbolism of Jesus's blood. Because it replenishes the soul and the body, it is drunk from Christ's wounds in fantastic imaginings and it is consumed in the Eucharist. Underlying it is the idea of blood as a healing elixir, well established in medieval European medicine.[91] And, most of all, one might say that the dryness of body and soul is a cue that releases the vision of the Passion, itself a culturally acceptable symbol that has a standard past and present, yet having deep motivational significance for the visionary, drenching her roots with rain. As Raymond of Capua observes of that compulsive consumer of the Eucharist, Catherine of Siena: she was "dry to look at but inwardly watered by rivers of living water and at all times full of life and happiness."[92] Yet none of these listings make sense except through the crucial act of "union" with Christ, in whatever manner that union is expressed, because it is union, merging, dissolving into the Other that permits the mystic to transform what one might call a "symptom" into a personal symbol, operating simultaneously on the level of culture and psyche. And the deepest expression of union with Christ is through rapture. I shall now explore even further the significance of *union* in the generation of "symbolic wounds" once again, this time moving to flagellation, the wounding of the body, and the stigmata.

I start with the meaning of union, not exclusively as divine marriage but as identification with Christ. In union the woman identifies with Christ without losing her own separate identity, which is also true of the marital sense of union. This is neatly put by God the Father himself to Catherine of Siena, when he says that Paul "had experienced what is to enjoy me without the weight of the body, because I made him experience it through the sense of union without actually being separated from his body."[93] When the union becomes intense, one is merged or dissolved into Christ, and it is here that the true mystical experience in Christianity occurs. This is what I suppose Thomas Merton meant when he says that although the two loves have "merged into one . . . the human soul and God, remain ever and absolutely distinct."[94] The ineffability of this experience of merging cannot be put into discursive language and hence the ecstatic has to depend on the language of mystical theology inherited from Pseudo-Dionysius. When one "identifies" with Christ, in our sense of that term, it is possible for the mystic to feel through her passion for Christ the other-passion of his wounds. Thus, cutting up of one's body in flagellation and the miracle of the stigmata, whether as actual opening of the body through wounds, an imagined opening like Catherine of Siena's stigmata, or a spiritual opening in the soul or in one's inner being, must, I think, be seen in relation to the woman's identification with Christ.[95]

Nevertheless, both fair and foul inhere in the symbolism of saint's self-inflicted wounds with their "surpluses of meaning." One can therefore say that the wounds of love are overdetermined by multiple motivations and meanings such that one cannot see them as organized in a logic-tight or rational manner, even though *we* can unscramble the meanings that inhere in the symbol or symbolic field though our logical and rational techniques. That is, *contradictory* meanings can inhere in the symbolic formation because these meanings emerge from different cultural, theological, and psychic domains and then converge together in the wounded body of the penitent. Take the case of flagellation. By flagellation I am identified with the sufferings of Christ who suffered for our sins; hence I punish my body as Christ suffered, although on my part it can also be a kind of penance for sinning. I might be possessed by the devil, who tempts me with sexual fantasies; hence by flagellating my body I am not only punishing the demons inhabiting it but also punishing myself for sinful desires. But other meanings and motivations coexist with the preceding ones, either separately or to form a complex. For example: the idea of unconsciously recognized sin can be related to the masochistic wishes of a repressed woman unable to seek a direct outlet for sexual desire. Finally, something even more significant occurs when flagellation entails wounding the body and bloodletting, which, I think, can, at least in many cases, be related to the deep motivation of the sufferer.

Raymond of Capua asked Catherine of Siena why she "disciplined herself with an iron chain three times a day." He soon found out: "When I asked her privately how she did this penance she confessed with some embarrassment that she took an hour and a half over each application, and that the blood used to run down from her shoulders to her feet."[96] Bloodletting is both real and imagined, as is Christ's flagellation, which produces streams of blood. So it is with the stigmata, where the five wounds of Christ, or a smaller number, reappear on the body of the woman and sometimes on that of the man, as in the prototypical case of St Francis. I suggest that these symbolic wounds, with their interpenetrating and nondiscursively organized meanings and motivations, can again be related to the dryness or aridity of the parched body, especially the clogged orifice of the mystic.[97] The dried up orifice is reopened in the wounds, deliberately inflicted or unconsciously reproduced in the body as stigmata.[98] Put in psychoanalytic terms, closed vaginal and womb orifices are displaced onto other parts of the penitent's body and her impure menstrual blood is released through the newly created bodily openings, just as in medieval physical medicine bad blood is released by bloodletting and leeching.[99] These elements of unconscious meanings and motivations cannot be separated from the ingestion of Christ's blood in communion and in the wounds of the Passion, including his bleeding heart that can fill the mystic's body with pure blood to replenish the impure pseudo-menstrual flow from the mystic's wounded body. To repeat the words attributed to Marie d'Oignies, "the life-giving blood washed and purified her" as it did everyone else. And this includes male mystics like Henry Suso (d. 1366), who, on a visit to a convent, spoke in the third person of his childlike devotion to Christ and then: "When the Servant [Henry Suso] was in the flower of his youth it was his long continued custom, when he was bled by the surgeon, to go at once to his beloved God on the cross. There he raised his wounded arm, and said with a deep sigh: 'Ah, Friend of my heart, remember that it is the custom for a man to go to his beloved when he has been bled, for some good blood. Now Thou knowest, dear Lord, that I have no other beloved than Thee. Therefore, I come to thee, so that Thou mayest bless my wound and make good blood for me.'"[100] Not quite what our female penitents wanted, but close.

With Suso we are back to the theme of medieval physical medicine where bad blood is released by bloodletting and leeching and then purified by Christ's good blood, his good will, and the flow of his sacraments. But bleeding cannot be performed on fasting women without endangering their lives, and, as we already know from Teresa's experience, even giving emetics can shrink the nerves, "causing such unbearable pains" (L, 174). Hence these women must resort to the fantastic leeching of blood through their imagined or real wounds. These elements of unconscious meanings and motivations circle back into the symbolism of the wounds, although the sum of the symbolic elements I have listed are not exhaustive, and, even if they were, they do not total or add up to the existential significance of the mystical experience for the protagonist. Just as it is not possible to wander into the labyrinth of another culture without being lost, so it is with attempts to enter into the hidden recesses of another's being.

HISTORICAL TABLEAUX: THE PARTICIPATORY
VISUALIZATIONS OF MARGERY KEMPE

Ah! how they scourge me! yet my tenderness
Doubles each lash; and yet their bitterness
Winds up my grief to mysteriousness;
    Was ever grief like mine? . . .

Nay, after death their spite shall further go;
For they will pierce my side, I full well know;
That as sin came, so Sacraments might flow;
    Was ever grief like mine?

But now I die; now all is finished.
My woe, man's weal; and now I bow my head.
Only let others say, when I am dead,
    Never was grief like mine.

—George Herbert, "The Sacrifice"

Margery Kempe provides a fascinating contrast from the fasting or ascetic visionaries of the previous discussion. She was born around 1373 in King's Lynn, a medieval port in Norfolk. Because she could neither read nor write, she dictated her "autobiography" to her amanuensis, a priest-scribe who was not always sympathetic to her spiritual quest. Perhaps because the text was dictated, she appears in the third person and is generally referred to as "this creature." Although *The Book of Margery Kempe* is inevitably interspersed with the comments of her scribe, critics generally agree it is her voice that is primarily heard in the text.[101] What is uniquely characteristic of Margery's relation to Jesus is her continual weeping and crying whenever she recollects his Passion.[102] I will deal with the events of her life in the next section but now focus on the historical tableaux or showings that depict her presence and participation in the life of the family of God.

Christ first gave Margery the gift of meditation and contemplation when he tells her to call him "Jesus, my love" and to desist from eating meat and instead consume his own flesh in the Eucharist (MK, 51). I shall deal with these events more fully later, but for now mention that Margery had no prior experience of meditation. She therefore asks him, "Jesus, what shall I think about?" for purposes of contemplation. Jesus urges her to think of his mother, "the cause of all grace that you have." And, sure enough, "at once she saw St Anne, great with child, and then she prayed St Anne to let her be her maid and her servant" (MK, 52). And, when Mary was born, it was Margery who looked after the child until she was twelve, serving her good food and drink and also "with fair white clothing and white kerchiefs," reminiscent, I might say, of the white clothes that Margery herself wore later. And it was Margery who informed Mary, "My Lady, you shall be the mother of God" (MK, 52–53). We now have a fascinating scenario: "The blessed child went away for a certain time—the creature remaining still in contemplation—and said, 'Daughter, now I have become the mother of God.'" I take it that, while Margery was in contemplation or meditation, the child Mary moved from the "dream-screen," as it were, and, when Mary returned to the screen (perhaps when Margery also returned to meditate after a recess), Mary was much older and had been impregnated by the Holy Ghost. Once again, Margery was witness to that great event. She fell down on her knees, saying, "I am not worthy, my lady, to do you service." But Mary urged her to continue and follow her.

"Then she went forth with our Lady and with Joseph, bearing with her a flask of wine sweetened with honey and spices. Then they went forth to Elizabeth, St. John the Baptist's mother, and when they met together Mary and Elizabeth reverenced each other, and so they dwelled together with great grace and gladness for twelve weeks. And then St John was born, and our Lady took him up from the ground with all reverence and gave him to his mother, saying of him that he would be a holy man, and blessed him." During the period when Margery was serving them, Elizabeth, reiterating similar sentiments made by Mary earlier, said, "Daughter, it seems to me that you do your duty very well." After this Margery went with Mary to Bethlehem "and procured lodgings for her every night with great reverence, and our Lady was received with good cheer" (MK, 53). And consider her role in the very birth of Jesus. She begged of Mary to give her white cloths and kerchiefs to swaddle her son, and when Jesus was born "she arranged bedding for our Lady to lie on with her blessed son. And later she begged food for our Lady and her blessed child. Afterwards she swaddled him weeping bitter tears of compassion, mindful of the painful death that he would suffer for the love of sinful men, saying to him 'Lord, I shall treat you gently; I will not bind you tightly. I pray you not to be displeased with me'" (MK, 53–54).

It seems that the history in which Margery participates triggers her compulsion to weep. Thus, on the twelfth day when the three kings came to worship Christ, "our Lady's handmaiden, *beholding the whole process in contemplation*, wept marvelously sorely." And, when the Magi wished to leave, "she cried so grievously that it was amazing." Later, when an angel commanded Mary and Joseph to leave for Egypt, she went with them, helping them to find lodgings day by day and "sometimes continuing weeping for two hours and often longer without ceasing when in the mind of our Lord's passion" and of her own sins. And, in true Christian fashion, she also wept for souls in distress and those in purgatory. At other times she wept "very abundantly and violently out of desire for the bliss of heaven, and because she was kept from it for so long" (MK, 54; my emphasis).

What is truly unique about Margery's visions is that they are more like the Hindu dream texts discussed by Wendy Doniger where time past and time present, and sometimes time future, are enfolded in the experience of the dreamer.[103] In Margery's case contemplation transports her to the past of the divine family and she becomes a participant in the birth of Mary and of Christ, though no reference is made to her being present at his death in this first tableau. Her visualizations are based on late medieval Christian models combined with her own inventiveness and perhaps with other popular background beliefs of her time. Franciscans encouraged visualizations of Christological history, even when they seem to go counter to the Gospels.[104] The exemplary model is St Francis, who had a vision of the bleeding Christ and then imitated Christ's wounds through his own stigmata, becoming, in effect, Jesus bleeding on the Cross. This is a strict imitation of Christ, though most people simply imitated his moral virtues and simplicity of living. Margery's case follows popular visualizations in mimicking and imaginatively reconstructing the past and often reinventing it.

Bonaventure himself encouraged popular visualizations of the life of Christ and the Passion in his own *Lignum Vitae,* or *Tree of Life,* where he urges the meditator not only to visualize events from the past but to actually participate in them imaginatively. Bonaventure does not, however, speak of visions; rather, one conjures past events in the mind or in the soul, but these are only highly developed forms of "normal visualization" wherein we shut our eyes and see in our mind's eye those persons and events we think or fantasize about.[105] His injunctions are repeated and further elaborated in detail (alongside additions to the Gospels based on popular Christianity) in handbooks, the most important being *Meditations on the Life of Christ,* once attributed to Bonaventure himself and having a greater impact on popular penitents than anything that he wrote.[106] It urges a nun affiliated with the Poor Clare's to contemplate Christ's life and crucifixion and then visualize it. Yet it goes beyond this stated goal and beyond Bonaventure's own examples to include inventions and reinventions of the past derived from popular religiosity and from pictorial representations in late medieval religiosity. Here are some of the scenarios that the penitent might visualize: the Virgin at the birth of John the Baptist, the ox on the journey to Bethlehem, the saddle and the column of the nativity, the adoration of the Magi and kissing the foot of the Christ child, and the whole Passion cycle.[107] It is not clear from the text whether this empathetic involvement in Christ's life might come from what one could call "normal visualization" or whether it also suggests that normal visualization combined with meditation or contemplation would lead the penitent to an actual vision. What is clear is that Margery Kempe not only recreated the histories found in *Meditations* but also added her own versions of history by the very act of being present in the past and witnessing events not mentioned in the Gospels.

There is no doubt that Margery's visions are also "showings," and therefore it might be instructive to compare her historical tableaux with that of her distinguished contemporary Julian of Norwich, whom she had met and whose work she had probably heard about. Julian also is shown the actual Passion of Christ in a bodily vision, but she does not claim she was present at the scene. Instead the original scene is recreated or represented as it actually occurred in the past through God's grace. The case closest to Margery's, as far as I know, is that of her illustrious predecessor Henry Suso, who participated in Christ's suffering by witnessing it and imitating it without ever being a participant in the Christological history.[108] Although Margery was once temporarily jailed for heresy and later suspected of Lollardism, her visions, like Julian's bodily ones, did not receive official condemnation. Like those before and after her, they were powerful ones, even though she does not explicitly describe them as something seen with the immediacy of her bodily eye, nor does she deny bodily visions that form this first tableau. It is God's gift of meditation that gives her access to that history. Nevertheless, one might ask: how could Margery have been a participant in it unless it was a bodily one?

Toward the end of the book (in chapter 78), we are told that for many years on Palm Sunday she had similar experiences "as *though* she had been at that time in Jerusalem, and seen our Lord in his manhood received by the people as he was while he went about here on earth" (224–25; my emphasis). In the earlier tableau she makes no such qualification; she was physically present at the scene of the nativity through Jesus's gift of meditation. But in this second series we are told very clearly that hers was not a bodily vision but a "spiritual sight." We are soon informed that her visions are refracted "in the sight of her soul," the locus of her spiritual sight whereby she has a vision of Christ's passion in the uttermost detail and hears his mother's sorrowful words: "Now, dear son, if you have no pity for yourself, have pity on your mother, for you very well know that no man can comfort me in all this world but you alone" (MK, 228). In a long dialogue between mother and son, Margery is once again reinventing history or redefining it in her own terms and that of her local culture. Perhaps it is because of the power of these historic visions that she feels the urge to get her "autobiography" written down. The visions of Christ's suffering also provide a rationale for her continual crying and lamenting, for who wouldn't if they were witnesses to the Passion?

The vivid second tableau continues after the long dialogue between mother and son. The mother and son then part; he goes to his Passion and death and his mother falls down in a faint. But what happened to Margery, who was present at the scene? "Then the said creature *thought* she took her Lord Jesus Christ by the clothes, and fell down at his feet, praying him to bless her, and with that she cried very loudly and wept very bitterly, *saying in her mind*, 'Ah, Lord, what shall become of me? I had much rather that you would slay me than let me remain in the world without you, for without you I many not stay here, Lord.'" Jesus asks her to remain here and rest with his mother and find comfort with her. He also comforts Margery with the prophecy of his return: "I shall come again, daughter, to my mother, and comfort both her and you, and turn all your sorrow into joy" (MK, 229; my emphasis). More history follows, but the qualifying word *thought* appears with greater frequency. "And then she *thought* that they followed on after our Lord, and saw how he made his prayers to his father on the Mount of Olivet, and heard the beautiful answer that came from his father, and the beautiful answer that he gave his father" (MK, 230; my emphasis). Her vision continues to unfold with Judas kissing Jesus and the Jews laying violent hands on the "lamb of innocence." "And very soon the said creature beheld with her *spiritual eye* the Jews putting a cloth before our Lord's eyes, beating him and buffeting him on the head. . . . And soon after, she saw them pull off his clothes and strip him all naked, and then drag him before them as if he had been the greatest malefactor in the world." While it is clear that she is a participatory witness of what happened in history, that history is seen through her spiritual eye, although very vivid and fresh "*as if they had been done in her bodily sight*" (MK, 231; my emphasis). In all these scenarios, and in those that follow, Mary Magdalene is both "model and rival" for Margery.[109]

These moving scenes are continued in the next chapter, for example, with Christ carrying the cross and the mother saying, "Ah, my sweet son, let me help to carry that heavy cross." And, when Margery saw the mother fall down and swoon, Margery also wept and sobbed at the "piteous sight." And once more we are given an explanation for her historical presence: "Later she went forth in contemplation" and saw "the Jews with great violence tear off of our Lord's body a cloth of silk, which had stuck and hardened so firmly and tightly to our Lord's body with his precious blood . . . and made the blood to run down all around on every side" culminating in his being nailed to the cross. Then we are switched back to the physical context of her church in England where she had these visions and where she continued to weep. Then the dream-screen moves back to the original scene when the Jews took up the cross with the Lord's body hanging on it and let it fall on the mortise so that "our Lord's body shook and shuddered, and all the joints of that blissful body burst and broke apart, and his precious wounds ran down with rivers of blood on every side, and so she had ever more reason for more weeping and sorrowing" (MK, 233).[110] And soon more qualifications:

> Then she *thought* she saw our Lady swoon and fall down and lie still. . . . Then this creature *thought* that she [Margery] ran all round the place like a mad woman, crying and roaring. . . . Then she *thought* she saw Joseph of Arimathea take down our Lord's body from the cross, and lay it before our Lady on a marble stone. . . . And the said creature *thought* that she continually ran to and from, as if she were a woman without reason, greatly desiring to have had the precious body by herself alone, so that she might have wept enough in the presence of that precious body, for she *thought* she would have died with weeping and mourning for his death, for love that she had for him.
>
> (MK, 234; my emphasis)

The second series of historical visions differ from the first by clearly indicating that Margery's visions were either spiritual ones or that she thought they were bodily ones when in fact they were not. Or that they were nothing but "normal visualizations." It is hard for me to believe that Margery thought her visions were a product of her multiple "thoughts" albeit derived from a meditative context. Something has intervened between the writing of the first tableau and the second, perhaps her being jailed for heresy and later suspected of being a Lollard. In which case, Margery herself is now scared into saying that her experiences were imaginary ones or at best emerging from her spiritual sight. Or, given the fact that the second series of showings are peppered with qualifications absent in the first, is it her priestly amanuensis who is scared into interjecting the qualifying phrases? If so, Margery is being converted into a dubious witness of history by the male cleric. Either way, the qualifying observations of the second tableau would retrospectively have the effect of sanitizing the unmistakable daring of the first.

Whether bodily or spiritual or imagined, Margery's visualization of her past life poses several problems that the Hindu or Mahāyāna visionary need not have worried about. A Mahāyāna meditator can enter into the past because his or her presence in history can easily be justified by the theory of rebirth. He would have no problem in inventing a history in which he was a participant. In spite of Bonaventure and *Meditations,* it is rare for a Christian mystic to participate in the life of the holy family as Margery does. Margery's case was especially vivid and

impressive and might in fact possess the taint of heresy. Hence the series of qualifications pertaining to the second set of visualizations that primarily deals with
the historical activity before, during, and immediately after Christ's passion.
There is no doubt of the power of Margery's first visualization; she is right there
at a historical event. The second is different. Margery, or more likely her scribe,
has almost no choice except to say that her visions were imagined ones, that she
thought she saw the death, suffering, and Passion of Christ. But this drains the
second tableau of the power of the first. From *my* point of view, I would say that,
owing to her fertile fantasy life, she *reinvented* a theory of reincarnation or reproduced it in her first tableau. This is not difficult, given the fact that ideas of reincarnation were circulating in Europe in popular culture and in heresies like that
of the Manichaeans and Catharists. Bonaventure and other Franciscans attuned
to popular religiosity, as well as the author of *Meditations* or Margery herself,
could have assimilated these floating mythemes into their world view with or
without being aware of it.[111] Be that as it may, Margery's complicated fantasy life
cannot be divorced from the one feature of her spiritual quest that commands
our attention: her constant weeping when any cue, however vague, reminds her
of the Christ's Passion. And her imagined or real historical tableaux led up to the
key event that produced rivers of blood in Christ's flesh and released a flood of
tears in Margery's eyes along with fits of uncontrollable weeping, which I will
now take up by relating them to her life history.

MARGERY'S GRIEF: A POSTPARTUM DEPRESSION AND ITS TRANSFORMATION

> Culture can influence the experience and communication of symptoms of de-
> pression. . . . For example, in some cultures, depression may be experienced
> largely in somatic terms, rather than with sadness or guilt. Complaints of
> "nerves" and headaches (in Latino and Mediterranean cultures), of weakness,
> tiredness, or "imbalance" (in Chinese and Asian cultures), of problems of the
> "heart" (in Middle Eastern cultures), or of being "heart broken" (among Hopi)
> may express the depressive experience. Such presentations combine features
> of the Depressive, Anxiety, and Somatoform Disorders.
>
> —*Diagnostic and Statistical Manual of Mental Disorders*, 4th ed.

What kind of person was Margery Kempe? This is a difficult question to answer,
because she showed little interest in her childhood and married life. She barely

mentions the fourteen children whom she produced. What is even more problematic is that she omits all reference to her mother, a relationship that might have had considerable bearing on her later life. She hardly engages with her own times except obliquely, since, like many visionaries and religious virtuosos, she is obsessively focused on her vocation and vision quest. We do know that when she was twenty she was married to John Kempe, a burgess of Bishop's Lynn. Her marriage was a loss of status for her because her own father was five times mayor of Lynn and held other honorable positions, whereas her husband seemed to have been nothing more than a small landowner.

The conception and birth of her first child has relevance to her own life because "she was troubled by severe attacks of sickness until the child was born" (MK, 41). With her labor pains, "she despaired of her life" and hoped to confess a sin she had harbored for a long time but does not tell us what it was. Some of her subsequent amours indicate it was a sexual sin that was tormenting her—so shameful a one that she could not even confess it. My hazardous guess is that it is the sin of adultery and that her first child was conceived in sin, a theme I will take up later. Her personal inability to be shriven is projected into the devil, "her enemy," who urged her not to confess as long as she was in good health. Instead she should perform penances. Following the devil's advocacy, she did penance and fasted on bread and water, but "would not reveal that one thing in confession" (MK, 41). Thus, when her child was born, and thinking she would die, she sent for her confessor, but she claimed he was rude and began to reprove her. The real sin obsessing her thus went unconfessed. Consequently, "this creature went out of her mind, and was amazingly disturbed and tormented with spirits for half a year, eight weeks and odd days" a long dark night of anguish. At this time she was a witness of "devils opening their mouths all alight with burning flames of fire, as if they would have swallowed her in, sometimes pawing at her, sometimes threatening her, sometimes pulling her and hauling her about" and attempting to undermine her Christian faith, her faith in God, in her parents, saints and her friends (MK, 41–42). She would like to have killed herself "and in witness of this she bit her own hand so violently that the mark could be seen for the rest of her life. And also she pitilessly tore the skin on her body near her heart with her nails, for she had no other implement . . . [because] she was tied up and forcibly restrained both day and night so that she could not do as she wanted." The preceding signs suggest a "postpartum depression" compounded by the guilt feelings for an unconfessed sin. In this first demonic attack she is not only punished by devils but she also punishes herself with acts of bodily self-hurt, itself a form of penance and expiation.

During this expiatory-punishment she had a conversion experience when Jesus appeared "clad in a mantle of purple silk, sitting upon her bedside, looking at her with so blessed a countenance that she was strengthened in all her spirits, and he said to her these words, 'Daughter, why have you forsaken me, and I never forsook you?'" Then immediately, the air opened up as "bright as any lightning, and he ascended up into the air, not hastily and quickly, but beautifully and gradually, so that she could clearly behold him in the air until it closed up again" (MK, 42). With this vision she grew calm and asked her husband for the keys of the buttery to obtain food and drink. She ate and drank as her bodily strength allowed and gradually began to recognize her friends and members of her household. But we are also told that she would not give up her "showy way of dressing," in spite of her husband's advice. She flaunted her fashionable clothes "so that she would be all the more stared at, and all the more esteemed" (MK, 43).

Now let me proceed with a psychocultural exegesis of Margery's psychic condition. Her ambivalence toward her relatively low status husband comes out when, chastised by him for her proud ways, she says she came from "worthy kindred" and that "he should never have married her," which is her way of saying that she shouldn't have married him (MK, 44). The marked ambivalence toward her husband compounds her feelings of guilt and further influences the development of her spirit attack. She behaves very much like the demons within her, insulting friends and family and acting out or abreacting her past like the priestesses in my Sri Lankan case studies. Newman mentions common features of a woman in the European Middle Ages afflicted by demons who "screams, rants incoherently, or howls like an animal; appears hostile and self-destructive, even homicidal or suicidal; has disturbing physical symptoms like those of epilepsy, for example, convulsions and facial contortions; and flees human society as far as possible, seeking out deserted wilderness spots or graveyards."[112] Margery also bruises her body; tearing her body near her heart with her nails suggests the guilt she feels is related to a matter of the heart. Her behavior is simply not feasible as "masochism"; these are acts of self-punishment for the unconfessed and nameless sin and perhaps other sins against significant others that also lie dormant in her unconscious thoughts and unhappily remain inaccessible to us also. Nevertheless, nameless sins can be given a name and a meaning as "devils." "Demonomorphic" representations of deep motivations such as guilt cannot be dealt with in medieval times except through what was available in the Church and often outside of it in popular culture. Once the motivation has a habitation and a name, then it is possible to deal with it and also deal with the emotions objectified in the demonic figures.

Then comes Jesus in his radiant form. With that vision she recovers and begins to eat ordinary food and reestablishes normal familial relations. The second chapter says that she came to her "right mind" through Jesus's grace and now "was bound to God and that she would be his servant" (MK, 43). Yet soon, out of "sheer covetousness," she took to brewing, but this business enterprise failed. She naturally thought that God has punished her and therefore promised her husband to reform her ways. But, in fact, she undertook another business, a horsemill that also failed and provoked popular scorn. It is then that she "asked God for mercy, and forsook her pride, her covetousness, and the desire she had for worldly dignity, and did great bodily penance, and began to enter the way of everlasting life" (MK, 45).

"One night, as this creature lay in bed with her husband, she heard a sound so sweet and delectable that she thought she had been in paradise. And immediately she jumped out of bed and said, 'Alas that ever I sinned! It's full merry in heaven.'" Here we see a door opening on to her fantasy life, a fun heaven, in contrast to her dull bourgeois existence. Thereafter when she heard mirth or melody on earth she would shed tears and sigh for the bliss of heaven and thus she was drawn to God. Consequently, sexual intercourse with her husband was "so abominable to her that she would rather, she thought, have eaten and drunk the ooze and muck in the gutter than consent to intercourse, except out of obedience." She informed her husband that, though she could not deny him her body, "my love and affection is withdrawn from all earthly creatures and set on God alone." It is not likely that Margery was disgusted with sex only after she heard the heavenly music; rather the hearing of the music was triggered by disgust at sex with her husband, even though she occasionally enjoyed it, a not unusual Christian attitude to sexuality. And she did produce fourteen children! But once her love was transferred to God, human love becomes the ooze and muck of the gutter. Hence she began "much weeping and sorrowing because she could not live in chastity" (MK, 46).

Meanwhile, Margery took to fasting and going to church at two or three in the morning and staying till noon and sometimes later. She obtained a hair cloth "and put it inside her gown as discreetly and secretly as she could, so that her husband should not notice it," and wore it every day, a statement about marriage if ever there was one! Making love with her hair shirt on would cause her pain; and it is unlikely that her husband was unaware of this irritating object when making love. Repelled by him, she nevertheless speaks of "temptations" that she felt were "the snare of lechery." This snare lasted for a period of three years. At this time she continued to weep and carried out penances because she felt that these temptations were sent by God to test her. During the first year of the three-year spell, sex with her husband was "painful and horrible to her," but that she would label this period one of "temptation" indicates that she did enjoy this repulsive practice.

In the second year of temptations, a man she knew and liked suggested that he would like to sleep with her so she could "enjoy the lust of his body," a mortal sin. In Margery's complicated reasoning, this was something the man suggested to test her, but "she imagined that he meant it in earnest." She was very troubled, and naturally the "devil put it into her mind that God had forsaken her, or else she would not be so tempted. She believed the devil's persuasions, and began to consent because she could not think any good thought" (MK, 49). But the man did not agree! We do not know the details of this convoluted relationship, but it is clear that she wanted sex with this man and, for whatever reason, he did not turn up for the assignation. That night as she lay in bed with her husband she felt "that to have intercourse with him was so abominable to her that she could not bear it." She, therefore, made up her mind to go back to her other man "if he would then consent to have her." But again he would not "for all the wealth in this world," and, to add insult to injury, he said he "would rather be chopped up as small as meat for the pot" than screw her.

Consider what is going on here: Margery rejects her husband and wants another man who rejects her, and she falls into a state of despair or depression, as if in hell. She was false to God because of her willingness to commit a mortal sin. Consequently, she was "shriven many times and often, and did whatever penance her confessor would enjoin her to do" according to the rules of the Church. For her part, she thought that God had abandoned her and she was "troubled with horrible temptations to lechery and despair all the following year, except that our Lord in his mercy, as she said to herself, gave her every day for the most part two hours of compunction for her sins, with many bitter tears." Thus her mourning continued "and she sorrowed as though God has forsaken her" (MK, 50).

Then something terrible and beautiful happened on the Friday before Christmas, that is, at Advent, the traditional time of penance. During the course of continual mourning and weeping and asking forgiveness for her sins and her trespasses, "our merciful Lord Christ Jesus—blessed may he be—ravished her spirit and said to her, 'Daughter, why are you weeping so sorely? I have come to you, Jesus Christ, who died on the cross suffering bitter pains and passion for you. I, the same God, forgive you your sins to the uttermost point." Christ adds that she will never suffer purgatory, or come into hell, for he has granted her contrition till the end of her life. "Therefore, I command you, boldly to call me Jesus, your love, for I am your love and shall be your love without end." And, most impressively, Jesus commands her to take off her hair shirt. Instead he will give her "a hair-shirt in your heart which shall please me much more that all the hair-shirts in the world." The protective barrier that she wore against the husband's sexual advances, which might have been removed if her hoped-for lover had really come to her, is now off. Instead she wears one in her heart. Then an injunction from Jesus: she should abstain from eating meat, and instead "of meat you shall eat my flesh and my blood, that is the true body of Christ in the sacrament of the altar" every Sunday that will cause "so much grace to flow into you" (MK, 51). Christ generously tells her to give up praying with many beads and instead "lie still and speak to me in thought, and I shall give you high meditation and true contemplation" (MK, 52). I have already discussed the visions she had through the power of contemplation bestowed by Jesus. For the moment, let me mention that she was commanded by Jesus to consult a certain anchorite who tells her that she will suck at Christ's breast. What Christ feeds her is symbolically milk, though in actuality Jesus says that it is his blood and his flesh that, every Sunday, she will consume at communion. It is Christ's act of nurture to the suffering child of God.[113] What about the hair shirt of the heart? It still constitutes a symbolic barrier, this time with Jesus in fact implying that she cannot truly be his spouse— at least not just yet. Jesus urges her not to eat meat; and she "must fast on Friday both from meat and drink," and sometime before Whit Sunday Christ will "suddenly slay your husband." Sharing a meal with meat and wine with her husband had been a habit with the couple and a symbol of the marital bond. When her husband desired sex on Easter Week, perhaps on April 26, 1413, she shouted, "Jesus help me" and never again could he approach her with carnal knowledge (MK, 56).[114] We know that she had mentioned Jesus's threat to her husband, three years earlier. Slaying the husband had a double meaning: as a real act of killing him and the symbolic killing of his desire, his castration, as it were. Hence, the fear of God as well as practical considerations (to be mentioned later) were perhaps instrumental in his refraining from sex. Now, eight weeks after living in chastity, she reminded him again of God's threat and pleaded with him to allow her "a vow of chastity at whatever bishop's hand that God wills." He agreed conditionally: first, they would still lie in the same bed, but abstain from sex; second, she should settle his debts before her planned trip to Jerusalem; and, third, "that you shall eat and drink with me on Fridays as you used to do" (MK, 59). I won't go into the details of what subsequently transpired, except that Margery agreed to redeem her husband's debts on condition that he renounces the marriage bed to "make my body free to God." This prompts her husband to say "May your body be as freely available to God as it has been to me" (MK, 60). But his second and third conditions explicitly make a domestic demand: both should maintain the social convention that they are still married and share the same board and bed.

It seems that underlying the religious motivations are very pragmatic ones. The year of the vow of chastity when she was around forty was also the year of Margery's father's death, and this gave her an inheritance that she could use to buy her husband.[115] But the redemption of her husband's debts apparently reduced her to poverty because from now on she would complain of her lack of money. She also begins pilgrimages to both local sites and to Jerusalem. With the father's death and the initial chastity agreement with her husband, God gives her another important instruction: "And, daughter, I say unto you that I want you to wear white clothes, and no other color, for you shall dress according to my will" (MK, 67). Christ himself clarifies the nature of this injunction: "the state of maidenhood is more perfect and more holy than the state of widowhood and the state of widowhood more perfect than the state of wedlock, yet I love you, daughter, as much as any maiden in the world" (MK, 84–85). The white cloth symbolically converts the widow into a maiden although in actuality both Margery and her God recognize that she is in reality a widow, although, as Jesus clarifies much later, "you are a maiden in your soul" (MK, 88). But, beyond that, white has other more general biblical meanings of purity and fellowship with Christ in many places, for example in Revelation 3, 4: "Thou hast a few names even in Sardis which have not defiled their garments; and they shall walk with me in white; for they are worthy." And 3, 5: "He that overcometh, the same shall be clothed in white raiment; and I will not blot out his name out of the book of life, but I will confess his name before my Father, and before his angels."

To seal the compact with Jesus, Margery goes to the bishop of Lincoln and tells him that she "was commanded in my soul that you shall give me the mantle and the ring, and clothe me all in white clothes. And if you clothe me on earth, our Lord Jesus Christ will clothe you in heaven," something the bishop could not ignore.[116] And he agreed on condition her husband concurred. Eventually, the husband joined the wife before the bishop in the formal renunciation of sex and the ratification of the earlier chastity agreement; any violation on his part would hereafter be a mortal sin. But, as far as the white clothes were concerned, the bishop introduced a proviso: "Pray to God that it may wait until you come back from Jerusalem, when you have proved yourself and are recognized" (MK, 70).

As Margery's story develops, the white clothes begin to accrue further meaning, a symbolic interplay between the white of chastity and the black of mourning and the colorful clothes of her early married life that contrasted with both the black and the white. Because Margery's book is without chronological sequence, we have to bring in material from her later accounts. We are told that once, when she is "newly delivered of a child" (long before the actual chastity agreement), Jesus told her not to have any more children and instead go to Norwich, the home of Julian, her contemporary (MK, 73).[117] "And this creature," Margery says, "was dressed in black clothing at that time," clearly implying that black clothes were not instigated by the death of her father but rather with the continual production of children (MK, 74).[118] It seems that at some point during this production process Margery gave up her colorful clothes for black ones indicative of mourning or a deep sorrow. Mourning and black clothes ought to take us back to her copious weeping, which now seems to have a further significance, as I shall demonstrate presently.

After she settled her husband's debts, she went to several pilgrimage places in England and later took a boat from Norwich and landed in the town of Zierekzee (in the Netherlands) on her way to Jerusalem. She received communion every Sunday and with it came fits of sobbing and weeping.[119] Instigated by her pilgrimage companions who resented her weeping and abstentions, her new confessor tells her that she should recommence eating meat and drinking wine, after her four-year moratorium. This she did for a short time, but she then implored him to excuse her from eating meat, owing to her earlier and more powerful compact with Jesus. Meanwhile, her companions cruelly mocked her for her unending weeping, which caused her "much reproof and shame." "They cut her gown so short that it only came a little below her knee, and made her put on some white canvas in a kind of sacking apron, so that she would be taken for a fool" and made her sit at the far end of the dining table away from the others (MK, 98). The significance of commensality is reasonably clear: sitting at table together and consuming meat and wine is an affirmation of normal domesticity and fellowship, something her husband had demanded much earlier. For ordinary citizens, Margery has violated those norms; so she must eat by herself as God's fool. There were others, however, who held this particular God's fool in high esteem. As for Margery, she would have known the popular tradition that Herod, who saw no miracles being performed by Christ, "thinking Him a fool, in derision he had Him dressed in white, and sent Him back to Pilate." And, like Margery, "He bore everything most patiently."[120] I am not sure whether Margery or her detractors were aware of Paul in Corinthians, 4, 10: "Here we are, fools for the sake of Christ, while you are the learned men in Christ."

Eventually Margery arrived with other pilgrims at the city of Jerusalem and, led by friars, she went to sacred places and then to the site where Jesus suffered his Passion (MK, 103). "And this creature wept and sobbed as plenteously as though she had seen our Lord with her bodily eyes suffering his Passion at that time." This was apparently a vision provoked by the site, nothing unusual in Christian visualizations. Like Julian's, she experienced a powerful vision as if it were something seen with her bodily eyes. At Calvary, the site of the crucifixion, she could not stand or kneel; she "writhed and wrestled with her body, spreading her arms out wide, and cried with a loud voice" at the fresh vision of Christ's suffering. And now with her spiritual sight she saw the mourning mother and St. John, Mary Magdalene, and many other mourners. Here she cried and kept roaring, but apparently *"this is the first time that she ever cried in any contemplation"* (MK, 104; my emphasis). Margery never used the word *cry* before, though she had been constantly weeping and sobbing and shedding copious tears. Her present "crying," while still in contemplation, involved fits of screaming and shaking that astounded people. Hereafter all sorts of cues would produce the image of the suffering Christ and with it her new form of lamentation, which went on for ten years in varying degrees of strength and frequency (MK, 313, n 8). Crying would occur at communion or when she saw a crucifix or if a man or beast had a wound or if a man beat a child before her or hit a horse with a whip or if she even thought of such things.[121] It seems as if associational thinking was her forte.

On her way to Rome from Jerusalem, when she was afraid of the perils of travel, God consoled her, "Don't be afraid." But Jesus insisted that his protection was conditional; she should be "clad in white clothes, and wear them as I said to you while in England." Her own wish is God's wish: "I shall obey your will; and if you bring me to Rome in safety, I shall wear white clothes, even though all the world should wonder at me, for your love" (MK, 112). What is happening here? Remember that in England God had urged her to wear white, but the bishop deferred the request until her return. The impatient Margery, however, will not wait. And again God urges her in effect to bypass the Church and obey his will. Earlier people had ridiculed her and made her wear a white sackcloth. By wearing white, she now literally covers up that earlier shame that was also Christ's shame when Pilate made him a fool wearing white. Her white clothes are thick with further symbolism, the white of maidenhood that in effect denies her marital status. But, in every instance, shame is something she courts because Jesus himself was thus taunted. I shall skip some details here and come to chapter 34 where the discourse on white clothes reappears.

In Rome she had a German priest as her confessor and an English one who was her enemy. At the latter's urging, the German priest asked her if she would obey his order, and, when she agreed, he said, "I charge you then to leave off your white clothes and wear your black clothes again." It is likely that during her confession she had told the priest of her promise to the English bishop to wear white only after her return. The good German priest probably held her to this promise.

The hostile English priest was naturally pleased and told her: "I am glad that you go about in black clothes as you used to do" (MK, 121). A later account retrospectively informs us that she did not comply with the request. In this account Jesus tells her to return to the German priest "and ask him to give her leave to wear her white clothes once again." The priest agreed when Margery convinced him it was the Lord's will. "And so she wore white clothes ever after" (MK, 128). The semiotics of clothing is analogous to the semiotics of wine and meat, the latter being an argument that Jesus and Margery have with the husband on bed and board.

The conversion to wearing white, the setting of Rome, the prior death of her father, and the symbolic slaying of the husband's desire set the stage for her wedding with Jesus and the approval of the divine Father himself. One cannot but assume unconscious equations at work: Jesus as the idealized substitute for the "slain" husband and God the Father for her own father, whose approval had been surely necessary for her earthly marriage. Thus, on Lateran's Day (November 9, 1414) in Rome, the divine Father, who, I think, appears for the first time in her text, tells her: "Daughter, I will have you wedded to my Godhead, because I shall show you my secrets and my counsels, for you shall live with me without end" (MK, 122). The entry of the Father-father results in another dilemma. Marriage with the Godhead is not what she, or, for that matter, other female virtuosos want, because "she had no [spiritual] knowledge of the conversation of the Godhead, for all her love and affection were fixed on the manhood of Christ, and of that she did have knowledge and would not be parted from that for anything" (MK, 122–23). With that Margery's associational thinking gets a fresh boost: when she saw mothers with children in Rome she sees the child Christ. "When she met a handsome man [she] wept bitterly for the manhood of Christ as she went about the streets of Rome, so that those who saw her were greatly astonished at her, because they did not know the reason."

Thus, though the Father spoke to her, she did not answer him "when he told her that she should be wedded to his Godhead." But Jesus, the second person of the Trinity, now intervenes and asks why she did not respond to the Father's words. The reason is clear: "She wept amazingly much, desiring to have himself [Jesus] still, and in no way to be parted from him."[122] The son therefore tells his father: "Father, excuse her, for she is still only young and has not completely learned how she should answer" (MK, 123). "And then the Father took her by the hand [spiritually] in her soul, before the Son and the Holy Ghost, and the Mother of Jesus, and all the twelve apostles, and St. Katherine and St. Margaret and many other saints and holy virgins, with a great multitude of angels, saying to her soul, 'I take you Margery, for my wedded wife, for fairer, for fouler, for richer, for poorer, provided that you are humble and meek in doing what I command you to do. For, daughter, there was never a child so kind to its mother as I shall be to you, both in joy and sorrow, to help you and comfort you. And that I pledge to you'" (MK, 123).

The marriage is couched in the form of an ordinary one, and, like a conventional husband, the Father demands obedience and humility in exchange for his love.[123] I want now to add my own addendum to Margery's text: by this time she would have removed the symbolic hair shirt of the heart that separated her from her divine spouse. This marriage, unlike the mundane Godless one, affirms the maternal aspect of the relation between the Father and his child Margery, a reflection of her relationship to her own father. The mother and saints were present in her soul, ensuring her newfound happiness with the Father and her "high devotion" to him. She sometimes sensed sweet smells and heard with her bodily ears and eyes sounds of melodies and saw "many white things flying all about her on all sides, as thickly in a way as specks in a sunbeam" a kind of divine bridal shower that appeared at different times and places (MK, 124). Then God gave her another token that lasted for sixteen years, the heat of the Holy Ghost, "which will burn away all your sins, for the fire of love quenches all sins." It burned in her heart like a material flame, even in cold weather. It is not clear whether it is the Father or the son or the Godhead itself that speaks to her at this time. But soon the Godhead disappears and the second of the Trinity takes over and comforts her, praising her for allowing him to speak to her for "if you said a thousand *paternosters* every day you would not please me as much as you do when you are in silence and allow me to speak in your soul" (MK, 125). An interesting statement, acknowledging that it is in silence or in meditation that Jesus speaks to her.

Jesus now brings the relationship from the high spiritual level in which it was couched to a more domestic idiom, because it is "appropriate for the wife to be on homely terms with her husband." "Therefore I must be intimate with you, and lie in your bed with you. Daughter, you greatly desire to see me, and you may boldly, when you are in bed, take me to you as your wedded husband, as your darling, and as your sweet son, for I want to be loved as a son should be loved by the mother, and I want you to love me, daughter, as a good wife ought to love her husband" (MK, 126–27). An interesting shift in Margery's imago of the deity has occurred. During the marriage with the Godhead, the Father speaks to her in his maternal role, but now the son appears and he wants her to be a kind of mother to him, in addition, of course, to being a spouse, both constitutive features of the imagined Christ for Margery. This provokes us to make the point that while Jesus and the Godhead are theologically consistent, the way they are imagined by the penitent, namely, their imagos, might change and shift around. Jesus says,

"Therefore you can boldly take me in the arms of your soul and kiss my mouth, my head, and my feet as sweetly as you want" (MK, 127). This is not an erotic statement. It is antedated in popular Catholic beliefs and formalized by Bonaventure, who urges the penitent to "embrace the divine manger [and] press your lips upon and kiss the boy's feet."[124] The personal symbolism here is thick with meaning: kissing the mouth, head, and feet is what loving and nurturing mothers or caretakers would do for an infant. In Margery's case, it is an expression of maternal love to the very son she had carefully tended in the historical scenario of his birth, suggesting, once again, the power of that recollection in her fantasized desire to cuddle Christ. One must not assume that in Margery's visions, as with dreams, there is a contradiction in her double imago of Christ as her conventional husband and her child. Such imagos are present even in our psychic lives when one's partner can be simultaneously imagined as spouse, lover, parent, and much more.

On her return to England, the discourse of chastity and whiteness once again reappears. It seems that, although Margery wore white in Rome, it was perhaps a temporary garb improvised for the moment—perhaps to cover the short sackcloth she was forced to wear—or she simply needed another set of clothes in England to replace worn-out ones. She therefore prayed to God, saying that if he creates thunder, rain, and lightning this will mean that she can fulfill his will to wear white (MK, 141). And, sure enough, the following Friday morning, as she lay in bed, she saw "great lightning, and heard great thunder and great rain" and she resolved to wear white clothes. But she was penniless now. Urged by her soul, she now does something that is integral to her character, the mix of spirituality and down-to-earth pragmatism. She went to a "worthy man" in Norwich, who welcomed her, and together they began to relate holy stories, and Jesus spoke to her soul continually, "speak to this man, speak to this man" (MK, 141). She asked him where she could find someone who could give her two nobles to buy white cloth until she could pay him back, and, sure enough, the worthy man agreed. The very practical Margery needed the money; she goes to a decent person and establishes a bond with him through shared storytelling, and then asks money from him indirectly. God urging him is now a refraction of her simple practical needs. Our worthy man "had a gown made for her from it [the white cloth], and also a hood, a kirtle and a cloak" converting Margery fully into the woman in white (MK, 142). The following Sunday she received communion in her new white attire, only to suffer once again the contumely of crowds because of the inappropriateness of the garb for a married woman and their intolerance of her "crying" (MK, 143).

These external signs of "crying" could easily be read by the public as the work of the devil: some thought she howled like a dog; others who knew her now shunned her, refusing to take her into their homes. Yet there were others who were amazed and invited her home to eat and drink and converse on religious matters. And one of them gave her money to fulfill her wish to go on pilgrimage to the shrine of St. James of Compostela in Spain. We noted that soon after she was put in prison as a heretic; and in a later visit to the Archbishopric of York, when she was suspected of being a Lollard, the archbishop himself said: "Why do you go about in white clothes? Are you a virgin?" (MK, 162). I shall skip her tribulations and humiliations, except to suggest that in some respect the public attitude to her was similar to that of Pemalingpa. Margery does not come from the peasant class, but neither was she an educated aristocrat or a member of the nobility. Aristocratic or wealthy women had fewer problems dealing with public skepticism; whereas Margery was dogged by them right through her life and could never obtain full public acceptance of her religious role or the authenticity of her visions. And her weeping, instead of resolving public ambivalence, only exacerbated it.

I omit many details of Margery's life, but I will mention one important event, when a young priest came to Lynn and read many books to her "such as the Bible with doctors' commentaries on it, St Bride's [St. Brigit's] book, Hilton's book, Bonaventura's *Stimulus Amoris, Incendium Amoris,* and others similar." The relationship went on for about eight years, and, as a result, this young priest suffered "many an evil word for her love." He also "supported her in her weeping and crying," a feature that generally produced public opprobrium for both of them (MK, 182). During this period Jesus made several presentations on the fates of those who were saved and those who were damned. While she rejoiced at those being saved, she could not bear the showings of the damned souls, almost certainly provoked by her own fears of being one of them. But this annoyed Jesus, who blamed her for disregarding his "secret counsels." Hence Christ peevishly withdrew from her mind all her good thoughts and contemplations and opened up her mind to evil thoughts—or so she imagined. This is, of course, a beautiful rationalization of her own "foul thoughts and foul recollections of lechery and all uncleanliness, as though she would have prostituted herself with all manner of people" (MK, 183). Thus, in spite of her resistances, she had visions of "men's genitals, and other such abominations." Among the latter were "various men of religion, priests and many others, both heathen and Christian, coming before her eyes so that she could not avoid them or put them out of her sight, and showing her their naked genitals." And then "the devil ordered her in her mind to choose which of them she would have first, and she must prostitute herself to them all" (MK, 184). These demonic incursions are reminiscent of the women in *Medusa's Hair* as well as those in the Tibetan tradition.[125]

Underneath God's punishment is simply her rationalization for the return of earlier fantasies provoked by sexual desire and guilt and, deeper down perhaps, the return of childhood repressions. But, while we cannot access the deeper infantile roots of her guilt feelings, we can read the more immediate one: her relationship with the young priest. I am not suggesting that the two of them had a sexual relationship; only that she was erotically tempted by close physical and emotional contact with him, triggering earlier feelings of sexual guilt, including the one she could never confess and could not fully exorcise. In other words, the immediate trigger for her devilish visions was the relationship with the young priest but accumulating feelings of guilt from her past released the trigger. Thus God withdrew her knowledge and her contemplations—those very things she learned from the priest—and sent the dreadful incubus visitations including that of Christian and heathen priests with their genitals exposed. The devil astutely inserted the thought into her mind that "she liked one of them better than all the others." Margery felt he spoke the truth; she could not say no and she had to do his bidding (MK, 184).[126]

Margery must have met many priests, including heretical ones, during her travels. But surely the one she liked best was the young priest, with whom she copulated through the incubus fantasy and against all her resistance. "These horrible sights and accursed thoughts were delicious to her against her will. Wherever she went or whatever she did, these accursed thoughts remained with her" even during sacrament or prayers. And, though she went to confession, she found no release and nearly fell into despair and blamed God: "where is now the truthfulness of your word?" Then immediately an angel visited her to say that God had not forsaken her, but, because she had ignored his previous secret counsels (regarding the fate of the damned), she will endure this punishment for twelve days "until you will believe that is God who speaks to you and no devil" (MK, 184). Although she does not give details of how this renewal occurred, the dark night of the soul, with its forbidden fantasies, gradually dissipated and holy thoughts returned. She could now engage in renewed conversations with the Lord: "Daughter, now believe indeed that I am no devil." And, of course, she was filled with joy and she said, "I will now lie still and be obedient to your will" (MK, 185). Following an orgy of indulgence, she can now go back to the soul's silence and don her habit of perfection.[127]

Having ensured Margery's compliance, Jesus permits her to relax her regime; that it is okay to eat meat again.[128] Margery responds with the usual idea that she will now have to face the scorn and shame of people who knew of her abstinence for years. But Jesus tells her not to worry, "but let every man say what he will." And, interestingly, when she told her confessors of God's will, they agreed. In her visions the mother mentions what must have been the thoughts of the son and of Margery by discoursing at length on the virtues of meat eating, adding that weeping and crying will "make you weak and feeble" (MK, 201). But a new pact is substituted for the old: following God's instructions, she makes a vow to fast once a week in worship of Our Lady. Very pragmatic reasons therefore underlie the wishes of the mother and the son, and these are simply refractions of Margery's own wishes and needs.

But consider the psychological implications of the return to meat eating in addition to the spiritual-pragmatic ones. Though Margery wears white clothes, she cannot really be converted into a virgin or maiden. At best the white clothes express her vow of chastity to Jesus, which is violated only in the fantasies I have just presented. She is his comfortably wedded spouse, not a virgin unacquainted with sexuality, writhing in rapturous delight. Eating meat and drinking wine, I noted, is a compact of the conjugal tie such that William Kempe insists on her continuing this compact at least on Fridays, even though they abstained from sex. At that time, Christ tells her not to eat meat and drink wine; this is the preliminary symbolic break of the conjugal tie with her husband. The hostility of her English confessor at Rome now takes on an added significance. He knew she was a married woman and therefore insisted that she return to consuming meat and wine, those symbols of conjugal felicity, which she ignores. However, when Jesus asks her to resume the consumption of meat and wine, he is in effect telling her that she is now *his* spouse. Conjugal harmony that never existed in reality in the human context has been transferred to the more appropriate spiritual one.[129]

It is time to end this long detour and get back to the psychodynamics of Margery's weeping, sobbing, later crying, and the wearing of black, this last occurring while she was still producing children. We do not know when her weeping commenced, but it is likely that it was with her first childbirth, along with other signs we have already discussed, and is associated with what nowadays we label a postpartum depression. The birth of the first child is a life crisis, exacerbated in those societies where marriages are arranged and where the woman marries at an early age and lives virilocally under some form of patriarchal authority. In this situation there are problems of meaning that emerge, especially the relative absence of familial love and care during this critical event. And, along with that, are associated resentments against one's husband and *his* family and the child about to be born, the instigator of the crisis of birth.

Many societies with patriarchal ideologies have institutionalized the return of the woman to her own parental home during this time and also, often enough, when the out-marrying woman suffers a serious illness. Even if the woman cannot go back to her parental home, her mother might be present in her husband's home at this time. Some homes, like Margery's, did not permit either arrangement, and this complicates the crisis of birth, aggravating the sufferer's loss of self-esteem and her self-pity. But, if there are further feelings of unconscious guilt and hatred against significant others and against one's own self, then the crisis might lead to feelings of profound sadness, melancholy, or "depression." Such feelings would surely have become worse if indeed my guess is correct that Margery's first child was conceived in adultery and hence the refusal to be shriven during the time of her illness. This son was the first person to whom she dictated her text.[130] She later had a good relationship with him, and, when he died, Margery continued to be friends with his wife.

These feelings of loss and depression can be objectified in several ways: as somatic signs or symptoms, such as Margery's "weeping"; as behavioral signs, such as her hurting herself; and as culturally familiar scenarios, such as attack by devils. All these are woven together in the fabric of her illness or postpartum life crisis such that the somatic and behavioral signs and the demonic attack together could be seen as constituting an overarching symbolic totality, though, for analytical purposes, one might separate them. By contrast, Western psychiatric nosology not only denies the psychic reality of the symbolic order for the patient but posits the symptomatology of modern and postmodern women patients as the norm for depression anywhere, relegating the rest of the world to the crude one-paragraph residual category of my epigraph, thereby inhibiting cross-cultural theoretical understanding of the postpartum life crisis.[131]

We do know that Margery recovered from her first illness, and this was clearly indicated by her reverting back to wearing colorful clothes. Then she engaged in two business enterprises and both failed. Further, complicating her life was her obvious dislike of her husband and the revulsion (cum desire) of the ooze and muck of intercourse. And then she begets so many children who, except for the eldest, are excised from her autohagiography. Concomitant with these events is her movement toward Christ and her fantasy of a fun heaven. I suspect that the continuing production of undesired children resulted in continuing postpartum life crises of different degrees of intensity. Somewhere during these co-occurring sad events she gave up flaunting her colorful clothes and donned the black garb of despair, while her weeping became worse. Our reconstruction is necessarily speculative and incomplete because we do not know whether there was another trauma, such as the death of the mother or a loved child, that might have compounded these events. A death in the family would be the initial reason for wearing the black of mourning, but not its continuation. All we know is that her fellow citizens thought of her as the woman in black. We do not know whether she wore black continuously or not. Compounding matters further was the cultural belief that "black bile" causes melancholy; if so, wearing black had an added symptomatic meaning that might have further overdetermined her choice of black clothes.

I find it fascinating that much later in life Margery was called upon to treat a woman who exhibited similar signs of melancholy but was also given to uncontrollable weeping, suggesting very strongly that in the medieval culture of her times the symptom of uncontrolled weeping might coexist with the other signs as a feature of the postpartum crisis. Let me recount this event. When Margery was once in church, a man came there in great distress because his wife had just had a baby and she had gone out of her mind. "She doesn't know me, or any of her neighbors. She roars and cries, so that she scares folk badly. She'll both hit out and bite, and so she is manacled on her wrists" (MK, 218). When Margery went to see her, the woman was comforted by her presence and asked Margery not to leave her. But when others visited her "she cried and said she saw many devils around them," whereas with Margery she saw only angels. "She roared and cried so, for the most part of both day and night, that people would not allow her to live amongst them, she was so tiresome to them. Then she was taken to a room at the furthest end of the town, so that people will not hear her crying. And there she was bound hand and foot with chains of iron, so that she should not strike anybody." Margery continued to visit her once or twice each day, and the woman would talk with her meekly *without roaring and crying*. Margery prayed to God everyday to restore the patient to her wits, and God answered in her soul that he would. "Then she was bolder to pray for her recovery than she was before, and each day, weeping and sorrowing, prayed for her recovery until God gave her wits and her mind again. And then she was brought to church and purified as other women are" (MK, 218). Margery's scribe thought this a miracle; but all the sensible husband of the woman did was to consult a religious virtuoso given to "roaring and crying," hoping that she would be able to cure another with similar signs of illness.

When the illness presents itself as part of a symbolic order, members of the society would generally know how to act upon it. Others in Margery's society might have gone to local curers or exorcists. Some cures will succeed and others will fail. For us, this fascinating case has other implications. First, it is clear that Margery's sadness has cultural antecedents. Her patient is the mirror image of herself when she suffered from her first postpartum crisis. Second, a religious specialist noted for her weeping, crying, and roaring effectively cures another with similar symptoms. Once the patient's symptoms disappear, she is brought to church and purified, though the actual techniques of curing will remain unknown to us. The end result is, however, clear: the goal of traditional healing everywhere is to bring the afflicted person back to the familial and social world that has been disrupted by illness, and this is what Margery achieved for her patient.

We know that the path of Margery's "cure" is different from that of her patient. Although suffering from similar signs of postpartum sadness, the denouement of Margery's melancholy took a different direction. Her wearing of black is fused to her weeping and sobbing, no longer as sadness or depression per se but as lamentation for the Passion of Christ. The occasion for changing from black to white occurred when she gave up sexual relations with her husband and made the decision to wear white, reverting back to symbolic maidenhood, all of which was sanctioned by her bishop. We have sketched the ups and downs of that initial decision. The culminating event is her marrying the Godhead and soon becoming both Christ's spouse and mother figure. But then another question surfaces: in becoming a mother of Christ, has she usurped the place of the Madonna without being consciously aware of it? Note that Margery implicitly obtains the mother's permission to be a mother to her son when she voluntarily makes a compact with Mary with the vow of fasting once a week in remembrance of her.

Margery's lamentation must surely have ontogenetic roots of which we know nothing; here the lack of information on Margery's mother is especially unfortunate. Guilt and remorse, repentance and expiation are the emotions that are expressed in the dark night of demonic attack in her case as in others. But guilt, we have often said, is an emotion that can rarely be verbally articulated. In her case it is expressed through various culturally appropriate signs and symbols during her postpartum periods, and even when the demonic attack fades owing to her relation with Christ, the key somatic sign or symptom remains. This is weeping and sobbing. But these are now transformed as weeping and sobbing at the suffering of Christ and then further intensified into "crying" when she visits Golgotha, the scene of his Passion. Guilt is never extinguished or fully expiated in her case. It emerges in demonomorphic representations and incubus visitations that both reflect guilt and also punish the sufferer and provides her a temporarily expiation, at the same time allowing an indulgence in her sexual fantasies and needs. And then she overcomes those dreadful visitations through her spousal and maternal relationships with Jesus, which also has its ups and downs. But Margery's lamentation and mourning never ends. From an uncontrollable sadness during and after childbirth and the continual production of children, her lamentation is transformed into another kind of mourning, a spiritual one for Christ's suffering. But she could neither emancipate herself from it nor avoid the contumely of her fellows. The somatic sign of weeping, sobbing, and crying continue to haunt her endlessly, giving her no respite.

Nevertheless, her crying has a *symbolic* power, which is vastly different from a somatic sign. Christ's grief is her grief. Unlike other Christian penitents, she becomes a player present during his dark travail. Without being fully aware of it, Margery has positioned herself as the human counterpart of Our Lady of the Sorrows and of the sorrowing Magdalene, the one who stood by Jesus when all other disciples had fled. How can one not be moved by her heartrending cry and her visionary tableaux of the suffering Christ? And yet I am not sure whether one can speak of Margery's anguish as "sublimation," because her original melancholy or sorrow is actually *intensified,* not overcome in her present grief. Nor is there a transmutation of the sorrow into something else, as was the case with Teresa's rapture. Her mourning for whatever-it-is never ends. Margery's suffering on Christ's behalf goes on to the very end of her life with only small spaces of tranquility. That tranquility, that fullness of peace, must, as with all Christian virtuosos, await the death of the body and the soul's final rest in Christ.

Book 5

CHRISTIAN DISSENT

The Protest Against Reason

HINGE DISCOURSE: THE OCCULT WORLDS OF
EARLY EUROPEAN MODERNITY

The only thought that philosophy brings with it, in regard to history, is the simple thought of Reason—the thought that Reason rules the world, and that world history has therefore being rational in its course. This conviction and insight is a *presupposition* in regard to history as such, although it is not a presupposition in philosophy itself. In philosophy, speculative reflection has shown that Reason is the *substance* as well as the *infinite power*; that Reason is for itself the *infinite material* of all natural and spiritual life, as well as the *infinite form*, and that its actualization of itself is its content....

Thus Reason is the *substance* [of our historic world] in the sense that it is that whereby and wherein all reality has its being and subsistence. It is the *infinite power*, since Reason is not so powerless as to arrive at nothing more than the ideal, the ought, and to remain outside reality—who knows where—as something peculiar in the heads of a few people. Reason is the *infinite content*, the very stuff of all essence and truth, which it gives to its own *activity* to be worked up.... Even if you do not bring to world history the thought and the knowledge of Reason, you ought at least to have the firm and unconquerable belief that the world of intelligence and self-conscious will is not subject to chance, but rather that it must demonstrate itself in the light of the self-conscious Idea.

—G. W. F. Hegel, *Introduction to the Philosophy of History*

I N BOOK 4 I HAVE dealt with the rich visionary traditions in medieval Christianity. The rest of this essay leaps over a couple of centuries to consider those who lived and worked under the shadow of the Enlightenment. This hinge discourse builds a rough bridge between the visions of Catholic penitents and those who experienced visions in the height of the age of reason, beginning with Blake and ending with new age visionaries. We now know that it is a mistake to think that Enlightenment and scientific reason simply supplanted the prior tradition of visionary thought, even in those countries that came under the rationalizing imperative of the various brands of Lutheran and Calvinist Protestantism. I begin my demonstration by interrogating E. P. Thompson's *Witness Against the Beast: William Blake and the Moral Law* in order to look at the antinomianism ("against the law") of the late seventeenth century, a form of radical dissent that refused to accept conventional Christian ethics, including the rule of the father and the authority of the Church.[1] My major focus, however, will be on Jacob Boehme, who, like his Catholic forbears, was a visionary and, like them, experienced a dark night of the soul and a spiritual awakening. In all of his writing, Boehme employed alchemical and occult thinking and reasoning that had considerable impact on English Behmenists ("followers of Boehme"), including Blake and, much later on, the philosophical and psychological treatises of Blavatsky and Jung, both of whom will appear in this essay.

Let me begin with Thompson. Focusing on the dissenting sects of the seventeenth century, Thompson says that, although they suffered persecution and decline, their ideas persisted into the next century and right into Blake's times as part of a widely prevalent discourse among the disaffected in London and its suburbs, the "masterless men," as they have been felicitously labeled.[2] Antinomianism of the seventeenth century is multifaceted, but Thompson engages with one facet, "carrying to an extreme the advocacy of grace, and bringing the gospel of Christ into direct *antagonism* to the 'covenant of deeds' or the 'moral law'" of the established Church (WAB, 13). Even seventeenth-century Calvinists were occasionally labeled antinomian, owing to their doctrines of election and free grace, although not in the next century. However, the idea of free grace, if not that of the elect and predestination, was important to non-Calvinist antinomianism of the interregnum (1649–1660) such as that of the Ranters, Diggers, Behmenists, and early Quakerism.[3]

Throughout the seventeenth and the eighteenth century, dissenting sects tended to advocate an opposition between the "Moral Law" and the "Everlasting Gospel," the latter a doctrine of love that replaced the ethical formalism ("moral law") of the Church and, according to Thompson, partook of the vocabulary of radical heresy. "The signatures of this antinomian sensibility will be found, not at two or three points in Blake's work, but along the whole length of his work, at least from 1790 until his death" (WAB, 19). According to Thompson, Behmenists like Jane Lead published many volumes of visionary writing during trance states in the late seventeenth century and employed "a vocabulary which seems to flash signals forward to Blake" (WAB, 37). Lead was the founder of the Philadelphian movement and was a friend of fellow Behmenist John Pordage, who was the primary theoretician of the Behmenists and Philadelphians in London. Pordage, according to Thompson, belonged to a circle that "defined four degrees of revelation: (1) Vision, (2) Illumination, (3) Transportation or Translation, and (4) Revelation," while female colleagues experienced ecstatic visions of "supercelestial life" (WAB, 38, 44). Thompson sums up the situation thus: "Philadelphian and Behmenist thought has a significance as a counter-Enlightenment impulse, as a reaction against the mechanistic philosophy of the time, and hence as a potential resource for alternative positions" (WAB, 39).

Thompson rightly points out that neither the Behmenist influence nor that of the Philadelphians, nor that of antinomian dissent, appear in Blake unless transformed by his visionary imagination. But surely this is one of degree, because most creative thinkers recast previous knowledge in terms of their own scheme of things. The visionary impulse was apparently one channel through which this adaptation or transformation of preceding thought occurred. A writer of the time noted of the Philadelphians that "their only Thirst was after visions, openings and revelations" (cited in WAB, 47). Although this visionary thirst was widespread in sectarian dissent, Thompson, like many others, downplays it in Blake. So it is with Blake's esoteric symbolism. Thompson discusses Blake's various borrowings from Proclus, Jacob Boehme (1575–1624), and Boehme's English contemporary Robert Fludd (1574–1637), then adding: "Blake *plays*, in his prophetic writings with some of these symbols and myths. I could myself wish that he played with them less. But he plays in distinctive ways. In his prose, even his visionary statements have a matter of fact quality, totally unlike [Behmenist] Theosophical visions" (WAB, 50). But those who have read the previous pages of this book would know that visions, however profound, can be stated in matter-of-fact prose, and they can also be invested with dense symbolic and poetic power, as much of Blake's prophetic work illustrates.

The problem with Thompson is that he thinks the dissenter group that truly influenced Blake was the Muggletonians, founded by John Reeve and his cousin Lodowick Muggleton, with Reeve as the "messenger" and Muggleton as the "mouth" or speaker of the word. This was Thompson's "missing vector" and the immediate model for Blake. Muggletonians, like other antinomians, were fiercely anticlerical, had no preachers or officers, and did not constitute a "church" or sect in any formal sense. They were dogmatically opposed to Reason and, following prominent antinomian discourse, believed in reified and oppositional categories or contraries such that Satan was the god of Reason and stood contrasted to faith, a distinction existing within human beings also. It is true that these ideas are prominent in Blake, but they are also found in other dissenters, especially those who, as Behmenists, received their inspiration from Boehme himself. While Blake refers to Boehme, Paracelsus, and to hermeticism, he makes no reference whatsoever to the Muggletonians. Further, and this is crucial, Muggletonians distrusted visions, whereas, for Blake, visions and visionary knowledge, we will demonstrate, was central to his work as a poet and painter. And, as with Boehme and Blake, there is a scholarly tendency to deny or down play their visions, in effect perceiving thinkers opposed to Reason through a lens of rationality, ignoring the centrality of visions in the genesis of their thought.

Contrary to Thompson, I think that not only Blake but also Blavatsky and her followers as well as Jung were in some way or other reacting against the rational imperative of the Enlightenment by harking back to Boehme and the hermetic and occult thinkers that influenced him. In dealing with these important thinkers, it is necessary to reaffirm that hostility to Reason is not to advocate un-Reason. Most of our opponents of Reason were rebelling against its reification as the only way to knowledge. Like human beings everywhere, our opponents of Reason could think rationally and logically in their everyday lives and in the commonsense worlds they inhabited using the normal speech of their times. Boehme explicitly opposed Reason, but by *reason* I think he meant "reasoning," that is, logical discourse employed to understand the nature and work of God. Boehme, unlike Blake, was not hostile to the rational imperative of the Christian tradition, not just the Protestant tradition but the prior Catholic thinkers represented by Pseudo-Dionysius, Scottus Eriugena, and Nicholas of Cusa (1401–1464).

Boehme did not hesitate to employ discursive language to express his opposition to "reasoning," even employing difficult concepts to express what he perceived through his clouded vision. Vision and intuitive understandings are "reason's prior," and Reason, especially conceptual thinking, we now know, is an imperfect vehicle to express the profundity of visionary thought. As with theologians of *via negativa*, Boehme's God can be *explained,* but not *apprehended,* through reasoning. In the work of Blake, Jung, Blavatsky, and others who will appear in the following pages, there are two broad features that express both continuity and difference with the Christian penitents of the preceding discussion, namely, their preoccupation with the large movement we might conveniently label hermeticism or occultism and with their particular experiences of the dark night of the soul. As far as the broad category of occultism is concerned, its most sophisticated expressions came with the rediscovery of the Jewish Kabbalah and the texts of hermeticism in the late fifteenth century, in the wake of the translation into Latin of *Corpus Hermeticum* (1464), that compendium of occult thought attributed to Hermes Trismegistus ("Thrice-Great-Hermes").[4] This was followed by the work of Paracelsus (1493–1541) and his disciples and of course Jacob Boehme, all of which constituted what came to be known in the nineteenth century as "esotericism." "Certain of Boehme's most characteristic figures resemble kabbalistic prototypes. In the wake of the Renaissance, Hermeticism, Neoplatonism, and Kabbalism became so thoroughly mingled with the alchemist, speculative, and mystical trends of thought sweeping Europe, that is no longer easy to trace individual strands of influence."[5]

For the thinkers of early modern times occultism did not possess the pejorative connotations that it has for many of us today. The other term, *hermeticism*, soon became a broad label that incorporated alchemy and astrology and forms of positive magic of the imagined magi as against negative magic such as sorcery and witchcraft, another obsession in the European Middle Ages. There were a large number of creative thinkers whose work spanned these horizons, and they include Paracelsus, Boehme, Cornelius Agrippa, and Heinrich Conrad Kunrath (Khunrath), mentioned by our new visionaries and their many followers and emulators in Europe and England.[6] Although dismissed by the later Enlightenment, these hermetic and alchemical thinkers constituted part of mainstream philosophy of the early modern period. Cartesian thought had little effect on diminishing their impact on the seventeenth century.

It is well known that major scientists of that century were as much interested in occult thought as they were in their own scientific disciplines. Charles Webster says that "Newton himself possessed a major edition of the works of Paracelsus," who represented "a significant element in a notoriously large section of chemical and alchemical works in the Newton library. The extent to which his alchemical works were annotated . . . gave rise to the celebrated epithet of Keynes that Newton was the last of the magicians," by which Keynes probably meant the magi of biblical prophecy.[7] What is important is not so much Newton's controversial commitment to alchemical thought as that "the literature of alchemy, hermeticism, and Paracelsian natural philosophy remained in vogue and was required reading among the serious scholars of Newton's generation."[8] Even an early rational philosopher like Francis Bacon (1561–1626), generally opposed to occult knowledge, was a believer in that segment of astrology that dealt with the impact of the stars, especially comets, on human life and history. And English Baconians "devised a means whereby physical astrology could be subject to precise experimental inquiry," as Jung did several centuries later, probably under their inspiration.[9] And although seventeenth-century England was chockablock with dissenter prophets, every serious scientific and philosophical thinker including Newton believed in the biblical prophecy that the end of the world was imminent, even though there was no consensus on actual dates.[10] Webster uses the term *physico-theologies* to describe the interpenetration of science and occult knowledge in the seventeenth and early eighteenth century.

To get back to the other distinctive feature of those virtuosos who appear in the rest of my essay: for most of them, a frightful trance illness and the dark night of the soul had spiritual meaning and consequence, but, except for Blake, it was not an explicitly Christian one. The devil does not appear in them. Nor does he appear in the powerful sonnets of Gerard Manley Hopkins when he wrestles with God. Satan does not intrude into Hopkins's despair, a despair that he overcomes with special poignancy in "Carrion Comfort."[11] It is as if the two important movements in Europe in early and late modernity had a profound impact on them: the Protestant Reformations and the revolution in scientific and philosophical thought after Descartes and Spinoza and British empiricism, all entailing in their differing ways the intrusion of skepticism into religious life and thought. These developments led to the demise of alchemical experiments as they gave way to modern chemistry.

Let us now return to Jacob Boehme who opposed Reason, or "reasoning," for understanding the divine presence in our lives. Early modern scientific rationality had no impact on his thought. Boehme died when Descartes was twenty-eight and the long shadow of Cartesianism had not yet fallen on Boehme's Europe as it did on Blake's. Boehme is an extraordinary complex theologian, difficult to summarize in a short exposition. To me his visionary experiences cannot be separated from his illness, which he defined as a state of "melancholy" that, in turn, released a profound Christian epiphany whose contents were later formulated by him in rational terms. "Melancholy" was defined in Boehme's time as one of four temperaments, and it cannot be equated with the modern psychiatric notion of depression or bipolar disorder. Boehme's melancholy is closer in time and in spirit to Albrecht Durer's somber depiction of an alchemist suffering from "melencolia" (1514). It should be remembered that Blake, who also suffered from "the pit of melancholy," had a copy of this painting "hung in his workroom until his death."[12]

Most modern commentators on Boehme I have read mention the *fact* of his visionary experiences but not their content or context with the notable exceptions of Howard Brinton, Evelyn Underhill, and, recently, Andrew Weeks.[13] Let me quote Evelyn Underhill's sympathetic account of Boehme's central transformative vision of 1600, the one best known to us: "Jacob Boehme . . . having one day as he sat in his room 'gazed fixedly upon a burnished pewter dish which reflected the sunshine with great brilliance,' fell into a inward ecstasy, and it seemed to

5.1 Albrecht Durer, *Melencolia* (1514). *Art Resource*

him as if he could look into the principles and deepest foundations of things.'"[14] Ignoring for the moment the obvious examples of our female penitents, there is the case of Nicholas of Cusa, who, during a return trip from Venice in 1437, records a similar religious revelation, "which he describes as a divine gift [that] brought him to a vision of the 'incomprehensible' and a way of speaking about the ineffable for which he says he had for years struggled unsuccessfully before receiving this illumination." Even though Nicholas does not spell out his vision, it is out of this experience that he received "from on high" the crucial concept of "learned ignorance."[15] And we should know by now that a brief time-bound experience such as a ray of light on the mirrored surface of a pewter dish might yield a huge time-expanded vision. No wonder Boehme can say: "I do not write of my own accord but by the witness of the Spirit which no one can withstand. It stands in its own strength and does not depend on our desire or will." And again, anticipating Blake, as it were: "I have always written as the Spirit dictated and left no place for reason."[16]

It seems that the vision triggered by the beam of light on Boehme's pewter dish was not an all-or-nothing episode.[17] This experience, or similar ones, were apparently repeated until around 1612 and mentioned in retrospect in "A letter to an Enquirer," a customs officer at Beuten in 1621. In it Boehme says that the gate (presumably the biblical strait gate) was opened for him and then:

> In one quarter of an hour I saw and knew more than if I had been many years to-gether at a University. . . . For I *saw and knew* the Being of all Beings, the Byss (the ground or original foundation) and Abyss (that which is without ground, or bot-tomless and fathomless); also the birth or eternal generation of the holy Trinity; the descent and original of this world, and of all creatures, through the divine wis-dom [Sophia]. . . . And I saw, and knew the whole Being in the evil, and in the good; and the mutual original, and existence of each of them. . . . For I had a thorough view of the universe, as in a CHAOS, wherein all things are couched and wrapt up, but *it was impossible for me to explicate and unfold the same.*
>
> Yet it opened itself in me, from time to time, as in a young plant: albeit the same was with me for the space of twelve years, and I was as it were pregnant (or breeding of it) with all, and found a powerful driving and instigation within me, *before I could bring it forth into external form of writing*; which afterward fell upon me as a sudden shower, which hitteth whatsoever it lighteth upon; just so it happened to me, whatsoever I could apprehend, and bring into the external principle of my mind the same I wrote down.[18]

"Saw and knew": this is the way of visionary knowledge, exemplified by the Buddha's own trance, in which *knowing emerges from seeing*. The short empirical frame of fifteen minutes of vision contained the essence of Boehme's thought, which he expounded and expanded in his later work. Boehme highlights the difficulty of "explicating" or explaining the visual experience, condensed ("couched and wrapt up") as it was. Opening up the vision to discursive and con-ceptual thought was a slow process as Boehme, "from time to time," began to un-pack the meanings of what he saw and then put them down in writing. It seems that the epiphany that Boehme first experienced in 1600 through the prism of that perverse pewter was repeated off and on for twelve years when *Aurora*, his first work, was written. The twelve-year period was a long dark night of the soul, glimpses of which appear in his early writing, especially in *Aurora*, "the sun rise" or "dawn," that beautiful metaphor we are already familiar with wherein the visionary comes close to awakening from his trance. Needless to say, the metaphor of daybreak is my interpretation of the term *aurora*: it is neither Boehme's nor his commentators. In Boehme's case, the ups and downs of his dark night involve a periodic thinning out, a dawning of truth, one might say. That truth, enfolded in layers and layers of meaning, is difficult to unravel, as Boehme joins others who have opened up their minds to aphoristic thinking in our metaphoric daybreak and then to more discursive forms of expression, initially in bits and pieces that are then welded into the whole represented in *Aurora*. Although the "pewter vision" seems absurd to those nurtured in scientific rationality, we now know that such a visionary experience could have released an "illumination" of great depth and significance.

Now let me hesitantly venture into Boehme's experience of the dark night of the soul from 1600, the date of his pewter vision, and 1612, when *Aurora* was completed, alongside what seems to be a "trance illness," although one or many it is difficult to say. No chronological sequence of his long illness is possible, but I shall focus on the glimpses that appear in his texts especially in chapter 19 of *Aurora*, heeding the fact that Boehme's recollections appear in retrospect, not as a description of the events as they occurred. There, in a key statement, Boehme says that he believed in the work of naturalists or artists who had measured the distance from earth to heaven where God dwells and discovered its shape and form, but his own revelation taught him otherwise owing to the power of the Holy Spirit. "But when this had given me many a hard blow and *repulse,* doubtless from the [holy] spirit which had a great longing yearning towards me, at last I finally fell into a very *deep melancholy* and heavy sadness, when I beheld and contemplated the great deep of this world, also the sun and stars, the clouds, rain and snow, and considered in my spirit the *whole* creation of this world."[19]

In his deep and prolonged melancholy, he witnesses in the spirit the world's creation and also the doctrine of the material world charged with spirit. Boehme also sensed an intuitive understanding of the theodicy, that problem of good and evil in relation to the awesome power of a loving God. Moreover, this knowledge, based on his experience of the violent life of his time, emerges in the epiphany, especially the idea it is the unjust person who reaps rewards rather than the pious. "But finding that in all things there was evil and good, as well in the *elements* as in the creatures, and that it went as *well* in this world with the wicked as with the virtuous, honest, and Godly; also that the *barbarous* people had the best countries in their possession, and that they had *more prosperity* in their ways than the virtuous, honest and Godly had" (A, 486–87). This troubled him exceedingly, and even the Scripture in which he was well versed was no help. Meanwhile "the devil [Lucifer] would by no means stand idle, but was *often* beating into me many heathenish thoughts, which I will here be silent in" (A, 487). Hegel points out this conflict nicely when he says that "this struggle characterizes all his writings and brings about the torture of his mind."[20]

Unfortunately, like many monks and male virtuosos but quite unlike our female penitents, Boehme does not bare his innermost thoughts during his confrontation with the devil. Boehme's devil is not Satan, but Satan's manifestation as Lucifer, the being of beauty and light and evil. The heathenish thoughts with which Lucifer tempted Boehme were perhaps homosexual desires, but this is only my guess. However, in his affliction, Boehme managed to raise his spirit up to God, and he began to "*incessantly* wrestle with the love and mercy of God, and not to give over, until he blessed me, that is, until he *enlightened me with his holy spirit*, whereby I might *understand* his will, and be rid of my sadness" (A, 487). Thus with the assistance of the spirit of God, "*suddenly* after some violent storms made, my spirit *did break through* the gates of hell" and then reached the "innermost birth and geniture of the Deity." Reborn in the very bosom of the deity, Boehme "was embraced with love, as a bridegroom embraceth his dearly beloved bride." This triumph of the spirit cannot be described in speech or writing, but he felt that it was "like the resurrection from the dead" (A, 488). In terms of our dominant metaphor, Boehme has become an awakened one.

Boehme does not and cannot describe the details of his spiritual crisis except in terms of its resolution, the presence of God within him and everywhere in all creatures, "even in herbs and grass." "And suddenly in that light my will was set on by a mighty *impulse*, to describe *the being of God*." Because he could not fully understand "the *deepest* births of God in their *being*, and comprehend them in my *reason*, there passed almost *twelve* years, before the exact understanding thereof was given me" (A, 488). In other words, Boehme took twelve years before he could put the ideas he received from the Spirit in reflective scribal form. The knowledge that comes to him originally is through illumination; yet even his later writing is a manifestation of God's will expressed through Boehme's rational re-presentation of his visions. And "though I should *irritate* or enrage the whole world, the devil, and all the gates of hell, I will look on and wait what the LORD intendeth with it" (A, 489).

Boehme's advice for those who would walk the same path is found in many places in his writing, but more forcefully in chapter 13, which deals with the fall of Lucifer's kingdom. Here Boehme says he had climbed in spirit up Jacob's ladder straight to heaven. But those who wish to reap this reward must suffer from frequent giddiness of the head and then "climb through the midst or centre of the kingdom of hell, and there he will feel by experience what a *deal* of scoffings and upbraidings he must endure," implicitly comparing his suffering to Christ's own humiliation on the cross (A, 314).

Boehme's dense and often enigmatic prose expresses his own difficulty in conveying the depth and the mystery of his experience through conceptual thought. Contradictions and confusions exist, and one can only sympathize with Boehme critics and scholars who try to create systemic order from his visionary "CHAOS, wherein all things are couched and wrapt up"! Boehme's chaos theory is not our ordinary sense of "chaos," but heralds the beginnings of order from the *prima materia*. That underlying sense of order has been spelled out sympatheti- cally by Andrew Weeks from his understanding of *Aurora*: "the inert lifelessness of elemental matter, the power of the sun and the power which like gravity, holds the world together; the omnipresent life-giving spirit; the meaning of Christ's presence in the bread and wine of Communion, the relations of faith and knowl- edge, the validity of extra-scriptural sources of truth, the reality of free will; the issues of war and peace and of justice and tyranny; the hidden God, the hidden meaning of Scripture, and the hidden forces operating in nature, the design of microcosm and macrocosm; the utopian freedom of the angels, and the oppres- sion and exploitation within human society."[21]

I will only deal with those aspects of Boehme's work that influenced the vi- sionaries who will soon appear in my essay. These are Boehme's redefinition of the Godhead by bringing in the virgin Sophia, the seven fountain spirits of God that exemplify the power and presence of spirit in the universe, the problem of the androgyny of God and Adam, and two issues that come from very early Greek and Christian thought, namely, the bothersome problem of the theodicy that I have already mentioned and the *unio oppositorum* or the conjunction of opposites that engenders a wholeness of spirit.[22]

With the decline in Mariological piety in the Middle Ages and the emotional void it produced, the imagery and beliefs associated with the Virgin Mary were employed by Boehme and his followers in the construction of the feminine in the persona of the virgin Sophia.[23] Sophia is intrinsically part of the Godhead, the feminine principle within God himself, although sometimes she appears, like the occasionally deified Mary, as part of a "quarternity." As with the Jewish Kabbalah, the "necessary balance of male wrath and female love within the godhead was the essence of Boehme's theology" (GM, 70). There is no notion of the ex nihilo creation Luther envisaged because, for Boehme, if you will pardon the pun, noth- ing can come out of nothing. Or, as Boehme himself put it, "Now, where noth- ing is, there nothing can be: All things must have a root, else nothing can grow" (A, 501). Yet his theology perhaps answers what Schreber thought unanswerable, namely, if God created the world, how did God himself come into being? Gibbons puts this central idea well:

> Everything derives from a totally transcendent godhead, which Boehme calls the Abyss (*Ungrund*). . . . The Abyss is a "nothing" which, in order to become manifest, "bringeth it selfe into a will." This will, corresponding to the Father in the Trinity, is itself incomplete, since all manifestation requires contrariety. It therefore calls forth an opposing principle, the desire, corresponding to the Son. These are Boehme's first two Principles, those of the fire-world and the light-world, "God's wrath-spirit" and "a Meek *love*-source." Boehme insists that these Principles are "not parted asunder" since "the Light dwelleth in the Fire." The interrelationship between these two produces a third Principle, corresponding to the Holy Spirit, in which the godhead becomes complete.[24]

(GM, 89–90)

It is through the Third Principle that the abyssal will become manifest in creation, because it is the "magia" of the Godhead. Into this dynamic notion of the Godhead, Boehme introduces a fresh dimension, that of Virgin Wisdom or Sophia. "Sophia stands eternally before God, a mirror in which he sees the wonders of his own Being," these being the seven "fountain-spirits" or qualities which are to provide the structure of the created world (GM, 90). Because I have already introduced Boehme's notion of Sophia, the Godhead, and the abyss, let us now dwell, admittedly in a schematic manner, on the foundational medical meaning of the seven qualities that have been neglected or downplayed by Boehme scholarship, which in my opinion not only refer back to Paracelsus but also to the earlier tradition of Galenic medicine.[25]

The basic idea underlying the seven qualities is found in chapter 8 of *Aurora,* which deals with the spirit of God present in the created world. "*All power* is in God the Father, and he is the *fountain* of all powers in his deep; in *him* are light and darkness, air and water, heat and cold, hard and soft, thick and thin, sound and tone, sweet and sour, bitter and astringent, and that which I *cannot* number or rehearse" (A, 148). These qualities can be subsumed under the seven, but four are the foundational ones and they are based on the medical theories of the time. These four are the astringent, the sharp or harsh quality; the sweet that "mitigateth the astringent, so that it is altogether lovely, pleasant and mild or meek"; then the bitter quality, which, if it is kindled too much, "is like a tearing, stinging, and burning poison, as when a man is tormented with a raging plague-sore"; the fourth quality, which expresses the divine power of God the Father as heat, "the true beginning of life, and also the true spirit of life," because it was out of heat and light that the son was created.[26]

Chapter 8 not only has a detailed account of these four fundamental qualities but also shows how they move in the body and in nature and transform themselves, just as metals and mineral substances are transformed in alchemical experiments and the medical theories of Paracelsus. Boehme says: "Now in the body these qualities are *mixed*, as if they were but one quality; yet each quality moveth or boileth in its own power, and so goeth forth." Let me demonstrate with a few examples how these transformations affect the human body in terms of the dry or astringent quality that will shrivel up the body but can be counteracted by the sweet, the watery or cooling quality. "For it [the astringent] drieth all the other powers [qualities], and *retaineth* them all through its infection or *influence;* and the sweet softeneth and moisteneth all the others, whereby they become daintily pleasant and mild or soft" (A, 160). That is, the qualities can be antagonistic such as the opposition between the sweet, the bitter and the astringent but they can be mixed and eventually lose their antagonist character. "When the sweet quality thus stretcheth or *wideneth* itself, and retireth from the bitter, then the astringent always presseth after it, and *would* also fain taste of the sweet: and always maketh the body, that is behind it, and *in* it, to be dry; for the sweet quality is the mother of the water, and is very meek, mild, soft and gentle" (A, 163). Again: while the sweet quality flies away from its bitter opposite as it does from the dry astringent quality, the latter two hasten up to the sweet, and refresh themselves from the sweet. Thus the sweet is a blending and "tempering" agent that softens and moisturizes the bitter and the astringent. When as in fatness the sweet is predominant then it happens that "fat creatures are always merrier and frolicker than the lean, because the *sweet spirit*, floweth more abundantly in them than in the lean" (A, 171).

Although his illustrative examples are from the work of the human body, Boehme makes it clear that these principles apply to all of nature. "This is the true springing or *vegetation* in nature, be it in man, beast, wood, herbs or stones" (A, 164). But stones and related substances are not like living matter in the creatural world. The astringent or harsh or contracting quality is predominant in stones, but without the revivifying power of heat, and for this reason one cannot kindle light in a stone, he says (A, 170). So is the black earth where the bitter is predominant; and it also contains the dryness of astringency. Thus, to produce fire out of the earth, some of the qualities it contains have to be realigned or removed or, as he says in his metaphoric language, "boiled out of it." And when this happens to earth one might be able to extract gunpowder from it. Perhaps to meet the objection that the aforementioned qualities are purely medical, Boehme constantly emphasizes the presence of the spirit of God in them—and sometimes of his antagonist. Thus, in respect of the capacity of gunpowder to create fire, he says that "this light is but a flash or a spirit of *terror*, wherein the devil in the anger of God representeth himself" (A, 170).

The next three fountain spirits of the Lord complicate the preceding picture, and I can only hint at their complexity. The fifth nurturing quality is love, the quality of God the father expressed through his son and found in varying degrees in creatural life wherein his love appears "*gracious, amiable*, blessed, friendly and joyful" (A, 181). Because the preceding four are God's own fountain spirits, love also basks in them. God's love makes all the other qualities soft, pleasant and joyful as the following example illustrates: "That friendly *courteous* love-light-fire goeth along in the sweet quality, and riseth up into the bitter and astringent qualities, and so *kindleth* the bitter and astringent qualities, *feeding* them with the sweet *love-sap*, refreshing, quickening and enlightening them, and making them *living* or lively, cheerful and friendly" (A, 181–82). The sixth quality is tone or sound, and this includes speech, not meaningless utterances but those that are comprehensible or intelligible. Tone also is dependent on the preceding qualities and their admixture. Sound or tone however is not confined to what occurs on earth but also in heaven as Boehme's Pythagorean image of the music of the spheres indicates: "What we call tones upon earth in song and sound, are very coarse compared with these extremely subtle heavenly tones, as with the soul inwardly sports in itself, and hears within pleasant and sweet tones, but outwardly hears nothing."[27] Hence these heavenly tones can only be heard by near-perfect beings, the Angels.[28]

All the previous six qualities ultimately devolve on the seventh, which is God's corporeality, the "corpus" that represents God's reign over the universe where the previous qualities are reconciled and divested of contradictions. They create what Martensen calls "wholeness, the complete One, the Uncreated Heaven, the Kingdom or harmony," all of which express the glory of God.[29] The seventh quality is embodied in the angels, who consequently represent that wholeness or perfection (A, 316). Ultimately all seven qualities can be subsumed under the first three principles, which constitute "'a tripartite apportionment of divine will: pure unmanifested energy (Father), reflected energy within matter (Son) and matter itself (Holy Spirit)'" (GM, 91).[30] The seven qualities are "bound and united with the *whole* God, that they should not qualify in any other way, either higher or brighter or more vehemently than God himself," which is what Lucifer did (A, 318–19). Boehme reminds us that Lucifer was the most beautiful of all the angels until he tried to surpass God, rising up against him, and this fault led to his fall. Concomitantly, the six qualities present in Lucifer when he was an angel realigned themselves, especially the "astringent quality [which] attracted or compacted the *body* too hard together, so that sweet water was *dried* up." Astringency then linked up with the bitter in the body of Lucifer making him the evil being he became for all Christians (A, 343). Boehme seems to tread not the path of the angels but that of anti-Lutheran and anti-Calvinist heresy, especially his reformulation of a key figure that influenced him, Paracelsus.

Let me now return to Boehme's reformulation of Paracelsus in his doctrine of the seven qualities. The two foundational principles of his doctrine are the presence of spirit in nature and the movement of the four primary qualities found in the natural world. Hence, if the four qualities in metals could be experimentally mixed, then it is in principle possible to create more subtle and precious substances from their combination and permutation. The ideal example comes from precious stones that embody the seventh quality and in this sense constitutes one model that alchemists strove for, namely, creating precious metal out of grosser ones. Although Boehme denied he was a "Chymist" (alchemist), he employs an alchemical vocabulary throughout. He also "claimed to know how to turn metal into gold if he desired" (GM, 75). Thus the four foundational qualities I mentioned are further complicated by Boehme's occult and alchemical thinking.

Once again a few examples might help us understand this aspect of his thought when he associates Saturn "as the 'dryer' of all forces" whose action creates stones and earth. Saturn is dry (*herb*) because it is primarily affected by the astringent and the bitter. "Mars bears a raging, storming, poisonous, and destructive force. The quality of Mars is bitter" and the tempestuous qualities of Mars are also found when bitter is prominent among humans.[31] The relation between the seven qualities and the planets and their effect on human beings is neatly summarized by Weeks in the following table.

1. Dry: Saturn: melancholy, power of death
2. Sweet: Jupiter: sanguine, gentle source of life
3. Bitter: Mars: choleric, destructive source of life
4. Water/fire: Moon, Sun: night/day; evil/good; temptation to sin/triumphant virtue
5. Love: Venus: love of life, spiritual rebirth
6. Sound: Mercury: keen spirit, illumination, expression
7. Corpus: Earth: totality of forces awaiting spiritual rebirth.[32]

What we have in Boehme is not the well-known homology of the microcosm with the macrocosm. Instead, the seven qualities and the spirit of God infuse in different degrees the then-known cosmos and all of material, vegetative, and human life, microcosm as well as macrocosm. "Thus God is one God, with seven qualifying or fountain spirits one in another, where always one guarantees the others, and yet is but one God" (A, 331). When Hopkins says that the nature is charged with "the grandeur of God" and that it is a kind of "Heraclitean fire," he is not only pointing to Heraclitus but also to Boehme. With Hopkins, as with Blake, it is no longer the father whose spirit permeates nature but, through his creation, the son, as Hopkins's beautiful last lines, with its alchemical symbolism, indicate.

> In a flash, at a trumpet clash,
> I am all at once what Christ is, since he was what I am, and
> This Jack, joke, poor potsherd, patch, matchwood, immortal diamond,
> Is immortal diamond.[33]

If, in principle, all persons are infused with the divine spirit, then there is no radical distinction among peoples, undermining a fundamental idea in virtually every form of Christian orthodoxy that excludes those who haven't received its revelatory truth. As Boehme says, "*whether* he be Christian, Jew or Turk or a Heathen; it is all the same to me; my warehouse shall stand open to anyone" (A, 313). This breath of fresh air went into the English dissenters of the seventeenth and early eighteenth centuries, including Blake:

> And all shall love the human form,
> In heathen, turk or jew;
> Where Mercy, Love and Pity dwell
> There God is dwelling too.[34]

There is nothing unusual in Boehme's transformation of the seven qualities in occult terms. Most thinkers of early modern Europe not only employed an alchemical vocabulary but also employed the vocabulary of astrology and other forms of occultism. It is a later quirk of fortune that terms like *occult, hermetic,* and *alchemical* were used interchangeably to characterize the creative work of this period. As we have noted, the term *esotericism* was used as a similar catchall term in the nineteenth century.[35]

Although Paracelsus is a key figure for Boehme, I think that as far as his oppositional dialectic is concerned it is closer in spirit with the earlier tradition of Galen (born c. 129 CE), who, as with the Indians, emphasized the oppositional nature of the humors and the way they interact in the human body.[36] We noted a similar feature in Boehme's doctrine of the four qualities that then become uni-fied in their admixture, in turn leading to good or bad consequences. In addition to Galen, Boehme was directly influenced by the earlier Christian tradition of *coincidentia oppositorum* in such thinkers as Nicholas of Cusa and Eriugena, and this aspect of his thought was passed on to both Blake and Jung. We will examine its significance further on in this essay, but, for the moment, reaffirm that union of opposites express wholeness, be it in medicine or alchemy or in the earlier Catholic thinkers, whereby elements, once separate, are fused into a new holistic conception. Thus fire and water in Behmenist thought share an ultimate identity a "*unio oppositorum* symbolized by marriage and androgyny" (GM, 84).

Let me now come back to Sophia, the feminine principle of the Godhead rejected by Protestantism, where it has an almost heretical implication. In Boehme's thought, marriage of the soul with Sophia was "the most common im-age for man's union with God," and he uses the conventional mystical language to explain this relationship when he says, "shee came and comforted mee, and married her selfe to mee."[37] For later Behmenists, Sophia appears in visions, as she did to Jane Lead, whose entire theological corpus was the product of inspired visions that were then revised and brought in line with a not-too-inspired prose. Lead's visions were often triggered when she was engaged in lonely walks in a grove or woods while sojourning in "a solitary country place." Here is the first of many visions recorded in her work, *A Fountain of Gardens*. "There came upon me an overshadowing bright Cloud, and in the midst of it the Figure of a Woman, most richly adorned with transparent Gold, her Hair hanging down, and her Face as the terrible Crystal for brightness, but her Countenance was sweet and mild. At which sight I was somewhat amazed, but immediately this Voice came, saying, Behold I am God's Eternal Virgin-Wisdom, whom thou hast been enquiring af-ter. . . . Out of my Womb thou shalt be brought forth after the manner of a Spirit, Conceived and Born again."[38] I find it hard to believe that Sophia did not appear to Boehme in similar fashion.

Perhaps the most startling of Boehme's thought for the established religions (Lutheranism, Calvinism, and Catholicism) is his resurrection of the original an-drogyny of human kind. We have already discussed the problem of androgyny in myth and dream, as well as psychically in those, like Schreber, who have had a felt need to develop an androgynous being in one's own body through fantasy, and the fantastic visionary realization of androgyny among Tibetan visionaries. An-drogyny has a kind of subversive quality as far as traditional Christian beliefs are concerned. Yet some argued that if Genesis 1:27 says both male and female were created in God's image then one can say God himself possesses an androgynous nature.[39] Further, "from the early Talmudic period onwards, this text [Genesis] has led some commentators to believe in the original androgyny of Adam and the duality of divine gender." And though such notions were more pronounced in Gnosticism and in the older hermeticism than in mainline Christianity, at least one major thinker, John Scottus Eriugena, "anticipated Boehme in seeing the Fall as a loss of androgyny which Christ was able to repair because he 'united the masculine and feminine in a single person'" (GM, 61). Thus Adamic androgyny is central to Boehme's theology and Theosophy. For him Adam apparently existed on a spiritual plane, and therefore "he could go through Earth and Stone, uninterrupted by anything" (GM, 95). One might add that Boehme's Adam had the kind of powers attributed to the Mahāyāna Buddhas and to Tantric virtuosos and, further, that Adam resembled the Jesus of the Docetic heresies who was also a spiritual being *without* physical characteristics and was not incarnate in the flesh.

In Boehme's conception, Adam had two falls. In the first, while Adam was still an androgynous being, he committed adultery by having intercourse with a stranger because his androgynous female counterpart, represented in the Virgin Sophia, refused to accept his sexual advances. He had thus violated the spiritual component of his being by turning from the heavenly spiritual side to the material. Hence Sophia or Divine Wisdom accused him of committing much sin and wickedness by betraying her and showering affection on a stranger (GM, 95–96). The original androgynous pair, being entirely spiritual, had been created to "converse and embrace each other, but not to experience desire or to copulate" (GM, 96). The consequence of this fall is that Adam entered a forty-day sleep when God removed heavenly wisdom from Adam's being. In this long sleep "his angelform and might lay on the ground and fell in helplessness."[40] According to Gibbons, this means that Adam has fallen from androgyny into gender (GM, 96). The fall from androgyny is also a loss of the complete image of the androgynous god that he originally possessed, the unity of what Boehme, borrowing an alchemical concept, calls "tinctures," the fiery masculine and the watery feminine.

After the second fall, the conventional one in Genesis, Eve inherits the watery tincture while Adam inherits the fiery. Following Paracelsus's thought, heterosexuality becomes the search for the lost wholeness, the original androgyny, but now expressed and recovered, however imperfectly, in the union of male and female, fire and water (GM, 95). The original state of androgyny, split as a result of the first fall, is renewed in the marriage of man and woman and in the androgyny of Christ. As Boehme puts it: "A man without a woman is not whole, only with a woman is he whole" (cited in GM, 84–85). Both falls entail a reinterpretation of Genesis 1:23–24, which says that in intercourse a "man will cleave unto his wife: and they shall be one flesh." But in the second fall Adam and Eve "were given the members for animal reproduction along with earthly intestines in which they could bag vanity and live as beasts."[41] If God gave Adam bestial form and endowed him with the "shape of Masculine Members," Eve was worse off (GM, 100). God in his "angry wrath" saw to it that she "became in one part of her soul, in her inner nature, a half-devil and in the other part, the external world, a beast."[42] Both Paracelsus and Boehme (and their followers) admit that man and woman were created from an original material matrix, but for both thinkers woman remains an inferior vehicle in relation to man. In Boehme she is especially gruesome. Sophia then can be seen as an escape from Eve's bestiality.[43]

Nevertheless, there is hope for the descendants of Boehme's Adam and Eve. In the sixth treatise on the "supersensual life," in *The Way to Christ* (1620), the student asks his master on the fate of humans after the imminent apocalyptic end of the world. The reply is that humans will be reborn in spiritual form, the very form Adam lost through his sexual desire. And then the master adds: "There shall be neither man nor woman, but all shall be like God's angels, androgynous virgins, neither daughter, son, brother, nor sister, but all one sex in Christ, all of one [piece] like a tree with all its branches, and yet separate creatures; but God all in all."[44] Many of our contemporary Christian fundamentalists might find our androgynous destiny rather reprehensible. Not for me!

Now let me return to the central feature of Boehme's thought, namely, the theodicy whereby he absolves God from the authorship of sin by making evil synonymous with the disharmony of the seven qualities. If "A letter to an Enquirer" and the sections from chapter 19 that I quoted earlier reflect Boehme's spiritual crisis of 1600 and after, then it seems that he wrestled with the problem of good and evil during that crucial period. It is likely that part of Boehme's motivation, whether consciously aware or not, in discovering the seven fountains or qualities through his visions is to resolve the theodicy. In a very interesting shift, "Boehme tells us 'the meek light [of the Second Principle] maketh the stearn nature of the Father meek, lovely, and merciful,' and the divinity is called God 'not from the Fires property, but from the Lights property.'" Hence "'the Father is onely called an holy God in the Son.'" For Gibbons, Boehme's God is conceived in a feminine stereotype rather than in the masculine stereotype of Calvinism. Boehme's God is meekness, and he is "'love and the Good,'" echoing I think an original Plotinian or Platonic concept. There is no angry thought in him, "'and Man's punishment was not but from himself'" (GM, 92). I find it hard to accept Gibbons attributing to Boehme the idea of God conceived in a feminine mold; this is true of Jesus, but everywhere Boehme's God is a wrathful being, though, as with orthodox forms of Christianity, he is also a loving God.

Boehme dilutes the theodicy among the seven agencies, which are subsumed under the three principles that are in turn subsumed in the Trinity, with the abyss usurping a good part of the role of God in the work of his creation. These are simply one of many stratagems Boehme employed to resolve the issue of unjust suffering he had to face during the brutal times in which he lived.[45] There is no doubt Boehme was sensitive to the oppression of the poor by princes, as this question by the student to the master in *The Way to Christ* indicates: "How will those fare on the day of such Judgment who thus torment the poor and the wretched, sucking their very sweat from them, oppressing them, drawing them down with force, viewing them as something to trample, so that they themselves may be important and may destroy their sweat in proud and vain voluptuousness?"[46] I am not sure whether the master's reply that God will eventually punish the oppressors could either ameliorate the suffering of the poor or truly console them. And how can one exempt God, who is both powerful and kind, for not helping the poor in the here and the now? It is extremely difficult for any Christian, Boehme included, admitting that the responsibility for sin and evil must in an ultimate sense rest with God. As I shall demonstrate later, a heretical and daring solution to the problem of theodicy is Blake, who simply ignores or dismisses the father and the moral law of the commandments and idealizes Christ as the androgynous being who is not born of the virgin, either Mary or Sophia. Another solution is through heretical movements such as Manichaeanism and Gnosticism, wherein, as Weber pointed out with respect to Zoroastrianism, unmerited suffering and evil become the work of a malign and powerful deity who stands opposed to a benevolent but not all-powerful God.[47] In the seventh treatise of *The Way to Christ,* Boehme comes close to such a solution that he thought fell within the frame of Christian orthodoxy.[48] Yet, as Robin Waterfield says, "Boehme never completely reconciled the wrath of God of which he was intensely conscious with the notion of the all-loving God of conventional Christianity."[49]

The seventh treatise in *The Way to Christ* is a question and answer session that begins with Reason, who, among other things, asks the following question: how could one know a God whom one has never seen and who's dwelling one does not even know? Reason begins to wonder why "all things are mortal and fragile." Reason poses the problem of theodicy, but Reason "is the natural [cultural] life whose ground is in a temporal beginning and end" and cannot come into the "supernatural ground where God is to be understood."[50] Boehme's natural life and conception of time is the "empirical time" (that we have discussed in the Buddha mythos). The "hidden God" cannot be found therein.

Thus Reason thinks there is no God who takes up the cause of sorrowing men. Perhaps the most pertinent question asked by Reason is the following. "Why has God created a painful, suffering life? Would it not have been better in this world without suffering and anguish, since He is the ground and beginning of all things? Why does He tolerate the disobedient will? Why does He not break evil so that good alone remains in all things?" And the answer: "No thing may be revealed to itself without contrariety. If it has no thing that resists it, it always goes out from itself and does not go into itself again. . . . Moreover, if there is no contrariety in life there would be no perceptivity, nor willing nor working, nor understanding, nor knowledge, for a thing that has one will has no divisibility. If it does not discover a contrary will that causes in it a drive to movement, it remains still. For one single thing does not know more than one [thing]; and if it is in itself good, it knows neither evil nor good, for it has nothing in itself that makes it perceptive."[51] Thus, to know evil, one has to have good and vice versa. Here Boehme falls back once again on the powerful Christian tradition of the union of opposites, but projected onto the attributes of God himself, in whom the whole epistemology of oppositions rests. What is in God is also in life and nature, which is compounded of good and evil and other opposites, and these oppositions ultimately rest in God and spring from his very being.[52] Without the one there is no way of understanding the other. "Evil, as a contrary will, causes the good, as will, to press again toward its own cause, toward God, and to become desirous again of the good, as the good will. For a thing that is good only in itself, having no anguish, desires nothing, for it knows nothing better in itself or for itself after which it can lust."[53] Moreover, anticipating another popular argument in Christianity, "the hidden God . . . reveals Himself in the mind of man, punishes injustice in his conscience and, by suffering, draws unjust suffering to Himself."[54]

Philosophers of salvation religions have been obsessed with the problem of theodicy as was Boehme. He too can only dilute the problem of the theodicy, but cannot resolve it, because the theodicy is *logically irresolvable*. One cannot grasp its ultimate irrelevance in the ground of Reason where philosophers have their home, but only when one is *thrown* outside of time into the "supernatural ground" where Boehme's hidden God has his being. (See the following note for my definition of "thrownness.")[55]

WILLIAM BLAKE AND THE THEORY OF VISION

I was more miserable than my work-a-day companions, because the very intensity of vision made the recoil more unendurable. It was an agony of darkness and oblivion, wherein I seemed like those who in nightmare are buried in caverns so deep beneath the roots of the world that there is no hope of escape, for the way out is unknown, and the way to them is forgotten by those who walk in light. In those black hours the universe, a gigantic presence, seemed at war with me.

—A. E. (George Russell), *The Candle of Vision*

Unlike some of our Christian penitents, Blake, like Boehme, gives us little life history or hagiography to fall back on. Yet, like the others mentioned in this essay, Blake is a visionary par excellence, defying Enlightenment rationality or what he, following Boehme, calls "Reason." I therefore propose to approach Blake by focusing for the most part on what he says about himself and what those who knew him say about his gift of vision. I will begin with three of Blake's prose works, two very brief early pamphlets, circa 1788, *There Is No Natural Religion* (first and second series) and *All Religions Are One,* followed much later by a third entitled *A Descriptive Catalogue* (1809), a detailed guide to some of his mature paintings exhibited in London in his brother's hosiery shop.[56] All three help us pin down some of Blake's elusive thoughts on the epistemological backdrop of his visionary experiences.

Natural Religion (first series) begins as a simple critique of deism, the religion of Enlightenment rationalists. Blake highlights the basic proposition of deism, thus: "Man has no notion of moral fitness but from Education. Naturally he is only a natural organ subject to Sense." That is, our perceptions are grounded in the physiology of our bodies and all we do and desire is limited by our physically determined perceptions. Even morality is a product of education (socialization), whereas for Blake it comes from our identity with Jesus. The falseness of these propositions is expounded in the second series where he maintains the very opposite of what he thinks is the Enlightenment position and perhaps of British empiricism from Locke to Hume: "Man's perceptions are not bounded by organs of perception; he perceives more than sense (tho' ever so acute) can discover" and "Reason, or the ratio of all we have already known, is not the same that it shall be when we know more" through nonrational means. Bounded perception, with its finite sense-derived knowledge, can only produce "the same dull round, even of a universe, would soon become a mill with complicated wheels," a critique of god and the universe caught in the mechanical movement of contemporary deism.

What transcends this dull clockwork idea of natural religion? Desire, or as Blake puts it elsewhere, energy: "The desire of Man being Infinite, the possession is Infinite and himself is Infinite."[57] And energy or desire can be sexually transformed in multiple ways, but never in the orthodox Christian sense of repressive sexuality and the idealization of chastity, most clearly seen in his later "proverbs of hell" and in his erotic paintings.[58] The application of the foregoing propositions, says Blake, yields the following conclusion: "He who sees the Infinite in all things, sees God. He who sees the Ratio only, sees himself only," which is a selfish and destructive position (CW, 98). It would seem that from Blake's viewpoint *I think, I am* puts the whole onus on the ego or the person or the individual being, not on God. Both these ideas, namely, the central critique of Reason and the selfish I, are almost certainly derived from Jacob Boehme's thoroughgoing critique of Reason and the need to annihilate the "I."

One can re-present Blake by saying that the measure of mankind is not man as a physically bounded being, a position that both Boehme and Blake criticizes. Instead, man is a container of God; and simultaneously God (Jesus) becomes man, the one refracted in the other. "Therefore God becomes as we are, that we may be as he is." Or again in his 1820 *Annotations to Berkeley*: "Man is All Imagination. God is Man and exists in us and we in him." Or: "What Jesus came to Remove was the Heathen or Platonic Philosophy, which blinds the Eye of Imagination, The Real Man" (CW 775). This same idea is beautifully expressed in Blake's famous interviews with Crabb Robinson when the latter queried Blake on the divinity of Jesus: "He [Blake] said—*He is the only God*—But then he added—'And so am I and so are you'" (BR, 310). In the same spirit, Blake speaks in an inspired voice in *Jerusalem* when the savior tells Albion (who in "petrific hardness" had turned away from universal love) to react to "the loves and tears of brothers, sisters, sons, fathers and friends," which "if Man ceases to behold, he ceases to exist," a triumphant paean exalting sensitivity to human suffering, a theme that runs through all of Blake's work (CW, 664). That sensitivity is beautifully expressed in the simple first stanza of "On another's sorrow," one of Blake's songs of innocence:

> Can I see another's woe,
> And not be in sorrow too?
> Can I see another's grief,
> And not seek for kind relief?

(CW, 122)

And in more abstract fashion later on:

> We live as One Man; for contracting our infinite senses
> We behold multitude, or expanding, we behold as one,
> As One Man all the Universal Family, and that One Man

We call Jesus the Christ; and he is in us, and we in him
Live in perfect harmony in Eden, the land of life,
Giving, receiving, and forgiving each other's trespasses.

(CW, 664–65)

The quotation from *Jerusalem* is anticipated in book 1 of *Vala* (c. 1797) with the same theme.[59] Both bring us naturally to the idea that "all religions are one," the epigraph of which reads, "The Voice of one crying in the Wilderness" (CW, 98). The biblical saying takes on an added significance if one regards the "wilderness" as the mechanical world of rationality in which Blake is fated to live or what we might label as the radical Euro-rationality of the later Enlightenment. Blake sums up his argument thus: "As the true method of knowledge is experiment [experiencing], the true faculty of knowing must be the faculty which experiences." It is the human experiential faculty that moves Blake. Seven "principles" follow from this initial argument, and I will comment on a few. The first principle says: "That the Poetic Genius is the true Man, and that the body or outward form of Man is derived from the Poetic Genius. Likewise that the forms of all things are derived from the Poetic Genius, which by the Ancients was call'd an Angel and Spirit and Demon [Daimon]." If Jesus and man are the same, that is, if constituted of the same essence, then Blake adds to that equation another component, Poetic Genius. This is nothing new, he thinks, because Poetic Genius was known to ancients as angel, spirit, or demon and hence constituted a continuing vision of the world.

The second principle asserts that, while all human beings are alike in "outward form," they nevertheless possess "an infinite variety" and this variety circles back to the common human unity, that is, their possession of Poetic Genius. The third principle, as I interpret it, says that, insofar as Poetic Genius lies dormant in all of us, we are impelled to speak the truth when it comes from the "heart," the place from which the voice of the Poetic Genius emerges. This means that philosophy is in trouble because it is divided into various "sects" or schools of thought that are adapted to the weaknesses of every individual. I take this to mean that they speak from Reason and education, not from the heart. The next three principles deal with the idea that each nation's religion is derived from "each Nation's different reception of the Poetic Genius," thus presumably explaining the different forms of the religious life that ultimately springs from a single source, Poetic Genius. And that source? "The true Man is the source, he being the Poetic Genius" (CW, 98). This, of course, harks back on the previous work where the true man is Jesus. Man being Jesus is imbued with the Poetic Genius, which means that Jesus is immanent in man and in Poetic Genius. Or, to put it in more familiar terms, they partake of the same essence originally emanating from the true God, Jesus.

The idealization of Jesus as man and as the only God means there is no need for the Trinity—or not all of its components. As with many other dissenters of the time, it is the Holy Ghost that is rejected outright because Jesus is the only true and living God and born from an unknown human being to the young Mary. But what about the father? What kind of world did he create? These two questions are expressed in a late text, *Vision of the Last Judgment* (c 1810): "Thinking as I do that the Creator of this World is a very Cruel Being, and being a worshipper of Christ, I cannot help saying 'the Son, how unlike the Father!' First God Almighty comes with a Thump on the Head. Then Jesus Christ comes with a balm to heal it" (CW, 617). In kicking God off his pedestal, Blake is resolving the theodicy in a radical manner. The father may be powerful, but he is certainly not kind, an idea that is beautifully expressed in the contrast between the Lamb (Innocence) and the Tiger (Experience), those "two contrary states of the human soul." But these opposites also have to be reconciled because the world must consist of both. Hence Blake's is not a Manichaean view of the world. He has rejected the father for the son who imbues his essence in all beings and especially in those like Blake who have shed the encrustations of sense perceptions and rejected selfhood. Visionary thinkers like Boehme have elaborate arguments against Reason's critique of theodicy, but it is inconceivable for them to envisage Blake's dissenter views of Jesus as the only true God.

Blake goes on to make the Behmenist claim that the essence of the deity permeates every aspect of life such that even material things like rocks and stones and trees are imbued with the life principle, abolishing the key distinction between mind and nature that has come into prominence in his time. Thus Enitharmom, the female emanation of Los, takes various guises, including that of Catherine Blake, and sings:

> For everything that lives is holy; for the source of life
> Descends to be a weeping babe;
> For the Earthworm renews the moisture of the sandy plain.

> (*Vala*, 2, 366–68; CW, 289)

These are older ideas traceable immediately to Swedenborg and further back to Boehme and Behmenists, rooted in medieval alchemical thought and Neoplatonism and, beyond that, in Plato's famed statement in *Meno* that "all nature is kin."[60]

The variety in the material world and the universe is no different from the variety among people and nations and their religions, although in essence they emanate from a single spiritual source and are then differentiated into variations. Although Blake's universe is bound together by spiritual kinship, there is an implicit idea that human beings alone possess Poetic Genius, which for Blake is the source and ground of inspiration and vision and the other qualities that come with it, imagination and intellect, the latter term not to be confounded with Reason. In most of Blake's writing intellect is opposed to Reason and is close to its medieval Christian meaning of the soul's capacity to mirror what Christ dictates or to passively register or cognize visions and thoughts as John of the Cross formulated it. Thus, for Blake, a "tear is an intellectual thing" because it emerges from spirit or from love; hence one can be "drunk with intellectual vision."[61]

While we all share the same essence and the same capacity for inspiration and vision, they are manifest in different degrees in different persons because inspiration and vision might remain untapped or poorly utilized. To unlock vision, the doors of perception trapped in the physical senses must be cleansed, opening the road to "excess" or "impulse." This in turn leads to a wonderful statement in *The Marriage of Heaven and Hell* where Satan speaks with the voice of the poet: "I tell you, no virtue can exist without breaking these ten commandments. Jesus was all virtue, and acted from impulse, not from rules," with "rules" being moral law, which for antinomian dissenters constituted the foundation of church and state (CW, 158). Rules also refer to the law of those who believe that everything we do arises from sense perception, as the Enlightenment rationalists did. In his *Annotations to Reynolds*, Blake says that when he was young he read Burke's *Sublime and Beautiful*, Locke's *Human Understanding*, and Bacon's *Advancement of Learning*. He felt "Contempt and Abhorrence" for them and for Reynolds then as well as now (in 1808). "They mock Inspiration and Vision. Inspiration and Vision was then, and now is, and I hope will always Remain, my Element, my Eternal Dwelling Place; how can I hear it Contemned without returning Scorn for Scorn?" (CW, 477).

Vision is a heavily loaded word, and in order to understand its multiple uses let me now go into the text of 1809, *A Descriptive Catalogue* when Blake was fifty-two and in full artistic form. The catalogue begins with Blake's painting: *The spiritual form of Nelson guiding Leviathan, in whose wreathings are infolded the Nations of the Earth.* This is followed by its companion picture: *The spiritual form of Pitt, guiding Behemoth; he is that Angel who, pleased to perform the Almighty's orders, rides on the whirlwind, directing the storms of war: He is ordering the Reaper to reap the Vine of the earth, and the Plowman to plow up the Cities and Towers.* And here are Blake's comments: "The two pictures of Nelson and Pitt are compositions of a mythological cast, similar to those Apotheoses of Persian, Hindoo, and Egyptian Antiquity, which are still preserved on rude monuments, being copies from some stupendous originals now lost or buried till some happier age. . . . The Artist has endeavoured to emulate the grandeur of those seen in his vision, and to apply it to modern Heroes, on a smaller scale" (CW, 565). Nelson and Pitt are not depicted in their natural forms but in their spiritual forms from models existing in the past.

To elucidate this important distinction, let me examine the two kinds of "vision" in Blake, Vision and vision (even though Blake did not consistently employ the distinction that I have just made). There is vision in a literal sense, reminding us of Tibetan quests to recover past "treasures" (one can use Blake's language and call the latter "stupendous originals" sequestered by Padmasambhava). Then there is Vision in the sense of our inspirational propensity emanating from the Poetic Genius and dependent on whether we could shed and cleanse our sense-based perceptions. Blake recognizes that Vision permits him to see forms of ideal artistic works ("stupendous originals") from the past. Thus the inspirational propensity or Vision permits Blake to have visions, that is, it opens up Blake's "expanding" eye, the "inner-eye" that other visionaries mention. If Tibetan treasure seekers sought to physically locate and retrieve the originals, Blake can only copy them, not possessing their gift of space travel. "The Artist having been taken in vision into the ancient republics, monarchies, and patriarchates of Asia, has seen those wonderful originals called in the Sacred Scriptures the Cherubim, which were sculptured and painted on the walls of Temples, Towers, Cities, Palaces, and erected in the highly cultivated states of Egypt, Moab, Edom, Aram, among the Rivers of Paradise, being originals from which the Greeks and Hetrurians [Helvetians] copied Hercules Farnese, Venus of Medicis, Apollo Belvidere, and all the grand works of ancient art" (CW 565). These incredible visions are unfortunately not described in any detail.

Given these assumptions, the famed Greek statues were not originals, and, except for the torsos, they "are evidently copies, though fine ones from greater works of the Asiatic Patriarchs." Hence "the Greek Muses are daughters of Mnemosyne, or Memory, and not of Inspiration or Imagination, therefore not authors of such sublime conceptions" (CW, 566). Blake ignores a further question that we might now prompt: wherefrom did the artistic "originals" of the ancient Asiatic patriarchs come? Did they derive from some previous models? This Blake does not answer, perhaps because it would lead him into an infinite regress or to a Platonic notion of ideal forms that he also resisted. Or more likely because Blake never really worked out (rationally) the implications of his doctrines. Neverthe-less, he had an intuitive grasp of an ideal reality underlying the artistic originals: "The antiquities of every Nation under Heaven, is no less sacred than that of the Jews. . . . How other antiquities came to be neglected and disbelieved, while those of the Jews are collected and arranged, is an enquiry worthy of both the Anti-quarian and the Divine. All had originally one language, and one religion: this was the religion of Jesus, the everlasting Gospel" (CW, 578–79).

It is clear therefore that Blake could access the original sculptural forms and create new works that are closer to the originals than the Greek copies. "Those wonderful originals seen in my visions, were some of them one hundred feet in height; some were painted as pictures, and some carved as basso relievos, and some as groupes of statues, all containing mythological and recondite meaning, where more is meant than meets the eye" (CW, 566). Those mythological mean-ings are the stuff of Blake's own recondite symbols in his prophetic works, and if *we* cannot understand their meaning it is not the poet's fault but ours, locked as we are in our physical perceptual apparatus and our reification of Reason. I might add that Blake's vision of the past is not confined to painting but also to poetry: "No man can believe that either Homer's Mythology, or Ovid's were the production of Greece or Latium" because they too are refractions or reformula-tions of original forms (CW, 565).

A Descriptive Catalogue also refers to Blake's illustrations to Chaucer and con-tains an important discussion about vision and re-vision. The characters in Chau-cer are based on the original forms mentioned earlier. Blake asserts that "we see the same characters repeated time and again, in animals, vegetables, minerals, and in men; nothing new occurs in identical existence." Consequently, "Accident ever varies" although "Substance can never suffer change or decay." What these statements imply is that visionary forms are of the same "substance," but his-tory, time, and accident affects how we represent them in the practice of art. (See book 3, note 48 for a discussion of "substance.") Original artistic forms are trans-formed in present practice. Hence "some of the names or titles are altered by time, but the characters themselves for ever remain unaltered, and consequently they are the physiognomies or lineaments of universal human life, beyond which Nature never steps. Names alter, things never alter." In his own practice, Blake has "varied the heads and forms of his personages into all Nature's varieties; the Horses he has also varied to accord to their Riders; the costume is right accord-ing to authentic monuments" (CW, 567).

Blake's model of God, of the human essence that is the divine essence, and of original forms open up the world of relativism and at the same time the universal world or essence or substance. He put this idea succinctly in his criticism of Swedenborg: "Essence is not Identity, but from Essence proceeds Identity and from one Essence may proceed many Identities, as from one Affection may proceed many thoughts," which seems to echo but not imitate Boehme's idea that diversity and contraries emerge from the outflow of God or the Eternal One or, employing an alchemical image, the *Mysterium Magnum*.[62] Whether we believe in Blake's idea of Essence/essence or not, he is surely right to see that there is no necessary contradiction between relativism and universalism, a distinction firmly entrenched in the human sciences today. One can rephrase Blake to say that relativism can spring from universalism, the particular from the universal, and, of course, the other way around.[63]

Let us now see how Blake's visionary consciousness developed and the manner in which vision is related to Vision, employing for the most part the important collection by G. E. Bentley, *Blake Records*. Blake biographies mention a very early childhood vision when at age four he was set screaming one day when God "put his head to the window."[64] We do not know whether this childhood event actually occurred or whether it is the hagiographical necessity to impute childhood visions to the adult visionary, much like "prophecies" made in reality *after* a momentous event are soon revised to look as if they occurred *before*. Other childhood visions might have some basis in reality, because Blake himself seems to have recollected "his first vision." "Sauntering along [on Peckham Rye], the boy looked up and saw a tree filled with angels, bright angelic wings bespangling every bough like stars. Returned home he related the incident, and only through his mother's intercession escaped a thrashing from his honest father, for telling a lie. Another time, one summer morn, he saw the haymakers at work, and amid them angelic figures walking."[65] Much later as an engraver's apprentice, working for long hours alone in Westminster Abbey, he saw "Christ and his Apostles among the tombs, and he both saw a great procession of monks and priests, choristers and censer-bearers, and heard their chant."[66]

It is during his stay at Felpham that we have clear record of Blake's more complex visions. Felpham was located by the sea and his patron and friend William Hayley, also a poet, owned a mansion there and urged Blake to reside in a beautiful cottage that was available for rent. To get a better understanding of Blake's motive in going there, let me quote from a letter written to George Cumberland on July 2, 1800. "I begin to Emerge from a Deep pit of Melancholy without any real reason for it, a Disease which God keep you from and all good men" (CW, 798). I will deal with this psychic malady later, but note that Blake felt the need to leave London for a more salubrious climate. He visited Felpham that same month and decided to move there for good with his wife and his sister. Prior to that move, he wrote a letter on September 12, partly in verse form, to his friend and fellow artist, the gentle John Flaxman, the key lines of which I quote:

Angels stand round my Spirit in Heaven, the blessed of Heaven are my friends upon Earth,
When Flaxman was taken to Italy, Fuseli was given to me for a season,
And now Flaxman hath given me Hayley his friend to be mine, such my lot upon Earth,
Now my lot in the Heaven's is this, Milton lov'd me in childhood and shew'd me his face,
Ezra came with Isaiah the Prophet, but Shakespeare in riper years gave me his hand;
Paracelsus and Behmen [Boehme] appear'd to me, terrors appear'd in the Heavens above
And in Hell beneath, and a mighty and awful change threatened the Earth.
The American War began. All its dark horrors passed before my face
Across the Atlantic to France. Then the French Revolution commenc'd in thick clouds,
And My Angels have to me that *seeing such visions* I could not subsist on the Earth,
But by my conjunction with Flaxman, who knows to forgive Nervous Fear.

(CW, 799; my emphasis)

This is a badly misunderstood letter-poem, owing to scholars confusing "vision" with "Vision." John Beer, like Thompson, thinks that this poem refers to Blake's reading of Milton and Shakespeare. "The American War broke out in 1776, so that if this is a chronological account we must suppose that Blake read all the authors he mentioned before he was eighteen."[67] The fact is that this is not a chronological account at all, but rather a visionary one coming in the aftermath of an illness (Melancholy) and the release of his "spirit." The quotation cited consists of four brief "movements." The first is based on the idea that Blake's spirit is in heaven, guarded by angels, but down below on earth are his friends blessed by heaven. The second movement lists these friends: Flaxman, Hayley, and Fuseli. The crucial third movement relates to Blake's ability to be in heaven, and, with that gift, he can conjure in visionary form several significant others in his spiritual life: Isaiah, Ezra, Shakespeare, Milton, Paracelsus, and Boehme. Especially significant for our understanding of Blake is Milton appearing in spiritual form as someone who had loved him from childhood (and continuing to appear right through Blake's life). For example, Crabb Robinson reports that Blake "spoke of frequently seeing Milton" (BR, 452). He not only gave Robinson a description of Milton but also that the great poet "had committed an error in his Paradise Lost, which he wanted me to correct" (BR, 543). Ezra with the Prophet Isaiah also appears in visionary form, followed by Shakespeare, who "gave me his hand" in comradeship. This is not surprising because *Blake Records* clearly prove that Shakespeare and many biblical and historical figures appear before Blake as visions he later painted. Then follows a showing of key hermetic thinkers who have influenced his writing, Paracelsus and Boehme, and they straddle heaven and hell, unifying opposites in Blakean fashion. The fourth movement is a metaphoric hell that comes naturally after the segments on heaven and earth. But it is a hell on earth that, as in a dream, the horrors of war in the American and French Revolutions appear before him in thick clouds, the latter a favorite Blakean image that can appear in benign form (as in the introduction to the *Songs of Innocence*) or in threatening form, as in this case and many others. He recollects in the letter that his angels have informed him of the danger of these visions because, in my reading, if his spirit is in heaven, how could he continue to subsist on earth without going mad? But, he tells Flaxman, his friends on earth, blessed by heaven, can "forgive nervous fear," that is, understand his troubled spiritual condition. Nevertheless, it is difficult to figure out whether "nervous fear" relates to being in two places in spirit or to his "melancholy" or both.

Another letter written to Flaxman on September 21, 1800, shows us the Blake household safely ensconced in Felpham, "a sweet place for Study, because it is more spiritual than London." Why so? "Heaven opens here on all sides her Golden Gates; her windows are not obstructed by vapours; voices of Celestial inhabitants are more distinctly heard, and their forms more distinctly seen, and my Cottage is also a Shadow of their houses" (CW, 802). Eleven days later, in a letter to Thomas Butts, another loyal friend, he mentions his "first vision of light," the opening of the heavens at Felpham, while sitting on its yellow sands during low tide.

> The Sun was Emitting
> His Glorious beams
> From Heaven's high Streams.
> Over Sea, over Land
> My Eyes did Expand
> Into regions of air
> Away from all Care,
> Into regions of fire
> Remote from Desire.

The light of the morning adorned the mountains of heaven in bright particles, and these "jewels of delight" shone "distinct and clear."

> Amaz'd and in fear
> I each particle gazed,
> Astonish'd, Amazed;
> For each was a Man
> Human-form'd. Swift I ran,
> For they beckon'd to me
> Remote by the Sea
> Saying: Each grain of Sand,
> Every Stone on the Land,
> Each rock and each hill,
> Each fountain and rill,
> Each herb and each tree,
> Mountain, hill, earth and sea,
> Cloud, Meteor and Star,
> Are Men seen afar.

By the difficult phrase "Men seen afar," he perhaps means that the material world is imbued with essence or spirit, except that I don't think Blake implies that they are imbued with Vision. He is close to Boehme and the neo-Platonic notion of the material world imbued with soul. In this vision the poet himself ascends in spiritual form ("my Shadow") to the streams of heaven's bright beams and from that visionary vantage he sees the village of Felpham down below beneath his "bright feet." Then his "expanding eye," or visionary eye, opens up new vistas, reminding us of the expansion-contraction of space and time he mentions in later works like *Jerusalem*.

> My Eyes more and more
> Like a sea without shore
> Continue Expanding,
> The Heaven's commanding,
> Till the Jewels of Light,
> Heavenly Men beaming bright,
> Appeared as One Man.

I take it that Blake is now saying that the heavenly particles who are men in the earlier part of the poem are now transmuted into a single man, once again implying the unity of the spirit we mentioned earlier. The visionary man who in later work appears as Jesus now addresses Blake using the kind of symbol system that has already appeared in his earlier prophetic works beginning with *Tiriel* (1789) and fully developed in the later great works, *Vala* (1795–1804), *Milton* (1804–1808), and *Jerusalem* (1804–1820). Blake's visionary man softly smiles and gives a typical enigmatic picture of his "fold" and its guardians, the lion and the wolf, the loud sea and deep gulf, that is, a symbolic representation of those opposites that are ultimately reconciled in Man. The voice gradually fades, but Blake remains there for awhile as a child, he says, for it requires a childlike imagination to see as he does, at least at this time of his intellectual and visionary development. He sees his friend Butts and his wife by "the fountains of Life" and then ends his letter-poem with the idea that his vision was a "showing":

> Such the Vision to me
> Appear'd on the sea.

(CW, 804–6)

It is also in Felpham that Blake's Poetic Genius received what other European visionaries have called auditions or locutions, voices heard in the spirit. In another letter, written on April 23, 1803, to Thomas Butts, he says:

> But none can know the Spiritual Acts of my three years Slumber on the banks of the Ocean, unless he has seen them in Spirit, or unless he should read My long Poem descriptive of those Acts; for I have in these three years composed an immense number of verses on One Grand Theme, Similar to Homer's Iliad or Milton's Paradise Lost, the Persons and Machinery intirely new to the Inhabitants of the Earth (some of Persons Excepted). I have written this Poem from immediate Dictation, twelve or sometimes twenty or thirty lines at a time without Premeditation and *even against my Will*; the Time it has taken in writing was thus render'd Non Existent, & an immense Poem Exists which seems to be the Labour of a long Life, *all produc'd without Labour or Study.*

(CW. 823; my emphasis)

Why, one might ask now, does Blake refer to one of his works as an immense poem comparable to the *Iliad* or *Paradise Lost*? Perhaps Northrop Frye is right that Blake was planning a huge epic that combined *Vala, Milton,* and *Jerusalem* but did not quite bring it off. I will, however, submit an alternative hypothesis later.[68] What is clear is that large chunks of texts were given to him as "spiritual acts" written in "slumber," that is, when rational or discursive thinking is in abeyance.

In this case the reference is to *Vala,* parts of which were composed in Felpham.[69] *Jerusalem*, at least in part, also seems to have been written in a similar manner. His address "To the Public" mentions that the poem was "first dictated to me," implying visionary dictation (CW, 621). In writing texts through spiritual dictation, Blake is simply following visionaries like Teresa and more immediately Jacob Boehme who, we have said, wrote as the Spirit dictated, outside the space of reasoning. But, I will soon argue that, as with Catherine of Siena, the visionary transmission was subject to later revision in his published text where the *model* of the vision or dream continues to operate.

THE CURE AT FELPHAM

> But what I dream about, the contents of the dream, may have a psychological explanation. It seems to me that my dreams are always an expression of my fears, not, as Freud thought, my wishes. I could build up an interpretation of dreams just as cogent as Freud's in terms of repressed fears.
>
> —Ludwig Wittgenstein, "Conversations with M.O'C. Drury"

Blake, we noted, came to Felpham afflicted with a "deep pit of melancholy." A letter written to Hayley on October 23, 1804, after he had left Felpham for London, suggests strongly that whatever spiritual distress or melancholy he experienced was somehow or other "resolved" during his stay in Felpham. "I have entirely reduced the spectrous Fiend to his station, whose annoyance has been the ruin of my labours for the last twenty years of my life. . . . I was a slave bound to a mill among beasts and devils; those beasts and devils are now, together with myself, become children of light and liberty, and my feet and my wife's feet are free from fetters" (CW, 851–52). Specter in Blake's thinking generally refers to the negativity of Reason, but "fiend" and "beasts and devils" also implies the traditional Christian representation of satanic forms. The reference is not only to the rheumatism from which his wife and perhaps Blake also suffered but also to his being a prisoner in metaphoric chains. It is Felpham that has produced his freedom. "O lovely Felpham, parent of Immortal Friendship, to thee I am eternally indebted for my three year's rest from perturbation and the strength I now enjoy." Consequently, the fiend (Satan) "who [once] domineered over me," is now a servant; and "he is even as a brother who was my enemy. Dear Sir, excuse my enthusiasm or rather madness, for I am really drunk with intellectual vision whenever I take a pencil or graver into my hand, even as I used to be in my youth, and I have not been for twenty dark, but very profitable, years. I thank God that I courageously pursued my course through darkness. . . . In short I am now satisfied and proud of my work, which I have not been for the above long period" (CW, 852). And then to Hayley again on December 4: "I have indeed fought thro' a Hell of terrors and horrors (which none could know but myself) in a Divided Existence: now no longer Divided nor at war with myself, I shall travel on in the strength of the Lord God, as Poor Pilgrim says" (CW, 935). Few seem to have noted that this divided existence included some erratic, even paranoid, behaviors that he exhibited during the period before 1804: his well-known fight with a soldier named Scolfield, his subsequent arraignment for sedition, his fantastic allegation that his friend and patron Hayley had tried to seduce his wife and then conspired with Scolfield to kill him.[70] I also think that the underlying decision to leave Felpham for London later on was at least in part, based on his paranoid fantasy regarding his friend and triggered by the Scolfield incident.

It is a pity that we do not have enough information on Blake's long twenty-year dark–night-of-the-soul experience, with its inevitable ups and downs of the spirit ("Melancholy"), periods of creativity and of despair or, one might say, transforming despair into creativity. But let us try to make something of it. Blake was born in 1757. He clearly says that the twenty-year period of suffering finally ended around 1804, although the healing process went on from 1800 to 1803, during his Felpham stay. Thus the commencement of his melancholy was in 1784 when he was twenty-seven. This was also the year his father died. It is this critical event that I think unleashed Blake's spiritual crisis. We do not know much about the father-son relationship except that Blake was threatened by his father when he confessed one of his childhood visions to him, and only the mother's intervention saved him. Frederick Tatham, who knew the Blakes during their last years and was especially close to Catherine, mentions that Blake's father did not send him to regular school for good reason. "Like the Arabian Horse, he is said to have so hated a Blow that his Father thought it most prudent to withhold from him the liability of receiving punishment" in school (BR, 510). Apparently, Blake never forgot the paternal threat of a blow (or more likely an actual one), and after his marriage to Catherine in 1782 (to which his parents objected) he left the parental home, deliberately stayed aloof from his parents, and indeed of his male siblings, except his youngest brother Robert.[71] Compounding the oedipal relationship was the terrible hatred he bore for his younger sibling John, born in 1760, three years after Blake, who was his parents' favorite. By contrast, Robert, born eleven years after William, was Blake's favorite, as we shall soon see. Thus it seems legitimate to assume that the infantile hatred for the parents, especially the father, was complicated by William's terrible sibling rivalry. In a letter poem to Butts written from Felpham in November 1802, he describes a vision where the dead males of his family appear along with John:

> And my Brother John the evil one
> In a black cloud making his mone[72]

The agonistic relation to the father is, I think, expressed in a long poem found in his *Notebook* but drastically edited and reduced to two stanzas in *Songs of Experience,* with the title "Infant Sorrow." The full poem was written around 1793, nine years after his father's death, and I use the version edited by Geoffrey Keynes (CW, 889–90).

> My mother groan'd, my father wept,
> Into the dangerous world I leapt,
> Helpless, naked, piping loud,
> Like a fiend hid in a cloud.
>
> Struggling in my father's hands,
> Striving against my swaddling bands,
> Bound and weary I thought best
> To sulk upon my mother's breast.
>
> When I thought that rage was vain,
> And to sulk would nothing gain,
> Turning many a trick and wile,
> I began to soothe and smile.
>
> And I sooth'd day after day
> Till upon the ground I stray;
> And I smil'd night after night,
> Seeking only for delight.
>
> And I saw before me shine
> Clusters of the wand'ring vine,
> And many a lovely flower and tree
> Stretch'd their blossoms out to me.
>
> My father then with holy look,
> In his hand a holy book,

Pronounc'd curses on my head
And bound me in a mirtle shade.

"Why should I be bound to thee,
O my lovely mirtle tree?
Love, free love, cannot be bound
To any tree that grows on ground."

O how sick and weary I
Underneath my mirtle lie,
Like to dung upon the ground,
Underneath my mirtle bound.

Oft my mirtle sigh'd in vain
To behold my heavy chain;
Oft my father saw us sigh
And laughed at our simplicity.

And so I smote him and his gore
Stained the roots my mirtle bore;
But the time of youth is fled,
And grey hairs are on my head.

Whatever difficulties one may have about the symbolism of the myrtle tree, the poem is a powerful expression of the loneliness of the infant, the father's pious hypocrisy that destroys childhood innocence, and the son's fantasized killing of the father who had bound him to the myrtle tree. If the myrtle tree is a symbol of the married state, as Keynes suggests, then the poem must have considerable personal meaning that we can only partially elucidate. What is clear is the father's hostility is the heavy chain that drags on the marriage, but the sighs of the married pair only provokes his father's laughter. The killing of the father occurred in the "time of youth," but now "grey hairs" are on his head. "Grey hairs" is not just about aging (he is now only thirty-six), but I think it is about guilt from the fantasized killing of the hated father when he was a youth. There was no doubt that the elder Blake was also a loving father, and this probably complicated Blake's feelings of oedipal guilt. Many of the poems of childhood in the *Songs of Innocence* and *Songs of Experience*, especially the sequences of the little boy lost and found, can also be read in the light of Blake's relation to his father. And so is the fascinating etching of "aged ignorance" in the late work *The Gates of Paradise*

(1818). Peter Ackroyd rightly says that even "stray remarks of those in authority over him are turned into permanent mementoes of humiliation and fear," a fear that I think is rooted in his agonistic relationship with his father.[73]

Although I think Blake's melancholy is a version of the dark night of the soul and its recovery, I can find only two indirect and opaque evidences for the initiatory symbolism of dying and awakening so characteristic of that experience. Yet let me make the most of it by quoting something that Blake wrote on an autograph album on January 16, 1826, the year before his death. "William Blake, one who is very much delighted with being in good Company. Born 28 Nov' 1757 in London and has died several times since" (CW, 781). By now the reader should know that we must take Blake's seemingly crazy statements seriously. I am sure he "died" and awoke from death several times during his twenty-year-long dark night of the soul, as did St. Paul in Corinthians 1, 15:31.[74] A glimpse of dying and awakening comes from *Milton*, if we assume that the text refers to Blake's personal experience of his spirit leaving the body for a moment, followed by a collapse (death) and return to the mortal body.

> Terror struck in the Vale [of Felpham] I stood at the immortal sound [of trumpets].
> My bones trembled, I fell outstrech'd upon the path
> A moment, and my Soul return'd into its mortal state
> To Resurrection and Judgment in the Vegetable Body,
> And my sweet Shadow of Delight stood trembling by my side
>
> (CW, 534)

Similarly, the model of dying and waking also occurs with respect to his mythic characters, which also I assume comes from his own personal experience. Thus, in *Vala* the god Los; his emanation Enitharmon; Tharmas, the deity associated with the senses and with painting; and the dark God Urizen, the apotheosis of Reason, all die only to awake sometime after.[75] In fact Urizen suffers a double death and resurrection in *Vala*:

> As the seed falls from the sower's hand, so Urizen fell, and death
> Shut up his powers in oblivion; then as the seed shoots forth
> In pain and sorrow, so the slimy bed his limbs renew'd,
> At first an infant weakness; periods pass'd; he gather'd strength,
> But still in solitude he sat; then rising, threw his flight
> Onward, tho' falling, thro' the waste of night and ending in death
> And in another resurrection to sorrow and weary travel.
>
> (CW, 316)

One can say of Blake's mythic figures that once born they too had "died several times since." Urizen's "waste of night" ending in death and the movement to "another resurrection to sorrow and weary travel" is a transformation into mythic thought of Blake's own experience of dying and waking in his own waste of night. Blake himself would continue to be born and die until his melancholy is progressively resolved during and after the Felpham period.

Three years after his father's death his beloved brother Robert died, without doubt further compounding his melancholy. Blake saw the ascent of Robert's soul at his death. From now on he had continuing spiritual conversations with Robert, consulting him in various matters, as he tells Hayley on May 6, 1800: "Thirteen years ago I lost a brother and with his spirit I converse daily and hourly in the Spirit and See him in my remembrance in the regions of my Imagination. I hear his advice and even now write from his Desire" (CW, 797). In these "dialogues with the dead," Robert imparts to his brother important technical information regarding relief etching and printing, which Blake later used.[76] Unlike the father who had been symbolically killed, the younger brother, both pupil and surrogate son, continued to live in Blake's visionary world.

In light of the preceding discussion, Blake's statement, which I quoted earlier, takes on added significance: "Thinking as I do that the Creator of this World is a very Cruel Being, and being a worshipper of Christ, I cannot help saying 'the Son, how unlike the Father!' First God Almighty comes with a Thump on the Head. Then Jesus Christ comes with a balm to heal it." The homely metaphor of the thump on the head refers, I think, to an actuality in childhood socialization, a form of punishment angry parents inflicted on their children, noted by Blake with respect to his own father. One might argue that in dethroning the Father Blake is also rejecting his own father. The resolution of the theodicy is simultaneously a resolution of an oedipal crisis. Hence Blake could explicitly inform Crabb Robinson that "he did not believe in the Omnipotence of God" (BR, 543).

It is true that Blake inherits some of these ideas from previous traditions, but they are now given personal meaning and significance through his real and fantasized relationship with his father. Father also refers to the priests (officiants at marriage) of the orthodox religions, with their holy book and hypocritical holy look, and he is the Father up there. My guess is that the "spectrous Fiend" who was the enemy of conjugal love and who Blake has subdued at last in Felpham is also the father and he is God and he is Satan combined. In his prophetic writings the god who appears is not the Christian God but, as with almost all of his mythic characters, consists of protean figures who can take many shapes, including the shape of a woman, even of Satan, whereas Blake's conception of Jesus remains much more consistent. Further, if god is not omnipotent, then Satan is also not the powerful being he claims to be. In Blake's writing, Satan sometimes appears in a positive light, at other times as negativity, or most often compounded of a variety of attributes and names just like the protean creator himself. Satan's empire is an "empire of nothing" (BR, 316), and in the famous verse-epilogue of *The Gates of Paradise* he is nothing but a dunce (CW, 771). Blake overturns once again the classic distinction between God and the devil, good and evil, operative in most of Christian history and, like virtue and vice, they are nothing but "Serpent Reasonings" (CW, 770).

Except for a few asides mentioned earlier there is no detailed account anywhere of Blake's twenty-year period of suffering. But let us see whether there are other oblique ways of making some sense of Blake's self-designated melancholy, the deep pit into which he fell, avoiding any modern diagnosis of melancholy as "depression." I doubt that Blake was thinking of the classic *Anatomy of Melancholy* by Robert Burton (1577–1640) either. That work describes the wide-ranging causes of melancholy, which, however, can occasionally be quite congenial as it was for Keats in his "Ode to Melancholy."[77] Given Blake's interests in Milton, I would think the appropriate model suitable to express his condition comes from *L'Allegro* and *Il Penseroso*, both of which he illustrated.[78] In the first poem, Milton invokes melancholy to flee so that joy could take its place.

> Hence, loathed Melancholy
> Of Cerberus and blackest midnight born
> In Stygian cave forlorn
> 'Mongst horrid shapes, and shrieks, and sights unholy!
> Find out some uncouth cell
> Where brooding Darkness spreads his jealous wings
> And the night-raven sings . . . [79]

Can the kind of mood that Milton evokes find its parallel in Blake? It appears in two poems written before 1804, *The First Book of Urizen* (c. 1794), contemporary with, or soon after *The Songs of Experience* and *Vala*. Both *Urizen* and *Vala* contain some of the characters inhabiting his prophetic books. In my view it is *Urizen* that best captures the poet's spiritual agony and must surely have been conceived when Blake's melancholy was at its height. Urizen is the dark god of Reason, modeled on Jehovah as well as on the biblical Satan, creating a terrifying world; the pitying and merciful deity, Los, modeled after Jesus but not equated with him; Enitharmon, who is Los's female counterpart (and some think based on Blake's own counterpart, Catherine); and their various spouses, creations, and "self-begotten" beings. These latter beings are sometimes known as the Eternals and are outside us as well as spiritually within us and coalesce into the eternal man, Jesus, who also is within us. The Eternals existed prior to "Urizen's travesty of Biblical creation," and they represent "an idealized alternative or antecedent to the hierarchical order consistently identified with Urizen."[80] The two poems, like the other prophetic ones, contain Blake's vision of the creation, destruction, and restoration of the world through various ages or eons, very much in the Hindu spirit, even though Blake had no knowledge of that religion. For me, these two poems and the graphic surreal paintings that illustrate their themes have been written in a tormented mood, and this mood is reflective of the poet's own dark night of the soul, or melancholy, which is also a period of "dying." The poems, like others of the same class, have no systemic organizational unity, and I can only use a few examples to illustrate my thesis.

The surreal paintings in *Urizen* beautifully match its dark poetry. The poem itself has images of the dark as a running motif. In the prelude to the poem, Blake invokes the Eternals and asks them to unfold "your dark visions of torment." He continues to speak of the "unknown, abstracted, brooding, secret, the dark power hid" wherein are contained "the black winds of perturbation." Then there is Urizen's "dark, revolving in silent activity," the "cold horrors silent, dark Urizen prepar'd"; Urizen speaks of the "depths of his dark solitude," the world within him is "a void, immense, wild, dark and deep"; he writes in books formed of metal, "the secrets of dark contemplation"; while the more positive god "Los, wept, howling around the dark Demon [Urizen]." All this language has the quality of "sounding, dark'ning, thundering" and comes from the "dark desarts of Urizen" where there is no light and where "all was darkness" (CW, 222–25). Bentley is surely right to say that "the spirit which dictated this strange work was undoubtedly a dark one" (BR, 486). Some of the poetry catches the poet's own terrible mood:

> In fierce anguish and quenchless flames
> To the desarts and rock he [Urizen] ran raging
> To hide; but he could not: combining,
> He dug mountains and hills in vast strength,
> He plied them in incessant labour,
> In howlings and pangs and fierce madness,
> Long periods in burning fires labouring
> Till hoary, and age-broke, and aged,
> In despair and the shadows of death.

(CW, 225)

The poem deals with the seven ages through which Urizen passed, each age being one of "dismal woe" that seems to echo the mood of the poet's melancholy. *Urizen* was printed in 1794, but surely the paintings and much of the poetry would have been conceived earlier. My guess is that the seven ages Urizen passed through symbolically represented the tormented years following the death of the father (1784).[81] The paintings that accompany the poem give a surreal and apocalyptic feel of the poet's own dismal woe. "There are in all twenty-seven designs, representing beings human, demoniac, and divine, in situations of pain and sorrow and suffering. One character—evidently an evil spirit—appears in most of the plates; the horrors of hell, and the terrors of darkness and divine wrath, seem his sole portion. He swims in gulphs of fire—descends in cataracts of flame—holds combats with scaly serpents, or writhes in anguish without any visible cause. One of his exploits is to chase a female soul through a narrow gate and hurl her headlong down into a darksome pit" (BR, 487). In *Urizen* the paintings are "scenes out of many visions," while the poems illustrate the tormented surreal quality of the art (BR, 487).

The cure at Felpham did not result in a shift to mirth (L'Allegro), to laughter, joy, and sport and tripping "the light fantastic toe." That kind of joy is not part of Blake's austere lifestyle. When he returned to London in 1803, he was so wholly preoccupied with his art he hadn't even time for walks to exercise his rheumatic limbs. His recovery entailed the transformation of the terrible pit of melancholy that had engulfed him into the kind of pensive, contemplative mood that Milton beautifully sketched in *Il Penseroso*.

> And let my lamp at midnight hour
> Be seen in some high lonely tower,
> Where I may oft out-watch the Bear
> With thrice-great Hermes, or unsphere
> The spirit of Plato, to unfold
> What worlds or what vast regions hold
> The immortal mind, that hath forsook
> Her mansion in this fleshy nook . . .[82]

The "high lonely tower" brings with it a fruition of spiritual experience:

> Till old experience do attain
> To something like prophetic strain.

I would like to think that Blake actually imagined himself in Milton's place when he read the concluding lines of *Il Penseroso*.

These pleasures, Melancholy, give,
And I with thee will choose to live.[83]

Blake, we noted, admits that the twenty-year period of illness beginning 1784 was a "profitable" one. That year, or thereabouts, produced a break between his early *Poetical Sketches* written during 1769–1778 (printed in 1783) and his later writing. In other words, illness saw the beginnings of enormous creativity, both in the more conventional stanza and rhyme forms and also in the bolder but obscure symbolic and prophetic works. I will illustrate Blake's marvelous powers of visualization with one example from *The Marriage of Heaven and Hell,* written during his night of prolonged "brooding darkness." The powerful apocalyptic imagery is derived from Revelation, but the images of doom are renewed and reinvented in the mind of the poet. Here Blake transforms Boehme's positive abyss into a terrifying reality reflecting the "black" mental hell of the protagonist cum poet.

By degree we beheld the infinite Abyss, fiery as the smoke of a burning city; beneath us, at an immense distance, was the sun, black but shining; round it were fiery tracks on which revolv'd vast spiders, crawling after their prey, which flew, or rather swum, in the infinite deep, in the most terrific shapes of animals sprung from corruption; and the air was full of them, and seem'd composed of them: these are Devils, and are called Powers of the air. I now asked my companion which was my eternal lot? he said: "between the black and white spiders."

But now, from between the black and white spiders, a cloud and fire burst and rolled thro' the deep, black'ning all beneath, so that the nether deep grew black as a sea, and rolled with a terrible noise; beneath us was nothing now to be seen but a black tempest, till looking east between the clouds and the waves, we saw a cataract of blood mixed with fire, and not many stones' throw from us appear'd and sunk again the scaly fold of a monstrous serpent; at last, to the east, distance about three degrees appear'd a fiery crest above the waves; slowly it reared like a ridge of golden rocks, till we discover'd two globes of crimson fire, from which the sea fled away in clouds of smoke; and now we saw it was the head of Leviathan; his forehead was divided into streaks of green and purple like those on a tyger's forehead; soon we saw his mouth and red gills hang just above the raging foam, tinging the black deep with beams of blood, advancing toward us with all the fury of a spiritual existence.

(CW, 156)

If Blake's visionary powers and creativity was not in doubt during his twenty-year period of suffering, we might want to ask the following question: what is the personal and psychic significance of the healing process that commenced in Felpham and culminated in 1804? I think the answer is clear. Blake states that he is no longer under the domination of demonic agencies but has them under his control, and, indeed, the father-devil-God himself is like a servant or a brother to him. This control also affected the quality of the writing during the Felpham and post-Felpham periods, as critics such as Northrop Frye and John Beer have noted. For Frye, *Vala/Zoas, Milton,* and *Jerusalem* represented the "final synthesis" of Blake's maturity; for Beer it is *Milton* and *Jerusalem* that led to an "intimation of sublimity."[84] Thomas Altizer adds: "Most of his biographers and critics are agreed that the revolutionary transformation that he underwent while working upon *Vala* and then beginning *Milton* and *Jerusalem* was probably initiated by a new and deeper conjugal relationship which he reached with his wife, Catherine," who provided a model for the deity Enitharmon of *Jerusalem.*[85] But I suggest that the changed relation with his wife is part of the larger inner transformation of Blake during the post-Felpham period.

We do know that the father and his nonhuman surrogates were hostile to conjugal love, and one must assume that this affected the relation between William and Catherine. But after Felpham, particularly after 1804, the father has been killed or subjugated, and Blake's melancholy cured or resolved in some fashion. The changed relation with the wife, the new mode of writing, the curing of the poet's melancholy, the "killing" of the father/Father, the emergent new confidence are all part of a single complex that involved overcoming the dark night of the soul and an awakening to a new period of creativity. In *Milton* (1804–1808), written on the back of the sketch for the design on no. 43, there is a fascinating, if enigmatic, statement: "Father and Mother, I return from flames of fire tried and pure and white" (CW, 535). What is interesting is that this sketch provoked Blake to write about his recovery, even though his parents were long dead, his father in 1784 and his mother in 1792, and could only appear to him in spirit form or recalled through memory. Whatever the symbolic significance of the painting no. 43, it obviously had personal meaning for the poet, who appears strong, muscular, and handsome, unscathed by the fires around him in a maṇḍala-like protective circle, shedding his old persona, depicted in the crouching figure below. No. 43 must be contrasted with several in *Urizen* where the same figure, with agonized expression, appears engulfed in flames, bound like Lear upon a wheel of fire.[86] The so-called evil spirit that Bentley speaks of is none other than Blake himself! Other paintings depict torment and the terrors of the soul. Blake has gone through the pit of melancholy and faced deadly red-hot fires, but has now

"Father and mother, I return from flames of fire tried and pure and white"

5.2 Painting no. 43, from *Milton* (1804–1808). *Art Resource*

5.3 (*Top*), 5.4 (*Bottom*)
Paintings from *Urizen* (1794).
Art Resource

emerged as a new being, "pure and white" in no. 43. The emergence of the inner qualities of purity and whiteness are depicted in the flames: the outer frame depicts red-hot flames whereas the inner frame surrounding the main figure has flames of white in a backdrop of gold. This painting, with its revealing note to his mother and father, shows at last a control, perhaps even a belated resolution of his oedipal conflicts and estrangement from his parents during his post-Felpham period

Along with this control there is a further development of his visionary powers. He can annihilate the self; the self dies and "spirit" takes its place, so that his spirit can move into the heavenly realms and back to earth. And, very significantly, he is more confident, assured of his Poetic Genius, and, to repeat his words, "proud of my work, which I have not been for the above long period." He is no longer defensive of his visionary powers; he can talk about them in a confident and matter-of-fact manner, ignoring the barbs of those who called him mad.[87] Not only are his visions under complete control but also, like other visionaries inhabiting this essay, he could also see things in a flash, whether or not he reproduced these visionary showings in his paintings and poetry. The style and esoteric symbolism of the post-1804 work might not have changed all that much; the spirit and conception of the prophetic project had changed and so did the persona of the artist.

ASIDE: THE WORK OF THE DREAM-EGO

Who is the third who walks always beside you?
When I count, there are you and I together
But when I look ahead up on the white road
There is always another one walking beside you
Gliding wrapt in a brown mantle, hooded
I do not know whether a man or a woman
—But who is that on the other side of you?
—T. S. Eliot, *The Waste Land*

I now want to raise the following issue: in nearly all the accounts of visions in this essay there is the notion of some entity that one might label spirit or soul or self or some kind of karmic force or an emanation of sorts that seems to move out of the visionary's body into another realm. Sometimes, as with Boehme and Blake, the visionary quest entails the movement of the spirit but not the soul, although it is not clear whether they cognize the spirit as a separate entity or as a refraction of the soul. To fully grasp the theoretical issue involved, let me get back to Freud's idea that dreams are "egoistic" in character, but without subscribing to his view that the "I" appears in all dreams. "Whether my own ego does not appear in the content of the dream, but only some extraneous person, I may safely assume that my own ego lies concealed by identification, behind this other person; I can insert my ego into the context" (ID, 323). It is likely that the dreamer appears in many meaningful dreams, either as himself or in some other guise, as in Nietzsche's vision where his dream persona split and "one became two" as Zarathustra passed him by. Yet one must envisage the possibility that, while the dream might have personal meaning to the dreamer, the dreamer himself need not always appear, changed or otherwise, in the dream. One can have a dream that terrifies the dreamer, projected outside him, as it were. Such a dream or nightmare might have deep personal meaning, like the objectified images of demons that appear in visions, without the dreamer appearing therein. Yet it is the case that often enough he appears in picture form in various guises, as the dreamer himself or masked in another persona. In which case one can say that the disguised being is, on the one hand, the dreamer and, on the other, a different being. And that other being can shift character, now appearing in this guise and now in another during the period of dreaming. Precisely for this reason the "I" or ego or self that is represented in the dream is not the everyday self or ego of the waking life. In a dream the waking ego or self is replaced by a hallucinatory ego, Scherner's "fantasy-I," or, as it is designated in Freud and in Jung and his followers, as the "dream-ego." For that reason I shall mostly use the familiar term *dream-ego* but occasionally remind ourselves of Scherner's more appropriate usage, the *fantasy-I.*

The preeminent characteristic of the dream-ego is its permeability. It can "dissolve" and transform itself in all sorts of ways, as, for example, when in one moment I am pictured here and in another there; in one moment the dream represents me in my normal manner and in the next my expression or clothes or demeanor changes as indeed the form and demeanor of others I see in the dream as well as conventional notions of place, time, and space. In the dream I can do things unimaginable in reality. I can fly and travel to other lands, unknown places, as dream travelers in the Western Pacific and everywhere else do.[88] So is it with visions or hallucinations, as was the case with Schreber when he observed that his fellow inmates "changed heads . . . and suddenly ran about with a different head."

A particular culture may have a theory that it is the soul or spirit or "self" or some other culturally defined entity that causes the dream, but, irrespective of the cultural theory, the dreamer acts very much the same everywhere insofar as he can do things inconceivable in normal life. Thus the Sambia, studied by Gilbert Herdt, believe it is a soul that experiences whatever happens in the dreamworld, but Sambia fantasies do not seem all that different from mine even though their dreams figures are products of the soul and hence "supernatural." "So events can be fantastic—for example, flying through the air, leaping rivers; copulating with forbidden persons; men entering evil places like caves or menstrual huts; snakes that turn into airplanes, having superhuman strength or being paralyzed by unreal terror."[89] I too can penetrate seemingly material spaces, but this is also what the shamans and Buddhist visionaries do in their cosmic journeys. Or when a Tibetan visionary dissolves into another hallucinatory being—a ḍākinī, a god, or a Bodhisattva—and sometimes into hallucinatory objects and even into a dream-created nothingness. Thus Giuseppe Tucci says of the Tantric virtuoso: "The mystic dissolves into the 'void' the real or imagined objects and instruments. After he has changed himself into a god, he emanates these objects from his mind until they fill the whole of space."[90] Hence the god has a "*māyā* body," or an illusory body, and this, as was the case with Blake's spirit, is a meditative transcreation of the dream-ego or fantasy-I that can penetrate mind created objects. One might even say that the mind-created objects in the dream are also hallucinatory creations, like the dream-ego itself and, often enough, a projection or emanation of the dream-ego. In a theoretical, if reductive sense, one can say that the dream-ego "emanates" all sorts of beings and things, creating them out of its own illusory "self," and this is most conspicuous in the visionary emanations of Tibetan Tantra as it is with Blake.

The *māyā* body of the Tibetan virtuoso appears in many meditative contexts. Germane to our discussion is its manifestation in Tibetan dream yoga. This is not to equate my notion of the dream-ego with the illusory body of Tibetan dream yoga, but the latter gives us a clue that the *māyā* body is a *form* of the dream-ego resurrected during the meditative experience. Thus, in the Kagyu and Nyingma traditions, the illusory body or *gyulus* is created out of intense meditative practice, but the practice of *gyulus* meditation must be conjoined with five other meditative disciplines. "Through *gyulus*, the illusory body, one is able to roam freely in various states of existence that require the other yogas: *milam*, to control the dream; *odsal*, a state where one experiences being absorbed into the Clear Light of the Void; *phowa*, transferring consciousness out of one's own body into other bodies or places; and *bardo*, entering the intermediate state between death and rebirth while still alive."[91] The point of dream yoga is not to enter into the dream and control it, as with contemporary Euro-American lucid dreaming and dream incubation (both partially inspired by dream yoga), but rather to recognize that sleep, dreaming, and waking are symptomatic of the movement between dying, *bardo* (Sanskrit, *antarābhāva*), and rebirth and therefore dream yoga is designed to help one control the actual intermediate stage or *bardo* when physical death occurs. Consequently, dream yoga is directed to the salvific interests of the meditator. The present Dalai Lama puts it thus: "At each state of the actual dying process there are internal signs, and to familiarize yourself with these, you imagine them during meditation in your daytime practice [of dream yoga and similar yoga]. Then in your imagination, abiding at the clear light level of consciousness, you visualize your subtle body departing from your gross body, and you imagine going to different places; then finally you return and the subtle body becomes reabsorbed into your normal form."[92]

How could these states, so characteristic of dream yoga as well as other meditative traditions of Tibet, be achieved via the physical body of the meditator? He must project through his meditative trance a form of the dream-ego—a more controlled form to be sure—that can take the place of the waking ego or will or waking consciousness. Once brought under control, the meditator then can create through his dream-ego, or *māyā* body, other emanations, or he can travel though the cosmos and then get reabsorbed into or return to the normal physical body, as did our Tibetan visionaries from the Nyingmapa tradition. Insofar as the dream-ego has a protean and insubstantial quality, it lacks enduring "self" or the idea of personhood. Or, avoiding the disputatious Buddhist criticism of some kind of enduring entity called the "self," one can perhaps more accurately say that the dream-ego has no body. It is not embodied. Hence the theoretical importance of the dream-ego or fantasy-I as it operates in the space-time of the dream, endowing the dreamtime with noetic significance. When the visionary spirit leaves the body, flies into the cosmos or the ancestral world, and relates to other beings living there, we can say, from a theoretical point of view at least, it is the transfigured form of the dream-ego that goes there. But one must make the proviso that meditative ascesis transforms the dream-ego into the illusory or *māyā* body or any other shape or form based on a particular society's cultural values. With this theoretical thrust, one can begin to understand the manner in which the dream-ego appears transformed in different cultural forms of spirit journeys. One can rephrase the issue thus: the dream-ego or fantasy-I can through the work of the passive intellect exhibit different degrees of symbolic remove. During dreaming its fantasizing can range from meaningless dreams to meaningful ones; it can transform itself *progressively,* into the dream-vision and the more elaborate visions I have described, and *regressively* into psychotic hallucinations and all sorts of states in between.

I have noted that the idea of the dream-ego, according to Freud, was first formulated in 1861 by Karl Scherner, a precursor of much of Freud's thinking.[93] Freud, however, did not make much of the distinction between the waking ego or self and its hallucinatory projection as the dream-ego. It was Jung who used the term in a theoretically significant sense in a 1920 essay, although unfortunately he also did not fully develop the concept in his later writing: "In a dream, consciousness is not completely extinguished; there is always a small remnant left. In most dreams, for instance, there is still some consciousness of the ego, although it is a very limited and curiously distorted ego known as the dream-ego. It is a mere fragment or shadow of the waking ego."[94] The idea that the hallucinatory ego is somehow or other a chip of the old ego of the waking consciousness was difficult for Jung to maintain, here and elsewhere, because for him "the ego is as psychic complex of a particularly solid kind."[95] Yet in this same paper he clearly informs us of the hallucinatory nature of the dream-ego when he says that "dream images enter like another kind of reality into the field of consciousness of the dream-ego." Why so? "In the waking state the psyche is apparently under the control of the conscious will, but in the sleeping state it produces contents that are strange and incomprehensible, as though they came from another world."[96] Freud himself might have found a place for the dream-ego in his insight that a part of the ego is submerged in the unconscious, but he did not equate this ego segment with the dream-ego as Jung did.[97]

Jung's idea of the dream-ego as a hallucinatory segment of the waking ego was developed further by his followers and more recently by the proponents of "lucid dreaming." Lucid dreaming refers to the ability to recognize that while one is dreaming one can control and direct the dreaming state. Many of us have experienced, admittedly rarely, the phenomenon of being aware during the space of the dream that we are in fact dreaming, then recognizing that "it's only a dream." Contemporary lucid dreaming provides techniques that permit us to enter into the dream and control it. It is no accident that lucid dream theorists have been influenced by Tibetan dream yoga without necessarily subscribing to its salvific or epistemological premises. I will take up lucid dreaming in more detail later, but will here mention the belief of most lucid dreamers, that it is the waking self, the conventional ego or "I," that acts as the agent controlling the dream's denouement. In my thinking, this is a mistake and what is at work in ordinary dreams or in lucid dreams is only the dream-ego or its emanations. It is the Western interpreter, whether a "dream-work specialist" or clinician or an ethnographer that converts the protean quality of the dream-ego into the "self," a prime Euro-American cultural value.[98]

Let me now get back to the operation of the dream-ego with an example from my own dreams. Some time ago I dreamt that I was bicycling in the village in which I was born but have rarely revisited during the last forty years. But in my dream there are two of us on bikes, me and someone else whom I could not identify but seem comfortable to be with. The village was similar to what I knew of it in childhood but also different, distorted as dreams are in varying degrees from the empirically real picture of everyday life. The village temple was on the wrong side of the road and a once familiar house cluster of my poorer kinfolk was there but not in the familiar place. The dirt road was steeper than I had known it in my childhood, and I noticed the rains had carved deep ridges everywhere on its slopes. Both of us were bicycling side by side avoiding the ruts on the road. Perhaps this scene was from memory's storehouse where, in childhood, when once bicycling I tried to avoid a rut on the mountain road and fell down, bicycle and all. Perhaps. But who was on the other side of me? I think he was my dream alter, the other of my dream-ego, in this case my "double," even though my double had no real physical resemblance to me. For Freud, this dream other is the "extraneous person" under whose identity the ego or self will hide. To my way of thinking this extraneous person is not me but my other-me, my dream alter or dream other or my double, as in the dream just listed. The dream other is then a special form of emanation of the dream-ego, but one that constantly keeps changing or transforming. When such transformations occur then my dream alter can take an independent form and cease its connection with me.

In Blake's prophetic poetry, the dream-ego can be transformed into what he calls "emanations" or the capacity to reproduce another form of oneself, either male or female. Thus the emanation of Los becomes the female Enitharmon and Enitharmon herself can emanate other forms of her shadowy being, such that she can be transformed into a harlot, a sinful creature, or a creative divinity. In this visionary transformation, Blake's dream other might develop into a "shadow," either a benign or grim kind of emanation or even a more frightening thing, "a spectral form." Thus one might say that these several emanations ultimately spring from Blake's own dream-ego but transfigured and making an independent entry into his mythmaking through his unique visionary inspiration.

Blake's idea of the dream other as shadow was inherited by Jung as the dark or unconscious side of one's being, but it also appears everywhere as a hallucination experienced by travelers lost in deserts and lonely spaces.[99] As with Blake, the spectral form of the dream other can appear in visions in every culture, as the following case from the Tibetan Kagyu tradition, the inventors of dream yoga, nicely illustrates. The reference is to Nāropa (1016–1100), the great Tibetan virtuoso, who though greatly learned was full of his own self-importance and had not fully understood the inner meaning of the Buddha's teaching until a hideously ugly old woman appeared before him. "The ugly physical characteristics of the apparitional woman were revealed to be reflections of his own mind," a spectral form of Nāropa's dream-ego, his fantasy-I, that deflated his arrogance.[100] Such cases remind us that the dream other appears in various guises or as multiple emanations in visions, in myth, fiction, and poetry, as in the epigraph of this section. Perhaps the best-known example is Hamlet's father's ghost, who is Hamlet's double representing or foreshadowing his own murderous desires.

The double or dream other appears in equally terrifying fashion in Joseph Conrad's short story "Karain: A Memory." Here Karain, a Malayan aristocrat, is haunted by the spectral form of the enemy he killed, and soon, unexpectedly, the specter appears beside him, his invisible footsteps following Karain. But there is no one there, the ghost or shadow being the guilty conscience of the murderer. The narrator of the tale saw the signs of torment on Karain's distraught face when he, unable to face his friend's ghost, fled to the white man's boat, a different cultural space where, Karain thought, the shadow would not appear. "His face showed another kind of fatigue, the tormented weariness, the anger and the fear of a struggle against a thought, an idea—a shadow, a nothing, unconquerable and immortal, that preys upon life. We knew it as though he had shouted it at us. His chest expanded time after time, as if it could not contain the beating of his heart. For a moment he had the power of the possessed—the power to awaken in the beholders wonder, pain, pity, and a fearful near sense of things invisible, of things dark and mute, that surround the loneliness of mankind."[101]

The spectral form of Karain's dream alter brings us to another feature of the dream. Because the thinking-I is in abeyance, the dream-ego or fantasy-I might well tap unconscious processes or deep motivations, including those that have been highlighted by both Freud and Jung, at least in principle. I say, "at least in principle" because one doesn't have to agree on what constitutes unconscious processes by these two creative thinkers. Nor does one have to agree that only deep motivations surface in the dream; hence, as we have already suggested, dreams can range all the way from the meaningful to the meaningless, from the tapping of deep motivations to the surfacing of harmless memories, from significant existential thoughts, reflected in the manifest dream, to wonderful bits of nonsense and so on, endlessly owing to the operations of passive cerebral activity and, I might add, depending on the personal sensitivity of the dreamer. I would say that, in Karain's case, his hallucination reflects his obsessive feelings of guilt. Similar motivations appear in all of us. For example, if I am undergoing an oedipal crisis, then I could expect oedipal conflicts to be expressed in symbolic form or as indirect representations in the dreaming process. So it is when I am being analyzed by a therapist of whatever theoretical orientation. Inevitably, I will dream those issues raised by the particular therapeutic school, facilitating therapeutic intervention and the eventual "cure," that is, giving meaning and existential significance to the life that has been disrupted by illness or distress. The preceding statement does not take a stand on whether one form of therapy works better than another or whether one provides better insights into life and existence than another. My stand only implies that a successful "cure" does not prove the theoretical validity of a particular brand of therapy. It only proves its efficacy.

Another powerful and yet sad and comic episode of the double is from *The Brothers Karamazov* where Ivan Karamazov, guiltridden over his parricidal motivations, has, during his gradually dawning self-awareness, a vision of a well-dressed yet poor relative, both devil and dream acquaintance, who sits by him. Ivan wants to kick and scold him and then says: "Because by abusing you, I abuse myself. . . . You are me with a different face; you keep telling me what I think and are unable to tell me anything new."[102] But the gentleman-devil disabuses him, assuring Ivan that he is not simply his double but a being who, often enough, appears in dreams. The sage devil later adds: "I heard a member of the government say that his best ideas come to him when he was asleep. Well, we are facing that problem now, too. I may be a hallucination of yours, but, just as in a nightmare, I can say original things that have never even occurred to you and I don't necessarily have to repeat your old ideas, even if I am nothing but a nightmarish figment of your imagination."[103] The dream-ego, in this case, emanates another being who can, as I suggested, take on an independent existence. Amusingly, and with deliberate irony, the devil goes on to inform Ivan that both of them share the same philosophy: *je pense, donc je suis.* He reminds the conscience-stricken Ivan that he no longer practices old-fashioned tortures, but rather employs moral punishments, such as a "guilty conscience," which, according to the devil, is a consequence of the "humanization of mores."[104] In similar vein, the pioneer of lucid dreaming, Hervey de Saint-Denys, records a terrifying dream where he is confronted by a monster, and when he asked the monster who he was, the monster replied: "Yourself."[105] The idea of the double, constantly shifting its shadowed form—now this and now that—is beautifully depicted in the terrifying hallucinatory imagination of Dostoyevsky's protagonist in his early novella, *The Double.*[106]

In spite of the omniprevalence of the shadow or double in European myths, dreams, and literature, it is Indic thought, owing to its fascination with illusion, that has fully developed the idea of the double or shadow (*chāyā*), as Wendy Doniger has shown in her pioneer work.[107] Dostoyevsky's own take on dreams is close to the Indic tales that Doniger recounts: Ivan thinks that he has a vision of the devil as a poor relation in flesh and blood; on the other hand, he thinks that the whole episode is a dream. The author himself hints at this possibility. When Ivan tries to wake up, he feels "as if his arms and legs had suddenly been fettered," which is the rare condition where dream paralysis persists for a moment into the waking state.[108] To compound the deliberate confusion, it is not only Ivan who is the dreamer but also the devil himself proclaiming that "while I walk about here on earth, I keep daydreaming. I love imagining things."[109] He insists that he is Ivan's nightmare, in both a literal and metaphoric sense. For Ivan himself, the whole episode hovers between the demands of everyday reality and the hallucinatory reality of dreams. Whereas the devil claims he is the one who imposes the dream on Ivan, but, on the other hand, he is, he says, a flesh-and-blood being, knowing full well, I suppose, that the Ivan of the dream is not a flesh-and-blood character anyway!

Among the various emanations of the dream-ego are all sorts of other beings that appear in dreams and in visions, and they also partake of the protean or quicksilver quality of the dream-ego and its other. That is, the dream-ego can produce multiple and varied emanations, not just beings, as we find in the dream-ego of the visionary who sees gods, ghosts, ancestors, demons. Everything in the dream, such as houses, scenes, places known and unknown, can be seen as emanations of a person's dream-ego in conjunction with the "thinking" that occurs through the work of the passive intellect. These beings and objects appear and reappear because time and space contracts or expands in mind-boggling ways. This is not only true of Viṣṇu; it is also true of the Christian God, but especially of the devil, who can appear to the visionary in many shapes and guises, only to disappear in the blink of an eye, then reappearing in some other form or voice. So was it with Dostoyevsky's suave gentleman-devil, who, having had a pressing invitation to a diplomatic party, wryly commented on the fix he was in: "So I had to dress in white tie, tails, gloves, the whole lot, as you can well imagine, although I was God knows how far away at that time and had to cross quite a lot of outer space to get to your earth. Of course, it is just a matter of a moment."[110] It seems to me that it is in dream and in vision that the camel can get through the eye of a needle, just as in the Buddhist text the troop of titans entered their city through the lotus stalk. I recently interviewed a Sri Lankan physician skilled in mantras in the area where I am currently engaged in fieldwork, and, in the course of the conversation, he said: "You know a demon can be huge and tall but he can go through one of the 'eyes' of a chair [through which the cane is inserted for weaving], and that is why it's so difficult to seize him and subjugate him."[111]

Let me now move from the dream-ego and its others to the way dreams are cognitively organized. One cannot live permanently in the dream; we shed it when we awake, unless it is a dream-vision. Even after we experience a vision we must come back to normal everyday life. It is only in the psychoses that the fantasy-I has invaded the spaces of the mind, more or less permanently rendering thoughts "incoherent." A dream as a protean thing is always in the making through passive cognition and yet might possess a form of "coherence" that is different from the logical or rational organization of thought based on what we have labeled I-thinking. Sometimes coherence further imposes itself on the dream when one awakes, which means that the dream as dreamt is near impossible to recover. What we have is the dream that a person relates to himself or to others, the dream text or script (the related dream or the written dream), though some scripts are closer to the phenomenal reality of the dream than others. To put it differently: the way pictures or visual images are put together in the dream is very different from the rational thinking consciousness, Boehme's or Blake's Reason.

One way to make preliminary sense of dream coherence is to examine the way that free associations are organized in the psychoanalytic session. Here the analysand lying on the couch is asked to bring as many associations as he can on a previous dream or a segment thereof. Free association ranges out from the recollected dream image or images into a wider arch of associations, and what provides coherence to the outflowing associations is that they center on the analysand and radiate from him. This is not to say that dreams are constituted of associations of this sort, only to assert that what we call coherence can exist outside the rules of discursive reasoning. In our example, free associations cohere around the particular dream segment the analyst urges his patient to consider. In daydreaming and in our daytime fantasy lives we, often enough, free associate in a similar manner (our thoughts "stray"), and some of our associational thoughts in fantasy might cohere around a single cue or trigger or a set of them while other associations might be less coherent or wildly incoherent.

Let me develop this idea further with one of my recent dreams that I have entitled "A Visit to Egypt."

I am traveling with my friend Eric Meyer in a car to Egypt and I am driving. We are at a hotel that had a name, but I could not remember it on waking. I buy a shirt or look at a shirt with the hope of buying one. We drive on a long, winding road that was suddenly flooded. I drive through the flood and hope that the engine will not stall. It is a tricky trip; on one side is a granite mountain and on the other what seemed like a precipice. The waters were everywhere, but I suddenly felt that my

eyes were somehow blinded, and I told Eric that I could not see ahead. Nevertheless, I continued to drive instinctively, often braking and worrying that I might
skid. Eric says nothing as he sits impassively in the front seat. We pass this area,
and at a certain point I park the car. The next scene is in a restaurant, and I am being served some food and drink I need, but of course I cannot speak the language.
I ask for the bill. A young man who I take to be a waiter comes up to me and gives
me the bill and, along with it, many notes and some coins that I took to be the local currency. I was looking puzzled, and the man seems to say that it is OK. I take
the money, and, as I near the exit of the restaurant, he gives me a packet with a
few white pills clearly seen through a small plastic wrap. The pills looked familiar
to me, and in the dream itself I recognized that these looked like the pills I swallow in the mornings. But there was another package whose contents could not
be seen underneath the small package. The waiter asks me whether I could take
these pills with me to the hotel where I'm staying and then what my name was. I
now realized that perhaps the package contained drugs, and that I was expected
to take it so that someone could then pick it up later. I was not sure how I should
reply, but I said "Dr. Obey," refusing to give my full name and using a familiar ab-
breviation instead. Then I noticed someone else was near me, but he was not Eric.
This man seemed to be a friend, and he gave a false name of my hotel to the waiter,
speaking to him in a confident manner. I had forgotten the name upon waking,
but it was an English name, something like "Oxford Hotel." I took the package,
and my helpful friend and I walked outside looking for the car and Eric. My helpful friend now drops out of the picture, and I am being chased by the waiter and
others while I go frantically looking for the car. But the car and Eric are not there
among the few parked alongside the road. I get panicky and run down a hillside
and now the scenery changes and seems somewhat familiar to me; it is thick scrub
jungle. Scared, I leap over rocks and gullies with two people following me over
these obstacles. They chase me and catch upon me, shouting at me, and then I feel
trapped and I am terrified as they close on me. I awake, and on waking feel a great
sense of relief.

I dreamt this dream the very night I had written on the "coherence" of dreams
in the Paris apartment where I was staying during January 2007, thanks to my
friend Eric Meyer who had arranged my visit. My dream could be a case of simple
wish fulfillment. If so, it is still fascinating that a dream did provide proof of my
hypothesis! I woke around 4.00 A.M. and carefully rehearsed the dream in the
hope of writing it down later in the morning, which I did around 9:30 A.M. Even
so, I have missed some parts of it, particularly the first part where I am in a hotel
with Eric and buying or thinking of buying a shirt.

Let me now pinpoint some of the day residues and earlier thoughts that went into the formation of the manifest dream. Eric is obvious and perhaps the immediate cue that triggered a set of associations leading to the formation of the dream. The hotel where the two of us stayed is simply a dream invention, yet not entirely. At the time of the dream, I have been living in an apartment complex owned by the University of Paris, but my dream had no connection with it. My wife and I did find a hotel near us for a friend who was to visit us in a few days, and, only the evening before, we returned to that street trying to familiarize the locale for ourselves. On the way back to our apartment, we bought a couple of items from a shop and passed other shops that had shirts for sale, but though they were attractive I had no interest in buying them. I was tempted, but their expense put me off. All this is woven into the first part of the dream. The other elements of the dream are woven from items from my memory's storehouse. Let me mention some. I don't know how Egypt came into the picture, although I have seen Egypt on TV ads and elsewhere and have recently read Madame Blavatsky's fantastic evocations of Egypt and her pyramids. Ages ago I traveled to Cairo, but my dream landscape was not Egypt at all. It seemed familiar, very much like the mountainside just before reaching the plains in which my hometown Kandy is located. But it is not a replica of it; the road was much broader than the Kandy road, the granite mountainside starker. And, while I have driven in shallow waters before, the dream's flooded road was deeper and fearful and something I had not yet experienced.

The hotel incident is central to the dream story and perhaps accounts for my forgetting details of the first part of the dream. The night before the dream, when my wife and I were watching TV, we sadly noted the indictment of a top UN official for accepting bribes. We were talking of unbridled greed endemic among those involved in the new capitalist global economy. I then thought to myself that, as an overarching concept, the Buddha's notion of *taṇhā*—greed, desire, or attachment—was a more philosophically profound idea than Michel Foucault's notion of "power" and then went on to reflect that perhaps none of us, as the Buddha said, were immune to greed and maybe I was too. I think it is this idea that is pictured in the dream, a critique of my own hidden desires, seemingly trivial (a few notes given by the waiter). Driving blindly down the road through floodwaters might have reference to my own greed but they also hark back to my own work dealing with greed or *taṇhā* as a universal human addiction. But near-blind driving might have other existential and personal implications I may have missed in my "blindness." The waiter speaking in a language I don't understand is a reflection of my poor French that I could read with some difficulty but cannot speak. More critically, once I accept the notes, I am forced to accept the "packet" and this is both a critique of my own greed and my ambivalence, if not exoneration (my reluctance to accept the illegal packet). The clear plastic through which the pills could be seen comes from my knowledge of recent airport security where one has to keep one's medications in a clear plastic bag. The packet might also express my fears that the medications I and others take often have side effects, and these have been highlighted in the media recently. The undisclosed packet behind the pills might indicate this fear. Even if this idea was part of the day's residue, there is no doubt that in my dream I thought of the packet as containing something illegal. Then there is my enigmatic "friend" who suddenly appears to help me out and soon disappears from the scene. Finally, the illegal act brings about a punishment, and I am chased by two men and then wake up in panic as soon as I am about to be captured.

The dream highlights an important feature of dreams noted by dream theorists, the idea that dream sequences can provoke anxiety and panic, which, when they become unbearable, forces one to waken. There are many other elements I am sure that constitute the manifest dream, but the sum of these elements is not the dream. The elements are transformed in many ways, as, for example, the mountain road is a composite formation of many roads in Sri Lanka, and so is the flood as is also the packet. They do not reflect an empirical reality at all. All the day residues and other elements are transformed into something new and strange, a dream narrative that, unlike verbal narratives, rarely have a tight organizational structure. If transformed into a story, a dream narrative might resemble a novel by Franz Kafka or Jorge Luis Borges, but then their stories are self-consciously constructed out of dream narratives or modeled on them. As with Kafka and Borges, James Joyce's *Finnegans Wake* is the artist's self-conscious and carefully thought-out production of a text that coheres in the manner of a dream narrative.[112] The dream narrative pastes pictures together, sometimes haphazardly, sometimes as in my dream with some "coherence" in its manifest content. As much as the coherence of free associations centers on the patient, so do dream images cohere around the dream-ego. What is striking in my dream, as with other dreams that have an interesting storyline or existential significance, is that the manifest dream is much more interesting that the latent dream thoughts!

Nevertheless, bits and pieces of the dream make no logical sense: what happened to Eric, and who was the person who appeared to help me at the restaurant's exit? On reflection, I can theorize and say that the third man is my dream alter, but that is my interpretation of the manifest dream, and someone else may not agree. But, as a "good guy," he is a kind of Everyman that every man can easily figure out! Consider the events in the hotel. My own interpretation of that sequence in terms of greed, punishment, and guilt is based on my prior dream thoughts. But these seemingly latent thoughts are not all that latent because I think of them all the time, especially during the period this essay is being composed, and hence *patent*, facilitating easy interpretation of the dream. The hotel event makes narrative sense, but enriched by my interpretation. Anyone reading my dream account will note its "coherence," even though it lacks any kind of rational enplotment. Some dreams may not cohere at all, and the images might appear more or less disconnected from each other or "incoherent." Incoherence would occur if, for example, I wake up while the dream is in the process of formation or if sleep is erratic, permitting ego consciousness to erupt, strongly or weakly, or owing to other conditions, psychological or neurological. I could have a dream with a tighter and more coherent narrative form than the one I have narrated, especially when the narrative work of the dream progresses into the night, but with an important proviso: some of the coherence or organizational unity might come through our waking recollection and the reworking of the dream. And that can happen in a few minutes after waking, even perhaps seconds later, although in some societies the reworking of the dream may even take years.[113] No dream is fully immune from this process of secondary revision or later "elaboration." One might even weave an organized story around the dream, but the dream itself is not an organized story. One of the striking differences between language and dream thoughts is the issue of coherence: who would disagree that a dream could be wildly incoherent and yet acceptable to us, a normal feature of dreams, but a wildly incoherent utterance is one that we associate with madness, intoxication, or some similar feature associated with cognitive disorientation.

Before we get further engulfed in creative chaos, let me now conclude by relating the implications of my two dreams to Blake's prophetic books. Blake's texts do not have a plot structure; nor are they logically woven together in an immediately intelligible sense. Nevertheless, they possess the kind of coherence, a preoccupation with patent existential issues leading to the thick symbolic formations of the sort that one notices in dream narratives and in the work of the authors I mentioned earlier. It is Ellis and Yeats who, with their characteristic insight, noted this feature of the prophetic books and related it to Blake's visionary imagination, although not necessarily to the dream mode. "Blake's visions coming to him in uncertain intervals during a long life, appearing now by night and now by day, suggested a vast symbolic myth to him, containing a whole language of names and personages, and telling by fits and starts a whole narrative whose apparent incoherence contains a unity of significance that becomes more astonishing and fascinating the more closely it is studied."[114] Ellis and Yeats add that in these texts there is no sign of "building up by ingenuity, of elaborating from a plot, expanding from a sketch."[115] "The fragments of which the whole is formed are often ill-joined and sometimes not joined at all, but . . . they bear every sign of having come straight to the mind in large segments at a time." However, they can be "reasoned over" or, in my language, rendered coherent through a process analogous to secondary elaboration.[116] In a later statement Yeats says that though Blake's prophetic works are chaotic when compared with his lyrics, they are "in every way more beautiful than the form chosen by Swedenborg or Boehme. It was even less chaotic in many ways than the 'Mysterium Magnum' and 'Aurora.'"[117] Blake's prophetic works are difficult to understand in the same sense as *Finnegans Wake*. In both the written text has a kind of coherence that I have associated with the dream, but in no way is the written work a prototype or refraction of the dream. *The dream is only the model for the written text.* That text is *crafted* at many degrees of remove from the dream, and the degree of remove varies from one writer to the next, with the complicated crafting of *Finnegans Wake* taking Joyce seventeen years to complete.

Take the case of *Vala.* It is subtitled "The Death and Judgement of the Ancient Man, a DREAM of Nine Nights." But it is *not* a dream; rather it is one modeled on the dream and possessing a similar coherence. Thus Blake's mature prophetic works are crafted with "dream-coherence" in the kind of cognitive model that Blake employs, as does Joyce or Kafka, toward the careful construction of the finished text. When a particular writer says, as does Blake, that his poem comes from a vision or dream, we must aver that it is a part-truth: the dream or vision is the preliminary text and the model for the finished product.

BACK TO BLAKE: THE WIDE REALM OF WILD REALITY

Our life is two-fold: Sleep hath its own world,
A boundary between the things misnamed
Death and existence: Sleep hath its own world,
And a wide realm of wild reality.
And dreams in their development have breath,
And tears, and tortures, and the touch of joy;
They leave a weight upon our waking thoughts,
They take a weight from off our waking toils,
They do divide our being; they become
A portion of ourselves as of our time,
And look like heralds of eternity:
They pass like spirits of the past,—they speak

Like Sibyls of the future: they have power—
The tyranny of pleasure and of pain;
They make us what we are not—what they will,
And shake us with the vision that's gone by,
The dread of vanish'd shadows—Are they so?
Is not the past all shadow?—What are they?
Creations of the mind?—The mind can make
Substance, and people planets of its own
With beings brighter than have been, and give
A breath to forms, which can outlive all flesh.
I would recall a vision which I dream'd
Perchance in sleep—for in itself a thought,
A slumbering thought, is capable of years,
And curdles a long life into one hour . . .
—Lord Byron, "The Dream"

While in Felpham Blake was aware of the fact that his spirit could rise up to heaven and also return to earth back and forth, from here to there and there to here. This kind of disjuncture might result in "nervous fear." I don't think one can understand Blake without recognizing that he can be in both places, as was the case with his predecessor Swedenborg. In this sense Blake was different from medieval penitents who might visualize heaven but do not enter its portals. A penitent's spirit goes to heaven permanently after death to be united with Christ. This is the goal of the normal Christian mystical path. Whereas Blake's spirit can be in both places, though when he is living on earth it is temporarily within the body. Even when spirit is within the body it has been freed from its encrustation of sense, which is the fate of ordinary people, an idea beautifully expressed by Blake's Milton in *Milton*:

Obey thou the Words of the Inspired Man.
All that can be annihilated must be annihilated
That the Children of Jerusalem may be saved from slavery.
There is a Negation, and there is a Contrary:
The Negation must be destroy'd to redeem the Contraries.
The Negation is the Spectre, the Reasoning Power in Man:
This is a false Body, and Incrustation over my Immortal
Spirit, a Selfhood which must be put off and annihilated alway.
To cleanse the Face of my Spirit by Self-examination,
To bathe in the Waters of Life, to wash off the Not Human,

I come in Self-annihilation and the grandeur of Inspiration,
To cut off Rational Demonstration by Faith in the Saviour,
To cast off the rotten rags of Memory by Inspiration,
To cast off Bacon, Locke and Newton from Albion's covering,
To take off his filthy garments and clothe him with Inspiration,
That it no longer shall dare to mock with the aspersion of Madness . . .

(CW, 532–33)

The text is reasonably clear, even for the reader who might not know the deeper symbolic significance of Jerusalem and Albion in Blake's thought, at least after 1804. Here we have Blake, after his recovery from the pit of melancholy, washing his spirit free of the body and the encrustations of Reason and memory's rotten rags, which, according to him, produced the not-so-inspired art of Greece. Reason is the negation, the specter that chokes vision and does not permit the union of opposites that is a sign of true creativity. Freeing the spirit from the body by annihilating the self will release Vision and inspiration. What is most important is that annihilation of the self must be permanent ("alway"). This is not the classic Christian abjection of the self before God or even the abdication of the self that sometimes occurs in the union with the deity. It is Boehme who is Blake's major precursor, one who in much of his work calls for the destruction of the "I" in one's relation to God and endorses, very much like the early Buddhists who also cut off rational discursive thought, the body's filthy garments as a precondition to the trance experience (*jhāna, dhyāna*).[118] Unlike the Buddhist denial of the self, Blake's is only a denial of ego, of selfhood, that releases the other kind of self, the spirit, thereby realizing his inspiration. Annihilation of the self "alway" does not mean he is permanently "in the spirit," but rather that he can achieve the condition, moving back and forth from the ordinary world into a spiritual realm.

Blake's idea that his purified spirit, divested of self, is both here and there, on earth and in heaven, is central to understanding Blake as visionary poet and painter. In Felpham this spirit's freedom from the body's dross produces "nervous fear," but not in *Milton,* where cleansing the body of Reason and self results in the true union of contraries, namely, body and spirit. One can put it more simply by saying that spirit takes the place of Blake's annihilated self. Instead of the self, Blake's body is a container of spirit. That spirit can leave the body at will and return at will. It is this spirit purified of self that permits Blake to bring forth the past into his visionary field. It permits him to grasp the visionary heads that I shall now discuss from the statements gathered by Bentley in *Blake Records.*

Here is Allan Cunningham, an old friend, who, in a short biography of Blake written in 1830, three years after Blake's death, says that "an ordinary gallery could not contain all the heads which he drew of his visionary visitants. That all this was real, he himself most sincerely believed." Unsurprisingly, his artist friends encouraged him to draw them. "The most propitious time for those 'angel-visits' was from nine at night till five in the morning; and so docile were his spiritual sitters, that they appeared at the wish of his friends. Sometimes, however, the shape which he desired to draw was long in appearing, and he sat with his pencil and paper ready and his eyes idly roaming in vacancy; all at once the vision came upon him, and he began to work like one possest" (BR, 496). What is striking about these visionary heads is that, unlike his paintings and poems, they are direct copies of what he saw and therefore required little revision. This does not mean that he completed his heads in one sitting, but, as with any human model, he could make his subject appear again and again. But they were *not* human models. These Blake eschewed: "Models are difficult—enslave one—efface from one's mind a conception or reminiscence which was better" (BR, 236).

Nighttime was propitious for recalling these visionary models because the dark envelops him in silence. Also at night he was probably in the "somnolent" or drowsy state that we know is conducive to showings (BR, 496). Allan Cunningham again noted: "He was requested to draw the likeness of Sir William Wallace—the eye of Blake sparkled, for he admired heroes. 'William Wallace!' he exclaimed, 'I see him now—there, there, how noble he looks—reach me my things!' Having drawn for some time, with the same care of hand and steadiness of eye, as if a living sitter had been before him, Blake stopt suddenly and said, 'I cannot finish him—Edward the First [Wallace's enemy] had stept in between him and me'" (BR, 496). And when a friend wanted Edward also painted, he forthwith complied, but Wallace had the face of a god, whereas Edward had a demon's aspect. Cunningham says that during these sessions Blake apparently never slept but "sat with a pencil and paper drawing portraits of those whom I most desired to see" (BR, 497).

In this way Blake drew many figures from the past during drowsy nights with "his eyes idly roaming in vacancy" (BR, 496). Once, Cunningham reports, he took a large book of paintings done directly from visions and, having opened it, said: "Observe the poetic fervour of that face—it is Pindar as he stood a conqueror in the Olympic Games" (BR, 497). And so Blake goes on and on producing a veritable gallery of heroes and rogues from the past, including the builder of the Egyptian pyramids! Another friend went to see Blake one evening and "found him sitting with a pencil and panel, drawing a portrait with all the seeming anxiety of a man who is conscious that he has got a fastidious sitter; he looked and drew, and drew and looked, yet no living soul was visible. 'Disturb me not,' said he, in a whisper, 'I have one sitting to me.' 'Sitting to you!' exclaimed his astonished visitor, 'where is he, and what is he?—I see no one.' 'But I see him, Sir, answered Blake haughtily, 'there he is, his name is Lot—you may read of him in the Scripture. *He* is sitting for his portrait'" (BR, 499). And should we be cynical when occasionally Blake converses with figures from the past, as when Crabb Robinson reports of his spiritual conversations with Voltaire? When Robinson asked in what language Voltaire spoke, Blake rejoined by saying: "To my Sensations it was English—It was like the touch of a musical key. He touched it probably French, but to my ear it became English," a translation that reminds us of the *ḍākinī* code of Tibetan visionaries, which is automatically translated into ordinary Tibetan (BR, 322).

These paintings, whether of faces from a historic past or the ghost of a flea, are showings apprehended through a visionary lens. A vivid description of the latter is found once again in an account probably reported by the painter John Linnell.

He [Blake] closed the book, and taking out a small panel from a private drawer, said, 'this is the last which I will show you; but it the greatest curiosity of all. Only look at the splendour of the colouring and the original character of the thing!' 'I see,' said I, 'a naked figure with a strong body and a short neck—with burning eyes which long for moisture, and a face worthy of a murderer, holding a bloody cup in his clawed hands, out of which it seems eager to drink. I never saw any shape so strange, nor did I ever see any colouring so curiously splendid—a kind of glistening green and dusky gold, beautifully varnished. But what in the world is it?' 'It is a ghost, Sir—the ghost of a flea—a spiritualization of the thing.'

(BR, 498)

John Varley, Blake's friend, was also a witness of this unusual sitter in its spirit form: "I called on him one evening, and found Blake more than usually excited. He told me he had seen a wonderful thing—the ghost of a flea! And did you make a drawing of him? I inquired. No, indeed, said he, I wish I had, but I shall, if he appears again! He looked earnestly into a corner of the room, and then said, There he comes! his eager tongue whisking out of his mouth, a cup in his hand to hold blood, and covered with a scaly skin of gold and green;—as he described him so he drew him" (BR, 498).

Blake's capacity to experience visions, his esoteric and sometimes undecipherable symbolism (that is, related to his visionary capacity), and the frustratingly incomplete or enigmatic poetic texts led his contemporaries to describe him as insane. Measured by standards of Enlightenment rationality, Blake must have seemed mad, as Swedenborg was also seen as mad by the same standards.[119] Crabb Robinson made this judgment even before he met Blake to interview him. "Of all the conditions which arouse the interest of the psychologist, none assuredly is more attractive than the union of genius and madness in single remarkable minds, which, while on the one hand they compel our admiration by their great mental powers, yet on the other move our pity by their claims to supernatural gifts. Of such is the whole race of ecstatics, mystics, seers of visions, and dreamers of dreams, and to their list we have now to add another name, that of William Blake" (BR, 448). Blake is mad because he belongs to a category of visionaries who by definition are mad. Robert Southey says that Blake "would have been the sublimest painter of this or any other country" but for his madness, such that some of his designs were "hideous, especially those which he considered as most supernatural in their conception and likenesses." He adds that Blake's "madness was too evident, too fearful. It gave his eyes an expression such as you would expect to see in one who was possessed" (BR, 399).

Similarly Robert Hunt, brother of the poet Leigh Hunt, noted in a hostile review that Blake was "an unfortunate lunatic" who would have been confined to an asylum but for his "personal inoffensiveness." His muse has produced "the furious and distorted beings of an extravagant imagination and his madness more largely; and thus exposed him, if not to the derision, at least to the pity of the public." The catalogue for Blake's famous illustrations to Blair's *Grave* was for Hunt a "farrago of nonsense, unintelligibleness, and egregious vanity, the wild effusions of a distempered brain" (BR, 216). This was a persistent theme among his contemporaries, men of lesser genius than Blake. When Charles Lamb heard "The Tyger" recited, he exclaimed, "the man has flown, wither I know not—to Hades or a Mad House," even while admitting it was a "glorious" poem.[120] It was the more talented fellow poet Coleridge who in an ironic statement sensed Blake's affinity with his own genius. "I have this morning been reading a strange publication—viz. Poems with very wild and interesting pictures, as the swathing, etched (I suppose) but it is said—printed and painted by the Author, W. Blake. He is a man of Genius—and I apprehend, a Swedenborgian—certainly, a mystic *emphatically*. You perhaps smile at *my* calling another Poet, a *Mystic*; but verily I am in the very mire of common-place common-sense compared with Mr. Blake, apo- or rather anacalyptic Poet, and Painter!" (BR, 251).

Unlike his poetic contemporaries, his fellow painters and sculptors were much more sympathetic and, at the worst, thought him "eccentric." Their characterization of Blake was perhaps an attempt to counter the image of the madman by positing another image, less unfavorable, as when his friend, the sculptor Flaxman, spoke of "his abstracted habits [*which*] are so much at variance with the usual modes of human life" (BR, 173–74; Bentley's parenthesis). The poet as an "abstracted" being must also have circulated among Blake's acquaintances, because the bookseller R. H. Cromer, in a nasty letter, criticized him as "altogether abstracted from this world, holding converse with the world of spirits!" (BR, 185) Fortunately, toward the end of his life, Blake developed strong relations with a group of young artists, known as "The Ancients," who, during the period from 1818 until the time of his death in 1827, loved, admired, and supported him.[121] They were all painters, and one of them, John Linnell, responded to the popular prejudice about him when he met Blake in 1818: "I never saw anything the least like madness for I never opposed him spitefully as many did but being really anxious to fathom if possible the amount of truth which might be in his most startling assertions I generally met with a sufficiently rational explanation in the most really friendly and conciliatory tone." Linnell adds that John Varley, painter and astrologer, believed in Blake's most "extravagant utterances." Yet both Linnel and Varley were willing to accept Blake's idea that everyone possessed these spiritual powers in greater or lesser degree, but, unfortunately, "they undervalued [these qualities] in themselves and lost through love of sordid pursuits— pride, vanity, and the unrighteous mammon" (BR, 257). I am not sure I would entirely disagree.

Another painter, James Ward, who met Blake often in the company of others, thought his visionary gifts seemed occasionally "peculiar," but often beyond the "comprehension of his fellow men." Ward, echoing an idea well-known to European visionaries of his time, added that these gifts were firmly established from the time that "the Saviour Christ was upon the earth, although our Established Church (to their shame), set themselves against it." Blake himself would sometimes hazard that "there are probably men shut up as mad in Bedlam, who are not so: that possibly the madmen outside have shut up the sane people," marvelously deconstructing the popular view of madness (BR, 268). Perhaps, he was thinking of Richard Brothers, a fellow visionary who also experienced visions but was foolish enough to claim he was a nephew to God the Father and was consequently incarcerated for some time in an asylum (proving that political undesirables get shoved into asylums and prisons then and now) (BR, 520).[122] Others among the Ancients simply treated Blake as a harmless eccentric found everywhere and generally well tolerated in British society. The consensus among his critics seems to have been that Blake was a mad genius, a not unusual diagnosis of genius, though not of madness.

In Blake's case, as with other visionaries, madness was easy enough to diagnose and judge because there were people confined to asylums who were undoubtedly psychotics and had visions and auditions. But, unlike those nowadays labeled schizophrenics, Blake had no difficulty in interpersonal relations. A gentle soul, although occasionally given to spurts of anger, he related well to others and was well known as a printer and engraver who could speak in a "normal" manner about his visions and his radical reformulations of Christian doctrine, aligning himself with other dissenting sects of his time, especially those inspired by Boehme and Swedenborg.[123] While everyone recognized his "genius," the qualifying term *madness* expressed contemporary views of Blake's self-conscious defiance of contemporary Euro-rationality or Reason. And, when one moved away from the conventional stanza forms and rhyme schemes of his *Songs of Innocence* and *Songs of Experience* and similar poems into his visionary and prophetic works, there was a further problem, a more legitimate one. In them Blake experimented with forms that flouted earlier conventions. These poetic forms and styles were admittedly innovative, but compounded by difficult and esoteric symbolisms, some of which only the poet seemed to fully understand. Even with a skeleton key or a dictionary of Blake symbols, the prophetic poetry has, often enough, a private and incommunicable quality, even though one can sense its richness. In my view this difficulty is not due to his madness or anything like it but owing to a peculiar form of *imagining* that went into his art, or a form of thinking that went totally contrary to Enlightenment rationality, which I will now hesitantly explore. This peculiarity was less apparent in his paintings, which often upset people owing to their content, but they were much more comprehensible than the prophetic poems.

Let me now bring together two interrelated propositions mentioned earlier. First, there is Blake's unremitting hostility to Reason. Second, Blake believed that his "spirit"—which is also the vehicle of Vision and Poetic Genius and ultimately the essence of Jesus—can be in heaven and in the body once it is cleansed of the ego and the falsity of physical perception. His spirit's outreach permits him to experience visions and also reach into the past. Swedenborg also had a similar capacity so that he could converse with angels, argue with philosophers and theologians of the past, and visit heavenly realms. But, unlike Blake, Swedenborg's visions can be didactic, rarely presented as directly experienced, and, as Ernest Benz pointed out, his later visionary debates with angels had a rational quality occasionally bordering on the pompous. Swedenborg's heavens are highly structured, even bureaucratized, places.[124] It is certainly true that he experienced visions, but he does not relate the manner or context of his experiences, unlike virtually all Christian virtuosos appearing in this book. His rational dialogues with angels and other beings remind us of his previsionary distinguished scientific career as an accomplished professional thinker. Blake was critical of Swedenborg's rationality, but the question is this: prior to Blake's revision or editing or reformulation of his visions or auditions as poetry, how did he *think* if he had deliberately renounced Reason? Or, better still, how did his visionary imagination work?

Let me therefore further explore the kind of visionary thinking Blake engaged in with an important account by Crabb Robinson in a letter to Dorothy Wordsworth on February 19, 1826.

> He is not so much a disciple of Jacob Behmen [Boehme] and Swedenborg as a fellow Visionary. He lives as they did in a world of his own. Enjoying constant intercourse with the world of spirits—He receives visits from Shakespeare Milton Dante Voltaire etc etc etc And has given me repeatedly their words in their conversations—His paintings are copies of what he sees in his Visions—his books—(and his MSS. are immense in quantity) are dictations from the Spirits—he told me yesterday that when he writes—it is for the Spirits only—he sees the words fly about the room the moment he has put them on paper And his book is then published—A man so favourd of course has sources of wisdom and truth peculiar to himself.
>
> (BR, 324)

Taking Blake's ideas seriously, let me now sum up the relation between Blake's paintings and poetry. What Robinson reports about Blake is that his paintings are copies of his visions and his writings are dictations from the spirits. Robinson's mistake lies in his distinction between two separate modes of artistic creation in Blake, the visionary mode that is confined to his paintings and the locution mode that is confined to his poetry. Robinson is obviously right that paintings must inevitably fall into the visionary mode, but he makes an erroneous distinction between what is obviously visual, namely, paintings, and what is obviously verbal, namely, poetry. This compartmentalization of the visual and the verbal is an error because, like other visionaries, Blake reexpresses in his writing what he sees in his visions or dream-visions and, like them, he sees and he hears spiritual voices, sometimes conjointly, sometimes separately. G. E. Bentley, the editor and commentator of *Blake Records,* is one of the rare modern critics who noted the fundamental, even foundational, significance of Blake's visions. "It seems probable that his imagination was primarily a visual one, and that he *saw* his visions before he translated them into words or pictures" (BR, 234).

It should be remembered that some of Blake's contemporaries self-consciously adopted the dream mode both in poetry and in painting, anticipating the later surrealists but harking back to painters such as Hieronymus Bosch, Pieter Breughel the elder, and Goya.[125] William Gaunt says of Blake's friend John

Fuseli: "He was a painter of dreams—his first big picture, completed in London before he went to Italy, was, significantly enough, concerned with Joseph's interpretation of dreams of the pharaoh's butler and baker (*Genesis*, 40)." A later painting, *Night Mare* (1781), when Fuseli was forty was a popular sensation and "depicted a woman asleep, her head thrown back, her arms limply hanging, while on her breast squatted a hideous furry little monster, catlike, dwarfish, demonic," and pushing through a curtain the "head of a white horse stared blankly into the shadowy room."[126] Two poets whose work Blake illustrated employed dreams as a source of their poetry, Edward Young's *Night Thoughts* and Robert Blair's *The Grave*. Gaunt says that "both poets imagined a trance-like state in which the mind traveled freely through scarcely imaginable distance and could 'dream of things impossible.' *The dream state, in fact, gave its own assurance of the independent life of the spirit.*"[127] But one might add that, as with poetry, the thinking-I reworks the dream without revoking it.

Having made this bridge between the visual and the verbal, let me further develop Blake's visionary thought in terms of what Blake imagines himself as an inspired being possessed of poetic genius. As we have already noted, man's god nature is clouded by dark shadows, spectral illusions consequent to living ensnared by Reason and material gain. But not the post-1804 Blake: he has annihilated the self, and his spirit is set free to move from heaven back to his body. But what is the spirit that moves outside the body and back, through voluntary action on Blake's part, at least after 1804? I have suggested that "spirit" is to the visionary what the dream-ego is to the dreamer, and, for convenience, let us call it that. During periods of his everyday life, Blake was under the domination of his spiritual dream-ego, which allowed him visionary journeys and contacts with angels and other spirits up there. Seymour Kirkuk, a young admirer, who knew Blake and his wife during the period 1810–1816 wrote: "His excellent old wife was a sincere believer in his visions. She told me seriously one day, 'I have very little of Mr. Blake's company; he is always in Paradise'" (BR, 221).

Given his rejection of self and living under the dominance of his dream-ego, how can Blake act in accordance with the Cartesian dictum I think, I am? Insofar as the Cartesian certitude is linked with the broader issue of Enlightenment rationality, Blake's rejection of Reason is inextricably tied to his implicit rejection of the self or ego. With that rejection, there follows, in my thinking, a reification of the dream-ego as spirit. Thus Blake's visionary powers, his annihilation of the self, his rejection of Reason and the centrality of spirit or the dream-ego are all part of a single complex. If he is under the domination of the fantasy-I or dream-ego, then Blake is, unsurprisingly, locked into the language and symbolic forms of Revelation, but transformed through his poetic genius. Hence his styles of versification, his incorporation of symbols and images from the past he has seen through his visions, and the whole parabolic mode of storytelling that exhibits what I have called dream coherence. Thus his poetry is visionary in both senses of the term *vision*. Even when spirits dictate texts I assume they express Blake's own visionary mode of thought operating through his dream-ego. During his Felpham experience, chunks of texts simply entered into his mind without any conscious cognition at all. In which case he is the recipient of the poem (sometimes an unwilling one), and the attribution of his writing and painting to the spirits simply explains what is going on within him through the operation of the passive intellect. Blake's visions and voices cohere as dreams cohere; but, just as dreams might make sense to the dreamer, so the pictures that float before Blake make sense to him, even if they do not fully make sense to his audience. The visual imagery is private, but it is not a private language. The private vision is reexpressed and reformulated in painting and prophetic poetry directed toward a public. Much as an outsider can make some sense of my manifest dream, so he can make some sense of Blake's prophetic poetry, even though much of it will remain obscure. Whereas, with almost all other virtuosos in my essay, the visionary scenario makes sense for anyone who knows the culture, and this includes the audience of the visionary.

Northrop Frye says that Blake's "prophecies form what is in proportion to its merits the least read body of poetry in the language."[128] Although Blake was passionately convinced of the truth of his visions and his cosmogony of creation, destruction, and rejuvenation, he never could persuade others to accept it—hence it would be impossible to create a community of believers on the basis of his mythic thought. He was quite unlike the founders of dissenting sects in this regard and of the many later established churches, congregations, or even small groups of the faithful of the sort that Madame Blavatsky created fifty years after Blake's death. It is therefore a mistake to impose a rational system on Blake's thought, as most critics have done, for example, when Thomas Altizer sees Blake through the prism of Hegel's *Phenomenology of Spirit*, something that would be unthinkable for Blake, given that Hegel was an out-and-out exponent of Reason, even though for Hegel, as for Blake, there is a healing of the Cartesian split between matter and spirit, mind and nature.[129] I can imagine Blake's spirit rising from his grave in protest, re-citing his own words: "I must Create a System or be enslav'd by another Man's. I will not Reason and Compare: my business is to Create" (*Jerusalem*, CW, 629). Blake's "system" is the very opposite of the systematization of thought one associates with Reason, and this includes his contemporary Hegel, and it has no connection with what we nowadays call system.

Only those who are labeled schizophrenics can remain in the dream mode. Blake has to live in the world of scarcity and want, and, to do so, he must act in terms of commonsense understandings and practical rationality in the lived world of his time. Thus he can act as a social being and relate to friends; even though he despised Mammon and the material world, he has to live in it. Fortunately, his wife, herself a visionary, had enough capacity to manage Blake's financial affairs to keep them economically afloat. The fact that Blake is *not* schizophrenic and not permanently under the domination of the dream-ego means that he can write another kind of poetry, when occasion demands, and that is during the spaces when his spirit or fantasy-I comes back to earth and occupies his phenomenal body and the waking I. Hence those wonderful lyric poems, the *Songs of Innocence and Experience*, the poems of the *Notebook,* and the *Pickering Manuscript*, all written before 1804 in traditional stanza form, and after that we have *The Everlasting Gospel* (1818) and perhaps *The Gates of Paradise*, completed circa 1818, also in comprehensible but thick rhymed verse. These poems are also inspired, but brought under the accepted rational conventions of poetic composition.

It is not surprising that his contemporary audience simply could not understand Blake's seemingly incomprehensible conversations because they were unable to figure out the assumptions behind his thinking. Consider this example from Crabb Robinson's interview when he called on Blake a year before his death. For Robinson, parts of his interview reflected "the same round of extravagant and mad doctrines," as, for example, when Blake had told him that "I have written more than Voltaire or Rousseau—Six or Seven Epic poems as long as Homer and 20 Tragedies as long as Macbeth" (BR, 321, 322). Here is Bentley, the modern editor of *Blake Records,* commenting on this sentence: "Blake's report of the bulk of his writings is also strange. Voltaire's works run into fifty volumes, while Blake's are contained in one. Only three 'Epic poems' of any length by Blake have survived, none of which is as long as the *Iliad* or the *Odyssey*, and no complete play by Blake is known. Unless Blake was grossly exaggerating here, his works must have been destroyed on a Herculean scale" (BR, 323).

None of Bentley's assumptions are valid when we relate Blake's extravagant talk to his spiritual ideology. Thus, in a letter written to John Flaxman on September 21, 1800, as soon as he arrived in Felpham, he says: "I am more famed in Heaven for my works than I could well conceive. In my Brain are studies and Chambers fill'd with books and pictures of old, which I wrote and painted in ages of Eternity before my mortal life; and those works are the delight and Study of Archangels. Why, then, should I be anxious about the riches or fame of mortality?" (CW, 802) In other words, Blake is saying that, unlike Voltaire, he had written his voluminous works "in ages of Eternity," and they are stored in his brain but not put down on paper, not yet at any rate. These storied thoughts and images appear before him or are simply dictated to him, as it happened at Felpham when parts of *Vala* were composed. Contrary to Northrop Frye, I think that when Blake told Butts that he had written an "immense number of verses," on the scale of the *Iliad* and *Paradise Lost*, he is thinking of what had already been conceived in the chambers of his brain but had not put down in writing. Thus Blake's sporadic and seemingly meaningless comments make sense from *his* point of view.

Unfortunately, Blake does not always help with a fuller exposition of his ideas, but even some seemingly crazy statements make for coherence, especially if we understand similar thinking in Boehme and Paracelsus and other hermetic philosophers whose work Blake was familiar with. Let me now proceed with an enigmatic statement that baffled Robinson and others and ignored for the most part by Blake biographers. As always, Blake told Robinson that "he copies his Visions," and sure enough, in answer to a question from Robinson, Blake said, "*The Spirits told me.*" "This led me [Robinson] to say 'Socrates used pretty much the same language. He spoke of his Genius. Now what affinity or resemblance do you suppose was there between the *Genius* which inspired Socrates and you're [sic] *Spirits*?' He smiled, and for once it seemed to me as if he had a feeling of vanity gratified. 'The same as in our countenances,' he paused. And [then] said, 'I was Socrates.' And then as if he had gone too far in that [he added], 'Or a sort of brother. I must have had conversations with him. So I had with Jesus Christ. I have an obscure recollection of having been with both of them'" (BR, 539; my slightly emended punctuation).

There is nothing unusual in Blake or other visionaries having had conversations with Christ or Socrates or having been with both. I suspect that his "obscure recollection" was in respect to Socrates, not Christ. In this conversation, Blake was on the defensive, yet he was gentle as always, because he knew that Robinson did not take his visionary ideas seriously. Hence his saying initially that he was Socrates and his later qualification that he was a sort of brother with whom he had conversations, as he did with his own brother Robert. Perhaps he thought "he had gone too far" for the unbelieving Robinson. But if Blake believed in a version of reincarnation, as some hermetic philosophers did, influenced as they were by Plotinus and Neoplatonism, then he certainly could have been Socrates or his brother surrogate for that matter.[130] A hint that Blake believed in some form of transmigration or even reincarnation comes from his friend John Varley, the astrologer and painter, when he witnessed Blake painting the ghost of the flea.[131] "During the time occupied in completing the drawing, the Flea told him that all fleas were inhabited by the souls of such men, as were by nature blood-thirsty to excess, and were therefore providentially confined to the size and form of insects" (BR, 373). Again, in "an enigmatic entry" made by Robinson, we have Blake saying that "he had committed many murders," which on the face of it seems crazy unless Blake was either thinking of visions or of a past existence (BR, 332).[132]

Blake's idea that a human being can be reborn as a flea is no stranger than Plato's own doctrine of reincarnation or metensomatosis, which later went into Neoplatonism. Blake does not provide enough information for us to surmise that he believed in a reincarnation theory, whereby an individual gets born and re-born in limited or endless cycles of existence. But, if we take his being Socrates seriously, then he did believe in a form of occasional reincarnation. Being an out-and-out opponent of Enlightenment rationality, Blake was not obliged to spell out his ideas in a systematic manner. Hence, once "when irritated by the exclusively scientific talk at a friend's house, which talk had turned to the vastness of space, he blurted out, 'It is false. I walked the other evening to the end of the earth, and touched the sky with my finger'" (BR, 302). There is nothing crazy or surprising in this statement, if Blake traveling across the earth was in a vision or a dream-vision. In which case, his experience was not that different from shamanic travels and the spirit journeys of Tibetan Buddhists or, for that matter, of the Buddha himself. Because Blake believed in the reality of his experience, he couldn't accept the idea of illimitable space. Blake's flat earth theory was simply an inference from his visionary travel to the end of our planet, an experience that for him was more serious than the experiments of those given to the apotheosis of Reason.

BLAKE'S PEERS: POETRY AND THE DREAMING

By "dream" I mean something which proceeds from the visionary spirit and the intellect mutually united, or via the illumination of the intellect acting beyond our soul; or through the undoubted revelation of some divine being after the mind has been cleansed and is tranquil. From this our soul receives genuine prophecies and furnishes us with an abundance of predictions. For in dreams we seem to ask questions, learn, gather information, make discoveries. What is more, many doubts, many debates, and many things our minds have never known, never foreseen, and never investigated are revealed in dreams. Images of places unknown to us, and the likenesses of people both living and dead, appear; the future is presaged and things are revealed which have hap-

pened somewhere else and which have become known by no means of report-
age known to science.

—Cornelius Agrippa, *De occulta philosophia*

There is no doubt that the visionary consciousness has dimmed with the advent
of the Age of Reason. Blake almost had no choice but to become a radical antirationalist if he wanted to be faithful to his visions. Or he had to be a madman.
Visionary women would soon be taken care of in new French hospitals, toward
the latter part of the nineteenth century, crowned by medical science as hysterics. How then could the lost visionary worlds be reenchanted in Western ideation? Through romanticism: the obvious and well-known answer. There were
attempts in European romanticism to penetrate a mystified world of nature,
not so much the cultivated garden of Andrew Marvell, but an imagined raw or
wild world of nature, or a return to the past worlds of ancient Britons both exemplified in Wordsworth and even more fully in German Romanticism. Blake's
romantic colleagues were hostile or contemptuous of his visions because for
them visions were seen or ought to be seen in lunatic asylums. Yet, if visionary
poets were a thing of the past, this was not so with dreaming poets. It seems
that with the threat of the closing up of the visionary worlds there occurs a
concomitant opening up or reopening of the world of dreams and, occasionally,
dream-visions.

This is not surprising, given the fact that, in all times and ages, dreams have
compelled human beings everywhere to puzzle out what some of them meant
or more generally pose questions of existential import: for example, is life itself something like a dream, something effervescent or illusory, and yet rich with
prognosticative meaning, as the Byron of my earlier epigraph thought? This idea
is invested with epistemological significance in Hindu and Buddhist thought
in the concept of *māyā* where the everyday world of illusion is compared to a
dream. But then the question must arise: if life is a dreamlike state, is there a reality beyond? And, with that question, there arises a whole series of philosophical and salvific issues addressed by the great Indian religions.

But dream provocations are surely not confined to Indian epistemologies.
They occur, I think, among the intellectually curious everywhere, especially
among thinkers, such as poets, philosophers, intellectuals, shamans, and all sorts
of religious specialists. Lesser beings must be satisfied by conventional manuals, dream books, and the like. It is thus not surprising that creative thinkers in
the West as elsewhere would give expression to existential concerns by comparing life with dreams. Examples abound in English literature: consider the well-
known lines of Ernest Dowson (1867–1900).

They are not long the days of wine and roses:
Out of a misty dream
Our path emerges for awhile, then closes
Within a dream.

Dowson's, like that of others, has to be a personal epistemology, not a religious one, because the latter is dominated by Christian epistemologies where such a view of life is tantamount to heresy. But that fear did not deter a better-known poet several centuries earlier to openly speak of the illusory nature of the world in a dreamlike apocalyptic vision which prophecies the world's end hour.

Our revels now are ended. These our actors,
As I foretold you, were all spirits, and
Are melted into air, into thin air:
And like the baseless fabric of this vision,
The cloud-capp'd tow'rs, the gorgeous palaces,
The solemn temples, the great globe itself,
Yea, all which it inherit, shall dissolve,
And, like this insubstantial pageant faded,
Leave not a rack behind. We are such stuff
As dreams are made on; and our little life
Is rounded with a sleep.

It therefore should not surprise us that with the decline of the visionary imagination poets should fall back on dreams and dream-visions. Let me document, briefly, with a few illustrations the sympathetic treatment of dreams in the romantic literature of the nineteenth century after Blake and before Blavatsky. Wordsworth, like other romantic poets, resurrects the dream imagination in several places, sometimes almost as a visionary experience or a waking dream, as in *The Prelude*. But, unlike Byron's wild reality, Wordsworth's were patriotic ones, and rare, yet acceptable to his peers.[133] Unsurprisingly, the dream-vision appears in the recollections of Wordsworth's mature years, when, in an earlier time, while roaming in the wilds of Sarum's Plain, the poet's "youthful spirit was raised," and he saw "in vision clear" the Druid past of Briton, thus:

Saw multitudes of men, and, here and there,
A single Briton clothed in wolf-skin vest,
With shield and stone-axe, stride across the wold;
The voice of spears was heard, the rattling spear

Shaken by arms of mighty bone, in strength,
Long mouldered by barbaric majesty,
I called on Darkness—but before the word
Was uttered, midnight darkness seemed to take
All objects from my sight; and, lo! again
The Desert visible by dismal flames;
It is the sacrificial altar, fed
With living men—how deep the groans!

We are back in nineteenth-century Europe's obsession with the imagined romantic past, in this case the Druids that Blake, more critically than Wordsworth, also both condemned and adored. The next movement unfolds Druid teachers appearing in a waking dream, the truth of which the poet takes for granted:

—gently was I charmed
Into a waking dream, a reverie
That, with believing eyes, where'er I turned,
Beheld long-bearded teachers, with white wands
Uplifted, pointing to the starry sky.[134]

Owing to my concern with detailed cases, I will now turn to John Keats, for whom, in his major poetry, the dream takes primary place. I use Keats as a model of what occurred to the post-Enlightenment visionary propensity as it transformed itself into dreaming in poetry, fiction, painting, and narcosis. Keats not only uses the model of the dream for his poetry but also idealized the drowsy dream state, perhaps what late nineteenth-century thinkers called the hypnagogic condition, the state in between waking and sleep, as the opening lines of "Ode to a Nightingale" suggests:

My heart aches, and a drowsy numbness pains
My sense, as though of hemlock I had drunk,
Or emptied some dull opiate to the drains
One minute past and Lethe-wards had sunk . . . [135]

This opening mood does something more than herald the drowsy harbinger of forgetful sleep. The metaphors of hemlock and opiate appearing here and elsewhere in his poetry indicates an emergent preoccupation of the nineteenth century that flowered in the middle of the next, namely, the new kind of poet or intellectual who consumes opiates in order to produce an induced "drowsiness" and high unobtainable through other means. Coleridge's famous poem is in fact entitled "Kublai Khan, or a visionary dream, a fragment," a product of a waking dream, but one induced by opium. And so is Keats's incomplete "The fall of Hyperion: a dream," a product of an imaginary or real opiate and written in 1819, a few months before his lungs began to bleed uncontrollably until his death two years later. Then there is the less talented Thomas de Quincey, who, in *Confessions of an English Opium-Eater,* mentions the highs (the *L'Allegro* kinds of pleasures, as he calls them) and the melancholy (*Il Pensoroso* feelings), that is, the painful depressive effects that follow ecstatic and drug-induced "mystical" pleasures. Not Keats though; he admired and longed for the soothing condition of sleep or the waking state of drowsiness.[136] Keats was acutely tubercular and knew he was dying and sometimes accepting of it, such that he "was half in love with easeful death," which came to him in 1821 at age twenty-six. The great odes were written two years before. His drowsy state might even have been induced, partially at least, by the medications he had to take, most surely laudanum, the popular herbal medication containing opium. "Ode to a Nightingale" concludes with the famous lines that proclaim his uncertainty regarding the reality of the nightingale's song:

Was it a vision, or a waking dream?
Fled is that music: do I wake or sleep?

A similar ambiguity is expressed in "Ode to Psyche" where the poet is not sure whether his vision of the goddess Psyche was a night dream or a waking dream.[137]

While Keats was preoccupied with the drowsy state and dreaming, there is little evidence that he experienced anything like Wordsworth's waking dream or that he incorporated his own dreams into his poetry. Even if the dreams that appear in his poetry were based on his own dreams, the man who experiences them has been submerged in the poet who creates. In this sense Keats represents a wider condition, of his century and the next, wherein dreams are either incorporated into poetry or painting or become a model or source of inspiration for creativity. Keats's poetry is full of dreams; the dreams of the protagonist and of others and dreams within dreams such that it is impossible for us to detect the dreaming poet in the dream images of the poem. Many dreams have a nightmarish quality, as, for example, "La Belle Dame Sans Merci," which combines the prejudicial theme of the femme fatale with that of the deadly succubus. The poem is a much anthologized one, and I will not deal with it here but move on to the lesser-known narrative poem "Lamia" (1919), where the succubus and her lover are painted in more sympathetic terms, even though it is not as powerful or moving a poem as the previous one.[138]

Lamia is the snake woman; the kind of being that destroyed the original magical Eden. Yet in "Lamia" it is the dry and corrosive voice and eyes of the rational sophist Apollonius that pierce the beautiful snake woman and destroy the magical enchanted world that she and her young lover had created for themselves. It is a poem that does not permit any choice between Reason and the visionary imagination; a vision without hope.

Let me briefly mention a few episodes from this fascinating narrative poem. The story begins with Hermes in search of a fair nymph. In the course of his search, the god rested on lonely ground when he heard a mournful cry that would evoke pity in any gentle heart. The voice said:

"Whence from this wreathed tomb shall I awake!
When move in a sweet body fit for life,
And love, and pleasure, and the ruddy strife
Of hearts and lips!"

What Hermes found was no maiden but "a palpitating snake," bright and lying in circular fashion in "a dusky brake," a kind of primeval garden. Then a beautiful description of the snake or lamia follows. The strange being had a head of a snake, but "she had a woman's mouth and all her pearls complete," a combination, one might say, of the serpent and Eve. Although her throat was serpent, she spoke human words to Hermes saying that she dreamt of him living in splendor in the realm of the gods. After a long and flattering description of the god, she asks him for a boon:

"I was a woman, let me have once more
A woman's shape and charming as before,
I love a youth of Corinth—O the bliss!
Give me my woman's form, and place me where he is . . ."

The poet now makes an interesting statement that the dream of gods or their dreaming is real. Thus it is through a dream that the god sees the snake woman.

It was no dream; or say a dream it was,
Real are the dreams of Gods, and smoothly pass
Their pleasures in a long immortal dream.

And in the continuing dream the god grants the boon to Lamia; after which follows a brilliant description of Lamia changing from snake to woman. I will skip
the details and move to her crying for her lost lover Lycius as she goes searching
for him toward Corinth, his home. But what kind of searching was this? The poet
tells us that in her serpent form (which continues to underlie her present virgin
beauty and grace) she has a "sciential brain" and when she was in her "serpent
prison house" she could "muse and dream" and send her spirit (or fantasy-I or
the dream-ego of our usage) forth into the world outside:

> How, ever, where she will'd, her spirit went;
> Whether to faint Elysium . . .

Or to the realm of the Nereids or where Bacchus lies reeling in his cups or to
Pluto's world. But, more strangely during her snake existence, she projects her
dreams outward as if through telepathy.

> And sometimes into cities she would send
> Her dream, with feast and rioting to blend;
> And once, while among mortals dreaming thus,
> She saw the young Corinthian Lycius
> Charioting foremost in the envious race,
> Like a young Jove with calm uneager face,
> And fell into a swooning love of him . . .

Thus Lamia fell in love with Lycius through her dream, indicating quite clearly
that the idea of dream and thought transference was known to Keats. It is this
dream where she sought her lover Lycius by wandering toward Corinth, the
place to which he would eventually return with his companions after a long sea
voyage. But for some reason Lycius left his friends and went over the solitary
hills, "thoughtless at first," and then, before the evening star appeared:

> His phantasy was lost, where reason fades,
> In the calm light of Platonic shades.
> Lamia beheld him coming, near, more near—
> Close to her passing, in indifference drear

Lycius was a real living human being, but seems to share some of the ephemeral qualities of a dream creation. It seems as if Lycius comes toward Lamia

through her telepathic dream projection, although Keats does not explicitly spell this out. Lycius soon appears before Lamia, tantalizingly close, but he cannot or couldn't see her. The poet continues: Lycius passes her by, "shut up in mysteries, his mind wrapp'd like his mantle," while her eyes follow his steps. She turns her neck "syllabling thus," that is, imploring him to look back. It seems that Lycius, whether a real or a dream-figure, is caught in the enveloping mystery of the dream. Instead of speaking normal speech, Lamia "syllables," that is, I suspect, a silent magical song or utterance that she transmits to her lover. And, of course, he turns back and is smitten, thinking her a kind of Naiad of the river or some other divine being and then, given the sad ending of the poem, saying, with unintended irony: "If thou shouldst fade thy memory will waste me to a shade" and therefore "for pity do not melt."

I am going to skip much of the text. Lamia and her lover move to Corinth, which is described in great detail. In the city they pass an old man, and Lamia is fearful of him. She asks Lycius who the man could be, and Lycius says he is Apollonius, his guide and counselor. They pass him by and move on. The couple begins to live together in a beautiful mansion that seems to be dream created, isolated from the rest of the city. Lycius knows her only as a divine creature, not as a lamia. At some point he wants to wed Lamia in an official ceremony in the city. She resists, but at last she consents, reluctantly, "in pale contented sort of discontent," telling Lycius that he must not invite Apollonius to the ceremony. When the wedding day arrives, the guests enter the fabulous dream palace, where they drink till their senses become numb. But then an uninvited guest appears, none other than Apollonius, the rationalist and sophist, whose "cold philosophy" the poet says makes all charms fly. Apollonius's world of cruel reality has no space for the wild reality of the dream world in which the lovers live. His eye penetrates Lamia; she becomes paler and paler, and Lycius knows it's the sophist that has wrought these changes. As she sat next to him, Lycius touches her body:

'Twas icy, and the cold ran through his veins;
Then sudden it grew hot, and all the pains
Of an unnatural heat shot to his heart.

The dream house begins to change, the music ceases, the garlands of myrtle shrivel, "voice, lute and pleasure ceased, a deadly silence step by step increased," and everyone feels the terror in their hair. And Lamia becomes paler and deadly white, withering like the dream house itself, while Lycius blames Apollonius:

> Corinthians! look upon that gray-beard wretch!
> Mark how, possess'd, his lashless eyelids stretch
> Around his demon eyes.

In the eyes of Lycius it is the sophist who is a demonic figure. But the enlightened realist responds, calling Lycius a fool: "And shall I see thee made a serpent's prey?"

> "A serpent!" echoed he, no sooner said,
> That with a frightening scream she vanished:
> And Lycius' arms were empty of delight,
> As were his limbs of life, from that same night,
> On the high couch he lay!—his friends came round—
> Supported him—no pulse, or breath they found,
> And in the marriage robe, the heavy body bound.

One might think this is a repeat of the theme of "La Belle Dame Sans Merci," but the beautiful Lamia is not quite without mercy, to put it mildly. She flees from the sophist's bleak, magical gaze of Reason. She has no other choice as she becomes a victim of Apollonius's Apollonian magic, which reminds one of another Apollonian rationalist magician, Prospero, the speaker of the earlier prophecy, beating a harmless monster into civilized submission and temporarily imprisoning a fairy creature, Ariel. Lamia must perforce leave her lover dead in his wedding shroud.

Book 6

THEOSOPHIES

West Meets East

THE VISIONARY TRAVELS OF MADAME BLAVATSKY: COUNTERING ENLIGHTENMENT RATIONALITY

> And immediately I was in the spirit; and, behold, a throne was set in heaven, and one sat on the throne.
>
> —Revelation 4:2

WHILE THE ANTINOMIAN MOVEMENTS in England were central to our understanding of Blake, one may ask how influential they were for Blavatsky, who was born and raised in Russia in the Orthodox Church. The late nineteenth century did not make it easy to be an antirationalist as Blake was. It was not only the impact of science that began to erode the field of visionary religion but also a galaxy of philosophers and thinkers who questioned the intellectual legitimacy of the Christian faith. This was the era of Herbert Spencer and John Stuart Mill, of Auguste Comte and Ernest Renan, of Ludwig Feuerbach and Karl Marx, of Charles Darwin and Thomas Huxley (inventor of the term *agnosticism*), not to mention the towering figure of Nietzsche, culminating in the fin de siècle of the anthropology and psychoanalytic search for religious evolution or development in such figures as Edward Tylor, James Frazer, and Sigmund Freud and their many associates and disciples. The death of God is the inevitable end product of this intellectual trajectory. The dilemma between Enlightenment rationality, or Euro-rationality, and religion was reflected in the two major founding figures of the Theosophical Society, and it is this movement, a pulling toward and a pushing away from the domination of the Enlightenment that I now want to briefly consider, especially in relation to the fate of the visionary consciousness at the end of that century.

The Theosophical Society was founded in 1875 in New York by its two leading figures, Colonel Henry Steel Olcott who was president for life and Blavatsky, the "corresponding secretary." Theosophy, literally meaning the "wisdom of God," had a long antecedent history in Europe. There were also many self-proclaimed Theosophists long before the formation of the Theosophical Society.[1] As we have shown in our earlier discussion, Jacob Boehme was one of the great Theosophists, known early in his career as "Theosophus Teutonicus." It is extremely likely that the term *theosophy* was much discussed by its founders, who thought it a suitable name for the new society and a mode of appropriating the prestige and ideas of Boehme. Like many other religious movements, the new Theosophy could broadly incorporate not only different interpretations of that term but also provoke many dissident movements that broke away from or were only peripherally linked to the main organization.

In this section I am going to focus primarily on Madame Blavatsky, the counterrationalist thinker and visionary, and make only passing references to Annie Besant, another major figure in the Theosophical movement. It was Besant who, after Blavatsky's death, carried on her legacy and took an active role in Indian intellectual, cultural, and political life, becoming the president of the Indian National Congress in 1917 by overwhelmingly defeating her rival Gandhi (who obtained one vote only).[2] Whereas Blavatsky and Besant were committed to a broad interpretation of the term *theosophy*, Olcott over the years became a convert to Theravāda Buddhism, which he, as did others of his time, recognized as a "nontheistic religion" consonant with modern science and reconcilable with Darwinism. Blavatsky was willing to admit she was a Buddhist, but defined the etymology of that word in her own unique manner, on occasion wrote it as "Budh-ism" or knowledge of "wisdom" ("Sophia"), thus simply equating Buddhism with Theosophy and at the same time leading Theosophy toward her own version of "esoteric Buddhism." Blavatsky did not deny Enlightenment rationality, but affirmed an alternative position, inventing a religious ideology that could coexist with scientific rationality but occasionally critiquing the latter, as she did Darwin and other "atheist" scientists. Wisdom always transcended and filled in the gaps that science had missed, a position many Christian intellectuals also subscribe to in our own times.

Blavatsky (1831–1891) was born in Ukraine and raised in a highly cultivated aristocratic family with influential political connections to the Russian ruling class.[3] Her mother, Helena Andreyevna, married an army officer, Peter von Hahn, at age eighteen (according to Russian reckoning) and had three children. Helena Petrovna, the eldest, was followed by a son who died and then a daughter, Vera, and another son born very late in 1840. Helena Andreyevna was a gifted writer of fiction, dying in 1842 at age twenty-nine. Because their father was stationed in different places, the children lived most of the time with Blavatsky's grandmother, Princess Helena Pavolvna, who was married to a wealthy and powerful government official, Andrey de Fadayev. Helena Pavolvna also was a highly educated woman who made a name in Russia in botany and archeology.

Early in her marriage, Blavatsky's mother was estranged from her husband, but Blavatsky apparently had a close relationship with her father. According to some accounts, her mother was somewhat aloof, too much involved in her own work. Blavatsky was educated at home by governesses, during which time she acquired a fair knowledge of English, French, and some German. She was also nurtured into the popular religious beliefs of her extensive array of servants who firmly believed in ghosts, spirits, and other kinds of spectral beings. Biographers mention Blavatsky childhood "visions," though their nature and content seems uncertain and perhaps only suggests the hagiographical imperative at work that I have mentioned in respect of Blake.

A significant event in Blavatsky's childhood socialization occurred when her grandfather Andrey de Fadayev was stationed among the Kalmucks in the province of Astrakhan for ten months. Because Peter von Hahn was out most of the time, his wife and children stayed in the Fadayev home. The Kalmuck people were Buddhists, and it is almost certain that Blavatsky became acquainted with Buddhist temples and lamas there and visited the palace of a Prince Tumen, a Kalmuck chief of Astrakhan. However, she was only a child of about five when she first met the Kalmucks and she could not possibly have had any grasp of their Buddhism at that time. After her mother died, the children had to move to Saratov, on the Volga, where her grandfather now was governor. On route the family once again visited the summer quarters of Prince Tumen, who warmly welcomed them. One account says that he "lived in a fabulous palace on one of the islands of the delta" of the Volga (C, 25). Blavatsky was about eleven, and this visit would have reinforced her earlier recollections of the Kalmucks, stimulated perhaps by a novel her mother wrote based on the life of the Buddhist Kalmucks.

At age eighteen, the very age that her mother married a man twice her age, Blavatsky, imitating her parental marriage, married a forty-two-year-old man in 1849. She confessed many times that she did not consummate this marriage, and we have to respect her claim. We do know that she left her husband soon after her marriage and, bearing his family name of Blavatsky, traveled for about a year in Egypt, Greece, and Turkey during the period 1849–1850. Blavatsky's fascination with Egypt was part of a continuing tradition in Europe from at least the middle of the eighteenth century, including the belief that religion had its origins there.[4] In Cairo she told a young American scholar that her ambition was to free mankind from mental bondage (C, 43). It seems that before age twenty she was already beginning to define her project on occult science, not surprising given her extensive reading of hermetic and occult literature in her grandfather's library, including, perhaps, whatever was known about Tibet at that time.

After her Egyptian visit, she spent some time in Europe and England but was in London in April 1851 with a friend, the Countess Bragration, "somewhere between the City and the Strand."[5] Here she claimed she had a vision of her master on the banks of the Thames near Ramsgate. Back in her hotel she sketched that scene with its water and sailboats and noted in French: "Memorable night! On a certain night by the light of the moon that was the setting at Ramsgate on August 12, 1851, when I met M [here follows the sign of the points of the triangle, the signature of M] the Master of my dreams," adding a note that according to the Russian calendar this was July 31 and her twentieth birthday.[6] We now have a name for her guru, M, or Master Moriya, the being whom she had for some time fantasized as the master of her dreams.

This account is however complicated by a recollection mentioned in a letter she wrote on March 1882 to a friend of her youth, Prince A. M. Dondoukoff-Korsakoff. Here she recounts some of her preceding experiences in Egypt and Turkey in the quest for the Red Virgin and the philosopher's stone whose union or marriage represented a fusion of soul and the spirit, at least at this point in her alchemical thinking. Apparently, in early 1851 in Constantinople, she needed money and contested in a steeple chase, but her horse reared and crushed her, and she was unconscious for six weeks. "I saw a man, a giant, dressed differently from the Turks, who lifted my tattered and bloody garments from under the horse and—nothing more, nothing but the memory of a face I had seen somewhere [in her earlier visions or dreams]."[7] She came back from Turkey depressed because she failed to find the sacred stone and was in London that same year with the Countess Bragration in Mivart's Hotel when, in order to escape her company, she records the following experience: "I escaped on to Waterloo Bridge, for I was seized with a desire to die. I had long felt the temptation approaching. This time I did not seek to resist it and the muddy water of the Thames seemed to me a delicious bed. I was seeking eternal repose not being able to find the 'stone' and having lost the 'Virgin.' The same mysterious personage [the 'giant'] woke me up and saved me and, to console me with life, promised me 'the Stone and the Virgin.' I *have them* now," implying that now (by 1882) she has the knowledge embodied in the Stone and the Virgin.[8] Whether the Ramsgate and Waterloo events were the same or two different episodes is not clear, but what is certain is that both were visions of her guru Master M. I am convinced that the suicide attempt was an actual event, not a fantasy, something that she was willing to admit in 1882, but not in 1851 at age twenty.[9]

The other account of an encounter with Master M is found in Blavatsky's reminiscence recorded by her friend Countess Constance Wachtmeister:

> When she was in London, in 1851, with her father, Colonel Hahn, she was one day out walking when, to her astonishment, she saw a tall Hindu in the street with some Indian princes. She immediately recognized him as *the same person she had seen in the astral.* Her first impulse was to rush forward to speak to him, but he made a sign to her not to move. She there stood as if spellbound while he passed on. The next day she went into Hyde Park for a stroll [to] be alone and free to think over her extraordinary adventure. Looking up, she saw the same form approaching her, and then her Master told her that he had come to London with the Indian princes on an important mission, and he was desirous of meeting her personally, as he required her cooperation in a work which he was about to undertake. . . . He also told her that she would have to spend three years in Tibet to prepare for the important task.[10]

According to Wachtmeister's version, Blavatsky had seen the master earlier in astral vision. This without doubt refers to her visions prior to 1851, but also very likely the Ramsgate/Waterloo ones. However, Wachtmeister's contention that the London meeting was a "real" one cannot be accepted at face value, even though this was the year of the Great Exhibition in Hyde Park held during May 1 to October 15 of that year. It was also known as the Crystal Palace Exhibition, a term that for Blavatsky must surely have sent memory waves to the Tibetan idea of the "crystal palace," the seat of the latent Buddha nature (see book 2, p. 114). A further stimulus: Indian dignitaries had gathered there, and the crystal palace was therefore an apt locale for Blavatsky to conjure up the hallucinatory Moriya. We cannot fully resolve these issues, especially the order of the visions. It should also be remembered that by this time Blavatsky had read extensively the hermetic literature, especially Paracelsus, on "astral" phenomena, which she later defined as sidereal force, that is, an "emanation from the stars and celestial bodies of which the spiritual form of man—the astral spirit—is composed."[11] This astral form is activated naturally during sleeping and dreaming or through the occult powers of adepts.

After her London sojourn she traveled extensively in North America and the Near East, after which, heeding the command of the master, she decided to go to India with the intention of moving on to Tibet. But this was not realized because she was not permitted to travel to Tibet via Nepal by the British resident (C, 50). Her travels in India and perhaps the Tibetan cultural regions were formative in developing her esoteric and invented Buddhist doctrines. These travels have been questioned by critics, but very likely her ambition to visit Tibet was partially realized during her second Indian trip, in 1856–57, when she managed to travel extensively in India and then to Kashmir and through regions bordering the Tibetan cultural region (Little Tibet) .[12] During one such trip, she was accompanied by a Tartar shaman who demonstrated his powers of leaving the body and directing his spirit (his astral soul or inner ego, according to Blavatsky) to visit other places, correctly identifying persons known to Blavatsky outside Tibet.[13] According to Cranston, she managed to visit "western Tibet," but the conditions in Tibet did not permit them to proceed further, and she had to return to India without fulfilling her dream of visiting eastern Tibet and Lhasa. She returned to Russia in 1858, and in the following year we have the first reports of a "strange illness" while visiting her father and her half-sister Lisa.

Her sister Vera explains these episodes thus: "Years before, perhaps during her solitary travels in the steppes of Asia, she had received a remarkable wound [in the region of the heart]. We could never learn how she had met with it. Suffice to say that the wound re-opened occasionally, and during that time she suffered intense agony, after bringing on convulsions and a death-like trance. The sickness used to last from three to five days, and then the wound would heal as suddenly as it had re-opened, as though an invisible hand had closed it, and there would remain no trace of her illness."[14] According to Vera it was "one of those mysterious nervous diseases that baffle science," but Blavatsky did not hide it from others and informed her relatives and friends about her "double life" during this first "trance illness."

Whenever I was called by name, I opened my eyes upon hearing it, and was myself, my own personality in every particular. As soon as I was left alone, however, I relapsed into my usual, half-dreamy condition, and became somebody else [Vera adds that she would not reveal the identity of this other person]. I had simply a mild fever that consumed me slowly but surely, day after day, with entire loss of appetite, and finally of hunger, as I would feel none for days, and often went a week without touching any food whatever, except a little water, so that in four months I was reduced to a living skeleton. In cases when I was interrupted, when I was in my other self, by the sound of my present name being pronounced, and while I was conversing in my dream life—say at half a sentence either spoken by me or those who were with my second me at the time,—and opened my eyes to answer the call, I used to answer very rationally, and understood all, for I was never delirious. But no sooner had I closed my eyes again that the sentence which had been interrupted was completed by my other self, continued from the word, or even half the word it had stopped at. When awake, and myself, I remembered well who I was, in my second capacity, and what I had been and was doing. When somebody else, i.e., the personage I had become, I know I had no idea of who was H. P. Blavatsky! I was in another far off country, a totally different individuality from myself, and had no connection at all with my actual life.[15]

This was in a little village in the Caucasus in Mingrelia, on the Black Sea, where Blavatsky lived for a while. From there she was dispatched in a boat to a town (Kutais) where there were doctors and a relative to take care of her. The servants in charge were terrified when they saw her "gliding off from the boat, and across the water in the direction of the forests, while the body of the same mistress was lying prostrate on her bed at the bottom of the boat."[16]

Let me focus for the moment on several features of Blavatsky's trance illness, bearing in mind this was the first one to be recorded. The most dramatic feature of her illness is the mysterious wound in the region of her heart. What must have occurred was a stigmata-type wound in the exterior of her body, reminding us of the wounds of love of Christian penitents. However, we do not have enough evidence to unravel their meanings in the emotional life of Blavatsky. It seems that she is being wounded in the region of the heart by the spiritual being who possesses her and whose identity she would not reveal. Could it have been a visitation by Master Moriya, whom she first met in her vision at Waterloo/Ramsgate and in Hyde Park in 1851 and even earlier in her dreams? If so, she refuses to discuss him with her friends, though she is quite open about other aspects of her illness, especially that she has a double with whom she identifies and through whose intercession she travels to far-off lands. It is certain that "Moriya" is derived from the Sanskrit *Maurya* meaning "peacock," a beautiful creature whose erotic significance is unmistakable. Blavatsky was a sexual prude and rarely talked about her erotic life, indeed scarcely mentioning eroticism in her work. In one visionary episode, John King, the buccaneer spirit popular with spiritualists, kissed her, but she did not like, she claimed, to be kissed on the mouth.[17] I suspect that the reason for not identifying Moriya as her visitant was because of her erotic relationship with this fantasized being.

It was after these illness episodes that she began to exhibit some of her remarkable spiritual powers before her friends, admirers, and relatives in Russia, including the production of "phenomena" that later made her famous in India. These included "raps" and bell ringing, materialization of objects and immobilizing furniture, such that "the news about the extraordinary phenomena produced by her spread like lightning, turning the whole town topsy-turvy."[18] The Theosophist W. Q. Judge claimed that Blavatsky herself told him that "this was a period when she was letting her psychic forces play, and learning to fully understand and control them."[19] It should be noted that during this time European psychics like D. D. Home were displaying similar powers.[20]

I will not deal with her other European and Middle Eastern travels, but move on to the year 1868, when she received a letter from Master Moriya urging her to go to Tibet. Heeding his summons, she claims to have traveled through the Karakoram range, north of Kashmir, and there in Little Tibet (Ladakh) she lived, according to her sister Vera, with another of her masters named Koot Hoomi (known generally to Blavatsky and all Theosophists as KH). According to one of Blavatsky's reminiscences, KH lived with his sister and mother in a "large wooden building in the Chinese fashion, pagoda-like, between a lake and a beautiful mountain."[21] Although Blavatsky's own personal guru was Master Moriya (Master M), most of her contact during this visit was with KH. Both masters were wanderers like Blavatsky herself, generally moving from one place to another on various missions and meeting with fellow brothers in different parts of the world or in the White Lodge where they congregated as a group. Her gurus were rarely present in the actual world, "but they can project their astral forms anywhere" and could therefore make their appearance before their devotees.[22]

The stay with KH and his sister was also a period of tutelage for Blavatsky. She not only received instructions on esoteric knowledge but also learned two languages, English and Senzar, the latter of which Blavatsky defined as "the mystic name for the secret sacerdotal language or the 'Mystery-speech' of the initiated Adepts all over the world."[23] It is in this secret language that the *Stanzas of Dzyan* was written. These stanzas described the origin of the universe and of human beings; *Dzyan* later developed into two better-known texts, *The Secret Doctrine* and *The Voice of the Silence*. Part 1 of the former text is an extended commentary on each line and stanza of the *Dzyan*.[24] I shall soon examine the context in which Master KH taught her English, the language she mostly used for writing and for translating or rendering the difficult Senzar language.

Her claimed second visit to Tibet (during or after her visit to Ladakh) is problematic. For her supporters, the event occurred in empirical reality, while her critics entirely discount it. My hypothesis, in consonance with the themes of this essay, is that Blavatsky's second trip to Tibet did in fact occur, but on the level of visionary reality, not as an empirical actuality. The question I pose now is this: when did that vision of the Tibetan sojourn first appear before her consciousness? It was not during her first trance illness and the episodes that followed, during the period 1859–1861, because the second Tibetan visit supposedly occurred only after that period, in 1869 according to her. A clue is provided by the second and more significant trance illness she suffered soon after she married Michael Betanelly in Philadelphia on April 3, 1875.

Betanelly was thirty-three years old and a native of Georgia, while Blavatsky was forty-four, although they had lived together in Philadelphia during the winter of 1874–75.[25] This union was also an unhappy one, and two months into the marriage she suffered from a severe illness. What seemed to have happened is that Blavatsky had a fall and injured her leg and had difficulty healing it, which resulted in a kind of "paralysis."[26] Two letters written on May 21 indicated that doctors wanted to amputate her leg.[27] But, soon afterward, she suffered from her second experience of a trance illness, probably in May or early June 1875. Her husband described the situation, in his own inimitable style, thus:

> All these days Madame was always the same: three or four times a day loozing power, and laying as one dead for two or three hours at a time, pulse and heart stopped, cold and pale as dead. John King [the buccaneer master] told truth right away in all. She was in such trance morning Monday and afternoon from three till six; we thought her dead. People say her spirit travels at that time, but I don't know nothing of it, and I simply thought several times, all was finished. It's very strange. Those who watch her, say that at night she gets up and goes right away in spirit room (sic) and that she goes strong on her leg, though in day she cannot move it or walk at all. Omniloff is the name of a Russian officer in Caucasus, was killed in last war with Schamile. I had [heard] of the name too.[28]

The background events are not clear. Her first unconsummated marriage to the elderly person was a failure; yet she continued to keep her married name. Some of her biographers claim that she had a second affair with another older man that ended in separation or divorce.[29] From our point of view, the critical event prior to her second trance illness is the death of her father to whom she was greatly attached. He had died on July 27, 1873, but unfortunately, on the orders of the masters, Blavatsky had left for New York on an emigrant ship, landing there on July 7. Thus there is no way that she could have been present at her father's funeral or be with him during his last days. We do not know when she heard about her father's death. Yet the feelings of guilt on the failure to attend a loved one's funeral is a familiar scenario in cases of spirit attack and the dark night of the soul, as I have demonstrated in *Medusa's Hair* and in this work. We do not know whether the previous trance illness was triggered by the death of a beloved person, but the most recent one certainly was. At this juncture marrying a younger man, someone with her own broad Russian background, might have provided her with some solace. It is likely that Blavatsky had an added feeling of guilt in wanting to leave her newly married spouse. Perhaps even earlier childhood anxieties and later betrayals of husbands or lovers might have been operative, but of these we know nothing. A puzzling reference is the one to the dead Omniloff, whose name she seemed to have mentioned, very likely someone who appeared before her during her illness, maybe even someone she had loved and lost.[30] She initially suffered a "paralysis" of her leg, but this was diagnosed as a physical condition. It was more likely a hysterical one, common enough in her time and provoked by the physical injury. One cannot rule out the fact that the physical injury itself might have been cured during her trance because minor injuries can be cured during hypnotic trances and even during lucid dreams.[31] What is clear is that she suffered an acute recurrence of her trance illness, wherein her spirit left the body and wandered in other lands.

During this period of spiritual "dying" and alienation, she not only encounters adepts but also acquires or reinforces some of her impressive spiritual powers, first obtained during her previous episode. In a letter written to her sister Vera she mentions that her Hindu teacher "has cured me completely." This might be a reference to both her trance illness and her leg. We know she could walk fairly well soon after, obviating the necessity for the amputation her doctor thought might be necessary. As in her earlier illness, she describes two beings within her, one of whom was "quite separable from me, present in my body. I never lose the consciousness of my own personality; what I feel is as if I were keeping silent and the other one—the lodger who is in me—were speaking with my tongue."[32] One must be careful of Blavatsky's use of language here. She has lost consciousness, but another "consciousness" has taken over her body. Needless to say, this is a specific manifestation of possession by spirits with which we are already familiar in this book and in the cross-cultural literature that is in turn a fantasized emanation of her dream ego, as the following admission indicates: "For instance, I know that I have never been in the places which are described by my 'other me,' but this other one—the second me—does not lie when he tells about places and things unknown to me, because he has actually seen them and knows them well. I have given it up: let my fate conduct me at its own sweet will; and besides, what am I to do? It would be perfectly ridiculous if I were to deny the possession of knowledge avowed by my No. 2, giving occasion to the people around me to imagine that I kept them in the dark for modesty's sake."[33]

She now makes a decision that other religious innovators also did, namely, proclaim her message to the world, something she refused to do during her previous illness. It is this wish that, I think, led her to form the Theosophical Society the very same year. The society became the instrument through which she hoped to spread her visionary knowledge to the world and very self-consciously convert the world, if not now, then later when her message would have been fully spread and understood. She now adds: "In the night, when I am alone in my bed, the whole life of my No. 2 passes before my eyes, and I do not see myself at all, but quite a different person—different in race, different in feelings. But what's the use of talking about it? It is enough to drive one mad. I try to throw myself into the part, and to forget the strangeness of my situation. This is no mediumship, and by no means an impure power; . . . it has too strong an ascendancy over us all, leading us to better ways."[34]

She informs her sister Vera that this No. 2 was her teacher: "I see this Hindu every day, just as I might see any other living person, with the only difference that he looks to me more ethereal and more transparent. Formerly I kept silent about these appearances, that they were hallucinations. But now they have become visible to other people as well. He (the Hindu) appears and advises us as to our conduct and our writing. He evidently knows everything that is going on, even to the thoughts of other people, and makes me express his knowledge. Sometimes it seems to me that he overshadows the whole of me, simply entering me like a kind of volatile essence penetrating my pores and dissolving in me," not unusual giving the fact that her master is ethereal and transparent, an astral being. When the master dissolves into the mistress, the two become one, then "we two are able to speak to other people, and then I begin to understand and remember sciences and language—everything he instructs me in, *even when he is not with me anymore.*"[35]

Several conclusions can be drawn from this somewhat fragmentary account of Blavatsky's dark night of the soul. The present trance illness has different existential implications from the first one of 1859, because she did not suffer a relapse. In the 1859 illness she had already developed a mastery over her trance states and her capacity to have visions, and the second episode reinforced these powers. Thereafter she could voluntarily enter trancelike states without any accompanying illness. She now clearly identifies the being within her as one of her Hindu masters, probably her guardian Master Moriya (Master M, sometimes familiarly referred to as "Boss"). She now begins to receive from the masters the kind of knowledge that went into *Isis Unveiled* and her later works. These communications of knowledge were from Master Moriya and the other powerful adept, KH, her tutor in Senzar and English.

It seems to me that these gurus were "composite images," that is, a fusion of known and imagined persons found in dream images and normal memories. Blavatsky was personally familiar with many living Hindu gurus through her sojourns in India; and the masters are composites of them fused into a new creation and then fixed in her mind.[36] Olcott also had visions of Master KH on several occasions, modeled on Blavatsky's descriptions of them, although for Olcott, but not for Blavatsky, this master had a Christ-like face, which was not surprising considering Olcott's strong Protestant background.[37] Similarly, one could argue that Blavatsky's visions of the Chinese pagoda-type mansion of the masters beside a lake was also a composite image based on prior memories based on her familiarity with Buddhist temples during her periods of contact with the Kalmucks. We have already met Prince Tumen, the Kalmuck chief, and mentioned his "fabulous" palace. In Marion Meade's somewhat cynical account, Tumen "lived in a white palace that was half-Chinese, half-'Arabian Nights' in décor" and this man spent "much of his day praying in a Buddhist temple he had erected nearby." Meade adds that this was a "water-encircled palace" with "its exterior fretted with balconies and fantastic ornaments."[38] Finally, one has to discount as literally true that Blavatsky spent three years in Tibet being initiated into the mysteries of the masters; rather, we have here the familiar visionary compression of time. To put it metaphorically: Blavatsky blinks her eyes and three years pass by, the standard time for initiation into the mysteries according to her.

To get back to our narrative: the second letter tells us about Blavatsky's own doubts that her visions might have been hallucinations. Yet, like other visionaries, she soon begins to recognize their noetic quality, to use, once again, William James's neat term. But, crucially, in Blavatsky's case, the master dissolving into the mistress is akin to Tibetan Vajrayāna adepts and treasure seekers. She is imbued with his essence, which then gives her the special powers she begins to exhibit more frequently from this date. The masters now begin to visit her every day. And finally the first letter to Vera helps us understand her visionary visit to Tibet when she says she has never been in the places that are described by my "other me." But, if the master dissolves in her, then surely the visits of her master to distant places are also her visits—no wonder she says that the master is her double, her No. 2. Thus her visits to Tibet, living with Master KH in Tibet and elsewhere, are visionary journeys familiar to shamanism and Tibetan Buddhism and perhaps even stimulated by her personal experience with the shaman who accompanied her during her first sojourn in Little Tibet and in other places.

The spirit journeys were real to her, as they were to other visionaries, but with an important difference. Christian penitents knew their bodily visions were real, but, at the same time, they remained visions, albeit of the past that had actually occurred, which they were privileged to reenvision. And Tibetan visionaries also knew that when they traversed the cosmos they did so in a meditative state such that after the journey was over they were back in their bodies, in spite of their belief that the places they visited and the divinities they met were empirically real or, more complicatedly, illusions of the empirically real or even illusions of illusions or their proxy forms. Blavatsky's was close to the Tibetan visionary experience, except that, at a certain point in time, she believed that, as a physical being, she had visited the areas depicted in her vision, even though she could easily have justified her presence there in terms of her possessing an astral body. While her equation of physical and empirical reality was closer to psychotic delusions where similar fusions of illusion and reality are made, I do not see Blavatsky even remotely as a madwoman. Such fusions of time and place only compel us to blur the distinction between normal and psychotic, especially as far as gifted religious virtuosos are concerned. The visions experienced during her trance illness recollect a past that, from *my* point of view, did not occur empirically, but not from Blavatsky's. From my point of view, I would say the vision was so powerful as to be imprinted in her mind and thereafter converted into an empirical reality. This merging of fantasy and reality is also, I think, true of her claim that she fought with Garibaldi in the battle of Mentana and incurred five wounds.[39] Merging of fantasy and reality is easy enough to envisage in the Tibetan Buddhism she was familiar with, because the real world is, often enough, seen as an illusion and the illusory world as "real." Blavatsky's visionary travels and knowledge acquisition has further implications for those who have dealt with her life and work. Her recall of past events constitutes a peculiar fusion of the imagined and the empirically real. Her critics could not grasp this because they were comfortable with the opposition between empirical reality and visionary unreality, the latter often enough equated with fraud or madness.

I now quote a fascinating letter written to her English disciple A. P. Sinnett on January 6, 1886, when she was in Wurzburg, after leaving India for good in 1885, upset at the report of the Society for Psychical Research condemning her as a fraud and a charlatan. Outside of the fact that the following dream-vision provides consolation during this troubled period, it also repeats, according to Blavatsky, some of her previous experiences, including her studying English and Senzar under the tutelage of Master KH:

> I went to bed and I had the most extraordinary vision. I had vainly called upon the Masters—who came not during my waking state—but now in my sleep, I saw them both, I was again (a scene of years back) in Mah. [Mahatma] K.H.'s house. I was sitting in a corner on a mat and he walking about the room in his riding dress, and Master was talking to someone behind the door. "*I remind can't*"—I pronounced in answer to a question of His about a dead aunt.—He smiled and said "Funny English you use." Then I felt ashamed, hurt *in my vanity*, and began thinking (mind you, in my *dream* or *vision* which was the *exact* reproduction of what had taken place word

for word 16 years ago) "now I am here and speaking *nothing but English* in verbal phonetic language I can perhaps learn to speak English better with Him." [She then says in this letter that is how she studied English in Tibet and adds] Then, in my dream still, *three months after* as I was made to feel in that vision . . . I took to him a few sentences I was studying in Senzar in his sister's room and asked him to tell me if I translated them correctly—and gave him a slip of paper with these sentences written in English. He took and read them and correcting the interpretation read them over and said "Now your English is becoming better—*try to pick out of my head even the little I know of it.*" He put his hand on my forehead in the region of memory and squeezed his fingers on it (and I felt even the same trifling pain in it, as then, and the cold shiver I had experienced) and since that day He did so with my head daily, for about two months.

The dream vision duplicating Blavatsky's long Tibetan sojourn into a few minutes now changes into a repetition of another episode that has to do with the writing of *Isis Unveiled*. "Again the scene changes and I am [at] 47 St, New York writing *Isis* and His voice dictating to me. In that dream or *retrospective* vision I once more *rewrote* all *Isis* and could now point out all the pages and sentences Mah. K.H. dictated—as those that Master did—in my bad English. . . . I saw myself night after night in bed—writing *Isis* in my dreams, at New York, positively *writing it in my sleep* and felt sentences by Mah. K.H. *impressing themselves on my memory* (my emphasis).[40]

This was a bad time for Blavatsky. She had left India owing to illness, the intrusion of the Society for Psychical Research, and the "Coulomb affair" in which a former employee and her husband denounced her to missionaries as a fraud and were expelled from the society in early 1884.[41] She was physically ill with kidney and liver ailments and was convinced that she had not much longer to live. In the letter she tells Sinnett that "everything went against me and I had but to die."[42] What about her dream-vision of learning English and Senzar from KH and her firm belief that the vision was simply a repetition of an event that actually occurred during her second improbable Tibetan sojourn? If, as I suggested, it is the trance illness in 1875 that produced the visionary journey, then the present dream repeats the prior vision, a return of the past vision. Further, while Blavatsky fans think that this second visit to Tibet occurred in empirical reality, we can inject some of our discredited commonsense doubts now. I assume that Master KH, originally from the Punjab, was a strange person to have taught English to Blavatsky. Blavatsky herself realizes some incongruity here, and that is why I think KH does not tutor her directly, but rather asks her "to try to pick out of my head even the little I know of it [English]." Blavatsky actually learned English in her Russian home through a Yorkshire governess; she then traveled through different parts of the world including England, the USA, India, and Egypt, where presumably she communicated with others in English. And then, before her marriage to Betanelly, she lived and interacted with Americans from July 7, 1873, till May or June 1875, the latter being the date of her trance illness. In other words, she would have had plenty of time to learn proper English before her first visit to India and certainly prior to her trance illness of 1875. Senzar, yes; but English surely is fantasy projection of her previous knowledge of English now attributed to Master KH in a truly "retrospective vision."

Now consider the second dream sequence, described in the letter of 1886, in which another "actual" event is once again repeated in the present "retrospective vision." Blavatsky dreams of her writing parts of *Isis* dictated by KH many years ago, and she sees herself "night after night in bed writing *Isis* in my dreams . . . writing it in my sleep." And she felt KH impressing sentences into her memory, presumably by pressing her forehead, as he had done during her visionary sojourn in Tibet. Blavatsky's "retrospective vision" of writing *Isis* therefore repeats an earlier event, which even she admits occurred on the level of a visionary or dream reality, providing added justification for our assumption that learning English from KH and her whole visit to Tibet were also visionary episodes, just like the writing of *Isis Unveiled*. That mode of writing should be familiar to us now as a way of formulating visionary knowledge unmediated by the cogito. But what is extraordinary is that in the dream that we have just considered she recollects writing all *Isis* during a dream episode that lasted, at the very most, a few hours, if not minutes, a fantastic task considering the text of *Isis*, in its present edition, is in two volumes adding up to 560 pages!

Olcott was with Blavatsky most of the time during their New York sojourn and helped her edit *Isis* in its final form. He says: "Her pen would be flying over the page, when she would suddenly stop, look out into space with the vacant eye of the clairvoyant seer, shorten her vision as though to look at something held invisible in the air before her, and begin copying on her paper what she saw" (ODL, 1:208–9). After she wrote down the reference, she would revert to her normal looks and posture until the master interrupted her with another reference. In another letter to her relatives she said:

> When I wrote "Isis" I wrote it so easily. . . . Whenever I am *told* to write I sit down and obey and then I can write easily upon almost anything: metaphysics, psychology, philosophy, ancient religions, zoology, natural sciences. . . . Why? Because *He who knows all* simply dictates to me. . . . My MASTER, and others whom I knew years ago in my travels . . . I address myself to *Them*, and one of Them *inspires* me,

i.e., he allows me to simply copy what I write from manuscripts, and even printed matter that pass before my eyes, in the air . . . and even He (the Master) is not always required; for, during His absence on some other occupation, He awakens in me His substitute in knowledge. . . . At such times it is no more *I* who writes, but my *inner ego*, my "luminous Self" who thinks and writes for me.[43]

The "inner ego" and "luminous self" of her dream-vision take us to the realm of the dream-ego or fantasy-I, as I have redefined it in this essay. They lead us to the being within her, one of her masters who can be both outside her in apparitional form and within her in spiritual form as a "volatile essence," infusing her through her very pores owing to his "transparent" and "ethereal" qualities.

The masters, however, are not infallible. Some admit mistakes they have made, partly, I suspect, because several of these masters or adepts are not only Hindu but also Chaldean and Egyptian, with the exception of buccaneer John King and the great Cambridge Platonist, Henry More (1614–1687), who at least must have been fluent in English! And mistakes can occur when Blavatsky puts down the thoughts that flow into her. During the period when *Isis* was being received by Blavatsky in New York, it was Olcott who took over the task of organizing her visionary imaginings into rational form.[44] Much later, when she had left India for good in 1885, Countess Constance Wachtmeister, who lived with her for a long time during her European sojourn, mentioned that Blavatsky asked her to check some bibliographical references from a friend in the Bodleian Library in Oxford. "It happened that I did know someone I could ask, so my friend verified a passage that HPB had seen in the Astral Light, with the title of the book, the chapter, page and figures all correctly noted."[45] Similarly, Hiram Corson, professor of rhetoric at Cornell, who knew Blavatsky and with whom she stayed for sometime noted, somewhat slyly: "She herself told me that she wrote them down as they appeared in her eyes on another plane of objective existence, that she clearly saw the page of the book, and the quotation she needed, and simply translated what she saw into English. . . . The hundreds of books she quoted were certainly not in my library, many of them not in America, some of them very rare and difficult to get in Europe, and if her quotations were from memory, then it was an even more startling feat than writing them from the ether."[46] This other realm of "objective existence" is the astral plane. In occult theory, according to Evelyn Underhill, one enters a new level of consciousness "where images of all beings and events are preserved, as they are preserved in the memory of man" and these can be revisualized through the gift of the "Astral Light."[47]

For myself who is not a believer in such a plane of existence, I am convinced that these quotations were in fact from a special gift of memory. The pages and references that floated in astral fashion before her in visionary form replicated those she had read in the past. She tells us that her maternal great grandfather "had a strange library containing hundreds of books on alchemy, magic and other occult sciences" and she had read them "with the keenest interest before the age of 15." Consequently, she could triumphantly proclaim that "neither Paracelsus, [Heinrich] Kunrath, nor C. [Cornelius] Agrippa would have anything to teach me [now]."[48] When she was sixteen, she came under the influence of a family friend, Prince Alexander S. Golitsyn, a famous freemason who had traveled in such places as Greece, Egypt, Iran, and India, spurring Blavatsky's own urge to wander into exotic lands (C, 35). It is hard to believe that she did not continue her reading in the course of her extensive travels where she met both scholars and religious virtuosos. Her library in New York, however, had only a modest collection of about a hundred books, but friends brought many volumes on occult and hermetic sciences for her to read.[49] If indeed her ability to conjure up her past readings in "astral" fashion is correct, then surely it is a "startling feat" and shows how little we know about what Nietzsche called mnemotechnique or the "technique for remembering things" that human beings possess.[50] Perhaps the visionary master placing his hand on her forehead in the region of memory might have assisted in her own memory recall. Pressing the forehead to elicit visions or memories is mentioned many times in our sample of visionaries and reminds us of the more authoritarian technique used by Freud to elicit visions from his hysterical patients. Remember that, when he was at the Palmer residence Blake *sensed* the return of young Samuel Palmer, but *visualized* him walking down the road and entering the gate only after he placed his hand on his forehead.

Toward the very end of her life she theorized the manner in which thoughts— not just images of pages—floated into her awareness field via the astral light: "Well, you see, what I do is this. I make what I can only describe as a kind of vacuum on the air before me, and fix my sight and my will upon it, and soon scene after scene passes before me like a successive pictures of a diorama, or, if I need a reference or information from some book, I fix my mind intently and the astral counterpart of the book appears, and from it I take what I need. The more perfectly my mind is freed from distractions and mortifications, the more energy and intentness it possesses, the more easily I can do this."[51] Again, in more practical terms, "Space and distance do not exist for thought, and if two persons are in perfect mutual psychomagnetic rapport, and of these two, one is a great Adept in Occult Sciences, then thought transference and dictation of whole pages become as easy and as comprehensible at the distance of ten thousand miles as the transference of two words across a room."[52] It seems as if Blavatsky has multiple ways of tapping into the astral, with or without the aid of the masters. "Pictures of a diorama" is a neat metaphor for "showings" that simply appear before the visionary, unmediated by the thinking-I.

THE PRODUCTION OF
PSYCHIC PHENOMENA

Visions are not everyone's forte, although several key figures of the Theosophical movement experienced them. Other Theosophists could communicate with the masters by formally corresponding with them in English, with Blavatsky acting as a medium of communication, generally in a cabinet in her house in Adyar nicknamed her "shrine." She herself says that "the shrine was thought of to facilitate the transmission, as now dozens and hundreds come to pray and put their letters inside."[53] And, sure enough, the masters' responses would appear in the shrine. She was initially reluctant to act as communicant to the masters on behalf of others but ultimately agreed to help some of her closest associates, especially Sinnett. KH's letters to Sinnett and other members of the Theosophical Society have been published. They are written in excellent English, sometimes with a masterly eye for commonplace expressions, as, for example, when Master M tells Sinnett, in a letter written in February 1882, "Put that conviction into your consciousness and let us talk like sensible men. Why should we play with Jack-in-the-box; are not *our* beards grown."[54] Sinnett himself derived much of his knowledge from these letters, on whose basis he wrote the popular *Esoteric Buddhism.*[55] It has been said by her enemies, and occasionally by a skeptical Theosophist like A. O. Hume, that these letters were forgeries by Blavatsky. But we know that because the masters are emanations from Blavatsky's dream-ego, and that she was infused with their spirit as Blake was in similar fashion, it is simply possible that it is the masters who are writing through her.[56] Blavatsky might have been mistaken in thinking that the masters (if they exist) can communicate through her through the astral plane, or through some other mode, but this does not make her a deliberate fraud or deceiver. She joins the ranks of shamans, spirit mediums, and other kinds of religious virtuosos who cram the ethnographic record and with whom Blavatsky felt a spiritual kinship. Moreover, Blavatsky can be credited with creating a model of communication with spiritual beings incorporated almost everywhere in new age religion as "channeling," not in séances as with spiritualism, but the communication of knowledge and sometimes whole texts through spiritual contact with such beings.

Let me mention two techniques among many others she employed for both letter and thought transference. As with communication through psychomagnetic rapport, these techniques need not tap into the astral realm, but only require the cooperation of the masters. "Take for instance this illustration as an instance: transmission by *mechanical* thought transference (in contradistinction with the conscious.) The former is produced by calling first the attention of a *chela* [disciple] or the Mahatma. The letter must be open and every line of it passed over the forehead, holding the breath and never taking off the part of the letter until bell notifies it is read and noted," bell ringing being a phenomenon in which Blavatsky was accomplished.[57] Now to the conscious mode of transmission: "The other mode is to impress every sentence of the letter (consciously of course) on the brain, and then send it phrase by phrase to the other person on the other end of the line," something that could also be performed by especially gifted persons without the mediation of masters.[58] In both instances, the letter must be burned before it reaches the receiver in what Blavatsky calls a "virgin fire" (where no matches or other conventional means of lighting are employed but is instead "rubbed with a resinous transparent little stone").[59] When this is successfully done, the letter is communicated to the receiver. These are not the only ways of communicating with the masters, but perhaps the way that many messages and letters were sent and received. I take it that the virgin fire and the transparent stone are symbolic representations of the Red Virgin and the philosopher's stone that she was seeking in her youth and now is blessed with.

Although Blavatsky says that any disciple could in theory practice these techniques, the reality is that it is she who does so in her shrine, located adjacent to her bedroom, a place conducive to "somnolence." One must assume that these techniques were taught by the masters, because they are strikingly similar to those employed by KH to teach English and Senzar and other occult knowledge during her trance visit to his residence in Tibet. In communicating with the masters, it is she who would then place the letter on her forehead and transmit it to the masters. My guess is that the placing of the letter on the forehead would produce a trancelike reaction in Blavatsky, and she would then unconsciously write down the Mahatmaic message to be delivered to the recipient. If so, there is nothing unusual in this because, as we have already noted, the method was similar to the manner in which her major books were composed. When she was accused by Hume and others of "forging" the Mahatma letters, she humorously defended herself by saying that she learned her English from a mahatma and "no wonder then that *my* English and the Mahatma's show similarity!"[60]

The production of letters was confined to the inner circle of the Theosophical Society, but other kinds of phenomena were popularly known and admired by the educated Indian middle classes, as they were earlier by her Russian relatives and friends. Olcott mentions, in his *Old Diary Leaves,* some of Blavatsky's occult powers and her capacity to produce "phenomena." She could sound the angel bells and raps that spiritualists also claimed, which Blavatsky performed long before she had her second trance illness. More impressively, she could produce telepathic faxes or what Sinnett calls "psychological telegraph." She could materialize objects and exhibit numerous other accomplishments, some of which I shall now list from Olcott's *Old Diary Leaves.*[61] As someone initiated into the mysteries, she could be a bearer of the masters' magnetism, but without them she could do little in the way of producing phenomena.

1. In New York, on one occasion while having tea, Blavatsky asked Olcott for the sugar tongs, and when he told her that he had packed them away, she reached her hand and picked up from near her chair a pair of nondescript tongs, though it had legs much longer than usual, "and the two claws slit like the prongs of a pickle-fork" (ODL, 1:345) Engraved therein was the cryptograph of Blavatsky's "boss," Master M (ODL, 1:346). This occult phenomenon is now given a scientific explanation ("an important law") by Olcott: "To create anything objective out of the diffused matter of space, the first step is to *think* of the desired object—its form, pattern, color, material, weight, and other characteristics: the picture of it must be sharp and distinct as to every detail; the next step is to put the trained Will in action, employ one's knowledge of the laws of matter and the process of its conglomeration, and compel the elemental spirits to form and fashion what one wishes to make. If the operator fails in either of these details, his results will be imperfect" (ODL, 1:346).[62] According to Olcott's law, Blavatsky had confused in her own mind two different types of tongs and a pickle fork and, consequently, the materialized object had no resemblance to an ordinary pair of sugar tongs.

2. On another occasion, Blavatsky took Olcott's ring, put it in the palm of her hand, and then, opening her hand, she showed him his own ring plus another that she had phenomenally produced, but quite different from Olcott's (ODL, 1:347).

3. During a discussion in India in December 1879, a noted German scholar, Dr. Thibaut, wanted to know why there aren't any longer *siddhas* ("perfected beings") who could do wonderful things like producing phenomena. Blavatsky got up and "setting her lips together and muttering something, she swept her right hand through the air with an imperious gesture, and bang! on the heads of the company fell about a dozen roses." Again, that very evening, while a discussion on Saṃkya philosophy and Max Muller's work was under-

way, she made a similar gesture and "down fell another shower of flowers; one rose actually hitting the Doctor on the top of his head and bouncing into his lap as he sat bolt upright" (ODL, 2:132). This is not simply a display of occult powers or magical prowess; Blavatsky is satirically commenting on what for her were useless abstractions by learned men, and she directs at Thibaut her own pointed dart!

When she was in such states, her face had that "strange look of power which almost always preceded a phenomenon." Once, when she commanded the flame of a lamp to go up and down, she said that "a Mahatma was there, invisible to all but herself, and he had just turned the lamp up and down while she spoke the words" (ODL, 2:134). William Q. Judge, the vice president of the society, who later broke away from the movement to form an independent American Theosophical Society, wrote in a letter to the Indian Theosophist Damodar Mavalankar on March 1, 1880:

I have seen her cause objects in the room to move without aid from anyone. Once a silver spoon came from the furthest room through two walls and three rooms into her hands before our eyes, at her simple silent will. Another time, she—or—he [the master] produced out of the wall a dozen bottles of paint that I had desired to use in making a picture in her room. At another time a letter was taken by her unopened, sealed, and in a moment the letter lay in her hand, while the envelope was unbroken; again the same letter was taken in the fingers and instantly its duplicate was lifted off it, thus leaving in her hands two letters, facsimiles of each other. Still further, her three-stoned sapphire ring was taken off, given to a lady who wanted it to wear for a while, taken away by her, and yet on her departure the real ring remained on HPB's finger, only an illusion was taken by the lady. And so on for hundreds of instances."[63]

Indian newspapers publicized Blavatsky's powers at great length, giving her national fame in India.

THE COLD SNOWS OF A DREAM: THE DEATH OF DAMODAR MAVALANKAR

Hermits upon Mount Meru or Everest,
Caverned in night under the drifted snow,

Or where that snow and winter's dreadful blast
Beat down upon their naked bodies, know
That day brings round the night, that before dawn
His glory and his monuments are gone.
—W. B. Yeats, "Meru"

I noted that, in addition to Blavatsky and Olcott, other members of the Theosophical Society had visions directly or indirectly linked to the masters. Thus Damodar, the early Indian convert, during the period he was being instructed by Blavatsky on the secrets of the occult, made in his sleep "a dash for the home of the Master among the Himalayas, but found, on arriving, that he [Master KH] too was away in the astral body. . . . The next minute Damodar found himself at Adyar, in the presence of both his Master and H.P.B" (ODL, 3:32).

But who was Damodar Mavalankar? He was born in September 1857 in Ahmedabad and belonged to a wealthy Maharashtra Brahmin family, but he gave up his wealth, caste status, and his child bride, renouncing his family's version of Hinduism, for Blavatsky's esoteric Buddhism. He joined the Theosophical Society after reading *Isis Unveiled,* which he felt was "a Key to the Mysteries of the Ancient and Modern Religion and Science."[64] His father gave him permission to join the society and adopt the renouncer or *sanyāsin* style of life. He assigned his ancestral estate to his father and saw to it that his wife Lakshmibai was provided for. Theosophists referred to Damodar as being frail and like a girl and often sick, which he was. Like others in our study, he also suffered from a trance illness, although the details are skimpy. "In his childhood Damodar had a very critical illness, and the doctors despaired of his life. While the family was expecting him to die at any moment, the lad had a vision which made a deep impression upon him. He saw as if in a dream a glorious personage who gave him a peculiar medicine and curiously, from that time, the boy began to recover."[65] A few years later, while engaged in meditation, he saw the same personage again and "recognized him as his savior."[66]

After renouncing his own family, he seemed to treat Blavatsky as his foster mother such that "her slightest word was to him law; her most fanciful wish an imperative command, to obey which he was ready to sacrifice life itself" (ODL, 2:212). That "sacrifice" did take place, as we shall soon see. According to Olcott, Damodar also could obtain telepathic faxes from his master and wander through space via his astral body. On one occasion, Olcott noted that when they were in Lahore in November 1883 Damodar met a master in his physical body, perhaps, in this case, as a "bodily vision" (ODL, 3:43). Again, while Damodar and Olcott were in Jamnu in Kashmir as the guests of the maharaja, Damodar left the palace on his own and could not be contacted for a few days. Blavatsky, however, calmed Olcott's anxiety by informing him that he had gone into a retreat with his master. He did return in three days (ODL, 3:54–55). Damodar mentions his receiving a letter, via Blavatsky, from Master KH, who, like M, signed himself not with a name but with three dots in the points of a triangle.[67]

Given his background, it is therefore not surprising to find Damodar giving us a fantastic description of a mahatmaic mansion sometime in 1881. The time was around 2:00 AM. Damodar went to bed after having locked the door to his room, and, after two or three minutes, he heard Blavatsky's voice summoning him. When he went to her, Blavatsky told him that "some persons want to see you" and urged him to go out without looking at her. He complied and "before I had time to turn my face I saw her gradually disappear on the spot and from that very ground rose the form of [his Master]." He saw others, also in Tibetan clothes. His master's voice informed Damodar to stand still and look at him fixedly. Then, he said, "I felt a very pleasant sensation as if I was getting out of my body," and, sure enough, he was transported to a "peculiar place." "It was the upper end of Cashmere at the foot of the Himalayas. I saw I was taken to a place where there were only two houses just opposite to each other and no other sign of human habitation."[68] Soon Master KH appeared and asked Damodar to follow him:

After going a short distance of about half a mile we came to a natural subterranean passage which is under the Himalayas. The path is very dangerous. There is a natural causeway on the River Indus which flows underneath in all its fury. Only one person can walk on it at a time and one false step seals the fate of the traveler. Besides the causeway there are several valleys to be crossed. After walking a considerable distance through this subterranean passage we came into an open plain in L—k [Ladakh?]. There is a large massive building thousands of years old. In front of it is a huge Egyptian Tau. The building rests on 7 big pillars in the form of pyramids. The entrance gate has a large triangular arch. Inside it are various apartments. The building is so large that it can easily contain twenty thousand people. I was shown some of these compartments. This is the Chief Central Place where all those of our Section [their lodge] who are found deserving of Initiation into Mysteries have to go for their final Initiation and stay there the requisite period. . . . The grandeur and serenity of the place is enough to strike any one with awe. The beauty of the Altar which is in the center and at which every candidate has to take his vows at the time of his Initiation is sure to dazzle the most brilliant eyes. The splendor of the CHIEF'S throne is incomparable. Everything is on a geometrical principle and containing various symbols which are explained only to the Initiate. But I cannot say more now [owing to an oath of secrecy].[69]

After this double vision—that of Blavatsky and the underground initiatory mansion—was over, Damodar found himself in bed. There he found Blavatsky summoning him and then disappearing, to be replaced by KH and some Tibetans.

Damodar's second vision is provoked by the master staring at him fixedly (or he at the master), and he is transported in spirit into the Himalayan mansion: a vision within a vision. The mansion itself is a variation of the "maṇḍala mansion" that Tibetan meditators envision. Initiation through visions is also to be expected in Tibetan Tantra. But what about the Egyptian pyramids and pillars? It seems that Damodar's vision does not come from his Hindu background, but is based on his prior knowledge of "esoteric Buddhism" and, of course, Blavatsky's ideas of Egyptian masters and their esoteric knowledge familiar to him from reading Isis and from conversations with Blavatsky herself, from discussions with other Theosophists, and from the masters, who would then refurbish that knowledge in their communications with Damodar. Damodar's vision is an idiosyncratic one; they are composite images based on bits and pieces of his personal knowledge and then beautifully and coherently woven. When Damodar found himself back in bed, he was naturally puzzled about the noetic significance of his vision and asked himself whether it was simply a dream or a hallucination. "If a reality, how could I traverse the whole of the Himalayas even in my astral body in so short a time?"[70] He is highlighting the difference between empirical time and space and the spatial and temporal vastness of his vision. "Perplexed with these ideas I was sitting silent when down fell a note on my nose. I opened it and found inside that it was not a dream but that I was taken in some mysterious way in my astral body to the real place of Initiation where I shall be in my body for the Ceremony if I show myself deserving of the blessing. My joy at that moment can be more easily conjectured than described."[71] It is clear that Damodar was not initiated in his vision, but he was promised a tantalizing picture of the initiatory site with its subterranean passages (the tunnels where, in mystery religions, the initiate must undergo a symbolic death and rebirth) and a foreknowledge of his own future and futuristic initiation in the glorious palace of his vision.

We therefore find Damodar determined to go seek the masters and their initiatory mansion in its physical actuality, in spite of his frailty and his worsening tuberculosis. With KH's and Blavatsky's blessing, he left Adyar on February 23, 1885. He halted in Varanasi for about two weeks and, wearing a cap given to him by KH (via Blavatsky perhaps), he wandered into the Himalayan snows with a group of coolies to carry his belongings and food. Olcott wrote: "The most disquieting rumors were circulated, soon after he left Darjeeling, about our dear boy's having perished in the attempt to cross the mountains. In the first week of July it was reported from Chumbai, Sikkim, that his corpse, frozen stark and stiff, has been found in the snows, and his clothing at a little distance." Such a reality was quite unacceptable to Olcott, who felt the "transparent improbability of his having thrown off his clothing in that climate merely to die." Such a rumor was simply spread by those who denied the existence of the initiatory mansion, the "White Lodge" (ODL, 3:271).

It is easy to trace Damodar's travels to the Tibetan border, because he left his small pocket diary with his coolies. We know that in Varanasi on March 9 he visited the ashram of Majji, a female ascetic whom Olcott, Subha Row (Rao), and Blavatsky had known earlier and with whom they had had many conversations. From there, he briefly described his journey to Calcutta, then to Darjeeling on March 30, and on to Sikkim, which he left on April 22. "Left Sikkim in the morning at about 10 o'clock. Reached Kabi (about half a mile from Longboo) at 3. P.M. Halted there for the day. The [master] said he had not yet fully known me, but that I am destined for some important work within the next month or two; that I must be a big Tibetan lama reincarnated in Tibet. The Karma is great." The following day the diary notes: "Took *bhāt* [rice] in the morning, and proceeded from Kabi alone, sending back my things with the coolies to Darjeeling" (ODL, 3:276). Kabi is in north Sikkim, and Damodar might have crossed over to Tibet. According to Olcott, who interviewed the head "coolie" or carrier, Damodar was to meet someone, probably a master, at a place two days walk from where they were now. He sent his clothes and other belongings to Darjeeling through his carriers and wandered into the mountains, followed, according to Olcott's imagination, by his Tibetan master. But what about his frozen, naked corpse found in the snows? What made him throw off the clothes he was wearing? There is some plausibility in the head carrier's statement that Damodar shed his clothes and went by himself alone to meet his Master, the Maker of his dream. The pragmatic Olcott simply thought that the death of Damodar might have been an illusion. "A Māyā of his body *may* have been left there to make it appear as if the pilgrim had succumbed; but that he reached his destination safely, and has ever since been under the protection of his Guru, I have reason to believe" (ODL, 3:278).

We know that Damodar shed his clothes which were found some distance from his body. Olcott thinks he would have changed into a flimsy ascetic garb, but does not mention how this piece of clothing would have prevented him from freezing to death. Hence my guess: Damodar shed his clothes because he was instructed to do so by his master, now a reified form or emanation of his dream-ego. But why? Like many other novices, he had to shed his worldly clothes before being initiated. It is possible that he wanted to be entirely naked prior to being reborn in a new status as an adept or he might in fact have worn an appropriate but flimsy ascetic garb after discarding his workaday clothes, as Olcott suggests he did. One must remember that Damodar, unlike some Himalayan ascetics, had no *yogic* training to withstand the rigors of the cold while being naked in the drifted snow and winter's dreadful blast beating on his bare body. A contemporary biological hypothesis might suggest that Damodar suffered from hypothermia, which leaves one disoriented and, like mirages to parched travelers lost in the desert, creates an illusion of bodily warmth that might then have tempted him to throw off his clothes. If so, whether naked or partially clad, he must surely have suffered from hypothermia, and his end must have come fairly fast. And, given his certainty of the truth of his dream and his visionary aspiration to realize his initiatory destiny, would he not have interpreted his bodily warmth as a gift of the master, and would he not have seen before him the beckoning mirage of the master, his dream other, or the beckoning mansion of his dream time?

Whatever faults Blavatsky might have had, cruelty was not one of them. Hence the question: why did she encourage the frail and faithful Damodar, coughing blood from his diseased lungs, to go into the freezing cold in search of the White Lodge of the masters? Olcott was away in Myanmar and could not give him any advice, but surely not Blavatsky, even though she herself was seriously ill and would leave India for good a few weeks after Damodar's departure. It seems certain that Blavatsky, contrary to many of her detractors and even some of the faithful, never wavered in her belief in the masters. She was convinced that Damodar's present earthly existence was his last and that he "was ready from his last birth to enter the highest PATH and [Damodar also] suspected it. He had long been waiting for the expected permission to go to Tibet before the expiration of the 7 years," when he would then become an adept himself.[72] One has to lead a pure and moral life during this period, but asceticism and bodily mortification were shunned.[73] "Happy Damodar! He went to the land of Bliss, to Tibet and must now be far away in the regions of our Masters," she prophesied.[74] So did Olcott. But in 1885 Olcott had perhaps begun to lose his awe of the masters, consequent to Hodgson's report to the Society for Psychical Research and the increasing conflicts among Theosophists, especially A. O. Hume's rejection of Blavatsky's masters and Blavatsky's own hostility to Hume. Nevertheless, the official position of the society was stated by Olcott and Subha Row in a notice sent to the *Theosophist* on July of the following year, stating "that we have positive news as late as the 7th of June that he has safely reached his destination, is alive, and under the guardianship of the friends whom he sought." Such "positive news" came from Blavatsky who saw him through her astral vision during January 4–6, 1886, when she was in Europe. His presence was further verified through Blavatsky's communications with the masters, although none of this correspondence has been preserved.[75]

Damodar was, on the one hand, a disciple of Blavatsky; on the other, he was nurtured in the Hindu thought of his parents and was living in a society where visions were perfectly expectable. Unhappily, he was a product of contradictory worlds. He was educated in Western thought and also raised in a conservative Brahmin family and at the same time, he was an admirer of the new Protestant Hinduism of Dayananda Sarasvati, who attempted to redefine the Vedas in modernist terms. Prior to all that, in late childhood, we noted that he was afflicted with a trance illness and began to see a guru whom he later retrospectively identified as a mahatma after reading *Isis* and joining the Theosophical Society. He was perhaps the only major figure in the Theosophical movement to practice the meditation he had known from his traditional religious training. His visions of masters and their fabulous abodes might have come from his meditative visions, but the masters were not the Hindu deities of his upbringing. We have already mentioned that Indian and Tibetan meditative disciplines need to have a guide or guru or a "true friend"—the representative of the rational consciousness—to direct the meditator away from visionary danger zones. But there was no such figure to guide Damodar. Blavatsky was a guru for sure, and a mother figure, but she was no guide who could safely direct the disciple through mind-created mazes. Damodar thought that the masters were his gurus; but these imaginary beings turned out to be just that, imaginary beings who led him to die in the Himalayan snows. All that knowledge gave Mavalankar was the illusion of power and the reality of powerlessness, the sweet and the bitter that some of us also have tasted in our own lives. Most of us have at some time or other awakened from the cold snows of our dreams, as Yeats did, but we do not treat the dream as a truth that can be implemented in the real world in which we live.[76] And even visionaries, we noted, for the most part, do not conflate the vision with the empirically real world of scarcity and want. Damodar's dream of a seductive future of becoming a knowledge-soaked adept led him to the Himalayan snows that cruelly shut him out of the gates of the initiatory mansion.

COLONEL OLCOTT AND THE RETURN TO EURO-RATIONALITY

Colonel Olcott was the president of the Theosophical Society and its organizational genius, whereas Blavatsky was its spiritual head and the inventor of its doctrines. She was scarcely interested in the day-to-day running of the society and its varied outreach activities in both Asia and Europe. Olcott's education and training was in science and agricultural technology. He had published several books and articles on agriculture, notably on sugar cane and celery, and was concerned like many American innovators with the practical application of science. He volunteered to serve during the Civil War and was given the job of investigating fraud in the army, a task he set out to do assiduously as was the case with every other task he undertook. Later on he was a member of a commission set up to inquire into Lincoln's assassination. After the war he took his law exams and as a professional lawyer he also wrote on insurance law and taxation. Olcott was forty-two in 1874 and a practicing lawyer when he decided to carry out what he thought were rigorous experiments to prove or disprove spiritualistic cases of communication with the dead; the evocation of flesh-and-blood apparitions from the past; and raps and other phenomena produced by William Eddy and his family in their farm in Chittenden, Vermont.

It is here that he met Blavatsky, but while the latter took for granted that there were occult mysteries governing the universe, she did not subscribe to the spiritualist view that the dead could be summoned through séances and made to appear in their material forms. Rather, she believed that the astral powers of the participants produced these forms and were expressions of occult powers that lay dormant within all of us.[77] Olcott initially believed in the reality of spiritualist phenomena and wrote twenty articles to the *New York Daily Graphic* between September and December 1874, then publishing them in book form the following year as *People from the Other World*.[78] The book was dedicated to Sir William Crookes, a well-known chemist and physicist, and Alfred Wallace, the independent codiscoverer of evolutionary theory, both believers in the reality of spiritualist phenomena. Soon enough, Olcott came to agree with Blavatsky and recanted his earlier views in a letter to the *New York Tribune* suggesting that the phenomena produced by séances were the work of "elementary spirits" or "embryonic or rudimentary men" who were nothing but products of natural occult laws misunderstood by spiritualists with their "poverty stricken mediums" catering to the "gaping crowd."[79]

Olcott's early role was to justify Blavatsky on the basis of empirical and rationalizing science. For him, *Isis* is a master work of science, and, with characteristic generosity, he proclaimed: "If any book could ever have been said to make an epoch, this one could. Its effects have been as important in one way as Darwin's first great work have been in another; both were tidal waves in modern thought, and each tended to sweep away theological crudities and replace the belief in miracle with the belief in natural law" (ODL, 1:202).[80] This last phrase represents the rational goal of Theosophy for Olcott, and I am suggesting that confronting

Theravāda Buddhism and Sri Lanka helped him to further that goal. Buddhism was for him the quintessential rational religion, and his Sri Lankan experience made him realize this. Parallel with his preoccupation with Buddhism, and not unrelated to it, was his increasing conflict with Blavatsky and her version of Buddhism, which was intrinsically connected with occult science. While Olcott knew something of Blavatsky's Buddhism, he admits that, prior to their visit to Sri Lanka and India, none of the mahatmas instructed Olcott on the key doctrine of karma. Though Blavatsky was, no doubt, familiar with it, Olcott says there is very little of it in *Isis Unveiled* and that Blavatsky believed reincarnation was a rare phenomenon. "She was not taught the doctrine of Re-incarnation [by the mahatmas] until 1879—when we were in India" (ODL, 1:280). It is true that the masters discoursed with Blavatsky at length on karma when they were in India, but Blavatsky was familiar with the karma theory from her early reading in her Russian homeland and firmly believed in it. But Olcott's own mind is clear: "In its plain exoteric, or orthodox form, I had got it in Ceylon and embodied it in *The Buddhist Catechism*, of which the first edition, after passing the ordeal of critical examination by the High Priest Sumangala Thero, appeared in July, 1881" (ODL, 1:284). Note the words *exoteric* and *orthodox*, both implicitly contrasted with the *esoteric* Buddhism that Blavatsky and Sinnett were engaged in at the time. Once the approval of the masters was given, Olcott rather grandiosely proclaimed that "the fundamental and necessary idea of Re-incarnation was launched on the sea of modern Western thought from the congenial land of its primeval birth [in 1881]" (ODL, 1:288).

I shall discuss in some detail Olcott's relation with Buddhism later on; suffice it here to state that as Olcott got more and more involved in Buddhism his relationship with Blavatsky became increasingly strained. This appears very clearly in volume 2 of *Old Diary Leaves*. Soon after the first visit to Sri Lanka (with Blavatsky), while they were in Simla, he spoke critically about her occult powers: "HPB kept on with her phenomena, some of them very trifling and undignified, I thought, but still such as to make half of Simla believe that she was 'helped by the Devil'" (ODL, 2:242). That the Sri Lankan experience had to do with his critical attitude is implied in Olcott's statements, later found in ODL. He wanted to go to Sri Lanka for the second visit and start a national educational fund to promote education for Buddhist boys and girls. The scheme had the approval of the mahatmas, and, when Olcott was ready to leave, "HPB fell out with me because I would not cancel the engagement and stop and help her on the *Theosophist*. Of course, I flatly refused to do anything of the kind, and as the natural consequence she fell into a white rage with me. She shut herself up in her room a whole week, refusing to see me, but sending me formal notes of one sort or another, among them one in which she notified me that the Lodge would have nothing to do with the Society or myself" (ODL, 2:293–94).

The Lodge was a Masonic idea adopted by Blavatsky and in this case perhaps referred to the Great White Lodge that was the abode of the masters. The threat was a powerful one and implied that Olcott might be ostracized by the masters. But he was undeterred: "I should carry it [the Sri Lankan work] through, even though I never saw the face of a Master again; that I did not believe them to be such vacillating and whimsical creatures; if they were *I preferred to work without them*" (ODL, 2:294, my emphasis). What seemed to be happening was that Blavatsky sensed Olcott's turn toward Theravāda Buddhism, away from the occult theosophy that she favored, and Olcott, for his part, made a strong statement about the masters. A serious breach seemed to have occurred, but Blavatsky, in characteristic fashion, ultimately turned around; and the mahatmas took a hand in the reconciliation.

Apparently, the masters appeared before Blavatsky and "exposed to her the whole situation" (ODL, 2:294). As Olcott rightly recognized, once Blavatsky's temper burned itself out, she felt guilty of her action with respect to her friend and, more pragmatically, worried that a break in their relationship might damage their life's work. These inner, and perhaps unconsciously recognized, doubts and fears are objectified in the appearance of the masters and their healing of the conflict. The effect of all this was nevertheless momentous: the two agreed "to reconstruct the Society on a different basis, putting the Brotherhood idea forward more prominently, and keeping the occultism more in the background, in short, to have a secret section for it" (ODL, 2:294). For Blavatsky's part, it is doubtful that she could move backstage in this fashion. Hence, when she left for Europe for good, she founded the EST (*The Esoteric Section* of the Theosophical Society) in October 1888, with Olcott's sanction, and in addition brought out a new journal, *Lucifer*, for the propagation of her philosophical and occult ideas. And, most importantly, she found a new and powerful disciple, Annie Besant, who would carry on after her death the Blavatsky heritage.

To pick up the thread of the narrative: Olcott left for Sri Lanka on April 23, 1881, but without Blavatsky. When he came back on December 19, a "rude shock" awaited him. "*HPB conveyed to me a most kind message from the Masters about my success in Ceylon, seeming to have completely forgotten the angry threats and even the written declaration that the Society would be abandoned by them if I went there, and that with them [mahatmas] nor with her could I have any further relations.*" Olcott was so profoundly shaken by this about-turn that the whole passage just quoted appears in italics in his text. He then switches back to ordinary type as he concludes: "Thereafter, I did not love her or prize her less as a friend and a teacher, but the idea of her infallibility, if I had ever entertained it even approximately, was gone for ever" (ODL, 2:326). In spite of this breach, Olcott stood by Blavatsky during two major crises: the denunciation of Blavatsky during the "Coloumb affair" and then by the Society for Psychical Research. Blavatsky understandably did not forgive Olcott, who she believed thrust her occultism on the investigators of the society. She thought he "behaved like an ass" and referred to him sarcastically in several letters.[81]

To sum up the subsequent developments: Blavatsky fell badly ill, left India for good in March 1885, and ultimately settled down in England. There she took charge of the Esoteric Section, while Olcott effectively controlled the Theosophical Society. The society, under Olcott's leadership, seemed to move in a Buddhist and less occult direction. It is likely that this too was one of the reasons for Blavatsky's discontent and her choosing Besant to carry out her mission. Besant hadn't the range of occult powers that Blavatsky possessed, but she was a firm believer in them and had considerable organizational skills. In addition to her open political message for the liberation of India within the fold of empire, she was also an uncritical believer in Hinduism. She idealized the Brahmins and even justified the division of Hindu society into the four hierarchical classes or *varnas*, all of which would have been unthinkable for Blavatsky.[82] Meanwhile, the relationship between Blavatsky and Olcott continued to be unpleasant, though often plastered over with politeness. In 1887 Olcott admitted that his letters to Blavatsky were "very harsh"; and equally harsh were her responses (ODL, 4:25). He also mentions a "violent letter" written by her describing him as a "vacillator" (ODL, 4, 78).

EPISTEMIC BREAKS: BLAVATSKY AND THE HINDU CONSCIOUSNESS

I now want to make the following suggestion: charismatic leaders like Blavatsky produce what might be called epistemic breaks through preexisting traditions of thought and consciousness, into which may be poured new sets of ideas or epistemes. The notion of epistemic breaks comes from Michel Foucault, and it is similar to Kuhn's idea of a paradigm shift that heralds a revolution in the sciences. I doubt that paradigm shifts ever occur in the messy disciplines that form the human sciences. And they are equally rare in religious traditions. For the most part, one can only speak of epistemic breaks here and there that permit the introduction of new ideational sets or epistemes, the success of which depends on a host of historical and sociological and emotional reasons that cannot be easily separated.

Consider the two major figures of the Theosophical movement. Olcott, in spite of his belief in mahatmas and spirit healing, was a product of the Enlightenment, continuing the Enlightenment's self-imaginings of rationality, unable to see its contradictions owing to its "rationalistic myopia." Blavatsky's was a more eclectic "vision," compounded of both Eastern and Western mysticism and hermetic thought, a prophetess full of crazy and brilliant insights but by no means given to experimental validation or conceptual systematization, though she did believe that her powers were rooted in a deeper "science" that had yet to await its full realization. If Olcott introduced a Euro-rational view of Buddhism to Theravāda Buddhist societies, Blavatsky's influence was quite different, its effect more on the Hindu consciousness, creating a space for a certain class of modern gurus and saviors to emerge into middle class and international prominence.

Let me begin with Olcott.[83] The vision of Buddhism that Olcott initiated was one rooted in Western oriental research and philology, American Protestantism, and by the thought of the European Enlightenment of the nineteenth century. His thinking is characterized by a strong intellectualism with two features. First, an empirical component that put a high premium on scientific validation and falsification, however farfetched these may seem to us on hindsight. He believed quite reasonably, I think, that such things as thought transference and telepathic communication existed and could be verified or falsified by empirically grounded scientific experiments (ODL, 1:138). Commonsense and pragmatism were intrinsic to his character; he was very American in this sense. He was an admirer of Edison, also a member of the Theosophical Society (ODL, 1:466). Soon after his arrival in India, he worked with Blavatsky on "the ideal of an Antetypion, or machine to rescue from Space the pictures and voices of the Past," an attempt to expand upon, refine, and empirically validate the idea of an astral plane (ODL, 2: 89). I suspect in this endeavor he was influenced by Edison, who not only was a firm believer in such things as extrasensory perception but also "constructed an electrical apparatus in an unsuccessful attempt to facilitate ESP."[84] Second, Olcott was also a believer in an Enlightenment rationality that had little sympathy for what was labeled in the West as "supernatural." He converted the idea of the "supernatural" into the "natural," thereby making the former amenable to scientific rationalization and experimentation and in that sense he firmly supported the work of the Society for Psychical Research. He believed in another realm of reality, the astral realm and the masters, but he thought of them as empirically existent and verifiable phenomena. He had little sympathy, even in his earliest spiritualistic days, for what one might call the religion of the heart. He was the rare case that fully exemplified an intellectualized Enlightenment split between mind and body, head and heart, thought and emotion. Thus, for Olcott, the rational and philosophical component of Buddhism was primary and the emotional elements—faith and devotion—were not intrinsic to the religion. For him the Buddha was a figure who fitted the thought of the European Enlightenment. Following the practice of nineteenth-century Indologists, the Buddha's own "Enlightenment" was Euro-rationalized, so to speak.

The text that deals with this transformation of Buddhism into its Euro-rational form is his *Buddhist Catechism,* which eliminated all forms of devotional religiosity and treated Buddhism as a religion consonant with science and modernity. Olcott's Buddhism, which has now become normative for many native Buddhist intellectuals, produced a breach in the traditional structure of knowledge and emotion. It is easy to show that, contrary to Olcott's assertions, Theravāda Buddhist thinkers and exegetes like Buddhaghosa (not to mention virtually every Mahāyāna thinker) believed in both the abstract philosophical teachings as well as the devotional and so-called miraculous aspects of Buddhism. For them there could not exist a radical disjuncture or split in consciousness. For example, virtually every Buddhist thinker literally believed in hells and heavens and that the Buddha was born in a "miraculous" manner, unsullied by impurity; and that he had the thirty-two marks of the Great Man (*mahāpuruṣa*). These were ideas that Olcott would have scoffed. I might add that almost all the postcanonical Buddhist literature written in the Theravāda Buddhist societies of South and Southeast Asia were not of a philosophical nature at all.[85]

If the epistemic break Olcott introduced into Sri Lanka was a Euro-rational version of Buddhism, Blavatsky's influence was quite otherwise. Let me first show her in relation to the European Enlightenment tradition. Blavatsky filled the spiritual void of the nineteenth century when Euro-rationality as well as colonialism was in its heyday. The world was beginning to contract and was on the brink of global communication, such that a Theosophist like Sinnett introduced the idea of telegraphic communication as a metaphor for communication with masters. Buddhism and Vedantic Hinduism were also beginning to be known in Europe through the influence of Schopenhauer, and Theravāda Buddhist texts were being translated, even though Tibetan Buddhism was still little known. Blavatsky's project was to create a new religious consciousness and a wisdom reli-

gion that brought Tibetan and Indic thought into the popular Western imagination, harmonizing it with the other great religions like Christianity, Islam, and
indeed most ancient religions, such as the Egyptian and Chaldean.

With the opening up of the world through imperialism, colonialism, and
emergent global capitalism, the time was ripe for the appearance a new universal religion that transcended atheistic science, and it is Blavatsky's implicit argument with the latter that led her to deny that her new religion was a religion![86]
In her introduction to *The Secret Doctrine,* she states that her esoteric philosophy
"reconciles all religions, strips every one of them of its outward, human garments, and shows the root of each to be identical with that of every other great
religion," another version of the "perennial philosophy."[87] In her version, there
was once a universal truth—the root truth, one might say—that later was lost,
and only bits and pieces manifested themselves in contemporary and ancient religions. She believed that many of these lost texts were hidden by their devotees
in subterranean caves and tunnels and would one day be discovered, perhaps
centuries hence. "The Secret Doctrine was the universally diffused religion of
the ancient and prehistoric world. Proofs of its diffusion, authentic records of
its history, a complete chain of documents, showing its character and presence
in every land, together with the teaching of all its great adepts, exist to this day
in the secret crypts of libraries belonging to the Occult Fraternity."[88] All she does,
she claims, is to discover a few of these texts and the truths enshrined in them
through occult means—very much, I might add, in the spirit of Tibetan treasure
seekers and others who appear in these pages.

During her time there was little space for female spiritual beings, at least in
Protestant Europe and the U.S., quite unlike the very Tibetan Buddhism that
Blavatsky self-consciously espoused. And, although she was a bit of a prude and
there is no trace of sexuality in any of her writings, she did not encourage a sexual Puritanism the way Olcott did, with his rigid Protestant background. And,
perhaps following Neoplatonic and Beheminist models, she believed that androgyny existed in evolution before humans split into male and female. It is the
new age religions, the heirs of Blavatsky that gave central place to female deities
and to sexuality in the newly emergent affirmation of womanhood and motherhood in the mid-twentieth century. And while Blavatsky mentions the importance of female deities, including Sophia, in the history of occult thought, she did
not produce a critique of male-dominated Protestantism.

Let us now move from Blavatsky's universal religion to examine her specific
contributions to Indian thought. To consider this issue, let me return to Olcott
and Blavatsky as they visited India to form the headquarters of the Theosophical
Society. Both of them were anxious to meet mahatmas, and they tried their best

to meet and confer with spiritually advanced yogis. One of the first they actually met was the yogini Majji (whom we have already met with Damodar) in 1879 in an ashram on the Ganges, a mile or two from the city of Varanasi. They wanted to see her do "phenomena," but she refused to show such things.

> Being a true Vedāntin, she spoke very strongly as to the folly of people's hankering after such comparatively childish distractions instead of enjoying the calm delight of reposing the mind with the realization of the ideals which Shankarāchārya's incomparable philosophy depicts. Go where you will throughout India, it will ever be the same experience, the most honored ascetics are those who decline to exhibit such powers as they may possess save under very exceptional circumstances. The wonder-workers are regarded as of a much lower degree, principally as black magicians, and as such appeal to the lower classes for patronage and notoriety.
>
> (ODL, 2:121)

When Olcott met the famous Dayananda Sarasvati, of the Arya Samaj, who had already given a Protestant and rationalizing stance to Hinduism, he got the same message (ODL, 2:222). And of course he knew that Theravāda Buddhist doctrine especially disfavors the unnecessary display of occult or psychic powers (ODL, 1:307). By 1893, with Blavatsky out of the way, Olcott fully endorsed both the Theravāda Buddhist and the neo-Vedantic position of the Arya Samaj and then made a general condemnation of psychics and of wonder-workers in 1898, nine years before his death: "In my thirty years experience in India, I have never found one person who had the reputation of being a real wonder-worker of the better sort who would show me phenomena, while, on the other hand they have almost invariably spoken slightingly of them as objects to be searched after and have directed attention to the real object of Yoga, the development and evolution of the Higher Self" (ODL, 6:292–93).

I think Olcott was only partially right. It is true that in the late nineteenth century serious Vedantic yogis and gurus shunned the display of occult phenomena, which they viewed as the preserve of unsavory saviors. Blavatsky also believed that the highest goal was spiritual development, but she showed very little overt signs of yogic spirituality. Instead, she was known to the Indian public mostly for her occult displays. As far as I know she did not practice Buddhist meditation in any serious sense (and neither did Olcott).[89] Olcott said that Blavatsky's occultism commanded the "adoring wonder of her Western pupils," but it "actually lowered her in the opinion of the orthodox pundits and ascetics of India and Ceylon, as marking an inferior spiritual evolution" (ODL, 1:306). No wonder that she moved away from Olcott and got more involved with the lodge and the Esoteric Section of the Theosophical Society. In my view, Blavatsky herself was influenced by Buddhist and Vedantic criticisms of her occultism and, in her last years, moved closer to the spirit if not the letter of Vajrayāna, as much as Olcott increasingly moved toward the spirit of Euro-rational Buddhism. She once claimed that she was a convert from Christianity to Buddhism, but added that "I am not even a Buddhist but some kind of a strange mixture, something incomprehensible."[90]

The relation between Olcott and Blavatsky is what Gregory Bateson has called schismogenesis. When one person in a dialectical relation to another affirms a particular value stance, the other person responds with an opposing stance, and this process develops into an incremental differentiation between the two that ultimately results in a schismatic opposition.[91] Thus, the more Olcott moved toward Theravāda, the more strongly Blavatsky moved toward her own conception of Vajrayāna. She, no doubt, studied whatever translations of Tibetan texts were then coming into prominence in the West and she had Theosophical disciples and followers who began to translate key texts, beginning with Evans Wentz's imperfect translation of Tibetan Buddhist texts, including the popular Tibetan Book of the Dead.[92]

But what about the production of phenomena a hundred years after Blavatsky? I know of gurus in New York City and elsewhere whose initial mode of confronting potential and actual disciples is through the display of "phenomena." As Sai Baba nicely put it, "miracles are my visiting cards."[93] The public display of psychic power is now sine qua non for advanced guruism, and it is Blavatsky, I think, who legitimated this space for Sai Baba and many other contemporary gurus who now are so much adored in the middle-class spirituality of South Asians.[94] When Blavatsky and Olcott arrived in India, their audience and readership consisted exclusively of the educated middle class. Later Theosophists, including Annie Besant, appealed to the same social stratum. Here also Blavatsky's contribution is hard to miss: it is she, more than anyone else, who through her writing and example gave currency to the common belief (now a cliché) on "Indian spirituality," as against the supposed materialism of the West, based on a larger distinction she made between material and spiritual civilizations. Finally, it is clear from the insightful work of Sumathi Ramaswamy that it was Blavatsky who gave wide publicity to the idea of Lemuria, initially formulated by the paleontologist Philip Sclater. Sclater wrote an influential work in 1858 arguing that, on the basis of the distribution of lemurs in Asia, Madagascar, and Africa, there must have existed a huge land mass that linked continents. He called this fantasized land mass Lemuria, perhaps based on imaginary dream creatures known as lemuri.[95] Ramaswamy documents the use of Lemuria in Tamil nationalism, with even serious scholars affirming, after Blavatsky, that Lemuria was the source of human civilization and that Tamil culture had its locus there.[96] The Lemurian age for new age religion was, along with the theosophical recasting of Atlantis, a period when "human beings had reached an exquisite level of spirituality."[97] Finally, one can argue that Blavatsky's preoccupation with symbolic formations and a pool of occult philosophies common to all ancient religions looks forward to Jung, who recast hermetical and alchemical thought in terms of a science of psychology that rejected the primacy of consciousness, even though he affirmed an idea of the self that, we shall soon see, had little to do with the ego of Enlightenment thought.

MODERNITY AND THE DREAMING

HINGE DISCOURSE: DREAM KNOWLEDGE IN A SCIENTIFIC WELTANSCHAUUNG

These problem solving dreams are not like my others. They have a lot of clarity—there's not the bizarreness of other dreams. These dreams have a narrator who's sketching the problem verbally. Then the voice is giving the solution. I'm also seeing the solution. . . . I keep a pencil and paper next to the bed to write down these dreams. That's the one way in which they are like other dreams—they're beads of moisture on a very hot stove. They'll evaporate in a second if I don't get them down. I take my notes into work and tell my team, "I've dreamed up a solution—literally. They've gotten quite used to doing things based on my dreams.

—Paul Horowitz, Harvard physicist[1]

I N THE PRECEDING discussions we have dealt with those visionaries who pitted themselves against Enlightenment rationality, or Reason, as many of them labeled it. Although the eighteenth century was the "age of reason," there were some like Blake who out-and-out opposed it, as did the antinomian sects that preceded him. The term *Enlightenment* was a late arrival in Europe and did not reach England until the nineteenth century, although the ideal of scientific and experimental rationality was firmly established by the end of the seventeenth century. And in the Enlightenment's heyday, in the nineteenth century, there was Blavatsky, who represented a fast-developing array of thinkers willing to accept some or all of scientific rationality, but advocating forms of inspired thought that transcended and superseded the iron cage of Reason. Similarly, the twentieth and twenty-first century represented attempts to reconcile the great historical religions—Buddhism, Christianity, Islam, Judaism, and the new forms of Protestant Hinduism—with science and the larger reach of Euro-rationality. During this process of reconciliation, forms of indigenous knowledge, such as Ayurvedic medicine in South Asia, drastically shrink in popularity and scope, unless they absorb the norms of scientific rationality and adapt themselves to it. In the universities of Sri Lanka, the "logic" taught in philosophy departments goes under the rubric of "[Western] logic and scientific method," not that of the great Buddhist logicians like Dignāga (c. 5 CE) and Dharmakīrti (c. 7 CE). And linguistic and language departments have little space for Panini in their syllabuses. Sri Lankan philosophy students know more about the thought of Hegel and Kant than about Nāgārjuna's epistemology, unless they take courses in the history of Buddhism or study in one of the specialized graduate departments of Buddhist studies. If Euro-rationality tends to swamp indigenous knowledge and inhibit its development in South Asia, its fate in the rest of the non-Western world must surely be worse, although in many small-scale societies the inroads of science had been predated by the more destructive inroads of the early Christian missions. As the nineteenth century progressed, Euro-rationality has become the dominant way of thought in modern intellectual and scientific disciplines and inevitably associated with irreversible social and economic "progress." The larger issue of the role of colonialism in bringing about this radical change is outside the purview of this essay.

What then is the fate of the visionary consciousness under the tyranny of the Enlightenment? As the nineteenth century progressed into the twentieth, the spaces for the visionary consciousness of the previous two centuries and, prior to that, of medieval European Christendom had shrunk badly. Surely people did have visions. William Christian has documented their persistence in Spain up until recent times. Yet the Spanish visions are mostly of the Virgin, and they lacked the complexity of their medieval counterparts.[2] And in the Protestant world, both in the U.S. and in Britain, there were continuing traditions of ecstatic religiosity in the evangelical churches, but, while prophetic messages and possession by the Holy Spirit continues, visions seem to have shrunk in scope and depth. Even within the Baptist evangelical tradition of contemporary enthusiasm, an occasional visionary would spring into sight, a good example being the African American Sister Gertrude Morgan (1900–1980), who not only experienced visions but also painted them in a house she significantly named "the Everlasting Gospel Mission."[3] Contemporary new age religions do not discourage visions, but only a few adepts experienced them, whereas most were attuned to "big dreams" and receiving messages ("channeling") from masters and other spiritual beings.[4]

With the impact of empiricism on Euro-rationality, a further consequence followed. The visionary propensity that flowed into prophecy in the previous centuries seems to have been crushed. Along with the medicalization of visions as hysteria there was a concomitant trend to empirically test or verify the so-called supernatural or other kinds of visionary experiences. Hence Colonel Olcott rushing to verify the truth of séances through science; hence the formation of the Society for Psychical Research (in 1882), which tried to disprove Blavatsky by employing techniques that seem to us today to be incredibly naive. In the larger context of the spread of Euro-rationality one can further appreciate Blavatsky defining her visions as real experiences, occurring on an empirical plane, and her futile and courageous attempt to deal with the triumph of empiricism.

I am now tempted to posit an unpopular hypothesis. I believe that although the space for visions have shrunk, not so with Western dreaming from the early nineteenth century to our own times. The conventional ethnographic wisdom is that in Euro-American thinking dreams are viewed as ephemera that vanish into nothingness with waking. Dreams are not significant of anything: oneiromancy is dead, dream sharing is something found in non-Western cultures, and so on. But is this version of the secularization thesis applicable to dreams? I suggest that in Euro-American cultures, when he has an especially good, or vivid, dream, a person will think about it himself and share it with a partner or with significant others. And, if it is really fearsome, he will try to shake it off and tell himself, "It's just a dream" and confide it with others as a way of coping with it. Dream sharing in this sense occurs everywhere, and it is on this basis that the more structured forms found in some cultures are erected. But I want to get beyond this idea and reaffirm that, with the decline of visions in the West, there is a concomitant interest in dreams beginning with the romantic movement and reaching its peak in our own times. I have already noted that alongside the dream are related phenomena such as the consumption of narcotics, initially with opium, employed both for domestic consumption and the control of colonized people, followed by attempts in the twentieth century to simulate visions through hallucinogenic substances.[5] Toward the end of the nineteenth century, parapsychology has taken hold in the Western scientific and pseudo-scientific imagination as an investigative tool for ESP and other "paranormal" phenomena. But one can think of these new preoccupations as a return of suppressed knowledge, that is, oneiromancy and the meaningful nature of dreams in a new guise. Let me tentatively explore these issues, beginning with dreaming.

In my thinking the nineteenth-century preoccupation with dreams went with their existential meaning for human beings, even if meaning and significance eventually came within the orbit of a scientific worldview. Dreams have always been significant to the visionary, but only as dream-visions that coexisted with ancient and continuing interpretations of dreams by ordinary people, for example, as omens of disaster or signs of good fortune. Handbooks on dreams existed everywhere in Europe and so did folk wisdom regarding dream prognostication. These conventional dream books would eventually be displaced by the scientific dream books written under the rationalizing imperative of the Enlightenment. But, interestingly enough, long before Freud, it is to the visionary Swedenborg to whom one must turn for a work interpreting dreams that seems to anticipate Jung, relating the dream to the spiritual problems that confront the dreamer and heralding his later visionary experiences. But Swedenborg's dream book was a private journal, unavailable to European thinkers, and Freud himself made no reference to him, although Jung did.[6]

Let me now examine the somewhat discredited secularization thesis originally enunciated by Max Weber, who posited the idea that, with the development of rationality in the West, there is a concomitant erosion of the worlds of enchantment, the magical garden cultivated by many a traditional society. This sociological version of the death of God has led to a host of critical scholarly works on whether this process occurs or not, whether the modern world in which we live is a disenchanted one or whether a reenchantment of the world occurs. The Nietzschean idea of the death of God makes sense in relation to the intellectual and scientific traditions of the West, along with the "radical Enlightenment," particularly as it manifests itself in nineteenth-century thought. By contrast, Weber's notion of the disenchantment of the world is a more general process applicable to our own times and not only among intellectual elites. Whether the world is or remains disenchanted is problematic and has to rethought against some fundamental ideas of Weber's own sociology of knowledge, specifically that human beings by their very nature (I would add, owing to the complexity of their neurological structures) must invest the world with meaning. This imperative to create meaning leads eventually to what Weber calls culture, the publicly accepted webs of significance we create in order to understand and grasp the worlds we live in.

In light of his own thought, I would recast Weber in the following way. I do not doubt that secularization in the Weberian sense does occur owing to the impact of rationality on our own thought and the institutions we have created in our modernity. But not irrevocably because human beings dissatisfied with the bleak worlds that emerge, or threaten to emerge or imagine might emerge, will want to reenchant the world, sometimes through religion, at other times through secular fantasies, creating a multitude of magical gardens. And yet others might want to fall back on religious worldviews, now heightened and rendered more meaningful than ever before. There is, as it were, a continuing cultural dialectic of disenchantment-reenchantment. New age religion and much of contemporary dreaming contends with both processes if one does not fall into the trap that the two processes of disenchantment and reenchantment are mirror opposites of one another. These two processes are not confined to our modernity or postmodernity either and occur in a much less dramatic manner whenever Reason is reified as the ruling power. And in our own times there is an area that we have neglected, an "inner-worldly" enchantment, borrowing a phrase from Weber, an enrichment of our private fantasy lives and acting them out in both creative and destructive ways.

Consider Nāgārjuna who, quite unlike contemporary language deconstructionists, was a deconstructionist of *existence*, postulating that in the quicksilver world of continuing change there is no still point, no god or God, no Self, no numinous hiding behind phenomena, no Being of any sort in the world or outside it. But then, parallel with this movement and against the antimetaphysical traditions of Theravāda, come the emergence or rereification of the fabulous worlds of the Bodhisattvas of Mahāyāna Buddhism and the enchanted cosmic spaces created by visionaries with power and faith. They then bequeath that magical heritage to others. Nāgārjuna leads us to the larger issue I have mentioned: where Reason reigns there must necessarily be an erosion of the magical garden, which then produces its reaction of enchantment, resulting in the ultimate coexistence of the two. We see this as well in our modern and postmodern world, where those who live and work in the world created by Reason can slip into arenas where Reason is temporarily in abeyance. But those alternate arenas have themselves come under the aegis of Reason and modernity, as we noted with respect to Buddhist meditation.

Because this essay is primarily concerned with visionary knowledge, I want to focus on dreaming and rational science. If the late nineteenth century saw the beginnings of the obsession with empirical verification of occult phenomena, we could say the same of dreams. Both forms of scientific knowing were in full bloom in the nineteenth century, especially in its third quarter, and from there flowered in the next century and into our own times. In this hinge discourse, I want to deal with the science of dreams, which combined empirical knowledge on dreams and a rationalized fallback on older views deriving prophetic and other forms of knowledge through dreams, both quests sometimes occurring simultaneously. With the triumphal march of empirical science and atheistic philosophies in the nineteenth century, the science of dreams and dreaming also flourished. Freud's dream book, as he himself recognizes, inherits many of the ideas of his scientific predecessors, whom he refers to at length.[7]

Freud's list of sources is impressive, considering the fact that he dealt primarily with German writers as well as a few writing in French. Between 1850 to

1900 (the date of the first edition of *The Interpretation of Dreams*), Freud refers to around seventy-five sources of scientific, philosophical, and psychological books and articles on dreams, of which fifty-nine were published in the last quarter of the century.[8] Freud only gives us a glimpse of the European preoccupation with dream studies at the fin de siècle, missing much of the literature of the period and especially the emergence in the nineteenth century of what nowadays we call lucid dreaming. I will treat lucid dreams at length later on, but will now consider Freud's introductory chapter, entitled, "The Scientific Literature Dealing with the Problems of Dreams," which details nineteenth-century thinkers who anticipated many of the issues taken up by dream studies in the next century, even though they did not deal with Freud's own concern with dreams and deep motivation and his innovative understanding of the dream work.

That first chapter begins with the contributions of nineteenth-century thinkers on the relation of dreams to waking life, some exploring the question of whether dreams and waking life are related, whether dreams are cut off from the waking realities, or whether they are interconnected. Much more fruitful are the discussions that follow on "memory in dreams," wherein several thinkers, including one of the founding fathers of lucid dreams (mentioned previously in book 5), Marquis Hervey de Saint-Denys, argue that dreams tap memories that are inaccessible to normal memory.[9] And this includes memories from earliest childhood, something with which Freud himself was preoccupied. In the same vein I. Strümpell says: "Dreams sometimes bring to light, as it were, from beneath the deepest piles of debris under which the earliest experiences of youth are buried in later times, pictures of particular localities, things or people, completely intact and with all their original freshness," a view that unfortunately eliminates what Freud later called "composite formations" that distort original memories (ID, 15). Some probe the idea of "day residues" as being always present in dreams, while others argue that waking events are not significantly operative in dream formation because dreams "plunge instead into the remote and almost extinct past," a vague anticipation of both Freud and Jung (ID, 19). By contrast, meaningful or not, in one of the first statistical studies, one investigator found that 11 percent of her sample bore "no visible connection with waking life" (ID, 19). Memory is, of course, central to both Freud and Jung and to almost all therapies employing dreams; and it is the late nineteenth century that laid the foundations for that research.

Innovative research on dream memory is followed by serious and important discussions on the physical, organic, and external stimuli that precipitate dreams, and here we have the beginnings of several key experimental studies on dreaming that flowered over fifty years later with the discovery of REM states.

To give just one instance: when, prior to sleep, the lips and tips of the nose were tickled, the subject (the experimenter himself) dreamt of a "frightful form of torture," without inquiring whether it was a kind of wish fulfillment or a self-fulfilling prophecy (ID, 25). Other experiments produced similar results, most dreams never directly repeating the external stimulus, but picturing it obliquely or symbolically in what Freud would later call an "indirect representation." This interesting discussion on external physical stimuli is followed by those arising from within the organism.

Some writers dealt with rather simple premonitory dreams that made indirect reference to the diseased organ within. "Pronounced disorders of the internal organs obviously act as instigators of dreams in a whole number of cases" (ID, 34). Thus heart and lung diseases and digestive ailments all send messages to the dreamer, because in these instances "the mind, being diverted from the external world, is able to pay more attention to the interior of the body" although it is not clear whether those who are perfectly healthy would not dream similar dreams. Freud says that "organic somatic stimuli upon the formation of dreams is almost universally accepted today," though much more systematic research needs to be done (ID, 37). Systematic research has indeed been initiated by contemporary neurologists, the prime example being Oliver Sachs's study of "neurological dreams," which can "show how sensitive a barometer dreaming may be of neurological health and disease than examination with a reflex hammer and a pin;" and it might provide information on "current states of body and mind."[10] Nineteenth-century research on physiological reactions in dreams is extremely interesting, although inconclusive until Freud developed his notion of "overdetermination." Thus, when Strümpell indicates that flying dreams are produced by the "rising and sinking of the lobes of the lungs at times when cutaneous sensations in the thorax have ceased to be conscious," he is perhaps ignoring that other motivations might also be associated with the production of those dreams (ID, 37–38).

Freud laments the fact that no significant research on the role of psychic stimuli in the production of dreams has appeared, and this includes major thinkers of the period such as Wilhelm Wundt. Yet, even while Freud underplays it, one of the most important discussions in the nineteenth century, in my view, pertained to the associational significance of dreams, that is, dream sequences interconnected through a web of associations. Given the importance of free associations in Freudian therapy, the role of associations in linking dream sequences together cannot be neglected, although obviously their centrality in dream formation ought to be contested. Thus one might argue that physical and organic stimuli lead to a triggering of a series of associations that then produces a dream with no direct connection to the original stimulus or, in my language, "symbolically removed" from the instigating cue.

Another theme that has continued down to our own times relates to why dreams are so easily forgotten. Most researchers subscribe to the idea that our ordinary daytime lives are full of "noise" or distractions, whereas in the night these stimuli are stilled, opening the way for dreams to occur. With waking and its distractions, dreams are forgotten, an idea that Freud himself criticized as inadequate, as he formulated the notion of repression, wherein unpalatable psychic motivations are pushed down to the realm of the unconscious from whence they spring in the first place. But other writers, notably Wilhelm Jensen in 1855, anticipated Freud's notion of secondary revision by asserting that dreams as dreamt are impossible or difficult of recall and that "even the most truth-loving of men is scarcely able to relate a noteworthy dream, without some additions or embellishments" (ID, 46). Hence coherence in dreams is something invented by the dreamer, who fills the gaps in the series of "dream-images" that make up the dream. Others emphasize something that Freud developed in detail later, namely, that in the immediate aftermath of the dream we produce organized or coherent dreams by introducing "causal chains" and "a process of logical connection which is lacking in the dream" as it is dreamt (ID, 47).

According to Freud's discussion, in the section on the "Psychological Characteristics of Dreams," the late nineteenth century introduced a series of innovative ideas that are with us today. Among these is the important thesis that, though dreams "think," they do so only in terms of images or pictures, a notion Freud borrowed wholesale from other German thinkers, most notably the famous Friedrich Schleiermacher, one of the founders of hermeneutics. Schleiermacher pointed out that "thought-activity takes place in *concepts* and not in *images*," an argument that Freud fully accepted: "We shall be in agreement with every authority on the subject in asserting that dreams *hallucinate*, that they replace thoughts by hallucinations" (ID, 49, 50). Other nineteenth-century thinkers, like H. Spitta, formulated the idea that dreams dramatize an idea from waking life, a reference to the narrative or story line that dreams might take (ID, 50). Earlier in the century, K. F. Burdach (in 1838) makes the important point on the passivity of the self during sleep: "Sleep signifies an end of the authority of the self. Hence falling asleep brings a certain degree of passivity along with it. . . . The images that accompany sleep can occur only on condition that the authority of self is reduced," a view that many major thinkers including Freud held, if, by "the authority of the self," we mean the ego of psychoanalysis (ID, 50). Whether as a function of the passive consciousness or not, the nineteenth century continued the traditional European idea—but by no means confined to Europe—that dreams might well be nonsensical, converting the dreamer into a fool (ID, 55); or the very opposite, where dreams might have deep symbolic meanings; or, as one writer put it, life events are given "re-interpretation in allegorical terms," a point made as well by one of Freud's patients (ID, 58). Another writer seems to anticipate Jung, or even Freud and some of his own nineteenth-century colleagues, when he says that *"when asleep we go back to the old ways of looking at things and of feeling about them, to impulses and activities which long ago dominated us"* (ID, 60).

I cannot deal with all the topics covered in Freud's introductory chapter except to note that which later became relevant to us, for example, the relation between dreams and mental illness and the role of wish fulfillment in dreams, this last being an idea Freud generously acknowledged he borrowed wholesale from W. Griesinger, writing in 1861. To me, however, one of the most interesting ideas come from K. A. Scherner and his concept of the fantasy-I, the presence of the "I" in the dream not as the ego of the waking life but as a fantastic or fantasized "I," the theoretical implications of which I have already discussed (ID, 84–85.) Reflecting back on the preceding account, it seems to me that Freud's key distinction between the manifest dream and its underlying latent meanings is something he inherited from his nineteenth-century predecessors.

Let me then reiterate my hypothesis: as a result of the march of science and rationality in the nineteenth century, one would expect dreams also to come within the purview of science. Freud remained firmly rooted in the weltanschauung of nineteenth-century science. A key chapter in the dream book, entitled, "The Psychology of the Dream–Processes" indirectly bears on the abandoned neurological model of his *Project for a Scientific Psychology*. Even when he wrote about historic episodes or figures, such as that of Leonardo da Vinci, or dealt with the rise of monotheism in ancient Egypt, he was firmly and self-consciously rooted in the diagnostic and interpretive rules of psychoanalysis, which for him remained a scientific paradigm. Yet many of his disciples partially or wholly abandoned this model for a greater preoccupation with myth, symbol, and allegory as providing access to "truths" normally neglected by the empirical sciences of the nineteenth century. Anyone familiar with the history of psychoanalysis knows the two most famous rebels who broke away from Freud were Carl Jung and Alfred Adler, with lesser beings such as Otto Rank, Theodor Reik, Wilhelm Stekel, and Emil Gutheil and, later, many others like Karen Horney and Eric Fromm, who partially or wholly broke away from mainline psychoanalysis. Alfred Adler, who focused on the neuroses that spring from inferiority and lack of self-worth, does not fit my model of a dreaming scientist, and I won't deal with his work except to say that he is one of the very few therapists who believed that the "will to power" had great motivational significance and was integral to the strivings of human beings in contemporary life. Freud never incorporated this facet of Nietzschean thought into his theory of unconscious motivation and consequently missed its expression, frustration, canalization, and the defenses erected in response to it in the life of his patients. One might say that its neglect led to the impoverishment of the psychoanalytic study of politicians, business tycoons, and terrorists, not to mention intellectuals. Freud simply refused to recognize that sexuality itself can be a mask for the will to power or, for that matter, the other way around.

Yet this preoccupation with the science of dreaming has another thrust when science is conjoined with the search for meaning. In our times this quest for meaning is part of a larger Euro-American movement of investing dreams with existential meaning, which in turn occurs in the context of the erosion of the magical garden and the death of god. To explore these themes, let me get back to Freud's opening statement in *The Interpretation of Dreams* that "there is a psychological technique which makes it possible to interpret dreams, and that, if that procedure is employed, every dream reveals itself as a psychical structure which has a meaning and which can be inserted at an assignable point in the mental activities of waking life" (ID, 1). Freud seriously believed in the nonsensical idea that dreams are never nonsense. Ever meaningful, Freud had to think about explaining *all* dreams in an age before modern probability theory was developed in the early twentieth century. Yet, while most nineteenth-century thinkers were almost entirely focused on the science of dreams, Freud and those who followed him were at the same time interested in the psychic and existential meaning of dreams, thereby retranslating traditional ideas of prophecy, meaning, and oneiromancy by bringing them within the purview of science or at least minimally accommodating them into a scientific worldview. But, more than this, without explicitly recognizing it, Freud, in dipping into dreams, also derived knowledge from them. By peering into his own dreams, he began to understand his inner life and oedipal conflicts and then employed his personal insights to understand psychic life in general. Thus one can justifiably assert that Freud discovered psychoanalysis, or at least its central features, through his own dreams, and in this sense he joins the ranks of those visionaries and dreamers who appear in this essay. Having discovered the central ideas of his theory through visionary dreaming (if not a "dream vision"), Freud then transformed them into a rational framework, just as some of our vision seekers did, relating the It to the I.[11]

If my hypothesis is correct, then, with the general acceptance of Enlightenment rationality, the propensity for visions dwindled, but their place was taken by dreams, which occupied a prominent role for the major English romantic poets mentioned earlier and, indeed, many more, all of whom fell under the sway of European romanticism. They then paved the way for later poets, painters, and novelists, up to our own times with, surrealism as the most powerful and obvious creative use of dream imagery. Freud simply represented a unique configuration whereby dreams are not only brought within the purview of science but also where the scientist dipped into his own dreams for psychic and human understanding, as, of course, Jung also did. Both opened the way for other therapists and dream theorists who understood the meaning of dreams in their own lives, before, while, or after reaching out to their patients irrespective of whether they followed Freud, Jung, Gestalt analysts, or existentialists and followers of Heidegger's thought, and all sorts of "analytical schools" that mushroomed after the 1960s.[12]

Freud was important for another reason. Dreaming poets and artists would scarcely raise eyebrows, unlike a Blake who experienced visions that only madmen were generally guilty of. But a dreaming scientist? What I think Freud represented in his own career is the penetration of dreams as a mode of knowing for those who were, like Freud himself, exemplars of scientific rationality. This public breach in the rational consciousness is neatly documented in Deidre Barrett's very readable account of a variety of intellectuals, including scientists, for whom dreams came to be a replacement for the older visionary consciousness.[13] I refer the reader to Barrett's work, but only illustrate this newer trend by referring to perhaps the best-known case of a dreaming scientist, August Kekulé (1829–1896).

Kekulé was a great chemist known for his formulation of the structural theory of chemistry and his discovery of the benzene ring that gave him the Nobel Prize. A modern-day chemist, Eduard Farber, says that "we need Kekulé's testimony today as a powerful reminder that chemistry advances not by experiments alone but by a process in which dreams and visions can play an important role."[14] Such a view was anathema to Enlightenment thinkers of the nineteenth century, and even today the very idea that dreams and visions can have significance in inspiring scientific insights is for most physical scientists something unspeakable. It was also unspeakable for the dreamer Kekulé. Hence he refuses to admit his dream hypotheses in his major scientific paper of 1865, which dealt with his discovery of the benzene ring. He only mentioned it in 1890 during the celebration of the twenty-fifth anniversary of that great discovery.[15] What is impressive is that even before his discovery of the benzene ring, when he was formulating his structural theory of chemistry, Kekulé used to have dream visions:

> During my stay in London I resided for a considerable time in Clapham Road. . . . One fine summer evening I was returning by the last bus, "outside," as usual, through the deserted streets of the city, which are at other times so full of life. I

fell into a reverie (Traumerei), and lo, the atoms were gamboling before my eyes! Whenever, hitherto, these diminutive beings had appeared to me, they had always been in motion; but up to that time I had never been able to discern the nature of their motion. Now, however, I saw how, frequently, two smaller atoms united to form a pair, how a larger one embraced the two smaller ones; how still larger ones kept hold of three or even four of the smaller; whilst the whole kept whirling in a giddy dance. I saw how the larger ones formed a chain, dragging the smaller ones after them but only at the ends of the chain. . . . The cry of the conductor: "Clapham Road," awakened me from [my] dreaming; but I spent a part of the night in putting on paper at least sketches of these dream forms. This was the origin of the "Structural Theory."[16]

It is clear that Kekulé was consistently dreaming of atoms whirling before him, but this is the first time that the dream unfolded itself in such a manner that it led him to formulate his structural theory. Although this dream is fascinating, Kekulé is best known for the dream-vision that helped him to win the Nobel Prize.

Something similar happened with the benzene theory. During my stay in Ghent I resided in elegant bachelor quarters in the main thoroughfare. My study, however, faced a narrow side-alley and no daylight penetrated it. . . . I was sitting writing my textbook but the work did not progress; my thoughts were elsewhere. I turned my chair to the fire and dozed. Again the atoms were gamboling before my eyes. This time the smaller groups kept modestly in the background. My mental eye, rendered more acute by repeated visions of the kind, could now distinguish larger structures of manifold conformation; long rows, sometimes more closely fitted together all twining and twisting in snake-like motion. But look! What was that? One of the snakes had seized hold of its own tail, and the form whirled mockingly before my eyes. As if by a flash of lighting I awoke; and this time also I spent the rest of the night in working out the consequences of the hypothesis.[17]

What Kekulé's statement implies is that his kind of creativity entails a complex relationship between the It and the thinking-I, that is, between the dream (Kekulé calls it a vision) and the afterwork following it, putting the intuitive grasp of the hypothesis within the frame of rational thought, as with my model of the Buddha's awakening.[18] Further, the cognitive reworking of the dream hypothesis is analogous to the "secondary revision" that Freud speaks about or, better still, to "secondary elaboration," as I have suggested. Kekulé clearly shows that he encouraged dreaming as a vehicle for insight, and the two rich dreams in particular provided him intuitive grasp of the structural theory and the benzene ring. These two dreams are culminations of an ongoing process of dreaming and daytime thinking. Thus it seems reasonable to suppose that the earlier dreams were products of prior rational thinking that went on in Kekulé's head. That is, the dream-visions have to be related to prior thoughts or "fantasy activity" or ideas incubating in his mind for some time and then symbolically re-presented through what he called his "mental eye," the alchemical image we have already mentioned. These earlier dreams were repetitive but, as with dreams, never identical. Between them and the two key dreams, Kekulé must inevitably have been thinking—consciously perhaps—about the significance of these dreams for his theoretical work. The two key dreams crystallized the earlier dreams and the concomitant fantasy in the symbolism of the moving atoms and the ouroboros. This is beautifully expressed in the second dream where the moving atoms gradually formed themselves into the hermetic symbol of the snake biting its tail. Kekulé was familiar with European alchemy and hermeticism and this knowledge might have affected the form and content of his dream, although it is not necessary to see it, as Jung does, as a welling forth from the deeps of the collective unconscious.[19] The meaning of the dream is not readily apparent to us, but it was to Kekulé, who soon after each dream not only put it into writing but also sketched the outlines of its possible theoretic significance. Kekulé himself put it neatly in his public confession in 1890 on the power of dreaming and its relation to rational reworking: "Let us learn to dream, gentlemen, then perhaps we shall find the truth. . . . But let us beware of publishing our dreams till they have been tested by the waking understanding."[20]

What I find especially fascinating in Kekulé's dream experience is that it provides one form of the process of visionary knowledge that helps us to understand the nature of "fantasy activity." Dream knowledge did not come to Kekulé "out of nothing," as Yeats would have it. It is preceded by Kekulé wrestling in his mind with his hypothesis but finding no answer; then the dream of ouroboros appears before him; he wakes and realizes the answer he was seeking; he then puts back that knowledge into rational form. Here is a circular form of knowledge derivation, with which one has grown familiar as the hermeneutic circle. The final rational solution closes the circle. But this is an oversimplification, since it does not deal with the complicated manner in which Kekulé's earliest thought processes would have worked. In actuality the scientist had been grappling with his thoughts in the rational mode for a long time: he dreams of atoms moving in a circle; but his initial dream could not have provided him with an answer; he continues to think his problem out in waking hours or in the fullness of "daybreak;" then dreaming once again; then back to rational thought. This process of dreaming and thinking goes on for some time; finally he dreams of the atoms circulating in the manner of the ouroboros, and the circle is closed with a rational solution of the problem.

There is no evidence that Kekulé gave any cosmic or religious significance to his dreams, even though he called them "visions" in order to indicate their seriousness. Eduard Farber, in his provocative article, not only makes the point that dreams had an important role in the development of chemistry but also refers to eleven scientists who derived inspiration from dreams and flashes of insight of the sort mentioned by Jacques Hadamard in his early study of mathematicians.[21] One such is Wilhelm Ostwald (1853–1932), who spent a long night with a friend persuading him to write a textbook on chemistry. "I . . . slept [only] for a few hours, then suddenly awoke immersed in the same thought and could not go back to sleep. In the earliest morning hours I went from the hotel to the Tiergarten, and there, in the sunshine of a glorious spring morning, I experienced a real Pentecost, an outpouring of the spirit over me. . . . This was the actual birth-hour of energetics."[22] What these dreaming scientists did not know is that dream-visions and "revelations" are as old as the hills and found in much more developed form in the early history of Europe and almost everywhere in the non-European world. For those like Ostwald, the power of the experience gave them virtually no choice but to incorporate the dream as a revelation of a truth *thrown* at them from their Christian faith. (See book 5, note 55 for "thrownness.") For others such as Kekulé, they must surely have been expressions of what I call "secular spirituality."

A POSTSCRIPT TO FREUD: REVISITING MANIFEST DREAMS AND LATENT THOUGHTS

An aged man is but a paltry thing,
A tattered coat upon a stick,
Unless soul clap its hands and sing, and louder sing
For every tatter in its mortal dress . . .
—W. B. Yeats, "Sailing to Byzantium"

Freud is a pervasive presence in this essay. As I have already mentioned, my Freudian empathy extends mostly to the "first topography" of *The Interpretation of Dreams,* which for me contains a flexible model of the mind, providing for many of us a basis for the further development of his thought without being fettered by the later tripartite division of ego, id, and superego. To be emancipated from that model is not to reject Freud's later thinking and insights. Instead, while embracing these, I reject the later neo-Cartesian model within which his thoughts are imprisoned. The model of the second topography, I believe, is peripheral to his great speculative works such as *Future of an Illusion, Beyond the Pleasure Principle, Civilization and Its Discontents, Moses and Monotheism,* and almost all his early case histories.

I now want to develop some of the ideas in the first topography, especially the important distinction Freud made between the dream as dreamt, or its manifest content, and the latent content, which reveals the various elements from the past that help to form the manifest dream. The latent content, or the dream thoughts, are those hidden in the dream, and this includes memories and day residues, sometimes troubling ones, sometimes of a harmless sort. It is a mistake to attribute to Freud the idea that dream thoughts always pertain to deep motivations. The famed dream of the "botanical monograph" has little to do with his dark dream thoughts; so it is with another famous dream about his patient Irma, even though a reanalysis suggests that it is less innocent than Freud made it out to be.[23] It is through the dream work that latent thoughts are converted into the manifest dream. Thus my dream "visit to Egypt" has a coherent narrative as its manifest content. Thereafter, I unravel the elements that went to form the manifest dream, namely, the latent contents or dream thoughts. For Jung, too, it is not the manifest content that matters but deep structures of the collective unconscious, those archetypes with historical roots brimming over with meaning. Yet I believe that we will never understand dreaming as a process or a special mode of "thinking" unless we try to figure out the manner in which the manifest dream gets constructed, beginning with an initial cue or cues that precipitate dream formation followed by other associations that in turn trigger bits and pieces from memory, which are then put together into pictures exhibiting degrees of coherence-incoherence owing to the operation of the passive intellect during sleep. For Freud, even absurd dreams can have a latent meaning, but, as I said earlier, disconnected and absurd dreams may remain just that for various reasons including the interruption of the dream. Students of the human sciences ought not to neglect the manifest content, a phenomenological enterprise that makes sense in terms of our own dreams but is extremely difficult to record in an ethnographic setting. It has nevertheless to be done even though, I will admit, the final answers to this question must lie with a neurophenomenology of the future.

On the face of it, manifest dreams seem to exhibit an enormous variety, an unmistakable relativism, such that two dreams are rarely identical, even though it is certainly possible that common themes or common symbols might appear within a culture or even cross-culturally. Recurrent dreams do occur, but they are not repeated in identical substantive form. Most ethnographers are interested primarily in the cultural structuring of dreams, but I find this obvious because the content of dreams must surely reflect features of the dreamer's culture! I believe that ethnographers are so firmly committed to assuming dreams as cultural formations that they will interpret them in terms of that very presupposition, eliding content deemed culturally irrelevant. The last observation prompts me to make the proposition that *any kind of interpretation of a dream entails a movement from the manifest to the latent,* from the immediately intelligible to its hidden meanings, both in terms of content and motivation, although not necessarily in the Freudian sense of deep motivations. This rule must also apply to conventional dream manuals found the world over. They too are a reaction to the extreme relativism of dreams by imposing fixed meanings on them, thereby facilitating interpretation and bringing about order from confusion. In general, popular dream manuals ignore the total dream and instead pick a few items from it, as, for example, when traditionally in Sri Lanka it is believed that if one sees a Buddhist monk in a dream it will harbinger a misfortune.

In this sense, dream manuals are no different from modern ethnographic and psychological attempts to understand the latent content hiding behind the manifest dream. I am not exempt from this rule either. On the theoretical level, my analysis is also a reaction to the impossible-to-tolerate nature of dream relativism. I personally believe, following the Freudian and Jungian assumption, that the underlying precipitates of the manifest dream can in special circumstances draw upon deep motivations or enduring structures that surface when consciousness is in abeyance. Bracketing these motivations for the present, I will now deal with existential themes that occur and recur in dreams as part of human experience, although the form in which they are represented in the manifest dream may exhibit cultural or personal dilemmas. In which case it is the manifest dream and my waking interpretation of it that is significant and not the "thoughts" that went into its construction, even though the manifest dream could not have occurred without precipitating latent thoughts. Let me illustrate this with a very brief and seemingly simple dream I dreamt in Delhi on October 31, 2008, long after this essay had been completed and, I foolishly imagined, finally dispatched to the publisher!

I will bestow on my dream the grandiloquent title of "tattered trousers"! Here is the dream scenario: I was opening the wardrobe that contained my clothes and I pulled out a pair of cotton trousers. The wardrobe seemed vaguely familiar as the one in our apartment in Delhi, but its contents were close enough to the one in Kandy, Sri Lanka, though never the same, as ever is the case with dreams. The particular pair of trousers was not one found in my home closet. It was full of holes and tears, and in the dream itself the thought came to me that termites had attacked it. The dream flashed at me a picture of the pretattered trousers, just regular old cotton trousers, nothing special, and I was shown, also in a flash, the closet full of other clothes including trousers. I was terribly, terribly upset, rendered anxious during the space of the dreaming, but didn't know why. When my dream wife examined it, she said it might not be termites. I was not persuaded, and so she looked inside the closet and said that it could be termites after all, although we never saw any.

That was pretty much the dream, or at least the segment that I remembered when I awoke. Yet on waking, still drowsily anxious, Blake's aphorisms from a poem I quote in this work in several places floated into my mind.

> Does the Eagle know what is in the pit?
> Or wilt thou go ask the Mole?
> Can Wisdom be put in a silver rod?
> Or Love in a golden bowl?[24]

My waking recollection is nothing unusual because, interested as I am in Blake, I recite these lines often and mull over their many meanings when I am by myself so that, as with many of my favorite poems, they have been engraved in memory.

Soon after waking I wondered why my simple dream disturbed me so much. Most people might say that the tattered pair of trousers is only what it means on the manifest level. But in my waking interpretation it signified much more. Many of us dream of death and dying in our old age or when stricken by illness or when confronted with the sudden loss of someone near and dear. Some of us might even develop into imaginary practitioners of death. What is more, I often reflect on the problem of physical decrepitude, decay, the skull beneath the skin, and the transience of life in Buddhist terms. In my waking reflection I realized that my trousers, already an old pair, now eaten by termites, are a symbol of physical decay, aging, death, and, by association or by metonymy, my own aged self. Existential issues such as these can only be *indirectly represented* in dream picturing. One can argue that my interpretation of the dream on waking takes me from the manifest to the latent. This is true, but, for me at least, latent thoughts of death and decay were *patent* ones, not necessarily buried deep in memory. The day residue was no residue, and the dream itself did not require a serious excavation of the past. I think this is true for many dreams of existential import.

On the theoretical level, I reflected that dreams are indirect representations in another, less obvious sense, in that they express in pictorial form ideas that have little to do with language, even though it is through language that I must later describe them. Rather than saying that language influences dream formation (a partial truth at best), I would say the reverse is truer: dreams affect language formation, not the grammatical or syntactical structure of language but what one might call thick metaphors and dense symbolic forms, often appearing in poetry and in our aphoristic thoughts.[25] It is on this level that one can say that language might circle back into the dream and the dream might circle back into language. But this is not a chicken-and-egg question: we were dreaming primates before we became speaking humans. Dreams therefore are prior to language, and in human life itself it is the former that is primary as far as the long-term circular causal interconnection between dreams and language is concerned. As with visions, our dreams compel us to recognize that the limits of language are *not* the limits of thought.

I cannot even say that an idea or theme that cannot or will not be expressed in language is reexpressed in the dream. This again is only a partial truth. In my dream the idea of decay and decrepitude can easily be spoken or written about, quite unlike Freudian deep motivations such as guilt or oedipal or castration anxieties and similar motivations, which often resist conscious formulation. The thinking that goes into the formation of a dream must be treated in its own right, as something quite different from language and from rational cognitive processes. My dream of the tattered trousers is simultaneously an indirect representation of my inner thoughts of decay and finitude, because a dream, as we have asserted, is not equipped to handle our instigating "dream thoughts" or fantasy activity in a cognitively rational mode. I would say that thoughts (and this includes deep motivations or primary process "thinking" as well as rational ones) circulating in my mind are expressed in picture form as symbolic or indirect representations with varying degrees of coherence-incoherence.

What about the Blake poem? The lines are from *The Book of Thel* and are foreshadowed in a longer work, *Tiriel*, both written around 1789. In the larger context of Blake's work I interpret the four lines later on in this essay as representing the "enigma of death." At the time of my recall I never connected these lines with the dream, but did so several hours *after* I had interpreted the dream on waking. It seemed to me that the dream itself, unconsciously to be sure, was the cue that triggered the remembrance of the poem. As for the Yeats quote of my epigraph, I included it only weeks later when it surfaced from memory's storehouse where it had been sequestered for quite some time. Nevertheless that poem might even have had a role in the very construction of the dream. That poem is part of the latent content, but the dream itself does not depend for its existential significance on the lines from Blake or Yeats. One might argue that my *interpretation* of the dream was affected by the poem, but, on the other hand, the dream is part of my larger interest in the Buddhist existential issues of death and decay. These issues are patent, that is, on the surface of my consciousness.

What I have been doing here is trying to beat dream relativism on two fronts. First, a speculative "theory" of dream formation through passive cerebration occurring when consciousness has been suspended, and, second, the idea that dreams, certainly not most, have a symbolic function, giving expression to existential concerns that all human beings must face at some time or other. It is this latter issue—the idea of universal existential meanings and motivations—that has led Freudian and Jungian analysts and others to postulate a doctrine of universal symbols appearing and reappearing within and across cultures. But, for me, what is universal is something that precedes symbolic formation, by which I mean *ideas* pertaining to universal existential issues—such as birth, copulation, and death—that are, for the most part, conscious. My ideas of death and decay are expressed through the symbolism of the termites and the tattered trousers, but I would hesitate to label this dream scenario a cultural formation or a universal symbol. This does not mean that existential ideas and motivations cannot be expressed through cultural meanings that are simultaneously personal or that some symbols might be universal. But such universalisms cannot be taken for granted and are much less pervasive than imagined. I cannot imagine a tattered pair of trousers eaten by termites could ever be a universal symbol even though the *underlying ideas* have universal existential provenance. Hence similar symbolic phantasmagorias could be dreamt by others and even incorporated into art, as with the Yeats poem of my epigraph. Further, for some of us at least, a disturbing dream on the enigma of death, dying, and human finitude, *thrown* at us at night, might lead to further reflections on the nature of existence that then might release serial or recurring dreams resonating with existential themes or aporias. Insofar as these themes are the concern of virtually all religions, one might say that through such dreams even a dreaming atheist, unbeknownst to him, might experience a form of "secular spirituality." It is Jung who pointed out serial dreams loaded with existential meanings when he analyzed the dreams of some of his sensitive subjects such as the Nobel laureate Wolfgang Pauli, who will soon make an appearance in this essay.

CARL GUSTAV JUNG AND THE "NATURAL SCIENCE" OF ONEIROMANCY

Lise literally shrieked with delight. . . . "By the way, let me tell you about a funny dream I had. It's night, I'am alone in my room, a candle is burning. Suddenly the room is full of devils, in every corner, under the table. . . . They want to come in and seize me. And they do get to me and are about to grab me when I suddenly make a sign of the cross and they reel back. They are frightened but they won't leave altogether; they wait in the corners and by the door. Suddenly I get a tremendous desire to say insulting things about God out aloud and I begin to shout foul words. . . . I have a marvelous time. It takes my breath away."

"I have that same dream sometimes too," Aloysha said.

"I can't believe it! Tell me, Aloysha, and please don't laugh—what I am going to ask you is very important. Do you really think it's possible for two different people to have the same dream?"

"Apparently it is."

"But it's so terribly important, don't you see?" Lise exclaimed in complete amazement. "It's not the dream that's important. It's the fact that you could have the same dream as I had. You never lie to me, so please don't lie now either—is it true? You're not making fun of me?"

"No, it's true."

—Fyodor Dostoyevsky, *The Brothers Karamazov*

Both Freud and Jung were imbued with the spirit of nineteenth-century science, but Jung, unlike Freud, could hardly be called a child of the Enlightenment, critical as he was of Enlightenment rationality. Freud's theoretical reference group was the physics of his time, but, while Jung considered his mature analytical psychology a "natural science," it was not modeled on the conventional natural sciences.[26] Ideals apart, practice tended to be different in both Jung and Freud. As Paul Ricoeur clearly shows, the very title of Freud's *The Interpretation of Dreams* indicates the prime place given to interpretation and "understanding" as against the causal explanatory models of empirical science he explicitly avowed.[27] And, in his major works, Jung even more radically brought back the old hermetic and alchemical thinking, albeit in a new analytical guise. Yet there is no escaping the fact that both, along with virtually every other thinker that will appear in the following pages, lived and had to contend with the scientific weltanschauung of their time.

My approach to Jung flows from my examination of his predecessors Blake and Blavatsky. I will initially acquaint the reader with key features of Jung's thought and then discuss in some detail his two dark nights of the soul and the many dream-visions he experienced in order to bring him in line with the other visionaries of my essay. I will use two texts as my primary resource. First, *Psychology and Alchemy*, published in 1944, although based on earlier papers, gives us an excellent account of Jung's mature thinking. That work heralded some of the most significant works of Jung's later opus, especially *Aion* (1951), *Mysterium*

Coniunctionis (1956), and his detailed formulation of synchronicity (1951). Second, absolutely central for my argument is his "confessional" *Memories, Dreams, Reflections,* written when he was eighty-one and containing accounts of his spiritual experiences along with his comments on the processes that lie outside the rational consciousness or the thinking-I.[28] *Psychology and Alchemy*, in addition to opening a window onto the "analytic psychology" he formulated in opposition to Freud's psychoanalysis, also gives us a summary of Jung's deep interest in alchemy, hermetic philosophy, and the occult as well as his mature thinking on dreams. These issues tie Jung with the visionaries of my essay rather than his well-known forays into psychological types, such as the introvert-extrovert distinction, which I will simply ignore.

Let me begin with Jung's somewhat drastic critique of the Cartesian cogito. He says that the Enlightenment imagined that "there was no psyche outside the Ego," and this has produced an "inflated consciousness [that] is always egocentric and conscious of nothing but its own existence" and further "is incapable of learning from the past, incapable of understanding contemporary events, and incapable of drawing the right conclusions about the future" (PA, 480). Jung attributes the terrible calamity of World War II, which, according to him, no one wanted, to this deadly ego inflation that in turn resulted in the swallowing up by ego of the many features of the unconscious. What he seems to be saying is that the dark, even murderous thoughts in the unconscious has been absorbed by the ego, waiting to be acted upon as in World War II, resulting in a tragedy for Europeans. Implicitly, Jung's thesis also contains a critique of the Freudian formula on the end result of the psychoanalytic cure: "Where id was there shall ego be." For Jung, ego and the unconscious should be in harmony with each other and the fullness of this harmony, as we shall see, lies in notions of individuation and the development of the self.

Thus, for Jung, there has to be a continuing interplay between consciousness and the unconscious, and in his thinking the "self" must be differentiated from the ego wherein Reason resides. The self is the broader concept that embraces and integrates both unconscious and conscious processes; it is, one might say, the totality of one's being.[29] Jung asserts: "Nobody realized that European man was possessed by something that robbed him of free will" owing to the Enlightenment's obsession with the ego. For this to change, one must recognize our possession of a psychic non-ego, that is, the self that ought not to be swallowed by the ego. As a later work put it: "I should like to mention that the more numerous and the more significant the unconscious contents are assimilated to the ego, the closer the approximation of the ego to the self, even though this approximation must be a never ending process. This effectively produces an inflation of the ego," which, according to Jung, is a "psychic catastrophe" because one cannot pollute the integrity of the self with the discursive rationality of the ego.[30]

In order to creatively dip into the unconscious, we must learn from the past, especially from the alchemists who in their experiments denied that consciousness was all. For Jung, alchemy becomes a model for analytical psychology. Jung imagines that the alchemist in his experimental work was engaged in something similar to analysis. The alchemical process, insofar as it is practiced in the laboratory, is a projection of the unconscious, but, because it is externalized in experiments, it does not deal with the internal processes within the individual, which is the work of analytical psychology. In his last book, *Mysterium Coniunctionis,* he says that alchemists "did not know that they were bringing psychic structures to light but thought they were explaining the transformations of matter."[31] It is left to the psychologist to unravel psychic processes implicit in alchemical experiments, although Jung is never very clear how alchemical experiments anticipated analytical psychology, even though he categorically emphasized the link in *Memories, Dreams, Reflections*: "I had very soon seen that analytic psychology coincided in a most curious way with alchemy. The experiences of the alchemists were, in a sense, my experiences, and their world was my world. This was of course a momentous discovery: I had stumbled upon the historical counterpart of my psychology of the unconscious. The possibility of a comparison with alchemy, and the uninterrupted intellectual chain back to Gnosticism, gave substance to my psychology" (MDR, 205).

Further clarification is available in Jung's idea that alchemy brings opposites together in such conjunctions as ego and psyche, male and female, being and nonbeing, and, in Chinese alchemy, the idea of yin and yang. In the European alchemist's lab such contrasts are chemically melted into a unity and "purified of all opposition and therefore incorruptible" (PA, 37). In other words, what Jung is saying is that alchemists, in fusing opposites to form a new whole, are in a sense doing what Jung himself is trying to do through his theory of individuation and the wholeness of the self. And then he adds: "I hold the view that the alchemist's hope of conjuring out of matter the philosophical gold, or the panacea, or the wonderful stone, was only in part an illusion, an effect of projection: for the rest it corresponded to certain psychic facts that are of great importance in the psychology of the unconscious. As is shown by the texts and their symbolism, the alchemist projected what I have called the process of individuation into the phenomena of chemical change" (PA, 482). For myself, I find it hard to accept the argument that alchemists were engaged in a Jungian kind of enterprise without being aware of it.

The point of psychological healing is therefore a kind of alchemical process that brings about wholeness achieved through a conjunction of opposites and a uniting symbol representing the idealized self that often has a numinous quality, such as the figure of the Buddha or God or the maṇḍala (PA, 476). "We are dealing with life-processes which, on account of their numinous character, have from time immemorial provided the strongest incentive for the formation of symbols. These processes are steeped in mystery; they pose riddles with which the human mind will long wrestle for a solution, and perhaps in vain." "Mystery" is not quite what Reason is about and hence his quotation from the alchemists: "Rend the books lest your hearts be rent asunder," in spite of the fact that alchemists were educated people and insisted on the importance of study (PA, 482). In the final sense, "experience, not books, is what leads to understanding." "Experience" in this sense takes Jung to the study of dream symbols that open up "the unknown regions of the soul." "The forms which the experience takes in each individual may be infinite in their variations, but, like the alchemical symbols, they are all variants of certain central types, and these occur universally. They are the primordial images, from which the religions each draw their absolute truth" (PA, 483). As is well known, Jung calls these primordial images archetypes a term borrowed from the alchemical tradition.[32] While consciousness is subject to change, as, for example, with ego inflation, the human psyche has not changed at all during thousands of years, and this collective or objective psyche (as against the variable personal psyche) will continue unchanged for thousands more. Jung's notion of the psyche or the unconscious provides an epistemological rationale for shared archetypes to appear right through human history.

What then is an archetype? In an earlier work, Jung says that, owing to our unchanged collective unconscious "certain motives repeat themselves in almost identical form. I have called those motives archetypes and by them I understand forms or images of a collective nature which occur practically all over the earth as constituents of myths and at the same time as autochthonous, individual products of unconscious origin. The archetypal motives presumably start from the archetypal patterns of the human mind which are not only transmitted by tradition and migration but *also by heredity*. The latter hypothesis is indispensable, since even complicated archetypal images can be spontaneously reproduced without any possible direct tradition."[33]

Jung rightly believes that the union of opposites has had a long history in Neoplatonic philosophies, in medieval Christianity, and especially in the work of Boehme and in the German tradition of alchemy culminating in the seventeenth century.[34] And they reappear later in Blake and Blavatsky and in veiled form in Claude Lévi-Strauss. Consider Blavatsky once again. For her, the empirical record of ancient civilizations contains certain mythic themes that have persisted throughout history, but modernity has dissipated them, and the task of Theosophy is to recover them with the help of the masters. Jung believed in some of these ideas, but, unlike Blavatsky, he wanted to ground his notion of forms or archetypes in a psychological science or an analytical psychology. Consequently, the way to verify the existence of archetypes is to document their empirical manifestation in dreams.[35]

Thus one of his most famous patients, Wolfgang Pauli, dreams archetypal myths that for the most part does not come from his personal knowledge or from his German and larger European tradition.[36] They must surely have been "spontaneously reproduced without any possible direct tradition" from an unknown historic or prehistoric past. Or as Jung states in another work, myths do not appear as well-formed stories or in their original forms in dreams, but only as "motifs" or "primordial images" or as "archetypes." They are "'autochthonous' revivals independent of all tradition, and, consequently, the 'myth-forming' structural elements must be present in the unconscious psyche." [37] Archetypes, insofar as they come from that past, permit Jung, as in Pauli's case, to understand—tentatively to be sure—the minds of one's ancestors, providing a strong appeal for those of us, in our disenchanted times, living out our quest for roots. Because archetypes are based on a common collective psyche, on heredity, and on a commonality of motives ("instincts"), they can be designated "natural symbols." [38] These natural symbols can be transformed in different ways, as, for example, by cultural traditions and the fantasy of patients, but their original form can be excavated through analytical psychology. Thus the circle or maṇḍala archetype can occur with substantive additions and accretions, but the circle itself remains unchanged.

One of Jung's most insightful concepts is that of the shadow, a key archetype that represents the dark side of the personal unconscious or psyche, which can manifest itself in various apparitional forms. In general, a man's shadow is personified by another man, a woman's by another woman or perhaps by the witch or the devil. "The encounter with the dark half of the personality, or 'shadow,' comes about of its own accord in any moderately thorough treatment" (PA, 31). So is the interesting notion of *anima*, the female within us males; and the *animus*, the male component within the female psyche, both of which provide a vehicle for human beings to revert in their dreams to a primordial archetype of androgyny.[39] These latter ideas seem to be rooted, much more than other archetypes, in human hereditary transmission.

A striking feature of archetypes is that they are "capable of endless development and differentiation" and therefore it is possible for one "to be more developed or less" (PA, 11). Thus the maṇḍala is the most complex because it expresses more fully than any other archetype the union of opposites. But it is a mistake to say that the maṇḍala archetype is exclusively Buddhist. "It seems to me beyond question that these Eastern symbols originated in dreams and visions, and were not invented by some Mahayana church father. On the contrary, they are among the oldest religious symbols of humanity," found in Christian as well as pagan thought, and may even have existed in Paleolithic times (PA, 96).

In Europe it is alchemy that attempts the reconciliation of opposites, as we have already seen. But this, in turn, produces another complication: Jung realizes that the conjunction of opposites is practiced in the laboratory by alchemists, not in normal conditions. Therefore, psychologically speaking, the alchemist "had no opportunity to identify himself with the archetypes as they appeared, since they were projected immediately into the chemical substance." An unclear statement: the alchemist creates the archetypes from chemical substances, but cannot relate psychologically to the product he has created, if indeed Jung is correct that the alchemical process represents a more general feature of the unconscious. "The disadvantage of this situation was that the alchemist was forced to represent the incorruptible substance as a chemical product—an impossible undertaking which led to the downfall of alchemy" and the rise of chemistry (PA, 37). Jung's account makes it clear that the alchemist was familiar with archetypal images in their sketches and drawings. Given his theory, alchemists would inevitably have dreamt about them, but apparently they could not consciously relate to what they dreamt and drew to their work in the laboratory, except unconsciously. Therefore it is left to Jung to resurrect the psychic meaning of the chemical union of opposites, missed by the alchemists.

Just as the alchemist joins together chemical substances in metals to create gold, so does the therapist who conjoins opposites to create wholeness. Moreover, while in alchemy the experimenter tries to make gold through chemical processes, the goal was not really gold but the discovery of the philosopher's stone, which would open up the world of occult knowledge. "In searching for it the alchemist was endeavoring to liberate the spirit believed to be congealed in matter, and in so doing preserving the bridge to nature—i.e. the unconscious psyche—which the Church, with its emphasis on sinfulness, was speedily destroying."[40] The therapist is the alchemist, but with a difference: one can dream archetypes, even the archetype of the self, but that would not necessarily lead to psychic or personal development without the intervention of the therapist who liberates the patient from the grip of a neurosis, most often through the analysis of his archetypal dreams. For the European alchemist, the philosopher's stone represented many meanings, among them the dominant idea of the *unio oppositorum* of body or matter and spirit, Adam and Eve, and many such conjunctions that then go to form a whole. Jung appropriates this powerful symbolism in the model of the therapist as alchemist who finds the symbolical stone in the unconscious, and the physician's alchemical task is to bring about a conjunction of opposites and realize the wholeness of the self as the goal of therapy.

Jung's idea of the archetypes of the collective unconscious led him, as Frieda Fordham rightly says, to the "natural religious function" that he thought human beings possess.[41] Thus, archetypes of the collective unconscious can be shown empirically to be the equivalents of religious dogmas" and they are found in some shape or form in all known religions because the conscious mind works and reworks these primordial images to constitute known religious beliefs (PA, 17). Hence archetypal dreams are so profound that they are "big dreams," a phrase that became popular with later dream theorists. It also seems that Jung is continuing his arguments with Freud, for whom religions are illusions, projections into the cosmos of familial images. Nevertheless, even if Jung is right that religions are built on archetypes, and, further, if archetypes are *not* the equivalents of religious beliefs, an idea he also affirmed, then specific religious beliefs still remain illusions (but not psychotic delusions) insofar as they are built on empirically demonstrable archetypes.[42]

Jung, as did Freud, noted that intensity of religious emotion can be canalized and sublimated into great creative art, just as it can be channeled into acts of unspeakable cruelty. The latter concern appears in *Answer to Job* (1952) and in his later thought where, like Blake, he sees the destructive and amoral side of God alongside the good. Yet, reading his Jung's work as a totality, Jung much downplays the destructive element of numinous archetypes, owing to the inherent paradox contained in the very idea of the numinous, which by definition cannot entail violence and evil.[43] Therefore, for Jung, any really good church provides outlets and ways of dealing with violence and cruelty when it arises. But is this true? Surely the experience of the Inquisition and the terrible wars conducted with the approval of churches point to the simplicity of such a position. Although Jung is not explicitly a believer in formal or orthodox Christianity, I shall later show that he did in all likelihood engage in a personal reformulation of Christianity, alchemy, and Indian religions and affirmed atheism and nonbelief as deadly things. In *Psychology and Religion* (1938), he made the point that "it would be a regrettable mistake if anybody should understand my observations to be a kind of proof of the existence of God. They prove only the existence of an archetypal image of the Deity, which to my mind is the most we can assert psychologically about God."[44] Yet, from a therapeutic point of view, many neuroses can be cured if a nonbeliever experiences a genuine conversion and goes back to the church to which he originally belonged. But what about those who do not wish to return to the church? Atheists and agnostics can also be cured if they open themselves up to an understanding of their dreaming archetypes, providing some hope for the hopeless.

Jung's discussion of this large question of cure led him gradually to the key theory of the "individuation process," the search for the other mysterious entity, "the whole man" or "wholeness" that we have already briefly mentioned, requiring the forging of creative links between the conscious and unconscious aspects of the psyche. Thus "it is the prime task of all education (of adults) to convey the archetype of the God-image, or its emanations and effects, to the conscious mind" (PA, 12). The mediatory archetype is the self, perhaps derived from the Upaniṣadic version that was also important to Blavatsky, namely, the idea that Self (*Brahman*) is the god within (*ātman*). Thus: "The experience could also be formulated as the finding of the God within or the full experience of the archetype of the self" (PA, 76). For modern man living under the shadow of the death of God, the solution is stated in *Psychology and Religion*: "A modern mandala is an involuntary confession of a peculiar mental condition. There is no deity in the mandala, and there is no submission or reconciliation to a deity. The place of the deity seems to be taken by the wholeness of man."[45] If so, the goal of the analyst is to help the patient to achieve the "individuation process," the search for wholeness, and this search, as always with Jung, must lead to the realization of the self. This central concern with the self is neatly stated in the following definitive statement: "The symbols of the process of individuation that appear in dreams are images of an archetypal nature which depict the centralizing process or the production of a new center of personality. . . . I call this center the "self," which should be understood as the totality of the psyche. The Self is not only the center, but also the whole circumference which embraces both conscious and unconscious; it is the center of this totality, just as the ego is the center of consciousness" (PA, 41).

This gives hope to sensitive atheists, provided they can creatively interpret (with the help of the therapist) the meanings of the archetypes of the self as they appear in dreams. Jung is at pains to show that the term *individual* in no way implies *individualism* or being ego-centered or egotistical. On the contrary, the individuated person is aware of his own uniqueness, such that in the therapeutic process the patient is "alone with his own self, or whatever else one chooses to call the objectivity of the psyche. The patient must be alone if he is to find out what it is that supports him when he can no longer support himself. Only this experience can give him an indestructible foundation" (PA, 28). Although alone, Jung's unique and, I might add, rare individual is sensitive of his bond with others.

Individuation and wholeness in this sense occur for the most part during the second half of adult existence, the first given to marriage, the bringing up of children, work, social obligations, and where, to use a Freudian metaphor, the world dominated by anangke or scarcity and want prevail. Often enough, around age forty, these no longer satisfy, and depression and mental illness might occur. Then a person begins the search for wholeness that endows meaning to existence by tapping the resources of the unconscious. Jung sees this as a quest or a journey during which "the traveler must first meet with his shadow, and learn to live with this formidable and terrifying aspect of himself: there is no wholeness without the recognition of the opposites. . . . If he is fortunate he will in the end find 'the treasure hard to attain,' the diamond body, the Golden Flower, the lapis, or whatever name and guise have been chosen to designate the archetype of wholeness, the self," thus universalizing the spiritual quest as did Blavatsky.[46] Insofar as atheists also could participate in this process of recovering wholeness, I would say that Jung provides for them a model of "secular spirituality." For Jung, the quest for wholeness is a difficult road because during crises the mind, while in sleep and in fantasy, is battered by all sorts of images that can drive one mad. I shall later show that the crises in the latter half of one's life are based on Jung's own experience of his mental breakdown and recovery after his break with Freud in 1913 and the start of recovery in around 1916, when he was forty-one! Insofar as wholeness cannot be achieved without suffering, Jung is aligning himself with the great tradition of mystical suffering in Christian penitential religion. Jung has now become the high priest of the cult of the self.

Jung strongly believed that it is possible for a person to identify with an archetype, but that too is a futile quest because the archetype also can become "inflated," and one might develop "an archetypal personality." Dreams, however, can creatively bring together archetypes, even without the conscious awareness of the dreamer, as was the case with the dream series of Wolfgang Pauli. In his case, as with other sensitive dreamers, "consciously the dreamer has no inkling of all this. But in his unconscious he is immersed in this sea of historical associations, so that he behaves in his dreams as if he were fully cognizant of these curious excursions into the history of the human mind. He is in fact an unconscious exponent of an autonomous psychic development, just like the medieval alchemist or the classical Neo-Platonist. Hence one could say—*cum grano salis*— that history could be constructed just as easily from one's own unconscious as from the actual texts" (PA, 86). Outside the extraordinary idea that history can be reconstructed from dream texts, albeit with a pinch of salt, a question I will take up later, there is a problem with Jung's elitism that effectively denies any creative understanding of archetypes except for unique individuals, especially those seeking guidance under a Jungian therapist who is, in effect, a living representation of the archetype of "the wise old man." Why so? Because "no doubts can exist in the herd" and, worse, "the masses are blind brutes as we know to our cost," echoing what might seem to be Nietzsche's more dubious ethics (PA, 481).[47]

Contrary to popular adaptations of his work, Jung believes that symbols emerging from the unconscious can take "grotesque and horrible forms." It is therefore necessary to have the therapist as guide, the person who himself has taken the same road and has the experience to calm the patient's turmoil (PA, 32). In confronting one's shadow or shadowed forms, the therapist guides the patient and helps him to tie the unconscious forces with consciousness and reconcile opposites. Obviously the Jungian guru is available only to those who are neurotic and seek a Jungian therapist. Consequently one might ask, what happens to the rest of us? Hence, I think, the shortcuts taken by post-Jungians, new age religions, and all those movements using the path of dreams as the royal road to wholeness. Jung's own answer to us is not very satisfactory:

> The psychological elucidation of these images, which cannot be passed over in silence or blindly ignored, leads logically into the depths of religious phenomenology. The history of religion in its widest sense (including therefore mythology, folklore, and primitive psychology) is a treasure house of archetypal forms from which the doctor can draw helpful parallels and enlightening comparisons for the purpose of calming and clarifying a consciousness that is all at sea. It is absolutely necessary to supply these fantastic images that rise up so strange and threatening before the mind's eye with some kind of context so as to make them more intelligible.
>
> (PA, 32–33)

Here lies the big gap between Blavatsky and Jung. Blavatsky, in *The Secret Doctrine,* produced a powerful ideology of the consciousness all at sea for a large, educated middle class, whereas Jung provides a therapy that only a very few can afford. Jung was sometimes contemptuous of Theosophy, precisely on the grounds that it encouraged naive beliefs, but he could not provide a theory of religion without a concomitant faith, even though he believed that faith is necessary for religion and affirmed that if religion permitted the reconciliation of opposites then it would serve us well.[48] This implies that most of mankind (the herd) is doomed to an unwholesome existence of unwholeness or nonwholeness. Nowadays, however, therapists influenced by Jung open up their practice to a much larger clientele, and, unsurprisingly, the Jungian quest for wholeness becomes a major preoccupation that transcends their rootedness in Jung's own thought.

Further, there is another unanswered question. Jung and Jungians express the positive nature of wholeness and the reconciliation of opposites, but what about the negativity of wholeness? That is, even intolerant fundamentalist religions are adept at reconciling opposites and claim to be restoring the wholeness of self, lost as result of modernity or postmodernity. One must, it seems to me, try to link up the idea of individuation and wholeness with its negative opposite, as in *Answer to Job,* written eight years after *Psychology and Alchemy.*

Jung is highly critical of the externals of Christianity, and religion in general, because they have "all God outside" and do not experience him in the soul (PA, 11). The word *soul* in Greek, we know, means "psyche," and psyche is, for Jung, the unconscious. Jung's dilemma is simply this: he constantly emphasizes that God is an archetype or at least a numinous refraction of the archetype of the self, of wholeness. But what does this mean in real life where God, if not dead, is believed only in a formal sense by many Christians? Jung is compelled to make a distinction between belief in the externals of religion (where God is dead) and real spiritual understanding of God, where he is alive as the god within, a theme that later became central to new age religions. "The Christ-symbol is of the greatest importance for psychology in so far as it is perhaps the most highly developed and differentiated symbol of the self, apart from the figure of the Buddha" (PA, 19).

Jung asserts that the Christ symbol agrees with "the psychological phenomenology of the self in unusually high degree," but not fully. "The self is a union of opposites par excellence, and this is where it differs essentially from the Christ-symbol. The androgyny of Christ is the utmost concession the Church has made to the problem of opposites," such that the opposition between light and darkness and between good and evil are left "in a state of open conflict," God and the devil becoming separate and irreconcilable entities. Whereas Jung affirms in a Hegelian mood: "The self, however, is absolutely paradoxical in that it represents in every respect thesis and antithesis, and at the same time synthesis" (PA, 19). In contrast with the God symbol, the maṇḍala archetype better expresses the reconciliation of opposites. In the psychic archetype of the self, as manifest in the maṇḍala, even such opposites as good and evil are united, whereas Christian symbolism "leaves the conflict open" (PA, 22). I think it is this issue that is taken up in *Answer to Job,* and that is why I suspect that in later life Jung could be seen as a spiritual person, strongly influenced by his own unique and idiosyncratic falling back on medieval Christian constructs such as that of the *coincidentia oppositorum* of Nicholas of Cusa and the hermeticism of such thinkers as Boehme and Paracelsus and, of course, Blake.

In extolling contraries, Jung is also implicitly criticizing a major visionary thinker, Swedenborg, who believed in correspondences rather than oppositions, that is, the idea that differing realities or realms are not in contradiction with each other but in harmony or correspondence. Swedenborg writes of the correspondence between earthly actions and their heavenly manifestations such that angels were once human and so were spirits in hell. They meet and talk of their experiences in these different realms, which are in correspondence with one another. Unlike Blake, there could not be a marriage of heaven and hell for Swedenborg.[49] Only correspondences matter: for example, the bond of conjugal love on earth is refracted in heaven, such that a happily married person enjoys that conjugal relationship forever. In Swedenborg's terminology, the latter is a "representative" in correspondence with the former. Thus, in his massive *Apocalypse Explained*, he is informed by heaven of the following: "Those who are in true conjugal love, after death, when they become angels, return to their early manhood and youth, the males, however spent with age, becoming young men, and the wives, however spent with age, becoming young women. . . . Marriages on earth correspond to marriages in the heavens; and after death people come into the correspondence, that is, comes from natural bodily marriage into spiritual heavenly marriage, which is heaven itself and the joy of heaven."[50]

While the idea of correspondence has a respectable genealogy in Christianity, this is not true of alchemy, which for Jung "endeavors to fill in the gaps left open by the Christian tension of opposites" (PA, 23). Hence, in contrast with most forms of orthodox Christianity and especially contemporary monotheistic fundamentalisms, Jung could insightfully affirm Boehme's idea that good and evil exists everywhere, even in nature: "In the last resort there is no good that cannot produce evil and no evil that cannot produce good." In Jung's elitist conception of religion, the work of therapy must give meaning and significance to the maṇḍala symbolism and other rich archetypes in the dreams of a patient, helping to calm the "consciousness that is all at sea."

Jung is sympathetic to paradox and equivocation, contradiction and contrast, which he believes underlie every religion including Christianity. "Has it not yet been observed that all religious statements contain logical contradictions and assertions that are impossible in principle, that this is in fact the very essence of religious assertion?" He buttresses his argument by quoting the famed paradox of Tertullian of Carthage, even though, strictly speaking, Tertullian was talking of miracle rather than the kind of paradoxes and "logical contradictions" with which Jung was concerned: "And the Son of God is dead, which is worthy of belief because it is absurd. And when buried He rose again, which is certain because it is impossible" (PA, 15). For Jung, paradox is "one of our most valuable spiritual possessions," and a religion becomes impoverished when it waters down paradoxes. "Non-ambiguity and non-contradiction are one-sided and thus unsuited to express the incomprehensible" (PA, 16).

Now it is time to consider Jung's extraordinary claim that one can read the dream as a historic or archival text in order to reconstruct a past, as he does in the dreams of Wolfgang Pauli. Initially, I will admit that the series of dreams Pauli dreamt are full of existential meaning and significance, but here I want to interrogate Jung to ask: can one read a dream as a historical text? Take Pauli's dream no. 20: "The globe. The unknown woman is standing on it and worshiping the sun" (PA, 84). This is related to an earlier dream no. 7 in which "the veiled woman uncovers her face. It shines like the sun" (PA, 57). The latter "vision" (Jung's usage) is the anima of the dreamer. And the sun is the illumination or enlightenment, quite unlike the rational consciousness that recognizes only "intellectual enlightenment." "It is clear, therefore, that a 'lighting up' of the unconscious is being prepared, which has far more the character of an *illuminatio* than of rational 'elucidation'" (PA, 57).

Most of Pauli's dreams are highly abbreviated or condensed by Jung for purposes of presentation. Unfortunately, this eliminates seemingly inessential details, not quite the way the dreamer himself would have dreamt his dream or recollected it soon after. Going back to the globe dream, the earlier symbols reappear in the later dream, but in "amplified form." Jung says that unless the conscious mind intervenes, the unconscious would simply continue to churn similar images, implying that these dream sequences to be meaningful require a coalition of the archetypal dream and the conscious mind that interprets the dream. Now for the "history" *cum grano salis* that Jung promises us. "The globe probably comes from the idea of the red ball. But whereas this is the sun, the globe is rather the image of the earth, upon which the anima stands worshipping the sun." Thus anima and sun are distinct "which points to the fact that the sun represents a different principle from that of the anima. The latter is a personification of the unconscious, while the sun is a symbol of the source of life and the ultimate wholeness of man" (PA, 84). The play of such opposites constitutes "enantiodromias," a neat term Jung claimed was derived from his reading of Heraclitus.[51] Enantiodromias are "characteristic of dream sequences in general" and, needless to say, of myth (PA, 84).

Note the link up here: non-Jungians might agree that the sun is symbol of the source of life, but many, including myself, would hesitate to see its connection with the "ultimate wholeness of man," although such an existential interpretation would have made sense to the dreamer, helping him to mend his fractured self. Some may agree with Jung that the sun "is an antique symbol that is still very close to [Christians]," while others might wonder how this could have significance for modern Christians, except of course through cultural memory via the movement of archetypes (PA, 84). The sun as the wholeness of man (and a symbol of the self, the signifier of that wholeness) is a Jungian interpolation that seems a forced or an a priori assumption that has no logical connection with the previous segment. The next sentence, however, brings history more clearly into the picture. "The dreamer's anima still seems to be a sun-worshiper, that is to say, she belongs to the ancient world, and for the following reason: the conscious mind with its rationalistic attitude has taken little or no interest in her and therefore made it impossible for the anima to become modernized (or better still Christianized.) It almost seems as if the differentiation of the intellect that began in the Christian Middle Ages, as a result of scholastic training, had driven the anima to regress to the ancient world" (PA, 84–86).

Regression here is not the Freudian one of the movement of the patient's desires to their childhood roots but rather more complex up and down movements of an anima to her historical roots. In this case, the anima symbol of the sun-worshiping woman sends roots, or regresses, to the ancient world. It is true, Jung says, that this anima continued to appear well into the renaissance, but it has the capacity to plunge or regress into an even earlier world, including the world of alchemical texts and experiments, and then to reappear in dreams. But note: the tracing of the historical regressive trajectory cannot be performed by the dreamer alone, even though in this case the dreamer is a highly educated scientist. It needs the skills and knowledge of someone like Jung to excavate the past in this manner. It therefore seems that the history of the archetype can only be known to a person already familiar with the history of the archetype as it appears in myth, in alchemical and other texts. If I did not know the history of the anima worshiping the sun, which is a history that comes from rational knowledge, how would I be able to excavate the history of that very anima? Less educated others must rely on the standard meaning of archetypal images, a catalogue of symbols that permits a modern oneiromancy to develop, for example, in Patricia Garfield's *The Universal Dream Key*.[52] In Pauli's dreams, contrary to Jung, it is the despised rational consciousness that deciphers the history of the anima worshiping the sun. Yet Jung seems to suggest something more: the patient's psyche has picked up the symbolic meaning of the anima through unconscious processes not clearly explained. Perhaps when these processes act in conjunction with the conscious ego the anima can revivify its history in the mind of the dreamer, leading him to re-cognize Jung's idea of individuation and the coming into being of wholeness and the integrated self. But what goes on here cannot be dissected by the rational consciousness as in the Freudian scheme, which, with all its weaknesses, can posit some rules of interpretation whereby one can point out how regression and symbol formation occur. Jung, though, has reasons for suspecting Reason in the diagnoses of dreams, yet the diagnosis itself can and must be stated in rational terms.

The historical reconstruction of archetypes is called "archetypal amplification," and this is what lay and professional Jungians and new age thinkers find useful. Amplification is generally "reserved for archetypal or big dreams, dreams more conspicuously involving deep springs of our nature, important events of the life cycle, and archetypal imagery."[53] These images appear sometimes clearly, sometime indirectly, as in the following dream recorded by a pair of Jungian analysts: "Usually [archetypes] present themselves in some fragment or variation of their theme and/or in a contemporary frame of reference. Thus a dreamer was warned by an electrician that he might be accidentally executed by a high tension wire if he did not stop fooling around. This was his symbolic encounter with the transpersonal lord of the thunderbolt and ruler of energies, Zeus."[54] Many Jungians and new age thinkers will probably agree with this interpretation, even though it would seem farfetched to some of us. A Freudian may interpret the dream as an expression of guilt feelings (and so could a Jungian). In fact, any kind of dream analyst will find it easy to interpret this dream within his or her own frame of reference or theory. And, unlike the slow process of Freudian therapy, patients might find a real attractiveness in being in touch with their historic past, in this case the Greek. Once again, I see Jung and Jungians engaged in a kind of "secular spirituality" that is meaningful to both patient and therapist, if not to the author of the present essay.

Sometimes interpretations by Jungians are plain nonsense, as, for example, the following dream reported by Edward Whitmont. "A middle-aged businessman in a state of depression dreamed: I was in a bed with a young girl and had just finished intercourse. Then I heard a voice saying in Hungarian—my mother tongue—that I did not deserve the *fa* or *fasz*. I was not sure which, perhaps both." Here is part of an extended and reasonable interpretation of the first part by Whitmont. "In Hungarian *fa* means wood, *fasz* means penis. Taken on the personal level, allegorically this dream might show the dreamer that he undervalues sexuality." But then the analyst says that in this particular dreamer "there was no question of any repression of sexuality or masculine aggressiveness." He "was a self-confident and successful go-getter and felt himself quite deserving of his successes both in and out of bed." But irrespective of Whitmont's misplaced assumption of sexual potency in go-getters, this particular dream yields a historical dimension. Here is Whitmont's "amplification" whereby the dream opens a new dimension of historical understanding:

The phallus that is also wood is a widespread cult object. At the spring festival Indian men dance with wooden phalli. In ancient Egypt the wooden phallus represented the generative power of Osiris, restored to life by Isis from death and dismemberment; his natural phallus was lost and Isis substituted a wooden one by means of which he begot a child, Horus, on her. The wooden phallus, then, is not naturally, unconsciously and automatically grown but deliberately created. It signifies creativity that is not of the flesh, of natural being, but of the striving of the spirit, of immortality. An analogous image is found in the phallus carved in antique grave monuments bearing the inscription 'Mortis et vitae locus' (the place of death and life). Purportedly this is a replica of the phallus which Dionysius, the god who dies and is reborn, erected before the portals of Hades.[55]

The hodgepodge history and the ethnography are badly dated, perhaps derived from Frazer and other late-nineteenth-century ethnologists. I cannot expect it to appeal to any but a very naive patient. And who is to know whether the simplistic characterization of the "Indian" who dances with the wooden phallus refers to Amerindians, South Asians, or some other brand of Indians?[56]

Now let me get back to the dreams of Wolfgang Pauli and their significance for the popular understanding of Jung. Jung had with him over a thousand of Pauli's dreams, but used only about four hundred. "I asked one of my pupils, a woman doctor, who was then a beginner, to undertake the observance of the process. This went on for five months. The dreamer then continued his observations alone for three months. Except for a short interview at the very beginning, before the commencement of the observation, I did not see the dreamer at all during the first eight months. Thus it happened that 355 of the dreams were dreamed away from any personal contact with myself," and this Jung thought helped Pauli to avoid knowing Jung's own views of archetypes (PA, 42).

This Jungian posture seems to me extraordinary naive. Young Pauli surely knew something about Jung's theory beforehand, as David Lindorff clearly demonstrates.[57] And more so after the initial dreams under the supervision of Jung's pupil Erna Rosenbaum, who was being analyzed by Jung while she was analyzing Pauli! After the first major round, it is not surprising that the patient would continue to dream Jungian dreams and write them down, many of them serial dreams, developing one theme after another, as with the series of dreams of the globe and the sun. Jung's naïveté was shared by Freud as well and concerns the well-known fact that, irrespective of theory or therapy, patients belonging to a particular therapeutic school will dream the dreams incumbent on that school. This is not to deny the significance of such dreams for the dreamer or for the therapeutic outcome. Indeed, I would say that successful outcome depends on the patient's acceptance of the therapist's interpretation. The patient and therapist jointly give existential meaning and significance to the interpretation, weaving the interpretation into his or her troubled life history. This is true of any form of "ritualized" curing, whether Freudian, Jungian, shamanic, or whatever.

Anthony Shafton rightly says, "It is not misleading to speak of Jung as spiritual teacher."[58] Or, as a discerning disciple and acolyte Jolande Jacobi put it, "Apart from its medical aspect, Jungian psychotherapy is thus a system of education and spiritual guidance, an aid to the forming of personality." She adds significantly: "Only a few are willing and able to travel a path of salvation."[59] I would add that Jung's spirituality is an oblique answer to Nietzsche: if god is dead, spirituality as the way of life of Jesus still remains open, as Nietzsche himself thought in *The Anti-Christ*. But more than this: Jung gave a famous seminar on Nietzsche's *Zarathustra* during the period May 1934 to January 1939.[60] Here, he says, when God is dead, the archetype is not extinguished because it reappears as the wise old man "to give birth to a new truth" and "that is what Nietzsche meant Zarathustra to be."[61] And so is Nietzsche's Superman, who is a kind of replacement for God;[62] and God is another replacement for the Jungian archetype of the "wise old man," as indeed the imagined Jung was for many Jungians.

Underlying these statements is that the god archetype is still within us, and we can await its resurrection or realization in some numinous guise or other.[63] And for Jung's disciples and followers, "spirituality" can be expressed either in eclectic religious form or in a secular guise that taps the creative sources of archetypes and the potentialities of the psyche. Once again it is Jacobi who puts this well. After listing a series of universal archetypes, she opens up a space for "secular spirituality," or, in her case at least, to give added meaning to her religious faith: "In every single individual psyche they [archetypes] can awaken to new life, exert their magic power, and condense into a kind of 'individual mythology,' which presents an impressive parallel to the great traditional mythologies of all peoples and epochs, concretizing as it were their origin, essence, and meaning and throwing new light on them."[64] No wonder then that Jungian therapy can be "a way of healing and a way of salvation." That is, in addition to healing psychic ills "it knows the way and has the means to lead the individual to his 'salvation,' to the knowledge and fulfillment of his own personality, which has always been the aim of spiritual striving."[65] Salvation in this sense is self-knowledge and the deep (one might say "spiritual") understanding of one's inner experience. This side of Jung opens a path to a more popular version of Jungian spirituality taken up by new age religion and by recent Christian reformulations of Jung.[66]

Although Jung did not idealize aristocratic values as Nietzsche did, he certainly applauded the solitary individual. Yet, unlike Blavatsky, Jung does not create a new religion for modern man but instead opens up a space for modern forms of spirituality to develop by drawing on all existing religions, especially mystical and apophatic Christianity, European hermeticism and alchemy, supplemented by Buddhism, Vedantic Hinduism and all manner of pagan and ancient beliefs. This is not all that difficult to do, because, for him, archetypes appear in all these forms of the religious life. And, like the medieval alchemist whom he idealizes, he also puts together from bits and pieces of the world's religions a form of spiritual wholeness, a kind of modern-day philosopher's stone that can never by itself constitute a path to salvation in any *religious* sense.

Let me now give one instance of many where Jung deals with the future of religion that bears his own stamp as a prophet. Max Zeller, one of Jung's disciples, was concerned with the consequences of World War II and the terrible burden of work where he had to deal with twenty or forty patients. He asks himself: "What are we doing, all of us [analysts]?"[67] Then in a hasty meeting with Jung, he mentions the following dream: "A temple of vast dimensions was in the process of being built. As far as I could see ahead, behind, right and left there were incredible numbers of people building on gigantic pillars. I, too, was building on a pillar. The whole building process was in its very first beginnings, but the foundation was already there, the rest of the building was starting to go up, and I and many others were working on it."[68]

In relation to Zeller's concerns, one would think that this dream is hugely overdetermined by the devastation of Europe (though not Jung's Switzerland) and the need for building a new Europe. Beyond that is Zeller's personal concern: tired of seeing endless patients, Zeller dreams of a renewal of Jungian psychology, a building that he and others are going to construct. But Jung's answer ignores these immediate concerns and deals with the synchronistic significance of the dream in predicting the future: "Ja, you know, that is the temple we all build on. We don't know the people because, believe me, they build in India and China and Russia and all over the world. That is the new religion. You know how long it will take until it is built?" When Zeller claimed not to know, Jung replied: "About six hundred years." And when Zeller asked how he knew, Jung's messianic response reminds us of Blavatsky's own future for Theosophy: "From dreams. From other people's dreams and from my own. This new religion will come together as far as we can see." Zeller wished him good-bye and adds: "there was the answer to my question what we, as analysts, are doing."[69]

Sometimes history, oneiromancy, and a kind of Blakean recapitulation of past historic scenarios come together in Jung. One of Jung's most fascinating mantic dreams occurred when he had built a house, or "Tower," by the lake in Bollingen near Zurich to which he could escape from his family home in Küsnact. He first envisaged it on the model of an African round hut because "primitive huts concretize an idea of wholeness," in this case a place where animals and humans can live together as his later experience in various parts of Africa in 1925 seemed to confirm (MDR, 224). On the basis of this idea, he created a two-story structure that was completed in 1923, two months after the death of his mother, and then he added a central structure in 1927. Finding this too primitive as well, Jung had another annex to the tower in 1931 where he could temporarily become a "homeless one," idealizing, as he often did, the space of solitude and the rejection of modern amenities, such as electricity and running water. This was even before he went to India in 1939, when he became familiar with people who had in their houses a small curtained off space into which the occupants could retreat to meditate. "I felt the Tower as in some way a place of maturation—a maternal womb or a maternal figure in which I could become what I was, what I am, and will be" (MDR, 225).

And here is the fascinating dream of 1924 after the first part of the tower had been completed, which suggests to me once again the power of the manifest dream:

> I awoke to the sound of soft footsteps going around the Tower. Distant music sounded, coming closer and closer, and then I heard voices laughing and talking. I thought, "Who can be prowling around? . . ." I opened the shutters—all was still. There was no one in sight, nothing to be heard—no wind—nothing at all.
>
> "This is really strange," I thought. I was certain that the footsteps, the laughter and the talk, had been real. But apparently I had only been dreaming. . . . I fell asleep again—and once more the same dream began: once more I heard footsteps, talk, laughter, music. At the same time I had a visual image of several hundred dark-clad figures, possibly peasant boys in their Sunday clothes, who had come down from the mountains and were pouring in around the Tower, on both sides, with a great deal of loud trampling, laughing, singing and playing of accordions. Irritably, I thought, "This is really the limit! I thought it was a dream and now it turns out to be reality." At this point I woke up.
>
> (MDR, 229–30)

Once again he opened the shutters, but, as before, everything was still.

The whole dream experience seemed real, but initially Jung could make nothing of it except that the peasant boys had come to see his tower. He ignored or dismissed the context of the dream as "compensation" for someone living alone, in silence, and receptive to communications from the past of the sort he had already experienced and documented in the Black and Red Books. Instead he felt compelled to recognize the dream as a reality, a "synchronistic" phenomenon where, in this case, Jung sees a scenario from the past through his "bodily eye" as with Christian penitents. Jung mentions two possible sources for the scenario. First, in a later reading he found an instance of a writer of a seventeenth-century chronicle who, while climbing a mountain, "was disturbed one night by a procession of men who poured past his hut on both sides, playing music and singing—precisely what I had experienced at the Tower" (MDR, 230). The writer was told that this was Wotan's army of departed souls. Second, "There actually existed, as I discovered, a real parallel to my experience. In the Middle Ages just such gatherings of young men took place. These were the Reisläufer (mercenaries) who usually assembled in spring, marched from Central Switzerland to Locarno, met at the Casa di Ferro in Minusio and then marched together. . . . My vision, therefore, might have been one of these gatherings which took place regularly each spring when the young men, with singing and jollity, bade farewell to their native land" (MDR, 231). Although neither of these examples says they were peasant boys, this might not be a serious objection because all these examples illustrate celebratory occasions. More seriously, he ignores the possibility that he might also have "discovered" this cultural phenomenon before his dream and the dream recaptured not as an event from the historic past but from Jung's reading of that past. I shall later show that Jung's vision, even though it might be from his reading, does not invalidate synchronicity or the acausal psychic interconnection between the dream and the historical event. Yet Jung's examples from his reading surely had its parallel in other European cultures, that is, of persons celebrating spring festivals and similar occasions, and, if so, would it be unusual for Jung, or any sensitive European dreamer, to experience this kind of vivid dream as a powerful one, perhaps helping him relate to similar events from the past as Jung did? If so, the dream is not so much a recapitulation of a historic past but Jung's imagination linking his dream with his historic past.

It should be apparent now that Jung's later theory and practice of analytical psychology contains an oneiromancy. I want to develop this aspect of Jung's thought further because it went into popular dream theory, dream therapy, and new age spirituality after the cultural revolution of the 1960s. Jung exemplifies in his work the larger cultural move in Europe and the U.S. that increasingly began to place emphasis on dreams, rather than on the visionary experience per se. For him, however, dreams come close to what we know as dream-visions, and Jung himself uses the two terms, *dream* and *vision*, interchangeably. The reason is quite simple: in his thinking, dreams have such deep meaning and noetic significance that they could be equated with vision, and it is this thinking that went into later Euro-American dream theory and practice.

ON SYNCHRONICITY

The theoretical bridge that connects dreams and oneiromancy is Jung's controversial idea of "synchronicity," which he developed in conjunction with his gifted patient Wolfgang Pauli, namely, the idea that events can be related in an acausal manner, quite unlike most of the physical sciences of his time, which would discount such relationships.[70] In his important paper "On Synchronicity," written in 1951, Jung says: "As its etymology shows, this term has something to do with time or, to be more accurate, with a kind of simultaneity. Instead of simultaneity we could also use the concept of a meaningful coincidence of two or more events, where something other than the probability of chance is involved."[71] Victor Mansfield, the Jungian physicist whom we met earlier, places it in the larger perspective of the new quantum mechanics that began to be developed during Pauli's time.[72] Mansfield recognizes that quantum mechanics does not prove synchronicity, but, by blurring the distinction between mind and matter it provides a philosophical or metaphysical justification or a provocative foundation for defending the reality of synchronistic phenomena as well as much of Buddhist metaphysics, such as "conditioned genesis" and its attendant doctrine of emptiness. Thus synchronicity can exist when a psychic and material or physical event are linked together in an acausal manner and further interconnected through meaning, especially where an event in the outside world is meaningfully connected to a psychic state.

To give a simple illustration: some time back, my research assistant came to my room and mentioned a shrine of an ancestral female deity in the town of Kosgoda, the word *kosgoḍa* literally meaning "a cluster of jackfruit trees." A few minutes later a female acquaintance entered our room bringing us a gift of jackfruit, and my assistant exclaimed, "Fantastic, what a coincidence!" A Jungian explanation would discount the idea of coincidence and instead posit that the two events are connected in an acausal manner and illustrates "synchronicity."[73] Mansfield is critical of Jung relating synchronicity to paranormal phenomena but such concerns are central to Jung's thought as it is for many adherents of new age religion. Jung would also include situations wherein identical thoughts or dreams appear or occur in different places at the same time, as with telepathic dreams, or when a sensitive visionary like Blake or Swedenborg senses in a flash an event occurring in the world outside.[74] Jung's notion of synchronicity contains a further implication that some key events from the past, especially archetypal ones, are ineradicable and can be intuited directly or indirectly by the gifted visionary. Jung's early work on astrological predictions would be entirely consonant with his broad conception of synchronicity.[75]

Mansfield uses two of Jung's examples of synchronicity to illustrate the idea of meaningful and acausal connectivity, including what he calls Jung's paradigmatic example—the case of the golden scarab—which highlights both synchronicity and archetype. It deals with a highly educated patient who intellectualized everything and was therefore psychologically inaccessible for treatment purposes. Her weapon of resistance was Cartesian rationalism and "an impeccably 'geometrical' idea of reality," another feature of Descartes's thought. Jung says:

> Well, I was sitting opposite her, with my back to the window, listening to her flow of rhetoric. She had an impressive dream the night before, in which someone had given her a golden scarab—a costly piece of jewelry. While she was still telling me this dream, I heard something behind me gently tapping on the window. I turned round and saw that it was a fairly large flying insect that was knocking against the window pane from outside in the obvious effort to get into the dark room. This seemed to me very strange. I opened the window immediately and caught the insect in the air as it flew in. It was a scarabacid beetle, or common rose-chafer (*Cetonia aurata*), whose gold-green colour most nearly resembles that of the golden scarab. I handed this beetle to the patient with the words, "Here is your scarab." This experience punctured the desired hole in her rationalism and broke the ice of her intellectual resistance.[76]

Mansfield rightly rules out accident, coincidence, and chance and also any form of causal connection between the reciting of the dream and the entry of the live scarab. But does this instance provide genuine evidence, if not proof, of synchronicity? I want to suggest that a *causal* connection might well exist between the two events, if we recognize that this patient, like many others who appear in my essay, is gifted with an exceptional, snail-horn sensitivity to sight, smell, and hearing, if not to the other two senses. Contrary to Jung's account of the two events bound together by synchronicity, I suggest that it was not Jung who first noticed the scarab knocking on the window. It was the patient herself who with her acute senses heard the presence of the creature—not consciously, of course. Her "awareness" of the scarab's presence was the associational cue that led her to recount the dream and not the other way around. But Jung thought differently: soon after the patient's dream he notices the scarab and, presto, he creates a hole in her rationalistic outlook and simultaneously proves the reality of synchronicity. Perhaps another analyst would not even have noticed the presence of the scarab, but Jung who had a scarab dream-vision in 1913, already knows that the scarab is an archetypal symbol of rebirth, in this case an awakening from a prior state of ignorance into a new kind of knowledge or insight (see p. 419).

In my opinion the other well-known case of attributed synchronicity cited by Mansfield follows, according to my reinterpretation, the identical logic of causality. "I walk with a woman patient in a wood. She tells me about the first dream in her life that had made an everlasting impression upon her. She had seen a spectral fox coming down the stairs in her parental home. At this moment a real fox comes out of the trees not forty yards away and walks quietly on the path ahead of us for several minutes. The animal behaves as if he were a partner in the human situation."[77] Is this also an example of acausal connection through meaning? Or, as in the previous case, does the patient sense the presence of the fox *before* the creature approaches the walkers, through her sensitivity to sound and smell and maybe her familiarity with the woods? Her special awareness then produces an immediate association that leads her to recount her dream of the spectral fox. The real fox then appears on the scene, and, because he is familiar with walkers in the woods, he calmly walks ahead of the two humans, behaving, according to Jung, "as if he were a partner in the human situation." The animal seems to have outfoxed the humans.

Thus, while I believe that some of Jung's insights into "synchronistic phenomena" are justified, many seem to me quite improbable. One kind of synchronistic phenomena is so common that it might be necessary to give it a separate designation. I refer to a situation where, to use Blavatsky's term, two minds are in "psycho-magnetic rapport," or, as Freud put it, "a kind of psychical counterpart to wireless telegraphy" occurs when two minds are in conjunction with each other.[78] Let me label this meeting of minds "psychic coevality," or simply "coevality" or "coeval phenomena," in contrast to Jung's more improbable idea of "synchronicity."[79] Take the case of the psychoanalytic situation of transference and countertransference occurring in the close physical confines of the therapeutic encounter. According to standard psychoanalytic theory, the patient unconsciously projects an image of a significant other on to the therapist; and the therapist might then project on to the patient his own countertransference. Projection as a psychic mechanism operates here, without doubt, but in the larger context of a communion of minds. One might say that the therapist and patient are in psychic communion with each other ("psycho-magnetic rapport"), providing insights into each other's hidden conflicts. Jung sensitively recognized this when he said that the "doctor and patient thus find themselves in a relationship founded on mutual unconsciousness," so much so that the patient's illness might be transferred to the doctor![80] A coeval phenomenon, in our limited usage, is an extreme instance of "transference" whereby ideas might be transferred from one person to another or shared among persons in close psychic communion. Freud had little sympathy with the occult, yet, on the basis of several fascinating case studies he was willing to grant "that there is such a thing as thought-transference."[81] Unlike Jung, Freud thought that genuine dream telepathy entailing the complicated dream work does not occur, but sometimes the condition of sleep permits thought-transference when "the mind remains passive and receptive," a point I have made for a variety of similar experiences![82]

Unfortunately, there are several problems with Freud's position. He makes the connection between telepathic thought transference and his own version of the transference and countertransference in both the patient and the analyst. But he did not push this line of investigation far enough. A few of Freud's early disciples did take up the challenge, particularly Helene Deutsch, who believed that the analysand's mind is *passive* during the analytic session, but also thought that the analyst has a duty to "receive passively the material" that the patient offers to him. "During psychoanalysis the psychic contact between analyst and analysand is so intimate, and the psychic processes that unfold in that situation are so manifold, that the analytic situation may very well include all such conditions which especially facilitate the occurrence of such [telepathic] phenomena."[83] When he is not taking down notes or otherwise involved, the analyst might let his concentration slip and take on the "somnolent" mood of the patient, opening a path for the transfer of ideas from the patient to the doctor. But why the neglect of Freud's early work on psychoanalysis that deals with patient-to-patient telepathy as well as his insights into the mind-reading capacity of "prophets"? I suspect this is due to the recognition that the back–and–forth telepathic communication of minds would seriously question the "objectivity" of the analyst. More importantly, a one-way or two-way telepathic communication of ideas might have drastic implications for the psychoanalytic theory of transference and countertransference.[84] Further, Freud was dismissive of dream telepathy and presumably of dream sharing, which ought to have been treated with the same seriousness and critical acumen as ordinary telepathy, although an unorthodox analyst, Jule Eisenbud, takes them more seriously. If telepathic transfer of ideas and thoughts occur, why should not dreams be transferred from minds engaged in psychic rapport as with Lise and Alyosha in the Dostoyevsky quotation of my earlier epigraph? By contrast, Jung was much more sympathetic to such phenomena, and his imprimatur was important for the fillip it gave to the testing and verification of telepathic dreams, as, for example, the experimental work of Montague Ullman.[85]

Therefore it is not Freud but his rebellious disciple Jung who opened the doors of modern oneiromancy by giving instances of dream prognoses of future events. These "forward-looking" or prospective dreams most often warn the dreamer of a disaster to come, not the kind of coeval dream where a hypersensitive person might dream of a terrible disaster to a near and dear one and, sure enough, about the time of the dream, the disaster in fact occurs. Jung records a fascinating case of dream synchronicity when he met a friend on the street, a mountain climber, who related the following dream. "I am climbing a high mountain, over steep snow-covered slopes. I climb higher and higher, and it is marvelous weather. The higher I climb the better I feel. I think, 'If only I could go on climbing like this for ever!' When I reach the summit my happiness and elation are so great that I feel I could mount right up into space. And I discover that I can actually do so: I mount upwards on empty air, and awake in sheer ecstasy." What is striking about this case is that Jung acted very much like a prophet when he warned his friend not to go mountain climbing alone, urging him to take two guides, though his friend scoffed at this idea: "Three months afterwards . . . he went on a climb with a younger friend, but without guides. A guide standing below saw him literally step out into the air while descending a rock face. He fell on the head of his friend, who was waiting lower down, and both were dashed to pieces far below. This was *ecstasis* with a vengeance."[86] Jung simply refuses to accept alternative possibilities outside the prognosticative significance of the dream, such as an unconscious acting out of the dream scenario; or an accident by someone given to taking chances, in dream and in reality, and not all that uncommon among mountain climbers.[87]

Jung records other prognosticative dreams where he believes that the principle of synchronicity operates when "the psyche at times functions outside of the spatio-temporal law of causality" (MDR, 304). Here is Jung dreaming about the death of his wife: "I dreamed that my wife's bed was in a deep pit with stone walls. It was a grave, and somehow had a suggestion of classical antiquity about it. Then I heard a deep sigh, as if someone were giving up the ghost. A figure that resembled my wife sat up in the pit and floated upward. It wore a white gown into which curious black symbols were woven." When he awoke it was three in the morning, and he thought the dream might signify a death. At seven came the news that a cousin of his wife had died in the morning (MDR, 303). This and other examples indicate that Jung joins the ranks of many religious virtuosos who appear in this work and for whom accident, coincidence, and chance do not make sense, although for Jung such things can be explained by synchronicity. And, in this case, he ignores the manifest dream of the death of his wife, thereby ignoring its possible connection with his many infidelities, especially the tumultuous relation with his patient and student Sabine Spielrein and the more stable yet peculiar open relation with Toni Wolff—the confidant, friend, and fellow analyst with whom he maintained a continuing intellectual and sexual relationship. His wife, Emma, seriously thought of divorcing her husband on three occasions. Instead of probing his own conscience, Jung delved into the latent synchronistic meanings of the dream.[88]

Perhaps the most powerful of Jung's own prognosticative dreams deal with the night before his mother died, quite unexpectedly, according to him.[89]

> The night before her death I had a frightening dream. I was in a dense, gloomy forest; fantastic boulders lay about among huge jungle-like trees. It was a heroic, primeval landscape. Suddenly I heard a piercing whistle that seemed to resound through the whole universe. My knees shook. Then there were crashings in the underbrush, and a gigantic wolfhound with a fearful, gaping maw burst forth. At the sight of it, the blood froze in my veins. It tore past me, and I suddenly knew: the Wild Huntsman had commanded it to carry away a human soul. I awoke in deadly terror, and the next morning I received news of my mother's passing.
>
> (MDR, 313)

Who would dispute that this is a very powerful nightmarish dream? But the existential significance of the dream depends on the meaning of the dream entering into Jung's "awareness" during the dreaming itself or soon after. The dream revealed to him that the wild huntsman was Wotan, the pre-Christian god whom the missionaries converted into a demon and, like other figures from the past, had been resurrected by German Romanticism. For Jung, Wotan is a manifestation of Mercury or Hermes, "a nature spirit who returned to life again in the Merlin of the Grail legend" and the *spiritus Mercurialis* of the alchemists, ideas he perhaps added on later reflection. The dream not only possesses a synchronicity with the death of his mother but also "says that the soul of my mother was taken into that greater territory of the self which lies beyond the segment of Christian morality, taken into that wholeness of nature and spirit in which conflicts and contradictions are resolved," although the manifest content of the dream does not indicate anything of the sort (MDR, 313–14). Yet the dream contains so much promise that it is virtually certain, had his mother not died, Jung could have incorporated the death of any known person or, for that matter, any disaster anywhere into the meaning of the dream. Further, Jung does not tell us of powerful dreams, which he surely must have had, but that possessed no prognosticative or synchronic significance.

He then uses these synchronistic dreams to make an important qualification. A person nearing death might dream of a myth or mythlike dream. But, instead of being fearful of the dark pit into which he will descend, he might begin to dream a myth of fulfillment whereby the dream conjures up "helpful and enriching pictures of life in the land of the dead." And then, in a marvelous Jungian version of Pascal's wager, he adds: "If he believes in them, or greets them with some measure of credence, he is being just as right and just as wrong as someone who does not believe in them. But while the man who despairs marches towards nothingness, the one who has placed his faith in the archetype [myth] follows the track of life and lives right into his death. Both to be sure remain in uncertainty, but the one lives against his instincts, the other with them" (MDR, 306). Here is Jung almost denying the difficult road to psychic and spiritual wholeness, ignoring the shadow, thereby opening his thought, once again, to new age and other forms of popular religiosity.

It is rare for Jung to move beyond what can be demonstrated empirically through dreams, and he had no doubts whatever about synchronicity. In general he refused to speak about his views of the afterlife except in his letters and in *Memories, Dreams, Reflections*. While *Memories, Dreams, Reflections* gives us details of his life that made sense to his work, there is little concerning his intrapsychic conflicts. Because many of his private journals are inaccessible to us, Jung's intrapsychic life, unlike Freud's, is a closed book. He might have been reluctant to publicly disclose his inner conflicts. Indeed he referred to *Memories, Dreams, Reflections* as "Aniela Jaffé's [editor's] project" and urged that it not be incorporated into his *Collected Works*. But, from our point of view, this work moves from discussions of synchronicity to Jung's more personal views of the afterlife and his visionary experiences. In the dream of his mother's death, she becomes for Jung a perfect incarnation of his ideal of the self. This mother was for him a mysterious figure, and Jung mentions a boyhood experience in which she appeared in visionary form. He used to sleep in his father's room, but from his mother's room came "frightening influences." "One night I saw coming from her door a faintly luminous, indefinite figure whose head detached itself from the neck and floated along in front of it, in the air, like a little moon. This process was repeated six or seven times" (MDR, 18). Now place this childhood vision against the dream of the wild huntsman that heralded his mother's death. The latter dream, on the manifest level, has no reference to his mother but not Jung's interpretation of it.

In his *interpretation*, he turns around the childhood vision of the mother's fractured body, restoring it to wholeness, endowing his mother with the fullness of the self that he so much admired, and then, as we shall soon see, enshrining that maternal wholeness in the tower he built at Bollingen.

JUNG'S PSYCHOSIS: WHEN THE DEAD AWAKEN

> Only those taught by the knowers of Truth can become knowers of Truth themselves, O Goddess. Those who are instructed by the ignorant remain ignorant.
> Only one who is pierced [by the Truth] can pierce [others]; one who is liberated can only release someone bound [in knots]; how can one who is not liberated, ever become a liberator?
>
> —*Kulārnava Tantra*, 13, 123, 124[90]

Jung experienced two major spiritual crises, the first around 1913 at age thirty-eight after his break with Freud, his father figure and guru and later in 1944 when he was sixty-nine. The first was for Jung the more fearful experience, and, like many others, I thought that a more detailed account of his illness would be found in the so-called Red Book that would have described his terrifying illness and might contain what might well be one of the most important documentations of the dark night of the soul. Apparently, neither Jung nor his heirs wanted any of Jung's private life exposed to the public, even though much of his life is now public anyway. It was after this essay was practically completed in its present form that the Red Book was published in a magnificent volume.[91] Even though Jung felt his unconscious fantasies and conflicts were productive for his later creativity, he refrained from public comments on this episode until the famous series of interviews during the period 1956–1958 that went into *Memories, Dreams, Reflections*. Both illness episodes are mentioned in this work, but, though Jung spoke extensively of his later trance illness, his account of the first illness is very sketchily described, without much concern for chronology in a chapter entitled "Confrontation with the Unconscious." But there is no way one can avoid confronting Jung's spiritual crisis, and I will rely mostly on the account in *Memories, Dreams, Reflections*. We now know that the Red Book was based on six earlier texts bound in black leather, now jointly known as the Black Book. The Black Book, as well as other material relevant for understanding Jung's illness, still remains unpublished in the Jung family archives. (See the following note for a detailed discussion of the Red Book.)[92]

Because this crisis, which both he and his colleagues and biographers have defined as a "psychosis," was precipitated by the symbolic killing of a father figure, I cannot avoid dealing with Jung's triangular agonistic relationship with three crucial authority figures in his life. First, there is his own father, the pastor Johann Paul Achilles Jung whom the son perceived as a distant figure in his life and about whom he speaks unfavorably in *Memories, Dreams, Reflections*. Second: another father figure, also for Jung an authoritarian persona, Eugen Bleuler, the director of the Burghölzli Mental Hospital where Jung worked as a junior doctor in 1901 after graduation from medical school at the University of Basel. Bleuler was a very distinguished psychiatrist and the inventor of the term *schizophrenia* (displacing the term *dementia praecox* favored by Emil Kraepelin). He was a strict disciplinarian who imposed a rigorous hospital routine, insisting on doctors being fully teetotalers and encouraging them to eat together with patients and generally act toward them without patronage. Jung worked with Bleuler at Burghölzli for nine years, and their mutual hostility "varied from the occasionally veiled remark to open hostile invective, often before shocked doctors or frightened patients" (BJ, 97). By the end of his stay there, Jung had become a highly respected scholar and psychiatrist, but Bleuler twice refused to recommend him for a professorial position at the university where Jung was privatdozent. A colleague at Burghölzli remembered the two antagonists locked in mortal combat and "fighting to the death" (BJ, 150). At the same time, Jung was indebted to Bleuler because it was his access to patients and later to the doctors who came to work with him at the hospital that was, partly at least, responsible for his early fame. Indeed Jung's first major work on *The Psychology of Dementia Praecox* (1908) was indebted to Bleuler's own seminal work on schizophrenia.

The third father figure for Jung was, of course, Freud. Freud and Jung (and Jung's wife Emma as well) referred to the relationship as one between father and son. Jung was to be Freud's destined heir. Jung chaired the congress held in Salzburg in 1908 that was to form the basis of the International Psychoanalytic Association, and he was appointed by Freud in 1909 as editor of the first major journal, *Jahrbuch für psychoanalytische und psychopathologische Forschungen* (*Yearbook for Psychoanalytical and Psychopathological Research*). The following year he became the life president of the International Psychoanalytic Association. The drama of their conflict has been well described and is I believe rooted in the authoritarianism of both Freud and Jung. Freud himself could scarcely brook dissent, and he wanted disciples to defer to his authority as the founder of psychoanalysis. Jung, for his part, was looking for the father he did not find in Paul Jung. Freud seemed to be such a figure, both loving and yet demanding abjection. Jung also could not get on with older authority figures, and he too, like Freud, wanted disciples. Jung not only demanded allegiance and abjection from his male disciples but would also insult or shame them in his seminars and confrontations. As was the case with Freud, friendships with male friends and colleagues became distant or hostile when disagreement over theoretical or substantive issues arose. The women were different. Jung's seminars were crowded with elite females for whom he provided intellectual stimulation they lacked in their mundane lives. Psychologically speaking, given his relationship with his own father and with Bleuler, the break with Freud seemed almost inevitable, particularly after his increasing disagreement on some of the major tenets of Freudianism. I think the break with Bleuler in 1909 anticipated the break with Freud, the signs of which coincidentally occurred at the same time.

Initially there was the issue of the role of sexuality in the generation of neuroses, especially hysteria, a kind of criticism that Freud was facing from some of his breakaway colleagues like Alfred Adler and from the general public. Jung believed that the libido was the seat of energy and that sexuality was simply one source of energy, not even the primary source. This is a view that Freud could hardly tolerate. Another was Freud's concern that Jung was beginning to believe in the empirical reality of the paranormal. The Freud-Jung letters give us glimpses of the enveloping, though still guarded, tension, as this letter from Freud dated April 16, 1909, suggests: "It is strange that on the very same evening when I formally adopted you as my eldest son and anointed you—*in partibus infidelium* [in the hands of unbelievers]—as my successor and crown prince, you should have divested me of my paternal dignity, which divesting seems to have given you as much pleasure as I, on the contrary, derived from the investiture of your person."[93]

The reference is to Jung's visit to the Freud household, when a huge noise was heard from the bookshelves and Jung attributed it to the kind of poltergeist phenomenon he seemed to have believed in. Jung predicted that a second noise would follow, which it did and without seeming agency. Freud was impressed at the time, but, on reflection, the letter said the noise was simply the product of the creaking boards of his bookshelves, which had to bear the weight of two huge Egyptian steles. Jung, of course, refused to accept such a simple empirical explanation. Even more significant was Jung's developing interest in myth and his conviction that dreams have a mythic component that would help the therapist understand the patient's problems as well as the nature of the unconscious as the repertory of mythic thought. This idea of the relation between myth, dream, and fantasy came from his knowledge of a psychotic patient Emile Schwyzer, admitted to Burghölzli on October 27, 1901, at age forty.[94]

Emile Schwyzer was analyzed by Johann Jacob Honnegar, who was referred to Jung as a patient by Freud and later became Jung's own research assistant, a not unusual combination in early analytic psychology. Honnegar was a talented and extremely intelligent patient, but Jung felt his illness was incurable. It was not surprising then that he escaped from his confinement at Burghölzli and committed suicide in 1911. This patient cum research assistant's patient was Schwyzer, whose delusions commenced when he was in London employed in a small job as a bank messenger. There was a family history of psychosis, but Schwyzer's delusions surfaced only when he was an adult. After he learned English and went to London, he developed hallucinations of being followed. He had informed his family that he did not write to them because they too were following him in London. Schwyzer also believed his family members would be killed by his imagined persecutors. In his delusionary state, he shot himself on the left side of the head and was admitted to a London hospital in 1882, later transferred to a hospital in Surrey where he stayed until 1887, when his parents had him admitted, back home, to a private hospital. Because they could ill afford the expense, Schwyzer was ultimately transferred to Burghölzli. Here he was known as the "solar phallus man" owing to an unusual and recurrent dream that Honneger, his patient therapist, recorded. The various doctors who treated him noted that he could not talk logically (not surprising given the damage to the left brain), although he was a good worker in the hospital kitchen. Most of his conversations were in a kind of archaic language, and his thoughts were expressed through his hallucinations. It was as if hallucinations took the place of rational discourse.

Among his many delusions, Schwyzer thought he was God and that he was obliged to distribute his semen in order to prevent the world from perishing. These visions-hallucinations-delusions were followed by his insistence that he could change the weather. "If asked how he did this, he would reply that the sun had a gigantic phallus, and if he looked at it with eyes half shut and moved his head from side to side, he could make the phallus move, thus creating the wind and, by extension, the weather" (BJ, 175). Because of Jung's interest in myth, he was intrigued by the patient's archaic language and visions and referred to this case in his 1912 work, *Wandlungen und Symbole der Libido*, translated in English as *The Psychology of the Unconscious*. However, I think, there is another unstated reason for Jung's interest. In his childhood, Jung had a dream of a gigantic phallus that also, according to his later interpretation, had a mythic quality (see pp. 414–15). In any case, Jung admitted that he couldn't understand this case until he read two well-known books on Mithraic ritual, Albrecht Dieterich's *Eine Mithrasliturgie* (1903) and another influential work by G. S. R. Mead, *A Mithraic Ritual* (1910). The former described a Mithraic liturgy where "a so-called tube, the origin of the ministering wind [was] hanging down from the disc of the sun" (BJ, 177). Jung also discovered an early German painting that showed a similar tube or hose-pipe descending from heaven where the Holy Ghost in the form of a dove flies down to impregnate Mary. In his 1912 book he mentioned this case and similar ones in order to show that a "universally human characteristic" existed and hence the appearance of similar myths everywhere. Although Freud was also interested in universal symbols, influenced by his student Wilhelm Stekel, who later became another rebel, any notion of myth dreaming and inherited symbolic forms was anathema to him and smacked of what he felt was Jung's preoccupation with "mysticism," a term that had pejorative connotations for Freud. In *The Psychology of the Unconscious,* Jung was now proclaiming the autonomy of his form of psychoanalysis, which would leave Freud's materialistic and empiricist psychology far behind.

"After the parting of the ways with Freud, a period of inner uncertainty began for me. It would be no exaggeration to call it a state of disorientation. I felt totally suspended in mid-air, for I had not yet found my own footing" (MDR, 170). Jung felt that his first obligation was to write down the fantasies that began to occur in 1912, when the confrontation with Freud was coming to a head and then continued for several years afterward. His earliest dreams during this period did not help him to overcome his disorientation. "One fantasy kept returning: there was something dead present, but it was also still alive. For example, corpses were placed in crematory ovens, but were then discovered to be still living" (MDR, 172). Jung says that these fantasies were "resolved" in a later dream of a lane of sarcophagi, some of which came from Merovingian times. In the dream, Jung saw another lane with a row of tombs that reminded him of old church burial vaults. They lay mummified in their antique clothes. One such person was a knight, and when Jung looked at him he moved and unclasped his hands. And then he walked to another body, belonging to the eighteenth century, that also moved when Jung looked at him, then on to a third corpse, dating from the previous century (MDR, 172–73).

Jung confessed to living under "constant inner pressure," admitting that there was "some psychic disturbance" within him, even a schizophrenic episode. He claimed, however, that he had some control over his psychosis, because he could go through the whole of his entire life detachedly and "with particular attention to childhood memories," a Freudian enterprise to which he seemed to have turned in order to check whether there was something in the past that was responsible for his present crisis. But nothing came of it. He then thought he should submit himself to the "impulses of the unconscious" (MDR, 173).[95] Under that decision, the first thing that came up to the surface was a childhood game from his tenth or eleventh year at a time he was passionately involved in playing with building blocks. "I distinctly recalled how I had built little houses and castles, using bottles to form the sides of gates and vaults. Somewhat later I had used ordinary stones, with mud for mortar. These structures fascinated me for a long time. To my astonishment, this memory was accompanied by a good deal of emotion" (MDR, 173). Why the emotion? Because he felt that these acts were creative ones and he must return to them and to that period of childhood, particularly since his adult creativity has dried up. He had to do it even though "it was a painfully humiliating experience to realize that there was nothing to be done except play childish games" (MDR, 174).

Then he began some fascinating activity, recapturing or creatively rebuilding his childhood games. He gathered suitable stones from the lake shore and from the water and soon started to build "cottages, a castle, a whole village" and then added a church but hesitated for awhile to build an altar. One day while searching for stones he found "a red stone, a four-sided pyramid about an inch and a half high" that had been polished by the action of the water. "I knew at once: this was the altar!" Whether he consciously realized or not, the red altar stone was an early representation of the philosopher's stone. He put it in the middle of the dome of the church, but for some reason he recalled "the underground phallus of my childhood dream," when he was between three and four years old and living in his father's vicarage near a castle and a meadow. This was the earliest dream he could recall and one that he could not shake off for a long time.

In this dream he was in the meadow when he suddenly discovered a dark, rectangular stone-lined hole in the ground with a stone stairway leading below, onto which he slowly descended. At the bottom was a round arch enclosed by a green curtain, very sumptuous. He pushed aside the curtain and "saw before me in the dim light a rectangular chamber about thirty feet long." The ceiling and floor were paved with hewn stones, and a red carpet was laid from the entrance to a platform on which lay a magnificent throne. Something was placed on the throne that he took to be a tree trunk twelve to fifteen feet high and about one and a half foot thick, reaching up to the ceiling. "But it was of a curious composition: it was made of skin and naked flesh, and on top there was something like a rounded head with no face and no hair. On the very top of the head was a single eye, gazing motionlessly upward." Above the head was "an aura of brightness," and, while the thing did not move, Jung felt that "at any moment it might crawl off the throne and might creep towards me. I was paralyzed with terror. At that moment I heard from outside and above me my mother's voice. She called out, 'Yes, just look at him. That is the man-eater!'" (MDR, 12) This intensified the child's terror, and he awoke sweating. Jung adds that he could not sleep for many nights afterward, and the memory of the dream continued to haunt him years later. It must be noted that the central symbol of this childhood dream had been drastically and unconscionably changed by Aniela Jaffé and Jung's daughter Marianne and her husband. Jung did not dream of a tree; this was a bourgeois substitution for the huge phallus Jung actually dreamt.[96]

Because Jung was a committed Freudian until his break with the master, it is hard to believe that he missed the obvious oedipal significance of his recollected dream. What seems clear to me is that, following his break with Freud, he gave the childhood dream a radically different interpretation. Because the object was a phallus, he converted it decades later into a ritual phallus, perhaps when he had fully developed the idea that myths and rituals were constituted of archetypes. And, in his blindness or willingness to ignore the Freudian psychodynamics of the dream, he—again much later—thought that while the man-eater was the phallus, "the dark Lord Jesus, the Jesuit, and the phallus were identical." The reference is to Jung's fear that as a child he had associated Jesus with people dressed in black coats led by his own father, the parson, who with others "busied themselves with the black box" or coffin; while the "Jesuit" was a traumatic vision he had of a figure with a black hat and female-looking garb that he identified as a Jesuit (MDR, 9–11).

Continuing his later interpretation he says that the phallus had an "abstract significance" and was enthroned "ithyphallically," that is, phalluslike and upright. The hole in the ground was a grave that in turn was an "underground temple whose green curtain symbolized the *meadow*, in other words the mystery of Earth with her covering of green vegetation" (none of which, however, appeared in the dream itself). And he adds once again, "I do not know where the anatomically correct phallus can have come from. The interpretation of the *orificium urethra* as the eye, with the source of light apparently above it, points to the etymology of the word phallus (shining, bright)." In his youth, presumably before his illness and break with Freud, he felt that the phallus was a "subterranean God," and this image reappeared whenever someone mentioned Jesus. During Jung's youth, Jesus seemed to him the god of death whose love and kindness "which I always heard praised, appeared doubtful to me, chiefly because the people who talked most about 'the dear Lord Jesus' wore black coats and shiny black boots which reminded me of burials"; they were also "my father's colleagues as well as eight of my uncles—all parsons" (MDR, 13). No wonder Jung as a child and youth simply loathed going to church (MDR 19).

Let me now restore the obvious Freudian meanings of this childhood night-mare that Jung refused to acknowledge, which haunted him through the years and reappeared when he was building the village and church, itself a restoration and restitution of a game engaged in around age eleven or twelve. The dream represents the dread of the father, his phallus, and this object is also a "man-eater," a cannibal monster surely familiar to European children from their fairy tales. The phallus is enthroned, and Jung mentions explicitly that it was "a king's throne in a fairy tale" (MDR, 12). Implicit here is the familiar symbolism of king = father, but the father-king is substituted by the horrible, huge, and upright enthroned phallus. It is the mother who tells him that the phallus is a cannibal, and we know from Jung himself that the parental relationship was a bad one. This is not to deny that the father was also occasionally a loving parent, but he represented something else for Jung—the black dressed parsons with their black boots who "busied themselves with the black box [coffin]." These many figures were not only Jung's relations who were pastors but also multiple representa-tions of his father, emanations of Jung's dream-ego, as were indeed the "Jesuit," also identified by him as the African, the "black man" whom every child fears (MDR, 14). The latter figures were bogeymen.

Jung slept with his father during his childhood, presumably also at the time of his phallic dream while his mother slept in a different room. He admits that the "dim intimations of trouble in my parent's marriage hovered around me" and he attributes his mother's illness and hospitalization as "something to do with the difficulty in the marriage" (MDR, 8). He adds that his own illness in 1878 (the details of which do not appear in *Memories, Dreams, Reflections*) was perhaps connected with the temporary separation of the parents when Jung was around three, or more likely a bit older, when he had his frightful nightmare. Later, dur-ing his school years, Jung referred to the "nocturnal atmosphere" of his home. "All sorts of things were happening at night, things incomprehensible and alarm-ing" (MDR, 18). I have already mentioned the frightening maternal influences and the dream of his fractured mother. It is this strange and mysterious mother who in the dream tells the child that the phallus is a cannibal monster.

We now have some preliminary insights into the nature of Jung's first dark-night-of-the-soul experience, about which the Red Book is mostly silent. Behind the break with Freud, his guru and his father figure, lies the actual dreaded fa-ther of his childhood, the cannibal ogre represented in the monstrous phallus. Hence Jung's recollection of the dream during his dark night while engaged in reenacting the childhood game. We noted that Freud referred to Jung as his son and crown prince and heir; then it must surely be that Freud's own fantasy would reinforce Jung's, namely, that he, Freud, is king! Hence the childhood dream of the enthroned phallus threw tentacles much later into Jung's troubled relationship with Freud. Further, because Freud was the discoverer of the phallus as an object of dread and desire and also of the father's phallus, representing the oedipal conflict, it was impossible for Jung to go back to the Freudian theory he had rejected. Hence his later continuing attempts to give the phallus archetypal and mythic meaning in accordance with *his* theory. During his deepening crisis of 1913 he goes back to childhood and reinvents the game of building castles and vaults of late childhood, which then triggers the memory of the dreaded phallus. But this game was a culmination of games he used to play even earlier and that must have made a deep impression on him. We must now turn to these games and their symbolic meanings.

"My first concrete memory of games dates from my seventh or eighth year. I was passionately fond of playing games with bricks, and built towers which I then rapturously destroyed by an 'earthquake'" (MDR, 18). The child, it seems to me, builds a castle or home or tower and then "rapturously" destroys it in a kind of earthquake, symbolically coping with a childhood trauma of a fractured home life, very much in the spirit of the game of *fort-da* played by Freud's much younger grandchild acting out a game of absence and loss, beautifully described in *Beyond the Pleasure Principle*.[97] Jung's is also a game about absence and loss, but, in his case, the attempt is to restore wholeness (that key word in the later Jung lexicon) of the home, its destruction and its restoration, again and again. In the later game, of the tenth or eleventh year, he is building castles and vaults this time, but no longer breaking them in an "earthquake." For some reason or other, when Jung was ten or eleven or twelve and his father was around forty-three, there must have been a restoration of domestic concord or a semblance of it. Or, more likely, Jung had learned to cope with his fractured family. During his emotional crisis, he is repeating that early symbolic act of "wholeness" and concord, a wish to heal the wounds caused by the split with Freud (and with his father and Bleuler). But in a special way: instead of the castles and vaults he builds a village with its church, an idealization of the very things he hated in childhood. It is a kind of adult *fort-da* ritual during a regression to childhood, a reinvention of an archaic game. For the altar he finds a stone, and the church is complete. But perhaps his symbolic actions mean something more: Jung is building his own church with its altar containing the stone that was the container of the kind of knowledge he was seeking. The game is an early anticipation of the actual building of his own tower after he overcame the dark night of his psychosis. The reenactment of the childhood game, with its village and church, is also an attempt to symbolically effect reconciliation with his father, though not reconciliation with the other father, Freud, and, behind Freud, the hated image of Bleuler. The building operations also flooded his mind with fantasies that he began to put down in writing and, perhaps following Blake's example, to paint.

The Red Book does not give many details about these early dreams and fantasies, but its editor, Sonu Shamdasani, provides us with a useful summary of twelve visions Jung experienced during 1913–1914, crucial years from our point of view (RB, 202).[98] Because some of these dream texts are not available to me, I will deal with the fantasies and dreams recorded in *Memories, Dreams, Reflections*, beginning with his experience during a train ride in October 1913 when he was "suddenly seized by an overpowering vision" that seems to have had prognosticative significance. "I saw a monstrous flood covering all the northern and low-lying lands between the North Sea and the Alps. When it came up to Switzerland I saw that the mountains grew higher and higher to protect our country. I realized that a frightful catastrophe was in progress. I saw the mighty yellow waves, the floating rubble of civilization, and the drowned bodies of uncounted thousands. Then the whole sea turned into blood. This vision lasted about one hour." The duration of the vision is questionable, because Jung was unaware of the distinction between empirical and visionary time that I have highlighted. However, after two weeks the vision reappeared more vividly and with the blood more emphasized, while an inner voice told him: "Look at it well, it is wholly real and it will be so. You cannot doubt it" (MDR, 175). It is strange he could say that "the idea of war did not occur at all" as the basis for the manifest dream when all of Europe was reeling with rumors of the First World War.

According to the reminiscences recorded in *Memories, Dreams, Reflections*, Jung, confronted with the "incessant stream of fantasies," thought he must not lose his head but find some way to understand these strange happenings, a not unusual concern on the part of a psychotherapist who had already written on the psychoses and defined his illness as one.[99] "I was living in a constant state of tension; often I felt as if gigantic blocks of stone were tumbling down upon me. One thunderstorm followed another." The childhood game of earthquakes had become a psychic reality in adulthood. He says that Nietzsche, Hölderlin, and many others have been shattered by them, but he endured them with "brute strength." In a bit of self-heroizing, Jung speaks of "a demonic strength in me" and adds that from the beginning "there was no doubt in my mind that I must find the meaning of what I was experiencing in these fantasies," these "assaults of the unconscious." Yet he had the "unswerving conviction that I was obeying a higher will, and that feeling continued to uphold me until I had mastered the task."

At first he attempted yoga exercises "to hold his emotions in check," but he wanted to find out what was happening inside him, not obliterate these emotions as Hindus did: instead he wanted to abandon restraint temporarily and allow "the images and inner voices to speak afresh" (MDR, 177). Because he did not understand what was going on, he "had no choice but to write everything down in the style selected by the unconscious itself," perhaps putting his fantasies into the writing that went into the Black Book (MDR, 178). This strategy was very important to him and to us in understanding him. In Jung's time, and with his experience at Burghölzli, it is inevitable that his illness could not be defined as a spiritual crisis but invariably as a psychosis. To achieve mastery over it, Jung deliberately decided to immerse himself in the terrors of the unconscious. What is striking about Jung is that by plunging into his unconscious, the source of his troubled fantasies, he overcame his psychosis by giving it mythic meaning and significance, not through his Christian heritage but through his reading of myth, ritual, and hermetic thought. As early as 1912 the voice of his unconscious had informed him: "Now you are free to unlock all the gates of the unconscious" (MDR, 171).

And then during the Advent of December 12, 1913, he had the following dream:

> I was sitting at my desk once more, thinking over my fears. Then I let myself drop. Suddenly it was as though the ground literally gave way beneath my feet, and I plunged down into dark depths. I could not fend off a feeling of panic. But then, abruptly, at not too great a depth, I landed on my feet in a soft, sticky mass. I felt great relief, although I was apparently in complete darkness. After a while my eyes grew accustomed to the gloom, which was rather like a deep twilight. Before me was the entrance to a dark cave, in which stood a dwarf with a leathery skin, as if he were mummified. I squeezed past him through the narrow entrance and waded knee deep through icy water to the other end of the cave where, on a projecting rock, I saw a glowing red crystal. I grasped the stone, lifted it, and discovered a hollow underneath. At first I could make out nothing, but then I saw that there was running water. In it a corpse floated by, a youth with blond hair and a wound in the head. He was followed by a gigantic black scarab and then by a red, newborn sun, rising up out of the depths of the water. Dazzled by the light, I wanted to replace the stone upon the opening, but then a fluid welled out. It was blood. A thick jet of it leaped up, and I felt nauseated. It seemed to me that the blood continued to spurt for an unendurably long time. At last it ceased, and the vision came to an end.
>
> (MDR, 179)

Jung naturally was "stunned by this vision," but he gave it an archetypal interpretation as "a hero and solar myth, a drama of death and renewal symbolized by the Egyptian scarab," ignoring the interesting details of the vision, not all of which Jung or I can interpret. But some, surely: the earlier red altar stone reappears in the dream as the red crystal in the womb-cave, the ideal of the philosopher's stone that Jung got a hold of but found hollow underneath, implying that the knowledge he seeks in the stone is as of now hollow or empty. Underneath the hollow was running water in which was the corpse of a young blond man with a wound in his head, that is, Jung himself with his symbolic head wound or psychosis. Even though he had rationalized the dream as a myth of renewal, he is then forced to admit that, if it were so, the dream should herald a new dawn, not the welling of blood that reminded him of his earlier apocalyptic vision. So he says: "I abandoned all further attempts to understand" (MDR, 179). Jung may be right, however, that the red newborn sun emerging from the waters might indicate the possibility of renewal. He surely knew that Advent was the time of penance and repentance, but did not give the dream any kind of penitential significance, a significance that clearly emerged in the next.

Six days later, still in the period of Advent, Jung had a vision where it seems to me that the blond young man of the previous dream reappears as the mythic hero Siegfried: "I was with an unknown brown skinned man, a savage, in a lonely, rocky mountain landscape. It was before dawn. . . . Then I heard Siegfried's horn sounding over the mountains and I knew that *we* had to kill him. *We* were armed with rifles and lay in wait for him on a narrow path over the rocks" (my emphasis). Siegfried was in a chariot filled with the bones of the dead, and, when the chariot sped down the precipitous slope, "we shot at him, and he plunged down struck dead." In the dream-vision itself Jung felt "disgust and remorse for having destroyed something so great and beautiful." He turned to flee, dreading that the murder would be discovered, but a huge rainfall came down and he knew all traces of the murder would be obliterated. "I had escaped the danger of discovery; life could go on, but an unbearable feeling of guilt remained."

After he woke from his dream he tried to fall asleep, but a voice within urged him to understand the dream at once. "If you do not understand the dream you must shoot yourself," a reference to the loaded revolver he kept on his night table. He began to understand the dream, but only as a drama being waged in the political world of Germany. Siegfried "represents what the Germans want to achieve, heroically to impose their will, have their own way. . . . The dream showed that the attitude embodied by Siegfried, the hero, no longer suited me. Therefore it had to be killed" (MDR, 180). Jung giving meaning to his own experience in this fashion might have had therapeutic benefits. Yet, there are two possible interpretations of this dream that Jung does not reckon with. First: because Jung himself was sometimes called Siegfried by his friends (the tall, handsome hero, talented and creative, on the way to discovering new truths), the dream could be understood as the killing of his undesirable self, his shadow. This fits with Jung's interpretation that the attitude signified by Siegfried no longer suited him, perhaps reminding him that in the Norse Völsunga Saga, as well as in the Wagner opera, *Siegfried* (or *Sigurd*) is the son of Sigmund! On the other hand, a Freudian interpretation is also seductive and that is Siegfried equals Sigmund, also a discoverer of new truths. Both interpretations could be conjoined: Jung has killed his alter ego Siegfried and at the same time killed Sigmund Freud. And note that when the decision to kill and the killing itself takes place, Jung drops the "I" and uses "we," that is, he and the brown-skinned savage, a shadow figure if ever there was one and a reappearance of the dwarf of the earlier dream! His later interpretation of the dream-vision as a political drama would be partially correct if one were to substitute "Freud" for the "Germans" of his interpretation. Jung's interpretation also cannot account for the disgust and remorse he experienced during the space of the dream, but would make sense if it is Sigmund cum Siegfried that he has killed, simultaneously killing his own alter, and that the dream took place during a period of Christian repentance. The last thought comes out in the aftermath of the dream when he speaks of the "overpowering compassion" he felt, as if "I myself had been shot: a sign of my secret identity with Siegfried, as well as that of the grief a man feels when he is forced to sacrifice his ideal and his conscious attitudes," but blind to the fact that his unconscious is also pointing to Freud (MDR, 180). Is it also possible that beneath the image of the German hero Siegfried there is a fantasy image of a Greek hero, his father Johann Paul Achilles Jung, and perhaps even Bleuler?

Although one must be wary of Jung's self-heroizing posture, one must also realize that to "plummet down" into the unconscious would have made sense to him. Jung's son Franz, interviewed by Linda Donn, had some pertinent things to say about his father's self-heroizing: "My father writes as if he chose. I believe he had no choice. Can you believe what it must be to think that you might be going mad? That you might fall forever into the void?"[100] Franz Jung adds: "For years after he and Freud parted, my father could do no work. He placed a gun in his nightstand, and said that when he could bear it no longer he would shoot himself. . . . For seven years he did nothing really except his painting."[101] And then: "Think of my mother, think of her. Can you imagine living with a man who slept with a gun by his bed and painted pictures of circles all day?"[102]

One must however qualify the son's view of the father that he did nothing but paint pictures of circles for seven years. Jung himself says that he could not read a scientific work or engage in intellectual activity for a period of three years and couldn't even talk of the material he coughed up from his unconscious, although the Red Book contains attempts to deal with them. "The material brought to light from the unconscious had, almost literally, struck me dumb" (MDR, 193). But he also admits that his "psychosis" lasted, in some form or other, till the end of the war, that is, around 1919, when he had turned the corner to full recovery. There is some evidence that the worst years were during 1913–1916. On January 16, 1916, he put down his first maṇḍala in the Black Book, although he was unaware of what it meant at this time.[103] In the beginning of August to the end of September of that year he began to draw "a series of twenty-seven mandalas in pencil in his army notebook, which he preserved" (RB, 206). These "pictures of circles," as his son called them, were once again a kind of creative game to control his inner turmoil and eventually bring about "wholeness." Jung's creativity did not completely dry up. He wrote some important scholarly articles, expressing the kind of inner transformation he gradually began to realize during his dark travail. However, he asserted that "it was only toward the end of the First World War that I gradually began to emerge from the darkness" when armistice was declared on two fronts as it were, in the war outside and the conflict inside (MDR, 195).

Let me now deal with Jung's aridity or dryness, or deadness of the spirit, with which Christian penitents were also afflicted, expressed in the many dreams of 1913 recorded in *Memories, Dreams, Reflections* of corpses, sarcophagi, mummies, tombs, and vaults. In these dreams, as I understand them, the corpses and sarcophagi represented the spiritually dead Jung, not yet awakened. But not quite dead, witness the signs of nascent life that emerge when Jung stares at the corpses. So with the following recurring dream, seen sometime between April or May till June 1914, just before the outbreak of the war. "I had a thrice-repeated dream that in the middle of summer an arctic cold wave descended and froze the land to ice. I saw, for example, the whole of Lorraine and its canals frozen and the entire region totally deserted by human beings. All living green things were killed by frost." Jung points out that, as with the first vision of devastation, he did not think this a prognosticative dream, the sort of dream that he would later describe as "synchronistic." Rather it had to do with himself clearly recognizing that he was "menaced by a psychosis." The icy landscape without greenery is another version of barrenness and deadness of the spirit. That very year, on April 20, he resigned as president of the International Psychoanalytic Association, and on July 10 the Zurich Psychoanalytical Association was renamed the Association for Analytical Psychology.

It is therefore not surprising that the third dream of the series gives a sign of hope, a possibility of revivifying life. "[A] frightful cold had again descended from out of the cosmos. This dream, however, had an unexpected end. There stood a leaf-bearing tree, but without fruit (my tree of life, I thought), whose

leaves had been transformed by effects of the frost into sweet grapes full of healing juices. I plucked the grapes and gave them to a large, waiting crowd." Here
perhaps is a truly prognosticative dream, the hope of a renewal of green life from
out of the barren cold, a hope fulfilled when he was invited by the British Medical Association to deliver a lecture in Aberdeen, "On the Importance of the Unconscious in Psychopathology" (MDR, 176). He was also seeing patients, but his
own state of psychic limbo is reflected in his attitude toward them. "I avoided
all theoretical points of view and simply helped the patients to understand the
dream images by themselves, without application of rules and theories" (MDR,
170). He suspended his Freudian rules of interpretation, but had not yet developed his own. It seems that with Jung, as with Blake and the many who appear
in this essay, the dark night of the soul is never an unmitigated nightmare but
consists of ups and downs; bleakness and aridity; dying and awakening, interspersed with periods of creativity represented by images of burgeoning life. In
Jung's case, he continued to perform his military obligations as a Swiss citizen
and give a few public lectures.

Were there further signs of emergent creativity and the gradual overcoming
of his psychosis? Let me mention a few. In his visions during the period of the
dark night, Jung began to meet with the sort of Theosophical gurus whom we
have already encountered. Let me begin with Philemon, one of the fantastic figures he frequently met in his visions. Philemon was a pagan, briefly mentioned
by Goethe in *Faust*, who "brought with him an Egypto-Hellenistic atmosphere
with a Gnostic coloration," as well as, one might add, a Blavatsky coloration
(MDR, 182).[104] Jung gives a beautiful description of Philemon, but let me focus on
his significance. "Philemon and other figures of my fantasies brought home to
me the crucial insight that there are things in the psyche which I do not produce,
but *which produce themselves and have their own life*" (my emphasis). Philemon was
outside of Jung, and, as time went on, he developed into a Theosophy-type master with whom Jung could carry on conversations and from whom he could learn
many things about the psyche. "Psychologically, Philemon represented superior
insight. He was a mysterious figure to me. At times he seemed to me quite real,
as if he were a living personality. I went walking up and down the garden with
him, and to me he was what the Indians call a guru" (MDR, 183). Many of his
Philemonic thoughts were incorporated into the Red Book, and Jung painted him
with wings and horns. He also had a vision of him as "an old man with horns of
a bull" and the "wings of a kingfisher," a Lucifer figure, but an illuminative one,
both physically and psychically (MDR, 183). Further, if, as I think, Philemon was
his dream alter, then it is not surprising that Jung would, without being aware
of it, invest him with a "lame foot," the distinctive biological anomaly of his un-

mentioned and unmentionable alter, Oedipus, the father killer (MDR 185). Jung says that in order to imprint this figure in his memory he painted Philemon, when, lo and behold, as he was thus preoccupied he found a dead kingfisher in his garden, a scarce commodity in Zurich at the time, indicating once again an initial awareness of synchronicity, but as yet without a theoretical understanding of that phenomenon.[105] Opposed to Philemon was another figure, Ka, a demonic and Mephistophelian persona, also painted by Jung. Much later he says he could integrate these two oppositional figures through the study of alchemy (MDR, 183). And then there was Salome who appeared with Elijah in a vision in which, once again, he plunged into the depths of his unconscious and there, at the edge of a "cosmic abyss," entered a moonlike crater, a land of the dead where he saw an old man with a beard and a beautiful girl. The old man told Jung he was Elijah, and the young woman Salome (MDR, 181). Salome was perhaps a composite image of the biblical Salome and the attractive Lou Salome, Nietzsche's friend, whom Jung had met in Freud's circle in Vienna. It was the Salome figure who gave him his first intuitive insight into the anima, the female side of a man's psyche. Jung thought that Salome was associated with Elijah for all eternity. Both had a black serpent living with them who, says Jung, "displayed an unmistakable fondness for me" (MDR, 181). Elijah was perhaps the precursor of Jung's later "wise old man" archetype, and it is not surprising that he was later transformed into Philemon.[106]

Along with the anima, Jung was also beginning to understand what would become one of his key archetypes, the shadow. The dark-skinned savage and the dwarf of his dreams were the shadow side of his own being now returning, in other guises, earlier images of parental pastors associated with deadness. Then, in his dark night, when he was wondering what he was really doing, a female voice within him replied that what he was doing was not science (MDR, 185). This imaginary conversation with the voice continued for some time and further reinforced his intuitive grasp of the nature of the anima. But more: the anima in this case was a dangerous force because it criticized Jung's paintings, which, according to her, indicated an artistic rather than a scientific sensibility, a criticism he was to accept in his recovery phase.[107] "Thus the insinuations of the anima, the mouthpiece of the unconscious, can utterly destroy a man. In the final analysis the decisive factor is always consciousness, which can understand the manifestations of the unconscious and take up a position toward them." But Jung eventually, long after his illness, brought back a positive image of his anima as a being who can communicate "the unconscious to the conscious mind. . . . For decades when my emotional behavior was disturbed . . . I would ask the anima: 'Now what are you up to?' . . . After some resistance she regularly produced an image. As soon as the image was there, the unrest or the sense of oppression vanished" (MDR, 187). He would also converse with the anima, as if in a dream (MDR, 188). My guess is that these communications with the anima ceased or at least declined after the termination of the Red Book in 1930 when the anima became a key theoretical construct.

What I find fascinating in Jung's fantasies of 1916, the beginning of the period of recovery, is the awakening of the dead and of the corpses of the earlier dreams and the stanching of the flow of blood that characterized many of his dream images. Jung mentions the ominous atmosphere in his house, which he clearly sensed as the supernatural presence of "ghostly entities" (MDR, 190). It was the children who were the first to confront the spirits of the dead, beginning with his eldest daughter who saw "a white figure passing through her room." The second daughter had her blanket snatched away, while the nine-year-old son had an anxiety dream. And then there occurred the poltergeist phenomenon on a Sunday at about five in the afternoon when the doorbell started ringing furiously, although there was no one at the door. "The whole house was filled as if there was a crowd present, crammed full of spirits. They were packed deep right up to the door, and the air was so thick it was scarcely possible to breathe" (MDR, 190). It should be remembered that Jung alone experienced the poltergeists, and it was he who connected the children's dreams and fantasies as a prelude to the poltergeist phenomenon. Deirdre Bair rightly points out that the children's dreams and fantasies were unsurprising given the deadly undercurrent of unexpressed familial tensions in the Jung household owing to the presence of Toni Wolff, in effect Jung's cowife (BJ, 293). At this point the visitations provide certitude for what Jung himself calls the "paranormal" and of which he claimed to have firsthand experience in his childhood, in his later life as a physician investigating séances during his first job at the Burghölzli, and when the poltergeists made noises during his visit with Freud in Vienna. But, before this, while still a medical student, the young Jung not only believed in séances and the spirits of the dead but also conducted several in his own home, with Helly Preiswerk, his cousin on his mother's side, as a medium.[108] And it is not surprising, given Jung's investigations into the paranormal, that he would later become an "honorary fellow of the *American Society for Psychical Research*."[109]

It was during the presence of the poltergeists that the enigmatic work, *The Seven Sermons for the Dead* (*Septem Sermones et Mortuos*), was written.[110] In this text, addressed to the ghosts beating on his door, Jung speaks with the voice of the Gnostic thinker Basilides (c. 2 CE) whose extant work appears only in fragments. Jung's voice gives a "coherent," but not rationally organized account, of some imagined features of Basilides's thought. I will leave others to investigate how far this text conforms to what is known of Basilides, and here focus on some features relevant to our argument.[111] As with other visionaries, Jung says that this text "began to flow out of me, and in the course of three evenings the thing was written," that is, unself-consciously or without the mediation of the cogito. Elsewhere he is reputed to have said: "there are certain things that I don't make, but that make themselves," that is, things that make themselves manifest in the Wittgenstein sense, reminding us of a similar phrase Jung mentioned earlier (MDR, 183).[112]

The text introduces us to the ghosts knocking on Jung's door. "The dead came back from Jerusalem, where they found not what they sought. They prayed me [Basilides] to let them in and besought my word, and thus I began my teaching" (MDR, 378). The "me" of the visionary voice is Jung-Basilides imitating the style of Nietzsche's *Zarathustra,* but without its poetic quality, with the exception of the aphorisms that appear in sermon 3 (MDR, 382–83). The ghosts, we later find out, were Christians, but the sermons don't give much consolation to a Christian believer. For example, in his first sermon Basilides tells the Christians he wants to free them "from the delusion that somewhere, either without or within, there standeth something fixed, or in some way established, from the beginning." Then, smacking more of Buddhist thought rather than that of Basilides, he adds: "Every so-called fixed and certain thing is only relative. That alone is fixed and certain which is subject to change" (MDR, 379). The rest of the sermon also provides no consolation to the ghosts. They stand on the side of the wall (presumably of Jung's house) and cry as if demanding an answer to Nietzsche's killing of the Christian god: "We would have knowledge of god. Where is god? Is god dead?" Basilides-Jung informs them that god is not dead, but "he is distinguished, however, from created beings through this, that he is more indefinite and indeterminable than they" (MDR, 382). And so it goes on. The second sermon ends with an affirmation of Basilides's Gnostic deity, the great God Abraxas, whom mankind and the ghosts have forgotten. Naturally, "the dead now raised a great tumult, for they were Christians" (MDR, 383). Similarly, as Basilides continues into sermon 4, the dead ask him: "Tell us of gods and devils, accursed one!" (MDR, 385) Basilides's answers once again are of little use to them. And, in sermon 5, "The dead mocked and cried: Teach us, fool, of the church and holy communion," only to receive an answer pertaining to sexuality, as, for example, in the following statement: "Man is weak, therefore is communion indispensable. If your communion be not under the sign of the Mother, then is it under the sign of the Phallos. No communion is suffering and sickness. Communion in everything is dismemberment and dissolution," an insulting reference to the consumption of the body of the wounded Christ (MDR, 387–88).

The final sermon affirms the one god as Abraxas, "the creator and destroyer of his own world." And Abraxas's guiding god is the star. "Prayer increaseth the light of the Star. It casteth a bridge over death. It prepareth life for the smaller world and assuageth the hopeless desires of the greater" (MDR, 389). A little more sermonizing and then a sort of miracle found in *Zarathustra*: "Whereupon the dead were silent and ascended like the smoke above the herdsman's fire, who through the night kept watch over his flock" (MDR, 389–90). In his later recollection, in *Memories, Dreams, Reflections*, he says: "As soon as I took up the pen, the whole ghostly assemblage evaporated. The room quieted and the atmosphere cleared. The haunting was over" (MDR, 191).

Although neglected by commentators, *The Seven Sermons* is for me a crucial document that anticipates the end of Jung's psychosis and the awakening of his dead soul. The fleeing of the Christian ghosts is a rejection of his father's religion and that of the many kinfolk of his father's generation who were Calvinist pastors. It is a break with Freudian theory, as it is with orthodox Christianity and the Nietzschean death of God. Instead Jung seeks truth in Gnosticism when he speaks in the voice of Basilides. God lives in Abraxas. It heralds the beginning of his serious interest in what was considered esoteric or occult or downright nonsense by his contemporaries, including Freud. He had been pierced and laid low by a psychosis, only to become a "piercer" of new knowledge. The haunting by his father and his mentor Freud was over. *The Seven Sermons* also anticipates his thinking on such things as the conjunction of opposites that he, at this time, attributes to Gnosticism.[113] It is a kind of charter myth promising the movement of his future thought both as a thinker and a healer. And that future thought, based on the understanding of his own unconscious fantasies, was exemplified in the gradual renewal of his scientific work from 1916 onward.

THE TOWER: THE DARK NIGHT OF THE TRANCE ILLNESS

> All those things whereof
> Man makes a superhuman
> Mirror-resembling dream
> —W. B. Yeats, "The Tower"

There is nothing to indicate that the high point of Jung's psychosis during the period 1914 to 1916 was a mystical experience in the broad sense of that term or, in any way, a religious one. He had effectively rejected his father's religion and the other fathers dressed in black who haunted him. He had not forgotten that he was an experimenter; someone who a few years ago helped to develop a "word association test" and had written in a scientific vein about mental illness. He was interested in séances and other occult phenomena and believed in them, but, as with the fellows of the Society for Psychical Research, he wanted to experimentally validate or prove their empirical reality. Nevertheless, one could say that the resolution of his psychosis, with his redefinition of the unconscious and that of his fantasies in mythic terms, expressed a form of secular spirituality, giving meaning and significance to a psychosis, investing that experience with mythic but no transcendent significance, as is beautifully expressed in his Red Book. Gradually, as his reading and experience widened, he became more and more sympathetic to spiritual experience in a somewhat more traditional sense, but we have no real clue as to Jung's own personal beliefs regarding the afterlife until a crucial event occurred in January 1944, at age sixty-nine, when he underwent another terrifying and transformative experience, a trance illness that gave him a sudden sense of salvific truths thus far hidden from him. Whereas the first was associated with a psychosis but later developed, in the Red Book, into what he self-consciously saw as an aesthetic exploration of the workings of the soul, the second had a more profound quality, a transcendental intimation of the revelatory power of the spirit.

I emphasize "transcendental" because big dreams are also for Jung a manifestation of spirit, once more in the secular sense of something profound emerging when I-thinking has been suspended and knowledge appears before the visual lens of the dreamer. Obviously, not all dreams are equally significant, but, for Jung, the truly meaningful ones contain archetypes emerging from the collective unconscious, especially those revealing a hidden past, a "history." One might call them myth dreams. Among these myth dreams are those that operate very much like charter myths, as I have already said. I will mention another dream charter that helps to bridge the psychosis of 1913 with the transcendental vision of 1944. And that was when Jung was in India as a guest of the British government from 1938–1939.[114]

After an exhausting time of new and crowded impressions, Jung fell ill with diarrhea, which landed him in the hospital and gave him a holiday from India: a holy day, as it turned out to be. While isolated there he had a revelatory dream of his search for the Grail, showing him that, while India was a profound influence, he was essentially a European being.[115] In the dream, Jung was with a large number of Zurich friends, sightseeing on a little island off southern England, at the further end of which was a medieval castle located on a rocky coast. Beyond its courtyard was a wide stone staircase and beyond that was a columned hall, dimly illumined with candlelight. Jung understood, in his dream, this to be the castle of the Grail and that there was to be a "celebration of the Grail here." Among his fellow tourists, there was someone who looked like the famous German historian Theodor Mommsen. This Mommsen figure could discourse in professorial style about the dead past, but he "was not conscious of the meaning of the legend, nor of its living presentness, whereas I was intensely aware of both" (MDR, 281). I shall skip a portion of the dream and deal with Jung mentioning that when the dream changed they were in the same place, but without the professor. He sensed a celebration was to occur that evening in a small uninhabited house, the sole one on the north side of the island. In the dream he felt that their task was to bring the Grail located there to the castle. After arduous hiking they arrived at the spot, but to reach the house itself they had to cross a kind of channel, although there was no bridge or boat. "It was very cold; my companions fell asleep, one after the other. I considered what could be done, and came to the conclusion that I alone must swim across the channel and fetch the Grail. I took off my clothes. At that point I awoke."

This dream according to Jung "wiped away all the intense impressions of India and swept me back to the too-long-neglected concerns of the Occident, which had formerly been expressed in the quest for the Holy Grail as well as in the search for the philosopher's stone," the latter representing the former (MDR, 282). This charter dream indicated that his real goal was not Indian spirituality—quite unlike Blavatsky, one might say—but rather to bring about a fusion of his Christian past, represented in the Grail, with the alchemical reading he had been immersed in for some time. Indian and pagan beliefs, I take it, continued to have a place in his belief world, but not as primary ones. "It was as though the dream were asking me, 'What are you doing in India? Rather seek for yourself and your fellows the healing vessel, the *servator mundi*, which you urgently need. For your state is perilous, you are all in imminent danger of destroying all that centuries have built up'" (MDR, 282–83). I assume that Jung would have realized that the pompous professor was his alter ego, the old scholastic Jung that now has to be replaced with the new historical role he, Jung, will initiate by bringing together his Christian and alchemical heritages. Jung was often called professor, owing to the many lectures and seminars he gave, although he never had a regular university professorship.

Jung claimed that his British travels ten years prior to his India visit convinced him the Grail was a living tradition in England. Now he realized that there was a consonance between the essentially Christian nature of the Grail myth and the research of the alchemists, both ultimately searching for some kind of "gold" or the philosopher's stone. And then, in a beautiful statement, he gives his vision of the continuing historicity of myth and its contemporary relevance through the workings of the collective unconscious. "Myths which day has forgotten continue to be told by night, and powerful figures which consciousness has reduced to banality and ridiculous triviality are recognized again by poets and prophetically revived; therefore they can also be recognized 'in changed form' by the thoughtful person. The great ones of the past have not died, as we think; they have merely changed their names" (MDR, 282). It is important to recognize that Jung emphasizes that manifest dreams of deep existential significance are those dreamt by "poets" and by the "thoughtful person," not Everyman. For example, I might select a random sample of Swiss men and women and study their dreams, but statistical surveys or relating dreams to culture are unlikely to shed light on big dreams. The implication is clear: a sensitive dreamer, already attuned to the significance of dreams, whether or not he believed in Jungian or any other theory, might have dreams thick with existential meaning demanding some form of interpretation.

The next great spiritual event was the 1944 trance illness, which occurred when he had broken his foot in a fall during a constitutional walk in January that year. This event was followed by a heart attack, that biological intimation of mortality, when he "hung on the edge of death" and was given oxygen and, of all things, "camphor injections." We do not know whether his state of unconsciousness was compounded or not by the intake of oxygen and camphor. "I had reached the uttermost limit, and do not know whether I was in a dream or an ecstasy" (MDR, 289). Either way, the dream or vision was a profound, life-altering one. It also showed that, in spite of his consciousness of being really European, Indic spirituality simply refused to be shoved aside.

It seemed to me that I was high up in space. Far below I saw the globe of the earth, bathed in a gloriously blue light. I saw the deep blue sea and the continents. Far below my feet lay Ceylon [Sri Lanka], and in the distance ahead of me the subcontinent of India. My field of vision did not include the whole earth, but its global shape was plainly distinguishable and its outlines shone with a silvery gleam through that wonderful blue light. In many places the globe seemed colored, or spotted dark green like oxidized silver. Far away to the left lay a broad expanse— the reddish-yellow desert of Arabia; it was as though the silver of the earth had there assumed a reddish-gold hue. Then came the Red Sea, and far, far back—as if in the upper left of a map—I could just make out a bit of the Mediterranean. . . . I could also see the snow-covered Himalayas, but in that direction it was foggy or cloudy. . . . The sight of the earth from this height was the most glorious thing I had ever seen.

After contemplating it for a while, I turned around. I had been standing with my back to the Indian Ocean, as it were, and my face to the north. Then it occurred to me that I made a turn to the south. Something new entered my field of vision. A short distance away I saw in space a tremendous dark block of stone, like a meteorite. It was about the size of my house, even bigger. It was floating in space, and I myself was floating in space.

(MDR, 289–90)

Jung claimed that he had seen similar stones in the Gulf of Bengal, some of which were used in temple architecture. His huge dream stone had an entrance that led to a small antechamber. Within the antechamber to the right sat a black Hindu in a lotus posture on a stone bench. "He wore a white gown, and I knew that he expected me" (MDR, 290). Inside to the left of the antechamber was the gate to the temple. There were innumerable niches on the walls with saucerlike cavities filled with coconut oil that contained lighted wicks, triggering a memory of oil lamps in the Palace of the Holy Tooth Relic in Kandy, Sri Lanka.

As I approached the steps leading up to the entrance into the rock, a strange thing happened: I had the feeling that everything was being sloughed away; everything I aimed at or wished for or thought, the whole phantasmagoria of earthly existence fell away or was stripped from me—an extremely painful process. Nevertheless something remained; it was as if I now carried along with me everything I had ever experienced or done, everything that has happened around me....

This experience gave me a feeling of extreme poverty; but at the same time of great fullness. There was no longer anything I wanted or desired. I existed in an objective form; I was what I had been and lived. At first the sense of annihilation predominated, of being stripped or pillaged; but suddenly that became of no consequence. Everything seemed to be past; what remained was a *fait accompli*, without any reference back to what had been. There was no longer any regret that something had dropped away or taken away. On the contrary: I had everything that I was, and that was everything.

(MDR, 290–91)

This fascinating episode is Jung's second and unique dark night of the soul. He enters the entrance of the rock, a temple of sorts, and at that moment suffers from a sense of being stripped or dispossessed. His former self has been wiped clean, as it were, and he is ready to enter the temple and its initiation chamber. Now comes the visionary experience of initiation, as he approaches the temple, where he feels "the certainty that I was about to enter an illuminated room and would meet there all those people to whom I belong in reality." If my reading is correct, Jung was hoping to meet other adepts; then "I would at last understand—this too was a certainty—what historical nexus I or my life fitted into." These are all very profound existential questions and have little to do with his scholarly work thus far. Scholarly work takes place within time, whereas Jung's experience of *thrownness* is outside time, as is normally understood—outside scientific or philosophical understanding. (See book 5, note 55 for the significance of "thrownness.") Once in the temple, he felt he would know "what had been before me, why I had come into being and where my life was flowing." He would have all the answers from people within, people who would know, he repeats, "about what had been before and what would come after," a search relating perhaps to an earlier incarnation and the fate of his soul after the present one had ended (MDR, 291). If, in the previous charter dream, he felt his true spiritual lineage was European, the current vision leaves that question open. Jung might be a systematic scholar with respect to his intellectual work and analytical psychology, but he was not a systematizer of his powerful existential dreams and visions. It is as if his salvific awareness and the apprehension of a transcendental reality refuse to be brought under the aegis of Reason.

To get back to his experience: while Jung was thinking over problems of existence (still in his trance), a bizarre experience occurred when an image floated up toward him from the Europe of his vision. "It was my doctor, Dr. H [Dr. Theodor Haemmerli-Schindler]—or rather his likeness—framed by a golden chain or a golden laurel wreath," the significance of which Jung readily grasped. And here is Jung's fascinating occult interpretation of this part of the vision, almost in the spirit of Blake or Blavatsky. "Aha, this is my doctor, of course, the one who was treating me. But now he is coming in his primal form, as a *basileus* [king] of Kos [the island shrine of Asklepios]. In [his current] life he was an avatar of this *basileus*, the temporal embodiment of the primal form, which has existed from the beginning. Now he is appearing in that primal form."

Several ideas are very clear here. Jung obtains visionary knowledge indicating that his friend and doctor has appeared in his "primal form" as a physician or "king" of the great Greek medical center and this means that Jung believes in some form of reincarnation. Whether the idea of "primal form" was borrowed from Blake or a Neo-Platonic source remains unclear. From a synchronistic point of view the apparition indicates that his doctor would die, that is, go back to his primal form. Jung adds that in the vision the two communicated in "mute" fashion. From this communion of two minds in their spirit forms, Jung inferred that "Dr. H had been delegated by the earth to deliver a message to me, to tell me that there was a protest against my going away," which is to say that, unlike his friend,

Jung is not going to die. "I had no right to leave the earth and must return. The moment I heard that, the vision ceased" (MDR, 292). Translating the previous visionary sequence in my terms, it seems as if Jung's dream-ego, to use a term that he favored, is experiencing these wondrous events, both painful and full, and in this state he meets his doctor, an emanation created by his dream-ego. When Jung heard the protest, presumably from the adepts he had mentioned earlier, the vision ceased because, it seems to me, he has to come back to earth, whereas he can enter the temple only when his spirit is finally released from his body.

We are not told the time span of the vision, but it was not long. Jung's sense of loss was so great that it took about three weeks for him to fully decide not to die. After his grand experience, the view of the city from his hospital bed was a fragmented one, like a painted curtain full of black holes or a tattered sheet of newspaper that meant nothing. The human world in which he now lived seemed like a prison where he was boxed in. "I had been so glad to shed it all, and now it had come about that I—along with everyone else—would be hung up in a box by a thread. While I had floated in space, I had been weightless, and there had been nothing tugging at me. And now all that was to be a thing of the past" (MDR, 292–93). The vision, then, was not only a temporary transcendence of the mundane world but also an intimation of the afterlife of the spirit. Naturally, Jung felt a profound ambivalence toward the doctor who brought him back to life. There was resentment and, with it, fear that the doctor himself might die, guilt feelings that Jung did not explicate except to say that the "terrifying thought came to me that Dr. H. would have to die in my stead." Jung tried to explain all this to the doctor, but naturally none of this made sense to the poor man. Hence Jung, on his part, became angry with the doctor and said silently to himself: "Why does he always pretend he doesn't know he is a basileus of Kos? And that he has already assumed his primal form? He wants to make me believe that he doesn't know." Jung is so enraptured and entrapped by his vision and its absolute truthfulness that he thinks the doctor should also have apprehended the same truth via his spirit meeting Jung's in cosmic space. But Jung's warnings couldn't possibly make sense to his doctor, who would simply have thought that Jung was suffering from a delirium. Jung's wife reprimanded him for being harsh on the doctor. She was, of course, right, says Jung, but at that time "I was angry with him for stubbornly refusing to speak of all that passed between us in my vision. Damn it all, he ought to watch his step. He has no right to be so reckless." He felt the doctor's life "was in jeopardy," and, sure enough, the vision proved to be true, because on April 4, 1944 ("I still remember the exact date"), Jung was permitted to sit up in bed. His doctor, however, became indisposed, took to his bed with septicemia, and did not leave it till he died. The visionary experience not only proved the truth of Jung's theory of synchronicity but also the truth of a spiritual existence after death, even though the details of that afterlife were not given to him in his vision.

During the weeks that followed, Jung often felt depressed during the day, weak and wretched because of the necessity of going back to this "drab world." In the evening he would fall asleep till about midnight. "Then I would come to myself and lie awake for about an hour, but in an utterly transformed state. It was as if I were in an ecstasy. I felt I was floating in space, as though I were safe in the womb of the universe—in a tremendous void, but filled with the highest possible happiness. 'This is eternal bliss,' I thought. 'This cannot be described, it is far too wonderful!'" (MDR, 293)

During these glorious days, Jung sees significant episodes from the past, just as female Christian penitents did. When he looked at his elderly nurse, she had a halo around her, and with this cue Jung was transported to the garden of pomegranates of the Jewish kabbalistic tradition, there witnessing a "mystic marriage" described in old texts with which he was already familiar. The fact that this, and the other visions he experienced in his hospital bed, might have come from his own erudition does not bother him. But it provokes us to question whether his earlier "historical visions" were also recapitulations of what he had read.[116] And, if such thoughts did occur, it would make no sense to him now. It cannot invalidate the noetic and genuine spiritual reality of the vision. Jung claims that he was present during this wedding, but wasn't sure of his exact role. "At bottom it was I myself. I was the marriage. And my beatitude was that of a blissful wedding." So with the next vision which took him to a Greek amphitheater: "And there, in this theater, the *hierosgamos* was being celebrated. Men and women dancers came onstage, and upon a flower decked couch All-father Zeus and Hera consummated the mystic union, as it is described in the *Iliad*" (MDR, 294). The reader of the preceding account might think Jung was mad. "Mad" he might have been, but delusional he was not. His was the madness of the saints.

And so on it went, night after night, during which, he said, "I floated in a state of purest bliss." Gradually, the visions began to fade, with the fading away of his illness. He says that "scarcely three weeks after the first vision they ceased altogether. . . . Although my belief in the world returned to me, I have never since entirely freed myself of the impression that this life is a segment of existence which is enacted in a three-dimensional boxlike universe especially set up for it." In contrast to the empty world to which Jung is forced to return, the absolute truth of the vision is never disputed by him. "It was not the product of imagination . . . the visions and experiences were utterly real; there was nothing subjective about them; they all had the quality of absolute objectivity" (MDR, 295). His experience was "the ecstasy of a non-temporal state in which present, past, and future are one," a merging of temporal opposites (MDR, 295–96). And, further, it was not a dream but a vision, thus making a qualitative distinction that in general he rarely made, even though for Jung dreams often enough had a visionary quality.[117]

Now let me make symbolic sense of the huge stone of his dream. As the dreamer says, it is from this kind of stone that Hindu temples were constructed, and the associational link with Hinduism shifts the vision to a meditating yogi in the inner chamber. But does the vision represent something more? I suspect that the stone is an "amplification," to use Jung's own term, of the idea of the philosopher's stone. The tower he built in Bollingen was also for Jung "a kind of representation in stone of my innermost thoughts and of the knowledge I had acquired. Or to put it in another way, I had to make a confession of faith in stone" (MDR, 223).

I mentioned that Jung considered the tower a place of meditation; he later reflected that they were like the curtained-off meditating chambers he saw in India. Remember that, in the annex he added in 1931, he had his own private room to which few were admitted: only he had the key. "In the course of the years I have done paintings on the walls, and so have expressed all those things which have *carried me out of time into seclusion, out of the present into timelessness.*" It became for him a "place of spiritual concentration" (MDR, 224; my emphasis). After his wife's death in 1955, eleven years after his transforming vision, he "felt an inner obligation to become what I myself am." What is fascinating is that the very first part of the tower was built two months after his mother's death in 1923, and, as we have already noted, the tower became a "maternal womb" or "maternal figure," and out of this matrix Jung himself felt as if he was "being reborn in stone." Thus the tower represented the maternal and the spiritual forces welling forth from the unconscious. He now added an upper story that represented his "ego personality," or the part of his rational being, "an extension of consciousness achieved in old age." He confessed he built it "in a kind of dream," and "only afterward did I see how all the parts fitted together and that a meaningful form had resulted: a symbol of psychic wholeness" (MDR, 225).[118] Jung in his self-conception has become fully whole, with the ego in harmony with the self.

The addition of the ego to the tower had, I think, personal meanings for Jung. After the trance illness of 1944, his relation to his wife was much more dependent which went along with his distancing Toni Wolff, who was appalled by Jung's commitment to the "paranormal." His wife's death left him desolate, and he gradually felt the need to get back to work and not be swamped by the forces of the unconscious. Assuming that the tower is a hugely overdetermined symbol and that the earlier parts represented the spiritual and maternal, the ego section represents his wife Emma, the one who managed Jung's domestic and financial affairs with consummate skill. When she died, Jung was distraught that his everyday life and the management of finances might end in shambles. Hence the further need to bring the ego fully into the picture both in the tower and within himself.

Once Jung is ensconced in the now lonely tower, earlier psychic experiences and fantasies become more real and psychologically and spiritually meaningful. Always sensitive to the "paranormal," he used to talk about his number two, the other being conjured up by his fantasies, just as Blavatsky did, number one being Jung himself. Fantastic figures from the past appeared in his dreams, and these dreams of his number two gave him further insights into the unconscious.[119] One of these fantasy figures was Philemon, who appeared in his first illness. During that earlier psychosis, he sometimes referred to these guru figures as "fantasies," but they become much more real in the tower, such that Philemon "comes to life again in Bollingen" (MDR, 225). Philemon becomes, in effect, not so much the conjured up fantasy of his "psychosis" but a spiritual being within Jung.

In 1950, six years after his trance illness, he made a "monument out of stone to express what the Tower meant to me" by adding an enclosure to his garden and, to do so, he ordered some stones from a quarry (MDR, 226). But, instead of the required triangular stone, a much larger square stone was sent, a huge square block about twenty inches thick. The mason wanted to send it back, but Jung felt this was his predestined stone, and he wanted it kept outside the tower. He chiseled into the stone a Latin verse by an alchemist, Arnaldus de Villanova (d. 1313), signifying that this was the *lapis philosophicus* despised by the ignorant. He also carved into the stone a small circle, like an eye looking at him, and in the center he engraved a small homunculus, as if it were the pupil of the eye. The circle within the stone is obviously the maṇḍala, the symbol of perfection. He engraved other Latin inscriptions, but the upshot of his efforts is clear: the stone is a representation of the philosopher's stone, the stone of knowledge (MDR, 226–27). I will take up later what I consider to be the homunculus in the center of the maṇḍala.

The stone reappears in the first dream of several he had before his death. He saw an enormous round block of stone standing on an unspecified place, and it bore the following inscription: "And this shall be a sign onto you of Wholeness and Oneness."[120] The stone of his trance vision of 1944 was close to the one he dreamt before he died, and perhaps the latter was structured on the basis of the former. Note that the dream stone of 1944 opens up to an initiation chamber. Had Jung died, he would have had access to the knowledge contained in the stone chamber, but this was denied to him, temporarily, of course. In some sense all the stones of his tower and of his dreams are lapis or philosopher's stones, and this includes the stone altar he constructed during his first illness or psychosis. But his last resurrection of the Stone indicated to Jung that he will soon be dead. Thus the dream contains a prognostication: another form of wholeness and oneness is something he will realize after death, the fulfillment of the message implicitly contained in the stone initiation chamber, the stone from which he will be reborn.

One must assume that during his trance illness Jung's spirit via his dream-ego would have left his body and soared to the cosmic heights he describes. Further, during the three weeks of visionary experience that followed, the spirit periodically left the body, rendering the body insensate. This is, of course, a form of death. When he *awakens* after that period, a change in his work and life has taken place. Although knowledge in the transcendental sense was denied him, Jung admits that "after the illness a fruitful period of work began for me. A good many of my principal works were written only then." And, more significantly, echoing the experience of others who have awakened from similar forms of temporary death, Jung says, "I no longer attempted to put across my own opinion, but surrendered myself to the current of my thoughts. Thus one problem after the other *revealed itself to me* and took shape" (MDR, 297; my emphasis). A terribly significant statement, which aligns Jung with the other visionaries of my essay. He is saying that his insights, more clearly than ever, emerge from "revelation," rather than from Reason, if by that word one means the emergence of knowledge through a form of surrender to something outside the cognizing ego. Reason, the ego that symbolically represents the top story of his tower reappears after 1955 as "secondary elaboration," when revealed thoughts have to be written down for public consumption.

Nevertheless, in Jung's later work there are degrees of systematization of thought. *Memories, Dreams, Reflections,* which opened his inner experiences to public consumption was close in spirit to his late affirmation of the importance of revelation. His last great works, *Aion* and *Mysterium Coniunctionis*, still seem to emerge from the top story of his renovated tower.[121] At best one might say that these two works were products of ideas that were "revealed" to him and then, as with other visionary thinkers, put into final rational form as scholarly treatises, very much in the manner of Madame Blavatsky. Unlike her, Jung was true to his promise. In these two works, he goes back to Europe's Gnostic, alchemical, and hermetic traditions rather than the Buddhist, Hindu, or Taoist, which now appear only as illustrative examples. Nevertheless, if Indic thought has been effectively banished from his scholarly treatises, they reappear in his trance illness and his personal experiences.[122]

Hereafter, Jung, still hesitantly, begins to talk of his views on the afterlife in two chapters entitled "On Life After Death" and "Late Thoughts." But why did he urge his interlocutor, Aniela Jaffé, not to include these and other thoughts in *Memories, Dreams, Reflections* in his projected collected works? Partly, perhaps, he was still worried about the norms of academic scholarship, which tend to exclude personal experiences of the numinous. But more, I think, because he had not yet formulated a philosophy or systemic exposition of his thoughts on life after death, on immortality, and on God. The initiatory door was closed to him, but thoughts did appear as revelations and sometimes, as with Blavatsky, directly from a spirit guru.[123] Jung could systematize his analytic psychology on the model of an imagined "natural science," even if his ideas came to him through intuition and dreaming. But he could never systematize his "inner experience," also derived from visions, dreams, and ecstatic trances that held the prospect of some form of the transcendence of the body and the material world, if not of salvation in its Christian sense. If a visionary experience occurs within a frame of a cultural tradition, then it can easily be systematized or given theological justification. But if one rejects that tradition or its main presuppositions, as Jung and Georges Bataille did, one would find it hard to give the visionary experience some sort of systemic meaning.

I now pose the following question. Where in Jung's lived existence is there a place analogous to the initiatory temple of Jung's vision? I suggest that it is the tower, that space of solitude where contemplation can take place without the intrusion of the world outside. Milton too, in *Il Penseroso*, had his imaginary tower where he fantasized retreating at midnight to converse with the mythic founder of hermetic philosophy, the "thrice-great-Hermes," and to commune with the stars.[124] And, in a beautiful coinage, he could "unsphere" the spirit of Plato, which, in turn, will open worlds unknown when the mind has left "this fleshy nook." So is it with W. B. Yeats, who actually bought an old castle, Thor Ballylee, his tower, as he called it, where he lived and wrote most of his major poetry. Here he could, with the aid of his mediumistic wife George, invoke the spirits of the past, beautifully depicted in "All Souls' Night," wherein the bubbling muscatel on the table evokes the memory of the dead.[125] The tower, then, is not simply a space for solitariness and contemplation or meditation, not only for the "sober ear," as Yeats said. For Jung, Milton, and Yeats, all of whom were influenced by hermetic thought, the tower is also kind of substitute for the older idea of the *axis mundi*, the pillar that links earth and sky, where the spirits of the past can come and commune with the occupant. Hence the profound importance of the alchemical stone for Jung. By placing the live stone outside his tower, itself a monument in stone, he has, in effect, consecrated the building into a kind of temple that, in synchronistic manner, represented his own self. But, more than that: the homunculus he carved in stone in the maṇḍala, which he felt was a kind of eye, is Jung's own fantasized self as the teacher of a new truth, the knowledge derived from the visionary eye, the gold he discovers in the modern philosopher's stone. Jung is in good company here, because, according to his ventures into alchemy, the philosopher's stone can be represented by a special human being, for example, Christ or Adam. And inasmuch as the gold sought by the alchemist is the king of metals, so it can represent the "king."[126] He was also surely familiar with Tibetan thought where a god or the disciple's guru is at the center of the maṇḍala. My interpretation is that the homunculus is Jung's fantasized self as a kind of guru who has proclaimed a powerful new truth to the world, a truth that will make sense to modern man in search of his soul.

Jung could now, in his old age, affirm another truth, a mystical apprehension of reality, in the spirit of Boehme and Blake, anticipating thinkers who with the blessings of quantum physics blurred the distinction between mind and matter and created a space for mystical thought. "At times I feel as if I am spread out over the landscape and inside things, and am myself living in every tree, in the plashing of the waves, in the clouds and the animals that come and go, in the procession of the seasons" (MDR, 225–26). Jung himself would claim he has inherited these ideas from his commitment to alchemical thought stemming from at least the time of Paracelsus up to the seventeenth century, the idea that metals and other inanimate objects have their own inner life or being, often generated from the heavens. "For Paracelsus the operative side of science involved bringing into action forces derived from the heavens. . . . Only mankind was granted to unleash the virtues hidden in stones, plants, words and characters," a view that is central to alchemy.[127] In a late work, Jung affirms the insights of the alchemists (and of Jung himself) of "a stone, which is no stone," of base metals and material objects imbued with spirit as a result of alchemical experimentation.[128] Through his new sense of spirit's interpenetration with nature, Jung must have imagined he had finally pierced the secret of the philosopher's stone, releasing the spirit congealed in the stone, not only abolishing the distinction between mind and matter but also affirming their interpenetration. The memorable words that end *Memories, Dreams, Reflections* demonstrate the spiritual significance of overcoming that distinction. "Yet there is so much that fills me: plants, animals, clouds, day and night, and the eternal in man. The more uncertain I have felt about myself, the more there has grown in me a feeling of kinship with all things. In fact it seems to me as if that alienation which so long separated me from the world has become transferred into my own inner world, and has revealed to me an unexpected unfamiliarity with myself" (MDR, 359).[129]

Book 8

CONTEMPORARY DREAMING

Secular Spirituality and Revelatory Truth

LUCID DREAMING: VISIONARY CONSCIOUSNESS
AND THE DEATH OF GOD

> By *inner experience* I understand that which one usually calls *mystical experience*: the states of ecstasy, of rapture, at least of meditated emotion. But I am thinking less of *confessional* experience, to which one has had to adhere up to now, than of an experience laid bare, free of ties, even of an origin, of any confession whatever. This is why I don't like the word *mystical*.
>
> —Georges Bataille, *Inner Experience*

TO ME LUCID DREAMING is the most interesting of the contemporary Euro-American obsessions with dreams, providing a kind of escape from the world of everyday reality into the dream realm. Several lucid dreamers experience what one might reasonably label dream-visions that provide insights into a transcendental reality, not based on any known religion but rather on an intuitive personal insight into such an imagined reality. In that sense they constitute another form of "secular spirituality" for those who have been disenchanted with traditional religion.

What is meant by lucid dreaming? The French dream theorist Michel Jouvet puts it thus: "A dream is lucid when the subject, while dreaming, knows he or she is dreaming. This peculiar state allows the dreamer a certain measure of control over the actual unfolding of the dream and a sense of freedom through being able to explore the dream world according to his or her own inclinations."[1] What is striking about lucid dreaming is that, like its Buddhist and Hindu precursors, it provides technologies for disciplining oneself in order to dream lucidly. A detailed account of these technologies is found in the work of an important theorist, Stephen LaBerge, whose pioneer work *Lucid Dreaming* was followed by

Exploring the World of Lucid Dreaming, written with his collaborator Howard Rhein-gold.[2] I find the second work especially interesting and deal with it here in some detail.

The range of technologies for achieving lucidity varies from simple ones, such as keeping a diary, to more complicated techniques influenced by Buddhism and fitting the needs of reasonably educated persons.[3] LaBerge and Rheingold say that "lucid dreaming requires concentration, which is nearly impossible to achieve with a distracted mind and tense body" and they provide simple step-by-step techniques (WLD, 53). Although the senior author was a student of a Tibetan guru at the Esalen Institute in 1970, most of his knowledge of Buddhist meditation seems limited to what is known as *samatha* (Sanskrit *śamatha*) modes of achieving relaxation and concentration through breathing, rather than on the more complex *vipassanā* or "insight meditation" found in all schools of Buddhism. The reason seems obvious: insight meditation is not only extraordinarily difficult, but it is also not necessary in training oneself for lucid dreaming. As the authors themselves say, "lucid dreaming is easier than you may think," which is, of course, not true of any serious path to salvation (WLD, 57).[4]

While lucid dreaming theorists have systematically employed the term *dream-ego,* most equate the fantasized "I" of the dream with the ego of the waking consciousness. Thus: "The person, or the dream-ego, that we experience being in the dream is the same as our waking consciousness. It constantly influences the events of the dream through its expectations and biases, just as it does in waking life. The essential difference in the lucid dream is that the ego is aware that the experience is a dream. This allows the ego much more freedom of choice and creative responsibility to find the best way to act in the dream" (WLD, 31).[5] The authors of *Exploring the World of Lucid Dreaming* recognize that the most lucid of lucid dreams occur during REM periods or the "paradoxical sleep" of Jouvet's formulation. In his experimental work, Jouvet makes the point that REM sleep is paradoxical because intense cerebral activity coincides with muscle atonia in both humans and animals; that is, in dreams high arousal is conjoined with almost complete paralysis of the body.[6] "Deaf, blind, and paralyzed, the individual becomes very vulnerable. He can only dream if he is in security, for only then can he plunge safely into deep sleep."[7] Hence the question: how does the cognitive activity of the ego operate given the fact that lucid dreamers know, as serious dream researchers do, that the body is paralyzed during REM periods when most lucid dreams appear to surface? If so, we must ask how the ego, the aspect of the mind that is intrinsically connected with the body and fully conscious (or mostly conscious in the Freudian model) could, in a condition of bodily paralysis, surface in the dream and deliberately engage in cognitive activity?

Jouvet seems to be aware of this problem, but he hedges his answer. Although a late believer in lucid dreams, he agrees with LaBerge and others that "dream cognition can be much more reflective and rational than sometimes assumed." But the explanation that he offers is both vague and theoretically unsatisfactory: "An *ego*, conscious of being conscious, and awake, is dreamed up by an unconscious self who cannot interfere, except by stopping the event by the slightest movement. The neurobiological interpretation of such phenomena is totally obscure."[8] A partial answer is provided by Jouvet himself when he says that, in contrast to the sensory splendor one associates "with periods of paradoxical sleep [REM], mental activity during slow wave sleep is generally more poorly recalled. It is closer to thinking than dreaming, less vivid, less visual, more conceptual, subject to greater voluntary control, more related to everyday life, and it occurs during lighter sleep."[9] This is to be expected: the hallucinatory ego does not simply drop in out of the blue; it evolves out of the thinking-I during light sleep or occasionally in day dreaming or during daybreak or in hypnagogic dreaming, that is, dreams that occur prior to the onset of deep sleep or prior to waking. But lucid dreams can apparently appear outside the conditions involving slow wave sleep, that is, during deep sleep and REM states. Even in these conditions it may in exceptional circumstances be possible for the ego to appear in the middle of dream, but I find it hard to document such instances. When I am feeling anxious during the dream, I might say, "this is only a dream," but whether this is the thinking-I that intrudes into the dream or a thought that registers in my passive consciousness is not something I can say for sure.

One has to seriously consider Ouspensky, a cult figure for new age dreamers, when he says that "if I pronounced my name in sleep, I immediately wake up" (cited in WLD, 135). This is confirmed by other dream thinkers, and one of the most prominent, Patricia Garfield, says that while it is not impossible to say one's name in a dream, "it *is* disruptive."[10] A name is an identity badge and designates an ego, a thinking-I, a live self-conscious being. No wonder that when I utter my name I wake up and the dream-ego dissolves into the ego of the waking consciousness. But not for LaBerge, who, in one of his early lucid dreams repeats, "I am Stephen, I am Stephen," and, presto, he continued to sleep and nothing unusual happened (WLD, 136). My guess is that simply saying "I am Stephen" was not good enough, given the dream scientist's patent wish to disconfirm Ouspensky. The dream-ego plays all sorts of tricks, and the utterance "I am Stephen" might send out a network of word associations, for example, toward some other Stephen he knew or even the famed Steven Daedalus, bypassing the dreamer Stephen LaBerge. If in his dream he loudly proclaimed, "I am Stephen LaBerge, the Stanford psychologist," I would bet my bottom dollar he would wake up! LaBerge is, however, willing to admit that it is impossible to engage in writing during lucid dreaming.[11] This is not surprising because writing is the discursive operation par excellence, although we now know that visionaries can write lengthy texts when they become passive receptacles for dictation from the spirit. I would say that the issue is not one of writing per se but whether writing involves the "I" of the waking consciousness. It seems that when genuine self-reflection enters, the dream will terminate "like a ghost that has been laid."

Let me get back to Jouvet's frank admission that neurological science cannot yet understand how the ego can function during paradoxical sleep when the body is paralyzed. Because science is not the only way to realize lucidity in interpretation, I am compelled to adopt an ascientific and intuitive grasp of the death of the ego under the conditions of body paralysis and the emergence of the dream-ego with its own form of passive cognitive functioning.

Let me begin with LaBerge. In the very first page of *Lucid Dreaming* he makes the point that "I was in full possession of my waking faculties while dreaming and soundly asleep."[12] But there is obviously one catch. That is, if the dreamer is fully conscious, then it would be possible for him to go about in his kitchen, make a cup of coffee, and still continue to dream.[13] Of course, it is possible to walk into the kitchen and make coffee, but only within the lucid dream itself. Hence it would be presumptuous for a lucid dreamer to say that it is his waking self rather than his hallucinatory ego that is engaged in kitchen activity. LaBerge is obviously aware of the impossibility of being fully conscious or awake during lucid dreaming, if by the terms *conscious* or *awake* one is equating one's imputed dream consciousness with everyday consciousness. Hence he must perforce qualify his earlier argument: "I say that dreamers are asleep in regard to the physical world because they are not in conscious sensory contact with it; likewise, they are awake to the inner worlds of their dreams because they are in conscious contact with them."[14] Thus it seems that LaBerge recognizes that one is not fully conscious in lucid dreaming, and, indeed, we can say that it would be impossible to be fully conscious given the fact that in REM dreams one is out of touch with the physical world outside and the body is temporarily paralyzed. All LaBerge can say is "So if you can say to yourself while dreaming that 'what I am doing just now is *dreaming*,' you are, if fact, conscious."[15]

The nature of being conscious in dreams was first formulated by Hervey de Saint-Denys, who insisted that "will" and "attention" are operative in lucid dreams as they are in waking life. But he adds some very important qualifications. In our ordinary conscious living, "free will" operates when we make ethical decisions, yet in a dream I might do things that I would not do in my everyday life, such as killing someone.[16] Further limitations on the work of the ego are evident in dreams. Most important for us is Saint-Denys's belief that although "the activity of the will is obvious in certain dreams, [it] does not mean that I believe it to be constantly present. . . . There are many others in which the association of ideas acquires such a vigorous spontaneous flow that the will is unable to hold it in check."[17] Thus, one can initially change the direction of the dream, but then, owing to the "association of ideas," the dream can take us in completely different directions from that envisaged by the conscious dreamer. Saint-Denys also says that under certain conditions, such as daydreaming, there can be "a passivity of the will."[18]

Let me now develop the implication of these ideas by considering one of Saint-Denys's fabulous dreams, long before lucid dreaming became fashionable.[19]

Last night I dreamed that my soul had left my body, and that I was traveling through vast spaces with the rapidity of thought. First I was transported into the midst of a savage tribe. I witnessed a ferocious fight, without being in any danger, for I was invisible and invulnerable. From time to time I looked towards myself, or rather towards the place where my body would have been if I had had one, and was able to reassure myself that I did not have one. The idea came to me to visit the moon, and immediately I found myself there. I saw a volcanic terrain with extinct craters and other details, obviously reproduced from books and engravings I had read or seen, but singularly amplified and made more vivid by my imagination. I was well aware that I was dreaming, but I was by no means convinced that the dream was entirely false. The remarkable clarity of everything I saw gave rise to the thought that perhaps my soul had temporarily left its terrestrial prison, an occurrence that would be no more remarkable than so many other mysteries of creation. . . . Immediately, I wished to return to earth; I found myself back in my bedroom. For a moment I had the strange sensation of looking at my sleeping body, before taking possession of it again. Soon I thought that I had got up and with pen in hand was writing down in detail everything I had seen. Finally I awoke, and a thousand details which had recently been so clear in my mind faded almost instantly from my memory.[20]

It is certainly the case that the dreamer is aware that he is dreaming, and let me assume for the moment that the will or ego operates during the dream when Saint-Denys says, "the idea came to me to visit the moon." He did visit that moon, but it seems to me that, even if the ego makes the decision to visit that planet the fantasy-I or dream-ego takes over when he says that his soul had left his body, permitting the dream-ego to travel through space with the rapidity of thought, moving from one cosmic realm to another, just as Blavatsky's did as she traveled through cosmic dream space into Tibet. Saint-Denys clearly says he was aware he had left his physical body behind and it was his dream body traversing the cosmos. It is hard to believe that the ego of consciousness could exist in the hallucinatory body of the dreamer. Although the thinking-I might instigate the dream, another form of cognitive functioning takes over: what I have labeled passive cerebral activity. In this particular dream, Saint-Denys's formulation "the idea came to me" might well denote the kind of "awareness" that I mentioned with respect to Buddhist meditation. Saint-Denys's thinking in his dream perhaps belongs to the larger class of experiences akin to the Buddhist "meditative awareness," rather than the "self-awareness" of the waking ego that lucid dreamers claim enters the space of the dream. His guess that "the passivity of the will" occurs in daydreaming ought to be extended to other arenas where the will or ego seems to be temporarily suspended, and this includes ordinary dreaming. We now know that, because it is almost impossible in normal discourse to report the dream in passive terms, the active "I think" enters into dream reporting. Consequently, the dreamer translates passive knowing or awareness into the active mode of conscious thinking. Here, as elsewhere, we are confronted with the "prison house of language" from which one cannot easily extricate oneself.

One can argue that, if ego consciousness is operative in the dream, it ought to create a rationally cohesive dream narrative. But all cases of lucid dreams confirm our hypothesis regarding dream coherence. In his dream Saint-Denys initially moves to a savage place; then he witnesses a fight, the details of which are not clear except that the dreamer was invisible to those fighting; then he visits the moon (or somewhere similar) where he sees volcanic craters; he returns to earth and into his bedroom, still in the dream; and so on till he wakes. There is a story here, but not one that is rationally organized or enplotted. Yet it is not incoherent. Let me add that when I dream I sometimes appear different from me in my waking life, and even people I know do not appear in their waking shapes in the dream. LaBerge has performed an interesting experiment where, in spite of claimed ego control, the dreamer's image gets distorted. "In one experiment, subjects were asked to carry out specific tasks in their lucid dreams, including finding a mirror in the lucid-dream setting and looking at the image in the mirror. . . . Subjects had no difficulty in finding a mirror and seeing a reflection, but more often than not, what they saw was somehow different from their waking reflection."[21] The so-called control supposedly exercised by the ego of conscious life is simply not there in the distorting mirror; rather, what we have here is the familiar hallucinatory work of the dream-ego in our sense of that term.

Saint-Denys mentions another interesting feature of his lucid dreams: "Even when I am perfectly conscious of the fact that I am dreaming, I find it extremely difficult to recognize that when some imaginary companion is sharing my illusions with me, he is only a shadow, forming part of the vision. I dream for example that I have climbed up the tower of a church with one of my friends and we marvel at the panorama which meets our gaze. I know very well that it is only a dream, but nevertheless I say to the friend who is with me: 'Please make sure you remember this dream, so that we can talk about it tomorrow when we are awake.'"[22] The friend or shadow in Saint-Denys's dream is the dream alter or other whose task it is to remind the dreamer to remember the dream that then is written down by Saint-Denys's own reflective consciousness.

In a previous discussion I pointed out the influence of Jung in the nonelitist oneiromancy of Euro-American modernity. So is it with lucid dreaming, with one important proviso, namely, its temptation to create a dream world in which the shadow can be erased. Dream therapy, if it is to be genuinely Jungian, must confront the shadow, and in that great drama there will be a play of opposites, an enantiodromia wherein such things as heaven and hell, yin and yang, good and evil will be married. So is it with the awakened ones in the religions I have dealt with: they too must meet the shadow or some form of the dark night of the soul, most often during their trance illnesses; so is it in forms of shamanism; and so in European myths where the dragon has to be met, confronted, and killed by the dream hero. For Jungians, dreams are part of a larger complex of symbolic formations wherein the visionary or dreamer confronts and overcomes the shadow side of his or her being. In some lucid dreams recounted in LaBerge and Rheingold, the dreamer of nightmares does confront the shadow, but without understanding what the shadow represents. In others, the shadow is simply wished away.[23] Consider the following dream where the dreamer confronts the shadow and erases it. "In the midst of a lucid dream I saw a series of grey-black pipes. Out of the largest pipe emerged a black widow [spider] about the size of a cat. As I watched this black widow, it grew larger and larger. However, as it was growing I was not the least bit afraid and I thought to myself 'I am not afraid' and I made the black widow vanish. I was very proud of my achievement since I had always been terrified of black widows. The earliest nightmare I can remember was about a large black widow which I couldn't escape. For me, black widows were a very strong symbol of fear itself" (WLD, 228).

Without doubt there is an immediate therapeutic benefit because this dreamer has lost the fear of black widows. The erasure of the shadow results in the erasure of a symptom. Yet the Jungian critique remains: has this dreamer really confronted his shadow, or, as a Freudian might put it, has the dreamer dealt with the ontogenetic meaning of the black widow; or even its existential significance, which thinkers like Ludwig Binswanger were concerned with? I am tempted to speculate that the symbolism of the "black widow," with its double meanings, is somehow related to a significant other in the dreamer's life. Unfortunately, LaBerge and Rheingold do not provide, in this case and in others, any information on the life of the dreamer.[24]

From the perspective of this essay, the most interesting of lucid dreams are those that give "intimations of a wider world," to use a chapter subheading from *Exploring the World of Lucid Dreaming*.[25] This wider world gives us a glimpse of a visionary transcendence of our everyday lives and might tempt seekers to use "lucid dreaming to take them to their spiritual goals" (WLD, 300). Let us see whether these goals can be realized by considering one of the most interesting and detailed lucid dreams of transcendence. Because of its length I shall quote only sections of the dream experienced by PK from San Francisco that I think are relevant for us in understanding the wider salvific claims of lucid dreaming.

> I am standing quietly alone in a room when I become aware that I am dreaming. . . . [PK thought of various options and then] I recall my intention of seeking the meaning of life and decide to pursue this task. Outside, the evening is clear and quiet with stars shining brightly. I float comfortably on my back, gazing up at the heavens. I notice the moon is not visible and assume it has already gone down. I'd like to see it, though, and figure that if I rise high enough I should be able to. Immediately I began to ascend, still in the same position. [The dreamer found himself up near some power lines, but this, PK decided in his dream, is not what he wanted. One can hardly blame PK if he misses the significance of the "power lines" that take him to another world.] I decide at this point to visit the moon. I hold my hands out in front of me and fly upward into the sky. Moving more and more rapidly, soon I sense a roundish shape appearing behind my hands. I lower my hand, expecting to see the moon. The shock of what I see is very dramatic and startling: It is not the moon at all, but quite clearly it is the planet Earth! It is an exquisitely lovely vision, a gem glowing in soft greens and blues with swirling whites against the sable sky.
>
> Quickly replacing the sense of shock is a feeling of great elation and I jump up and down in space, clapping my hands and shouting joyfully. I've always wanted to be out here—I feel a thrilling rush and a sense of accomplishment. . . . I shift my focus to my surroundings: I am floating in the midst of a vast, limitless darkness that is at the same time brilliant with countless stars, and very much alive. This aliveness is somehow almost audible: I feel I am "hearing" with my entire being, sensing the "deafening silence" as in a deep forest. This is an exquisitely wonderful place to be.

Now I am beginning to move away from the stars and Earth, which becomes smaller and smaller until it disappears. Soon I am seeing entire solar systems and galaxies, moving and spinning harmoniously, growing smaller and smaller as they, too, gradually fade into the distance. I hover in space totally amazed. There is a profound sense of eternal energy everywhere.

Again I remember the experiment [of lucid control] and decide to try a question. I feel rather uncertain of how to put it and wish I had given more thought to formulating the question. But the moment seems most auspicious and I don't want to miss this opportunity, so I ask, "What's the meaning of the Universe?" This sounds too presumptuous so I rephrase the question, and ask, "May I know the meaning of the Universe?"

The answer comes in a wholly unexpected form. Something is emerging from the darkness. It looks like some kind of living molecular model or mathematical equation—an extremely complex, three-dimensional network of fine lines glowing like neon lights. It's unfolding itself, multiplying, constantly changing, filling up the Universe with increasingly complex structures and interrelationships.

This growing movement is not erratic but consistent and purposeful, rapid but at the same time unhurried, determined. When it has expanded beyond me, continuing to multiply, I think of returning to the ordinary world.

When almost back, I call out a very sincere "Thank you! Thank you!" to the Universe for the spectacular vision. I awake with wonder, excitement and delight, as well as a renewed and deeply moving respect for the Universe.

This experience left me with a renewed feeling of awe and respect for the nature and splendor and creative energy force of the Universe. It's as if I was seeing the invisible relationships connecting all things—the intimate molecular level superimposed over the vast and limitless Universe. This was indeed a powerfully moving and impressive event. It also led me to believe that in some way, I, too, am a unique and essential part of whatever is going on here—the Divine is within as well as without.

(WLD, 279–82)

There is no doubt that this is a powerful dream, but similar ones have been dreamt of before by Europeans, for example, the dream-vision of Henry Vaughan (1622–1695), mentioned in an earlier epigraph and based perhaps on Pythagorean and Platonic prototypes with which he was familiar.[26] Both the revelatory message and the substance of the dream exhibit striking similarity with Jung's vision during his trance illness. We do not know whether PK was familiar with his European past, but without doubt he is strongly influenced by current science fiction and movies and perhaps he is aware of LaBerge's characterization of lucid dream travelers as "oneironauts" with its obvious connection with "astronauts." Unfortunately, we are told nothing about PK's life or even gender.[27] Assuming he is a male, we note that he is interested in the search for the meaning of life and a wish to be "up there." It is most likely that PK must have pondered the meaning of life, as most of us do, and, if so, the existential wish is beautifully realized in the dream. It is not surprising that PK feels that his is a privileged vision, not just an ordinary dream but one commanding a sense of awe, from the beautiful view of planet earth to the galaxies and the mathematical power lines that surely would give the visionary dreamer a sense of mystery and permit him to project notions of "some kind of living molecular model or mathematical equation—an extremely complex, three-dimensional network of fine lines glowing like neon lights." Nevertheless, it is doubtful there is anything in the dream to suggest that the dreamer is in "some way" a part of "whatever is going on here." It is an insight or awareness occurring during the dreaming itself or more likely a postdream inference based on prior "fantasy activity." Having made that inference, the dreamer then makes a further interpretive leap, "the Divine is within as well as without." That is, the dream provides a projective screen for a kind of numinous or transcendental interpretation. If a similar dream was dreamt by a Tibetan visionary, he would be able to anchor the dream to his own Buddhist epistemology. This then is the problem with the "intimations of a wider world" by lucid dreamers. That wider world is a hint, an intimation at best, of another reality, and it is left to the dreamer to figure out what that reality is, an extremely difficult task because, as with Jung and Bataille, the dream is not encompassed within a larger, culturally intelligible religious worldview. Indeed many of the examples of such "intimations" that LaBerge has collected seem to me quite shallow. A final point: when PK *reports* the dream, it seems that the self-conscious I is operating, but the likelihood is that thoughts appeared in the dream through the operation of passive cerebral activity.

LaBerge is aware of the complexity of the salvific problem and tries to address it in his work, but he is on the horns of a dilemma. On the one hand he wants to affirm that oneironauts might have intimations of a mystical or transcendental order, but on the other he is aware that this might be difficult, if not impossible, to realize. Let us see how LaBerge himself realizes something transcendental in one his "most memorable and personally meaningful lucid dreams" (WLD, 294).

> Late one evening several years ago, I found myself driving in my sports car down a dream road, delighted by the vibrantly beautiful scenery, and perfectly aware that I was dreaming. After driving a short distance further, I saw a very attrac-

tive hitchhiker on the side of the road just ahead. I hardly need to say that I felt strongly inclined to stop and pick her up. But I said to myself, "I've had that dream before. How about something new?" So I passed her by, resolving instead to seek "The Highest." As soon as I opened myself to guidance, my car took off into the air, flying rapidly upwards, until it fell behind, like the first stage of a rocket and I continued to fly higher into the clouds. I passed a cross on a steeple top, a star of David, and other religious symbols. As I rose still higher, beyond the clouds, I entered a space that seemed a limitless mystical realm: a vast emptiness that was overflowing with love, and unbounded space that felt somehow like home. My mood had lifted as high as I had flown, and I began to sing with ecstatic inspiration. The quality of my voice was truly amazing—it spanned the entire range from deepest bass to highest soprano. I felt as if I were embracing the entire cosmos in the resonance of my voice.

(WLD, 294–95)

An impressive experience undoubtedly. The dreamer does not take the road to hedonism enticed by the girl hitchhiker, a typical scenario for someone owning a sports car. That path is easy to take because the dreaming author has told us earlier that "the lucid dreaming state tends to be a hotbed of sexual activity" owing to "increased vaginal blood flow or penile erection" during REM periods (WLD 171). Naturally, he seeks the upper road journeying into what he calls "The Highest." This wonderfully vague term takes us to the philosopher's abstractions noted earlier, but also I think contains an argument with new age religions that emphasize a "higher self."[28] However, unlike the higher self, "The Highest" aims at, or shows the path to, the realization of a transcendental goal. Yet "no assumptions need be made about the 'The Highest' except that whatever it is, it is hierarchically speaking, prior to everything else, and also more valuable than anything else" (WLD, 293). LaBerge, with his knowledge of Tibetan Buddhism, knows that to reach the "highest" one must relinquish ego control and yield to "something beyond the ego" and engage in "surrender" to it. And, while the Buddhist meditator will agree, this will be hard for the lucid dreamer who claims to control the dream through the work of the ego. Hence "despite having surrendered ego-control of the direction of your dream, you must maintain lucidity," but how this can happen is not clear from the lucid dreams he recounts. There is a way out, though, a Jungian-type solution that fits neatly with much of Western thought, including recent new age religions. Instead of the workaday ego of everyday life, one must say: "I surrender control to my true self," that is, finding out "who you truly are" (WLD, 293). LaBerge wants to have the Tibetan cake and eat it too because he surely knows that, in any ultimate sense, Buddhism rarely recognizes any form of the self unless it is a false or illusory self. But LaBerge assumes that if one surrenders to the true self then the path to the "highest" is available to the lucid dreamer. I take it that the "highest" means a pathway to salvation that the awakened ones of my essay have generally thought of as a hard road full of deep ruts, strewn with obstacles. Therefore, as far as salvation is concerned, I will say this of lucid dreaming: one can always leap over the edge of the razor.

Although he strives for the highest, LaBerge honestly believes that if, in a dream, someone "experiences some transcendental reality, whether God, the Void, Nirvana, and so on," it necessarily "does not allow us to conclude that the dreamer actually experienced that transcendental reality" (WLD, 295). A puzzling statement: if one does experience a transcendental reality in a dream, why is it not a *real* transcendental reality, especially as LaBerge and others want to convince us that "life is a dream" and that lucid dreams gives us intimations of transcendence? (WLD, 279) To me the answer is simple enough: the cases described by lucid dreamers hardly give *us* any indication that they have in fact experienced a transcendental reality. Hence LaBerge's dilemma: he also seeks the highest, but is forced to recognize that the sought-after salvific goal eludes the dreamer. To complicate matters, some studies have found that "more than 80 percent of those who believed in a personal deity found God in their dreams represented as a person" and "more than 80 percent of those who believed in an impersonal divinity experienced the Divine as something other than a person" (WLD, 296). No doubt the dreamers concerned would have felt that dreams verified their sense of God, or divinity, but the study clearly indicates that lucid dreamers simply dream what they are already predisposed to believe, hardly an intimation of salvation or a reaching out to the "highest."[29]

The salvific dilemma is not only confined to LaBerge and lucid dreamers but also applies to many involved in the contemporary dream movement. Let me frame the issue somewhat bluntly by putting together the scattered references to the death of God mentioned in this essay. As we have suggested, the late nineteenth century saw not only the high point of capitalist and colonial expansion but also the triumph of Enlightenment rationality, the death of God and the encroaching disenchantment of the world along with various ways whereby one could restore bits and pieces of the magical garden. Dreams are of course one route, but none of the Romantic poets and composers or the emerging opium eaters thought that such forms could open the royal road to salvation. One had to fall back on reinterpretations of traditional Christianity or reaffirm the ideal of an abstract principle governing the universe or resort to the new forms of ecstatic, even quietist evangelical religions or simply remain enlightened agnostics, nonbelievers. This period also saw the opening up of alternative salvific possibilities, with the increasing knowledge of Indian religions, mostly Buddhism and the abstract theistic religiosity of Vedanta that was soon popularized by Swami Vivekananda in the early twentieth century.

By contrast, the late nineteenth and early twentieth century saw the rapid spread of meditational practices among the lay intelligentsia, not only in today's Buddhist nations but also among Euro-American Buddhists. Let me remind the reader that Buddhist "insight meditation" (*vipassanā, vipaśyanā*) attempts to diagnose the human condition, to recognize the illusory nature of the self and all structures of existence, and for some this might include nirvana. It is intrinsically related to Buddhist existential understandings of the world, especially the Four Noble Truths and the ultimate realization of nirvana along with the cessation of rebirth. Yet contemporary Euro-Buddhist meditation, including that of middle-class Asians, is a much more shortened, communally oriented retreat, in the double sense of that term, from the labors of modern society.[30]

One of the earliest attempts to modernize meditation was the work of the Myanmar monk Bhikkhu Sadayaw, who invented a form of Buddhist meditation that dispensed with the preliminaries of calming (*samatha*) and produced a rationalized technology of insight meditation divested of devotional practices, Buddhist cosmological understandings, as well as many doctrinal underpinnings. In a further radical move, he said that monks were not necessary for teaching *vipassanā* and, indeed, non-Buddhists might also benefit from it—moves that touched the heart of modernity. One of Sadayaw's pupils from Sri Lanka founded a Buddhist meditation at Kanduboda that provided meditation courses in English as well as formal certification.[31] Another influence was John Kornfield, a major figure in training Americans as *vipassanā* instructors. In 1981 Kornfield founded the Spirit Rock Meditation Center in California, where nine of the regular teachers are (or were) trained psychotherapists.[32] Kornfield's meditative programs were based on that of Goenka, who radically shortened Sadayaw's arduous three-month program to ten-day retreats (sometimes longer, but not more than thirty days). Goenka came from a wealthy Indian business family, and his techniques not only gained ground among educated native Buddhists but also spread quickly among Euro-Buddhists.[33]

What we have here is an extremely interesting give and take between Buddhism and Euro-American modernity. The monk Sadayaw was prompted to invent his abbreviated form of *vipassanā* meditation because European businessmen who had no time or energy for the rigors of the traditional meditative disciplines sought him out. The felt white man's need was taken up by Goenka and exported to the West, where it remains, to this day, the dominant Theravāda form of *vipassanā* meditation. This abridged *vipassanā* was brought back from

Europe to the Theravāda societies of South and Southeast Asia among which it found a home with the middle classes striving to achieve a Buddhist balance while living in an increasingly fragmented and competitive modernity and, in some nations like Myanmar and Sri Lanka, in the context of collective violence and brutality that seem to openly flout every brand of Buddhist ethics. However, it was not Theravāda meditation and thought that had the most lasting and popular impact on contemporary Europe and America but rather Vajrayāna, which received an enormous fillip with the conquest of Tibet by the Chinese and the subsequent Tibetan diaspora.

Tibetan Buddhism also had to confront Euro-American modernity. As everyone knows, there was an explosion of knowledge of Vajrayāna, both in the popular as well as academic presses, and it was taught in major religion departments in universities. But, like Theravāda, its meditative asceses were also mutated in its adaptation to the West. Even the present Dalai Lama encourages mass meditation rallies and drastically shortened forms of retreats. The epistemology underlying Tibet's meditative disciplines has also to be watered down to make sense to the Euro-American middle classes.[34] While the complex salvific beliefs and particularly Mahāyāna and Vajrayāna epistemology are available to those who seek them, this difficult knowledge is not the forte of most. It is with reference to the amended or simplified vision of Tibetan Buddhism that we have to interrogate LaBerge and others who want to engage in Tibetan practices and yet retain such Jungian ideas as wholeness and the unity of the self impossible to justify in most forms of Buddhism.

I have already shown that while lucid dream theory claims to have been influenced by Tibetan dream yoga, the latter has little affinity with lucid dreams. But this is not LaBerge's position. He knows that lucid dreams are not a "complete path to enlightenment," but they might show the dreamer such a path. "I see it primarily as a signpost pointing to the possibility of higher consciousness, a reminder that there is more to life than people are ordinarily aware of, and an inspiration to seek a guide who knows the way" (WLD, 300). But there is no guide, only detailed and simple technologies for achieving lucidity with a culminating exercise for seeking the highest. In a typical modernist move, the guidebook takes the place of the guide.

LaBerge apparently got interested in lucid dreams after hearing a Tibetan guru named Tarthang Tulku, founder of the Nyingma Institute in Berkeley, lecture at the Esalen Institute. For LaBerge, Tibetan Buddhism is a kind of philosophical underpinning and a mythic charter for the lucid dream movement. Especially influential was the Tulku's openness mind doctrine, in which he says: "Dreams are a reservoir of knowledge and experience, yet they are often overlooked as a vehicle for exploring reality" (WLD, 10). The Tulku goes on to formulate prescriptions that would appeal to lucid dreamers, Jungians, and new age religions: "We begin to see less and less difference between the waking and dream state" and the awareness based on dream practice can "help create an inner balance" (WLD, 285). Thus "advanced *yogis* are able to do just about anything in their dreams. They can become dragons or mythical birds, become larger or smaller or disappear, *go back into childhood and relive experiences*, or even fly through the air" (WLD, 286; my emphasis). Outside the temptations these adventures might hold for oneironauts, there is no need for Freudian therapy, it is implied, because one can go back to childhood and relive experiences and presumably bring them under control. It looks as if the Tulku has been reading new age religious literature, where such theories abound, and he brings them back into the circuit of his already watered-down-for-the-West Tibetan beliefs, as, for example, when he says that we can use dreams to develop a "flexible attitude" or "change ourselves as well" and "create an inner balance."[35] In similar vein, he has incentives for us living in our everyday world of scarcity and want: "even the hardest things become enjoyable and easy. When you realize that everything is like a dream, you attain pure awareness. And the way to attain pure awareness is to realize that all experience is like a dream" (WLD, 286). The Tulku is one of the many Indian and Tibetan gurus who have adapted their Buddhism to the needs of Euro-Americans, in his case Nyingmapa-Vajrayāna made palatable for an intelligent Western audience.[36] There is a lot more advice given by the Tulku, which ends with the significance of "union," one that impressed LaBerge. "With the dawning of this Divine Wisdom, the microcosmic aspect of the Macrocosm becomes fully awakened; the dew-drop slips back into the Shining Sea, in Nirvanic Blissfulness and At-one-moment, possessed of All Possessions, Knower of All-Knowledge, Creator of all Creations—the One Mind, Reality Itself" (WLD, 288). Buddhist texts, as well as Platonic and Christian literature, as we have shown, occasionally use an obscure language of dialectical oppositions, but rarely at this level of obscurantism.

EROTICISM AND THE DREAM-EGO

We noted that LaBerge's dream-ego refused to yield to possible erotic temptations provided by the hitchhiker. But because such temptations have to be accepted and transformed into a salvific idiom of redemption in Vajrayāna, I must now ask how the transmuted and sublimated erotic desire found in Tibetan religion appears in lucid dreams. Hugh Urban has demonstrated the manner in which Tibetan Tantra has been adopted by American hedonisms, but for me some of these hedonisms are extremely innovative and authentically American![37] I will illustrate the American uses of Tantra in the work of Patricia Garfield, a major practitioner, theorist, and popularizer of lucid dreams who has shown us the way to sustained orgasmic pleasure through dreams, including some ludic forms of lucidity.

Tibetan dream yoga, as exemplified in the work of the Theosophist Evans-Wentz, is the main inspiration for Garfield and is a kind of charter myth for her form of lucid dreaming.[38] Garfield used a method of relaxation combined with autosuggestion to produce prolonged lucid dreams that ranged from zero to a high of three per week (WLD, 79–80). She says that "orgasm is a natural part of lucid dreaming" and "experience convinces me that conscious dreaming *is* orgasmic," a view contested by other lucid dreamers (cited in WLD, 171).[39] Garfield's technology of lucid dreaming produces fantastic orgasmic dreams wherein "the source of stimulation and the partners vary, but the energy flow is constant."[40]

> Most often, Zal [Garfield's husband] is my lover. But he is not always so—images of other men, imaginary or real, appear. Once, I confess, it was my father, although I had to tell myself repeatedly that his image was part of myself that I had to integrate—the father part—to make intercourse possible. Other dream lovers have included a kind of male angelic creature, a rare woman, or half man-half woman, and myself. Animals, plants, and objects all become more sexualized in my lucid dreams. A pink rose-bud, a sparkling fountain, a pipe with its bowl warm from being smoked, and many other such things have served as sexual implements in lucid dreams.
>
> I have been made love to by some strange beasts in these dreams. The ultimate of the animal-intercourse series was a strange sort of horse-goat who made love to me from behind. It might have been frightening, but I was amused to see, by peeping over my shoulder, that the tip of his grey beard was like Zal's and the edge of the Ben Franklin-style spectacles he wore were like those Zal wears.
>
> Sometimes I am my own lover in lucid dreams. Once, like a hermaphrodite, I found I possessed a penis myself and by bending into a circle could take the silky organ into my own mouth to climax. More often, I am airborne while the waves of sexual energy rise higher, and at some ultimate moment the tension is broken by a body movement. I will be climbing upward or hovering in the air, and suddenly arch backwards into orgasm. Or I lie upon my stomach as I float and merely lift my legs up behind me as I burst. During these ecstatic episodes, I often gaze upon beautiful sights. Once, for example, I watched a golden yellow egg that hung in the air near me; it was etched with a castle scene, an intricate tiny world. Or I roll over

and over, spinning in space. Once, as I lay on my back in the air, I circled round and round clockwise. At the instant of orgasm, I opened and shut my fingers rapidly as my body shattered. Often I will bring on the orgasm by ascending to great heights and then turning, plummet back to earth or ocean. On impact with land or water, I explode into orgasm.[41]

The wonder-evoking orgasms of Garfield's cavorting dream-ego constitute some of the most fabulous of erotic dreams that I have read about (and unhappily never experienced), the high point, one might say, of American Tantra. Most striking to me is her open honesty and refusal to hide under some kind of ethical or psychoanalytic mask. Like LaBerge, she invokes Tibet to understand her orgasmic dreams and other vivid ones as well, and one of her gurus is Tarthang Tulku Rinpoche, who is also LaBerge's inspiration. Her dreams blend Tibetan Vajrayāna beliefs with her own personal dream imagery in an extremely creative way, authentically American but remote from the epistemological reality enshrined in Tibetan doctrinal texts.[42] Like many a new age thinker, she is a true bricoleur picking her ideas from other sources here and there, from the Senoi, from American Indians, and from ancient Greeks, but woven into the fabric of her vision of a personal maṇḍala or, as she has put it, "the way of the dream mandala" inspired by Tibet.[43]

To me these dream orgasms have deep implications. I believe they are important for understanding incubus visitations, found almost everywhere in the ethnographic record. When I once asked a Sri Lankan woman why she wants to get rid of the incubus when it offers her indescribable pleasures, the reply was obvious. In Buddhist societies, as well as the Christian and everywhere else, the incubus visit is an unnatural affliction, the work of the devil or one of his disciples.[44] Hence the torture the woman suffers as she undergoes orgasmic pleasure. It seems that Garfield's example suggests that one can experience wonderful pleasure, but only if the ethical taboos that religions or secular ideologies have forced upon us can be ignored, erased, rationalized, or otherwise removed. Then only will the principle of uninhibited hedonistic pleasure be fully realized. However much Garfield says that anyone can experience these pleasures, I can only interject some doubt. They can only do so if they extinguish the ethical work of the conscience or the censor in whatever shape or form such forces or mechanisms intervene in our lives. Lucid orgasmic dreams such as Garfield's are those of sexually liberated women and men of our times—or those waiting to be liberated or those who think they are liberated.

Garfield's liberating and libertine experience provides us with another insight regarding the already emerged Euro-American divinization of orgasmic sexuality, not so much in dreams but in everyday life. In films and in popular fictional narratives, this is explicitly recognized. But largely unrecognized is the implication of whether flesh and blood beings can maintain orgasmic pleasure with a partner without running out of steam, as it were, or when custom becomes stale as partners become familiar with each other; when they bring forth children who provide another kind of love or, as the Bible promises us, when desire itself shall fail or when recognition inevitably dawns on us that every living being withers with age. But Garfield gives us hope: these most pleasurable dream orgasms can go on presumably unabated even with our failing human capacities. But then the Brontë question resurfaces for many of us who might want to take this route: it might get us hooked into lucidity's opiate, a draught that makes our workaday world an empty or boxed-in space, to use Jung's metaphor.

Garfield's eroticism provides insight into forms of dream-visions where neither the incubus nor her kind of orgasmic and uncomplicated lucidity is present. In shamanic visions or dreams one can marry a dream woman or man. Following our ethnographic foci, let me deal with Buddhist shamans in Myanmar documented by Melford E. Spiro in his pioneering work *Burmese Supernaturalism*.[45] Myanmar people are highly ambivalent about their shamans, but they are also necessary for curing and counter sorcery rituals that the official Buddhist religion seems to denigrate. Shamans can be recruited from either gender, but they are mostly women. They often contract a supernatural marriage with a male or female deity or *nat*, a term that is derived from the Sanskrit *nātha*, "lord."

While the Buddha is the head of the Myanmar pantheon, all the deities below him are collectively identified as *nat*s. Immediately below the Buddha are the Hindu-derived gods or *deva*s who are protectors of the Buddha's dispensation or *sāsana*. One rarely enters into erotic relations with these superior beings, but below them there exist a collectivity of thirty-seven *nat*s who are either the pre-Buddhist deities or heroes who have been deified; further down are other types of *nat*s, including nature spirits. Most shamanic erotic relations are with one of the thirty-seven *nat*s. In theory it is the *nat* that initiates the seduction by appearing in dreams. Sometimes the shaman resists, but eventually complies when all sorts of disasters hit him or her or family members. Thus, one female shaman in Mandalay was propositioned by a *nat* in a dream when she was seventeen, but she resisted the call and married a human husband that very year and later had two children by him. Soon she began to be punished by the *nat* in a variety of ways, especially with illnesses and loss of income. At last, at the age of thirty-seven, at the insistence of the *nat*, she divorced her husband and married the *nat*. She not only became free of her symptoms but also recovered the property she had lost. She had been married to the *nat* for six years at the time of Spiro's fieldwork, but she had not yet taken a human husband although the *nat* had no objection.[46]

In another case, a male shaman was loved by his *nat* when he was twenty-five, but at fifty-six he still has not been able to marry her because he had insufficient funds for a *nat* wedding. So she beat him on the back of his head with a wooden sandal and caused him other kinds of abjections.[47] One can sympathize with the plight of the shaman, because the wedding itself is expensive and has to be conducted in grand style. Spiro describes the standard ceremony in fascinating detail. For our purposes, we note that the wedding has to be held in either a *nat* shrine, designated a "palace," or in an improvised structure that symbolically, I think, recreates the "palace," the abode of both deities and kings. At a crucial point in the marriage ceremony the bride or groom and the *nat* enter a bridal chamber, which, among other things, contains two beds. While music is played, a feeding rite takes place in which a shaman feeds the divine lover. This is followed by a wedding ceremony proper. For example, if the shaman is female she returns home where "for seven days, she remains secluded with her nat husband. She does not leave her room, and no one else may enter it. At the end of this period of seclusion she emerges to resume her normal life. She is now known, however, as a *nat kadaw*, a *nat* wife."[48]

The *nat* lover appears to the shaman either in dreams or when he or she is possessed by the lover, especially during religious festivals for the *nats*. In the latter instance, the possessing *nat* informs the shaman about the *nat*'s erotic wishes. I assume that it is not the *nat* who is motivated to love the shaman, but it is the shaman who is motivated to love the *nat*. These motivations are extraordinarily complex, but, owing to the absence of detailed case histories, I will refrain from speculating about them, although the reader will note that they are related to the marital problems of the shaman as well as unsatisfied erotic desire. In addition to the cases already cited, I cite two other cases from Spiro.

1. U Maung Maung was first loved by the nat Ma Ngwei Daun when, at the age of twenty-five, he attended a *nat* festival. She appeared to his dream as a beautiful woman and asked him to have sexual intercourse with her. Although he had taken a human wife only two months previously, he divorced her at the bidding of his *nat* spouse. Ma Ngwei Daun is married to a *nat* husband, U Min Kyaw, who, although consenting to the marriage between his wife and U Maung Maung, always interferes when the latter attempts to have sexual relations with her. Consequently, U Maung Maung has still not succeeded in consummating their relationship.[49]

2. Daw Ei Khin was sixteen when the Mahagiri *nats* ["Great Mountain Lords"] appeared to her in a dream. Five or six years later, she was possessed by U Min Kyaw. Thereafter, as if "deranged," she "drifted about" the village in a trancelike state, barely eating or drinking. Prior to becoming possessed, she had been married and had borne a child, but U Min Kyaw, jealous of her husband, forbade her to resume sexual relations with him. The latter had to become a "servant" of the *nat*, doing his (i.e., his wife's) bidding. She does not suffer from sexual deprivation because she has sexual relations in her sleep with her *nat* husband.[50]

Let me now review our erotic dream material to briefly consider the spectrum of erotic visitations in the dream life. Take the case of simple erotic dreams, those that most of us have had in the course of our lives, in which we have had sexual relations with erotically desirable, even tabooed, partners. There is no doubt whatever in these cases that it is the dream-ego or fantasy-I that engages in erotic activity. These erotic engagements could sometimes be anxiety provoking or disturbing; at other times they are entirely pleasurable. With dream incubi-succubae (or with the devils in the medieval European cases) there is a change when guilt and anxiety become associated with the erotic pleasures of the dream-ego such that incubus dreams often have the quality of a nightmare. With the Myanmar dreams there is a qualitative shift. I suspect that ordinary Myanmar men and women have incubus dreams, but shamans do not, the dream tempter being a divine being, perhaps even a guardian deity or on the way to becoming one after the shaman has married the *nat*. In the Myanmar dream visitations also it is the shaman's dream-ego that engages in sexual activity, during sleep, not with the flesh-and-blood spouse but with a deity who is simultaneously a member of the pantheon and a dream creation, a culturally patterned emanation of the dream-ego. Even when the *nat* possesses the shaman, the possessing spirit is a transformed and reified version of the dream-ego.

What often complicates the relationship between the deity and the shaman is the latter's ambivalent relationship with the human spouse and sometimes the fear and dread of marrying a divine being, a king or queen of sorts, given the fact that the shaman herself is an ordinary member of the society. What is unthinkable in social reality is possible in the dream reality, but not without its angst. There are hints in Spiro's case studies of the dark-night-of-the-soul type of experiences, particularly when the shaman resists the call of the *nat* to engage in eroticism and marriage. Once the shaman's ambivalence is resolved, a glorious marriage takes place in a palace of the gods that cannot be remotely matched by anything in the mundane world. Most likely, this also applies to the erotic experience itself, a pleasure that is heightened because it is a deity one marries and therefore the experience is something beyond orgasmic pleasure. It does, however, bear a resemblance to Tibetan erotic union with divine consorts, ḍākinīs, and other deities. The differences are also clear: in Vajrayāna, spiritual eroticism is overwhelmingly a concern of male lamas and monks, quite unlike Myanmar shamanic marriages. But what is unthinkable in Myanmar Buddhism (or in mainline Theravāda or Mahāyāna) is the belief that Tibetan spiritual eroticism with a divine or a human consort can and often does lead the adept to the path of salvation. As with the Tibetan, the Myanmar examples also imply that "spiritual eroticism" is, after all, another form of eroticism, however sublimated, simply because sublimation is not a single thing, and the work of sublimation might well succeed as often as it might fail.

EDWIN MUIR: A MYTH DREAMER OF DEATH AND TRANSCENDENCE

> Remember now thy Creator in the days of thy youth, while the evil days come not, nor the years draw nigh, when you shalt say, I have no pleasure in them. . . . Also when they shall be afraid of that which is high, and fears shall be in the way, and the almond tree shall flourish, and the grasshopper shall be a burden, and desire shall fail; because man goeth to his long home, and the mourners go about the streets; Or ever the silver cord be loosed, or the golden bowl be broken, or the pitcher be broken at the fountain, or the wheel broken at the cistern. Then shall the dust return to the earth as it was: and the spirit shall return unto God who gave it.
> —Ecclesiastes 12:1, 5–7

For some the waking dream is but another kind of dream; for others it can be invested with visionary meaning, a dream-vision, as with Wordsworth, or, for others, an intermediate state between waking and dreaming whose visionary significance is at best uncertain or ambiguous. The case of Edwin Muir—literary critic, poet, mystic, and translator (with Willa, his wife) of Kafka—seems further proof that Enlightenment modernity cannot totally block out the visionary consciousness among intellectuals as long as it can be related to dreaming. It is no accident that Muir was familiar with physical isolation and the spaces of silence, born and raised as he was in the remote Orkney Islands off Scotland in a deeply religious Calvinist community. His autobiography is a fascinating document for my purposes because it illustrates a religiously musical thinker who is at the same time a modern poet and critic trying to reconcile his visionary experiences with his Christianity, not the one in which he was born and raised but an eclectic conception of God and of the immortality of the soul and the terrifying reality of death that came from the interpretation of his dreams and visions.[51]

As a young man, Muir had rejected the Calvinism of his childhood and was for some time a socialist, then becoming enamored of Nietzsche around 1919, at age thirty-two, perhaps as a kind of moral revaluation of the consequences of World War 1. He claimed that the "idea of the transvaluation of all values intoxicated me with a feeling of false power" (AA, 118). After he was converted into a Nietzschean worldview he had Nietzschean dream-visions. But soon, especially after severe mental "dejection," he went into Jungian psychoanalysis and then experienced dreams, visions, and trances that "began to come in crowds" (AA, 151). Whereas Muir's "dejection," and the dreams that followed, seem like the familiar trance illness, or a version of the dark night of the soul, there is no description of these experiences in his autobiography. His visionary experiences were not hostile to what he called mythological dreams, which, for Muir, but not for his strangely skeptical Jungian analyst, provided intimations, if not proof, of personal immortality. At the same time, he could continue to play both Nietzschean and Jungian language games when, for example, he says about one of his powerful dream-visions that "it was not 'I' who dreamt it, but something else which the psychologists call the racial unconscious, and for which there are other names" (AA, 158). It is not surprising that Muir felt obsessed with time and imagined he was 250 years old and that, spiritually speaking, he was born before the industrial revolution (AA, 289–91). If the visionary interpretations of his hysterical patients were denigrated by Freud's own rational consciousness, and if Schreber's were relegated to paranoia, not so with Muir, who could speak to those willing to listen, or read about, his visions in his sane autobiography as much as Schreber did in his maddening *Memoirs*. And, in the spirit of this essay, Muir could clearly indicate the bases for his and others' visionary experiences: "No autobiography can confine itself to conscious life, and that sleep, in which we pass a third of our existence, is a mode of experience, and our dreams a part of reality" (AA, 39).

In Muir, as with virtually every visionary who appears here and in the cross-cultural record, the distinction between dream and vision gets blurred. For Muir whether he has dream-visions or plain visions do not matter because he deals "with a class of experiences which the disbeliever in immortality ignores or dismisses as irrelevant to temporal life." And he sketches the contexts of these occurrences: "They come when I am least aware of myself as a personality molded by my will and time: in moments of contemplation when I am unconscious of my body, or indeed that I have a body with separate members; in moments of grief or prostration; in happy hours with friends; and, because self-forgetfulness is most complete then, in dreams and day-dreams and in that floating, half-discarnate state which precedes and follows sleep" (AA, 45). In these moments, when will and consciousness are out, even fleetingly, he discovers his true self and his certainty of immortality. But he also hints at the kind of dream-visions that are now familiar to us, what he calls waking dreams or walking trances, that is, visionary experiences occurring during the day where one could also have dreams, just as one could during the night. His daytime or nighttime dream-visions appear with considerable lucidity, even though he was not a "lucid dreamer" in the sense of having control over and directing the denouement of the dream. Muir's waking dreams or trances are not the deep meditative trances of Buddhist virtuosos, neither are they the ecstatic trances of shamans and men and women in states of possession in which one can be out of consciousness for much longer periods of time, sometimes hours. But with waking dreams, such as Wordsworth's or Muir's, one is out only for a moment or for the briefest span of time, as, for example, when Muir is traveling by bus and sees the passengers masked as animals. The true Christian virtuoso might speak of this fleeting moment of visionary consciousness with "immediately I was in the spirit."

One evening around six, still during the period of his Jungian analysis, Muir had come home after working in the office feeling ill, and he lay down on the couch in the sitting room with his face to the wall while his wife Willa was grading exams and turning over papers that seemed to make a "curiously loud noise in the room." "Then my breathing too grew louder and—this is the only way I can describe it—deliberate at the same time, as if I were breathing because I had willed it, not because I could not help it: the first act or rehearsal of breath" (AA, 152). Those familiar with breathing exercises in Indian meditation will recognize an affinity here.

> I felt my breast rising and falling, and something pressing upon it which I flung off and drew back again. This turned into a great, dark blue wave of sea-water, advancing and receding. A dark blue seascape opened on the lighted wall before me, a dark blue sky arched over it; and as if I had slipped out of my body I was standing on the shore looking at the waves rolling in. A little distance out a naked woman was posted; the waves dashed against her, washing up to her breasts and falling again; but she never moved; she seemed to be fixed there like a statue rising out of some other dimension.
>
> Then everything vanished and I was at the bottom of the sea, with the waves far above me. When I came up again—all this time I was lying on the couch listening to the rustling of the papers behind me—the sea and the sky were perfectly

white like paper; in the distance some black jaded rocks stuck out of the stagnant water; there was no color anywhere but black and white. I began to swim at great speed (at this time I had not yet learned to swim) towards the nearest rock. Round me countless creatures were circling and diving, glass-colored in the white sea: long cylinders about the length of a man, without heads or tails, mouths or eyes. I reached the rock and put out my hand to draw myself up, when one of these creatures fixed itself by the upper end, which seemed to have a little sucker, to the middle of my brow just above my eyes. Filled with rage, I kicked the creature with my bare toes; at last I kicked through it, and it fell like a broken bottle into the sea. All this time I had no fear. I pulled myself to the top of the rock.

(AA, 152–53)

The dream continues into long sequences, with breaks in between, "but the pictures followed one another at such a speed that I could not catch all of them." Gradually the dreams take on more the character of a "mythological dream" when Muir sees in rough woodland a troop of low-browed, golden-haired creatures like monkeys and, in the distance, a procession of white-robed female figures moving slowly as if to the tune of a silent music. "I remember coming to what I thought was the green, mossy trunk of a fallen tree; as I looked at it I saw that it was a dragon, and that it was slowly weeping its eyes into a little heap before it: the eyes were like brooches, ringed blue and red and white, hard and enameled, so that they tinkled as they fell. All these seem natural to me; each pair of eyes as they fell appearing to be pushed out by other eyes behind them" (AA, 153).

After another break in the dream Muir found himself in a wild and rocky place wherein was located a huge palace. He tried to get in, but couldn't. But he managed to enter through a three-foot square opening near the door. The place apparently had been deserted for some time. Muir climbed the balustrade and, raising his hands, dived down below, but he managed to get hold of scaffolding and climbed up again, "hand over hand, at great speed, with the ease of an ape." He went up and up till his head touched the ceiling and broke through it. "Above, there was a broad terrace lined with cypresses; night had fallen, and the dark blue sky was glittering with stars. Tall, robed men were walking with melodramatic stateliness along the terrace, under the trees."

Then follows a dream segment that appears after a few more breaks in the dream when Muir says, "I caught the dream again and I was standing beside a little mountain pool fringed with rushes" (AA, 154). He saw two clouds like scraps of paper floating toward each other and for the first time he was afraid but could not explain why. That felt fear clearly anticipates the next episode.

The two clouds met, blazed up, and turned into an angry sun. The sun began to revolve across the sky. As it revolved two serpents, one red and the other yellow, broke through its crust and began a furious locked battle. Still revolving, bearing the battling serpents with it, the sun burst into flames and in a moment turned to ashes. Black now, it went on wheeling across the paper-white sky. Then it stopped; its periphery trembled and quivered, and I saw that it was legged like a centipede. It began to come down diagonally towards me, walking on an invisible thread like a spider. As it came near I saw that it was a fabulous creature with an armored body and a head somewhat like the prow of a sailing ship, the head being partly that of a woman and partly that of a bird. Its body was jointed in the middle, and looked like two enormous tortoises one on top of the other. I saw now that I was naked and holding a broad sword in my hands. I lifted up the sword, swung it over my shoulder, and struck the creature on the brow. The blow made no alteration. I raised the sword again and struck harder, but the stroke merely pushed the head back. In a fury I thrust the sword into the beast's side at the joint of the armor; then it turned its head and *smiled* at me. This inflamed my fury past all bounds; I twisted the sword round and round; the mail burst open; something with white wings, robed in white, fluttered in the sky; and the creature drew its torn mail round it like an umbrella shutting, thrust its beak into the ground, and shot out of sight.

. . . The next I remember is seeing countless angels flying up in the air, going through absurd and lovely evolutions, looping the loop, hiding behind the edges of the clouds: the whole sky was filled with them. I watched an ordered formation of them flying over a still stretch of water, so that I could see them reflected in it as they passed above me in their flight. Then I was in the air, and when I was a little distance up someone took my hand: it was my wife. We flew up, now and then dropping extravagant curtsies to each other in the air, with a wide and light sweep, keeping our wings still. After a while I noticed that the wing on the shoulder next to her had fallen off, and looking at her I saw that the wing on her corresponding shoulder had disappeared too, so that we were mounting the air on two wings. After we had flown like this for a while we looked down and saw a great crowd ranged in concentric rings beneath us, and in the middle of it a gigantic figure clad in antique armor, sitting on a throne with a naked sword at his side. We flew down and settled on his shoulder, and bending behind his neck kissed each other.

(AA, 154–56)

Muir says that "when this waking dream, or trance, or vision ended I was quite well; all my sickness had gone," a condition of well-being that can be demonstrated for other visionaries also (AA, 156). Yet, Muir's analyst had little sympathy for the patient's view that the dream "seemed to point to immortality." He scoffed at the idea that a revelation had been neatly arranged for his patient and instead pointed to the sexual symbolism in the tubular animals, the two-handed sword, and the dragon shedding its tears. Initially, Muir did not want to interpret the dream and he told his analyst, that the vividness and rapidity of the flow of pictures made the dream "more exhilarating than any I had found in actual life or in poetry." Even the obvious sexual symbols mentioned earlier "did not seem applicable to the dream, which was unearthly, or rather unhuman, and so in a sense unsexual." All this he tried, hopelessly, to convey to his analyst (AA, 156).

This experience was followed by several "similar dreams or walking trances especially when I was about to fall asleep" (AA, 157). I will not mention them here except to say that some of them were awesome or frightening while others were like the cosmic dreams of lucid dreamers. Muir told his analyst that he could stop these "waking dreams," by which he meant those dreams he experienced during the day. The analyst urged him to do so, and "my waking dreams ceased at once, and have never come back again" (AA, 158). Muir also informed his analyst of the duration of his long myth dream: "it might have been half an hour [or] it might have been no more than a few minutes. But I felt it took far less time than the time required to put it into words" (AA, 156).

Let me now focus on the dream just recounted. Muir's dream sequence was highly scripted to fit his autobiography, yet one must take it seriously because it is the dreamer who gives the dream symbols a personal and cosmic significance—more in the spirit of Jung than his Jungian analyst was willing to recognize. Although Muir felt that some sequences eluded interpretation, he tried to connect them into a reasonable whole later on in life. Let me quote parts of his interpretation: "The analyst himself never returned to it again, and his theory that the dream was a myth of the creation does not satisfy me; for while the first part of it points back to the beginning of things, with the first large breathings, the undifferentiated creatures, and the absence of fear (as if consciousness had not yet begun, and fear with it), the last part extends beyond time altogether; and the battle with the wheeling sun, which, after running through all its revolutions, becomes the sphinx, is the last battle with time, after which time, having gathered its torn mail around it vanished into the grave which timelessly waits for it, releases the spirit to eternity." On the whole, Muir feels that there is a pattern to the dream, and it expresses human beginnings and ends, that is, of man's evolution and ultimate destiny. Some parts of the dream, such as that of the palace, were incomprehensible to him; but the existential implications of others were clear enough. "The sun in its revolutions and transmutations is a fantastic image of time, and that is probably why its first appearance evoked my first sense of fear. The woman or statue at the beginning, whom I saw when I still was so far from human consciousness that I could swim among the headless, eyeless sea-creatures without fear, as if I were one of them, seemed to belong to another millennium, and to be a prophecy of a remote future age; as if, long before the existence of mankind, the animal soul were dreaming of it and yearning towards it." The female figures and golden-haired animals had the same prophetic quality, while his attempt to fling himself down a height had two meanings. An immediate meaning is the analyst's injunction to him to come down to earth, and to the real world, but "it also brings to mind images of the Fall and of the first incarnation" of Adam (AA, 159). Given this train of interpretation, it is not surprising that Muir thinks that the armored figure in the last part of the dream was Jehovah surrounded by angels (AA, 160).

People have dreamt what Muir called mythological dreams in every place under the sun, but for Muir the myth is not a copy of something from Revelation, although modeled on it. This means that a myth is never dreamt in its pure form, as it were, because it is locked into the dreamer's motivations and gets "distorted," just as an ordinary dream narrative might be distorted owing to unconscious motivations, prior dream thoughts, and the culture of dreaming prevalent among a particular group. In Muir's case, we know too little of his early childhood conflicts, his sexual and marital relations, to relate his dream to his deep motivations. But then we are forced to ask another question: are deep motivations even relevant to the formation of this dream or other myth dreams with deep existential import? In Muir's case we can't even rely on a professional interpreter of dreams such as Muir's analyst, as he converts the dream into one acceptable to his own ideological framework. Yet this was not acceptable to someone like Muir to whom the dream-vision is a revelation of a truth, as his own interpretation makes clear. It is not surprising that, while he claimed to have benefited from his analysis, Muir was nevertheless relieved when circumstances compelled him to terminate it and he could go his own way. In the medieval past of his own Christian tradition, the revelation of a truth must be consonant with Church dogma, or at least not in contradiction to it, as much as modern dreams must conform, or be made to conform, to the dogma of a particular school of analysis. We have seen that, among Christian mystics of the Middle Ages, visions have to be mediated by a spiritual guide who can direct the interpretation in such a manner that it does not offend the religious sensibility of parishioners or clash too strongly with the teachings of the Church. And so it is even with our modernity and postmodernity where the guide or professional dream interpreter directs the patient or dreamer to an ideologically acceptable mode of understanding, although, for those of us living in a scientific weltanschauung, the interpretation, like all historical interpretations, must compel us to accept "evidence" for the substantiation of a theoretical assertion.

As I see it, Muir's battle with the monster is a primordial Western myth model, though by no means unique to Europe. In Muir's case he cannot kill the sphinx or monster of the apocalypse. He thrusts his sword into the monster, and the monster smiles. It is as if the violent act is no answer to whatever spiritual or salvific goal he is seeking. From the wounded coat of armor of the monster a winged white robed being is born, following, it seems to me, the poet's own rebirth. After some time, countless angels appear all aflutter, a further intimation of peace and of Muir's salvific aspirations. Remember that, prior to that dream segment, Muir found himself in the windowless palace, which was barred to him but that he nevertheless entered through a small opening, then diving down and rising up to the ceiling he broke in a rage. Muir cannot explain this episode, which to me, at least, seems pregnant with the symbolism of rebirth, another motif in both dreams and myths. And, as he "awakens," he sees the enigmatic robed men (like the earlier white robed women) whose pictures perhaps derive from Wordsworth's The Prelude and further down the lane of time from the prototype apocalyptic myth in Revelation 7:9–14, though similar images appear elsewhere in both Christianity and maybe in other religious traditions also.[52] And Muir's dream, in part or as a totality, would have an apocalyptic feel for the Christian conscience of his readership—the feel, if not the substance of Revelation that Muir taps in his own unique interpretation. I also find it surprising that Muir thinks that the dragon and the sphinx in his dream are completely "self-created" rather than a standard part of his own cultural repertoire.

The tearful and seemingly harmless dragon reappears in more terrifying form in the later sequence as the strange serpent-monster the dreamer must subdue. This dream element can be framed in terms of a popular myth model of medieval chivalry, a myth model that can be reconciled with the Christian battle between good and evil. But Muir's monster proves to be harmless, as it transforms itself into another peaceful being. After the pseudo-combat is over, it seems reasonable that the myth dream should reveal the liberation of the dreamer when there appears a figure on the throne who indeed could be Jehovah but, given the previous sequence, appropriately dressed as a knight in armor and surrounded by angels (clothed in bourgeois forms pictured in British calendars) alongside whom the joyous Muir and his wife float kissing each other. One wing of his wife and one of his falls off, but they fly together on their joint wings, united together in love, until they settle on the shoulders of the knight Jehovah in divine matrimony.

What I have speculatively highlighted are some of the elements of the dream that emerge from the so-called racial unconscious that Muir speaks about, that is, mythemes emerging into the field of the vision from the dreamer's cultural and historical past. As with all dream narratives, these mythemes are incorporated into the dream as a "coherent" account, though not a rationally organized one in which all the parts seem to fit into a whole. It seems to me that the first two dream sequences dealing with the waves and the statue-like woman, followed by the creatures circling and diving in the white sea, cannot be easily reconciled with the rest as a total vision. There are also dream sequences that Muir could not recall. The interconnections between the remembered sequences are made by Muir, who is both the dreamer and the interpreter combined, a common enough phenomenon. For Muir, the vision or waking dream brims over with existential meanings owing to its unmistakable revelatory quality. It is the curse of our modernity, and the scientific weltanschauung in which we live, and from which we cannot escape, that forces intellectuals like me to question his interpretation and to place within quotation marks the "truth" he and other awakened ones like him have discovered. But then we have to return to our assertion that all truths, including scientific ones, must be provisional, for otherwise, as the Buddha said, we will be trapped in the "bodily knot of adherence to the dogmatic assertion of truth."[53]

Let me shift my focus and get back to the idea that Muir is a myth dreamer, but one who was not permitted to fully dream his myth. What do I mean by this statement? His was not an ordinary dream, but one emerging from a trance that occurred after an illness, something out of sync with our bourgeois modernity. So is it with the other waking dreams that followed. Hence Muir's analyst, a kind of "sophist," would have none of it. According to Muir, his analyst, concerned "for the health of my mind" might have figured that he was "too close at this stage [of the analysis] to the border-line between sanity and insanity," even though Muir himself did not "for a moment believe it" (AA, 158). And that is why I say that he was not permitted to fully dream his myth, quite unlike Kekulé who continued to dream of whirling atoms until one night they formed into an ouroboros. Unlike a scholarly dream-investigator, Muir is not interested in the dream as dreamt, but rather its revelatory meaning and power. His is a concern of a truth about the world on the basis of the dream. Before our world became disenchanted, someone like him might have *communicated* his myth dream to others, and through processes of continual dreaming and secondary elaboration and feedback from his listeners he might have forged a myth that could have gone into a repertoire of a culture's mythic corpus. Nonetheless, Muir at least has the privilege of putting down his vision in his autobiography. But he had to confess that he "used the trance for a poem, but a poem seems a trifling result from such an experience."[54] This was too bad. It wasn't quite the way of myth dreamers like a Blake or a Kafka or a Borges. They could transmute the myth dream into works of great art, a kind of transcreation in principle open to all people, including those in the time of our own modernities.

Even though Muir thought he put a stop to his waking dreams, some visionary experiences seem to force their way into his consciousness, especially at night. I want to mention one brief unstoppable vision that stared at him from the mirror on the wall and sent frightening roots into his Christian past, into a childhood nursery rhyme now laced with terror, into the human experience of death and dying, and into the revelation of renewal:

> Spent an evening [August 13, 1938] in Edinburgh talking with A. and L. about immortality. When I returned to the hotel I sat down on my bed and stared at myself in a long mirror on the wall. My face, especially the bony ridge of forehead, came out, and I saw the skin and flesh shriveling from it, and the bone underneath; a terrifying, absolute vision, like Time being stripped off. And simultaneously a feeling of journeying on beyond Time with that forehead as a prow, and an assurance that the naked bone, there, would flower into new flesh and sprout new hair, fragrant and beautiful beyond conception. At the same time a feeling that I was doing a dangerous balancing feat on the edge of a precipice, that I had gone too far, and that it is not wise to play with death for the sake of immortality.

Yet, one might ask, how is it possible to avoid playing with death if one is interested in immortality? Because for many religious virtuosos, the salvation quest, in whatever form it might be expressed, must surely mean "practicing death," as such diverse thinkers as Socrates and the Buddha seemed to have realized.[55] Muir's skull is for a Buddhist skeptic like me a visual recognition of our bodily decrepitude, not so much an intimation of our immortality but a pointer to our mortality. It is a play with death, although a Christian culture like Muir's would hold out the promise of reburgeoning life while a Buddhist one like mine might give it a different existential slant in conformity with its own salvific presuppositions: "impermanent are all conditioned things."

A few years before Muir's death dream, Yeats records a similar dream of a skull in his *Autobiographies*:

> Molly Allgood [Maire O'Neill, Irish actress] has just told me of their pre-visions. Some years ago, when the company were in England on that six-weeks' tour, she, Synge and D— were sitting in a teashop, she was looking at Synge, and suddenly

the flesh seemed to fall from his face and she saw but a skull. She told him this and it gave him a great shock, and since then she had not allowed images to form before her eyes of themselves, as they often used to do. Synge was well at the time. Again last year, but before the operation and at a time when she had no fear, she dreamed that she saw him in a coffin being lowered into a grave, and a "strange sort of cross" was laid over his coffin. (The company sent a cross of flowers to his funeral and it was laid upon the grave.) She told this to Synge and he was troubled by it. Then some time after the operation she dreamed that she saw him in a boat. She was on the shore, and he waved his hand to her and the boat went away. She longed to go to him but could not.[56]

Such dreams of death, dying, parting, and the skull beneath the skin have been developed fully in both Christian and Buddhist thought, but, insofar as they are part of our "species being" they can appear in other guises in other cultures. If so, does one need an archetype to understand these experiences, as Carl Jung, the great dreamer of archetypes, asserted? Molly Allgood's first vision of the skull beneath the skin was, Yeats said, when Synge was well. In which case Allgood seemed to have sensed that Synge was sick, although it was not evident on the surface. And the vision, unsurprisingly, was enough to scare Synge himself. Whether Allgood's other dreams were premonitory ones or not we cannot

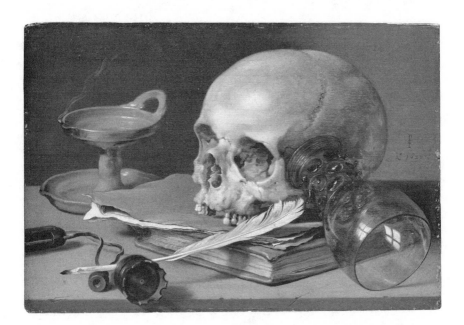

8.1 Pieter Claesz, *Still Life with Skull and Writing Quill* (1628). *Art Resource*

say for certain. If indeed she knew Synge was sick, then her dreams while being prophetic, would be self-fulfilling prophecies, but meaningful nevertheless because they forebode the enigma of death. That enigma was put well by Blake in the "motto" to his early poem *Thel,* which I will quote, but with (perhaps) a forgivable change in the last line, a line that thrusts its aerial root upward to my epigraph from Ecclesiastes and a taproot down into the enigma of dying that heralds the ethnographer's own farewell:

Does the Eagle know what is in the pit?
Or wilt thou go ask the Mole?
Can Wisdom be put in a silver rod?
Or Death in a golden bowl?[57]

ENVOI—INTIMATIONS OF MORTALITY

The Ethnographer's Dream and the Return of the Vultures

Far from the famed memorial arch
Towards a lonely grave I come.
My heart in its funereal march
Goes beating like a muffled drum.

—Yet many a gem lies hidden still
Of whom no pickaxe, spade or drill
The lonely secrecy invades;
And many a flower, to heal regret,
Pours forth its fragrant secret yet
Among the solitary shades.
—Charles Baudelaire, "Ill-Luck," *Les Fleurs du mal*

I WROTE THIS ENVOI with the hope that it would ease the burden of having written a long work. But, as with joys that happen to us, burdens never cease until the clock that keeps ticking away the passage of time within our frail bodies comes to a stop. Yet had I been living in another world or another time and place I might have used another epigraph for this ending. Or, for that matter, if I believed that nothingness can mean something else, as our negative theologians and Buddhist thinkers have formulated, giving that nothingness a transcendent reality. For some of us, nothingness does not appall. I have always liked to think that I could confront my journey's end with Buddhist equanimity, but one really can't predict such an outcome with certainty. We know that pain can kill anyone's resolve. And it saddens me to imagine leaving the voices of those I have loved and the many small pleasures that life gives us, like the view of the sun rising beyond the mountains overlooking my balcony at dawn, the fragrant scent of jasmine from the garden, the herons flying low over the evening river. But then, one might ask, what is there to miss when one is dead? And yet, without being one of them, I can relate to religious virtuosos who can creatively transform nothingness or thingness into the fullness of meaning in their visions, their dreams, and even in their nightmares. We all know that anyone, even a nonbeliever, can speak of doing something creative with the movement of the spirit. That is, one can speak of spirit in a metaphorical sense to designate acts of creativity: writing a poem or inventing something new, such as a machine or a scientific formula one scribbles in one's mind, or creating a recipe for a dish or living through one's art or dreaming a big dream or (perhaps) even writing a book or simply living compassionate lives without being trapped by what Buddhists have called *taṇhā*. But in this essay I have added something more to this well-known idea of creativity, something that is still part of our unique species-bound endowment. As I see it, some of our profoundest insights of the spirit emerge from processes of thought outside the rational cogito even though the final act of creativity might entail a coalition between the It and the I, my model being the awakened Buddha. I suggested that it is a mistake to think that the *It* does not think. It does not think discursively. It is in the sphere of the It that dreams and visions have their beginnings and their ends. And it is here the various guises of the spirit have their home and here the realm where Spirit holds court.

Much of our thinking, fantasies, and dreams might possess the coherence I attributed to the operation of passive cerebration or the workings of the passive intellect. I have some sympathy for lucid dreamers of whatever culture even though I am not enamored of modern or postmodern hedonistic lucidities. While many dreams are meaningless, and fragments of memory coming to us in the dawn watch might remain disconnected, others can be meaningful for those sensitive to hearing the voices of the spirit, whether we are religious or not. For me such happenings occur when egoistic thinking has been temporarily silenced and the phantasmagorias conjured by my dream-ego coalesce into something profound, a vision, if you will, of the past or of the passing or of the coming into being. Or when aphoristic thoughts hit me from the space of the silence.

Edwin Muir asks the question: "Why, seen from a distance, do the casual journeys of men and women, perhaps going on some trivial errand, take on the appearance of a pilgrimage? I can only explain it by some deep archetypal image in our minds of which we become conscious only at the rare moments when we realize that our own life is a journey" (AA, 212). Roads and journeys are part of human experience, I suspect, from the time when homo became sapiens, if not earlier, and it would be surprising if the imagery of roads and journeys does not take on symbolic significance in our waking lives, our forays into art and literature, our dreams and visions, and the labyrinths of our nightmares. The symbolic meanings we invest in roads and journeys depend not on some Jungian archetype but on our cultural and religious heritage as well as our personal desires and wishes and our intimations of dying. I, for one, cannot dream of Christina Rossetti's poetic allegory of the uphill road and the spiritual haven at the end of it.[1] I have dreamt of other roads and other places, but my journeys, unlike that of many a dreaming nun, never ended in a heaven-haven of the reward. They were dreams of someone who has always lived with uncertainty and questioned the self-assurance of those who take for granted that death is followed by a life of eternal bliss. Or, for that matter, those who comfortably think there isn't any such thing. I have no solution to the problems of salvation, but can only speak of my own prejudices. Being a Buddhist of sorts, there is little prospect for me of an unchanging bliss at the end of the road; nor do I care for the near-permanent bliss of the Bodhisattva aspirant flying into the western paradise—or for any such paradise. For me, death is not to be found in a golden bowl.

I remember vividly one pattern in my youthful dreams repeated time and again, without too much variation, that of roads amidst green hills and open spaces and people in little Sri Lankan houses helping me to reach the right forested paths, through which I have dream-hiked so many times, that seemed so real I sometimes think I have actually been on those journeys in my ordinary unlucid existence. Later, as an ethnographer, I have been on forest roads many a time, but not in the symbolic ones of my dreams. Then, as I began to gray and the shadow of Thanatos began to fall over Eros, I used to dream of culs-de-sac leading to a nowhere. I suspect that signals from the body sent messages via the brain to my dreaming mind, but my dreams were never a direct reflex of my bodily state but overdetermined by multiple motivations, meanings, and memories. And only a few of these body-messages were transmuted into symbolic forms expressing existential dilemmas, such as those I recorded for Edwin Muir. I rarely wrote down my dream journeys and have never spoken of them except in this book.

One of the earliest of these symbolic messages from the body was at age sixty on the night of August 10, 1990, when I was first told that the blood tests I took might be an intimation of a serious disease, but that I could afford to wait and see. Fourteen years later, in the late autumn of my life, that intimation of mortality became a reality when I was diagnosed with a death-threatening illness. My dream might seem an ordinary one to the reader, but not for me. Perhaps that is why I wrote it down and why I want to leave it largely uninterpreted, leaving you—my reader, my twin, my other—to make whatever you can of it.

I was going down a reasonably well-paved road in Sri Lanka with Her. I thought I was going to my uncle's at a place that was once a village and where I used to go as a child during school holidays. The scenery was beautiful and fitted the low country landscape with rice fields and an undulating hill or two. But the colors were not Sri Lankan—not the green of my youthful dreams but russet and other earth colors, also familiar to me as autumnal hues from my life in the States. I was not sure whether I was in a car or not (I think I was), but the road ended as if it had been damaged. As we neared this point we passed fields full of birds, but what was striking was the large number of vultures of the sort that heralded the Delhi of my vision and simply not part of my familiar Sri Lankan landscape. I pointed this out to Her, my dream alter or the feminine part of my own self or a composite form of my wife or mother or my anima or perhaps one of the many apparitions of the spirit. Whoever it was I cannot truly say. I only said, "Look, how strange and ugly are all those creatures." They were ugly in a sense—tall necks and fat bodies—but their colors were not unpleasant. We got off the road because it did not seem to go anywhere and tried to go across some fields, but now we saw so many of them, not the large vultures we were scared of but many small ones that we could get past. Then I looked up and saw a car coming from the opposite direction. I saw it drive up to the place where the road had ended by skirting the outside of the road and then moving back into it. We felt relieved; the road apparently was damaged in just this one place, and we could get off the road for a little while and pick it up later. I awoke as others have awoken in their dreams, their visions, and their psychoses from the ins and outs of the death and rebirth of the spirit. But to say this is not to equate my dreams with the profounder workings of the spirit recorded in this essay. One must bow down low before the Awakened One to recognize one's own inadequacies. The dream roads I walked then and now were meaningful to me, but, ill luck or no, they never once had me *thrown* on the road to Damascus.

NOTES

INTRODUCTION

1. For an excellent account of these skeptics of reason, see Richard H. Popkin, "The Revival of Greek Scepticism in the Sixteenth Century," in *The History of Scepticism from Savonarola to Bayle*, rev. ed. (Oxford: Oxford University Press, 2002), 17–43. Sometimes this Greek movement is labeled Pyrrhonianism after the supposed founder Pyrrho (c. 3 BCE).

2. For a summary version of the Cartesian cogito, see Peter Markie, "The Cogito and Its Importance," in *The Cambridge Companion to Descartes*, ed. James Cottingham (Cambridge: Cambridge University Press, 1992), 140–73.

3. Cited ibid., 144.

4. For a similar paradox in Spinoza, see book 3, n. 48.

5. My parody of Hegel's famous phrase, "Cunning of Reason"; see W. G. F. Hegel, *Introduction to the Philosophy of History*, trans. Leo Rauch (Indianapolis: Hackett, 1988), 35.

6. For a recent important account of the various phases of the European Enlightenment see Jonathan Israel, *Radical Enlightenment: Philosophy and the Making of Modernity, 1650–1750* (Oxford: Oxford University Press, 2002). The phrase "rationalistic myopia" of an "incurable sort" is from Peter Gay, *The Enlightenment: The Rise of Modern Paganism* (New York: Vintage, 1968), 83.

7. Israel, *Radical Enlightenment* is an important but difficult book to digest, whereas I find "Radical Enlightenment," in Charles Taylor, *The Sources of the Self: The Making of Modern Identity* (Cambridge: Harvard University Press, 1989), 321–67, an extremely readable and well-written account of the development of scientific rationality in Europe.

8. Here also I am much more sympathetic to Popkin, who, in *History of Scepticism* (242–53), argues that Spinoza built his system on the basis of Cartesian thought while, at the same time, being highly critical of it.

9. Walter Gratzer, *The Undergrowth of Science: Delusion, Self-Deception, and Human Frailty* (Oxford: Oxford University Press, 2001) has documented cases of scientific foibles and illusions, but limits himself to "pathological science." Gratzer only touches the tip of the iceberg, ignoring for the most part the work of labs in industrial, military, and pharmaceutical complexes, where self-delusion, deception, and greed are only thinly veiled; he totally ignores the corruption of scientists by power and monetary greed.

10. Ernest Benz, *Emanuel Swedenborg: Visionary Savant in the Age of Reason,* trans. Nicholas Goodrick-Clarke (West Chester, PA: Swedenborg Foundation, 2002), 279. Daytime visions with eyes closed are the fourth among five kinds of visions that Swedenborg discusses, the fifth and the least powerful being dream-visions (277–81).

11. William James, *The Varieties of Religious Experience* (New York: Penguin, 1985), 381.

12. Emile Durkheim, "Individual and Collective Representations," in *Sociology and Philosophy,* trans. D. F. Pocock (New York: Free Press, 1974), 1–34.

13. Francis Crick, *The Astonishing Hypothesis: The Scientific Search for the Soul* (New York: Scribner, 1994), 1.

14. Karen Kaplan-Sohms and Mark Sohms, *Clinical Studies in Neuro-psychoanalysis: Introduction to Depth Neuropsychology* (London: Karnac, 2000), 88–89. This is an excellent but difficult introduction to a new discipline. For another interesting work, see Mark Sohms and Oliver Turnbull, *The Brain and the Inner World: An Introduction to the Neuroscience of Subjective Experience* (New York: Other Press, 2002).

15. Antonio R. Damasio, *Descartes' Error: Emotion, Reason, and the Human Brain* (New York: Putnam, 1994). Damasio neatly sums up his argument: "In short, there appears to be a collection of systems in the human brain consistently dedicated to the goal-oriented thinking process we call reasoning, and to the response selection we call decision making, with a special emphasis on the personal and social domain. This same collection of systems is also involved in emotion and feeling, and is partly dedicated to processing body signals" (70).

16. Antonio Damasio, *Looking for Spinoza: Joy, Sorrow and the Feeling Brain* (New York: Harcourt, 2003). Damasio says that "a simple neurological explanation for the rise of ethics, religion, law, and justice is hardly viable. It is reasonable to venture that neurobiology will play an important role in future explanations. But in order to comprehend these cultural phenomena satisfactorily we need to factor in ideas from anthropology, sociology, psychoanalysis, and evolutionary psychology, as well as findings from studies in the fields of ethics, law and religion" (159–60). Unfortunately Damasio's project hasn't even begun to take shape. Nevertheless, I can relate to neurobiologists, as against academic psychologists, because the former are comfortable with detailed case histories. In my thinking it is this discipline that can really begin to relate the visions of the unusual people that inhabit this essay to the operations of the brain without reducing the former to the latter.

17. Freud used *secondary revision* and *secondary elaboration* as synonymous, whereas for me secondary revision is the immediate reworking of the dream, perhaps even without conscious awareness, and elaboration is a more complex cognitive process.

18. Jacques Derrida, *Of Spirit: Heidegger and the Question* (Chicago: University of Chicago Press, 1989).

19. My critique of postmodern writing is not applicable to poststructuralist thinkers such as Michel Foucault who can write clearly and insightfully.

20. I want to make it clear that my essay is not a response to Richard Dawkins's *The God Delusion* (London: Bantam, 2006). I had written most of my essay long before Dawkins's book, which I read only recently. I admire Dawkins's work on evolution, especially his most recent and clearly written book, *The Ancestor's Tale.* By contrast, *The God Delusion* does not excite me, uninterested as I am in debunking Christianity or any other religion. Admittedly, Dawkins's work is cogently argued, but in the days of my youth I read a very similar

work by a predecessor, the nineteenth-century American anti-Christ and atheist Robert G. Ingersoll, who does not appear in Dawkins's bibliography. And many more will appear before we are done with this question. This is not the place to make any detailed criticism of Dawkins, but I shall point a few issues that struck me as I read the book.

Dawkins's criticisms are primarily directed against Christian fundamentalist Evangelicals, mostly in the U.S., and those naive enough to believe in Creationism as a kind of scientific alternative to Darwinism. Most Christians do not need Creationism to believe in both and, like human beings in general, find no great cognitive dissonance in having contradictory beliefs. Many nonreligious beliefs and all sorts of political ideologies are not only false but also contradict other views or ideologies that we simultaneously adhere to. For Dawkins, there are members of our species who "clutter their minds with beliefs that are palpably false," without asking the obvious question whether such beings knew whether their ideas were false or whether they had empirical evidence or commonsense experience that seemed to them at least to validate their beliefs (165). We might think that some of these validations of religious truths are examples of self-fulfilling prophecies. Many human societies have cosmological doctrines, notions of the origin of the world and of the gods that, from a strictly scientific point of view, seem untrue. And that goes for much of philosophy. I can enjoy reading Plato or Plotinus but I would say that their beliefs about the world or the afterworld are false from our contemporary perspective. Were Platonists then and now mired in ignorance? Or could we say that, even though their ideas were false, they did have some insights into the human condition, as do philosophers in general? And, if so, why not Christianity, especially the gospel of Jesus and the many Christian philosophers who were, I would think, propagators of both truths and falsehoods? I am with Dawkins in condemning those who turn their back on the achievements of Darwinism, but that does not entitle us to turn our back on complex religious beliefs, even if their foundations could be seen by scientists to be false.

I can only partially endorse Dawkins's view that Christianity has been instrumental in great acts of cruelty. But then he goes on to make the naive proposition that, unlike religious wars, no war has been fought on the basis of "atheism." It surprises me that Dawkins would even make this argument, given its absurdity. Christianity and other religions have been with us for ages and possess a powerful ideology, a church, and millions of followers socialized within it. Not so with the term *atheism*, which came into popular use only in recent times; atheism does not have organizations or congregations that can mobilize large numbers. It lacks an ideology; and that is why nationalism, whether the Nazi variety or some other, can be mobilized to wage wars. In other words, even if you had fanatic atheists, you will not find them able to summon an army! Even atheistic doctrines like communism did not wage revolution on the basis of atheism but on an ideology based on Marx, holding up the capitalist classes as evil along with a populist hope for the masses of redemption from poverty and tyranny. Dawkins is obviously right that cruel wars have been waged in the name of religion, but he does not recognize that the name of religion is sometimes a cover-up for more blatant nonreligious motives, for example, plunder or territorial aggrandizement. Further, it seems to me that cruelty is much more endemic in wars fought without the invocation of religion. I would say that the God of Christianity has little to do with the two terrible world wars, not to speak of the unspeakable cruelty of revolutionary movements like the Russian or Chinese. The Crusaders seem like nice guys in comparison. Further, in decrying the nature of the God of the Old Testament, Dawkins is blatantly unfair by Jung, whom he credits with a belief in the God syndrome. Jung is a much more complicated thinker, as the readers of my essay will note. He was a more astute critic of the God of the Old Testament than Dawkins, especially in his late work *Answer to Job*, which I discuss later. As far as the general issue of human violence is concerned, whether of the Old Testament God and other deities or the wars waged on their behalf, I would assert that our understanding would much benefit from evolutionary biology, if one rejects the idea that biological explanations are by themselves sufficient.

I think the critique that Dawkins is a nineteenth-century thinker is well taken. His response is to admit it and ask, what's wrong with that? I agree that one can be proud to be an intellectual descendant of the great thinkers of the nineteenth century. But there is a deeper issue when it comes to Dawkins's nineteenth-century view of societies outside the West. His thought is rooted in the mostly discredited writings of James Frazer and others like him. No wonder he has some peculiar views of non-Western societies. He praises the Australian aborigines for their knowledge of nature and their physical capacity to weather extremes of climate and then points out their commitment to sorcery and other irrational beliefs (164–65). The latter conclusion is quite correct, except that reading Dawkins one would think that practices such as sorcery and witchcraft are confined to Australians and New Guinea folk, whereas any anthropology student would know they are found everywhere in the world, including a few centuries ago in England and Europe, even in the heyday of the Enlightenment. Moreover, Dawkins does not mention the extremely complex religious beliefs of the Aborigines and of course their art and what ethnographers have called their "kinship algebra." His chapter "The Roots of Religion" is one of the shallowest accounts of that interesting subject that I have read. We are back to my earlier critique: religious beliefs may be false, but their complexity and richness is something that tells us about the human spirit, and we might, if we have open minds, as Dawkins would surely agree, learn something about life and death and existence from them, a lot more, I would add, than one could from science. Science as it is now practiced can tell us very little about existential meanings for which we have to turn to art, literature, and philosophy, including the philosophical thinking of religious virtuosos. We do not have to be in bondage to the latter to read discriminately about their views of life and the world.

21. Baruch de Spinoza, *Theological-Political Treatise* (*Tractatus Theologico-Politicus*), in *Spinoza: Complete Works,* ed. Michael L. Morgan, trans. Samuel Shirley (Indianapolis: Hackett, 2002), 404–15. Spinoza's *Complete Works* is hereafter abbreviated as E because I focus primarily on his *Ethics.* For a good example of Spinoza's biblical criticism, consider his account of the variations in prophecy based on differences in temperament, style, and imagination among prophets: "[If] the prophet was of a cheerful disposition, then victories, peace and other joyful events were revealed to him; for it is on things of this kind that the imagination of such people dwells. If he was of a gloomy disposition, then wars, massacres, and all kind of calamities were revealed to him. And just as the prophet might be merciful, gentle, wrathful, stern and so forth, so he was more fitted for a particular kind of revelation. In the same way, too, revelation varied with the type of imagination. If the prophet

was a man of culture, it was also in a cultivated way that he perceived God's mind; if he lacked an orderly mind, in a disorderly way" (407).

22. For a good overview, see Charles B. Schmitt, "Perennial Philosophy: From Agostino Steuco to Leibniz," *Journal of the History of Ideas* 27:505–32. See also Antoine Faivre, *The Eternal Hermes: From Greek God to Alchemical Magus,* trans. Jocelyn Godwin (Grand Rapids: Phanes, 1995), 39.

23. Aldous Huxley, *The Perennial Philosophy: An Interpretation of the Great Mystics, East and West* (New York: HarperCollins, 2004 [1945]), 21. The work itself is a selection of writings from the world's mystical virtuosos with a running commentary by Huxley that, from a theoretical point of view, is not very useful.

24. Needless to say that my critique of Hegel and other philosophers has been anticipated by the Young-Hegelians, especially Ludwig Feuerbach (1804–1872), whose well-known study *The Essence of Christianity* placed humans, instead of God, at the center of the stage. Yet this led Feuerbach to search for the human essence that Marx criticizes in no. 6 of his "Theses on Feuerbach," in Karl Marx and Frederick Engels, *The German Ideology*, ed. C. J. Arthur (New York: International, 1995), part 1, 123–25. "Feuerbach resolves the religious essence into the human essence. But the human essence is no abstraction inherent in each single individual. In its reality it is the ensemble of social relations" (122). In the same period, Marx wrote his famous statement on religion in his "A Contribution to the Critique of Hegel's Philosophy of Right," in Karl Marx, *Early Writings,* trans. Rodney Livingstone and Gregor Benton (London: Penguin, 1992), 244 (243–57): "Man is *the world of man,* state, society. This state and this society produce religion, which is *an inverted consciousness of the world*, because they are an inverted world." Then, in a statement that anticipates Malinowski's view of myth, he adds: "Religion is the general theory of this world, its encyclopedic compendium, its logic in popular form, its spiritual *point d'honneur*, its enthusiasm, its moral sanction, its solemn complement, and its universal basis of consolation and justification." And finally the key sentence: "It is the *fantastic realization* of the human essence since the human essence has not acquired any true reality."

25. Gregory Bateson, *Steps to an Ecology of Mind* (New York: Ballantine, 1972), 345.

26. Czeslaw Milosz, "There Is No God," in *Second Space,* trans. Czeslaw Milosz and Robert Hass (New York: Harper Collins, 2004), 5.

27. Hans Georg Gadamer, *Truth and Method* (New York: Continuum, 1975).

28. G. E. Bentley Jr., *Blake Records* (Oxford: Clarendon Press, 1969), 303. This work will be abbreviated as BR.

1. THE VISIONARY EXPERIENCE

1. William James, *The Varieties of Religious Experience* (New York: Penguin, 1985), 388.

2. Ibid.

3. By *hypnomantic* I refer to those states where a person is in a trancelike condition (*hypno*) and makes inspired utterances (*mantic*).

4. William James, in *The Varieties of Religious Experience* (380–81), lists four crucial features of the mystical experience, one of which is its truth value or "noetic quality." The others are "ineffability," "transiency," and "passivity." James does recognize that mystical states still

survive and quotes a number of his friends who experienced them. Unhappily, they are brief states, and I suspect that James's definition of mystical states as "transient" comes from the contemporary cases he lists.

5. Ulrich Im Hof, *The Enlightenment,* trans. William A. Yuill (Oxford: Blackwell, 1997), 4, makes the point that "the English term 'Enlightenment' does not make its appearance until the nineteenth century, when it vies with the expression the Age of Reason." Im Hof adds that the French equivalent *Lumières* came even later, while the German expression *Aufklärung* generally meant "illuminate" and was employed to characterize a historical era only around the 1780s, but was "not widely accepted, however, until the nineteenth century" (5). Kant's view of the age of Enlightenment appeared in 1783 entitled "Was ist Aufklärung?" ("What Is Enlightenment"?).

> If the question is put in the form: are we living in an enlightened age? then the answer is no, but we are indubitably living in an age of enlightenment. As things now stand in the main, we have a long way to go before men may be fit to employ their own reason in matters of religion confidently and justly without the guidance of another. But there is manifest evidence that a field has been opened up to them where they may freely use that faculty, and that the obstacles to universal enlightenment or the emergence of mankind from its self-imposed minority are gradually diminishing, and in that sense this is an age of enlightenment.

Cited in Im Hof, *The Enlightenment,* 165.

6. The first meaning of *odana* is from the *Pali-English Dictionary,* published by the Pali Text Society, and the second from Paul B. Courtright, *Ganeśa: Lord of Obstacles, Lord of Beginnings* (New York: Oxford University Press, 1985), 56.

7. The purity of Suddhodana's seed is found in the origin myth of his Śākya clan. It says that four brothers, rejected by their stepmother, retire into the forest accompanied by five sisters. Under the guidance of the sage Kapila, they found the city of Kapilavastu, the Buddha's birthplace. Each of the four brothers marries a younger sister; they then place their eldest sister in the position of their mother and thus become the founders of the Buddha's own clan, the Śākyas. This myth could be interpreted to mean that the Śākyas originally belonged to the same blood, but unfortunately it is also based on brother-sister incest, an unnatural act, according to Indic thought. However the absolute purity of the line can only be maintained if the Śākyas continued to marry within the lineage, compounding its incestuous origins. For an good summary of this myth see, E. J. Thomas, *The Life of the Buddha: As Legend and History* (Delhi: Motitlal Banarsidass, 1993), 8–9.

8. *Mahāpadāna Sutta* ("The Sublime Story"), *Dialogues of the Buddha* (Dīgha Nikāya), in three parts, trans. T. W. and C. A. F. Rhys Davids (London: Pali Text Society, 1959), part 2, 14–16 (4–41). Hereafter this text will be abbreviated as Dial.

9. The popular *Jātaka Nidāna* says that the deities thought thus: "Prince Siddhārtha's time for Enlightenment is drawing near; let us show him the Omens [signs]." In similar vein, the great Buddhist savant Aśvaghoṣa says that the four signs were created by the gods. See *The Story of Gotama Buddha (Jātaka Nidāna),* trans. N. A. Jayawickrama (Oxford: Pali Text Society, 1990), 78; Ashva-ghosha [Aśvaghoṣa], *The Life of the Buddha,* trans. Patrick Olivelle (New York: New York University Press, 2008), 69. According to this text, the first three

signs were created by the gods and therefore only the Bodhisattva could see them. The fourth sign of the renouncer was also created by the gods, but here I feel that the text indicates a visionary experience. For example, prior to the fourth sign the Bodhisattva enters into his first trance in a state of "mental stillness." Then soon: "a man approached him wearing a mendicant's garb / unseen by any of the other men." After presenting a brief dialogue between the mendicant and the prince, the poem goes on to say: "Having said this, he flew into the sky, / even as the son of the king looked on; / for he was a deity who in that form / had seen other Buddhas and had come down / to arouse the attention of the prince" (131).

10. It is interesting that Theravāda Buddhists have ignored the etymology of Rāhula, the diminutive of Rāhu, Saturn, the deity that, according to Indic thought, swallows the moon. Aśvaghoṣa in Olivelle, *The Life of the Buddha* (51), is more in tune with Mahāyāna and Vedic thought and recognizes the etymology of Rāhu.

11. Jayawickrama, *The Story of Gotama Buddha,* 82.

12. The traditional or orthodox Vedic scheme of things refers to the four stages of life known as the āśramas: the student, householder, hermit, and renouncer. In general, the older literature extolled the householder life for Brahmins.

13. My understanding of liminality is based on the classic work of Arnold Van Gennep, *The Rites of Passage,* trans. Monika B. Vizedom and Gabrielle L. Caffee (Chicago: University of Chicago Press, 1960); and the equally well known paper by Victor Turner, "Betwixt and Between: The Liminal Period in Rites de Passage" in Victor Turner, *The Forest of Symbols* (New York: Cornell University Press, 1967), 93–111.

14. *Mahāsīhanāda Sutta* ("Greater Discourse on the Lion's Roar"), *The Collection of Middle Length Sayings (Majjhima-Nikāya),* vol. 1, trans. I. B. Horner (London: Pali Text Society, 1987), 103–4.

15. Ibid., 104–5.

16. Ibid., 107.

17. *Mahāsaccaka Sutta* ("The Greater Discourse to Saccaka"), trans. Bhikkhu Ñāṇamoli and Bhikkhu Bodhi, *The Middle Length Discourses of the Buddha: A New Translation of the Majjhima Nikāya* (Boston: Wisdom, 1995), 339 [332–43].

18. Jayawickrama, *Story of Gotama Buddha,* 89.

19. There are many versions of this event, but I have used the version in the popular *Jātaka Nidāna.* Aśvaghoṣa, more in tune with the larger tradition of Indian myth, has the milk rice given to the Buddha by Nandabalā, daughter of a chief of cowherders—nurturant, milk-producing folk. Aśvaghoṣa follows the tradition that Nandabalā offered the meal the very night the Buddha gave up asceticism; see Olivelle, *The Life of the Buddha,* 365.

20. *Bhayabherava Sutta* ("Discourse on Fear and Dread"), Ñāṇamoli and Bodhi, *The Middle Length Discourses,* 105 (102–7).

21. Ibid. The idea that true knowledge or direct knowledge comes from trance vision is found everywhere in Buddhist texts that deal with these experiences. For example, in the very first sermon of the Buddha ("Setting in Motion the Wheel of the Dhamma"), following his awakening delivered in the Deer Park: "This, bhikkhus [monks] is the middle way *awakened* by the Tathāgata [Buddha], *which gives rise to vision, which gives rise to knowledge,* which leads to peace, to direct knowledge, to enlightenment, to Nibbāna [nirvana]" (my emphasis). See *The Connected Discourses of the Buddha: A New Translation of the Saṃyutta*

Nikāya, 2. vols., trans. Bhikkhu Bodhi (Boston: Wisdom, 2000) 2:1844 (1843–1847), abbreviated hereafter as SN. It is certainly true that these kinds of refrains are repeated in many places in the Buddha's discourses, but they should not be seen as pure convention. Rather their constant repetition emphasizes the importance of the direct apprehension of knowledge through visionary insight. Going back to the previous text, the Buddha breaks down the various aspects of the Four Noble Truths, and, after mentioning each aspect, he employs the following refrain: "Thus, bhikkhus, in regard to things unheard of before, there arose in me vision, knowledge, wisdom, true knowledge, and light" (SN, 1844). The refrain is repeated twelve times in this short text, clearly confirming our view that Buddhist knowledge (in this case the Four Noble Truths) occurred in the context of awakening and vision. Other texts have as a refrain the phrase "the consummation and perfection of direct knowledge"; direct knowledge is like "true knowledge," that which is received through insight and vision. A good place to see the significance of "direct knowledge" is *Mahāsakuludāyi Sutta* ("The Greater Discourse to Sakuludāyin") in Ñānamoli and Bodhi, *The Middle Length Discourses,* 629–47.

22. See *Mahāsakuludāyi Sutta* where the Buddha clearly states that these techniques and knowledge are available to his meditating disciples. "Again, Udāyin, I have proclaimed to my disciples the way to create [through trance states] from this body another body having form, mind-made with all its limbs, lacking no faculty. . . . And thereby many disciples of mine abide having reached the consummation and perfection of direct knowledge" (643).

23. This and the preceding quotations are from Ñānamoli and Bodhi, *Bhayabherava Sutta* from *The Middle Length Discourses,* 105–6.

24. Olivelle, *The Life of the Buddha,* 405.

25. The popular *Jātaka Nidāna* (99) says that during the second watch the Bodhisattva purified his divine eye and in the third watch he discovered the doctrine of conditioned genesis. Aśvaghoṣa, in Olivelle, *The Life of the Buddha,* mentions the classical position in the second watch, but says that conditioned genesis and not the Four Noble Truths were discovered in the third watch. However, in Aśvaghoṣa the Four Noble Truths are effectively incorporated in the doctrine of conditioned genesis. In the Pali traditions and the current practice in Sri Lanka, the night is divided into three watches, whereas Aśvaghoṣa mentions a fourth "dawn watch" where the gods celebrate the Buddha's awakening. This is found in canto 14, but while it is incomplete in the Sanskrit versions it is available in Chinese and Tibetan. The older translation by E. H. Johnston, *The Buddhacarita or Acts of the Buddha* (Delhi: Oriental, 1972 [1936]) has canto 14 with the title "Enlightenment" (203–17). The reference to the fourth watch is on p. 213.

26. Although this fascinating doctrine has been dubbed a "causal" theory by many translators and commentators, one must recognize its difference from classical Newtonian physics or any notion of necessary and sufficient conditions where it is generally assumed that one can "explain" a phenomenon by its antecedent cause. This causal theory has little in common with Buddhist causality, which emphasizes the interconnectedness of the world of reality, that phenomena cannot be isolated and treated as an independent or dependent variable. Every variable, one might say, is dependent on another.

27. The popular tradition in stories and in temple paintings and frescoes focus primarily on Buddha's conquest of Māra and his daughters. So is it in some of the doctrinal texts, as in Mārasaṃyutta, SN, 195–220. Aśvaghoṣa has a marvelously detailed description of the

battle with Māra's hosts presented as horrifying nightmare-like dream images, but not the temptations of Māra's daughters in Olivelle, *The Life of the Buddha,* canto 13, titled "Victory Over Māra," 373–413.

28. Freud has a brilliant discussion of the "compulsion to repeat" that he relates to the nature of organic existence in general, to childhood, and, more specifically, to the neuroses. See especially *Beyond the Pleasure Principle, Group Psychology and Other Works, Standard Edition of the Complete Psychological Works of Sigmund Freud,* ed. James Strachey (London: Hogarth, 1981), 18:18–23. The *Standard Edition* is hereafter abbreviated as SE.

29. Henry Steel Olcott, *Old Diary Leaves: The History of the Theosophical Society,* 5 vols. (Adyar, Madras: Theosophical Publishing House, 1974), 2:169, hereafter abbreviated as ODL.

30. For more details, see my discussion of the three Enlightenments in *Imagining Karma: Ethical Transformation in Amerindian, Buddhist, and Greek Rebirth* (Berkeley: University of California Press, 2002), 283–87.

31. "The Brahmajāla Sutta: The Supreme Net," *The Long Discourses of the Buddha: A Translation of the Dīgha Nikāya,* trans. Maurice Walsh (Boston: Wisdom, 1995), 67–90.

32. For those unfamiliar with this enigmatic thinker and visionary, let me say that in normal life our eyes, tongue, ears are narrowed; in visions they are expanded. This text is an utterance by Lucifer, Molech, Elohim, Shaddai, Pahad, Jehovah, and Jesus, the "seven eyes of God" and representing the works of Providence, while Ulro represents gross mundaneity. Ulro's eyes see only the chaff, the dust, and the dregs; he represents conventional morality ("chastity"), which Blake rejects. In true visions, such as those seen by Blake, there is an expansion of time and space because the organs of sense have been perfected. Similar powers are found in the Demon, a creative and yet wrathful being in *The Four Zoas,* 5:121–124, in *Blake: Collected Writings,* ed. Geoffrey Keynes (Oxford: Oxford University Press, 1992), 308, hereafter abbreviated as CW. The text continues: "His eyes, the lights of his large soul, contract or else expand; / Contracted they behold the secrets of the infinite mountains, / The veins of gold and silver and the hidden things of Vala, / Whatever grows from its pure bud or breathes a fragrant soul. / Expanded they behold the terrors of the Sun and Moon, / The Elemental Planets, and the orbs of eccentric fire."

33. In several texts, the Buddha himself says that the divine eye is "purified and surpasses the human," as in "The Greater Discourse to Sakuladāyin," Ñānamoli and Bodhi, *The Middle Length Discourses,* 646 (629–47). Some texts say that the purification of the divine eye occurred during the second watch.

34. Sigmund Freud, *The Interpretation of Dreams,* SE, vols. 4 and 5, 498, hereafter abbreviated as ID. This example is not from Freud's own cases but one recorded by Justine Tobowolska in a thesis entitled "Etude sur les illusions de temps dans les rêves du sommeil normal" (Paris, 1900).

35. Freud himself thought of the unconscious as "timeless," and it seems reasonable to suppose that the products of unconscious ideation should also be timeless. However, I would qualify this idea by affirming that in dreams and visions we are transported into a different "realm" where our normal culturally structured ideas of time (and of space) do not operate or are suspended. For a good account and critique of Freud's concept of the unconscious as timeless, see André Green, "Space(s) and Time," chapter 10 of his *Key Ideas for a Contemporary Psychoanalysis,* trans. Andrew Weller (London: Routledge, 2006), 173–86 (165–86).

36. Śāntideva, *The Bodhicaryāvatāra* (Realization of the Path of Awakening), trans. Kate Crosby and Andrew Skilton (New York: Oxford University Press, 1998), 54.

37. Daniel Paul Schreber, *Memoirs of My Nervous Illness,* trans. Ida Macalpine and Richard A. Hunter (New York: NYRB, 2000), 76, hereafter abbreviated as M.

38. It was repeatedly mentioned in Schreber's visions that "the work of the last fourteen hundred years had been lost—this figure presumably indicated the duration the earth had been peopled with human beings—and that approximately only another two hundred years were allotted to the earth—if I am not mistaken the figure 212 was mentioned." Here note that he is giving a date for the end of the world; just as the Buddha gave a date for the end of his religion and of course as have Christians right down the ages.

39. Srimad Bhagavatam, *The Wisdom of God,* trans. Swami Prabhavananda, (Hollywood: Vedanta, 1943), 190.

40. Wendy Doniger, *Other Peoples' Myths: The Cave of Echoes* (New York: Macmillan, 1988), 2.

41. Julian of Norwich, *Revelations of Divine Love,* trans. Elizabeth Spearing (London: Penguin, 1998), 33.

42. Ibid.

43. Michael Aris, *Hidden Treasures and Secret Lives: A Study of Pemalingpa (1450-1521) and the Sixth Dalai Lama (1683-1706)* (London: Kegan Paul, 1989), 43, hereafter abbreviated as HTS. The use of the trope of the myrobalan (*Terminalia belerica* or *Phyllanthus embilica*) is found in many Buddhist texts and refers to "the creative power of thought, which in high levels of meditative praxis can materialize the unseen worlds in the manner of the myrobalan berry concretized upon the palm of the hand." See *The Lion's Roar of Queen Śrīmālā,* ed. and trans. Alex and Hideko Wayman (Delhi: Motilal Banarsidass, 1995), 52, n. 94.

44. This is during the culmination of the "generation stage" of *sādhana*, but it should be borne in mind that we are dealing with a text, not the actual practice of the textual instruction. See Roger Jackson, "The Kalachakra in Context," in *The Wheel of Time: The Kalachakra in Context,* ed. Geshe Lhundub Sopa, Roger Jackson, and John Newman (Madison, WI: Deer Park, 1985), 32 [1–50]. Focusing on the tip of the nose is one mode of Buddhist meditative concentration.

45. Thomas Cleary, trans. *The Flower Ornament Scripture: A Translation of the Avatamsaka Sutra* (Boston: Shambala, 1993), 819.

46. Ibid., 820–21.

47. Ibid., 129. These examples and similar ones abound in chap. 27 of this massive text (pp. 1627) entitled "The Ten Concentrations" (812–62). The Buddha's own powers are described at length in chap. 33, "Inconceivable Qualities of the Buddha" (908–32). Some of these have a "holographic" quality that has impressed Western physicists and neurologists. "All buddhas put the mountains, oceans, forests, and buildings in all worlds in all universes into a single pore for all future ages. . . . The pores on a buddha's body being equal in number to all beings in the cosmos, they place the same number of great adamantine mountains in each pore, and, holding all those mountains, walk in the ten directions, entering all worlds in space" (926). For an attempt to bring in *The Flower Ornament Scripture* and mystical thought in general within the frame of holographic models, see Ken Wilber, "Reflections on the New-Age Paradigm" in *The Holographic Paradigm and Other Paradoxes,* ed. Ken Wilber (Boston: Shambala, 1985), 249–94.

48. Friedrich Nietzsche, *Beyond Good and Evil: Prelude to a Philosophy of the Future,* trans. Walter Kaufmann (New York: Vintage, 1966), 24.

49. Ibid.

50. Sigmund Freud, "The Ego and the Id" in SE, 19:23 (12–66). I feel that Freud must have meant Id and not ego in this instance. Or that he could not use the term *Id* because the Id cannot reason. Perhaps Freud meant the segment of the Ego that is submerged in the unconscious.

51. Sigmund Freud, *New Introductory Lectures on Psychoanalysis,* SE, 22:72 (5–157). Freud first referred to Groddeck's work on medicine in his encyclopedia article on "Psychoanalysis" written in 1923, in SE, 18:250 (235–54); Groddeck's own work, *Das Buch vom Es* (*The Book of the It*) was published in 1923 in Vienna. We do not know whether Freud employed it when, in the same year, he wrote *The Ego and the Id.* Perhaps he was familiar with Groddeck's ideas much earlier. If Freud was indebted to Groddeck, Groddeck was also profoundly influenced by Freud, at least in his 1923 work. For the English translation see Georg Groddeck, *The Book of the It,* trans. V. M. E. Collins (New York: Funk and Wagnall, 1961). There are some memorable passages in it, for example: "I hold the view that man is animated by the Unknown, that there is within him an 'Es,' an 'It,' some wondrous force which directs both what he himself does, and what happens to him. The affirmation 'I live' is only conditionally correct, it expresses only a small and superficial part of the fundamental principle 'Man is lived by the It'" (16). Once again we have a thinker who affirms the "passive" nature of the "It."

52. "Grant me an old man's frenzy, / Myself must I remake / Till I am Timon or Lear / Or that William Blake / Who beat on the wall / Till Truth obeyed his call. " From "An Acre of Grass," W. B. Yeats, *The Collected Poems of W. B. Yeats* (New York: Macmillan, 1956), 299.

53. From Europe in CW, 241. For a painting of the serpent see William Blake, *Blake's "America: A Prophecy" and "Europe: A Prophecy"* (New York: Dover, 1983), 36.

54. James uses noesis as an experience that carries with it the stamp of "truth," and it comes close to the Greek sense of *noesis* or *episteme.* Plato uses *nous* or *noesis* or sometimes *episteme* to designate one's knowledge of a realm of Being that is opposed to the world of coming-into-being or becoming where one is enmeshed in ordinary beliefs or doxa.

55. This idea of the dream-ego is derived from K. A. Scherner, *Das Leben des Traumes* (Berlin: 1861), from which Freud borrows extensively. Actually, Scherner uses the phrase "das verlehendigte Phatasie-Ich uder die Person des Träumers," and the key words *Phantasie-Iich* and *Person des Träumers* are best translated as "phantasy-I" and "dreaming person." The first edition of the recently translated *Interpretation of Dreams* employs the term *dreaming self.* See Sigmund Freud, *The Interpretation of Dreams,* trans. Joyce Crick (Oxford: Oxford University Press, 1999), 71. I haven't been able to discover whether Freud himself used the term *dream-ego* in any analytical sense. However, the idea of the dream-ego is important for Jung and for my later analysis of dreams and visions. I am grateful to my friend Heinz Muermel of Leipzig University for translating large portions of Scherner's text for me.

56. A. E. (George Russell), *The Candle of Vision: Inner Worlds of the Imagination* (New York: Avery, 1990 [1918]), 4. A. E. clearly shows that rich visionary experiences haven't totally died out in modern times; some of his visions remind me of Jung's and those of lucid dreamers that I discuss later on in this work.

57. Josef Breuer and Sigmund Freud, *Studies in Hysteria,* SE, 2:276, hereafter abbreviated as SH.

58. See SH, 214–22 for Breuer's extensive discussion of Anna O.'s case history. Freud decided, in the case of "Lucy R.," to dispense with "somnambulism" but retain the "cathartic method," according to SH, 108.

59. John of the Cross, "Spiritual Canticle," in *John of the Cross: Selected Writings,* ed. and trans. Kieran Kavanaugh (New York: Paulist Press, 1987), 249 (211–83).

60. Ibid., 119.

61. *Meister Eckhart: A Modern Translation,* trans. Raymond B. Blakney (New York: Harper and Row, 1941), 110.

62. Ibid., 119.

63. Gananath Obeyesekere, *Medusa's Hair: An Essay on Personal Symbols and Religious Experience* (Chicago: University of Chicago Press, 1981).

64. According to ID, 293, composite formations or structures constitute "one of the chief methods by which condensation operates in dreams." One can, however, argue that "composite formations" is the chief method in the work of condensation or even assert that it is the work of condensation.

65. I do not want to belittle Freud's crucial formulation of unconscious motivation known as the primary process, but rather emphasize that a kind of cerebral activity occurs during the primary process, not just during the secondary process where cognitive I-thinking takes place as the result of the work of the ego. There is little space in classical psychoanalysis for "passive cerebral activity" during the primary process, even though Freudians use the phrase *primary process thinking.* Passive cerebration exhibits variations as conscious reasoning also does. Thus, primary process motivations might overwhelm passive cerebral activity as it does active cerebration of the thinking-I.

66. The Buddhist *kalyāna mitra* is analogous to the guide or "spiritual director" (or mystagogue) that helps the penitent through the travails of the "dark night of the soul." Both Saint Teresa and John of the Cross have fairly extensive discussions of this kind of spiritual guidance.

67. H.D. [Hilda Doolittle], *Tribute to Freud* (New York: New Directions, 1984 [1956]), 14.

68. James, *Varieties of Religious Experience,* 380–81. James gives several examples of the authority that the mystical experience has over someone. For example: "Saint Ignatius confessed one day to Father Laynez that a single hour of meditation at Manresa had taught him more truths about heavenly things than all the teachings of the doctors put together" (410). So is the case of Jacob Boehme, which I discuss later in this essay. One of the best examples is that of St Thomas Aquinas, the intellectual's intellectual of Catholicism, who after a single mystical experience after Mass, could say "all I have written seems like so much straw compared with what I have seen." Cited in Walter Kaufmann, *Critique of Religion and Philosophy* (New York: Anchor, 1961), 162. Aquinas experienced what I have discussed as "thrownness" in book 5, note 55.

69. *Mahāpadāna Sutta* ("The Sublime Story") in Dial. 2, 7.

70. *Janavasabha Sutta* ("The Janavasabha Story") in Dial. 2, 237–38 (237–52).

71. *Kevaddha Sutta* ("Discourse to Kevaddha") in Dial. 1, 277 (276–84). For another text that deals with this issue of supernormal powers and with less ambivalence, see *Sangarava* ("Discourse to the Brahmin Sangarava") in *The Book of Gradual Sayings (Anguttara Nikāya),* trans. F. L. Woodward, (Oxford: Pali Text Society, 1989), 1:151–56.

72. Jung uses "incubation" in many places, but especially relevant is his reference to Paul's sudden conversion in C. J. Jung, "The Psychological Foundations of Belief in Spirits," in *Structure and Dynamics of the Psyche: Collected Works,* 8 (Princeton: Princeton University Press, 1969 [1920]), 307 (301–18). Here he says: "Although the actual moment of conversion often seems quite sudden and unexpected, we know from experience that such a fundamental upheaval always requires a long period of incubation."

73. In some forms of Mahāyāna Buddhism, visionary knowledge reformulated in abstract or conceptual terms is given technical recognition in what is known as *prstalabdha jñāna.* This term is used in the Yogācāra school of Buddhism and referred to in two texts, *Trimśikā* (the "thirty verses" of Vasubandhu) and the *Mahāyānasūtrālamkāra* (the "ornament of Mahāyāna sūtras" commentary). My friend Maithrimurthi puts it thus: "The Awakened One after having obtained his *nirvāṇakalpajñāna* (transcendental insight) reflects or analyzes it conceptually after having returned to the reality or the diversity of the normal world (which perhaps exists only as a conceptual truth)."

74. Any good text on Buddhism will give a more detailed presentation of the Four Noble Truths. I recommend the extensive and authoritative discussion in Walpola Rahula, *What the Buddha Taught* (New York: Grove, 1974).

75. *Dhammacakkappavattana Sutta* ("Setting in Motion the Wheel of the Dhamma") in SN, 2, 1843–1847.

76. "The Sun" in *Saccasamyutta* in SN, 2, 1862 (1861–1862).

77. Nietzsche, *Beyond Good and Evil,* hereafter abbreviated as BGE.

78. Friedrich Nietzsche, *Twilight of the Idols/The Anti-Christ,* trans. B. J. Hollingdale (London: Penguin, 1990), 61. Note that the subtitle of *Twilight* is *How to Philosophize with a Hammer.* This work and *The Anti-Christ* were written in late 1888, just before Nietzsche's final emotional collapse.

79. Ibid., 48.

80. As others have also noted, one might even suspect that the true agenda behind the *Discourse* is an elaborate detour for proofs of God's existence—not the God of the Bible but the abstract God of the philosophers, as this statement from the fifth discourse suggests. "I have always remained firm in the resolution I made not to suppose the existence of any other principle than that which I have just used to demonstrate the existence of God and the soul," Rene Descartes, *Discourse on Method and the Meditations,* trans. F. E. Sutcliffe (London: Penguin, 1968 [1637]), 61.

81. Nietzsche assumes that a living being seeks to discharge its strength, and the master drive under which other drives are subsumed is the will to power, which then prompts him to formulate another aphorism: "Life itself is the will to power" (BGE, 20). And the philosopher's will to truth is nothing but the will to power, a wide enough concept to embrace forms of human creativity as well as destructiveness. It should not surprise us if the posthumous compilation, entitled *The Will to Power,* contains some of the most telling critiques of Descartes in the section "Belief in the 'Ego.' The Subject," in *The Will to Power,* trans. Walter Kaufmann and R. J. Hollingdale (New York: Random House, 1968), 267–82; see also the section entitled "Against Causalism," 293–300. Consider the penetrating statement in Aphorism 483, 267–68: "Through thought the ego is posited; but hitherto one believed as ordinary people do, that in 'I think' there was something of immediate certainty, and that this 'I' was the given *cause* of thought. . . . However habitual and in-

dispensable this fiction may have become by now—that in itself proves nothing against its imaginary origin: a belief can be a condition of life and nonetheless be false." In the very next aphorism he says the notion that there is something that thinks "is simply a formulation of our grammatical custom that adds a doer to every deed" (268).

82. For a great man's visionary experiences while sitting on the lavatory seat, see Erik H. Erikson, *Young Man Luther: A Study in Psychoanalysis and History* (New York: Norton, 1962), 204–6.

83. In "The Daffodils" (1807), *William Wordsworth: The Poetical Works,* ed. Thomas Hutchinson, revised by Ernest de Selincourt (Oxford: Oxford University Press, 1951), 149: "Full oft, when on my couch I lie / In vacant or in pensive mood, / They flash before the inward eye / Which is the bliss of solitude." The bliss of solitude is achieved through memory, the recollection in tranquillity of a witnessed beauty, like the host of golden daffodils that inspired his much anthologized poem.

84. *Conversations with Nietzsche: A Life in the Words of His Contemporaries,* ed. Sander L. Gilman, trans. David J. Parent (New York: Oxford University Press, 1991), 163, hereafter abbreviated as CN.

85. For another translation of this important passage, see Ronald Hayman, *Nietzsche: A Critical Life* (London: Phoenix, 1995), 275–76.

86. Ibid., 274.

87. Ibid.

88. It is a pity we do not know Nietzsche's attitude to visions, even though he was sympathetic to Dionysian ecstasies. However, we do know that Nietzsche was highly critical of all forms of spiritualism, to which, apparently, Lou Salome was addicted. Nietzsche took Lou Salome and Paul Rée to a séance in Leipzig in order to prove to Lou that it was all nonsense. See Rudolph Binion, *Frau Lou: Nietzsche's Wayward Disciple* (Princeton: Princeton University Press, 1968), 90, 74.

89. Cited in James L. Jarrett, ed., *Jung's Seminar on Nietzsche's Zarathustra* (Princeton: Princeton University Press, 1998), 10, n. 10.

90. The Blake poem that comes immediately to my mind is "Auguries of Innocence" where one can sense the aphoristic thinking that went into the construction of the well-known opening lines: "To see the World in a Grain of Sand / And a Heaven in a Wild Flower, / Hold Infinity in the palm of your hand / And eternity in an hour" (CW, 431). More directly, it is "Laocoön" that is in effect a series of aphorisms strung together.

91. Cited in Jacob Boehme, *The Way to Christ,* ed. and trans. Peter Erb (New York: Paulist Press, 1978), 12. In the commentary on the psalm, Luther says of *excessus:* "It is the transfiguration (*excessus*) which martyrs achieve just as the transfiguration of Christ, Moses and Elijah as discussed in Luke 9" (Ibid.).

92. Bernard McGinn, *The Flowering of Mysticism: Men and Women in the New Mysticism* (New York: Crossroad, 1998), 103.

93. In "Epistle to Dr. Arbuthnot," Alexander Pope, *Collected Poems,* ed. Ernest Rhys (London: Dent, 1939), 257 (252–64). "The Muse but serv'd to ease some friend, not wife, / To help me through this long disease, my life."

94. Ironically, in this context, one must note that Dostoyevsky was one of Nietzsche's favorite writers.

95. Richard Schacht, "Introduction," in Friedrich Nietzsche, *Human, All Too Human,* trans. R. J. Hollingdale (Cambridge: Cambridge University Press, 1996), vii–xxiii.
96. Lou Salome, *Nietzsche,* ed. and trans. Siegfried Mandel (Urbana: University of Illinois Press, 2001), 24 and passim.
97. Cited in Hayman, *Nietzsche,* 267.
98. *Cūlasakuladāyi Sutta* ("The Shorter Discourse to Sakuladāyin") in Ñāṇamoli and Bodhi, *The Middle Length Discourses,* 655 (654–662).
99. *Bahudhātuka Sutta* ("The Many Kinds of Elements") in Ñāṇamoli and Bodhi, *The Middle Length Discourses,* 927 (925–930). Rahula, in *What the Buddha Taught* (53), has an even more succinct translation of this formula: "When this is, that is /This arising, that arises / When this is not, that is not / This ceasing, that ceases." Given the fact that this is a key doctrine in Buddhism, there are several memorable texts, especially in SN in the book known as *Nidānavagga* ("The Book of Causation"). Within that book, there is a section entitled "Nidānasaṃyutta" ("Connected Discourses on Causality") where the Buddha speaks to the assembled monks on dependent origination (SN, 1, 533–723). What is striking about this text is the Buddha saying that the genesis of conditioned genesis occurred to him while he was still "not yet fully enlightened [awakened]" (537). Unfortunately, there is no uniformity in the Buddhist texts as to the meanings of "awakened" and "fully awakened." Some texts maintain that he was fully or perfectly awakened after the first trance experience under the bodhi tree. The section in which he says that he discovered this complex doctrine before he was fully awakened has this fascinating conclusion: "'Origination, origination'—thus, bhikkhus, in regard to things unheard of before there arose in me vision, knowledge, wisdom, true knowledge and light," suggesting once again that the context of discovery was during the first awakening (539).

    Critics might point out that this could mean that the statements made by the Buddha could refer to a time prior to his first awakening. There are other texts where the Buddha reminisces about his preawakening life, but it seems to me that most of these clearly indicate that this was when he was a young man. Thus, in the famous *Ariyapariyesanā Sutta* ("The Noble Search"), the Buddha says: "Bhikkhus, before my Enlightenment, while I was still an unenlightened Bodhisatta, I too, being myself subject to birth sought what was also subject to birth." This indicates that his ruminations on life's ills started before his "enlightenment" (that is, before his first awakening). The next paragraph makes it very clear that these thoughts arose in him when he was still living at home: "Later while still young, a black-haired young man endowed with the blessing of youth, in the prime of life, though my mother and father wished otherwise and wept with tearful faces, I shaved off my hair and beard, put on the yellow robe and went forth from home life to homelessness," incidentally giving us a glimpse of the human Buddha before he became the Buddha of myth. See Ñāṇamoli and Bodhi, *The Middle Length Discourses,* 256. There is no reference to conditioned genesis in this text.

    One text says the Buddha sought several gurus but found no satisfaction. He left them and reached the Magadha country where he sat in a delightful grove near a flowing river. There he achieved his awakening. The text however gives no description of his spiritual struggle. Another text, *Mahāsaccaka Sutta* ("The Greater Discourse to Saccaka"), in the same collection, makes a similar point: "Here, Agnivessana, before my enlightenment, while I was still only an unenlightened Bodhisatta, I thought: 'Household life is crowded and dusty; life gone forth [renunciation] is wide open" (335). It is clear that references like these are about the Buddha when he was still a householder. These do not contradict the account of the four signs which helped him to recognize the limitations of the "household" life. It seems to me that the four signs is a powerful mythicization of the real-life incidents previously mentioned.

100. "Analysis of Dependent Origination" in *Nidāna Saṃyutta*, SN, 534–36 (my emphasis). This text is followed by even more elaborate discussions. The aphoristic formula of conditioned genesis is once again stated in a text entitled "The Ten Powers" (552) and expounded at length in his many discourses to monks.

101. John D. Ireland, trans., *The Udāna, Inspired Utterances of the Buddha* (Kandy: Buddhist Publication Society, 1990), 13. The repetition of these verses in forward, backward, and reverse manner is surely based on a well-known strategy of memorizing texts.

102. Tenzin Gyatso (The Fourteenth Dalai Lama), *The Universe in a Single Atom* (New York: Broadway, 2005), 47.

103. See the section titled "On Personal Identity" in David Hume, *A Treatise of Human Nature*, ed. David Fate Norton and Mary J. Norton (Oxford: Oxford University Press, 2005), 164–65. Hume disagrees with metaphysicians who think there is something called the self and that every moment we are conscious of it and of "its continuance in existence; and are certain, beyond the evidence of a demonstration, both of its perfect identity and simplicity." If there is a stable self it should be found in "some one impression," but unfortunately life is "nothing but a bundle or collection of different perceptions, which succeed each other with an inconceivable rapidity, and are in a perpetual flux and movement" and therefore there is no stable self to be found in these. He adds that there isn't "any single power of the soul, which remains unalterably the same, perhaps for one moment. The mind is a kind of theatre, where several perceptions successively make their appearance; pass, repass, glide away, and mingle in an infinite variety of postures and situations." However, it would be a mistake to take Hume's general discourse on empiricism ("the experimental method of reasoning into moral subjects") as in any way "Buddhist."

104. Nietzsche, *Twilight of the Idols/The Anti-Christ,* 163.

105. For example, see Ludwig Wittgenstein, *Culture and Value,* trans. Peter Winch (Chicago: University of Chicago Press, 1984), 18e: "What a Copernicus or a Darwin really achieved was not the discovery of a new theory but of a fertile new point of view."

106. "Here I am, a one time professor of philosophy who has never read a word of Aristotle!" in M. O'C. Drury, "Conversations with Wittgenstein," in Rush Rhees, ed., *Recollections of Wittgenstein* (Oxford: Oxford University Press, 1984) 158 (97–171). Heidegger's absurd comments are in Martin Heidegger, *What Is Called Thinking?* trans. J. Glenn Gray (New York: Harper and Row, 1968), 75.

107. This sense of guilt appears in Wittgenstein's homosexual relationship with Francis Skinner; see Ray Monk, *Ludwig Wittgenstein: The Duty of Genius* (London: Vintage, 1991), 428; see also 376, 380, 403, 426–28.

108. Ibid., 114.

109. Ibid., 314–15, for the unpleasant details. This self-hatred was combined with a sense of guilt that was expressed in the so-called confession of 1937 he showed to several people, one of whom was Fania Pascal. In her recollection, one aspect of the confession pertained

to his Jewishness: "He understood that most people who knew him, including his friends, took him to be three-quarters Aryan and one-quarter Jewish. In fact the proportion was the reverse, and he had done nothing to prevent this misapprehension." See Fania Pascal, "Wittgenstein, A Personal Memoir" in Rhees, *Recollections of Wittgenstein,* 35 (12–49). In several places *Culture and Value* has a more positive but still ambivalent view of Jews, if not Wittgenstein's own Jewishness, see especially 13e and 18e.

110. Wittgenstein's love affair with the bomb is in *Culture and Value,* 48e–49e: "The hysterical fear of the atom bomb now being experienced, or at any rate being expressed by the public almost suggests that at last something really salutary has been invented. The fright at least gives the impression of a really effective bitter medicine. I can't help thinking: if this didn't have something good about it the philistines wouldn't be making an outcry. But perhaps this too is a childish idea. Because really all I can mean is that the bomb offers prospect of the end, the destruction, of an evil,—one disgusting soapy water science. . . . The people now making speeches against producing the bomb are undoubtedly the scum of the intellectuals."

111. Pascal, "Wittgenstein," 42.

112. Monk, *Wittgenstein,* 521.

113. Wittgenstein, *Culture and Value,* 17e.

114. Monk, *Wittgenstein,* 526.

115. For a detailed account of the relation between forest and āśrama and the complicated perception of the forest in Hindu thought, see Romila Thapar, "Perceiving the Forests: Early India," *Sontheimer Memorial Lecture* (Pune: Sontheimer Cultural Association, 2002).

116. See "The Unicorn's Horn," in *Sutta Nipāta,* trans. H. Saddhatissa (London: Curzon, 1987), 4, (4–8). Total isolation in the forest is impossible for a meditating monk because he has to leave his retreat and go into villages to beg for alms, and this means establishing some form of contact and communication with the laity. Theravāda does not advocate extreme isolation, but a very important early Mahāyāna text, the *Ugraparipṛcchā,* recommends that the Bodhisattva-aspirant living in a monastery "should avoid contact with all other human beings," more extreme than earlier monastic traditions. In this text, specially qualified monks are urged to leave the monastery for the wilderness, although they might return on occasion. See *The Bodhisattva Path: Based on the Ugraparipṛcchā, a Mahāyāna Sutra,* ed. and trans. Jan Nattier (Delhi: Motilal Banarsidass, 2007). The *Ugra* "allows four exceptions to its ideal of perpetual isolation," that is, to go into town to a monastery to listen to dharma, to associate with mature humans, to worship the Buddha image, and to associate with other beings" (132–33 and 82–83). These exceptions, according Jan Nattier, hide as much as they reveal, and it is likely that forest monks enjoyed the company of fellow renunciates, not to mention lay folk on whom they were dependent for alms. *Ugra* is a key text written in Sanskrit sometime before 2 CE but translated and analyzed by Nattier from a Tibetan version. The text straddles the Theravāda and related early traditions with the Mahāyāna and is indispensable for understanding all of these traditions and their interpenetration. Although advocating the path of the Bodhisattva, *Ugra* makes no reference to key Mahāyāna ideas, including the doctrine of Emptiness, and is close in ideation and spirit to the Theravāda and Sarvastivāda and other early schools (see chapter 7, "Telling Absences: What Is Not in the *Ugra*," 171–92). One of the fascinating features of this text is that it permits the male layperson (but never females) to adopt

the Bodhisattva path, although he should look upon the lay life with disgust, especially in relation to his wife. It urges the serious lay aspirant to eventually join the monastic order. The reason is also clear: no layperson can ever hope to become a fully awakened one (108–31).

117. Drury, "Conversations with Wittgenstein," 153.

118. Monk, *Wittgenstein*, 534.

119. These references are found in Ludwig Wittgenstein, *Tractatus Logico-Philosophicus*, trans. D. F. Pears and B. F. McGuinness (New York: Routledge, 1974), 69–70.

120. Monk, *Wittgenstein*, 166.

121. Wittgenstein, *Tractatus*, 5.

122. Outside of his own *Memoirs*, I recommend the following books on Schreber, beginning with the one I like best, Zvi Lothane, *In Defense of Schreber: Soul Murder and Psychiatry* (Hillsdale, NJ: Analytic, 1992); Louis A. Sass, *Madness and Modernism: Insanity in the Light of Modern Art, Literature, and Thought* (Cambridge: Harvard University Press, 1992), and *The Paradoxes of Delusion: Wittgenstein, Schreber, and the Schizophrenic Mind* (Ithaca: Cornell University Press, 1994); Eric L. Santner, *My Own Private Germany: Daniel Paul Schreber's Secret History of Modernity* (Princeton: Princeton University Press, 1996); and W. G. Niederland, *The Schreber Case: Psychoanalytic Profile of a Paranoid Personality* (Hillsdale, NJ: Analytic, 1984).

123. If childhood really mattered for Schreber, one must look at the life and work of his father, Moritz Schreber (1808–1861), well known for his regime of child training, which encouraged a very Spartan or Junker style. Virtually every writer on Schreber has an account of his famous father and the impact of his system of cruel child training on the son. In Moritz's scheme, children were threatened "with the Schreber *Geradehalter*, a contraption on boards and straps, if they did not sit up straight. He had a system and a manual for everything—the cold-water health system, the system to cure harmful body habits, indoor gymnastic systems for health preservation, outdoor play systems, the lifelong systematic diet guide" (Rosemary Dinnage, "Introduction," in Schreber, *Memoirs*, xii [xi–xxiv]). The older son, Gustav (1839–1877), who never married and possibly suffered from syphilitic paresis, committed suicide with a shot through the head. Paul's father himself went into bouts of deep depression for a period of about ten years, perhaps caused by head injury owing to a fall from a ladder. The three daughters apparently lived fairly normal lives, but obviously not the second son, Paul.

Paul was highly educated and earned a doctorate in law in Leipzig in 1869, passing the bar exam the next year. He worked as a judge in Leipzig until 1877 and afterward for two years in Berlin. It was in 1878 that Paul married Ottolie Sabine Behr, from a theater family, a woman to whom he was dependent right through his life, even though the relationship was a rocky one, especially because Sabine had several miscarriages and had no children. After his marriage, he stood as a candidate for the Reichstag, from his district of Chemnitz in 1884, but was badly defeated. This brought about his first breakdown, when he was hospitalized in Professor Flechsig's Psychiatric Hospital at Leipzig University from December 8, 1884, to June 1, 1885, though Schreber himself described the breakdown as a result of overwork. On this first illness, Schreber had only favorable impressions of Flechsig, even though he claimed mistakes were made. "My wife felt even more sincere gratitude and worshiped Professor Flechsig as a man who had restored her husband to her; for this reason she kept his picture on her desk" (M, 45–46). After a period of convalescence at Ilmenau Spa, he came back to Leipzig and was appointed as a presiding judge, or *Andgerichtsdirector,* at Leipzig followed by two important appointments. First as presiding administrative judge, or *Landgerichtssprösidant,* of the District Court of Freiburg; then, on July 5, 1893, as *Senatspräsident* of the Supreme Court of the Kingdom of Saxony in Dresden, a highly prestigious appointment.

The job as *Senatspräsident* did not last very long. Schreber dreamed of a return of his illness, and then imagination invented another fantasy of great psychological significance when, in a kind of hypnagogic state, he had the "idea [*Vorstellung*] that it really must be pleasant to be a woman succumbing to intercourse," something he says was foreign to his nature (M, 46). Owing to crippling anxiety and sleeplessness, his new attack had a "menacing character" such that during an anxiety attack he made preparations to use a towel to commit suicide and later even attempted to commit suicide by hanging "from the bedstead with a sheet" (M, 50). He had to get back, on his wife's encouragement, to Professor Flechsig who then committed him to the "Asylum." From November 21, 1893, for a period of nine years, Schreber lived in institutions for the mentally insane. These were in Flechsig's Hospital from November 21, 1893, to June 14, 1894; then for a brief period of about two weeks in Pierson's Asylum, followed by incarceration in a public hospital, the Royal Public Asylum at Sonnenstein, between June 29, 1894, and December 20, 1902. In his preface, Schreber says that the main part of the *Memoirs,* that is, chapters 1–22, were written in the period February to September 1900; postscripts 1–8 in the period October 1900 to June 1901, the second series of postscripts at the end of 1902, all during his stay in the public asylum whose chief was Guido Weber.

Both Flechsig and Weber were firm believers that mental illnesses were entirely due to neurophysiological causes, and the treatment Schreber received from them probably reminded him of his own father's hideous techniques of child training. The asylums of the sort in which Schreber was incarcerated were total institutions, made memorable by Irving Goffman, *Asylums: Essays on the Social Situation of Mental Patients and Other Inmates* (London: Pelican, 1968). They entailed the stripping of a person's physical attire and his sense of self-worth. Schreber mentions these techniques of humiliation and dispossession at great length in his *Memoirs.*

In 1899 Weber wrote a report to the court to make Schreber's incompetency permanent. Schreber contested this, and the lower country court refused to make it permanent. But Weber's second report was sent to the Dresden district court, which confirmed his incompetency. This was followed by Schreber's fine piece of reasoned writing where he made a writ of appeal to the higher court of Dresden on July 23, 1901. On July 14, 1902, the Royal Supreme Court of Dresden rescinded the earlier court decision in what I think ought to be considered a classic judgment on behalf of the mentally dispossessed (M, 405–40). Free at last, Schreber had a period of calm with his family, living first with his mother and then in his own house with his wife and adopted daughter, Fridoline. He published his *Memoirs* in 1903 and also engaged in legal work and led a seemingly normal social life. But on May 14, 1907, his mother Pauline died at age ninety-two; four months later, his wife suffered a stroke, leaving her with a speech disorder. These events precipitated his last and final illness, which lasted for four years, 1907–1911. Schreber died in April 14 at the Leipzig-Dosen Asylum, and his wife died the following year.

124. Schreber deals with several other issues in Christianity, which he says have to be taken on faith because they are outside the realm of rational understanding. Thus logical questions of the following sort must remain unanswerable, such as if God created the world, how did God himself come to be? So are ideas of eternal damnation and the resurrection of the flesh (M, 17).

125. Similarly, a nonpsychotic modern visionary, A. E. (George Russell), notes in his preface to *The Candle of Vision* that a distinction must be made between "self-begotten fantasy and that which came from a higher sphere" (n.p.).

126. The order of the world is a powerful construct in Schreber. Originally god himself was part of the order of the world, but now he seems to be outside of it. "In any case the whole idea of morality can arise only within the Order of the World, that is to say within the natural bond which holds God and mankind together; wherever the Order of the World is broken, power alone counts, and the right of the stronger is decisive" (M, 66). When Flechsig committed soul murder on him, the order of the world was disrupted. But god also conspired in this treachery. Thus: "The Order of the World reveals its very grandeur and magnificence by denying even God Himself in so irregular a case as mine the means of achieving a purpose contrary to the Order of the World." Eventually, through suffering and deprivations he will triumph "because the Order of the World is on my side" (M, 67).

127. For a detailed discussion of Schreber's description of nerves, soul, and God, see chapter 1, entitled "God and Immortality" (M, 19–32).

128. Another aspect of soul murder is Schreber's belief, not without foundation, that he was Flechsig's guinea pig, and Flechsig, "like so many other doctors, could not resist the temptation of using a patient in your care as an object of scientific experiments apart from the real purpose of cure" (M, 9). Perhaps Schreber had read Nietzsche because he refers to the "lust for power" of his two psychiatrists, Flechsig and Weber (M, 9).

129. Lothane, *In Defense of Schreber*, 378.

130. Ibid., 379; see also M, 210.

131. See especially M, 61–68.

132. "Paranoid imagination" is not clinical paranoia in my usage. Rather I refer to someone who develops a characterological suspiciousness of others because of the fear, imagined or real, of people or groups among whom he lives. This fear can be projected into imaginings that are difficult to distinguish from clinical paranoia. Thus a member of a stigmatized ethnic community living in fear of the police and the dominant political order might develop a "paranoid imagination." For a discussion of the paranoid imagination of white settlers living in fear among imagined cannibals, see Gananath Obeyesekere, *Cannibal Talk: The Man-eating Myth and Human Sacrifice in the South Seas* (Berkeley: University of California Press, 2004), 251–54.

133. Plato's Aristophanes describes the original human condition, which was that of the hermaphrodite, in *The Symposium,* trans. Alexander Nehemas and Paul Woodruff (Indianapolis: Hackett, 1989), 193a. According to Aristophanes, the hermaphrodite is unfairly vilified today, but was once a holistic creation in which the sexual features of both genders were unified. "Each human being was completely round, with back and sides in a circle; they had four hands each, as many legs as hands, and two faces, exactly alike, on a rounded neck. Between the two faces, which were on opposite sides, was one head with four ears. There were two sets of sexual organs, and everything else was the way you'd imagine

it from what I've told you. They walked upright, as we do now, whatever direction they wanted. And whenever they set out to run fast, they thrust out all their eight limbs, the ones they had then, and spun rapidly, the way gymnasts do cartwheels, by bringing their legs around straight" (Ibid., 189e–190a).

2. MAHĀYĀNA

1. These verses are not in consecutive order, but I have chosen them from the "Dedication" section of Śāntideva's poem that appears at the very end, verses 7, 9, 18, 19, 25, 44, 47, and 55. See Śāntideva, *The Bodhicaryāvatāra* (Realization of the Path of Awakening), trans. Kate Crosby and Andrew Skilton (New York: Oxford University Press, 1998), 138–43.

2. The Theravāda texts were written in Pali, whereas another set of texts belonging to the earliest stratum of Buddhism, known as the *Sarvastivāda,* was composed in Sanskrit. The Theravāda had a comprehensive canon whereas only a few *sūtras* from the *Sarvastivāda* are extant.

3. For a good discussion of these *skandhas*, see Walpola Rahula, *What the Buddha Taught* (New York: Grove, 1974), 20–28.

4. Jay L. Garfield, trans. and commentary, *The Fundamental Wisdom of the Middle Way* (Oxford: Oxford University Press, 1995), 68.

5. For a convenient listing of these perfections, see Richard H. Robinson and Willard L. Johnson, *The Buddhist Religion: A Historical Introduction* (Belmont, CA: Wadsworth, 1997), 100–1. Mahāyāna texts sometimes contain a lot more *pāramitās* than the standard number of six or ten. Theravāda in general mentions ten perfections.

6. Sadhatissa, *Sutta Nipāta,* trans. H. Saddhatissa (London: Curzon, 1987), 16.

7. There have been at least three thinkers with the name Nāgārjuna, and Buddhist historiography has fused them together. However, contemporary scholarship agrees that the great Nāgārjuna was born in South India sometime in the second century. He wrote several works, including some hymns, but his *Mūlamadhyamakakārikā* is what interests us here. There are several translations and commentaries of this work but for the general reader I recommend the one by Garfield, *The Fundamental Wisdom*; another work one might want to consult is David Kalupahana, *Nāgārjuna: The Philosophy of the Middle Way* (Albany: State University of New York Press, 1986). Kalupahana's important contribution is to show the continuities between the Buddhist thinking of the Theravāda canon and Nāgārjuna's work. However, he tends to downplay Nāgārjuna's innovative and creative genius.

8. Etienne Lamotte, in his classic work, *History of Indian Buddhism* (Louvain: Peeters, 1988 [1958]) has a good, readable account of the *dharmas* in the early schools of Buddhism (594–99). For the debates on unconditioned *dharmas* or unchanging ones, see his discussion (608–9). For an excellent discussion of the *dharmas* in all schools of Buddhism, see Upali Karunaratne, "Dhamma (2)" in *Encyclopedia of Buddhism,* vol. 4 (Colombo: Government, 1979), 453–69. As far as the early Theravāda Abhidharma was concerned, Karunaratne says: "The Theravadins have thus developed the *dharma*-theory to a point where *dhammas* [*dharmas*] are considered ultimate and real; ultimate in the sense that it is *dhammas* alone which obtain in the ultimate analysis of existence; and real in the sense

that they possess their own characteristics. The latter statement should be understood in a qualified sense, because there is no difference between the *dharma*s and their characteristics: the characteristics themselves are the *dhamma*s" (459).

9. Robinson and Johnson, *The Buddhist Religion*, 88.

10. Garfield, *Fundamental Wisdom*, 69. This quote is from chapter 24 of the text and entitled "Examination of the Four Noble Truths," one of the least enigmatic chapters in *Fundamental Wisdom*, and I encourage reading it for its critique of essentialism. Although one might not agree with the specific examples Nāgārjuna lists in his criticisms, one can understand clearly what he is getting at. For example consider his views on the Noble Truth of Suffering or *dukkha* (70): "If it is not dependently arisen / How could suffering come to be? / Suffering has been taught to be impermanent, / And so cannot come from its own essence. If something comes from its own essence, / How could it ever be arisen? / It follows that if one denies emptiness / There can be no arising of suffering. If suffering had an essence, / Its cessation would not exist. / So if an essence is posited, / One denies causation."

11. For a fascinating account of the interplay between the two forms of meditation, see Tsong Khapa's important text *Lam rim chen mo*, translated by Alex Wayman as *Calming the Mind and Discerning the Real: Buddhist Meditation and the Middle View* (Delhi: Motilal Banarsidass, 2004 [1978]).

12. See the section on "foulness as a meditation subject" in Buddhaghosa, *The Path of Purification (Visuddhi Magga)*, trans. Bhikkhu Ñāṇamoli (Kandy: Buddhist Publication Society, 1975), 185–203.

13. Śāntideva, *The Bodhicaryāvatāra*, 39.

14. S. Beyer, "Notes on the Vision Quest in Early Mahāyāna," in Lewis Lancaster, ed., *Prajñāpāramitā and Related Systems: Studies in Honor of Edward Conze* (Berkeley: University of California Press, 1977), 340 (329–40).

15. A. K. Warder, *Indian Buddhism* (New Delhi: Motilal Banarsidass, 1979), 361.

16. Cited in Janice Dean Willis, ed. and trans., *On Knowing Reality: The Tattvārtha Chapter of Asaṅga's Bodhisattvabhūmi* (New York: Columbia University Press, 1979), 27–28.

17. Beyer, "Notes on the Vision Quest," 237–39.

18. One of these powers is *ṛddhi*, described in Har Dayal, *The Bodhisattva Doctrine in Buddhist Sanskrit Literature* (New Delhi: Motilal Banarsidass, 1978 [1932]), 112.: "Being one, he becomes many; having become multiple, he becomes one; he enjoys the experience of becoming visible or invisible; he goes unimpeded through a wall, a rampart or a mountain . . . he can reach as far as the Brahma-world with his body." But this power, also attributed to the Theravāda Buddha and the arahants, is surpassed by the Mahāyāna Bodhisattva as he is represented in the literature. For example, he can emit flames; he can show the Buddha fields and its inhabitants to monks and other creatures; he can perform alchemical magic by transmuting the four elements into one another, such as water into earth; he can reduce and expand the volume of things, such that a mountain can be made small as an atom and vice versa, and, more to our purpose, "he can create a phantom body, which may be similar to or different from himself" (113–14). These powers according to Mahāyāna theory depend on the stages or *bhūmi* (lit. earth or field) of the Bodhisattva's career consisting initially of seven *bhūmi*, later ten, also discussed in detail in Dayal,

The Bodhisattva Doctrine, 270–91; and Edward Conze, *Buddhist Thought in India* (Ann Arbor: University of Michigan Press, 1996), 234–37.

19. Tāranātha, *History of Buddhism in India,* trans. Lama Chimpa and Alaka Chattopadhyaya (New Delhi: Motilal Banarsidass, 1970), 156–59.

20. A very good and persuasive argument on this topic is Paul Harrison, "Mediums and Messages: Reflections on the Production of Mahāyāna Sutras," *Eastern Buddhist* 35, no. 2 (2003): 115–51.

21. For a discussion of the Pudgalavādins, see Conze, *Buddhist Thought in India,* 122–34.

22. Robinson and Johnson, *The Buddhist Religion,* 86.

23. The Sanskrit *prasaṅga* means "reductio ad absurdum" according to T. R. V. Murti; and Prāsaṅgika refers to the school of Madyamaka dialecticians who resort to this method. See T. R. V. Murti, *The Central Philosophy of Buddhism: A Study of the Mādhyamika System* (London: George Allen and Unwin, 1980), 348.

24. Ibid., 89.

25. As Willis puts it in her "Introduction" to *On Knowing Reality,* 17 (3–66): "Nāgārjuna's negative approach resulted in many followers' misinterpreting śūnyatā as unqualified nihilism. It was largely to correct this misunderstanding of the meaning of śūnyatā that Asaṅga wrote his philosophical works." Willis's translation and introduction will give the general reader a feel for Asaṅga's philosophy.

26. Lambert Schmithausen, *Ālayavijñāna: On the Origin and the Early Development of a Central Concept of Yogācāra Philosophy,* 2 vols. (Tokyo: International Institute for Buddhist Studies, 1987), 1, 2. The present Dalai Lama, in a "Mind and Life Conference" convened by him in 1992, does not agree that *ālayavijñāna* (or "foundation consciousness," as he defines it) contains the sense of "unconscious." He asserts that the "difference between foundation consciousness and the psychoanalytic unconscious is that *ālayavijñāna* is manifest to consciousness. . . . The [psychoanalytic] unconscious is concealed, but what becomes manifest is not the unconscious itself, but rather the latent imprints, or propensities, that are stored in the unconscious. On the other hand, what is stored in the foundation consciousness can become conscious, and the foundation consciousness itself is always present." See "Dreams and the Unconscious" in *Sleeping, Dreaming, and Dying: An Exploration of Consciousness with the Dalai Lama,* ed. Francisco J. Varela (Boston: Wisdom, 1997), 86–87. However, one can argue that if *ālayavijñāna* is accessed through "yogic experience of the subliminal layer of the mind," then storied unconscious thoughts might surface during that process.

27. Alex Wayman, *The Buddhist Tantras: Light on Indo-Tibetan Esotericism* (Delhi: Motilal Banarsidass, 2005 [1973]), 42.

28. *The Lion's Roar of Queen Śrīmālā,* ed. and trans. Alex and Hideko Wayman (Delhi: Motilal Banarsidass, 1995), 44.

29. Ibid., 48.

30. Ibid., 92.

31. Ibid., 106.

32. Ibid., 45. Warder in *Indian Buddhism,* 402, says that the *Śrīmālā* posits the *tathāgatagarbha* as a kind of "absolute," or "the ultimate unchanging reality." This reality is not the self, however, and *Śrīmālā* attempts to link the "womb" or matrix of the Buddha with the idea

of Emptiness, owing to its absolute purity. But this might simply be a way of reconciling this notion with the fundamental belief of Mahāyāna in the emptiness of Emptiness.

33. *Tantra,* like the word *sūtra/sutta* literally means "thread." Although the formalization of these into a whole or system of Tantrism is a product of Western scholarship, it is nowadays an indispensable designation. Tantrism is a very complex system of beliefs and any attempt to define it is going to be misleading. It is best to describe its multiple manifestations rather than give an essentialist definition.

34. The four Tantric orders are Nyingmapa, Kagyudpa, Śakyapa, and the main order to which the Dalai Lamas belong, the Gelukpa. Each tradition has its unique body of texts in addition to those they share. Samuel, in *Civilized Shamans,* 227, writes: "Thus the Śakyapa specialize in the Hevajra Tantra, the Nyingmapa specialize in the various so-called Old Tantras and *terma* [treasure] cycles, and the most important Kadyudpa and Gelukpa Tantras are Guhyasamāja, Cakrasaṃvara and Kālacakra." For a very readable account of the political and religious domination of the Gelukpa, see Geoffrey Samuel, *Civilized Shamans: Buddhism in Tibetan Societies* (Washington: Smithsonian Institution Press, 1993), 499–552; and John Powers, *Introduction to Tibetan Buddhism* (Ithaca: Snow Lion, 1995), 402–30.

35. These are the vase initiation, secret initiation, knowledge initiation, and word initiation. These kinds of initiation are discussed in Tantric texts, but as they are not directly relevant to my argument I refer the reader to a convenient summary in Powers, *Introduction to Tibetan Buddhism,* 234–38.

36. *Abhiśeka* is consecration and generally refers to the anointing of a statue during religious rituals or the anointing of a king. In the Tibetan case, it is best translated as "empowerment." *Dīkṣā* is also translated as "initiation," and this usage is acceptable when it deals with traditional rites of passage, as, for example, the wearing of the sacred thread that makes the initiate "twice born." Agehananda Bharati, *The Tantric Tradition* (New York: Doubleday Anchor, 1965), 185–86, notes that the content of a *dīkṣā* "must be a *mantra* of some sort, or that a *mantra* must be part of its content. A person may be initiated into the use, say, of a *maṇḍala,* a *yantra,* or into the performance of a *yajña* (ritualistic sacrifice), but along with it a *mantra* is invariably imparted. There is an important difference between *dīkṣā* and *abhiśeka* 'anointment'; the latter never requires the conferring of a *mantra* on the neophyte." I don't know how systematically this distinction is followed in actual practice. For most purposes one could translate both *dīkṣā* and *abhiśeka* as "empowerment." Wayman, in *The Buddhist Tantras,* 60, put it thus: "The word 'initiation' is the translation of the Sanskrit word *abhiśeka,* which is rendered into Tibetan as 'conferral of power' (*dban bskur*)."

37. Cited in Bharati, *The Tantric Tradition,* 106.

38. Samuel, *Civilized Shamans,* 235–36. See also Powers, *Introduction to Tibetan Buddhism,* 227–29, for a more detailed discussion of this key symbol.

39. This is known as "deity yoga" and, according to Roger Jackson, "the most important—and indeed the defining—characteristic of tantra is the practice of deity yoga" through *sādhana,* the techniques associated with the meditation on the guru or on the deity. He adds: "A *sādhana,* the context in which deity yoga usually is practiced, involves, at the very least, the following elements: (1) taking as one's spiritual refuge the Buddha, Dharma and Sangha; (2) generation of the altruistic intention to attain enlightenment or bodhicitta; (3) cultivation of immeasurable love, compassion, sympathetic joy, and equa-

nimity toward other beings; (4) reduction of one's ordinary appearance to emptiness; (5) generation of oneself in the form of the deity, pure in body, speech, and mind; (6) absorption of the actual deity or gnosis being (*jñānasattva*), who is called from its abode, into the imagined deity or pledge being (*samayasattva*); (7) initiation by the deities; (8) repetition of mantras that effect the welfare of sentient beings and symbolize the deity's speech; and (9) dissolution of the divine form into emptiness—from which one usually arises as the deity often in simpler form." See Roger Jackson, "The Kalachakra in Context," in *The Wheel of Time: The Kalachakra in Context,* ed. Geshe Lhundub Sopa, Roger Jackson, and John Newman (Madison, WI: Deer Park, 1985), 20, 23 [1–50]. For a more technical study of *sādhana* in both Mahāyāna and Tantra, see Stuart Ray Sarbucker, *Samādhi: The Numinous and Cessative in Indo-Tibetan Yoga* (Albany: State University of New York Press, 2005).

40. Sri Dharmakirti, *Mahāyāna Tantra: An Introduction* (New Delhi: Penguin India, 2002), 79.

41. The primary text I use is Tulku Thondup Rinpoche, *Hidden Teachings of Tibet: An Explanation of the Terma Tradition of Tibetan Buddhism* (Boston: Wisdom, 1997), abbreviated as HTT. For a more detailed genealogy of the Nyingma tradition, see Tulku Thondup Rinpoche, *Masters of Meditation and Miracles: Lives of the Great Buddhist Masters of India and Tibet* (Boston: Shambala, 1996); and an even more specialized account is the classic work of Dodjom Rinpoche, *The Nyingma School of Tibetan Buddhism,* 2 vols. (London: Wisdom), 1991.

42. According to one tradition, Padmasambhava believed that a descendant of the king would destroy Buddhism, and hence the necessity to conceal the teachings. When the texts were hidden, Padmasambhava named the persons who would discover the treasures. See Erik Pema Kunsang, trans., *Dakini Teachings: A Collection of Padmasambhava's Advice to the Dakini Yeshe Tsogyal* (New Delhi: Rupa, 2007), xxxiii.

43. In the Theravāda traditions, the Buddha did some of the following: banished or controlled the indigenous demons; consecrated the land in several ways, but especially by placing his footprint in the Buddhist land (Sri Lanka, Thailand, Myanmar); and sanctified later pilgrimage centers by visiting them. In Tibet, Padmasambhava outdoes his predecessor by multiplying these acts. Tulku Thondup Rinpoche puts it thus: "He [Padmasambhava] tamed the entire land, both central Tibet and its outskirts. It was the land of demons and rākṣasas but he blessed it as a source of the Dharma and a noble land. Guru Rinpoche turned most parts of the land into meditation places and blessed them to have qualities equal to those of vajra-sacred places (of India). As proof he left behind rocks in the form of Hum-letters, foot-prints on four rocky mountains, hand-prints on four lakes and so on, which can still be seen" (HTT, 120–21).

It was once believed that the indigenous religion was what is known as Bön, but scholars now believe that Bön is the non-Buddhist religion of Tibet, but not a pre-Buddhist one. It has a complex canon and some of its texts are obviously borrowed from Buddhism; additionally it has its monks and novices, temples and stūpas. Like Vajrayāna, it also has a tradition of sequestered texts that await discovery by tertons. Whether pre-Buddhist or not, ancient shamanic elements are found in Bön, as they are in Buddhism. For a convenient account of Bön, see Powers, "Bön: A Heterodox System," chapter 16 in his *Introduction to Tibetan Buddhism,* 431–47.

44. Symbolic scripts or codes will appear in other contexts also in the course of this essay. For Tibet and for the Indic area I suppose these symbolic scripts are part of a larger lin-

guistic form of what is sometimes called *sandhyā bhāṣā,* or "evening language," a "coded language" where you have either a perfectly straightforward text given a kind of abstract interpretation or when a set of words are employed to designate something outside of its accepted meaning. For a Western analogy, one can mention the case of the Song of Songs as an example of the first; the second type is found in popular usage in South Asia, for example, as the language of the threshing floor or forest language where one employs words that are not normally in daily use and have meanings specific to the context of farming or hunting. For an excellent discussion of coded language in Indic and Tibetan sources, see Ronald Davidson, "Siddhas, Literature, and Language" in *Indian Esoteric Buddhism: A Social History of the Tantric Movement* (New York, Columbia University Press, 2002), 257–77 [236–92].

45. Cited in the "Introduction" in Susan Noffke, trans. *Catherine of Siena: The Dialogue* (New York: Paulist Press, 1980), 13–14.
46. HTS; Janet Gyatso, *Apparitions of the Self: The Secret Autobiographies of a Tibetan Visionary* (Princeton: Princeton University Press, 1998), hereafter abbreviated as AS.
47. Some of these treasure texts might be worthless, but such significant texts as the Tibetan Book of the Dead were discovered through this process (AS, 148).
48. For an account of Longchenpa's visions, see David Germano and Janet Gyatso, "Longchenpa and the Possession of the Ḍākinīs" in *Tantra in Practice,* ed. David Gordon White (Princeton: Princeton University Press, 2000), 239–65.
49. *Civilized Shamans* is an important book, but, unfortunately, Samuel sees Buddhist visions and related experiences as evidence for shamanism rather than Buddhism absorbing and integrating shamanism into its own system of beliefs. Whether integrated or adopted, Buddhist visions can take on an independent course and can be doctrinally and theoretically justified, especially in Mahāyāna. A more discrete tradition of shamanism that coexists with Buddhism is found in Mongolia, as Walther Heissig explores in *The Religions of Mongolia,* trans. Geoffrey Samuel (Berkeley: University of California Press, 1980).
50. This text is named "Reflection about the world" and is in the section entitled "The precipice" in SN, 2, 1864–65. I have, however, recast the discourse in dialogue form. I also use the term *monk* instead of *bhikkhu* of the original translation.
51. The following is the definition of a "waking dream" from the Chāndogya Upaniṣad, cited by Wendy Doniger O'Flaherty, *Dreams, Illusion, and Other Realities* (Chicago: University of Chicago Press, 1984), 16: "When someone dreams while he is awake, as when he sees two moons or a mirage in the water, that is called a waking dream."
52. Samtem Gyaltsen Karmay, *Secret Visions of the Fifth Dalai Lama* (London: Serendia, 1988), 15, hereafter abbreviated as SV.
53. This same point is well made by Samuel, *Civilized Shamans,* 278–79.
54. In this work I use Blavatsky's term *phenomena* rather than the technical terms favored by investigators of the paranormal. A recent investigator classifies "phenomena" as consisting of "materializations" and "apports." "Materializations (assuming they really occur) are cases where objects seem to be produced out of nothing. Apportations (sometimes called 'teleportations'), on the other hand, would be cases where already existing objects disappear from one location to another." See Stephen E. Braude, *The Gold Leaf Lady and Other Parapsychological Investigations* (Chicago: University of Chicago Press, 2007), 2.

55. Renée Weber, "Field Consciousness and Field Ethics" in Ken Wilber, "Reflections on the New-Age Paradigm" in *The Holographic Paradigm and Other Paradoxes*, ed. Ken Wilbur (Boston: Shambala, 1985), 41 (35–43).

56. The locus classicus of Australian aboriginal "dream-time" is W. E. H. Stanner, "The Dreaming" (1953), republished in Stanner, *White Man Got No Dreaming: Essays, 1938-1973* (Canberra: Australian National University Press, 1979), 23–40. I do not know enough of Aboriginal religion to deal with this issue and only use "dream-time" as a trope to describe certain forms of visionary dreaming.

57. Tulku Thondup Rinpoche has a fine account of the spiritual genealogy of the Longchen Nyingthig tradition of Buddhism in *Masters of Meditation and Miracles*. Tulku Thondup is himself a representative of this tradition.

58. The "ḍākinī of primordial consciousness" is of course Yeshe Tsogyel, who, as mentioned elsewhere, is the consort of both the king, Trisong Detsen, and the guru, Padmasambhava. It is a cosmic union and a polyandrous one, the latter a well-known form of marriage in Tibet.

59. The poem is found in the Pickering Ms. and reproduced in CW, 429. Here are the first three stanzas: "The Maiden caught me in the Wild, / Where I was dancing merrily; / She put me in her Cabinet / And locked me up with a golden Key. This Cabinet is form'd of Gold / And Pearl and Crystal shining bright, / And within it opens into a World / And a little lovely Moony Night. Another England there I saw, / Another London with its Tower, / Another Thames and other Hills, / And another pleasant Surrey Bower.

60. The mytheme of the descent into some underworld through a lotus stalk seems to have been well known in Indian thought, as Doniger O'Flaherty shows in *Dreams, Illusion, and Other Realities*, 94–95.

61. For me, one of most interesting examples of mirroring is from the founder of the Mormon faith, Joseph Smith. Prior to the discovery of the Book of Mormon, young Smith and his comrades used a stone known as the "seer-stone" to actually discover treasures supposedly sequestered by the ancients. Later on, Joseph Smith used the same stone to see the actual Mormon Scriptures contained in gold plates deposited in the woods. He dictated their contents to his amanuensis, adopting the following technique, according to a contemporary: "I will now give you a description of the manner in which the Book of Mormon was translated. Joseph Smith would put the seer stone into a hat, and put his face into the hat, drawing it closely around his face to exclude the light; and in the darkness the spiritual light would shine. A piece of something resembling parchment would appear, and on that appeared the writing." Cited in David Persuitte, *Joseph Smith and the Origins of the Book of Mormon* (Jefferson, NC: MacFarlane, 2000), 81. Persuitte is unfortunately a hostile critic, but the account is confirmed by a practicing Mormon and a professional historian, Richard Lyman Bushman, *Joseph Smith, Rough Stone Rolling: A Cultural Biography of Mormonism's Founder* (New York: Knopf, 2005), who has a good description of the "seer-stone" on pp. 48–54. The case of Joseph Smith ought to persuade scholars of Mormonism to interpret his visionary experiences in terms of the paradigm sketched in my essay. The text written in an ancient script on the gold plates (undecipherable for most people) is translated by Smith into coherent English, reminiscent once again of Tibetan techniques whereby ḍākinī scripts get transformed into Tibetan. Unfortunately, Joseph Smith suffered the fate of Madame Blavatsky, as I show later, with people who think her a fraud

and those who implicitly believed in her prophecies. Persuitte treats Smith, unfairly I think, as a fraud, as did Max Weber who thought him possibly to be "a very sophisticated type of deliberate swindler." See his discussion of "charismatic authority," in Max Weber, *The Theory of Social and Economic Organization,* trans. A. M. Henderson and Talcott Parsons (Glencoe, IL: Free Press, 1947), 359. By contrast, Bushman, writing under the guise of objective history, sees him as "genuine," warts and all, which raises a question as to why sophisticated persons, including scholars, would accept Joseph Smith's visions as containing a true history of the past inscribed in genuine but nonextant gold plates!

62. "The Statues," in W. B. Yeats, *The Collected Poems of W. B. Yeats* (New York: Macmillan, 1956), 323.

63. Samten Karmay, in his introduction to the second edition of *Secret Visions,* says that the first Dalai Lama was considered to be an incarnation of Avalokiteśvara, and this identity is also inherited by the Fifth Dalai Lama (no page reference given).

64. For a brief discussion of the Kadampa order, see Samuel, *Civilized Shamans,* 466–70. According to Samuel, it was Atiśa who brought about a creative synthesis of pre-Buddhist shamanism with Buddhist Tantra. Powers says that the founding of the Kadampa lineage is attributed to Atiśa's disciple Dromdön (1004–1064), "and the result was a new school that could transmit the yogic teachings of Milarepa and his predecessors and preserve them within a monastic framework" (Powers, *Tibetan Buddhism,* 350).

65. The best example that I am familiar with comes from a late biography of Guru Ḍākinī, the Sky Dancer, also known as Tsogyel, the consort of Padmasambhava and as such the "embodiment of the female Buddha" and published in *Sky Dancer: The Secret Life and Songs of the Lady Yeshe Tsogyel,* trans. Keith Dowman (Ithaca: Snow Lion, 1996), xiii. However, it was actually written in the eighteenth century by an inspired Tantric yogin named Taksham Nuden Dorje through a "mind treasure," a term that indicates a direct revelation from Padmasambhava and Lady Tsogyel herself. It is very likely based on earlier traditions of Tsogyel and perhaps indicates genuine female experiences of the dark night of the soul, prior to becoming a Bodhisattva. I will quote one of her experiences: "At first my voice developed a stammer, quantities of blood and pus oozed out of a rent in my neck, my throat became twisted, parched and paralyzed, and various swellings of blood and pus erupted. I came close to death. But finally, however much I used my voice, there was no discomfort. My enunciation was distinct, and the sweet tones of my voice were mellifluous" (74). With this change, she received various *siddhi* powers including visionary powers. But then this temporary awakening does not completely extinguish her suffering and soon after when she was concentrating to obtain other powers there was a relapse that also had to be overcome: "At first my nerves ached, my vital energy flows were reversed, my seed-essence was paralyzed, and the horror of death's proximity overcame me, but I continued to practice indifferent to these reverses." She continues: "After some time the deities manifested themselves and I gained control over psychic nerves, vital energy flows and seed-essence; the flows of the four rivers of birth, old-age, sickness and death were dammed; and I was granted the title 'Siddha'" (75).

66. For a brilliant account of such a cosmic battle, see Derek Freeman, "Shaman and Incubus," *Psychoanalytic Study of Society* 12:315–43.

67. It should be noted that Jigme Lingpa himself practiced sorcery when, in 1788, he was summoned with other lamas to "perform destructive rituals on Hepo Ri, a sacred moun-

tain near Samye to deflect the growing conflict between Tibet and the Gurkhas. He was later asked repeatedly to construct wrathful *mdos* devices and to do divinations to benefit the state." His autobiography records his ambivalence and probably his sense of guilt when he says that "that he is against black magic, that he feels regret about killing enemies, and that by conducting these rites he will harm himself" (AS, 135).

3. THE COSMIC "IT"

1. This is "the third proof" in proposition 11 in Spinoza's *Ethics,* part 1 in *Spinoza: Complete Works,* ed. Michael L. Morgan, trans. Samuel Shirley (Indianapolis: Hackett, 2002), 222 (217–43).

2. Blake, *The Laocoön,* CW, 776.

3. William James, *The Varieties of Religious Experience* (New York: Penguin, 1985), 399.

4. Ibid., 64.

5. Pierre Hadot, *Plotinus; or, The Simplicity of Vision,* trans. Michael Chase (Chicago: University of Chicago Press, 1993), 112. I have dealt with Plotinus at length in my book, *Imagining Karma: Ethical Transformation in Amerindian, Buddhist, and Greek Rebirth* (Berkeley: University of California Press, 2002), and I will excerpt freely from that text.

6. Hadot denies that he is attempting to "Christianize" Plotinus, but this is in effect what he does. Christianization is apparent in his notion of "grace" when he quotes one authority, Ravaisson, with respect to Plotinus: "Life is Grace because God is Grace" (51). So is his appropriation of Henri Bergson's *élan* as a Plotinian conception. And, worse, his refusal to recognize the reality of Plotinus reincarnation doctrines surely indicates this same Christian prejudice.

7. For a clear exposition of the *Enneads, see* Dominic J. O'Meara, *Plotinus, An Introduction to the Enneads* (Oxford: Oxford University Press, 1966); for a more specialized account, see Lloyd P. Gerson, *Plotinus* (London: Routledge, 1998).

8. See Plato, *Republic,* trans. Desmond Lee (London: Penguin, 1987), 299–309, containing his discussion of "The Philosophical Ruler." Plato's *Parmenides* is entirely devoted to a discussion of the One, and, while Plotinus takes his bearing from this text, his is a much more sophisticated and meaningful discussion. For a brief account of the sources for Neoplatonic ideas, see R. T. Wallis, *Neoplatonism,* 2d ed. (London: Gerald Duckworth, 1995), 32–36.

9. Plotinus, *The Enneads,* trans. Stephen MacKenna, abbr. ed. (London: Penguin, 1991), 5.1.6 (354), hereafter abbreviated as Enn.

10. O'Meara, *Plotinus,* 36.

11. *Ennead II* puts it thus: "All things must be joined to one another; not only must there be in each individual part what is well called a single united breath of life but before them, and still more, in the All. One principle must make the universe, a single complex living creature, one from all; and just as in individual organisms each member undertakes its own particular task, so the members of the All, each individual one of them, have their individual work to do." *Plotinus,* trans. A. H. Armstrong, 7 vols. (Cambridge: Harvard University Press 1966–88). See Armstrong, *Ennead II,* 71.

12. MacKenna, "Extracts from the Explanatory Matter in the First Edition," xxxiv (xxvi–xli), in *The Enneads.*

13. O'Meara, *Plotinus,* 43.

14. Once again, Hadot, I think, is mistaken in assuming that Plotinian mystical union is available to all of us. Surely, this is so in principle, but in effect only to sages who are willing to shed the body's dross and move upward toward Nous and the One, but even here there is no path that is sketched and made available to the sage. This was left to later Christianity and Islam.

15. Armstrong, *Ennead III,* 145–47.

16. Ibid., 149.

17. This point is made by John Dillon in his summary of Plotinus's "Our Tutelary Spirit" in Enn., 166.

18. I have used MacKenna's very readable translation of this passage from *Ennead III,* 148. For a more accurate translation, the reader may wish to consult Armstrong's translation in *Ennead III,* 83. For example, MacKenna's phrase that deals with "a woman wronged" is more accurately rendered by Armstrong as "one who has raped a woman will be a woman in order to be raped." Yet I believe that MacKenna nicely captures the spirit of Plotinus.

19. I have already noted that in Plotinian thought, as with Buddhism, the automatism of punishment results in the degradation and demotion of animals. Hence one could be Plotinus now, now a horse; or an "ox-soul which was once a man." However, it is not clear how the horse can rebecome Plotinus or an ox can reemerge as a man (unlike in Buddhism where this can happen when one's bad karma is over). As far as animal rebirths are concerned, "the degradation," says Plotinus, "is just" (Enn., 3:3, 161).

20. See my detailed discussion of this section of Plato's *Republic* in *Imagining Karma,* 240–48.

21. Enn. 4:8, 334; see also Armstrong's clearer translation in Plotinus, *Ennead IV,* 397.

22. Hadot, *Plotinus,* 64, 69. I am now tempted to posit Indian influence on both eschatological and soteriological levels. With Plotinus there is greater indication of Indian thought with respect to the salvation quest itself that, epistemically speaking, broke the Platonic apotheosis of reason and the contemplation of the sublime beauty of ideal forms. Indian ideas were floating in the first centuries of the Christian era in Gnostic thought, or there might have been a more direct influence from his predecessor Numenius and Plotinus's teacher Ammonius Sakkas, who apparently were receptive to Indian ideas. According to his biographer Porphyry, Plotinus "became eager to investigate the Persian methods and the system adopted among the Indians" (quoted in MacKenna, *Enneads,* civ). It would not surprise us if Plotinus self-consciously adopted Upanishadic and Buddhist ideas into his scheme of things as he did Platonic ones. What is striking about Plotinus is his rare attempt to describe the indescribable—the reach of the Good, the numinous—in a philosophical discourse, something that the Buddha refused to do. Plotinus does not give up the task of describing the indescribable even though he realizes that the soteriological vision "baffles telling" because active ratiocination and egoistic thinking cannot prevail there.

23. Once again I think Hadot has it wrong when he says that Plotinus's vegetarianism was for hygienic reasons and not for reasons of asceticism, imputing to him a modernist view of vegetarianism. Plotinus derives his vegetarianism from his prior Pythagorean inheritance where vegetarianism is intrinsically related to reincarnation. As with Empedocles, it is wrong to eat an animal who is an ancestor. It should also be remembered that Por-

phyry, Plotinus's student and biographer, was also a vegetarian and wrote a book on the subject. See *Imagining Karma,* 204–7, 228–29 for details.

24. I think these visual experiences of a bright light have a neurological base, but they get articulated to cultural traditions and personal motivations. Neurology cannot be divorced from culturology. There are many examples in recent work on near death experiences where the light changes into a "being of light," generally identified with Jesus. Many examples are found in Phillip H. Wiebe, *Visions of Jesus: Direct Encounters from the New Testament to Today* (New York: Oxford University Press, 1997). For a good example, see the case of Marian Gallife (49–50); see also the chapter entitled "Defining the Light" in Mark Fox, *Religion, Spirituality and the Near-Death Experience* (London: Routledge, 2003), especially 103–8 (98–141). I find many of the interpretations of the "being of light" utterly problematical, if not naive. The reader will note other Christian examples of shining light in the course of this essay, for example, when Teresa has the experience of Jesus in a light brilliant as that of the sun; or Angela of Foligno, who has a similar vision of Jesus, which "surpasses the splendor of the sun" (see book 4, no. 61). And note Freud's hysterical patient who had a vision of "the sun with golden rays" and identified it with God (p. 40). See also the Buddhist examples of the "vision-producing radiant light" (p. 115). These experiences are given theoretical meaning in Tibetan Buddhism in discussions of the "radiant light" that emerges like the sun during certain stages of the meditation process. For a good discussion see *The Life and Teaching of Nāropa,* trans. Herbert V. Guenther (Boston: Shambala, 1995), 65 and 188–97.

25. See Richard Gombrich, *Theravāda Buddhism* (London: Routledge, 1994), 62–63, and, more recently, "Everything Is Burning: The Centrality of Fire in the Buddha's Thought," unpublished MS, 12 pp.

26. Walpola Rahula, *What the Buddha Taught* (New York: Grove, 1974), 36.

27. Here are some key references to nirvana in early Buddhist texts one of which is entitled "Unconnected Discourses on the Unconditioned [nirvana]" (SN, 1378–79) in which the Buddha concludes: "Bhikkhus, I will teach you the truth, and the path leading to the truth. . . . I will teach you the far shore . . . the subtle . . . the very difficult to see . . . the unaging . . . the stable . . . the undisintegrating . . . the unmanifest . . . the unproliferated . . . the peaceful . . . the deathless . . . the sublime . . . the auspicious . . . the secure . . . the destruction of craving . . . the wonderful . . . the amazing . . . the unailing state . . . Nibbāna . . . the unafflicted . . . dispassion . . . purity . . . freedom . . . the unadhesive . . . the island . . . the shelter . . . the asylum . . . the refuge." These vague affirmations are not all that different from similar ones with respect to Brahman in the Upaniṣads.

28. "The Shorter Discourse to Malunkyaputta," in *The Middle Length Discourses of the Buddha: A New Translation of the Majjhima Nikāya,* trans. Bhikkhu Ñānamoli and Bhikkhu Bodhi (Boston: Wisdom, 1995), 534–35 (533–36).

29. Bu Ston (1290–1364), the Tibetan scholar of Buddhism, records a debate between the supporters of the Indian learned tradition of Kamalaśila and the Chinese supporters of instant awakening in which the Chinese makes the following point, which reminds us of Schreber's "not-thinking-of-anything-thought": "Whoever does not think anything, the one who does not ponder will become completely liberated from saṃsāra . . . he is instantly enlightened." Cited in Paul Williams, *Mahāyāna Buddhism* (London: Routledge,

1994), 194. Hereafter *Mahāyāna Buddhism* will be abbreviated as MB. Note also that in popular Buddhism, in Theravāda societies, one can simply realize nirvana by being born in the dispensation of the next Buddha, Maitreya, eons hence, of course, and listening to his sermons.

30. In John D. Ireland, trans., *The Udāna, Inspired Utterances of the Buddha* (Kandy: Buddhist Publication Society, 1990), 21.

31. James, *The Varieties of Religious Experience,* 64, 65.

32. *The Ten Principal Upanishads,* trans. Shree Purohit Swami and W. B. Yeats, 2d ed. (London: Faber and Faber, 1938), 94. The Purohit and Yeats rendering is easy to read, but for a more scholarly translation see Chāndogya, 6:13, in Patrick Olivelle, *Upaniṣads* (New York: Oxford, 1996), 154–55.

33. Śāntideva, *The Bodhicaryāvatāra* (Realization of the Path of Awakening), trans. Kate Crosby and Andrew Skilton (New York: Oxford University Press, 1998), 52.

34. Hadot, in *Plotinus*, speaks of the "amorous emotion which leads the soul towards Beauty itself." He also says that the Plotinian conception of unity with the Good is very much in the manner of the Christian mystic's use of the Song of Songs. Consider the passage in *Plotinus* VI 7, 22 where, according to Hadot, the soul is said to be infected with "Bacchic madness" from which love is born (52). Here is Armstrong's translation where Plotinus describes the soul colored by Good: "Then the soul, receiving into itself an outflow from thence, is moved and dances wildly and is all stung with longing and becomes love. Before this it is not moved even towards Intellect, for all its beauty; the beauty of Intellect is inactive till it catches a light from the Good, and the soul by itself 'falls flat on its back' and is completely inactive and, though Intellect is present, it is unenthusiastic about it. But when a kind of warmth from thence comes upon it, it gains strength and wakes and is truly winged; and though it is moved with passion for that which lies close by it, it naturally goes on upwards, lifted by this giver of its love. It rises above Intellect, but cannot run on about the Good, for there is nothing above." Hadot's discussion ends at this point, but let us continue with Plotinus's abstract philosophical discourse which, it seems to me quite remote from the language of the Song of Songs and Bacchic eroticism. "But if it remains in Intellect it sees fair and noble things, but has not yet quite grasped what it is seeking. It is as if it was in the presence of a face which is certainly beautiful, but cannot catch the eye because it has no grace playing upon its beauty. So here below also beauty is what illuminates good proportions rather that the good proportions themselves, and this is what is lovable. For why is there more light of beauty on a living face, but only a trace of it on a dead one, even it its flesh and proportions are not yet wasted away? And are not the lifelike statues the more beautiful ones, even if the others are better proportioned? And is not an uglier living man more beautiful than a beautiful man in a statue. Yes, because the living is more desirable, and this is because it has soul; and this is because it has more the form of good; and this means it is somehow colored by the light of the Good, and being so colored wakes and rises up and lifts up that which belongs to it, and so far as it can makes it good and wakes it" (Armstrong, *Ennead VII,* 155–59). As Armstrong rightly says, this is the language of Plato's Phaedrus, although Hadot is right to insist that Plotinus is much more of a mystic than Plato, if by mystic one means nontheistic mysticism. I find there is a paradoxical movement in Hadot's discussion. First, the active sense of the soul as feminine seeking union with the One, as with Christian mystics; and

along with this is the language of the Song of Songs, when Plotinus says that the soul "searches," "runs," and "jumps" (in Plotinus, *Ennead V*, 5, 8, 6 [p. 56], although Armstrong's translation of *Ennead V* on p. 179 does not reveal this activity of the soul.) For similar but totally nonerotic language use, there is Jacob Boehme's description of the movement of the Abyss in book 5, n. 24.

On the other hand Hadot reaffirms the idea that the "soul's highest state is complete passivity" (56). Here I agree with him, and also his statement that when Plotinus "describes a state of passivity, he is inviting his readers to bring about this passivity in themselves" but I am not sure how Plotinus's profound philosophical exhortation can bring this about (57). I can also agree with Hadot that "Plotinus' spiritual life consists in tranquil confidence and peaceful gentleness," but once again remind ourselves that, contra Hadot, similar states occur in Buddhist meditation. Further, if Buddhism provides a technology for achieving this condition, not so with Plotinus.

35. *Vajrayāna* literally means "diamond vehicle," in theory a further development of *Mahāyāna*, "the great vehicle." The *vajra*, or diamond, is a metaphor for the hard shining nature of the truth of Tantra; it further represents the awakened mind of the Buddha. In Hinduism the *vajra* is the thunderbolt of the Vedic god Indra and later of Viṣṇu, but in Tibet it is often represented as "scepters made of metal, bone, or some material with five prongs at one end. A straight vertical prong in the center is surrounded by four curved ones. They are commonly held in the right hand during tantric rituals and visualizations, while the bell is held in the left hand. In conjunction with the bell, the vajra symbolizes the method aspect of a Buddha's enlightenment, the skillful means he adopts in order to benefit others." See John Powers, *Introduction to Tibetan Buddhism* (Ithaca: Snow Lion, 1995), 229.

36. In *Imagining Karma*, I have discussed the whole problem of conceptual language. I borrow the term *conceptualism* from medieval scholastic philosophy, but give it a different twist.

37. *Imagining Karma*, 38–39.

38. Ibid., 40–41.

39. The Buddha uses similar language in respect of the *Unconditioned* or nirvana; see, for example, SN, 1378–79, see also n. 27.

40. Cited in Michael Sells, *Mystical Languages of Unsaying* (Chicago: University of Chicago Press, 1994), 44. For a modern example of not-so-profound language by an influential philosopher, see Martin Heidegger, *What Is Called Thinking?* trans. J. Glenn Gray (New York: Harper and Row, 1968): "The will is delivered from revulsion when it wills the constant recurrence of the same. Then the will wills the eternity of what is willed. The will wills its own eternity" (104), and so on, in obscurantist language that might, however, make sense to Heidegger addicts.

41. Elaine Scarry, *The Body in Pain: The Making and Unmaking of the World* (Oxford: Oxford University Press, 1985); for fine accounts of stories related by victims of torture, see E. Valentine Daniel, *Charred Lullabies: Chapters in an Anthropography of Violence* (Princeton: Princeton University Press, 1996).

42. When it comes to dreams, we will later demonstrate, the situation is even worse because dreams are fluid, constantly changing character. Hence it would be folly to deal with the grammar of dreams as David Foulkes, a major dream theorist, does in *A Grammar of Dreams* (New York: Basic Books, 1978). Foulkes's assumption is that the structure of dreams, like

the structure of a sentence, is propositional, and that they have a "verbal-propositional structure precisely because they are generated by mental systems which employ verbal codes" (15). Foulkes uses dream texts or dreams related by a dreamer but these recollected texts are by definition "propositional" and would inevitably slant the argument in the direction of language "grammar." I show later that a dream is systematized or rendered grammatical in different degrees in the very act of telling, but especially in scribal reflection.

43. Quentin Lauer, "Hegel," *The Encyclopedia of Religion,* ed. Mircea Eliade (New York: Macmillan, 1987), 6:247 (244–49).

44. The relevant text is from the Bhūridatta Jātaka in E. B. Cowell, ed., *The Jātaka or Stories of the Buddha's Former Births* (London: Pali Text Society, 1981), 5 and 6:110. The text reads as follows: "He who has eyes can see the sickening sight; / Why does not Brahma set his creatures right? If his wide powers no limits can restrain, Why is his hand so rarely spread to bless? / Why are his creatures all condemned to pain? / Why does he not to all give happiness? Why do fraud, lies, and ignorance prevail? / Why triumphs falsehood,—truth and justice fail? I count you Brahma one th' unjust among, / Who made the world in which to shelter wrong."

45. Max Jammer, *Einstein and Religion* (Princeton: Princeton University Press, 1999), 43–44.

46. Ibid., 47.

47. Israel, *Radical Enlightenment,* 160.

48. In proposition 11, part 1 of *Ethics,* the existence of God is stated thus: "God or substance consisting of infinite attributes, each of which expresses eternal and infinite essence, necessarily exists" (E, 222). "Substance," in Western philosophical discourse, is the ground of Reality from which everything else is generated through extension. It includes such notions as the idea of prima materia and its extension in the generation of nature. Or, as David Hume puts it in *A Treatise of Human Nature* (ed. David Fate Norton and Mary J. Norton [Oxford: Oxford University Press, 2005], 158), extension refers to the "modification of one simple, uncompounded, and indivisible substance." Similarly, Descartes believed in a two-substance theory: matter, which is opposed to mental processes, the latter a different kind of substance opposed to matter. Spinoza abolishes this distinction in that there is one Substance that could also be conceived of as nature or God. This is presented in the preliminary definitions of Substance that begins *Ethics.* These definitions are followed by "axioms" in the style of Euclid's geometry, and God as Substance is inferred from these definitions and axioms (E, 217–18).

God for both Spinoza and Descartes is an Absolute rather than the creator of orthodox Christianity, although both had to maintain some idea of providence for fear of prosecution or persecution by church and state. Descartes's idea of two substances, matter and mind, was based on earlier conceptions of body and soul, God and the world although, as with Spinoza, there is only one ultimate substance, God. Spinoza always maintained his notion of an abstract God or entity, and in one of his last letters, written seven months before his death, he summed up his thesis: "Simply from the fact that I define God as an Entity to whose essence existence belongs, I infer several properties of him, such as that he necessarily exists, that he is one alone, immutable, infinite, etc." (letter no. 83, July 15, 1676, E, 958). Brilliant as Spinoza is, the trouble with his kind of method is that the whole elaborate edifice collapses if one disagrees with the basic assumption of substance and the definitions and propositions that follow it or if one shows them to be false. This is David Hume's strategy when he says that Spinoza's notion of an indivisible substance from which everything else flows is "a hideous hypothesis" and then demolishes the idea of God as substance on empirical grounds. Hume further inquires whether "all the absurdities, which have been found in the system of Spinoza, may not likewise be discover'd in that of theologians" (Hume, *A Treatise of Human Nature,* 159). Nevertheless, the idea of substance, or substances, is different from the theologians' God although, it carries with it the same logical vulnerability, a kind of vulnerability that underlies much of European thought, insofar as the philosophical edifice rests on some taken-for-granted truth, as for example Hegel's idea that reason is substance.

Parts 1 to 4 of *Ethics* is Spinoza's "system," argued from the assumption of substance and carried out with such rigor that it gives him an opportunity to criticize in devastating fashion the whole edifice of the Catholic Church and all forms of religious beliefs in Christianity, Judaism, and Islam, and, indeed, popular beliefs everywhere. In his system everything is causally determined, and no knowledge can exist outside of reason and science, all of which are deduced from substance or God. Thus Spinoza unsparingly criticizes free will, the divine right of kings, deities, and supernatural figures that inhabit the cultural landscape, all forms of magic, and, above all, the biblical miracle that the churches thus far set such store by. There is very little of the creator left after this devastating attack. Nevertheless for an ethnographer like me, much more appealing than his system is the more open argumentative discourse of his later *Tractatus Theologico-Politicus* (1670), which employs a much more inductive method using actual biblical texts to make his judgments without depending on "axioms." Here Spinoza's criticisms involve a total demolition of biblical "superstition" and miracle, including such things as the central mystery of the resurrection and the notion of a providential God in the traditional sense. The *Tractatus* is a paean celebrating freedom of conscience and the affirmation that Spinoza's God is truly universal and available to all who live righteous lives. It also makes sense to think of Spinoza as the founder of the hermeneutics of suspicion, and it is the *Tractatus* that best exemplifies this critical stance. Yet if religious beliefs are products of ignorance, then what remains as far as faith is concerned?

Pushed to the wall, it seems to me that Spinoza has to fall back on a version of the Absolute. It is here that I disagree with Jonathan Israel, for whom Spinoza's substance or God is nothing but Nature in its modern sense. I think one can substitute reason, in later Hegelian fashion, instead of nature and still make sense of the propositions that flow from his notion of substance or God. Yet to substitute reason for nature also does not make sense because it is God that constantly appears in Spinoza's thought, even if that God can be said to represent laws of nature and exemplifies reason. I am also reluctant to attribute to Spinoza and his followers the "evolutionary hypothesis" Israel attributes to them, based on his conviction that God or substance is "nature." It is certainly true that the Enlightenment, after Spinoza, employed what Charles Taylor calls "Enlightenment naturalism," where nature becomes a kind of replacement for God, not only the God of Christianity but also the deism of the time. For a discussion of Enlightenment naturalism, see Charles Taylor "Radical Enlightenment" and his "Nature as Source," in *The Sources of the Self: The Making of Modern Identity* (Cambridge: Harvard University Press, 1989), 355–67. Yet it is one thing to affirm the importance of Spinoza and his immediate followers in creating the later naturalism but another to affirm that Spinoza's own God is nothing but a reification of nature. Spinoza says in the *Tractatus* that "God's decrees and command-ments, and consequently God's providence, are in truth nothing but Nature's order," and the "greater our knowledge of natural phenomena, the more perfect is our knowledge of God's essence, which is the cause of all things" (E, 450). But soon we realize that God is more than nature; one loves him, but in an abstract intellectualist sense, I suspect in the same way that one nowadays appreciates a work of art: "So he who loves above all the intellectual cognition of God, the most perfect Being, and takes special delight therein, is necessarily most perfect, and partakes most in the highest blessedness" (E, 428).

Thus underlying Spinoza's idea of nature is that of an essence or an entity or Abso-lute, and it is in the concluding part 5 of his *Ethics* that Spinoza tries to grapple with this idea. According to Israel, part 5 of *Ethics* "has an enigmatic and inscrutable quality," and it does not have the "air of inevitability and logical cogency" that his system in general exemplifies. But to me the enigma needs unraveling. I think that Spinoza is posed with a dilemma that he must contend with, namely, the public view of him (and that of the Jew-ish and Christian establishments) as an out-and-out atheist, a sacrilegious thinker, and, strangely enough, an idolater. Any true atheist has to deal with the attribution of nihil-ism or Nothingness, which for many modern-day atheists would be unproblematic. One dies to become the food of worms. That is all there is to it. But nihilism can be a problem for anyone living in a culture that is permeated with beliefs regarding God, the after-life, and doctrines of salvation, all held by philosophers and intellectuals with special intensity, many of them defying compromise. Nevertheless, Spinoza's is not simply an intellectual response to the fear of purported nihilism, because it is unlikely that Spinoza and those who immediately followed him personally believed that their philosophical thinking was nihilistic. In Spinoza's case he inherited a prior tradition of Greek thought in which one could believe in an abstract God or a Good that could reconcile the notion of an Absolute with ethics, both soteriological and worldly. I would say that if Spinoza's God is nature or reason, pure and simple, rather than a representation of those attributes, his God would be a nihilistic deity or no deity at all. Part 5 of *Ethics* is an attempt to think through these problems, but it is an incomplete project or a project that resists comple-tion, which is true of much of what we do, including my essay. And I would add that Spinoza dying at age forty-four meant that his project had to be incomplete almost by necessity.

One can phrase Spinoza's problem thus: if everything rests on God, as Spinoza clearly states everywhere in his system, and if he is not the personal God of Christianity, how does one conceptualize the deity, and how does one know that he exists? Spinoza's con-ceptualization and intellectual comprehension of God is brilliant, but how does he deal with God's existence, and, if he exists, what are the qualities he possesses? These are the issues that Spinoza tries to grapple with in the conclusion of *Ethics*. I can only hint at the manner in which Spinoza's engages in this daunting task.

Spinoza, we know, postulated three ways of knowing. The first kind of knowledge, derived from the operation of the senses (as with British empiricism), is imperfect ow-ing to the limitations of sense. Hence it is impossible to grasp the nature of God or of the world through sense perceptions. The second way of knowledge is through rigorous deductive reasoning from the primary desideratum of substance or God, as stated earlier.

That is the major enterprise of *Ethics*. But reasoning in this sense, while providing true knowledge of the world, has its limitations. Reason, while it is the work of God or his gift, is body and time bound. It consists of duration and, when the body dies, duration ends, and with it reason. Yet, if this was all, Spinoza's would be a nihilistic project: we die to become the food of worms. But Spinoza does not accept this nihilistic position, and therefore there is the third path of intuitive knowledge, which is knowledge of God's existence and, inextricably connected with it, the knowledge of existence after death. One cannot grasp the knowledge of God's existence through reason but, as with Descartes's cogito, only through intuition. But Spinoza's is not the kind of visionary truth that we deal with in this essay but an intuitive apprehension of truth he tries (hopelessly, I think) to justify in terms of reason.

In part 5, propositions 14 to 36 attempt to give meaning and content to the notion of God. A few illustrations will suffice to demonstrate this. Spinoza begins with one's love for God, but without the slightest taint of eroticism. Although one loves him, God tends to be indifferent to us. He is "not affected with any emotion of pleasure or pain" and "strictly speaking God does not love or hate anyone" (E, 17:371). The God who suffers no pain or pleasure is within us and insofar as that is the case we cannot express pain or pleasure in our relation to God, nor can that relation be tainted with envy or jealousy. Thus "nobody can hate God" (E, 18:371), and, moreover, "he who loves God cannot endeavor that God should love him in return" (E, 19:372). But, as far as human beings are concerned, this constant feeling of love toward God that is in our minds is mediated through the body because, unlike the Cartesian conception, mind cannot be separated from the body. Logically, it would seem that because the body cum mind can exist only during the duration of the body, both must disappear when human beings die. But Spinoza refuses to accept this position, and part 5 attempts to deny nihilism and provide some sense of immortality to mind after the demise of the body.

Spinoza tries to resolve the dilemma by getting back to God, and herein lies the difficult or unclear argument about the continuity of some form of existence after death, beginning with proposition 22 and best expressed in the proof based on that proposition: "God is the cause not only of the existence of this or that human body but also of its essence, which must therefore necessarily be received through God's essence by a certain eternal necessity, and this conception must necessarily be in God" (E, 22:374). This means, Spinoza implies, that mind consists of duration—our time-bound existence—and can last only as the body lasts, and that is what our scientific knowledge derived from the second path tells us. But proposition 23, along with others, tell us something more: God, unlike human beings, is not mortal, and therefore he possesses an essence, and this essence is also found in us. This is a kind of conventional wisdom that is found in nonatheistic traditions also, such as Blake's. If God's essence is found in us, then it surely cannot be in the body, but, rather, in the mind. Hence "there is a definite mode of thinking which pertains to the essence of mind, and which is necessarily eternal" (E, 23:274). But, given Spinoza's scientific knowledge on the finitude of the body of which mind is a part, the question now arises: how do we know that there is some such essence within our minds? In the "scholium" to proposition 23 he says that "we feel and experience that we are eternal," even though he cannot demonstrate what he means by a sense of feeling and experience. Thus there is no "logical proof" for this kind of knowledge, yet "we nevertheless sense that our mind, insofar as it involves the essence of the body under a form of eternity, is eternal, and that this aspect of its existence cannot be defined by time, that is, cannot be explicated through duration" (E, 23:374). The idea is clear enough: if we partake of the essence of God, who is eternal, then we also (our minds) must have an eternal essence. But these deductions cannot be from reason, the second way of knowledge, because that path of knowledge is built on human mortality. Thus there is no way to accommodate God's essence within us, and its certainty (albeit of a non-Cartesian sort), except through the "highest virtue," which helps us "to understand things by the third kind of knowledge," that is, intuitive knowledge (E, 25:375). Our mind therefore is a part of eternity because it contains the essence of God who is eternal.

It seem to me that at this point the Cartesian problem of intuitive understanding resurfaces: if the highest kind of knowledge is via the third intuitive path, how can that be reconciled with the certainty of knowledge that comes from the second path of reason, the primary mode of knowledge that underlies virtually everything Spinoza writes about? Spinoza's resolution of this problem is no different in principle from Descartes when he says that it is through desire or conatus or will that is not hostile to reason. Our desire to know God and the eternity of mind flows from the second and certain way of knowledge. We desire to know of God and his existence, the eternality of his essence within our minds through the path of rational knowledge, as proposition 28 (E, 375) says: "The conatus, or desire, to know things by the third [intuitive] kind of knowledge cannot arise from the first kind of [sense based] knowledge, but from the second." But the problem with this argument is that the second form of sure knowledge assumes the existence of God (or substance or nature), from whom everything flows, but that knowledge is in fact derived from the third, intuitive kind of knowledge. Proposition 32 tells us that the third kind of knowledge "is accompanied by the idea of God as cause." It therefore seems perfectly sensible for Spinoza to assume the third path of knowledge is the highest mode of knowing because the whole edifice of his system rests on the assumption of God, who can only be known intuitively! As far as I know, Spinoza does not deal with the circularity of his argument, which anticipates the later formulation of the hermeneutical circle. More important, Spinoza's thinking on the certainty of God's existence is very Cartesian, and, like the Cartesian, it illustrates the paradox of dogmatic reason, namely, the ultimate source of reason lies in God or substance, which can be apprehended only intuitively, and thus intuition becomes the primary (the third) mode of knowledge.

To add to these complications, Spinoza cannot tell us much about God within us and God's role in any form of the afterlife. As I have suggested, this is a continuing problem with any reified Absolute, and it comes out clearly in Spinoza's notion of our love of God. From the third kind of knowledge "there necessarily arises the intellectual love of God" (E, 32: 377), and that is "eternal," not bound by duration or time. It also means that this love persists after the demise of the body. But how is that love generated? The answer is that "God loves himself with an infinite intellectual love" and the implication is therefore that his essence in our minds contains that very same love. Earlier propositions have already told us that God does not express emotions in respect of humans, but now we know that his is a pure intellectual love that constitutes our very being, and we direct that love towards him who cannot love us! This intellectual love that we have toward God is what the Holy Scriptures call blessedness, or "glory," but "properly [should] be called spiritual contentment, which in reality cannot be distinguished from glory" (E, 36: 378–79). It seems logical that because God is eternal the intellectual love we have for him is eternal and "nothing can destroy it." When the mind understands this love, "the less subject it is to emotions that are bad, and the less it fears death" (E, 38–39:379). But, although we might not fear death, we know nothing about the eternality of the mind following death. Further, although the idea of blessedness is derived from the Scriptures, the loving and caring God of the Scriptures cannot exist for Spinoza. His God is in the great European tradition of the Absolute, but his attempts to give it emotional salience remains at the "intellectual" level, at best a kind of serene joy or blessedness. The last proposition sums it all: "Blessedness is not the reward of virtue but virtue itself. We do not enjoy blessedness because we keep our lusts in check. On the contrary, it is because we enjoy blessedness that we are able to keep our lusts in check" (E, 42: 382). I suspect this is what the Greek skeptical philosopher Sextus Empiricus, who had come into prominence in sixteenth-century Europe, called quietitude. "Men of talent perturbed by the contradictions in things and in doubt as to which of the alternatives they ought to accept, were led on to inquire what is true in things and what is false, hoping by the settlement of this question to attain quietitude." See Sextus Empiricus, *Outlines of Pyrrhonism*, trans. R. G. Bury (Amherst, NY: Prometheus, 1990) 19. Sextus Empiricus also deconstructs the idea of God (186–90), but does not leave any room for an Absolute either. The problem with Spinoza's God or absolute is this: I doubt that even Spinoza can enjoy access to this God or enjoy the blessedness he or it is supposed to give us.

49. Cited in Jammer, *Einstein and Religion,* 73.

50. In epistle 3, 163–68, in Alexander Pope, *Collected Poems,* ed. Ernest Rhys (London: Dent, 1939), 240.

51. For a good discussion of current existential theories of dreaming and psychotherapy, see Anthony Shafton, *Dream Reader: Contemporary Approaches to the Understanding of Dreams* (Albany: State University of New York Press, 1995), especially the section entitled "Existential Dream Psychology: Boss and Others," 140–57.

52. Charles Taylor, "Providential Deism," in Charles Taylor, *A Secular Age* (Cambridge: Harvard University Press, 2007), 221–69. The resultant moral and existential dilemma is highlighted by Taylor, who poses the following question: what remains of God after the eclipse of deism, using that term very broadly to describe Enlightenment notions of the Absolute? "God remains the Creator, and hence our benefactor, to whom we owe gratitude beyond all measure. We are grateful for his Providence, which has designed for our good; but this Providence remains exclusively general: particular providences and miracles are out. They would . . . defeat the kind of good which God has planned for us" (233).

53. Vic Mansfield, *Tibetan Buddhism and Modern Physics: Toward a Union of Love and Knowledge* (West Conshohocken, PA: Templeton Foundation, 2008), 63.

54. David Bohm, *Wholeness and the Implicate Order* (London: Routledge, 1980), 156, hereafter abbreviated as WIO.

55. Bohm says that relativity theory was the first to challenge the vision of unchanging particles in Newtonian physics. Einstein's idea is that the particle concept is no longer primary in his unified field theory. In terms of the theory of relativity, Bohm adds that "the idea of separately and independently existent particles is seen to be, at best, an abstraction furnishing a valid approximation only in a certain limited domain." But would

Einstein defend the following point that Bohm does? "Ultimately, the entire universe (with all its 'particles,' including those constituting human beings, their laboratories, observing instruments, etc.) has to be understood as a single undivided whole, in which analysis into separately and independently existent parts has no fundamental status." This is obviously not Einstein's position, and Bohm admits that "Einstein was not able to obtain a generally coherent and satisfactory formulation of his unified field theory." And, worse, Bohm says: Einstein's field concept "which is his basic starting point, still retains the essential features of a mechanistic order, for the fundamental entities, the fields, are conceived of existing outside of each other, at separate points of space and time, and are assumed to be connected with each other only through external relationships which indeed are also taken to be local, in the sense that only those field elements that are separated by 'infinitesimal' distances can affect each other" (WIO, 221). What is striking about this assertion is there is no justification on the basis of Einstein's unified field theory for either a flow in Bohm's sense or a unified wholeness.

56. It is the quantum theory that gives a more serious challenge to the mechanistic order, going far beyond what is postulated by the theory of relativity, especially the three features that follow. I quote Bohm, WIO, 223:

1. "Movement is in general discontinuous, in the sense that action is constituted of indivisible quanta (implying also that an electron, for example, can go from one state to another, without passing through any states in between).

2. "Entities, such as electrons, can show different properties (e.g., particle-like, wavelike, or something in between), depending on the environmental context within which they exist and are subject to observation.

3. "Two entities, such as electrons, which initially combine to form a molecule and then separate, show a peculiar non-local relationship, which can best be described as a non-causal connection of elements that are far apart (as demonstrated in the experiment of Einstein, Podolsky and Rosen)." He adds that the laws of quantum mechanics are statistical and "do not determine individual future events uniquely and precisely."

Relativity requires continuity, strict causality or determinism and locality whereas "quantum theory requires non-continuity, non-causality and non-locality. So the basic concepts of relativity and quantum theory directly contradict each other," and, therefore unsurprisingly, the two theories have not yet been able to be "unified," and indeed, says Bohm, such unification seems impossible. Hence what is needed is a "qualitatively new theory, from which both relativity and quantum theory are to be derived as abstractions, approximations and limiting cases."

57. So is it with the Cartesian grid. Bohm says he wants to deal with order that, however, is basically indefinable because everything we do is permeated with it. In physics "the basic order has for centuries been that of the Cartesian rectilinear grid (extended slightly in the theory of relativity to the curvilinear grid). . . . The Cartesian order is suitable for analysis of the world into separately existent parts (e.g. particles or field elements)," but in relativity and quantum theory the Cartesian model faces serious obstacles (xvii).

58. Chapter 2, which contains Bohm's theory of language, is perhaps the most disappointing one in the whole book. In the rheomode he turns the conventional syntax of English

around (and, in his conception, that of all other languages) and suggests a "new gram-matical construction, in which verbs are used in a new way" and also new syntactical rules, a new vocabulary and a word order (WIO, 51). There is not the remotest possibility that human beings will use this language in any form; ordinary language use is so much a part of living that it is futile to invent new forms impossible of realization. Here Bohm joins the company of those who have invented such games of language as Esperanto and Volapük, and surely his has even less chances of succeeding. Outside of a few examples, nowhere does Bohm apply his view of language to his own writing, for obvious reasons, namely, the anticipated bafflement of his readership.

59. The idea of changing the world through changing our fragmented way of thinking is spelled out in the question and answer session with his disciples and published as David Bohm, *Thought as a System* (London: Routledge, 1994).

60. J. K. Krishnamurti and David Bohm, *The Ending of Time* (New York: Harper, 1985).

61. Gregory Bateson, *Angels Fear: Towards an Epistemology of the Sacred* (New York: Macmillan, 1987), 53.

62. Bohm says that even if one accepts the traditional physics of ultimate particles, you are forced to recognize that "we will never measure all of them simultaneously, for the in-teraction between the observing apparatus and what is observed always involves an ex-change of one or more indivisible and uncontrollably fluctuating quanta" (WIO, 89). Even if there were "subquantum" laws operating, there would be no way of verifying them by "any kind of conceivable kind of measurement" to show "that these laws were really operating." "It is therefore concluded that the notion of a subquantum level would be 'metaphysical,' or empty of real experimental content." So with Niels Bohr, who "retained the notion of indeterminism in quantum theory as a kind of irreducible lawlessness in nature" (WIO, 93). This means that lawfulness is evident on the level of particles but not in quantum theory. However, one can have statistical laws. "Instead of relating to observable deterministic and indefinitely analyzable set of laws, we relate these same phenomena by the quantum theory, which provides a probabilistic set of laws that does not permit analysis of the phenomena in indefinite detail" (WIO, 95).

63. Karl H. Pribram, "What the Fuss Is All About," in Ken Wilbur, ed., *The Holographic Paradigm and Other Paradoxes* (Boston: Shambala, 1985), 31 (27–34).

64. See Wilbur, "A New Perspective on Reality," in *The Holographic Paradigm*, 6 (5–14). Wouter Hanegraaff, in *New Age Religion and Western Culture: Esotericism in the Mirror of Secular Thought* (Leiden: Brill, 1996), has a nice summary of the hologram and its significance: "Holography is originally a technique for making three-dimensional representation of objects. Laserlight is reflected onto a photographic plate from two sources: one source consists of light reflected directly by the object itself, the other consists of light reflected from the object to the plate by way of a mirror. The interference of these two beams on the photographic plate produces a pattern of apparently meaningless swirls, the so-called 'holographic blur.' This blur has no similarity whatsoever to the object. However, when a laser beam is shined through this holographic film, a three-dimensional image of the original object appears behind it. . . . Firstly, holography suggests that it is possible to convert objects into frequency patterns, and frequency patterns back into objects. The object is implicitly present in the seemingly chaotic frequency pattern. The latter appar-ently possesses a hidden order that can be regarded as the 'deep structure' underlying

the object in its manifested form. Secondly, there is not a simple one-to-one relationship between the object and the blur, so that each part of the blur would contain the information needed to reconstitute the corresponding part of the object. Instead, if the film is cut into pieces each fragment appears to contain all the information needed to reconstitute the complete object (although the smaller the fragment, the vaguer the image). In other words, the whole is present in each of the parts. This property of the hologram is difficult to reconcile with commonsense assumptions about the continuum of absolute space associated with the Cartesian/Newtonian world view" (139–40). Hanegraaff goes on to discuss in great detail the appeal of holography to new age intellectuals.

65. Pribram, "What the Fuss Is All About," 33 (27–34).

66. Ibid., 31.

67. Itzhak Bentov, "Comments on the Holographic View of Reality," in Wilbur, *The Holographic Paradigm,* 137.

68. Pribram, "What the Fuss Is All About," 34.

69. Unfortunately, neither Bohm nor Pribram seem to have a good grasp of "Eastern religion." Much of that knowledge comes from a popularizer like Alan Watts, a friend of Pribram and from Krishnamurti, a more sophisticated thinker, a friend of Bohm's but no scholar of Buddhism or Hinduism.

70. Wilbur, "Introduction," *The Holographic Paradigm,* 4 (1–4).

71. Ibid., 10–11.

72. Hanegraaff, *New Age Religion,* 175.

73. In an extremely interesting discussion critical of the new physicists, Wilbur also spells out what he believes are the essential features of mysticism as manifest in his version of the perennial philosophy. See Ken Wilbur, "Physics, Mysticism, and the New Holographic Paradigm," in Wilbur, *The Holographic Paradigm,* 157–86.

74. Quoted in Hanegraaff, *New Age Religion,* 147.

75. Gregory Bateson (1904–1980) is a truly original thinker in modern anthropology, and his earlier work, *Naven* (1936), is one of the classics in our field. In his later years he was engaged in extremely creative work on human and animal communications, strongly influenced by contemporary cybernetics and the "systems theory" that emerged from it, spelled out in Jurgen Reusch and Gregory Bateson, *Communication: The Social Matrix of Psychiatry* (New York: Norton, 1951). But, unlike most systems theorists, Bateson's version of cybernetics ranged from the very elementary form of a thermostat to extremely complex systems, including the evolution of life itself and, beyond that, to realms outside the domain of most cybernetic investigations, such as love and hate, religion and magic, areas central to the human sciences but generally ignored by the physical and natural sciences. He is especially interesting because he downgrades the Cartesian idea of the "self" as a separable entity and, like the physics metaphysicians of this essay, he tries to link his Western thought with epistemologies stemming from what he labels the "Orient" and spelled out in *Angels Fear.* I will only deal with the outlines of his thought, especially in his work *Steps to an Ecology of Mind* (abbreviated as EM). For details of his life and work, see David Lipset, *Gregory Bateson: The Legacy of a Scientist* (Englewood Cliffs, NJ: Prentice Hall, 1980).

I will focus primarily on his earlier cybernetic models and his provocative applications of them in terms of his theory of the ecology of mind. Bateson bids us consider the example of the steam engine, which, in the vocabulary of engineering, contains a *governor*, a misleading term, he says, because it implies a "self" or ego that propels the system. The reality is that the message from the governor must go through the whole cybernetic circuit. Even in this simple model, thinking or mental processes are not something found exclusively in the governor, or self, but rather in the flow of messages that unites the several interacting parts of the system to form a whole. Mental process does not exist in any single unit of the cybernetic circuit but in the whole circuit. Bateson makes inferences from this idea of a larger whole to postulate the idea of "determinative memory" and "Immanent Mind." Thus mind and memory are not located in the ego or self that thinks but immanent in the systemically interrelated whole. Following the same logic, he says that it is wrong to say that a more complex machine such as the computer by itself possesses mind or mental characteristics, because, like the steam engine's governor, the computer is part of a larger circuit that includes the human being and the whole environment from which information is received and upon which messages from the computer have effect. It is the total system with its flow and inflow of messages "that may legitimately be said to show mental characteristics. It operates by trial and error and has creative character" and, one might add, a teleological or purposive thrust (EM, 317).

What is striking about Bateson's work is his ethical concern when he extends his cybernetic model to the more complex ecological system that is being destroyed by human beings in their exploitation of the environment. Unlike those who blamed the capitalist order or unbridled greed for these violations, Bateson blames the Christian creator as the main culprit and adds that in Christian thought evolution is a downward movement conceptualized as the "great chain of being" where God or Supreme Mind is on the top of the chain or ladder. "If you put God outside and set him vis-à-vis his creation and if you have the idea that you are created in his image, you will logically and naturally see yourself as outside and against the things around you. And as you arrogate all of mind to yourself, you will see the world around you as mindless and therefore not entitled to moral or ethical consideration. The environment will seem to be yours to exploit. Your survival unit will be you and your folks or conspecifics against the environment of other social units, other races and the brutes and vegetables" (EM, 462). His is a neo-Lamarckian critique of both Christian epistemology and contemporary capitalist development.

Instead of the Christian God, Bateson reintroduces Immanent Mind which in his thinking is a kind of equivalent of "god." "The cybernetic epistemology which I have offered you would suggest a new approach [different from the great chain of being idea]. The individual mind is immanent but not only in the body. It is immanent also in pathways and messages outside the body; and there is a larger Mind of which the individual mind is only a sub-system. This larger Mind is comparable to God and is perhaps what some people mean by 'God,' but it is still immanent in the total interconnected social system and planetary ecology" (EM, 461). And more: because this new ecology of mind is the true reality, then I or my conscious self is diminished, but that little fall, one might say, can be compensated or "tempered by the joy of being part of something much bigger. A part—if you will—of God" (EM, 461–62). With this conception of mind, there occurs an important epistemological shift wherein the primary locus of Immanent Mind must necessarily lie in its larger order from the mentalist processes of the governor and the steam engine to the world in which we exist and have existed in the past, from protozoa to human beings engaged in communicative relationships of some sort or other.

"Cybernetic epistemology," as Bateson calls it, has implications for dealing with the despoiling of the earth's resources and the threat of global warming. This "crisis in the ecology of mind" leads us to an understanding of the "pathologies of epistemology." Because human beings are part of a total systemic order in which Immanent Mind prevails, it follows that destruction of the earth's resources entails the destruction of systemic order but without a cybernetic self-correcting movement or feed-back to restructure that order. In other words, our ecological destructiveness results in the "madness" of God. Yet, while Bateson might provide a theory that would justify our taking a stance in respect of ecological degradation, he does not face up to an obvious criticism, namely, can the notion of Immanent Mind as an epistemological ground mobilize human beings to save the environment? For this to happen, people have to accept Bateson's god, a dubious eventuality. Moreover, could not one believe that we are bound each to each and to others and to larger orders of nature and ecology without the concept of Immanent Mind or of a cybernetic model? After all, our knowledge of ecological destruction comes from the work of committed scientists and political activists who may or may not have any view of Immanent Mind and, worse, who might be either Christian or even atheistic believers. And there is the further hope that committed peoples and governments might open up our consciences and our self-interests, so that we can at least begin to think of a new order leading toward a respect for ecology without subscribing to the notion of Immanent Mind. These criticisms apply to Bateson's larger ethical concerns rather than to his theory of mind and Immanent Mind per se.

Bateson's ethics, however, deploys another kind of hope when he believes that "patches of sanity" still survive. "Much of Oriental philosophy is more sane than anything the West has produced, and some of the inarticulate efforts of our young people are more sane than the conventions of the establishment" (EM, 487). Bateson was fully attuned to the sixties in the U.S., and many in the counterculture saw him as one of their gurus, living and working at the Esalen Institute, helping to create a spiritual view of the universe, guided by a rational epistemology not hostile to science, inverting the traditional notion of the deity and creating a space for the emergence of "Oriental philosophy," which, in combination with the idealistic aspiration of the youth, might open up a way of saving the world from the "insanity" of ecological destruction. Bateson died in 1980 and was spared the sight of that idealistic youth, nurtured in the sixties, giving way to a youth almost everywhere in our world, including the so-called Orient, succumbing to the very forms of exploitative "development" he lamented.

My guess is that in his self-conception Bateson considers himself to be a thinker working toward a form of "secular spirituality" grounded on a scientific worldview that is out of sync with Christianity but better attuned to "Oriental philosophy." Yet, because Bateson is a kind of sphinx, there are probably issues that will remain unclear. Thus mind is, as it were, created when the cybernetic network is in motion. It is not entirely clear to me whether mind exists in the system when it is not working, as for example when the thermostat or computer is idle. If the latter, then it is difficult to conceive of "Immanent Mind" existing when the flow of messages do not exist, because it is in the pathways of communication that Bateson's mind lies, not in any unit in the system. Nevertheless, his thinking implies that in some sense mind exists outside the units that constitute the whole, and this would include the thermostat, all existing, as it were, outside the flow of messages and indeed possessing "determinative memory" rather than the more reasonable position that mind exists only when the system is functioning. But the latter position cannot provide a space for Immanent Mind or God.

In his later work, *Angels Fear*, Bateson says that a stone that belongs to nonliving matter "does not respond to information and does not use injunctions and trial and error in its internal organization. To respond in a behavioral sense, the stone would have to use energy contained within itself, as organisms do. It would cease to be a stone." In order to cease to be a stone understood in terms of "impacts" and "forces," it must somehow or other "make and receive news" (17). The stone, when it is part of nonliving matter, cannot send or receive messages. But let me suppose in terms of Bateson's earlier argument that, when a mason works on the stone, it is part of a cybernetic network, a receiver and giver of messages. One can therefore impute mental process to the mason, his chisel or other instruments, the stone, and back to the mason in a circular movement. Obviously in my example Immanent Mind at best resides in the cybernetic process as it operates. Can we therefore say that the man and the stone and the instruments are also permeated with mind, and, further, can one ask whether the cybernetic process makes the stone and the instrument nonmaterial? Hence my criticism: the human being is a key feature of the cybernetic complex that propels the system, whether of the steam engine, the computer, or the man chiseling the stone. In all these cases information is finally circling back to the human being or governor. If one has to use the idea of mind, then it is the human mind, if at all, that is changed by the operation of the system. Bateson does not and cannot accept these criticisms, which, from his point of view, inhibit understanding his own model of the mind.

Bateson's larger project of dealing with the ecological system is put tantalizingly before the reader, but remains an enticement, not even the beginnings of a thesis. He wants eventually to deal with communicative regularities in the biosphere and he believes that one can use the word *god* once again to describe these regularities. However, his new god is something above and beyond the Immanent Mind of the smaller systems. The regularities he plans to uncover could be said to be the work of a god that Bateson, somewhat playfully, suggests might be called Eco! "There is a parable which says that when the ecological god looks down and sees the human species sinning against the ecology . . . he sighs and involuntarily sends the pollution and the radioactive fallout" (ibid., 142). Eco therefore is Bateson's own invention to take the place of Anangke, an example of another force that acts involuntarily. "It is no use to make sacrifices and offer bribes. The ecological god is incorruptible and not mocked" (ibid., 143). I would pose another parable for Bateson's ghost: did the Eco god presiding over radioactive fallout destroy Hiroshima? For myself, I reject this horrible being or nonbeing, and so will most of my readership, I am sure.

With his analysis of larger systemic orders, it seems as if Bateson might modify the simple cybernetic model with which he began. The answer is ambiguous at best when he concludes with his critique of the linear trajectory of logical reasoning as against the circular one he proposes (that resembles, one might add, the less pretentious model of the hermeneutical circle). On a structural level, Bateson's Immanent Mind or his Eco god in *Angels Fear*, in its very abstraction, joins the class of absolutes that appear in the history of Western thought, some too abstract and unappealing and some meaningful like Plotinus's or Einstein's and flourishing with various degrees of meaningfulness among intellectuals and scientists of the nineteenth century and after. I would say that Bateson is a prisoner of that prior discourse and that his "god"—whether the Immanent Mind or his Eco god—is a preconception to which he gives a rational foundation in contemporary cybernetics or systems theory, making it relevant both to our scientific weltanschauung and the contemporary world in which we are fated to be witnesses of ecological disasters. While his cybernetic model might have some appeal, his conception of Immanent Mind or the Eco god is empty of emotional content.

But what about new age religionists who seem to look with favor upon Bateson and to whom he showed distinct sympathy? Just as with their appropriation of Mahāyāna Buddhism, they must radically modify Bateson's abstract God, a mind without human or humane attributes, a being who refuses to intercede in human affairs and has no sense of righteousness. They must fill that being with enchantment or use it to justify or provide a charter for the beliefs they have already reformulated from Tibetan and pagan traditions. For my part, I will repeat that Bateson is reacting to the death of god by inventing a form of "secular spirituality." I could substitute *spirit* and *spiritual* when Bateson talks of mind and mental processes without substantially altering his argument. But that, for Bateson, would be unthinkable. Or would it be heresy?

76. In addition to Mansfield's *Tibetan Buddhism and Modern Physics*, there has been a recent surge of publications linking quantum physics to Buddhism, much more sympathetic to that union than mine. See for example B. Allan Wallace, *Hidden Dimensions: The Unification of Physics and Consciousness* (New York: Columbia University Press, 2007).

4. PENITENTIAL ECSTASY

1. Stephen Toulmin and June Goodfield, *The Discovery of Time* (Chicago: University of Chicago Press, 1982), 131.

2. "Jane Mary of Maillé was often raised two cubits off the ground by angels, and once by St. Ives of Brittany;" so was Flora of Beaulieu: "once singing *Veni creator Spiritus* when all of a sudden, in the presence of all the sisters in her congregation, she was carried into rapture and raised up more than two cubits from the ground, where she remained hanging for some time." See Richard Kieckhefer, *Unquiet Souls: Fourteenth-Century Saints and Their Religious Milieu* (Chicago: University of Chicago Press, 1984), 155.

3. Ibid., 158.

4. The short text will be abbreviated as ST and the long text as LT, both from Julian of Norwich, *Revelations of Divine Love*.

5. It should be remembered that "bodily vision" was in fact a visionary experience for both Julian and Angela of Foligno and many other penitents. Teresa however reformulated her visions in much more orthodox Augustinian terms, claiming that she never experienced bodily or corporeal visions, only imaginative or spiritual ones. This is also the position of Teresa's disciple John of the Cross, who makes the point that bodily or corporal visions

might well occur but are not of much value and urges the devotee not to pay attention to them. Indeed, John of the Cross, like most male theologians and mystical thinkers, is wary of visionary experiences, as was the Buddha. "These images [such as Christ crucified], just as the corporal objects of the exterior senses, cannot be an adequate, proximate means to God." ("The Ascent of Mount Carmel," in *John of the Cross: Selected Writings,* ed. and trans. Kieran Kavanaugh (New York: Paulist Press, 1987), 106 [41–153]). Again: "But when there is question of imaginative visions or other supernatural communications apprehensible by the senses and independent of one's free will, I affirm that at whatever time or season they occur (in the state of perfection or one less perfect) individuals must not desire to admit them, even though they come from God," in effect undermining female ecstatic religiosity, including that of his mentor Teresa (125). He urges people not to "place their eyes on interior imaginative visions;" instead "they must instead renounce all these things" (126). For a learned discussion of these issues, see Father Karl Rahner, "Psychological Problems of Visions," in *Visions and Prophecies* (London: Burns and Oates, 1963), 31–43.

Augustine's own theory of visions are derived from Paul in Corinthians 1, but further developed by him. I shall briefly state Augustine's argument that Frank Tobin neatly formulates in his essay "Medieval Thought on Visions," in *Vox Mystica: Essays on Medieval Mysticism,* ed. Ann Clark Bartlett (Cambridge: D. S. Brewer, 1995), 41–53. The three kinds of visions that appear and reappear in our visionary texts are derived from Augustine's distinction between corporeal or bodily and spiritual and intellectual visions. Corporeal or bodily visions refer to our ordinary act of seeing, whereas *visio spiritualis* is the conjuring up of someone or thing already known by the imagination; thus if I know that Jesus existed I can conjure him up spiritually. By contrast, intellectual visions, or *visio intellectualis,* occurs when I can conjure up in my mind something that never existed or something that is so abstract it has no images readily associated with it, Tobin's example being "love," which has no images similar to it. *Visio intellectualis* is, therefore, totally immaterial, and it gives us true knowledge, whereas *visio spiritualis* is the highest form of visionary experience. But, for Augustine, and for many others, spiritual or imaginative visions are troublesome because they imagine an absent material object and therefore could lead to false visions or illusions. This, one might add, is not unique to Christianity, but everywhere, because spiritual visions cannot easily be judged as genuine or spurious. Augustine attempts to deal with this problem by reformulating Paul and making a distinction between mind and spirit, between *mens* and *spiritus.* "Augustine takes *spiritus* to signify that step in the process of cognition in which the images of things are in the soul but hence not yet been grasped and turned into knowledge of the *mens,*" thereby, says Tobin, creating a dark place in the soul where images exist but is not comprehended by the intellect (44). Spirits also can enter this dark space, but, because the body, and materiality in general, is inferior to the soul, the image in the space of the soul is superior to the material object it represents. But, the question is, if these images of absent material objects are what the soul cognizes, where do these physical objects come from? They come from things we have experienced and now stored in memory, apropos of Plato; things that we have not experienced but know to exist, such as places and beings; things that do not exist but which we make up. Normally we do not confuse objects with their images except during intense focusing of our thoughts or during illness (for example, delirium) or during the intervention of a good or evil spirit. Now Augustine can develop his notion of ecstasy where one is cut off from one's physical surroundings: "In the state of ecstasy the attention of the spirit/soul (*intentio animae*) is altogether turned away and cut off from the senses and its gaze utterly directed to images (*visio spiritualis*) or to things so immaterial that they cannot be rendered in images (*visio intellectualis*)" (44). It should be noted that these formal categories or norms of correct visionary experience, whether they be of Augustine or St. John of the Cross, are simply bypassed or ignored by the penitents in their ecstatic passion.

6. Rudolph M. Bell, *Holy Anorexia* (Chicago: University of Chicago Press, 1985), 163, hereafter abbreviated as HA.

7. *The Collected Works of St. Teresa of Avila,*, trans. Kieran Kavanaugh and Otilio Rodiriguez, vol. 1, containing two texts, *The Book of Her Life* and *Spiritual Testimonies* (Washington, DC: Institute of Carmelite Studies, 1987), 237: "One day when I was at Mass, this most sacred humanity in its risen form was represented to me completely, as it is in paintings." *The Life or Book of Her Life* will be hereafter abbreviated as L.

8. See Gananath Obeyesekere, *Medusa's Hair: An Essay on Personal Symbols and Religious Experience* (Chicago: University of Chicago Press, 1981), especially part 1, 13–51, which deals with my theory of "personal symbols," those symbolic formations that operate on the level of culture and psyche at the same time, tapping both public (or cultural) values and unconscious or deep motivations.

9. Catherine's biographer Raymond of Capua says that Catherine "had come to know and value the lives and way of life of the holy Fathers of Egypt and the great deeds of other saints . . . and had felt such a strong desire to do what they did that she had been unable to think about anything else." See Raymond of Capua, *The Life of Catherine of Siena,* trans. George Lamb (New York: Kenedy, 1960), 26. See also Henry Suso, *The Life of the Servant,* trans. James M. Clark (Cambridge: Clark, 1982), 45.

10. As Paul Lachance puts it in *The Spiritual Journey of the Blessed Angela of Foligno According to the Memorial of Frater A* (Rome: Pontificium Athenaeum Antonianum, 1984), 51, there was in medieval female mysticism a "downplaying of marriage in favor of virginity and a spiritual union with Christ. Marriage was considered something of a handicap to salvation, a remedy for concupiscence, and a concession to human weakness. Physical sexuality had no real place in the life of perfection. The superior form of life was, therefore, virginity or continence."

11. Caroline Walker Bynum, *Jesus as Mother: Studies in the Spirituality of the High Middle Ages* (Berkeley: University of California Press, 1984), 15.

12. See "Women Mystics in the Thirteenth Century," ibid., 170–262.

13. Raymond of Capua, *The Life,* 179.

14. *The Life by Jacques de Vitry,* trans. Margot King as *Two Lives of Marie D'Oignies* (Toronto: Peregrina, 2002), 147.

15. Cathleen Medwick, *Teresa of Avila: The Progress of a Soul* (New York: Doubleday, 1999), 45.

16. Barbara Newman, "Possessed by the Spirit: Devout Women, Demoniacs, and the Apostolic Life in the Thirteenth Century," *Speculum* 73.3 (July 1998): 733–70. Newman argues that while the evidence is mostly from hagiographical texts, there is little doubt that in the thirteenth century monks have taken over the role of nonreligious exorcists, although I imagine the latter also continued to exist. What is striking about Newman's material

is that the demons are controlled by monks in such a manner that they become agents for vindicating the power of the Church and the orthodoxy of the time. Not just by their submission to authority but also by their acts of preaching and proclaiming God's powers and virtues! Satanic beings have been tamed, but not fully: "At the same time, however, demoniacs as social actors not only parodied the authority of charismatic saints; they also reveled in a freedom like that of licensed fools" (768).

17. Bynum, *Jesus as Mother*, 15.

18. Ibid. 143.

19. Gerard Manley Hopkins, "Thou art indeed just, Lord," in *The Poems of Gerard Manley Hopkins*, ed. W. H. Gardner and N. H. MacKenzie, 4th ed. (Oxford: Oxford University Press, 1984), 106.

20. According to Bell, St Veronica (1660–1727) is an extreme case of holy anorexia, but a re-examination of his data suggests a different picture. She entered a convent in 1677 at age seventeen and then engaged in extreme ascetic practices for a five-year period, including rigorous fasting. Some of her practices were voluntary; others were ordered by her superiors in what is an extreme example of patriarchal brutality. She was asked to clean floors with her tongue, and also the chicken coop; she had to eat meager food and some she welcomed, these being spider webs and spiders themselves and cat's vomit with her plate of food. Yet, this regime gradually lessened after five years and was over by 1685. We know that by 1688 she is eating in Spartan fashion, but a healthy diet. Thus for most of her life, a forty-two-year period from 1685 to 1727 when she died, there was no fasting. It therefore made sense for her to discourage others from practicing extreme asceticism. Bell notes: "Although she herself experienced the crown of thorns, mystical marriage with Jesus, and stigmata, she carefully warned the young women in her charge against seeking such extreme signs of supernatural grace" (HA, 80). For details on this fascinating case study, see HA, 58–81.

21. The dozens of books on Teresa are much too permeated with hagiography to be useful for the critical reader. I suggest the well-written biography, *Teresa of Avila*, by Medwick; other accounts that I found eminently readable are Victoria Lincoln, *Teresa: A Woman* (Albany: State University of New York Press, 1984); and Stephen Clissold, *St. Teresa of Avila* (London: Sheldon, 1979).

22. In her *Life* she says that she was less than twelve years when her mother died; this is not so and is probably a refusal to recognize the coincidence of her real age and the age in which her mother had married (L, 56).

23. The average age of marriage for a woman in Tuscany was around fifteen and for men around thirty, according to Lachance, *The Spiritual Journey*, 52–53. The age of marriage for women was probably much less in other places, including the Spain of Teresa. In Teresa's case, the depressing family models of marital life were contrasted with the romantic literature, which both her mother and she read, about "amoral heroes . . . and high-born damsels who abandoned themselves so readily to their guilty amours" (Clissold, *St. Teresa*, 17).

24. These are well known as anger, envy, sloth, pride, covetousness, gluttony, and lust, but in reality included much more. Some sexual fantasies could easily be categorized as "lust."

25. She does not identify this cleric, who we know was a priest of Becedas, named Pedro Hernandez (L, 469, n.2).

26. I strongly suspect that this is Francisco de Salcedo, a steadfast friend and confidant, and he was known as *cabelloro santo* owing to his piety. But there isn't the slightest doubt that this relationship was more than friendship on Teresa's part. She refers to him several times as the married gentleman. None of the commentators whom I have read see the connection, which to me seems obvious. This older person seems to have been an oedipal father figure for Teresa.

27. In chapter 32, as Teresa was engaged in business matters relating to the founding of the Carmelite convents, she has a vision of psychic hell when, while in prayer, "I suddenly found that, without knowing how, I had seemingly been put in hell." This was not a punishment, however, but a piece of knowledge that God wanted to give her. The experience took place "within the shortest space of time," which means we are in the realm of waking dreams or trances. "The entrance it seems to me was similar to a very long and narrow alleyway, like an oven, low and dark and confined; the floor seemed to me to consist of dirty, muddy water emitting a foul stench and swarming with putrid vermin. At the end of the alleyway a hole that looked like a small cupboard was hollowed out in the wall; there I found I was placed in a cramped condition. All of this was delightful to see in comparison with what I felt there" (276). In this fetal position, along with the impurities of the womb, she reverts back to terror, but with a moral purpose. The lord wanted her to see the place from which he had freed her (277). Naturally she felt in this closed space a constriction and suffocation "as if the soul were continually being wrested from the body" and being torn to pieces. She says she cannot describe the "burning and crumbling" and, worse, "that interior fire and despair." The walls of the womb-place closed in on her; there was no light, only "blackest darkness," as the walls "closed in on themselves and suffocated everything." The lord did not show any more of hell at that time, but she saw frightening visions as "punishment for some vices" (277). But now she does not feel the pain or the fear. It is as if terror has been converted to blessedness because these terrors are visions of what she had avoided and in fact "secrets that the Lord, because of who He is, desired to show me about the glory He will give to the good and the suffering that will go to the evil" (279).

28. Beginning with chapter 14, several verses deal with the trope of the waterer and the garden in order to explicate the role of prayer and the replenishment of dryness. These discourses are, however, conducted on a purely abstract level as theoretical discussions of the soul's union with God and because of their formal nature they are not very relevant for us. However, when Teresa says in chapter 11 of *Life* (110–19) that she reflected on such things as water, fields, and flowers, which reminded her of the Creator, we are in the realm of generation as opposed to the dryness of body and soul. These originally biblical images were beautifully developed by Bonaventure, and from him it went into the popular biblical tradition. See "Tree of Life" in *Bonaventure: The Soul's Journey Into God, The Tree of Life, The Life of St. Francis,* trans. Ewert Cousins (Mahwah, NJ: Paulist Press, 1978), 120, 155 (117–75).

29. "I was once in an oratory, and he appeared to me in an abominable form at my left side. Because he spoke to me, I looked particularly at his mouth—which was frightening. It seemed that a great flame, all bright without shadow, came forth from his body. He told me in a terrifying way that I had really freed myself from his hands but that he would catch me with them again" (L, 264). This happened twice; and when Teresa threw holy

water at his direction, he never returned. But her "terrible interior and exterior pains" did not cease. The other sisters were scared; the lord however "wanted me to understand it was the devil because I saw beside me a black, very abominable little creature, snarling like one in despair that where he had tried to gain he had lost" (L, 264–65). She laughed and was not afraid any longer. The sisters were in despair because "I was striking myself hard on the body, head, and arms. What was worse was the interior disturbance, for I wasn't able to feel calm of any sort." She says there is nothing "the devils flee from more—without returning—than holy water. They also flee from the cross but they return." Why? The holy water not only chases the devils but also cools her dryness and with it her soul is consoled and refreshed. She notes that this has happened often: "Let us say the relief is like that coming to a person, very hot and thirsty, on drinking a jar of cold water; it seems the refreshment is felt all over." Because this holy water has been blessed its power to refresh is greater than ordinary water. When the nuns brought holy water and she threw it at the devil "he instantly went away and all the illness left me as if it were taken away by hand, except that I remained weary as though I had been badly beaten with a stick" (L, 265). Once when she was in the choir "there came upon me a strong impulse toward recollection. I left the choir so that others wouldn't notice, although all of them heard the striking of loud blows near the place where I was; I heard some coarse words next to me as though the devils were plotting something, although I didn't understand what" (L, 266). I assume that these coarse words were sexually loaded ones.

It is important that witnesses must authenticate these visionary experiences even if they were of the devil. Another instance is fascinating: she mentions a person who had been living in mortal sin but had not confessed or made amends otherwise. But he told Teresa of his sins, and Teresa persuaded him to go to a confessor, which he did. Teresa also engaged in a correspondence with him and persuaded her sisters to pray for him, even though they did not know who this person was. Now comes this statement: "I begged His Majesty to mitigate those torments and temptations and that those devils would come to afflict me, provided that I would not offend the Lord in anything" (L, 266–67). It's seems to me that Teresa's sexual desires are really on the surface and in this case her correspondence with the sinner has activated them again, whether or not she was attracted by the sinner or by the sin itself. "As a result, for a month I suffered severe torments; it was during this time that these two things I mentioned happened" (L, 277). The two things refer to the previous experiences of loud noises and the coarse words of the devil. The sinful man is, I suspect, the "married gentleman" in the previous chapter who reappears now, and her guilt therefore is not just that this gentleman has committed a mortal sin but that Teresa herself is attracted to him and cannot get rid of her feelings. Obviously she still corresponds with him: "he wrote to me, for I told him what I was going through during that month. His soul was fortified, and he was left completely free" (L, 267). The irony here is that the sinner might have been freed from his affliction, but the saint was not.

30. This caused her great affliction, but while she did not have any vision of Christ she did hear this: "Do not fear, daughter; for I am, and I will not abandon you; do not fear" (L, 221). Thus assured, Teresa becomes a kind of warrior fighting the devils who afflicted her. "I took a cross in my hand, and it seemed to me truly that God gave me courage because in a short time while I saw I was another person and that I wouldn't fear bodily

contact with them [the devils]; for I thought with that cross I would easily conquer all of them. So I said: 'Come now all.'" Not only was she not afraid of them but they were afraid of her, she thought; "I pay no more attention to them than to flies" (L, 222). In the next chapter she mentions the tribulations she had in founding the Discalced monastery of St. Joseph, and the Lord told her: "Why are you afraid? Do you not know I am all-powerful? I will fulfill what I have promised" (224). And now, like the Sri Lankan ecstatics in *Medusa's Hair:* "At other times the Lord warns me of some dangers I'm in, or of other persons, and about things of the future—three or four years in advance very often—all of which have been fulfilled" (L, 225).

31. In her theoretical discussions Teresa follows the orthodox position that "bodily visions" do not appear to the genuine mystic but in fact they do appear as in this case. As always, there is a gap between the theory of the mystical experience and the reality of it, best exemplified in John of the Cross's theoretical description of the dark night of the soul or the stages of ascension of the soul to God and the actual experience of ascension that leaps across these formal stages. In Teresa's case there is her famous allegorizing of "The Interior Castle" of the seven dwelling places of the interior spiritual life, with God residing in the center of the main dwelling place, which simply does not find an experiential parallel anywhere in her or any other nun's actual spiritual journey.

32. I have in effect dealt with the sublimation of orgasm into rapture with reference to Teresa's insistence that her experience of God wounding her heart is not a bodily one but one of spiritual agony and pleasure combined. Jacques Lacan has taken the Bernini sculpture as an orgasm, but also something more, while some Lacanian feminists have interpreted Teresa's rapture as a kind of visceral bodily reaction, rather than a matter of the heart. I have recently read Amy Hollywood, *Sensible Ecstasy: Mysticism, Sexual Difference, and the Demands of History* (Chicago: University of Chicago Press, 2002). On pp. 201–2 she mentions Luce Irigaray's critique of the baroque excesses of Bernini's statue of Teresa in seeming sexual ecstasy. "By reasserting the violence of Teresa's experience and by emphasizing the site of the transverberation as the viscera (stomach or womb) rather than her heart (Teresa describes the arrow as piercing the heart so deeply it reaches into her entrails and pulls them out), Irigaray upsets the boundaries between inside and out." "Rather than in her heart" is simply not correct, because the many references I have quoted (and others I have not) refer to the piercing of the heart and soul as the relevant or primary act rather than entrails. Father Kavanaugh, whose most recent translation of *Life* I use here, ignores the word *entrails*. He tells me, in a personal communication of October 24, 2005, that "in this passage entrails is used metaphorically to denote the deepest part of our emotional being." Nevertheless the literal translation by Allison Peers, in *The Life of Teresa of Jesus, The Autobiography of Teresa of Avila,* trans. E. Allison Peers (New York: Doubleday, 2004), 244–45, is worth quoting: "In his hands I saw a long golden spear and at the end of the iron tip I seemed to see a point of fire. With this he seemed to pierce my heart several times so that it penetrated to my entrails. When he drew it out, I thought he was drawing them out with it and he left me completely afire with a great love for God. The pains was so sharp that it made me utter several moans; and so excessive was the sweetness caused me by this intense pain that one can never wish to lose it, nor will one's soul be content with anything less than God. It is not bodily pain, but spiritual, though the body has a share in it—indeed, a great share." Even if one wants to interpret the piercing and disem-

bowelment as literally true, it surely has a biological component because deep feelings of fear or love produce pain or a burning in one's bowels. Here is Alison Weber's note to me, which, in my opinion, deals with this issue very well: "The original Spanish does indeed use the word 'entrañas' or entrails. But these were considered the seat of the emotions, much as today we say 'I felt it in my heart.' The seventeenth-century lexicographer Sebastián de Covarrubias gives this gloss: 'Everything the animal has inside itself in its belly, such as its heart, liver, lungs and spleen. . . . By allusion it means what is hidden, such as the entrails of the earth.' I expect Father Kieran was trying to find the emotional rather than the physiological equivalent. Peers' translation does seem more forceful." I think Alison Weber and Father Kavanaugh as well as Teresa are drawing on an Old Testament tradition, nicely highlighted by Moses Maimonides, the twelfth-century Jewish thinker: "In phrases like 'my bowels are troubled for him' (Jeremiah xxxi, 20); 'The sounding of thy bowels' (Isaiah lxiii, 15), the term 'bowels' is used in the sense of 'heart;' for the term 'bowels' is used both in a general and in a specific meaning; it denotes specifically 'bowels' but more generally it can be used as the name of any inner organ, including 'heart.' The correctness of this argument can be proved by the phrase 'And thy law is within my bowels' (Psalms 11:9), which is identical with 'And thy law is within my heart.'" Cited in Mary Douglas, *Natural Symbols* (New York: Vintage, 1973), 13. That God would literally disembowel Teresa is to me, as to Father Kavanaugh and Alison Weber, quite untenable. Such disembowelment during quartering is generally employed in medieval times in respect to animals and, of course, criminals and those guilty of treason, witness the phrase *drawn and quartered.*

33. This compact with Jesus is finally sealed in her visionary marriage to him in the monastery in Beas in 1575 and recorded in her "Spiritual Testimonies." "Our Lord told me that since I was His bride I should make requests of Him . . . and as a token He gave me a beautiful ring, with a precious stone resembling an amethyst but with brilliance very different from any here on earth, and He placed the ring on my finger" (L, 404).

34. See also book 3, p. 144, for a similar hypothesis. The most detailed attempt to give verbal expression to the "indescribable" nature of rapture and vision is in *The Interior Castle,* the text that is addressed to nuns for whom these difficult personal experiences must be made ideologically intelligible. Teresa recognizes the difficulty of this task, but nevertheless undertakes it. She rightly says that the allegorization of the mystical experience can never capture the power of that experience. This text deals with the mystical experience, but also contains useful guidelines for nuns who try to give theological meaning to their own mystical states, helping them to distinguish the genuine from the spurious. For details, see "The Sixth Dwelling Places," in *The Interior Castle,* in *The Collected Works of St. Teresa of Avila,* vol. 2, trans. Kieren Kavanaugh and Otilio Rodriguez (Washington, DC: Institute of Carmelite Studies, 1980), 359–426.

35. "I stretched out on the floor and the nuns came and held me down; nonetheless, this was seen" (L, 174). "When one sees one's body so elevated from the ground that even though the spirit carries it along after itself, and does so very gently if one does not resist, one's feelings are not lost. At least I was conscious in such a way that I could understand I was being elevated" (L, 175).

36. Once again the discussion of locutions in *Life* is closer to her personal experience. It is "experience near," whereas the elaborate discussion of the forms of locution in 370–78 of

The Interior Castle is "experience distant." This is also true of her discussions of union and rapture in the latter work.

37. For a good account of this "feminist" viewpoint, see Carol Slade, "Teresa's Feminist Figural Readings of Scripture," chapter 2 in her *St. Teresa of Avila: Author of a Heroic Life* (Berkeley: University of California Press, 1995), 39–64. To me it is somewhat problematic to think of Teresa as well as other female saints as *feminists,* a term that would have made no sense to them. Rather, one could see them as expressing a point of view of the religious experience of women, denied by the Church and the authority of Pauline and Augustinian texts. In this sense female discourse appears as a counter to the dominant male ones, but often they have to be clothed in attitudes of subservience, sometimes in indirect fashion and through a constant referral to confessors regarding the validity of direct communication with Jesus. Thus, in Teresa's address to the nuns known as "The Meditation on the Song of Songs," she affirms, as everywhere else, women's intrinsically weak nature, yet at the same time asserts that God "was able to give fortitude to many saintly girls . . . so they were able to suffer many torments, since they were determined to suffer for them." And she adds that "His Majesty enjoys having His works shine in weak people." See *The Collected Works,* 2:238. For a study that seriously considers these issues, see Alison Weber, *Teresa of Avila and the Rhetoric of Femininity* (Princeton: Princeton University Press, 1990).

Weber points out the denial of Teresa's womanhood during her beatification and canonization proceedings. She is referred to as "a virile man," who "endured all conflicts with manly courage;" some said she ceased to be a woman. Teresa is said to have transformed the "congenital inferiority of her sex" thereby being able to "rectify nature's error." She was treated often enough by the male priestly authorities as a *mujercilla,* that is, a "little woman" of the sort that got into easy ecstasies; at other times even more pejoratively as one of the *alumbrados,* or "illuminists," who, inspired by the word of God, claimed to understand Scripture through ecstasy (these citations are from Weber, *Teresa of Avila,* pp. 17–27). Weber has some deadly examples of those who seemed to defy papal authority: a stigmatic Magdalena de la Cruz was investigated in 1546, and, in spite of support by royalty and by ordinary people, she "was condemned to perpetual silence and imprisonment in a convent outside of Cordoba" (44). These cases multiplied after the 1500s, an example being Isabel de la Cruz, sentenced to lashes and life in prison. Public popularity did not immunize penitents from papal criticism and indeed might have been a trigger that accelerated that criticism. This might be the case with Teresa as well, despite her influential connections. As Weber says, "The Book of her Life was in Inquisitorial hands for thirteen years. In 1550 her confessor ordered her to burn her meditations on The Song of Songs, and in 1589, seven years after her death, theologians of the Inquisition urged that all her books be burned" (35). One can hardly blame Teresa for yielding to patriarchal authority. Because accusations could be deadly, Teresa had to contend with them by admitting her inferior and weak female nature everywhere in her work, sometimes excessively so, as when she refers to herself as living in "a sea of evil" as "a filthy scum" and "the weakest and most wretched of all who have ever been born" (49). Weber is citing E. Allison Peers, *Studies in Spanish Mysticism,* 2 vols. (London: Sheldon, 1927), 1:149–50. I might add that in *The Interior Castle* the text is explicitly addressed to fellow nuns, Teresa speaks of "our womanly dullness of mind," an astonishing self-caricature in so bright a person (19). These downright self-demeaning references might indicate fits of depression, as Peers thought, but more likely this is familiar self-abnegation before those in power. This discourse is different from that of female "weakness" and unworthiness, which also emerges in her prose but can be read both as a concession to patriarchal authority and as an expression of humility before Jesus. As many feminist scholars have pointed out, one has to read between the lines of her text to properly understand how she subverted that authority through her actions and the religious language in which she expressed her love of Jesus.

38. Cited in the "Introduction" to *The Interior Castle* in *The Collected Works,* 2:268 (263–79).

39. This idea appears all the time in both Teresa and other female mystics. Thus Teresa says, "When the Lord suspends the intellect and causes it to stop, He Himself gives it that which holds its attention and makes it marvel; and without reflection *it understands more in the space of a Creed that we can understand with all our earthly diligence in many years*" (L, 121; my emphasis).

40. St. John of the Cross, *The Dark Night of the Soul,* ed. and trans. Rev. Benedict Zimmerman (Cambridge: Clark, 1973), 143. Regarding "somnolence" of the soul, John of the Cross says: "It is enough for us here to know that the interior acts and movements of the soul, if they are to be divinely influenced by God, must be first of all lulled to sleep, darkened and subdued, in their natural state, so far as their capacity and operations are concerned, until they lose all their strength" (150).

41. Medwick, *Teresa of Avila,* 104; see also 205–6.

42. Multitudes of ecstatics were everywhere in Europe in medieval times and in Spain itself variously known as *beatas* (holy women, often ecstatics), *alumbrados* (those who receive scriptural "illumination" directly from Jesus), *dejados* and *mujercillas* ("little women," a contemptuous reference to heretical female ecstatics).

43. For a bold attempt to psychoanalyze female ecstatics, see Antoine Vergote, *Guilt and Desire: Religious Attitudes and Their Pathological Derivatives,* trans. M. H. Wood (New Haven: Yale University Press, 1988). Vergote examines the "pathological derivatives" such as obsession neuroses and hysteria in the ecstatic rhapsodies of nuns, but, more important, he is sympathetic to those nuns such as Teresa who have managed to transform and sublimate their sexual guilt and desire in a creative direction. See his chapter "The Mystical Enjoyment of Teresa of Avila: Displaced Eroticism or Sublimated Libido" (153–67). As with Freud, I think that Vergote also does not deal with "sublimation" adequately. Yet I am sympathetic to his critique of those who want to reduce visions and ecstasies to a pathological infrastructure, as, for example, when he says "that the entire personality of the individual in question cannot be reduced to a psychopathological category" (189).

The equation of female spirit possession worldwide and the mysticism of possessed female saints as victims of "hysteria" comes from a very long tradition in the West and is given clinical validation in the pioneering work of Jean Charcot and Pierre Janet in Paris in the late nineteenth century. Freud attended Charcot's seminars and came under his influence in his early work with Breuer on hysteria. The impact of Charcot on Freud is insightfully dealt with in a short essay by J. B. Pontalis, "Between Freud and Charcot: From One Scene to the Other," in *Frontiers in Psychoanalysis: Between the Dream and the Psychic Pain,* trans. Catherine Cullen and Philip Cullen (London: Hogarth, 1981), 13–22. For a good critique of the treatment of demonic possession and ecstasy in the West as hysteria, see

Cristina Mazzoni, *Saint Hysteria: Neurosis, Mysticism and Gender in European Culture* (Ithaca: Cornell University Press, 1996). Unfortunately, Mazzoni is totally unaware of the extensive work on possession by ethnographers from almost every part of the non-European world and their critiques of those who pathologize religious beliefs. It seems to me that historians of religion often ignore the intellectual world outside of theirs knocking on the door.

44. The classic work that affirms the truth of visions is Evelyn Underhill, *Mysticism: The Nature and Development of Spiritual Consciousness* (Oxford: One World, 2000 [1911]); see also Mark Fox, *Religion, Spirituality and the Near-Death Experience* (London: Routledge, 2003).

45. See some of the examples in Phillip H. Wiebe, *Visions of Jesus: Direct Encounters from the New Testament to Today* (New York: Oxford University Press, 1997), 55, 56–57.

46. For example, Thomas Merton says that some of St. Lutgard's visions might have been formed in a space outside the beholder, or the image of a body might be formed in the eye of the visionary beholder: both are forms of bodily vision. Then he deals with two other alternatives to account for Lutgard having visions of the soul of two deceased persons, Pope Innocent and Simon, an abbot. This kind of vision might be an imaginative one, that is, one formed inside the mind or imagination without any cue from the eye or exterior senses. Or more likely it could be spiritual vision, wherein her intellect would have been "directly illuminated by the divine light." "Spiritual or intellectual visions reveal to the soul, in a sudden blaze of intuition." Thomas Merton, *What Are These Wounds: The Life of a Cistercian Mystic, Saint Lutgarde of Aywières* (Milwaukee: Bruce, 1950), 61. See also n. 5, this chapter.

47. Most accounts of European saint mysticism have been by Christian believers, and hence they simply ignore larger theoretical issues. Even with modern intellectuals, autobiographical studies are vitiated by a theoretical relativism. A good example is Mazzoni, *Saint Hysteria,* mentioned in n. 43. Like feminists such as Luce Irigaray, Mazzoni believes that males are not capable of dealing with women's voices, a critique that has dangerous implications. Further, she criticizes thinkers like Simone de Beauvoir and even Lacanian analysts such as Luce Irigaray and Julia Kristeva for not understanding female mysticism on its own terms, that is, in terms of the worldview of the mystic and the reality of their own experiences. This kind of analysis simply carries relativism to such an extreme that any nomological or theoretical understanding of religious ecstasy is rendered impossible. Mazzoni almost seems to say that one needs to be a sympathetic woman and a believer to grasp the reality of the visionary experience. If we carry this logic to its inevitable conclusion, then it would seem that whites cannot truly write about blacks, women about men and vice versa, and that true ethnographic knowledge comes from members of a particular group or nation writing about themselves and so on.

48. Ludwig Wittgenstein, *Culture and Value,* trans. Peter Winch (Chicago: University of Chicago Press, 1984), 2e. His insight is more akin to Melanie Klein's and one I suspect comes from Wittgenstein's own troubled childhood.

49. In my work *Cannibal Talk: The Man-eating Myth and Human Sacrifice in the South Seas* (Berkeley: University of California Press, 2004), 255–65, I have made the point that in Fiji, as among the Aztecs, the human sacrifice is in fact infused with the spirit of the god on whose behalf the sacrifice is made. Thus in consuming the human sacrifice one is in fact eating the god in a sacramental meal. When the god is eaten directly, without an inter-

mediary sacrificial victim whether human or animal, there is no way except to eat the invisible god through a substitutive yet powerful symbolism. Nevertheless, whether in Fiji, where there is a human sacrificial victim, or in Christianity, where the victim is Jesus who is god and man, the eating of the god infuses the participant with the essence or spirit of the deity, hence its enormous power.

50. Jacob Boehme, *The Way to Christ,* ed. and trans. Peter Erb (New York: Paulist Press, 1978), 151

51. Raymond B. Blakney, trans. *Meister Eckhart: A Modern Translation* (New York: Harper and Row, 1941), 181.

52. Jacques de Vitry, Marie d'Oignies's hagiographer, uses the term *spiritual food* to describe the life-sustaining nature of the Eucharist. "As long as her soul was so full and copiously overflowing with spiritual food, it did not allow her to accept any refreshment from corporeal food." See King, *Two Lives of Marie D'Oignies,* 65.

53. *Angela of Foligno: Complete Works,* trans. Paul Lachance (New York: Paulist Press, 1993), 186.

54. Kieckhefer, *Unquiet Souls,* 29.

55. *Angela of Foligno,* 142–43. And so does Catherine of Siena in Raymond of Capua, *The Life,* 191: "I prayed to him continuously to take me from the body of this death, that I might be more closely united with Him." Although God denied her request in this instance, two years before her death he granted her wish "to be freed from the bonds of the body and united with Christ" (320).

56. King, *Two Lives of Marie D'Oignies,* 73.

57. Frank Graziano, *Wounds of Love: The Mystical Marriage of Saint Rose of Lima* (Oxford: Oxford University Press, 2004), 60.

58. King, *Two Lives of Marie D'Oignies,* 135.

59. Susan Noffke, trans., *Catherine of Siena: The Dialogue* (New York: Paulist Press, 1980), 30. Catherine's biographer Raymond of Capua perhaps expresses the conventional view that in spite of a starvation diet the penitent remains physically strong, a feature we noted in Marie d'Oignies also. Raymond gives several examples of Catherine dragging heavy loads in her weakened condition without much effort, a miracle according to him. "There seemed to be two Catherines in her, one that suffered in a state of exhaustion, and another that toiled in the spirit, and the latter, fat and healthy of heart, sustained and strengthened the weakened flesh" (Raymond of Capua, *The Life,* 57). As Christ puts it: "Drink, daughter, the liquid from my side, and it will fill your soul with such sweetness that *its wonderful effects will be felt even by the body which for my sake you despised*" (148; my emphasis).

60. The notion of the "surplus of meaning" is everywhere in Paul Ricoeur's work, but especially dealt with in *Interpretation Theory: Discourse and the Surplus of Meaning* (Fort Worth: Christian University Press, 1976), in the section entitled "Metaphor and Symbol," 45–69.

61. Angela of Foligno, once again, is a good example. She sees in the host the figure of Christ himself, just as she had seen him in an earlier vision, the neck and throat shining "with such splendor and beauty that it seems to me that it must come from God; it surpasses the splendor of the sun," Lachance, *Angela of Foligno,* 146. On another occasion she sees the Christ Child aged about twelve in the host (147).

62. Raymond of Capua, *The Life,* 170–71.

63. Ibid., 171.

64. Lachance, *Angela of Foligno,* 128; my emphasis.

65. Cited in Lachance, *The Spiritual Journey,* 150–51. When Jesus asks Lutgard of Aywières what she really wants from him, she responds, "I want your heart," to which Jesus answers: "Rather, it is I who wish your heart." This interchange of hearts might have theological and mystical significance, but surely its erotic meaning is inescapable as it is when the pseudo-Cupid pierces Teresa's heart. And one must remember that when Lutgard was a beginner and an adolescent "the crucified Christ appeared to her when she was on her way to Matins and allowed her to drink from the wound at his side," Bernard McGinn, *The Flowering of Mysticism: Men and Women in the New Mysticism, 1200-1350* (New York: Crossroad, 1998), 165. These examples can be multiplied. Gertrude of Helfta, according to Bynum, did not stress Christ's sacrifice but rather "it is a stress on the blood that Christ feeds us in our most intimate union with him or a stress on the union itself." Bynum adds: "Gertrude's devotion to Christ's wounds and especially to his heart, which culminated in her receiving (inwardly, not visibly, we are told) the stigmata and the 'wound of love.'" Bynum, *Jesus as Mother,* 192. Similarly, Christina Ebner's visions occurred during mass, and therefore it is not surprising that Christ allowed her to "suck from the wounds in his divine heart, as the bees do from flowers" (Kieckhefer, *Unquiet Souls,* 173).

66. Lachance, *Angela of Foligno,* 155.

67. Ibid., 200.

68. There follows a fascinating episode described in great detail in Julian's Long Text. Christ revives the "dead" Julian with his life-giving blood, but this blood is from Jesus's own wounded body as he lay dying on the cross. The blood gushing forth from his wounds means that Christ loses a vital substance from his body, and Julian describes in harrowing and obsessive detail the changes undergone by the body of Jesus as a result. In a sense, God dies to redeem Julian of Norwich and humankind in general, and it is therefore expectable that the blood that gushes from his dying body should revivify Julian's. Specially striking is that Jesus's body is drying up as a result of the loss of blood that wets Julian's. Let me give the reader a feel for this description of the drying body of the dying Christ. "After this, Christ showed the part of his Passion when he was near death. I saw his dear face as it was then, dry and bloodless with the pallor of death; and then it went more ashen, deathly and exhausted, and, still nearer to death, it went blue, then darker blue, as the flesh mortified more completely. . . . It was a sorrowful change to see this extreme mortification, and, as it appeared to me, the nose shriveled and dried, and the dear body was dark and black, quite transformed from his own fair living colour into parched mortification" (LT, 16:64–65). And when the blood had been drained from his body, some moisture still remained but a cold dry wind worsened his condition and "gradually dried the flesh of Christ as time passed. And though this pain was bitter and sharp, it seemed to me that it lasted a very long time, and painfully dried up all the vitality of Christ's flesh. So I saw Christ's dear flesh dying, seemingly bit by bit, drying up with amazing agony" (LT, 16:65). Julian's obsession with Christ's dryness is, I suspect, a projection of her own dryness. She says: "I saw in Christ a double thirst, one bodily, the other a spiritual one," and this I think is her own thirst (LT, 17:65). Then she goes into a detailed description of Christ slowing dying and drying on the cross, his blood "baked with dry blood," and so on, till the crown of thorns was placed on his head. "And then I saw what it was because it began to dry, and to lose some of its weight and congeal about the garland of thorns. . . .

The garland of thorns was dyed with the blood and the other garland of wounds, and the head, all was one color like dry, clotted blood. . . . Ah! His pain was hard and grievous when the moisture was exhausted and everything began to dry and shrink. The pains that were revealed in the blessed head were these: the first done to the dying body while it was moist; and the second a slow pain as the body dried and shrank with the blowing of the wind from without that dried him more" (LT, 17: 66).

69. In Hinduism this poses little theological anxiety because God is often represented in statuary as *ardhaneśvara,* the composite form of male and female.

70. Lachance, *Angela of Foligno,* 163.

71. Ibid.

72. Raymond of Capua, *The Life,* 146.

73. Ibid., 147.

74. David Gordon White, *Kiss of the Yoginī: Tantric Sex in Its South Asian Contexts* (Chicago: University of Chicago Press, 2003), 85, see also 75–76, 84, 109.

75. Raymond of Capua, *The Life,* 148.

76. An extreme example is from Francesca de' Ponziani (d. 1440), who sensed the devil's presence through his smells. The devil brought in a putrefying male corpse and "pressed her down onto the corpse and she could feel its flesh shedding away under her. . . . Francesca remained haunted by this macabre scene, and to the aversion she always felt about the male touch was now added a vivid sense all men smelled like corpses and that their odor had gotten inside her body" (HA, 138–39). One way to insult the devil and banish him is to scold him for his shit smells. Thus Jacob Boehme's exhortation in Boehme, *The Way to Christ,* 258: "Fie, you stinking hangman's servant, how you stink in your lodging. Cloaca smells the same as you do." Jung reports a personal experience of olfactory and auditory hallucination, which is recorded in Roderick Main, *Jung on Synchronicity and the Paranormal* (Princeton: Princeton University Press, 1997), 63–68. Jung is in London in a quiet house in the summer of 1920 when in drowsy torpor he was awoken several nights by foul smells and sounds of footsteps. He attributed it to the house being haunted; his nose could sensitively pick up smells emanating from some previous dead occupant! He also admits that previously he has had a number of "psychic smells" of "hallucinatory distortions" (68). He further believes the capacity to smell things out in this manner comes from one's phylogenetic heritage, mostly dormant, but in certain conditions that capacity could be reactivated.

77. Obeyesekere, *Medusa's Hair,* 25, 78, 94–98.

78. Ibid., 89.

79. Michael Sells, *Mystical Languages of Unsaying* (Chicago: University of Chicago Press, 1994), 118.

80. Angela of Foligno, in Lachance, *Angela de Foligno,* 126, mentions family members who had been a "great obstacle" to her, these being her mother, her husband, and all her sons, every one of whom died "in a short space of time." She "felt a great consolation when it happened." The benign reference in Matthew 10:37–39 reads: "He who does not forsake wife, children, brothers, sisters, money, goods and all that he has, indeed even his earthly life, and follow me, is not worthy of me."

81. The phrase "delightful pain" is from *The Interior Castle* in *The Collected Works,* 2:368; the same page says that the soul in love with Jesus "dissolves with desire."

82. The phrase is from Hopkins, "God's Grandeur," in *The Poems of Gerard Manley Hopkins*, 66.

83. Kieckhefer, *Unquiet Souls*, 155.

84. Milton Rockeach in *The Three Christs of Ypsilanti* (New York: Knopf, 1965) interviewed three inmates in the Ypsilanti hospital in Michigan who claimed they were Christ. Their claims were so outrageous that no one could take them seriously. But they, like some of our visionaries, claimed the capacity for bilocation and translocation and, like some Buddhist visionaries, stated that they had shamanic power to go through walls and perform other miracles (75–76).

85. Carlos M. N. Eire, *From Madrid to Purgatory: The Art and Craft of Dying in Sixteenth-Century Spain* (Cambridge: Cambridge University Press, 1995), 404.

86. Fray Diego de Yepes, *Vida Santa Teresa de Jesús* (Paris: Garnier Hermanos, 1847), 316.

87. Medwick, *Teresa of Avila*, 246. For a good summary of these events, see Eire, *From Madrid to Purgatory*, 411–12.

88. For a not untypical biomedical interpretation of her vaginal bleeding, see Efrén de la Madre de Dios and Otger Steggink, *Tiempo y vida de Santa Teresa*, 2d ed. (Madrid: Biblioteca De Autores Cristionos, 1977), 974: "An uncommon hemorrhage was, in effect, her mortal illness. Like we already said in the first part of this narrative, it was 'a visceral spill of frightening proportions,' that resulted from, it seems, a uterine carcinoma, as the most competent of doctors later confirmed." I am indebted to Julia Frydman, a Princeton graduate, for translating this into English, and to Cathleen Medwick, who provided me with much of the bibliographical information on Teresa's final illness.

89. The idea of progression and regression in symbolic forms has been brilliantly explored by Paul Ricoeur, *Freud and Philosophy: An Essay on Interpretation* (New Haven: Yale University Press, 1977), based on the two movements in psychoanalytic theory, that of regression and sublimation. I have further developed this idea in my notion of "symbolic remove," where I deal with symbolic forms that are close to their ontogenetic roots and those progressively removed from them in Gananath Obeyesekere, *The Work of Culture: Symbolic Transformation in Psychoanalysis and Anthropology* (Chicago: University of Chicago Press, 1990), especially the section entitled "Symbolic Remove and the Work of Culture," 51–68.

90. Lachance, *Angela of Foligno*, 176.

91. Marina Warner, *No Go the Bogeyman: Scaring, Lulling, and Making Mock* (London: Chatto and Windus, 1998), 130–32.

92. Raymond of Capua, *The Life*, 157.

93. Noffke, *Catherine of Siena*, 153.

94. Merton, *What Are These Wounds*, 14.

95. Jesus, in Catherine's vision, took out a nail and put it in the middle of her palm and pushed it so hard that she felt it was hit by a hammer. In Raymond of Capua, *The Life*, 175, she says: "And so, through the grace of my Lord Jesus Christ, I now have a wound in my right hand, and though it is invisible to others I can feel it, and there is continual pain from it."

96. Raymond of Capua, *The Life*, 55. In flagellation the body of the penitent might not actually bleed, and it would be foolish to assume that every flagellant is "menstruating." Sometimes, even if actual bleeding does not occur, the penitent imagines through this self-inflicted wound her identification with Christ being flagellated and bloodied. In other

cases, like that of Catherine of Siena and Marie d'Oignies, the penitent actually draws blood. Thus, it is said of the latter: "She would then beat herself with a discipline three hundred times and would offer herself up as a sacrifice by a long martyrdom. At the last three strokes, a copious flood of blood would pour forth which thus would become the seasoning [the spice] for the other strokes," King, *Two Lives of Marie d'Oignies,* 69.

97. My references to symbolic wounds here and elsewhere come from Bruno Bettelheim, *Symbolic Wounds: Puberty Rites and the Envious Male* (New York: Collier, 1971). Bettelheim's psychodynamic hypothesis is that in male subincision and similar bloodletting acts in New Guinea and Aboriginal Australia the person is suffering from "vagina envy" or attempting to identify with the mother. Whether we accept this interpretation or not, it seems to me that the idea of "male menstruation" is probably a reasonable interpretation. Subincision and genital mutilation among males in Highland New Guinea and among Australian Aborigines have multiple motivations and meanings, but a common cultural theme that animates them is that impure blood, most often female blood in the male body, is drained through these forms of bloodletting. Among both males and females in New Guinea, nose bleeding has a similar function. There is an extensive literature on this subject for New Guinea, and I recommend the following articles from Gilbert H. Herdt, ed., *Rituals of Manhood: Male Initiation in Papua New Guinea* (Berkeley: University of California Press, 1982): Philip L. Newman and David J. Boyd, "The Making of Men: Ritual and Meaning in Awa Male Initiation" (275–276); and Terence E. Hays and Patricia H. Hays, "Opposition and Complementarity of the Sexes in Ndumba Initiation" (220–221). On nose bleeding see Gillian Gillison, *Beyond Culture and Fantasy: A New Guinea Highlands Mythology* (Chicago: University of Chicago Press, 1993), 183–84; and, especially as an imitation of menarche, Gilbert H. Herdt, *Guardian of the Flutes: A Study of Ritualized Homosexual Behavior* (New York: McGraw-Hill, 1981), 244–45. Ian Hogbin has a graphic account of a similar fantasy in relation to subincision in *The Island of Menstruating Men: Religion in Wogeo, New Guinea* (Scranton: Chandler, 1870), 86–91.

So is it with our female penitents, but unconsciously and unbeknownst to them. For my own previous work on this subject see *Medusa's Hair,* 150–59, where I discuss the case of Abdin, a male ritual specialist who, in a trance state, menstruates through his mouth in fantasy.

98. In the case of Dorothy of Montau, Kieckhefer, *Unquiet Souls,* 211, n. 14, thinks that the mystic suffered from a pemphigoid condition, "a severe dermatological affliction characterized by sudden eruption of blisters along the trunk and extremities, with itching and stinging sensations." Whether the medical interpretation is correct or not, Dorothy herself interpreted these wounds as given by Christ; moreover, these wounds "festered, swelled up, then burst open; again, they sometimes bled vehemently and freely" (27). Naturally, these bloody wounds were interpreted by her biographer as stigmata.

99. Regarding the clogging of the menstrual flow and bloodletting to ease that condition, Robert Burton (1577–1640) in his *Anatomy of Melancholy,* 2:237, refers to the physician Trallanius practicing medicine in Rome in the sixth century as saying: "If there have been any suppression or stopping of blood at nose, or hemrods [hemorrhoids], or women's months, then to open a vein in the head or about the ankles." Robert Burton, *Anatomy of Melancholy,* 3 vols. (New York: Everyman's Library, 1964).

100. Suso, *Life of the Servant,* 110.

101. Margery Kempe, *The Book of Margery Kempe,* trans. B. A. Windeatt (London: Penguin, 1988), hereafter abbreviated as MK.

102. There were other mystics whose lives seem to parallel Margery's, the most relevant being Marie D'Oignies. In chapter 62 Margery mentions that she had heard of her, but one cannot be sure whether Marie was a model for Margery. Marie D'Oignies did not cry as Margery did, but she did shed profuse tears night and day, making the very church floor wet and forcing her to constantly change her veils. See King, *Two Lives of Marie D'Oignies,* 60. Margery's crying cannot be divorced from her very personal life history, as I demonstrate in the next section. On the cultural level she is following a popular tradition of holy tears "invented by medieval Christians who created a Mother of Sorrows to weep for the Man of Sorrows. The Magdalene—lover and weeper, redeemed by her tears—and the Virgin—the old woman crying at the foot of the Cross or holding in her lap her crucified Son—were powerful figures in medieval spirituality." See Clarissa W. Atkinson, *Mystic and Pilgrim: The Book and the World of Margery Kempe* (Ithaca: Cornel University Press, 1981), 58. That tears should be shed in the penitent's search for the Lord is not surprising, and a good theological formulation is given by Catherine of Siena in the dialogue in a section on "Tears" in Noffke, *Catherine of Siena,* 161–83. Unfortunately, except for cases like Margery's, we cannot relate tearing to the penitent's psychic life.

   Crying for the Lord appears in other traditions also: thus Mata Amritanandamayi, a contemporary devotee of Krishna and of the Mother, used to weep profusely, according to Brahmachari Amirtatma Chaitanya, *Mata Amritanandamayi* (Quilon, Kerala: Mata Amritanandamayi Mission Trust, 1988), 39–57 and 32. Her sorrow also, like Margery's, has a basis in her own personal life, one of being beaten constantly by her own mother and then ultimately reaching out to the fantasized Mother of Hindu thought. Her deep need for mother's love is reflected in her drinking milk directly from the udder of a cow, the latter a symbol of the Mother Goddess.

103. This issue is discussed at length by Wendy Doniger O'Flaherty, *Dreams, Illusion, and Other Realities* (Chicago: University of Chicago Press, 1984).

104. For a good account of this popular Franciscan tradition, see Denise Despres, *Ghostly Sights: Visual Meditation in Late-Medieval Literature* (Norman, OK: Pilgrim, 1989), 19–53.

105. This is beautifully expressed in several places in "The Tree of Life" in Cousins, *Bonaventure,* 158: O my God, good Jesus, / although I am in every way without merit and untrustworthy, / grant to me, / who did not merit to be present in these events / in the body, / that I may ponder them faithfully / in my mind / and experience toward you, / my God crucified and put to death for me, / that feeling of compassion / which your innocent mother and the penitent Magdalene / experienced / at the hour of your passion.

106. Isa Ragusa and Rosalie B. Green, eds., *Meditations on the Life of Christ: An Illustrated Manual of the Fourteenth Century* (Princeton: Princeton University Press, 1977).

107. This version of the meditation manual dates from the end of the thirteenth century and is couched in the form of advice given by a Franciscan monk to a Poor Clare. The original text was probably composed during the second half of the thirteenth century by a Franciscan monk, Giovanni de San Gimignano, according to Despres, *Ghostly Sights,* 34. Basically, meditations tell the penitent to contemplate or meditate on the life of Christ and particularly on the passion. The contemplator has to remain in solitude or, if not actual solitude, "at least in the mind" (275). Three different types of contemplation are

mentioned, but, as with many Christian texts, no serious technical advice is given, the assumption being that intense thought or concentration on events in Christ's life will produce the visions. "With your whole mind you must imagine yourself present and consider diligently everything done against your Lord and all that is said and done by Him and regarding Him. With your mind's eye, see some thrusting the cross into the earth, others equipped with nails and hammers" (333). The meditation schedule is also stated. It must last one week and begins Monday with the "flight of the Lord to Egypt" and ends from the Resurrection to the end," and this schedule should be carried out every week. "Converse freely with the Lord Jesus and . . . strive to place His life . . . inseparably in your heart" (388).

108. God urges Suso to imitate him, but Suso was afraid to do so (Suso, *Life of the Servant*, 42). So he practiced several exercises in order "to sink into Christlike sympathy with all that his Lord and his God, Christ, has once suffered." In order to so he walked from one corner to the other of his cell and tried to create an empathy with Christ's suffering by imitating it. These walking exercises, perhaps combined with meditation, merged into his walking with Christ until he was brought to Pilate and thereafter to the Cross and then to the scene of the crucifixion. In all of these it is Suso's imagination that is self-consciously at work, not an actual participation in the Christ drama in a historical sense. "And he imagined it all to himself as vividly as he could, and said a little prayer: *Hail, our King, son of David*, and then let Him pass on" (43). When Christ was nailed to the cross, Suso also "did penance, nailing himself with heartfelt love to his Lord on the cross" (44). Suso's is a spiritual exercise brought about by physical exercise in which he deliberately cultivated an imitation of Christ's suffering. Thus he nails himself as Christ does; but this is quite different from Margery actively participating in the Christ history and dreaming a past that actually occurred.

109. Barry Windeatt, *The Book of Margery Kempe* (Cambridge: Brewer, 2004), 19. Windeatt continues: "The saint [Mary Magdalene] has an especially close relationship with Christ and his mother; she is witness to the Crucifixion and Resurrection, and becomes a patron of the gift of tears, a contemplative and an evangelist. When Christ mentions Mary Magdalene's love for him, Kempe exclaims with mixed humility and ambition: 'I wolde I wer as worthy to ben sekyr (sure) of thy lofe as Mary Magdalene was' to which she receives an extraordinary divine reassurance of her own equality with Mary Magdalene in Christ's affections."

110. As I said earlier, "rivers of blood" pour forth from the wounds of Christ, and this idea is not unusual in the meditation texts of Christianity. Thus, *Meditations* refers to the "rivers of His most sacred blood [that] flow from His terrible wounds" (334). Margery was probably familiar with its contents.

111. That reincarnation appears in Manichean religion is well known, but perhaps the most powerful heretical movement in Margery's time in Europe was the Cathar heresy. A recent study of medieval heresy makes the point that Catharism believed in the continual purification of the body until death and the spirit's final release. "Those who did not attain purification in one life might pass, by metempsychosis, from body to body, even through animals." See Arthur L. Wakefield and Austin P. Evans, *Heresies of the High Middle Ages* (New York: Columbia University Press, 1991), 47. This aspect of Catharism has a striking resemblance to Indian doctrines, particularly that of the Ājīvikas that I discuss in

Gananath Obeyesekere, *Imagining Karma: Ethical Transformation in Amerindian, Buddhist, and Greek Rebirth* (Berkeley: University of California Press, 2002), 102–8.

112. Newman, "Possessed by the Spirit," 738.

113. Margery's visions occur in meditation or contemplation or in a state of somnolence or sometimes when her soul is silent even though the world outside is bustling. These meditative contexts are mentioned several times in chapter 85. For example: once in prayer "her eyelids kept closing together, as though she would have slept" when an angel appeared and showed her the book of life wherein her name was engraved (MK, 249). Elsewhere her condition is described as a "kind of sleep" (MK, 250).

114. The date is Windeatt's inference and is found in MK, 305, n. 2.

115. Ibid. The same note tells us that records at Lynn indicated that her father was ill on December 19, 1412, and was dead by December 1413.

116. It was this same bishop who asked her to write down her experiences. But she said it was not God's will that they be written down now; and they were written only twenty years later. Windeatt says that "the mantle and ring would indicate the taking of a vow of chastity before a bishop" (M. 307, n. 5).

117. She goes to several priests to find out if her revelations were genuine and ultimately to Julian of Norwich who confirms that they were from the Holy Ghost. And, among other things, Julian tells her that "when God visits a creature with tears of contrition, devotion or compassion, he may and ought to believe that the Holy Ghost is in his soul. St Paul says that the Holy Ghost asks for us with mourning and weeping unspeakable" (MK, 78). Naturally, this would further prove to Margery that her compulsive weeping is a religious experience.

118. There is little doubt that Margery loved her father, but her mourning for his death could simply be channeled into the normal pattern of mourning and weeping that characterized her life. Hence, any attempt to link her mourning pattern with Freud's famous thesis in "Mourning and Melancholia" (SE, xiv, 243–58) is difficult to establish, particularly because we have no information on the death of Margery's mother.

119. "And she received communion every Sunday, when time and place were convenient for it, with much weeping and violent sobbing, so that many people marveled and wondered at the great grace that God worked in his creature" (MK, 96–97).

120. Ragusa and Green, *Meditations*, 328.

121. These "cryings" were acute when Margery was in Jerusalem and in Rome: "Then once a day, afterwards daily, once she had fourteen in one day, and another day she had seven" and so on (MK, 105). When she felt the urge, she tried to hold it for a while, so as not to offend others, some of whom thought she was afflicted by an evil spirit. But then the crying that had been suppressed burst forth louder than ever. These became less when she was at home, about once a month.

122. There is good reason for the woman to be fearful of the Godhead, as a much later chapter indicates. Here Jesus makes a speech (in her soul because the word of God is not uttered for others to hear) from the authority of the Godhead itself. He says the planets are obedient to his will and "see how I send great flashes of lightning that burn churches and houses. You also sometimes see that I send great winds that blow steeples and houses down, and trees out of the earth, and do much harm in many places, and yet the wind may not be seen, but it may well be felt" (MK, 222). The message is clear in Margery's

fantasizing: her suffering may not seem reasonable, but neither is it reasonable that the Godhead should send winds and storms to batter churches and houses. And then a marvelous passage in which God tells her how he illumines the soul of the devotee. "And just so, daughter, I proceed with the might of my Godhead. . . . And as suddenly as the lightning comes from heaven, so suddenly I come into your soul, and illumine it with the light of grace and of understanding, and set it all on fire with love, and make the fire of love to burn there inside, and purge it clean from all earthly filth. And sometimes, daughter, I cause earthquakes to frighten people so that they should fear me" (MK, 222). This is Job's problem. It is beautifully illustrated in Kempe's older contemporary Geoffrey Chaucer (1343–1400) in "The Franklin's Tale" that describes poignantly the dilemma of a maiden waiting for her knight and husband to return from overseas and fantasizes her ambivalence toward him in terms of grisly black rocks that she fears might destroy his ship. "Eterne God, that thurgh thy purveiaunce / Ledest the world by certain governaunce, / In ydel, as men seyn, ye no thyng make. / But, Lord, thise grisly feendly rokkes blake, / That semen rather a foul confusion / Of werk than any fair creacion / Of swich a parfit wys God and a stable, / Why han ye wroght this werk unreasonable?" See *The Poetical Works of Chaucer,* ed. F. N. Robinson (Cambridge: Houghton Mifflin, 1933), 165 (163–74).

123. Of this wedding Atkinson says in *Mystic and Pilgrim,* 47–48: "In this episode, the language of a contemporary English wedding service was combined with the common visual imagery of a mystical wedding (frequently portrayed in paint and glass) to denote the spiritual reality of union with God in terms available to the imagination of Margery Kempe." But as B. J. Gibbons puts it, "at times, the relationship between Christ and the soul seems to exemplify the advice of contemporary conduct books. The soul-wife must be obedient, humble, patient; her will 'must be melted into the will of the husband,' whose needs are given absolute priority." See, B. J. Gibbons, *Gender in Mystical and Occult Thought: Behmenism and Its Development in England* (Cambridge: Cambridge University Press, 2002), 67, hereafter abbreviated as GM.

124. See "Tree of Life," in Cousins, *Bonaventure,* 129.

125. This is Lady Tsogyel, the Sky Dakini mentioned earlier in book 2, n. 65. Here Tsogyel mentions "demons [who] projected themselves as charming youths, handsome, with fine complexions, smelling sweetly, glowing with desire, strong and capable, young men to whom a girl need only glance to feel excited. They would begin by addressing me respectfully, but they soon became familiar, relating obscene stories and making lewd suggestions. Sometimes they would play games with me: gradually they would expose their sexual organs, whispering, 'Would you like this, sweetheart?' and 'Would you like to milk me, darling?' and other such importunities, all the time embracing me, rubbing my breasts, fondling my vagina, kissing me, and trying all kinds of seductive foreplay. Overcome by the splendor of my *samādhi,* some of them vanished immediately; some I reduced to petty frauds by insight into all appearances as illusions; by means of the Bodhisattva's meditation that produces revulsion, I transformed some into black corpses, some into bent and frail geriatrics, some into lepers, some into blind, deformed, dumb or ugly creatures, and without exception they all vanished." See Dowman, *Sky Dancer,* 78.

126. The common rationale for demonic attacks is that God sends these fiends to test the penitent. This piece of conventional Christian wisdom is communicated very neatly to Catherine of Siena by God himself in Noffke, *Catherine of Siena,* 88: "You see, then, that

the demons are my ministers to torment the damned in hell and to exercise and test your virtue in this life." This is a very comforting rationalization both for Kempe and for Catherine. In Catherine's case also, Raymond of Capua mentions the hordes of devils "rousing so many vile thoughts in her mind" and how she "would have fled up hill and down dale like St. Jerome to escape from those abominable monsters and obscene visions" (Raymond of Capua, *The Life*, 93). "He [the devil] brought vile pictures of men and women behaving loosely before her mind, and foul figures before her eyes, and obscene words to her ears, shameless crowds dancing around her, howling and inviting her to join" (91–92). Barbara Newman in "Possessed by the Spirit" (743) mentions a hagiography of Lutgard of Aywières wherein a nun was repeatedly raped by an incubus who not only defiled the nun's body but also tempted her to prostitute herself in a public brothel. Incubus visitations were common in the thirteenth century, according to Newman, but surely also common before and after. In Margery's case, as in many others, the incubus is a mask for an already desired but tabooed male or for unfulfilled sexual desires.

127. Her suffering probably affected the priest, her friend, who fell sick, and she was "stirred in her soul to look after him, on God's behalf." People thought he will die, and so she went off to Norwich and at the Churchyard of St. Stephen's she cried beside the grave of the good vicar buried there and who had been her confessor and guide. An event here is worth noting: a lady wanted to have Margery for a meal. She went to see her in the church; and here Margery saw an image of the *pieta* and began to cry loudly and weep bitterly. The priest told her, "Woman, Jesus is long since dead" to which she replied, "Sir, his death is as fresh to me as if had died this same day, and so, I think, it ought to be to you and all Christian people" (MK, 187). The effect of this was her priest-friend recovered.

128. This is in chapter 66, MK, 96–98.

129. In the latter portions of her book there is again more evidence that, unlike Teresa, she was not given to erotic raptures. She enjoys conjugal bliss with Christ in heaven where she will live with him, as Jesus says, "everlastingly as my beloved darling, as my blessed spouse, and as my holy wife" (MK, 254).

Again, in chapter 87, it is clear she has no sensual experience with God in this world, but only as a heavenly reward: she wants no other joy on earth except mourning and weeping for his love but "I know that it will be truly joyful to be with you in heaven" (MK, 256–57).

130. This however was not a satisfactory version and had to be rewritten in proper English by her scribe.

131. From the nineteenth century onward, psychiatry has been afflicted with the compulsion to classify mental illnesses endlessly, as is evident in the modern *Diagnostic and Statistical Manual of Mental Disorders*, leading up to what is known as *DSM-IV*. This compulsion to classify is the obsessional neurosis of modern psychiatry.

5. CHRISTIAN DISSENT

1. E. P. Thompson, *Witness Against the Beast: William Blake and the Moral Law* (New York: New Press, 1993), hereafter abbreviated as WAB.

2. "Masterless men" refers to those persons dislocated after the breakdown of feudalism in England, people without a master or patron and congregating in cities. For the most part, they formed the rank and file of the new dissident movements of the seventeenth century, ably documented in Christopher Hill, *The World Turned Upside Down: Radical Ideas During the English Revolution* (London: Penguin, 1991). The term comes from Thomas Middleton's play *The Mayor of Queensborough* (1661).

3. Jacob Boehme himself is hostile to any notion of predestination, and I am not sure why the English Behmenists should have adopted this position.

4. Antoine Faivre puts the dates as follows: the Jewish Kabbalah after the Diaspora of 1492; the rediscovery of the *Corpus Hermeticum,* which was brought to Florence in about 1460 by Leonardo da Pistoia, a monk returning from Macedonia; and then translated into Latin by Marcilio Ficino. See Antoine Faivre, *The Eternal Hermes: From Greek God to Alchemical Magus,* trans. Jocelyn Godwin (Grand Rapids: Phanes, 1995), 98.

5. Andrew Weeks, *Boehme: An Intellectual Biography of the Seventeenth-Century Philosopher and Mystic* (Albany: State University of New York Press, 1991), 49.

6. For an extremely useful set of excerpts from alchemical, hermetic, and occult thinkers, see P. G. Maxwell-Stuart, ed. and trans., *The Occult in Early Modern Europe: A Documentary History* (London: Macmillan, 1999).

7. Charles Webster, *From Paracelsus to Newton: Magic and the Making of Modern Science* (New York: Dover, 1982), 9.

8. Ibid., 9–10.

9. Ibid., 32. For Jung's views on astrology, see book 7, n. 75.

10. Here are some of the dates submitted by scientists and major thinkers of the time: 1666, 1655, 1688–1700, 1715, 1716. "Whatever specific date was favored, the scientists firmly believed that the ordained 6000 year span of life of the cosmos was ending and the way was being prepared for spiritual and possibly physical changes," Webster, *From Paracelsus to Newton,* 36.

11. Gerard Manley Hopkins, "Carrion Comfort" in Gerard Manley Hopkins, in *The Poems of Gerard Manley Hopkins,* ed. W. H. Gardner and N. H. MacKenzie, 4th ed. (Oxford: Oxford University Press, 1984), 99.

12. Peter Ackroyd, *Blake* (London: Random House, 1996), 377.

13. Howard H. Brinton, *The Mystic Will: Based on a Study of the Philosophy of Jacob Boehme* (New York: Macmillan, 1930); Evelyn Underhill, *Mysticism: The Nature and Development of Spiritual Consciousness* (Oxford: One World, 2000 [1911]); Weeks, *Boehme.* An early sympathetic study of Boehme is in G. W. F. Hegel, *Lectures on the History of Philosophy: Medieval and Modern Philosophy,* trans. E. S. Haldane and Frances H. Simpson (Lincoln: University of Nebraska Press, 1995). In this work Hegel says that it was "through him that Philosophy first appeared in Germany with a character peculiar to itself," but also considers him to be an unsystematic and barbarous thinker (188, 189 [188-216]. A short but convenient modern account is in Peter Ackroyd, *Blake,* 150–56.

14. Underhill, *Mysticism,* 58.

15. Lawrence Bond, "Introduction" to Nicholas of Cusa, *Selected Writings* (New York: Paulist Press, 1997), 5, 6 (3–84). Nicholas of Cusa says that knowledge of "learned ignorance" did not come from Dionysius and other "true theologians" but directly from God. We now

know that the earlier thoughts ("phantasy activity") did affect the content of visionary knowledge, but not the special truths or insights that visions proclaimed.

16. Cited in the "Introduction" by Erb in Jacob Boehme, *The Way to Christ,* ed. and trans. Peter Erb (New York: Paulist Press, 1978), 8. With Boehme I am not entirely sure whether he means it literally or metaphorically when he says that his works were given to him by the spirit, even though I opt for the former interpretation.

17. The earlier visions of Boehme, as expressed in the account by his contemporary Abraham von Franckenberg, is summarized in Weeks, *Boehme*, 9 and 40–42; and in Hegel, *Lectures on the History of Philosophy,* 189–90.

18. "Letter to an Enquirer" in Robin Waterfield, ed., *Jacob Boehme* (Berkeley: North Atlantic, 2001), 64 (parentheses belong, I think, to the editor).

19. "Concerning the Created Heaven, and the Form of the Earth, and of the Water, as also concerning Light and Darkness," chapter 19 in Jacob Boehme, *The Aurora,* trans. John Sparrow (London: John M. Watkins, 1914), 486. The full title of the work in German is *Die Morgenrothe au Aufgang,* sometimes translated as *Aurora, that is, the day-spring.* Hereafter *Aurora* will be abbreviated as A.

20. Hegel, *Lectures on the History of Philosophy,* 194.

21. Weeks, *Boehme,* 44.

22. In addition to Weeks's book, much the following discussion here will be dependent on GM.

23. Sophia can be traced back to the Old Testament, especially to Proverbs. For an insightful discussion of Sophia's origin and her fusion with the cult of Mary, see Carl G. Jung, *Answer to Job* (Cleveland: Meridian, 1961 [1952]). Everywhere in *Answer to Job,* Sophia appears as a force that humanizes the wrath of God, especially chapters 3 and 4, 56–74, 75–78.

24. Weeks argues in *Boehme,* 148, that "abyss" has Gnostic connotations and might not be an adequate translation of *Ungrund,* and he prefers to retain the German term. "It is noteworthy that Boehme's *Ungrund* often behaves as a subject: it 'seeks,' it 'longs,' it 'sees,' and 'finds.'"

25. For a further understanding of Boehme's notion of the seven fountain spirits of God, we must consider Paracelsus, who straddles the occult and alchemical world and of medicine that rejected the dominant Galenic tradition for a more empirically oriented discipline. Among his many contributions, Paracelsus, in his empirical work, formulated the idea that both male and female emissions determine the formation of the fetus, opening up physiology for the modern understanding of reproduction. But both Paracelsus and Boehme were also interested in alchemy and indeed Paracelsus's medical system was based on three principles or elements—mercury, sulphur and salt—although these were not synonymous with the modern senses of these terms. Paracelsus uses these terms instead of the exclusive Galenic reliance on the four elements and the humors derived from them. For him the main purpose of alchemical medicine was to create herbal and chemical remedies to cure diseases and he was the founder of what he called spagyrics or herbal alchemy. To give a modern example: in vegetable spagyrics "the 'sulphur' consists primarily of the essential oil and other volatile substances; the 'mercury' consists of ethyl alcohol which is a matured form of the sugary sap of plants; and the 'salt' consists of minerals and other substances that remain when the plant is burnt." See John Michael Greer, *The New Encyclopedia of the Occult* (St. Paul: Llewellyn, 2003), 446. In herbal alchemy

these elements are brought together and combined and recombined sometimes in simple but at other times in extremely complicated ways. In principle the alchemical process is not all that different from the later chemistry, but in seventeenth-century chemistry the "esoteric" or occult elements underlying alchemy were gradually rejected, leading to the development of a modern experimental science in the universities. The example previously given illustrates a very simple form of herbal alchemy, but it is also illustrative of the alchemical process in general, as is the case with Indian medicine and alchemy.

26. The quotations in the preceding paragraph are from different sections of A, chapter 8, 147–87.

27. Hans L. Martensen, *Jacob Boehme,* trans. T. Rhys Evans (New York: Harper, 1949 [1885]), 90.

28. Once again, an example from human life will help us understand the relation between intelligible sound and the preceding qualities although here, as in many other places, Boehme is not the model of clarity. "Observe, the word BARM [warm hearted or merciful] is chiefly formed upon thy lips, and when thou pronounceth BARM, then thou shuttest thy mouth, and snarlest [makes a rattling noise] in the hinder part of the mouth; and this is the astringent quality, which environeth or encloseth the word; that is, it figureth, compacteth or contracteth the word together, that it becometh hard or soundeth, and the bitter quality separateth or cutteth or distinguisheth it" (A, 174–75). "When however you say BARM-HERTZ [heart], the latter syllable springs from the heart and rises to the surface in speech through the operation of the quality of heat resident in that organ" (A, 175).

29. Martensen, *Jacob Boehme,* 51.

30. The seven qualities are extraordinarily complicated, as is the case with Boehme's three principles and other concepts. For a good discussion see Weeks, *Boehme,* chapter 4, "The Three Worlds," especially 93–114; and Martensen, *Jacob Boehme,* 46–64.

31. Weeks, *Boehme,* 72.

32. Ibid., 73. I have slighted rephrased Weeks.

33. Gerard Manley Hopkins, "That Nature Is a Heraclitean Fire and of the Comfort of the Resurrection," in Gerard Manley Hopkins, in *The Poems of Gerard Manley Hopkins,* ed. W. H. Gardner and N. H. MacKenzie, 4th ed. (Oxford: Oxford University Press, 1984), 106.

34. This is from "The Divine Image" in *Songs of Innocence, CW,* 117. Others also, including followers of Swedenborg, had similar ideas. E. P. Thompson mentions Richard Coppin, a late antinomian follower of the Ranters who "affirmed that the ministers of orthodox churches were 'evil angels, reserved under the chains of darkness,' and he distinguished between two opposed ministrations or 'contrarieties': that of the law ('a ministration of wrath, death, the curse, hell, and condemnation') and that of the Gospel (a ministration of love, joy, peace, life, light, heaven and salvation')". He also affirmed the right of women to preach and his Universal Restoration would take in Heathens, Pagans, Turks, Jews and Infidels (WAB, 56). Whether or not Blake got his idea of the equality of human kind from the dissenters or not, the original source of that inspiration is Boehme.

35. Worse, the European term *esoteric* was transferred to characterize a whole complex movement in Buddhism influenced by Tantra without critically examining whether this term and its opposite, *exotericism,* or *orthodoxy,* were appropriate to the Buddhist historical tradition. Blavatsky, I shall show later, used the term *esoteric* to describe her occult theosophy. According to the Oxford English Dictionary, the term *esoteric* and its opposite

exoteric in its Greek sense was first used by Lucian (born c. 125 CE) to describe Aristotle's work. The popularization but perhaps not the introduction of the term *esotericism* into discourse, according to *The Encyclopedia of Religion,* is due to the influence of nineteenth-century Jewish mystic Eliphas Levi. See Antoine Faivre, "Esotericism," in *The Encyclopedia of Religion,* 5:156–63. I am not sure how or when or why the term *esoteric* was used to designate Vajrayāna and other forms of Tantrism.

36. The Indian theory may help us further understand Boehme's balancing of opposites in his medical metaphors. Ayurvedic physicians in South Asia generally subscribe to the principle that all substances have medicinal value. Even poisons such as mercury could be detoxified and used in medical prescriptions and alchemical experiments. Any decoction is composed of vegetable or chemical substances that contain the four elements of the universe that Indians shared with the Greeks, namely, earth, fire, water, and air. Among Greeks the dominant elements are manifest in the human body as humors: earth (black bile), air (the same humor), fire (yellow bile), and phlegm (water). These humors are found in the food we eat, and they are transformed in the body into other qualities, such as blood and semen. In Europe the secondary and tertiary derivatives of the four elements are also represented in the four temperaments: melancholic (black bile), phlegmatic (phlegm), choleric (yellow bile), and sanguine (blood). In India, the earth element is pretty much ignored, and we have fire (bile), water (phlegm), and air (wind). Any decoction should entail the proper balancing (*saṃyoga*) of the medical substances to suit the bodily humor or humors that have been upset. Thus, if the element of fire manifesting itself as bile is the principal cause of my illness, I will need food and medications containing the watery humor to oppose the roused element of fire. And so forth, in more and more complicated balancing of the properties contained in the medical ingredients, just as in European herbal alchemy and indeed in alchemy in general. Except that in most forms of Indian medicine, as with Galenic and Hippocratic medicine, the elements in the prescription have intrinsic value and are not dependent on the infusion of those substances with "spirit," quite unlike Paracelsus and Boehme. For details see Gananath Obeyesekere, "Science, Experimentation, and Clinical Practice in Ayurveda," in Alan Young and Charles Leslie, eds., *Paths to Asian Medical Knowledge* (Berkeley: University of California Press, 1992), 160–76. However, once we move from classical Ayurveda to Hindu alchemy, the problem changes and alchemical substances can be imbued with "spirit." The interconnection of the two traditions of alchemy is long overdue. For an excellent and readable account of Hindu alchemy, see David Gordon White, "Why Gurus Are Heavy," *Numen* 31 (1984): 40–73; and his more detailed study, *The Alchemical Body: Siddha Traditions in Medieval India* (Chicago: University of Chicago Press, 1996).

37. Cited in Julia Hirst, *Jane Leade: Biography of a Seventeenth-Century Mystic* (Oxford: Ashgate, 2005), 72.

38. This work was written in 1697 with the inimitable title *The Fountain of Gardens: watered by the Rivers of Divine Pleasure, And Springing up in all the Variety of Spiritual Plants; Blown up by the Pure Breath into A Paradise. To which is Prefixed A Poem, Introductory to the Philadelphian Age, called Solomon's Porch, or the Beautiful Gate to Wisdoms' Temple.* My reference is on p. 18 of the 1697 edition, which I assume was published by the author. I cannot discuss this work here except to say that it is a wonderful record of Lead's visions during a six-year period beginning April 1670 and ending in December 28, 1676. For a detailed discussion

of Jane Lead, see Hirst, *Jane Leade.* Hirst points out that Lead not only entered into the conventional mystical marriage with Christ but also Sophia united with her soul and literally became her soul mate. She becomes the bride of Sophia and this, according to Hirst, has homoerotic meaning and content (74). Additionally, Hirst points out that Jane was searching for the "philosopher's stone," which "becomes a metaphor for spiritual transformation and salvation. On December 9, 1676, Jane recorded in her spiritual diary the word of God saying, 'in you is intombed a Precious Stone, a White Stone, that hath the Virgin's Name engraven on it'" (53). For a further discussion of Lead's visions, see *Jane Leade,* chapter 4, "Visions of Sophia" (59–70).

39. Genesis 1:27 says: "So God created man in his own image, in the image of God created he him; male and female created he them;" and then in 1:28 "And God blessed them, and God said unto them, Be fruitful and multiply." This contrasts with the more popular idea that the woman was created from Adam's rib, Genesis 2:20–23.

40. Boehme, *The Way to Christ,* 146–47.

41. Ibid., 147.

42. Ibid., 148.

43. For another, slightly different interpretation, see Weeks, *Boehme,* 114–121 and 121–126, on "The Androgynous Adam" and "The Noble Virgin of Divine Wisdom [Sophia]."

44. Boehme, *The Way to Christ,* 187.

45. The outbreak of the Thirty Years War was in 1618, and while Boehme's visions and his *Aurora* were before this event, he wrote most of his major work during the period of the war. But even prior to this event Boehme's world was not a pleasant place. Gorlitz where he lived "was a center of heterodox teachings and the town and surrounding countryside had known a succession of wandering preachers who spread heresies of various kinds and who gave authorities great cause for alarm," says Waterfield, *Jacob Boehme,* 22. Violence was reflected in the harsh justice of the times with executions, corporal punishments, and quartering. For a good account of this troubled period, see chapter 1, "Upper Lusatia" in Weeks, *Boehme,* 13–34.

46. Boehme, *The Way to Christ,* 191; for further details see Weeks, *Boehme,* 130–35.

47. Max Weber, "The Social Psychology of World Religions," in *From Max Weber,* trans. Hans Gerth and C. Wright Mills (New York: Oxford University Press, 1976), 274 (276–301). This position was first anticipated in the writing of the Rotterdam philosopher Pierre Bayle (1647–1706), who "resolved" the theodicy by affirming the Manichaean position of a good and an evil deity, which was more in tune with human experience than the Christian, as Popkin points out in Richard H. Popkin, *The History of Scepticism from Savonarola to Bayle,* rev. ed. (Oxford: Oxford University Press, 2002), 293.

48. Jacob Boehme, "The Seventh Treatise. The Precious Gate on Divine Contemplation," in Boehme, *The Way to Christ,* 194–212.

49. Robin Waterfield, *Jacob Boehme,* 31.

50. Boehme, *The Way to Christ,* 194.

51. Ibid., 195–96.

52. A similar point is made by Jung in *Answer to Job,* 28: "Yahweh is not split but is an antinomy—a totality of inner opposites—and this is the indispensable condition for his tremendous dynamism." Again: "All opposites are of God, therefore man must bend to this burden; and in so doing he finds that God in his 'oppositeness' has taken possession of

him, incarnated himself in him. He becomes a vessel filled with divine conflict" (110). Jung was attracted by the oppositional drama or *enantiodromia* between Good and Evil, but whether his is any more satisfactory explanation of Christian theodicy is doubtful.

53. Boehme, *The Way to Christ,* 197.

54. Ibid., 195.

55. Heidegger is the immediate source for "thrownness" (*Geworfenheit*), but I want to disengage that term from the philosophical aspects of Heidegger's *Dasein* for a more specific idea, not necessarily hostile to his usage, wherein a visionary or mystic is hit or *thrown* by some kind of supernatural or unknown force with a startling suddenness, a force that is almost physical, providing him or her spiritual insights into the ultimate nature of things or of the world or of the ground of Being, often but not always of a salvific kind. Thrownness of my usage is what James meant by the mystic as someone "grasped by superior powers" but "graspedness" doesn't sound right to me! Schreber had a sense of thrownness but not so much as a salvific intimation as was the case with Boehme and many others. The ideal typical case in the Christian tradition is Paul's experience of being thrown on the road to Damascus. I want to use this term very sparingly, without reference to the many traditions where one can collapse after being hit by some supernatural force, demonic or divine, unless the experience provides insight or shatters one's mundane illusions. Hence, not all forms of "trance-illness" induce thrownness. I believe that a form of thrownness is also seen in the sudden illumination or *satori* of Zen. On a more secular level, I will demonstrate this idea in Jung's trance illness in book 7 of this essay.

56. Ackroyd, *Blake,* 300, says that "hardly anyone came" to this exhibition.

57. William Blake, "There is no natural religion," CW, 97.

58. This has been well put by Thomas J. Altizer in *The New Apocalypse: the Radical Christian Vision of William Blake* (Aurora, CO: Davies, 2000 [1967]), 18. "Blake, who passionately identified himself with Jesus, came to look upon the doctrine of the virgin birth as blasphemous and insisted in *The Everlasting Gospel* that Jesus himself was neither chaste nor taught chastity, for the sexual organs are 'Love's temple that God dwelleth in,' and the sexual act of the 'Naked Human form divine' is that on which 'the Soul Expands its wing.'" Altizer further points out that, long before Freud and Nietzsche, Blake noted the effects of "repression" in the following "proverbs of hell" Altizer has culled from *The Marriage of Heaven and Hell.*

> He who desires but acts not, breeds pestilence.
> The cistern contains: the fountain overflows.
> Expect poison from the standing water.
> Damn braces: Bless relaxes.
> Sooner murder an infant in its cradle than nurse unacted desires. (20)

I could add many more from the same text, as, for example, when it harks on the Bible only to overturn its orthodoxy: "The nakedness of woman is the work of God" (CW, 151); "The head Sublime, the heart Pathos, the genitals Beauty, the hands and feet Proportion" (CW, 152). "Those who restrain desire, do so because theirs is weak enough to be restrained; and the restrainer or reason usurps its place and governs the unwilling" (CW, 149).

Peter Ackroyd, in *Blake* (296), has a superb discussion of Blake's erotic paintings in the *Four Zoas* (Vala) that I had missed in my earlier draft. There are "hermaphroditic figures with huge phalli, a woman reaching to caress a huge penis of a man while masturbating on a dildo, a small boy with an erection as he watches a scene of love-making, there are also sketches of anal penetration, fellatio, defecation and group sexuality. But the central motif is the erect phallus. It was clear from his earliest writings that he trusted the energies of sexual freedom and, at least in theory, believed in the possibility of complete sexual license." He rightly points out that "the image of the hermaphrodite, with penis and vagina, is an ancient one—for Blake it represents in literal form that time before the sexes were divided and human faculties thereby distorted or degraded."

59. The reference is to *Vala,* "Night the First," ll. 469–75, CW, 277. "Then those in Great Eternity [Eternals] met in the Council of God / As one Man, for contracting their Exalted Senses / They behold Multitude, or Expanding they behold as one, / As One Man all the Universal Family; and that One Man / They call Jesus the Christ, and they in him and he in them / Live in Perfect harmony, in Eden the land of life, / Consulting as One Man above the Mountain of Snowdon sublime."

60. Plato, *Meno,* 81 C, in *Five Dialogues: Euthyphro, Apology, Crito, Meno, Phaedo,* trans. G. M. A. Grube (Indianapolis: Hackett, 1981).

61. The first quote is from "The Grey Monk," CW, 683; the second from the letter to Hayley, October 23, 1804, in CW, 852.

62. "Annotations to Swedenborg's Divine Love," in CW, 91. Boehme's idea of the outflow from God to create diversity and contradiction or opposites is found everywhere in Blake's work. *Mysterium Magnum* or "Great Mystery" is an idea that Boehme probably borrowed from Paracelsus and used as the title of his last work.

63. Blake, not being a systematic thinker, never developed this notion, but for me this is a central idea that needs further rethinking. One needs to link two main currents in Western thought, represented by those who believed in the primacy of Reason and the possibility of natural laws as against those who denied this. In the century before Blake relativist thinking was represented by Cornelius Agrippa and Montaigne among many others. Perhaps closest to Blake's time is Giambattista Vico (1668–1744) in his *Scienza nuova* (*The New Sience*), even though Blake and much of Europe were unfamiliar with Vico's thought. For a good discussion of this issue, see Isaiah Berlin, "The Counter-Enlightenment" in *Against the Current: Essays in the History of Ideas* (Harmondsworth: Penguin, 1979), 1–24; and Berlin's other essays on Vico in the same volume.

64. Mona Wilson, *The Life of William Blake,* ed. Geoffrey Keynes, rev. ed. (London: Oxford University Press, 1971), 3.

65. Alexander Gilchrist, *Life of William Blake,* ed. Ruthven Tod (London: Dent, Everyman's Library, 1942 [1863]), 6.

66. Wilson, *The Life of William Blake,* 5.

67. John Beer, *Blake's Visionary Universe* (Manchester: Manchester University Press, 1969), 24.

68. Northrop Frye, *Fearful Symmetry: A Study of William Blake* (Boston: Beacon, 1962), 314–15.

69. In my earlier version I thought that the reference was to Milton but on reading Peter Ackroyd's *Blake* I realized the reference is to *Vala.* According to Ackroyd (250–51), the first thirty six pages were written in Lambeth, but the rest of the poem was written in Felpham.

70. This important incident occurred on August 12, 1803, when the war with France had just begun and tensions were high. According to Blake, a soldier named Scolfield was invited by his gardener without Blake's knowledge to assist him in his work. Blake says he politely asked Scolfield to get out of the garden, but when the man refused a verbal duel ensued, with the soldier uttering "abominable imprecations" and "some contempt to my Person." Blake took him by the elbow and pushed him off his premises, but the man kept hurling insults and threatened him. "I perhaps foolishly and perhaps not, stepped out at the Gate and putting aside his blows took him again by the Elbows and keeping his back to me pushed him forwards down the road about fifty yards." If Blake simply stayed inside his premises, nothing would have come of the incident, but even pacifists can get angry when they are gratuitously insulted! In this case it was a pacifist, who, I will soon show, had paranoid fantasies in his troubled mental state or melancholy.

Scolfield and a comrade of his named Private Cock [sic] accused Blake of sedition by insulting the king and the armed forces and especially saying "Damn the king" which was at that time a terribly serious crime. But, at the trial, numerous witnesses testified on Blake's behalf, while the court had only Scolfield's word and that of his comrade. Scolfield made a wild accusation against Blake, whom he called a "military painter" instead of a miniature painter. Scolfield's accusation did not carry much conviction because as a sergeant he had been demoted for drunkenness. I refer the reader to the details of this case in *Blake Records,* but suffice it here to state that Blake was acquitted on January 11, 1804, after a spirited defense by his counsel, who referred to him as "a pacific, industrious, and deserving artist" (BR, 145). In his evidence, Scolfield said that his wife came up to him when they were in the garden and said that "the King of England would run himself so far into the Fire, that he might get himself out again, and altho' she was but a Woman, she would fight as long as she had a drop of blood in her—to which the said—Blake said, My Dear, you would not fight against France—she replyed no, I would for Bonaparte as long as I am able" (Wilson, *William Blake,* 176).

During this whole period it was Hayley who was his support and help. Yet, in his *Notebook* Blake has the extraordinary poem entitled "On H—y's Friendship": "When H—y finds out what you cannot do, / That is the very thing he'll set you to. / If you break not his neck, 'tis not his fault, / But pecks of poison are not pecks of salt, / And when he could not act upon my wife, / Hired a villain to bereave my life."

This is clearly a reference to Hayley attempting to seduce his wife, and, when that failed, Blake thinks he hired Scolfield to kill him. Ellis and Yeats, who quote these lines, have shown the utter impossibility of Hayley hiring the soldier to kill Blake, although he might have tried to flirt with Blake's wife. More likely, these were paranoid suspicions Blake harbored during the last phases of his melancholy. See Edwin John Ellis and William Butler Yeats, eds., *The Works of William Blake,* 3 vols. (London: Bernard Quaritch, 1893). Volume 1, which I use here, is entitled *Memoir;* 56–85, has a detailed account of these events and their later expression in his poetry. It seems however that Blake changed his fantasized views on Hayley's betrayal of trust. Yet, according to Bentley "as time went by, Blake became more and more convinced that the trial was not an isolated accident, but an event of national or cosmic significance;" and according to Gilchrist "he used to declare that the Government, or some high person, knowing him to have been of the Paine set, 'sent the soldier to entrap him;' which we must take the liberty of regarding as a purely visionary [paranoid?] notion" (BR, 146).

71. Allan Cunningham puts it thus: "His marriage, I have heard, was not agreeable to his father; and he then left his roof and resided with his wife in Green Street, Leicester Fields. He returned to Broad Street, on the death of his father" (BR, 482).

72. "To Thomas Butts, 22 November 1802," in CW, 817 (816–19). According to Frederick Tatham, John was a baker's apprentice; he then enlisted as a soldier and after leading a reckless and dissolute life died young, sometime between 1793–1801 (BR, 509). Note again the symbolism of "black cloud" in this quotation.

73. Ackroyd, *Blake*, 62.

74. The Corinthian reference states: "I protest by your rejoicing which I have in Christ Jesus our Lord, I die daily." Blake was familiar with Neoplatonism from the translations of Thomas Taylor, but I doubt he knew Empedocles who makes similar statements in relation to reincarnation, for example, "many times dying mortal men," from fragment 105 of *Purifications* that I have cited in Gananath Obeyesekere, *Imagining Karma: Ethical Transformation in Amerindian, Buddhist, and Greek Rebirth* (Berkeley: University of California Press, 2002), 217.

75. For a fuller exposition of these and other mythic beings in Blake's "system" there is little choice but to rely on a text such as S. Foster Damon, *A Blake Dictionary: The Ideas and Symbols of William Blake* (New York: Dutton, 1971); or D. J. Sloss and J. P. R. Wallis, *The Prophetic Writings of William Blake*, vol. 2 (Oxford: Clarendon, 1964). However, one must remember that it is a mistake to reduce Blake's protean figures into a single persona.

76. According to Ellis and Yeats, in *The Works of William Blake*, 1:35, the technology imparted in the dream vision was simple and practical. "The poems and designs to be printed were drawn and written on metal plates with a varnish chiefly composed of pitch and turpentine which would resist acid. Then the plate was placed in the corrosive bath and all the rest of the metal was deeply bitten away until the letters and designs stood up so high that a roller with printing ink could be passed over them, and the plate used to print from, as the casts of the type and wood-blocks are used now. It was etching reversed."

   The phrase "dialogues with the dead" I borrow from the excellent study by Piers Vitebsky, *Dialogues with the Dead: The Discussion of Mortality Among the Sora of Eastern India* (Cambridge: Cambridge University Press, 1993), in which the dead continue to have conversations with the living through the medium of an entranced shaman.

77. Robert Burton, *Anatomy of Melancholy*, 3 vols. (New York: Everyman's Library, 1964), 1:202 f. deals with the multiple causes of melancholy: effects of witches and magicians, stars and planets, parental influence, bad diet, drunkenness, idleness, extremes of sleeping and wakefulness, passions and perturbations of the mind, the work of humors and so on. He rarely discusses the "pit of melancholy" that Blake mentions, although I suppose extremes of "black bile" could lead to that condition. For Burton—as for Blake, Milton, and Keats—melancholy can also induce a contemplative and philosophical mood, quite unlike the "depression" of contemporary psychiatry. So is it with Buddhist meditators, as I show in my speculative essay "Depression, Buddhism and the Work of Culture in Sri Lanka," in Arthur Kleinman and Byron Good, eds., *Culture and Depression* (Berkeley: University of California Press, 1985), 134–52.

78. It should be noted that Blake illustrated several passages from both of Milton's poems around 1816, as is evident in *Descriptions of the Illustrations to Milton's "L'Allegro" and "Il Pensoroso"* in CW, 617–19.

79. "L'Allegro" in H.C. Beeching, *The Poetical Works of John Milton* (London: Cambridge University Press, 1952), 20.

80. Jon Mee, *Dangerous Enthusiasm: William Blake and the Culture of Radicalism in the 1790s* (Oxford: Clarendon, 1992), 174.

81. Blake seems obsessed with the seven ages of dismal woe; it is repeated in *Milton* (CW, 492–93).

82. Beeching, *Poetical Works of John Milton*, 26.

83. Ibid., 28.

84. These are *Vala* or the *Four Zoas, Milton,* and the great epic work, *Jerusalem.* According to Geoffrey Keynes, the earliest manuscripts of *Vala* were probably written in 1795 but revised during the Felpham period and up to 1804. The extensive and continuing corrections are seen in the manuscript pages. The poem was never completed, giving way to *Milton* and *Jerusalem.* The first title indicated the dream like quality of the text: *Vala Or The Death and Judgement of the Ancient Man, A DREAM of Nine Nights by William Blake 1797.* The capitalization of "dream" is Blake's and one that I take seriously. The second title that now has been shortened to *Vala or the Four Zoas,* originally read *The Four Zoas, The torments of Love and Jealousy in The Death and Judgement of Albion the Ancient Man,* suggesting that some serious revisions had taken place between the first and second versions of the text (CW, 263). Blake had another interesting title for the poem scribbled in the back of one of his drawings: "The Bible of Hell, in Nocturnal Visions collected, Vol. 1. Lambeth" (CW, 897). The reference to "The Bible of Hell" is found in the conclusion of *The Marriage of Heaven and Hell:* "I have also *The Bible of Hell,* which the world shall have whether they will or no," suggesting strongly that the idea of writing *Vala* was at least conceived during 1790–1793 (CW, 158). "Nocturnal visions" picks up the theme of "dream" in the first title. *Vala* was never completed and neither was *Milton.*

    Northrop Frye suggests that *The Four Zoas* was a revision of the original *Vala.* And that this revision contained the much more complex symbolism that one associates with *Milton* and *Jerusalem.* It seems that Blake had an idea of a very large epic, but from "this nebulous epic the *Milton* and *Jerusalem* we now have were precipitated" (Frye, *Fearful Symmetry,* 314–15). Beer says: "In *Milton,* he wrote of the visitation of the poet which we call inspiration; in his final long work, *Jerusalem,* he is concerned with mankind's incessant longing for eternity. *Milton,* which had been planned to exist in twelve books was completed in two, and it is clear that he finally intended *Jerusalem* to be his long desired epic poem. But to order the latter poem was more difficult than to order *Milton;* it needed a pattern which would succeed, where *Vala* had failed, in presenting a mythological interpretation of human existence" (Beer, *Blake's Visionary Universe,* 172).

85. Altizer, *The New Apocalypse,* 88.

86. Blake was thoroughly familiar with the reference to Lear and Cordelia, as is evident in his water-color of "Lear and Cordelia in prison" in the Tate Gallery #N05189, part of his "illustrations to Shakespeare."

87. The new-born confidence was noted by Reverend Thomas Dibdin in 1816: "I soon found the amiable but Illusory Blake far beyond my ken or sight. In an instant he was in his

'third heaven—flapped by the wings of seraphs, such as his own genius only could shape, and his own pencil embody.... Never was such 'dreamings' poured forth as were poured forth by my original visitor" (BR: 242–43).

88. See the essays in Roger Ivar Lohmann, ed., *Dream Travelers: Sleep Experiences and Culture in the Western Pacific* (New York: Palgrave Macmillan, 2003) for interesting accounts of dream travel.

89. Gilbert Herdt, "Selfhood and Discourse in Sambia Dream Sharing," ed. Barbara Tedlock, *Dreaming: Anthropological and Psychological Interpretations* (Santa Fe: School of American Research, 1992), 58–59 (55–85).

90. Giuseppe Tucci, *The Religions of Tibet,* trans. Geoffrey Samuel (Berkeley: University of California Press, 1980), 54.

91. Serenity Young, *Dreaming in the Lotus: Buddhist Dream Narrative, Imagery and Practice* (Boston: Wisdom, 1999), 121. For another brief but clear review of the "six teachings" of the Kagyu tradition, see Donald S. Lopez Jr., "Foreword" to W. Y. Evans-Wentz, *Tibetan Yoga and Secret Doctrines* (Oxford: Oxford University Press, 2000), a–p, j–k.

92. Francisco J. Varela, ed., *Sleeping, Dreaming, and Dying: An Exploration of Consciousness with the Dalai Lama* (Boston: Wisdom, 1997), 128.

The central concept of Tibetan soteriology is that of the "subtle body" or the spiritual body that exists alongside the actual physical body. Let me very briefly sum up its more important features. There are three main channels in the subtle body, the major one being the central channel. Radiating from it, like the spokes of an umbrella, are the right and left channels as well as the four principal channel wheels or *cakra* that are connected to them. The central channel is also called the channel of nonduality and sometimes designated *Avadhūti,* the shaker of nonduality. Beginning at a point between the eyebrows, the central channel ascends in an arch to the crown of the head and then descends straight downward to the tip of the sexual organ. Branching out with no intervening space are the left and right channels, white and red in color respectively, the left designated as the sun and the right as the moon, each channel beginning with the left and right tips of the nostrils. Unlike the central channel, these are the channels of duality: the right is the female one and deals with the subjective; and the left male channel is the channel of objective reality. On waking the winds move the channels producing the separation of the subject and object world where duality prevails. Both male and female channels ascend to the crown of the head on either side of the central channel. At this point the left channel curves a little bit to the right, separating slightly from the central channel and rejoining it at the genitals from where it functions with the aid of wind to eject sperm, blood, and urine. Similarly, the right channel below the navel curves slightly to the left and ends in the anus where it functions to eliminate feces and break wind. There are elaborate descriptions of the right and left channels coiling round the central channel and forming the channel knots that are centered in the four *cakra*s or "wheels" of the subtle body designated as the navel wheel, the heart wheel, the throat wheel, and the crown wheel. I shall skip the details except to note that there are in all seventy-two channels that pervade the body. The important distinction is that while the left and right channels have to do with bodily functions, not so with the central channel.

The movement of the subtle body is performed by five principal and five secondary wind-mind pairs that cognize the outside world and inner subjectivity. The five principal winds are responsible for breathing, digestion, movement, speech, passing of feces and urine, menses, and ejaculation. There are other functions of the winds, but they are not relevant for our understanding of Tantric eroticism. Relevant for us are that the winds cause the movement of two kinds of drops or *bindu* (Sanskrit) or *tigle* (Tibetan), the red drops coming from the mother and the white drops from the father's semen.

My own guess is that *bindu* or *tigle* is based on an important Ayurvedic concept, *ojas,* that is, the final distillate of all the *dhātu*s or essences of the body. *Ojas* is also the distillate of "semen," and in both men and women and it is located in the heart, according to the great Sanskrit physician Caraka, and "from the heart as root, ten great vessels carrying *ojas* pulsate all over the body." Without *ojas* "no life of creatures exists, which is the essential essence of embryo and also the essence of its nourishing material." Caraka, *Caraka-Samhita,* ed. and trans. Priyavrat Sharma (Varanasi: Chaukhambha Orientalia, 1981), 237.

The white drops has its principal seat in the head-*cakra* which constitutes "the male 'pole' of the body" and the "'melting bliss' of sexual arousal" and also constitutes the waking state. The red drop of the mother is at the navel-*cakra*; it is the female pole and functions to warm the body, create the heat of sexual arousal and orgasm, and digestion of food. I cannot deal with the significance of the subtle body for Tibetan erotic soteriology in this essay, largely owing to the absence of case studies dealing with the experiential application of the scheme in the lives of actual meditators.

93. K. A. Scherner, *Das Leben des Traumes* (Berlin, 1861), see book 1, n. 55, for a brief statement of Scherner's ideas.

94. Jung, "Belief in Spirits," in *Structure and Dynamics of the Psyche: Collected Works* (Princeton: Princeton University Press, 1969 [1920]), 8:306.

95. Ibid.

96. Ibid.

97. There is a larger problem that emerges from Freud's discussion that part of the ego is unconscious. The moment one makes this assertion then we remove ourselves from the "I" of the waking consciousness. An "I" that is unconscious must be by definition almost a "hallucinatory"one. I doubt whether the Freud's unconscious "I" is the same as the "dream-ego," even though we can perhaps state that the dream-ego can find a home in the unconscious segment of the ego.

98. I use the term *Euro-American* advisedly; perhaps *Anglo-American* is the better term. There are huge issues involved in any discussion of a reified entity called "the self." American scholarship, including ethnographic research, explicitly or implicitly believes in such a notion and is given great theoretical significance in the work of G. H. Mead and symbolic interactionism in general. I do not have the time or expertise to discuss this issue, but, given my Buddhist background, I resist the localization of the "self" within a person. At best I would say that individuals have a sense of "I-ness," but whether this is the same as the "self," a core being within the person, is problematic. For a good discussion of this issue from the point of view of both French and psychoanalytic language games, see J. B. Pontalis, "The Birth and the Recognition of the 'Self,'" in *Frontiers in Psychoanalysis: Between the Dream and the Psychic Pain,* trans. Catherine Cullen and Philip Cullen (London: Hogarth, 1981), 126–47. I think Pontalis not only raises the problematic of the "self" in relation to the "ego" in psychoanalysis but he also brings out the whole issue of language use in the construction of the "self." For myself, I find it hard to translate many of the

"self" concepts into my own language, Sinhala, and I suspect into other Indic languages. Perhaps *personhood* might be a better term than *self*, but I am not sure whether this is simply transferring the problematics of *self* onto another term. Among British thinkers it is David Hume that treated the "self" and identity as a constantly changing phenomenon, as I point out in book 1, n. 103.

99. In addition to Jung, Wilhelm Stekel and his disciple Emil A. Gutheil have given many examples of the shadow, the dream alter, or double. Emil A. Gutheil in *Handbook of Dream Analysis* (New York: Washington Square Press, 1966), 131, says that the dream-other can appear in various forms, for example, as a companion, fellow traveler, or hitchhiker. "I am driving along on a dark foggy, rainy night, road very bad and covered with snow and ice. A hitch-hiker stops me and I let him in. He starts to tell me that without him I am lost and I feel frightened. He tells me that I am going crazy, I shout, 'you get out!' He is then out on the road behind me, looking very sorry, and I see that he is a little replica of myself, only shabbier. I gather all my courage and drive on. To my great elation, I now can see much better and awake with the feeling that I will get rid of my neurosis."

100. John Powers, *Introduction to Tibetan Buddhism* (Ithaca: Snow Lion, 1995), 347. For another interpretation of Nāropa's vision that does not contradict that of Powers, see *The Life and Teaching of Nāropa*, trans. Herbert V. Guenther (Boston: Shambala, 1995), 24–25.

101. Joseph Conrad, "Karain: A Memory," in *Stories and Tales of Joseph Conrad* (New York: Funk and Wagnalls, 1968), 174 (159–197).

102. Fyodor Dostoyevsky, *The Brothers Karamazov,* trans. Andrew R. MacAndrew (New York: Bantam, 2003), 855.

103. Ibid., 857.

104. Ibid., 863.

105. Hervet de Saint-Denys, *Dreams and How to Guide Them,* trans. Nicholas Fry (London: Duckworth, 1982 [1867]), 95. Saint-Denys thinks that this confrontation must contain deep psychological meaning, but he does not unscramble it.

106. Fyodor Dostoyevsky, *The Double,* trans. Constance Garnett (Mineola, NY: Dover, 1997 [1917]).

107. For a detailed discussion of the shadow in Indian myth, see Wendy Doniger O'Flaherty, *Dreams, Illusion, and Other Realities* (Chicago: University of Chicago Press, 1984), 81–122.

108. Dostoyevsky, *Brothers Karamazov,* 872. Because the body is paralyzed during REM dreaming, this condition on rare occasions might briefly continue into the moment of waking.

109. Ibid., 856.

110. Ibid., 858.

111. On April 23, 2007, in Pitakumbura, Bibile, Sri Lanka.

112. Much of early Surrealist literary writing (I resist the word *stories*) have a similar character as, for example, Andre Breton, "Soluble Fish" (1924) in *Manifestoes of Surrealism,* ed. and trans. Richard Seaver and Helen R. Lane (Ann Arbor: University of Michigan Press, 1993), 51–109.

113. Thus Douglas Hollan notes that Toraja folk in Sulawesi might occasionally have especially vivid dreams that they will remember for long periods because it is believed that dreams might contain some prognosticative significance. It seems likely that Toraja would in time rework the dream and its interpretation according to developing life events. See

Douglas Hollan, "Dreams, Aging, and the Anthropological Encounter in Toraja, Indone-sia," in Lohmann, *Dream Travelers,*169–87.

114. Ellis and Yeats, *The Works of William Blake,* 1:95.

115. Ibid.

116. Ibid.

117. W. B. Yeats, *Uncollected Prose by W. B. Yeats,* ed. John P. Frayne (New York: Columbia University Press, 1970), 282–83.

118. The annihilation of the "I" is one of Boehme's constant injunctions and is very conspicu-ous in *The Way to Christ* (178), as when the Master speaks to his student on the contrast between love and the "I": "Love hates the 'I' because the 'I' is a dead thing and [the two] cannot stand together, for love possesses heaven and dwells in itself, but the 'I' possesses the world with its being and also lives in itself." See also 128, 136, 350–36.

119. Ernest Benz, in *Emanuel Swedenborg: Visionary Savant in the Age of Reason,* trans. Nicholas Goodrick-Clarke (West Chester, PA: Swedenborg Foundation, 2002), 217, says: "His con-temporaries' suggestion that he was mad—even Kant refers him to the asylum—threat-ened Swedenborg's work and even his life." His visions were supposedly a product of brooding and several clergy wanted to arraign him. His insanity was a danger to society. "He should therefore be deprived of his freedom and confined to an asylum."

120. Cited in Wilson, *William Blake,* 336.

121. G. E. Bentley has extensive discussions of the Ancients and their relationship to Blake in part 5 of BR, entitled "The Ancients and the Interpreter, 1818-1825," 256–347.

122. Richard Brothers, born in the same year as Blake, was an extremely interesting figure whose visions proclaimed his supposed madness. Jon Mee in *Dangerous Enthusiasm* (29) says that Brothers, in his most famous work, *A Revealed Knowledge of the Prophecies and Times,* claimed, as with others in this essay, "that the two volumes of his book were writ-ten under the direct inspiration from God." Mee shows us convincingly that Brothers and others like him were well known in the political and religious landscape of the time (20–40).

123. In BR 34-38, Bentley says that in the winter of 1788–1789 Blake became seriously inter-ested in Swedenborg, having bought copies of *Heaven and Hell* and *Divine Love* and *Divine Wisdom.* He attended the inaugural conference of the New Church, which, in its mani-festo, rejected all the doctrines of the old churches, Catholic and Protestant. Key features of the manifesto affirmed the truth of Swedenborg's divine revelations and reaffirmed the Theosophical doctrine (perhaps from Boehme) that the only valid form of worship is that "addressed to the Divine Humanity, Jesus Christ," a doctrine central to Blake. And especially significant was the idea that "All can be saved, even the heathen, if they live charitable lives." Later on Blake was hostile to both Swedenborg and Swedenborgians, as his critique of 1790 indicates, and especially Swedenborg's doctrine of predestination. Blake never joined the New Church of Jerusalem, but Bentley rightly says that his attitude to Swedenborg remained ambivalent, accepting some of his ideas and rejecting others.

124. Benz, *Emanuel Swedenborg,* 314–17.

125. Albrecht Durer (1471–1528) mentions an awesome dream that he later painted, although I have not been able to locate it. "In the year 1525 . . . I saw in my sleep many great waters falling from heaven. The first struck the earth about four miles away from me with a terrific force, with tremendous clamour and clash, drowning the whole countryside. . . .

When I awoke I was so frightened that my whole body trembled and for a long while I could not regain my composure. So when I got up in the morning I painted it as I had seen it." Quoted in Maxwell Stuart, *The Occult in Medieval Europe* (London: Macmillan, 2005), 19–20.

126. William Gaunt, *Arrows of Desire: A Study of William Blake and His Romantic World* (London: Museum, 1956), 63.

127. Ibid., 59 (my emphasis).

128. Frye, *Fearful Symmetry,* 3.

129. Altizer, *The New Apocalypse,* 26–29, 62–67.

130. According to Northrop Frye, Blake believed he was a reincarnation of Milton, whether literally or metaphorically is not clear. In *Fearful Symmetry,* 316, he points out that "Milton, in eternity, determines to 'go to Eternal Death,' which means physical life, and after a long struggle he enters this world and reincarnates himself in Blake."

131. According to my usage in Obeyesekere, *Imagining Karma* (xxii), "transmigration" is where the soul at death migrates to another form of sentient existence and stays there without seeking further reincarnation.

132. Blake was thoroughly familiar with the work of the Neoplatonist Thomas Taylor, who wrote extensively on Pythagoras and Neoplatonism, and it is possible that Blake learned about reincarnation from him. See also n. 74.

133. Byron's poem as a totality is worth reading. In my epigraph I have quoted only 26 lines of a long dream poem of 206 lines. The poem itself is based on a dream series or scenarios. Byron uses the dream to deal with the lives of two star-crossed lovers. It is not a great poem, but beautifully illustrates the uses of dreams by a new generation of poets. After the theory of dreams is presented in the lines of my epigraph, Byron introduces, in section 2, his two lovers, the young adolescent falling in love with an older woman who treats him as a brother but not a lover (perhaps not unrelated to Byron's own incestuous relation with his half-sister). She loves another man. The two persons move apart and, beginning in section 3, there is a refrain that runs through up to section 8: "A change came over the spirit of my dream." This refrain indicates the shifting frames of the dream and is used by the poet to indicate the shifting frames of the narrative constructed on the basis of the dream. There is no happy ending here: the woman realizes too late that she really loves the youth, but she is now married and so is he, but both are unhappy in their marriages. Her fate is a deep distress and his a melancholy, a "fearful gift," however, because it is a "telescope of truth" baring the cold reality of a tragic existence. Section 9 is the short summary that ends the poem: "My dream is past; it had no further change, / It was of a strange order, that the doom / Of these two creatures should be thus traced out / *Almost like a reality*—the one / To end in madness—both in misery" (my emphasis).

134. *William Wordsworth: The Poetical Works,* ed. Thomas Hutchinson, revised by Ernest de Selincourt (Oxford: Oxford University Press, 1951), 582–83. For a similar and more fabulous vision of his Gaelic ancestors by a modern visionary, see A. E. (George Russell), *The Candle of Vision: Inner Worlds of the Imagination* (New York: Avery, 1990 [1918]), 34–36.

135. John Keats, "Ode to a Nightingale," in John Keats, *Complete Poems,* ed. Jack Stillinger (Cambridge: Harvard University Press, 1982), 279.

136. The poem to his friend John Hamilton Reynolds, entitled "Dear Reynolds, as last night I lay in bed," describes a series of dreams, some probably dream visions that he experi-

ences and among them funny images of "Voltaire with casque and shield and habergeon / And Alexander with his night cap on / Old Socrates a tying his cravat" and then more conventionally romantic ones followed by anxious or fearful dreams. See Keats, *Complete Poems*, 179–82. Keats also has several poems idealizing sleep, the best known perhaps is the early poem, "Sleep and Poetry," where he contrasts the dream state with the world of waking reality when awake: "The visions all are fled—the car is fled / Into the light of heaven, and in their stead, / A sense of real things comes doubly strong, / And, like a muddy stream, would bear along / My soul to nothingness." The poem also establishes a connection between sleep and opiate when Keats speaks of "sleep, quiet with his poppy coronet." Again, in a later and more interesting poem, "Sonnet to Sleep" he uses similar images: "O soothest Sleep! If so it please thee, close / In midst of this thine hymn, my willing eyes, / Or wait the Amen ere thy poppy throws / Around my bed its lulling charities." See ibid., 37–47, for "Sleep and Poetry," and 275, for "Sonnet to Sleep."

137. Keats "Ode to Psyche," ibid., 275–76. More significant is his unfinished "The Fall of Hyperion: A Dream," where he is not sure whether his is a dream or a vision, a blurring of genres that occurs everywhere. I regret space does not permit the analysis of this important poem.

138. The portions of "Lamia" that I quote here is from *Complete Poems*, 342–59.

6. THEOSOPHIES

1. For a discussion of the origins and significance of "theosophy," see Hans L. Martensen, "Character and Postulates of Ancient Theosophy" (15–36), in *Jacob Boehme*, trans. T. Rhys Evans (New York: Harper, 1949 [1885]), which still remains a clear and convenient exposition; so is Antoine Favre's article "Theosophy" in *The Encyclopedia of Religion*, 14:465–69.

2. See Herman A. O. de Tollenaere, *The Politics of Divine Wisdom* (Uitgevertij: Katholieke Universiteit Nijmegen, 1996), 85. For an overview of Besant's life and career, read Anne Taylor, *Annie Besant: A Biography* (Oxford: Oxford University Press, 1992); for her work in India, the earlier work by Arthur H. Nethercot, *The Last Four Lives of Annie Besant* (Chicago: University of Chicago Press, 1963) still remains useful. A recent critical appraisal of her life and work is that of Gauri Viswanathan, *Outside the Fold: Conversion, Modernity, and Belief* (Princeton: Princeton University Press, 1998), especially chapter 6, 177–207.

3. For details of Blavatsky's early life, I rely, for the most part, on two sources, Marion Meade, *Madame Blavatsky: The Woman Behind the Myth* (New York: Putnam, 1980), a hostile reading of her life; and Sylvia Cranston, *HPB: The Extraordinary Life and Influence of Helena Blavatsky, Founder of the Modern Theosophical Movement* (New York: Putnam, 1993) which, as the subtitle indicates, tends toward the adulatory. This work will hereafter be abbreviated as C. For a good summary read, *H. P. Blavatsky: Collected Writings, 1874–1878*, ed. Boris de Zirkoff (Wheaton, IL: Theosophical, 1966), 1:xxv–lii.

4. Jon Mee, in *Dangerous Enthusiasm: William Blake and the Culture of Radicalism in the 1790s* (Oxford: Clarendon, 1992), 126, mentions several mid-eighteenth-century writers, for example, William Warburton, who believed that the Egyptians invented state religion, and John Toland who said that "in Egypt Men had first, long before others, arrived at the vari-

ous beginnings of Religions" and, smacking of Blavatsky, asserted that "they preserv'd the first occasions of Sacred Rites conceal'd in their secret writing" (127).

5. A. P. Sinnett, *Incidents in the Life of Madame Blavatsky* (London: George Redway, 1886), 61.

6. For the picture of Ramsgate, see the reproduction in Cranston, *HPB*, 46.

7. H. P. Blavatsky, *H. P. B. Speaks,*ed. C. Jinarajadasa, 2 vols. (Adyar: Theosophical, 1986 [1951]), 2:66. There is a confusion of dates here because she claims that the Constantinople episode was in 1851 and she says that she was at Mivart's HHotel "years later." Actually, she was at Mivart's HHotel in 1851; perhaps she meant "it seems years later." One cannot rule out the possibility that the Constantinople episode and the "steeple chase" were also visionary events.

8. Ibid., 66–67.

9. Later in life, Blavatsky told Constance Wachtmeister (in *H. P. Blavatsky,* 1:4) that the Ramsgate episode was a "blind" and that the "first interview with him [Moriya] had been in London as she had previously told me." This is very likely. She probably wanted to cover up her attempted suicide in Waterloo, and she used Ramsgate as a blind. In a letter written to Dondoukoff-Korsakoff, around August 1881, Blavatsky says she met the master in London only twice and the second was an interview with him that clearly refers to the event where she met her master in person in Hyde Park (*H. P. B. Speaks,* 2:20). If so, the first visit of the master was a composite of the Ramsgate and Waterloo visions, but further evidence is needed before one can make a final judgment. Mivart's Hotel, where she stayed, was on Brook Street, in the heart of London, and is now the Claridge. It is within easy reach of Waterloo Bridge, whereas a trip to Ramsgate would have been more complicated.

For an attempt to resolve contradictions in Blavatsky's accounts, see Jean Overton Fuller, *Blavatsky and Her Teachers: An Investigative Biography* (London: East-West, 1988), 8–9. Fuller as well as Blavatsky's supporters think that she saw Master M in the astral at Ramsgate or Waterloo, but in the flesh in London in Hyde Park. Moriya was the "master of her dreams," and she had visions and dreams of him for a long time before this event. It is hard to believe that he suddenly appeared in flesh and blood in Hyde Park, although he could surely have appeared astrally!

10. Constance Wachtmeister, *Reminiscences of H. P. Blavatsky and "The Secret Doctrine"* (Wheaton, IL: Theosophical, 1976 [1893]), 44. Wachtmeister says that Blavatsky was with her father on this occasion, but there is some confusion here also. In a letter written to Sinnett, Blavatsky seems to deny that she visited London with her father in 1851. "Visit to London? I was in London and France with Father in '44 not 1851." She reaffirms that during 1851 she was with the Countess Bragation and that she "lived in a big hotel somewhere between City and Strand." Letter no. 61 (c. 1885), in *The Letters of H. P. Blavatsky to A. P. Sinnett,* ed. and transcribed A. T. Barker (Pasadena: Theosophical University Press, 1973 [1925]), 150 (148–56).

11. H. P. Blavatsky, *Isis Unveiled,* 2 vols. (Wheaton, IL: Quest, 2000 [1877]), 1:168. The astral form becomes free when our body is insensate as in sleep and trance and similar states. "It then *oozes* out of its earthly prison, and as Paracelsus has it—'confabulates with the outward world,' and travels round the visible as well as the invisible worlds" (179). For further details read 167–79.

12. Fuller in *Blavatsky and Her Teachers,* 13, and other Theosophists believe that this first Tibetan visit was not in 1856, as Blavatsky claimed, but either in 1854 or 1855. Because the

date 1856 is significant for Blavatsky, I will simply use her own recollection of the event. Blavatsky often mentions her Tibetan travels, though my guess is that, for her, upper Kashmir, Sikkim, and Ladakh were all part of Tibet.

13. For a good account of her meeting with the Tartar shaman, see Sinnett, *Incidents,* 69–72.

14. Ibid., 134. A physician was summoned, and the patient collapsed before him unconscious. Suddenly, the doctor (Vera claimed) "saw a large, dark hand between his own and the wound he was going to anoint. The gaping wound was near the heart, and the hand kept slowly moving at several intervals from the neck down to the waist." No wonder the physician was terrified and implored that he not be left alone with this patient! (134).

15. "Letter to her relatives," written in 1861, in John Algeo, ed., *The Letters of H. P. Blavatsky* (Wheaton, IL: Theosophical, 2003), 10. This is letter no. 1 in Algeo's edition, and he quotes only part of Blavatsky's letter; the rest in note 1. I have restored the full letter here.

16. Sinnett, *Incidents,* 148–50.

17. This incident is reported in n. 28, this chapter.

18. Sinnett, *Incidents,* 81–82; for details see *Incidents,* 80–111.

19. Cited in Cranston *HPB,* 65.

20. See Stephen E. Braude, *The Gold Leaf Lady and Other Parapsychological Investigations* (Chicago: University of Chicago Press, 2007), 37–46. One of Home's earliest displays of psychokinesis was in 1852, under reasonably well-controlled conditions, and Braude is convinced that there was no hoax involved (40–41).

21. *The Theosophical Forum,* May 1936, 343–46, cited in Cranston, *HPB,* 99.

22. Ibid.

23. H. P. Blavatsky, *Theosophical Glossary* (Los Angeles: Theosophical, 1990 [1892]), 295.

24. In H. P. Blavatsky, *The Voice of the Silence* (Pasadena: Theosophical Society, 1992 [1889]), vi. She says: "The work from which I here translate forms part of the same series as that from which the Book of Dzyan were taken, on which the Secret Doctrine is based." In H. P. Blavatsky, *Two Books of the Stanzas of Dzyan* (Adyar: Theosophical, 2002), 1, Blavatsky introduces the text thus: "An archaic manuscript—a collection of palm leaves made impermeable by water, fire, and air, by some specific unknown process—*is before the writer's eye*" (my emphasis). According to *The Voice of the Silence,* these kinds of verses were originally written on disks or engraved on thin oblong squares; the earlier quotation suggests they were written on treated palm leaves. Like the treasures sought by Tibetan virtuosos, these kinds of texts were seen by Blavatsky astrally and memorized by her and then reproduced for our benefit. In *The Secret Doctrine,* Blavatsky explains the etymology and esoteric origins of *Dzyan.* These were the "secret doctrines" coming down from ancient times and also known to the Buddha. The Buddha's teachings had two aspects, the public version that we now possess and a private esoteric wisdom he imparted to initiates, a select circle of the *arhats* (*arahants*) of Buddhism, who received this wisdom in an initiation conducted by the Buddha "at the famous Saptaparna cave (the Sattapanni of the Mahavansa), near Mount Baibar." This cave is mentioned in the Mahāvaṃsa, but not as an initiatory site. See H. P. Blavatsky, "Introductory" to *The Secret Doctrine: The Synthesis of Science, Religion, and Philosophy* (Pasadena: Theosophical University Press, 1999 [1888]), xx (xvii–xlvii). She traces the etymology of *Dzyan* from *dan* or *Jan-na,* which presumably is based on *Dhyāna,* the Buddhist word for meditative trance, later adapted by the Chinese as *ch'an.* The esoteric term is *Dzyan.* Here Blavatsky, like other innovators, has reinter-

preted traditional texts and corrected the "errors" found in them, something she does at great length everywhere in *The Secret Doctrine*.

25. C. Jinarajadasa, in *H. P. B. Speaks*, 1:96, says he was an Albanian; maybe an Albanian born in Georgia; Meade, *Madame Blavatsky*, 116, says he was Armenian and a native of Georgia.

26. In a letter to Francis J. Lippitt, written sometime in February 1875, Blavatsky says that "[I had] nearly broken my leg by falling down under a heavy bedstead." See *H. P. B. Speaks*, 2:163.

27. One letter was to H. P. Corson and the other to Colonel Olcott, in Algeo, *The Letters of H. P. Blavatsky*, 164–65 and 165–71 respectively.

28. "Bettanelly to General F. G. Lippitt, June 18th, 1875" in *H. P. B. Speaks*, 1:93–94. During her stay in the U.S., Blavatsky was often visited by John King, the buccaneer spirit who was popular in spiritualist séances. "Saved my life three times, at Mentana, in a shipwreck, and the last time near Spezia when our steamer was blown to pieces and out of 400 passengers remained but 16 in 1871, 21 of June. He loves me." *H. P. B. Speaks*, 1:84. In an undated letter, written probably in mid-April 1875, she says that John King cured her leg completely and urged her to rest for three days, but she neglected his injunction and the leg reverted back to its diseased condition (75). John King visited her during her trance, according to Betanelly, but the dominant being who possessed her was her Indian guru Master Moriya. Most likely it was Master Moriya who cured her finally. Betanelly mentions a séance that several friends had performed during Blavatsky's illness. John King appeared in them and tried to kiss Blavatsky and she resisted because "she hates when he kisses on the lips" (*H. P. B. Speaks*, 2:94).

29. According to Meade, in *Madame Blavatsky* (68–93), this was an actor Agardi Metrovitch. Meade says she had a sickly son from him or from another lover, and Blavatsky doted on him. But the child died in infancy. Although a prude, it is likely that Blavatsky had several affairs, but Meade is a hostile biographer, and one cannot rely entirely on her account. I am much more sympathetic to Blavatsky's own admission that she was, in a gynecological sense, incapable of bearing children, in which case the child was someone adopted by her, as she claimed. The child died prematurely. See also K. Paul Johnson, *The Masters Revealed: Madame Blavatsky and the Myth of the Great White Lodge* (Albany: State University of New York Press, 1994), 33–37.

30. In a séance conducted on June 23, 1875, during Blavatsky's illness, the medium mentions him with the statement "Omniloff is now with Madam." To the question on Blavatsky's condition, the response was "Better but very weak." See Algeo, *The Letters of H. P. Blavatsky*, 187.

31. For examples see, Stephen LaBerge and Howard Rheingold, *Exploring the World of Lucid Dreaming* (New York: Ballantine, 1990), 276–78, hereafter abbreviated as WLD.

32. "Letter to V[era] de Zhelihovsky, [June 1875]," Algeo, *The Letters of H. P. Blavatsky*, 192.

33. Ibid.

34. Ibid.

35. "Letter to V de Zhelihovsky," dated June 1875, in Algeo, *The Letters of H. P. Blavatsky*, 191 (my emphasis).

36. Johnson, in *The Master's Revealed*, makes the point that the so-called masters were real people whom Blavatsky had met and then fictionalized in her writings. I find this an implausible hypothesis and a product of a simplistic empiricism that, in spite of Johnson's

sympathetic treatment of Blavatsky, effectively puts her in the company of charlatans and frauds.

37. Olcott gives other examples of encounters with Mahatmas in the first two volumes of ODL. While he was cooperating with Blavatsky on the writing of *Isis Unveiled*, Olcott retired to his room in the night when "there came a gleam of something white in the right hand corner of my right eye." And then this vivid vision: "I turned my head, dropped my book in astonishment, and saw towering above me in his great stature an Oriental clad in white garments, and wearing a head-cloth or turban of amber-striped fabric, hand-embroidered in yellow floss-silk. Long raven hair hung from under his turban to the shoulders; his black beard, parted vertically on the chin in the Rajput fashion, was twisted up at the ends and carried over the ears; his eyes were alive with soul-fire; eyes which were at once benignant and piercing in glance; the eyes of a mentor and a judge, but softened by the love of a father who gazes on a son needing counsel and guidance. He was so grand a man, so imbued with the majesty of moral strength, so luminously spiritual, so evidently above average humanity, that I felt abashed in his presence and bowed my head and bent my knee as one does before a god or a god-like personage" (ODL 1:379). Theosophy's own project was outlined by this Master: of the great work to be done for humanity and the mysterious and unbreakable tie that bound Blavatsky and Olcott.

Then in 1878, on his way to India with Blavatsky, he stopped in London and there, while walking in Cannon Street with two others, he saw a master once again. "I recognized the face as that of an Exalted One; for the once seen can never be mistaken. As there is one glory of the sun and another glory of the moon, so there is one brightness of the average good man or woman's face, and another, a transcendental one, of the face of an Adept . . . the inner light of the awakened spirit shines effulgently," citing Corinthians 1:15, 41, perhaps without being aware of it (ODL, 2: 5). When they went to see Blavatsky, a friend, Mrs. Billing, ran into this same Mahatma near HPB's room, "a very tall and handsome Hindu, with a very piercing eye which seemed to look her through," the standard guise of these Hindu Mahatmas (ODL, 2: 5). Soon after this experience in London, Olcott, while riding in a horse cart in India, saw a Mahatma in "his white turban, and dress, mass of dark hair dropping from his shoulders, and full beard;" and he vanished in an instance like "one of the lightning flashes" (ODL, 2:145). At critical points in his life, it is this special guru who appears before him and gives him advice to resolve crises. Perhaps because of his scientism, Olcott does not recognize that his Mahatmaic guru acts very much like the *iṣṭa devata* or guardian deities in Indic thought and spirit familiars found in many other religions. In another instance it is not clear whether it is Blavatsky or a disciple that has the vision. In this case, Blavatsky persuaded Moolji Thackersey [Mulji Thakarshi], the first Indian Theosophist and a wealthy landowner, to go with her in a carriage to a beach in Bombay, and there she created a beautiful "*māyāvic* house," "with a rose garden in front and a fine bungalow with spacious Eastern verandahs in the back ground. . . . HPB had walked straight up to the house, had been received cordially at the door by a tall Hindu of striking and distinguished appearance, clad entirely in white, and had gone inside" (ODL, 2:43). Since Moolji confirmed all this, Olcott decided to go with him and retrace the route, but of course the *māyāvic* house had disappeared. Olcott says such houses are actually used by gurus and *chelas* (disciples) for conferences, and they are guarded by elementals and protected by a "circle of illusion" or "*māyāvic* engirdlement" (ODL, 2:45).

38. Meade, *Madame Blavatsky,* 30. Meade's description is supposedly based on an account by Blavatsky but no reference is given and I have not been able to track it down.

39. According to Blavatsky, she "had fought with Giuseppe Garibaldi's army at the battle of Mentana, which had taken place thirteen miles northeast of Rome on November 3, 1867, and claimed that she had been wounded five times: her left arm was broken in two places by a saber stroke, she had a musket bullet embedded in her right shoulder and another in her leg. Finally she had been left for dead in a ditch." Meade, *Madame Blavatsky,* 91. I suggest this was also a visionary experience, which she, at some point, conflated into a real experience, although in Blavatsky's case it is difficult for the analyst to disentangle the empirically and historically real with the visionary real. The idea of being wounded five times, I suspect, comes, without her being aware of it, from the five wounds of Christ. If the wounds she received at Mentana were a real event, she must have made a remarkable recovery, because she was at Florence in Christmas of that year, according to Fuller, *Blavatsky,* 22. She also claimed that John King, the spirit buccaneer, cured her wounds, and this might account for her quick recovery! In a letter addressed to Sinnett, she tells him "not to speak of Mentana and do not speak of MASTER I implore you." She seems reluctant to talk of the Mentana episode, and the reference to the master, who was probably John King, whose kisses on the mouth she does not seem to favor. See letter no. 61 in *The Mahatma Letters to A. P. Sinnett,* ed. A. Trevor Barker (Pasadena: Theosophical University Press, 1925), 153. I have not been able to trace this reference in the second edition of the letters that I use in the rest of this essay.

40. H. P. Blavatsky's letter (no. 111) in *The Mahatma Letters to A. P. Sinnett,* ed. A. Trevor Barker, 2d ed. (London: Rider, 1948), 478–79. Such transmission of knowledge from some known or unknown source became very popular in new age religions and was known as "channeling," perhaps inspired by Blavatsky. For a good discussion of modern channeling, see Wouter Hanegraaff, *New Age Religion and Western Culture: Esotericism in the Mirror of Secular Thought* (Leiden: Brill, 1996), 23–41.

41. For a summary of the Coulomb affair and the investigations of the Society for Psychical Research, see Cranston, *HPB,* 265–84. See also the reinvestigation of the affair by an officer of the Society for Psychical Research, Vernon Harrison, *H. P. Blavatsky and the SPR: An Examination of the Hodgson Report of 1885* (Pasadena: Theosophical Society Press, 1997). Michael Gomes, *The Coulomb Case* (Fullerton, CA: Theosophical History, 2005) has an excellent overview of the Coulomb affair.

42. Blavatsky's letter (no. 111) in *The Mahatma Letters,* 478.

43. Letter to her relatives written late 1887 in Algeo, *The Letters of H. P. Blavatsky.* In a letter to her skeptical sister Vera, written in late 1877, she says: "Open Isis wherever you please, and decide for yourself. I am telling you the truth: it is the Master who is explaining showing all this to me. . . . Pictures, ancient manuscripts, and dates pass before me: I am merely copying them and write with such ease that instead of its being an effort, it is the greatest pleasure" (394–95).

44. In a fascinating chapter, entitled "Isis Unveiled," Olcott gives details of the manner in which the work was written (ODL, 1:202–19), and, interestingly enough, the "most perfect of all were the manuscripts which were written while she was sleeping" (211). By "most perfect" he meant the thoughts expressed in *Isis,* not the manner in which these thoughts were organized. Some of the complications during transmission from the masters to Bla-

vatsky were noted by Olcott, especially the differences in literary style and presentation. She obtains various texts from the masters, but she has to cut and paste them together, something she was not good at. Olcott says that "the copy that was turned over to me for revision was terribly faulty, and having been converted into a great smudge of interlineations, erasures, orthographic corrections and substitutions, would end in being dictated by me to her to rewrite" (ODL, 1:243, see also ODL, 1:208). Sometimes several "intelligences" or "alter egos" were involved in the production of a text using her body "as a writing machine." These were occasions, says Olcott, when her own personality "melted away" and she was "somebody else." At other times, she was simply an amanuensis taking down texts. Blavatsky had little patience in reading proofs, which made for some terrible mistakes. Editorial work therefore was absolutely necessary, but often done in haste to meet a publisher's deadline (ODL, 1:250–52).

45. Wachtmeister, *Reminiscences,* 26–27.

46. Cited in Michael Gomes, *The Dawning of the Theosophical Movement* (Wheaton, IL: Theosophical, 1987), 114–15.

47. Evelyn Underhill, *Mysticism: The Nature and Development of Spiritual Consciousness* (Oxford: One World, 2000 [1911]), 155. Underhill immediately adds: "On this theory prophecy, and also clairvoyance—one of the great objects of occult education—consist in opening the eyes of the mind upon the timeless Astral World; and spiritualists, evoking the phantoms of the dead, merely call them up from the recesses of universal instead of individual remembrance."

48. C. Jinarajadasa, *H. P. B. Speaks,* 2:63. This is a bit of a strange statement because the impact of these hermetic philosophers, at least Paracelsus and Agrippa, especially the former, appear all the time in her own work, for example, in chapter 6 of *Isis Unveiled* (162–206) and elsewhere; and Paracelsus appears prominently in *The Secret Doctrine.* However, it is entirely possible that she had fully read and assimilated their thought before age fifteen and incorporated that knowledge into *Isis.* Heinrich Kunrath is also an alchemical and hermetic scholar who, as far as I know, is barely used by Blavatsky in her two major works, but extensively referred to by Jung.

49. These books are listed by Boris de Zirkoff, the editor of *Isis Unveiled,* 1:16.

50. Nietzsche wrote insightfully on such techniques of remembering, something that one inherits from human prehistory, a terrible and uncanny facility. "One burns something in so that it remains in one's memory: only that which does not cease to give pain remains in one's memory." Nietzsche seems to think that only traumatic episodes or events are burned into memory, but perhaps we need to extend his argument to other techniques whereby the past is imprinted in memory and facilitates visionary recall, as in the case of Blavatsky. "In a certain sense the entirety of asceticism belongs here: a few ideas are made indelible, omnipresent, unforgettable, 'fixed,' for the sake of hypnotizing the entire nervous and intellectual system with these 'fixed ideas'—and the ascetic procedures and forms of life are means for taking these ideas out of competition with all other ideas in order to make them 'unforgettable.'" Friedrich Nietzsche, *On the Genealogy of Morality,* ed. and trans. Maudemarie Clark and Alan J. Swensen (Indianapolis: Hackett, 1998), 37–38). The rendering of mnemotechnique as a "technique for remembering things" is from the translation by Douglas Smith, *On the Genealogy of Morals* (Oxford: Oxford University Press, 1996), 42.

51. Wachtmeister, *Reminiscences,* 25.

52. Blavatsky, "My books," in *Lucifer,* May, 15, 1891, 241–247 and reprinted in *H. P. Blavatsky,* 13:196. Presumably this letter was written before her death on May 8, 1891, and published afterward.

53. Ibid., letter no. 138, 470

54. Sinnett, *The Mahatma Letters* (no. 43), 262.

55. A. P. Sinnett, *Esoteric Buddhism* (London: Trubner, 1883). Blavatsky was aware of the criticisms of this work by scholars who had pointed out that there was neither esotericism nor Buddhism in it. She countered criticisms by defending Sinnett and insisting the only problem was the title of his work and that the book was in fact a survey of her own work, *The Secret Doctrine.*

56. For A. O. Hume's skepticism of Blavatsky, read the account by Johnson, *The Masters Revealed,* 234–41. Hume was a British civil servant who was one of the early organizers of the Indian National Congress and took up the cause of home rule, but not independence. He seemed to have a profoundly ambivalent relationship to Blavatsky, so that he became an assistant to Richard Hodgson who led the inquiry by the Society for Psychical Research to "test" Blavatsky's proclaimed powers. While Hume scorned Blavatsky's occult powers and also those of Damodar, the senior Indian Theosophist, he himself believed in masters, but only those of his own "lineage." Hume wrote seven volumes of "history" that I think were, like Blavatsky's, based on visionary voices.

57. Letter no. 128, written from Adyar on March 17 (no year given) in Sinnett, *The Mahatma Letters,* 470–71.

58. Ibid., 471.

59. Ibid.

60. Blavatsky, "Letter no. 111," written in Wurzburg and dated January 6 1886, in *The Mahatma Letters,* 480. The handwriting expert Vernon Harrison, who convincingly refuted most of the Hodgson report, says that there were several kinds of handwriting represented in the *Mahatma Letters* that he examined in the British library. They seemed to be from different hands, and only a few of them were Blavatsky's. But why didn't Mahatma KH have a single handwriting? Harrison recounts the Theosophist defense, saying that the Mahatmas, like modern leaders, had "secretarial" assistance; they dictated to others who wrote on their behalf. The alternative possibility, which is close to mine, is also mentioned by Harrison: "What may have come through her head in trance, dislocation or other forms of altered consciousness is another matter; but writing so made cannot be classed as either fraud or imposture." See Harrison, *H. P. Blavatsky and the SPR,* x.

61. For a convenient summary of her later skills in producing phenomena and a "theoretical" explanation of them, see the chapter entitled "Recent Occult Phenomena" in A. P. Sinnett, *The Occult World* (London: Theosophical, 1984 [1881]), 37–134; and 83 for psychological telegraphs. This book is "affectionately dedicated" to "The Mahatma K.H."

62. The elemental spirits are those that govern the four elements, namely, earth, air, fire, and water, those constituents from which the material world is created. One of the most famous listings of elemental spirits is Paracelsus, "who defined the elementals in the terms used ever since: gnomes, the elementals of earth; undines, elementals of water; sylphs, elementals of air; and salamanders elements of fire," John Michael Greer, *The New Encyclopedia of the Occult* (St. Paul: Llewellyn, 2003), 151.

63. Sven Eek, ed., *Damodar and the Pioneers of the Theosophical Movement* (Adyar: Theosophical, 1978), 47.

64. Ibid., 5.

65. Ibid., 4–5.

66. Ibid., 5.

67. Damodar, "Letter to William Q. Judge," ibid., 57–58.

68. Ibid., 60–61; see 58–62 for the full letter to Judge written on June 28, 1881.

69. Ibid., 61

70. Ibid.

71. Ibid., 61–62.

72. Ibid., 10.

73. The moral training during these seven years has been described by Sinnett, *Occult World,* 23–29.

74. "Letter no. 137," Sinnett, *The Mahatma Letters,* 468.

75. Eek, *Damodar,* 18.

76. The Yeats reference here is to "The road at my door," W. B. Yeats, *The Collected Poems of W. B. Yeats* (New York: Macmillan, 1956), 202.

77. Initially, Blavatsky considered herself to be a believer in "spiritualism," but soon enough she used the term *occult science* instead. She claims that when she admitted to being a "spiritualist" she meant the "ancient spiritualism" of adepts and not its modern variety. The details of her acceptance and rejection of spiritualism is found in the letters published in New York newspapers from October 30, 1874, to July 8, 1875, and republished in *H. P. Blavatsky,* 1:30–93.

78. Henry Steel Olcott, *People from the Other World* (Hartford: American, 1875).

79. Letter to the *Tribune,* September 17, 1875, 3, cited in Gomes, *The Dawning,* 80.

80. Blavatsky herself had no use for Darwin. Her notions of the evolution of races and of the spirit had little to do with the origins of species and natural selection and indeed could scarcely be reconciled with Darwinism. Wallace, however, being more attuned to the very spiritualism that Blavatsky had rejected, was impressed by "the vast amount of erudition" and the "refinements" of style; and he thought that *Isis Unveiled* would "open up to many spiritualists a whole world of new ideas." Cited in Cranston, *HPB,* 160.

81. Blavatsky, "Letter No. 133," probably written in 1882, 460. In letter 141 of *The Mahatma Letters* (485) she refers to his "blessed self-confidence and—pardon—his vulgar but all powerful *cheek.*"

82. Nethercot in *The Last Four Lives of Annie Besant* (217) mentions a powerful visionary experience of Besant's that transported her in 1913 to Shambala in the Gobi Desert to meet the "great King," who warned her of the dangers facing her, but that she should have no fear or anxiety. "Do not let opposition become angry. Be firm, but not provocative. Press steadily the preparation for the coming changes and claim India's place in the Empire." This vision, says Nethercot, "controlled the rest of Annie Besant's life" and possibly reinforced her idea that India should not claim full independence but remain within the empire. Besant's political ambitions to lead India were thwarted by the rise of a new leadership under Gandhi and Nehru; but her influence in resurrecting the Hindu past has yet to be assessed, especially in relation to the rise of movements like the BJP, spearheaded

by the middle class. It should be remembered that Nehru joined the Theosophical Society at age thirteen!

83. For details of Olcott's contribution to Buddhism, see my paper, "The Two Faces of Colonel Olcott: Buddhism and Euro-Rationality in the Late Nineteenth Century" in *Buddhism and Christianity: Interactions Between East and West*, ed. Ulrich Everding (Colombo: Goethe-Institut, 1995), 32–71.

84. Montague Ullman and Stanley Krippner, *Dream Therapy: Scientific Experiments in the Supernatural* (New York: Macmillan, 1973), 157.

85. Olcott is generally silent about his Buddhist faith in the first two volumes of ODL, that is, up to 1883. From around 1887 onward (that is, toward the end of vol. 3 of ODL and after), Olcott unequivocally and publicly voices his open profession of Buddhism and speaks of his Sri Lankan friends as "my co-religionists" (ODL, 3:371). We do not know the inner motivations that went into this public proclamation: perhaps the influence of the Sri Lankan monk Sumangala, his friend; his extensive reading of Buddhist texts for the preparation of *The Buddhist Catechism*; the equalitarian ideology of doctrinal Buddhism that appealed to his American egalitarianism; and perhaps his belief that here was an arena where he could bring about crucial social and educational changes. In volume 4 of ODL the references to his profession of Buddhism are everywhere. For example, in 1887 he was given the sacred thread by the Hindu Pandit Vidyasagara and asked to dine with him, "a case without precedent, as I was a declared Buddhist" (ODL, 4:1). He begins to quote Buddhist texts, such as the *Dhammapada*: "One is the road that leads to wealth, another the road that leads to Nirvana" (ODL, 4:3) The increasing success of Buddhism in meeting the missionary challenge and creating schools spurred his enthusiasm further. A Japanese Buddhist refers to him as "a Buddhist of many years' standing"; and Olcott refers to "resistless power of the Buddha Dharma that would be pitted against the forces of irreligion and moral revolt" (ODL, 4:90). Theosophy itself posed no problem for Olcott, though it did to his monk consultants who eliminated all references to Theosophy in *The Buddhist Catechism* when Olcott consulted them. He calls himself "a Theosophist and a Buddhist" (ODL, 4:258). Olcott now is so much of a Buddhist that in 1897 he administered the five precepts to Dr. J. M. Peebles to "make him a Buddhist." He says that "under a commission from Sumangala and the Kandyan High Priests, I am empowered to administer to such as wish to enter into Buddhism," when of course anyone could administer these precepts. In the same year, nine years before his death, he retrospectively and sentimentally imagines that he "became a Buddhist at New York" (ODL, 6:154).

86. I was fascinated to note the subtitle of Jeffrey Kripal, *Esalen: America and the Religion of No Religion* (Chicago: University of Chicago Press, 2008). Theosophy, I think, anticipated this "religion of no religion."

87. Blavatsky, *The Secret Doctrine*, xx.

88. Ibid., xxxiv.

89. K. Paul Johnson, *Initiates of the Theological Masters* (Albany: State University of New York Press, 1995), 63, makes the point that Blavatsky practiced a form of "concentration on the brow chakra" based on the Radhasoami faith, but I find no evidence in Blavatsky's works that she engaged in serious meditation. She did practice forms of concentration, but they were highly eclectic or invented ones I would think.

90. This statement is from a letter to Prince A. M. Dondoukoff-Korsakoff on June 25, 1882, when she was in Bombay in *H. P. B. Speaks,* 2:87.

91. Gregory Bateson, *Naven,* 2d ed. (Stanford: Stanford University Press, 1965); the discussion on schismogenesis is found in chapter 13, 171–97.

92. Donald S. Lopez has a powerful critique of Evans-Wentz's work, and the fact that he knew little or nothing of the Tibetan language. Lopez's criticism is found in chapter 2 ("The Book") of his *Prisoners of Shangri-La: Tibetan Buddhism and the West* (Chicago: University of Chicago Press, 1999), 85. The book's popularity is in Lopez's view a product of the West's search for spiritual meaning. This is correct, but I don't see this as something wrong! Also Lopez dumps all later translations of the Tibetan Book of the Dead in the same orientalist category, generally based on the respective authors' political and religious views of Tibetan religion rather than the quality of the translation. We are not told which translation is closest to the originals; perhaps academic politics are involved.

93. Cited in the "Introduction" to Erlendur Haraldsson, *Miracles Are My Visiting Cards* (Bangalore: Sai Towers, 2006), n.p.

94. The Sai Baba cult has a global outreach and has been documented by both devotees and scholars or even scholarly devotees. For a convenient and useful account, read Smriti Srinivas, *In the Presence of Sai Baba: Body, City, and Memory in a Global Religious Movement* (Hyderabad: Orient Longmans, 2008). Srinivas's is a good description of the movement, but avoids any criticisms, letting the movement speak for itself. She does not discuss seriously the class-based significance of the movement and its economic ethics, although she reminds us that the Sai Baba cult group is both locally and globally almost overwhelmingly middle class, with a large support from the business community. Srinivas, however, rightly puts emphasis on the good works done by the Sai Baba movement, such as hospitals, universities, and other philanthropic activities.

 There is no doubt of the charisma of Sai Baba, but how this is created or reinforced by the production of phenomena is well documented in Haraldsson, *Miracles.* Haraldsson, like many educated persons, says that, while there is no proof regarding Sai Baba's paranormal powers, there is plenty of informant evidence to suggest its genuineness. But neither Haraldsson nor anyone else asks how mental concentration, or whatever, could produce complicated machines like Swiss wristwatches, and, as far as I know, no one has tracked down these objects, if they have had some kind of registration number, to an original source. This is true of the production of Indian sweets or personal ornaments like rings and necklaces and also statues, sometimes made of gold. The fact remains that Sai Baba can produce gold statues through concentration, but not gold nuggets that might help India's poor. Instead he seeks the help of philanthropists for his genuine social work and educational projects. So it is with his producing large quantities of food. In my view two things are obvious in Blavatsky's and Sai Baba's materialization of objects. First, there is a limited repertoire of phenomena that can be produced. Second, there is no real difference in principle between the production of phenomena and what paranormal investigators call "teleportation," that is, the movement of objects, such as furniture. It is possible that the phenomena that Blavatsky and Sai Baba produce are moved from somewhere else, through what means we do not know. This is true of Blavatsky's flying roses or Sai Baba's more wide-ranging productions. I have no position to take in Sai Baba's case, but I am reluctant to label Blavatsky a "fraud."

95. For an account of lemuri, see the fantastic zoology of dream creatures in Jorge Luis Borges, *The Book of Imaginary Beings,* trans. Andrew Hurley (New York: Viking, 2005), 124.

96. For further details, see Sumathi Ramaswamy, *The Lost Land of Lemuria: Fabulous Geographies, Catastrophic Histories* (Berkeley: University of California Press, 2004). Ramaswamy has beautiful discussions of the various maps of Lemuria.

97. Shirley MacLaine, *Going Within: A Guide for Inner Transformation* (New York: Bantam, 1989), 127.

7. MODERNITY AND THE DREAMING

1. Interview reported in Deirdre Barrett, *The Committee of Sleep: How Artists, Scientists, and Athletes Use Dreams for Creative Problem Solving—And How You Can Too* (New York: Crown, 2001), 108.

2. William A. Christian, *Visionaries: The Spanish Republic and the Reign of Christ* (Berkeley: University of California Press, 1996).

3. For an account of her life and mission and a sampling of her paintings, see William A. Fagaly, ed., *Tools of Her Ministry: The Art of Sister Gertrude Morgan* (New York: American Folklore Museum, 2004).

4. Shirley MacLaine is one of those new age thinkers who mentions her visions in her many books. Especially fascinating is series of visions when she had a spiritual acupuncture treatment from a fellow religionist Chris Griscom. Griscom pierced MacLaine's forehead, shoulders, and ears with thin golden acupuncture needles with an ancient Chinese doctor, in spirit form, guiding or helping her, permitting MacLaine to see past incarnations of her mother and then herself and also of Atlantis before it sank! "The pictures came in front of my mind as though I were watching a film inside of my own head." Shirley MacLaine, *Dancing in the Light* (New York: Bantam, 1985), 329. She justifies most of this in terms of modern quantum physics and other forms of contemporary scientific knowledge. In another session, recorded in chapter 16 (345–63), she meets her alter who is also simultaneously a highly advanced spiritual being. "I saw the form of a very tall, overpoweringly confident, almost androgynous human being. A graceful, folded, cream-colored garment flowed over a figure seven feet tall, with long arms resting calmly at its side. . . . The eyes were deep, deep blue and the expression was supremely kind, yet strong. It raised its arms in outstretched welcome." This being introduced him/her self as "I am your higher unlimited self" (350). MacLaine, perhaps following Theosophical practice, referred to this being as HS. She has extensive conversations with HS that produce new knowledge on a variety of spiritual matters.

5. After the sixties there have been both scientific and personal experiments using hallucinogenic substances, especially LSD. My own prejudice is to ignore "mystical experiences" derived from the ingestion of such substances, even though they might show resemblances to visions during meditative and nondrug induced conditions. The classic work that influenced much of later thinking on visions induced by drugs is Aldous Huxley's fascinating experiences with mescaline in *The Doors of Perception and Heaven and Hell* (New York: HarperCollins, 1994 [1954]). Huxley believes that drug-induced substances clear the doors of perception and help realize Blake's ideal that "everything would appear

to man as it is, infinite." My own prejudice is that Huxley's is not Blake's way at all and that drug induced "visions" are best compared to dreams than to Blake's visions or that of the visionaries who appear in this essay. For a survey of these experiences and the place where they were used for serious personal, scholarly, and soteriological reasons, see the important study of Esalen in Jeffrey Kripal, *Esalen: America and the Religion of No Religion* (Chicago: University of Chicago Press, 2008).

6. Swedenborg's *Journal of Dreams* was first published in a Swedish edition of 1859 and an English translation appeared ten years later. The edition I am familiar with has a running commentary by Wilson Van Dusen and is entitled *Swedenborg's Journal of Dreams, 1743-1744* (New York: Swedenborg Foundation, 1986).

Swedenborg, as we know, was a distinguished natural scientist and author of many learned treatises on metallurgy, crystallography, and related sciences. In his middle age, he had visionary experiences and a new revelation that led him to reject science. The *Journal* was one of three personal accounts he kept, but only the last survived, with some of Swedenborg's sexual dreams expunged by unknown persons. It was written when he was fifty-three and indicates his spiritual turmoil and is especially interesting because Swedenborg himself interpreted his dreams in these terms. Although it was a kind of travel diary, it is most significant as a collection and interpretation of dreams. Several key pieces of information are available in it. For example, we are told that he has renounced sex and admitted that prior to this he has been obsessed with it. Here is a diary entry: "Of my delights during the nights. Wondered at myself for having nothing left to do for my own honor, so that I was even touched. Also at not being at all inclined towards the sex, as I had previously been all my life. How I was in waking trances all the time" (17).

We have no information on the content of these waking trances except that another entry states they were "wakeful ecstasies almost the whole time" (19). He mentions that he had until now resisted the "spirit." And then a dream: "How I set myself against the power of the Holy Spirit, what happened thereupon; how I saw hideous specters, without life horribly shrouded and moving in their shrouds, together with a beast that attacked me, but not the child." Unfortunately, Swedenborg does not interpret this wonderfully frightening dream, but he did interpret several dreams that followed, including this one: "Descended a great staircase, which ended in a ladder; freely and boldly; below there was a hole, which led into a great abyss. It was difficult to reach the other side without falling into the hole. There were on the other side persons to whom I reached my hand, to help me over, wakened." And then his cryptic but meaningful interpretation: "Signifies the danger I am in of falling into hell, if I do not get help" (25). This dream cum interpretation suggests what I have stated elsewhere, namely, a dream has especial significance not in itself but when it is interpreted by the dreamer and that can appear at the point of waking or later. This same dream could be interpreted as meaningfully by a Freudian or a Jungian or an existential analyst.

7. I have used Freud's first chapter on "the scientific literature dealing with the problem of dreams," as a convenient way of dealing with the subject. For a more exhaustive and eminently readable account, see J. Allan Hobson, *The Dreaming Brain: How the Brain Creates Both the Sense and Nonsense of Dreams* (New York: Basic Books, 1988), 23–51. Hobson unfortunately is thoroughly hostile to psychoanalysis and to any phenomenological understanding of dreams, believing that dreams must be exclusively understood in physiologi-

cal terms, without realizing that if one explains dreams as a neurological phenomenon, which it is, it does not militate understanding them in symbolic or existential terms.

8. I have used here the new translation of the first edition of Sigmund Freud, *The Interpretation of Dreams*, trans. Joyce Clark (New York: Oxford University Press, 1999). For the rest of my discussion of Freud's first chapter I will revert to the authorized standard edition.

9. Freud had no access to Saint-Denys's book, but had to rely on references to him by others. Saint-Denys (1822–1892) is a pioneer in the study of dreams, which he started recording at the age of thirteen. His discussion of memory is entitled "Dreams and Memory," in Hervey de Saint-Denys, *Dreams and How to Guide Them,* trans. Nicholas Fry (London: Duckworth, 1982 [1867]), 26–33. He also believed that wish fulfillment underlay the motivation for most, if not all, dreams, but, unhappily, Freud missed this reference. "Since the dream is the representation in the mind's eye of what occupies our thoughts, as I have so often said, in the dream we would immediately see the image of what we had voluntarily thought of; in other words, we would have dreamt what we wished to dream" (52).

10. Oliver Sachs, "Neurological Dreams" in *Trauma and Dreams,* ed., Deidre Barrett (Cambridge: Harvard University Press, 1996), 212 (212–16). What is striking about Sachs's examples is that a neurological disease might be indirectly represented in symbolic form in dreams. A fascinating example is from a patient stricken with "an acute encephalitis lethargica" in 1926 who dreamed "she was in an inaccessible castle, but the castle had the form and shape of herself; she dreamed of enchantments, bewitchments, entrancements; she dreamed that she had become a living sentient statue of stone; she dreamed that the world had come to a stop; she dreamed of a death which was different from death. Her family had difficulty waking her the next morning, and when she awoke there was intense consternation: she was parkinsonian and catatonic" (213–14). Sachs goes on to give other examples where dreams seem to recognize the onset of a disease before that condition becomes known to the patient and doctor.

11. For an important study of the role of dreams in Freud's self-analysis, see Didier Anzieu, *Freud's Self-Analysis* (London: Hogarth, 1986), especially the chapter "Discovery of the Oedipus Complex" (175–251).

12. For a detailed discussion of these various schools, see Anthony Shafton, *Dream Reader: Contemporary Approaches to the Understanding of Dreams* (Albany: State University of New York Press, 1995) part 2 (59–235), entitled "Schools," which is devoted to these psychologists. Very recently, after this book was completed, I read Somu Shamdasani, *Jung and the Making of Modern Psychology: The Dream of a Science* (Cambridge: Cambridge University Press, 2003), which gives a very much broader background than mine on the scholarly work on dreams in the nineteenth century, and those interested in this topic should read his chapter 5, "Night and Day," especially 100–40. Shamdasani's book deals with the making of modern psychology, but, in spite of its title, does not deal with the significance of dreaming in the genesis of Jung's psychology. The work is also vitiated by an anti-Freudian bias, such that the term *Freudian legend* appears in somewhat derogatory fashion in his characterization of Freud. He also seems to blame Freud for ignoring the historical development of psychology, ignoring the fact that few creative thinkers had the time and energy to uncover antecedent background material that more professional historians later did. For example: does he expect Darwin to have given us an intellectual history of evolutionary thought prior to his discovery of the origins of species? As

Shamdasani himself admits, much of psychoanalysis was "hidden history" till he and others like him unraveled it for us (xii). Shamdasani traces the Jung's scholarly genealogy to major European thinkers, but misses Jung's own self-reflection regarding the genesis of his thought, and that is the significance of alchemy and of such thinkers as Paracelsus and Cornelius Agrippa in the formation of his key ideas, rather than Kant or Hegel and mainline European philosophers. Shamdasani has almost nothing to say on the significance of alchemy on Jung's work, which seems remote from that of the formal genealogy he sketches for us. However, Shamdasani has a fine last chapter, entitled "The Ancient and the Modern," that deals, among other things, with the impact of several modern thinkers on Jung's thought, especially Lucien Lévy Bruhl and ethnographers of the later nineteenth and early twentieth centuries (271–352).

13. Barrett, *The Committee of Sleep.*
14. Eduard Farber, "Dreams and Visions in a Century of Chemistry," *Kekulé Centennial* (Washington, DC: American Chemical Society, 1966), 129 (129–39).
15. It is unlikely that Kekulé knew of Freud's work, which, for the most part, appeared after Kekulé's death in 1896, but as a highly educated scientist he was probably familiar with the increasing scientific literature on dreams in Germany and France.
16. O. Theodor Benfey, "August Kekulé and the Birth of the Structural Theory of Organic Chemistry," *Journal of Chemical Education* 38, no. 1 (January 1958), 22 (21–23).
17. Ibid.
18. For a good account of the ratiocinative processes that preceded the formation of Kekulé's major work, see Alan J. Rocke, "Hypothesis and Experiment in the Early Development of Kekulé's Benzene Theory," in *Annals of Science* 42, no. 3 (July 198): 355–81.
19. Here is Jung's version of Kekulé's dream vision, which he interprets as an archetype of the collective unconscious. "Thus Kekulé's vision of the dancing couples, which first put him on the track of the structure of certain carbon compounds, namely the benzene ring, was *surely* a vision of the *coniunctio,* the mating that had preoccupied the minds of the alchemists for seventeen centuries. It was precisely this image that had always lured the mind of the investigator away from the problem of chemistry and back to the ancient myth of the royal or divine marriage; but in Kekulé's vision it reached its chemical goal in the end, thus rendering the greatest imaginable service both to our understanding of chemical compounds and to the subsequent unprecedented advances in synthetic chemistry." See C. G. Jung, *The Practice of Psychotherapy: Essays on the Psychology of the Transference and Other Subjects* (New York: Pantheon, 1954), 168. I am not familiar with the specific dream mentioned by Jung. The crucial one from Kekulé's viewpoint was the atoms forming into the ouroboros. Of course this image too could in Jung's thinking be a manifestation of the *coniunctio,* but surely not mating. Kekulé dreaming of the dancing couples, if ever he did, is important for Jung because it represents the "mystic marriage" or *hierogamos,* something that Jung himself dream-participated in his later life (see p. 434). My guess is that Jung badly misread Kekulé's dreams.
20. Cited in Rocke, "Hypothesis and Experiment," 380.
21. Kekulé's dreams produced considerable hostile reaction from positivist chemists, but also led to the beginnings of serious rethinking of the nature of scientific hypotheses. One of the earliest attempts was by a notable mathematician Jacques Hadamard, *An Essay on the Psychology of Invention in the Mathematical Field* (New York: Dover, 1945). While Hadamard

is sympathetic to visions, he is primarily interested in broader intuitive flashes of understanding that he relates to the unconscious and the various layers within it. In relation
to Henri Poincaré, he makes the point that ideas incubate in the unconscious and then
a flash of understanding occurs, an idea that Jung also noted. Poincaré was apparently
chatting with a companion waiting for a bus when "the idea passed through his mind for
less than a second, just the time to put his foot on the step and enter the omnibus" (36).
This is true of all of Poincaré's illuminations, according to Hadamard, as it is true of some
visionary and aphoristic insights.

22. Farber, "Dreams and Visions," 136. More recently, the *New York Times* of March 10, 2005,
reported a similar revelation by another distinguished scientist and Nobel laureate. "Dr
[Charles H.] Townes often recalls that he came up with the idea that would become the
laser while sitting on a Washington park bench [Franklin Park] in 1951. In his 1966 article
he [says] there was little difference between such epiphanies, when the subconscious
hits upon a solution to a problem, and the religious experience of revelation." His book,
How the Laser Happened: Adventures of a Scientist (New York: Oxford University Press, 1999),
55–56, briefly refers to this episode, which seems more like an aphoristic insight or a
thought that hit him from the space of the silence, rather than a vision.

23. The dream of the "botanical monograph" is on ID, 169–76 and 281–84. The famous Irma
dream that Freud dreamed on July 23–24 is worth reading in full in ID, 106–21 in conjunction with Didier Anzieu's analysis in *Freud's Self-Analysis*, 131–56. It is used by Freud to
illustrate his central theme of wish-fulfillment in dreams. Freud has a detailed account
of the latent thoughts that precipitated the manifest dream, but none of them, at least in
his reading, pertain to deep motivations or even sexual fantasies. There has been a lot of
commentary on this dream by critics and I will hint at some of them. For example: critics
have pointed out that Freud himself says that he did not fully reveal all the motivations
that went into the dream, there is a "gap" in the analysis and admits that he is not entirely frank in filling this gap (ID, 120–21). A clue is provided by one element in the dream
wherein Freud's friend Leopold "was percussing her [Irma] through her bodice" (ID, 107);
and Freud, in examining his dream thoughts, referred to a "celebrated physician who
never made a physical examination of his patients except through their clothes." He then
immediately adds: "Frankly, I had no desire to penetrate more deeply on this point" (ID,
113). But we can, if we recognize that the male figures in the dream are his dream alters.
Irma was a beautiful widow, and if one interprets the dream as Freud's own sexual fantasy
(expectable in the analytic transference) then the dream would require reinterpretation.
If the "gap" can be filled with Freud's sexual fantasies regarding his patient Irma, much
of the symbolism of the dream has to be rethought. For example, in the dream Irma refused to open her mouth, and Freud relates that dream element to women who refuse to
open their mouths if they had false teeth. But when Irma ultimately opened her dream
mouth, he noticed a "big white patch" and also "extensive whitish grey scabs upon curly
structures which were modeled on the turbinal bones of the nose" (ID, 107). In his examination of the latent thoughts, he refers to his fears that his daughter, who was ill at that
time, might have contacted diphtheria. He therefore thought, based on day residues, that
the throat scab in the dream was a diphtheria membrane. This is possible. But it does
not invalidate another association to which Freud paid scant attention and that is his
friend Fleiss, who, according to Freud, made some remarkable nosological correlations

(if I might be permitted a pun) between the turbinal bones of the nose and the vagina (ID, 117). If so, one can treat Freud peering into Irma's mouth with its scabs and white patch as his peering into her vagina, giving added significance to the well-known phenomenon of the displaceability of orifices! It now looks as if the injection his dream alter and friend Otto gave Irma with a dirty syringe (also part of the manifest dream) could surely have been Freud's fantasy of penetration. In which case other elements of the dream, such as Irma's pains in the throat (vagina) and stomach and abdomen, can be attributed to the consequences of Freud's fantasy of intercourse, that is, her pregnancy. Freud honestly admits that "pains in the throat and abdomen and constriction of the throat played scarcely any part in her illness" and wonders "why I decided this choice of symptoms in the dream but could not think of an explanation at the moment" (ID, 109). All this, of course, indicates the vulnerability of dream analysis.

24. The quotation is entitled "Thel's motto" from an early poem (1789) by Blake, *The Book of Thel,* CW, 127 (127–30). This moving poem deals with the Virgin Thel, the embodiment of innocence and the youngest daughter of the Seraphin, soon to be confronted with experience, namely, death and transience. And, in her conversation with the cloud, the flower, and the worm, she begins to understand the nature of life. "Dost thou, O little Cloud? I fear that I am not like thee, / For I walk through the vales of Har, and smell the sweetest flowers, / But I feed not the little flowers; I hear the warbling birds, / But I feed not the warbling birds; they fly and seek their food: / But Thel delights in these no more, because I fade away; / And all shall say, 'Without a use this shining woman liv'd, / Or did she only live to be at death the food of the worms?'" And then the wonderful response by the cloud: "Then if thou art the food of the worms, O virgin of the skies / How great thy use, how great thy blessing! Every thing that lives / Lives not alone nor for itself" (CW, 129). These images continue in the poem. According to S. Foster Damon, in *The Blake Dictionary* (401), the clod of clay with its worm represents the mother and her baby, but I think it also echoes the beautiful lines in *Job* 17.14: "I have said to corruption Thou art my father; to the worm Thou art my mother and my sister." Here is Damon's summary of the conclusion: "Through the Imagination (the Northern Gate), she enters the future land of death, and from her own grave-plot hears a voice lamenting the power of the five senses, especially the voice of awakening sex. Thel is terrified, and 'the Virgin' flees back to her vales of Har." Algernon Charles Swinburne's interpretation of the poem is perhaps more meaningful. The Virgin, sick of life owing to the presence of death, is informed by the lily, the cloud, and the worm that "the secret of creation is sacrifice; the very act of growth is a sacrament; and through this eternal generation in which one life is given for another and shed into new veins of existence, each thing is redeemed from perpetual death." But Swinburne misses the point that the poem ends with the Virgin, fleeing from the world in horror. "The Virgin started from her seat, and with a shriek / Fled back unhinder'd till she came into the vales of Har [her home]." For the Swinburne quote, see D. J. Sloss and J. P. R. Wallis, eds., *The Prophetic Writings of William Blake,* vol. 2 (Oxford: Clarendon, 1964 [1926]), 267.

25. See book 3, n. 42, for my critique of David Foulkes, *A Grammar of Dreams* (New York: Basic Books, 1978), where he makes a case for the "propositional" structure of dreams.

26. Jung affirmed in several places that, when dealing with the psyche, one cannot use the methodology one associates with the analysis of the body, which is an implicit criticism

of British empiricism. For example, in *The Practice of Psychotherapy*, he says that "we are not dealing here with the body—we are dealing with the psyche. Consequently, we cannot speak the language of body-cells and bacteria; we need another language commensurate with the nature of the psyche, and we must have an attitude which measures the danger and can meet it" (190).

27. This is the major thrust of Paul Ricoeur, *Freud and Philosophy: An Essay on Interpretation* (New Haven: Yale University Press, 1977). For a revaluation of this work with respect to ethnography and another look at Freud's "metatheory," see my discussion in "Freud and Anthropology: The Place Where Three Roads Meet," in Gananath Obeyesekere, *The Work of Culture: Symbolic Transformation in Psychoanalysis and Anthropology* (Chicago: University of Chicago Press, 1990), 217–84.

28. C. J. Jung, *Psychology and Alchemy*, trans. R. F. C. Hull, 2d ed. (Princeton: Princeton University Press, 1980 [1944]), hereafter abbreviated as PA; C. G. Jung, *Memories, Dreams, Reflections*, ed. Aniela Jaffé (New York: Vintage, 1983), is based on conversations with Jung in 1958. It will be abbreviated as MDR. In my first draft on Jung, I relied exclusively on MDR for my discussion of his three visionary episodes, but since then I have read the fine study by Deirdre Bair, *Jung: A Biography* (New York: Little Brown, 2003). According to Bair the "protocols" that contained the original interviews with Jung were highly edited by Aniela Jaffé and Jung's daughter Marianne and her husband, but I have no choice but to use MDR, which does have Jung's own approval. I have had no access to the protocols; consequently I have relied on Bair's references to them. Hereafter Bair's work will be abbreviated as BJ.

29. For a readable exposition of Jung's difficult and often vague concept of the self, see Jolande Jacobi, *The Psychology of C. G. Jung* (New Haven: Yale University Press, 1973 [1942]), 126–35. On p. 130 Jacobi has a diagram that illustrates the centrality of the self and its relation to the ego, to the "persona" and to the "shadow," the animus and the anima, although it seems to me that Jacobi's is too rigid a formalization of Jung's more open models.

30. C. J. Jung, *Aion: Researches Into the Phenomenology of the Self* (Princeton: Princeton University Press, 1979 [1951]), 23.

31. C. J. Jung, *Mysterium Coniunctionis: An Inquiry Into the Separation and Synthesis of Psychic Opposites* (Princeton: Princeton University Press, 1976 [1963]), xvii.

32. According to Jolande Jacobi, Jung borrowed the term *archetype* from the *Corpus Hermeticum* and from Pseudo-Dionysius. See *Complex, Archetype, Symbol in the Psychology of C. G. Jung*, trans. Ralph Manheim (Princeton: Princeton University Press, 1974 [1959]), 34. This work also discusses in detail Jung's sometimes confusing notions of the archetype.

33. C. G. Jung, *Psychology and Religion* (New Haven: Yale University Press, 1962 [1938]), 63–64; my emphasis.

34. Of the latter, Antoine Faivre, in *The Eternal Hermes: From Greek God to Alchemical Magus*, trans. Jocelyn Godwin (Grand Rapids: Phanes, 1995), 44, says: "It was, in fact, in seventeenth century Germany that the greatest number of alchemical works were printed with illustrations and figures. . . . He (Mercury) reigns as the master of reconciling opposites, and guiding our active imagination, in numerous examples from Michael Maier's *Atalanta Fugiens* (1617) to Adolpe C. Beutes' *Philosopische Schaubühne* (1706)." See also n. 113, this chapter, for a brief account of binary opposites in Western thought.

35. Jung claimed that "I investigate yearly some fifteen hundred to two thousand dreams ... " See C. G. Jung, "General Aspects of Dream Psychology" (1916), republished in *Dreams* (Princeton: Princeton University Press, 1974), 33 (23–66).

36. Pauli won the Nobel Prize for physics in 1945, for work done in 1925. For a good readable account of his important contribution to physics, see David Lindorff, *Pauli and Jung: The Meeting of Two Great Minds* (Wheaton, IL: Quest, 2004).

37. C. G. Jung and C. Kerényi, *Essays on a Science of Mythology: Myths of the Divine Child and the Divine Maiden* (New York: Harper Torchbooks, 1963 [1949]), 71. Here Jung expresses some bizarre views of primitive mentality that were popular in the West but were already being questioned by social anthropologists. "Primitives" are a generic type and they are under the sway of the unconscious and "the primitive mind is far less developed in scope and intensity." Nevertheless, occasionally Jung comes close to what we have labeled passive cerebration. "The primitive cannot assert that he thinks; it is rather that 'something thinks in him.'" He "does not think consciously, but that thoughts appear" (72). I show later that during his trance illness of 1944 Jung comes close to this position in respect of his own thoughts, but I am not sure whether it led him to revise his notion of primitive (or for that matter Western) mentality. Unless he is saying that in respect of our dreams and visions we are like primitives living under the domination of the unconscious.

38. For a detailed discussion, see Jung's chapter 3, "The History and Psychology of a Natural Symbol" in *Psychology and Religion*, 78–114.

39. The idea of primordial androgyny and its archetypal manifestation is discussed by Jung in several places, but a convenient summary is provided in a section entitled "The Hermaphroditism of the Child," in Jung and Kerényi, *Essays on a Science of Mythology*, 92–96.

40. Frieda Fordham, *An Introduction to Jung's Psychology* (Hammondsworth, Middlesex: Penguin, 1964 [1953]), 81. This work still remains a good short introduction to Jung and contains a preface by the master himself, but equally useful is Jacobi, *The Psychology of C. G. Jung*.

41. Fordham, *An Introduction to Jung's Psychology*, 69.

42. Jung adds that archetypes of the unconscious "can be shown empirically to be the equivalents of religious discourse" but with important qualifications. The expressions of the unconscious are "natural" and not formulated dogmatically, implying that archetypes are utilized by religion and given dogmatic meaning. For example, Christ is a figure of Christian dogma, but the God archetype on which it is based can be interpreted according to time, place, and milieu so that it can be filled with dogmatic figures from other religions, as for example Purusha, Atman, Hiranyagarbha, or the Buddha. "The religious point of view, understandably enough, puts the accent on the imprinter, whereas scientific psychology emphasizes the typos, the imprint—the only thing it can understand" and it "stands as the symbol of an unknown and incomprehensible content." The reason is that the typos "is less definite and more variegated than any of the figures postulated by religion" (PA, 17). The typos never coincides with the figure from religious dogma, but Christian and non-Christian figures can be included under the rubric of the typos, and Jung would say they are generated out of the typos.

43. In *Answer to Job* (Cleveland: Meridian, 1961 [1952]), Jung makes the point that Christ, the son, and paradoxically Satan as well is responsible for softening the wrath of the father (98–99). Ironically, the son not only redeems humanity but also redeems the father, which

is close to Jacob Boehme's position. The work as a whole attempts to answer God's unfair and immoral (from the human viewpoint) treatment of Job. Gradually the brutal and "savage" deity that inflicted unfair punishments on Job is humanized and rendered a more loving God, although he still retains his wrathful aspect.

44. Jung, *Psychology and Religion,* 73. Jung's work has been appropriated by Christians, Buddhists, new age Pagans, and others but it is doubtful whether any of this is true to Jung's own interests. Jung's attitude toward Christianity, in addition to *Answer to Job,* comes in his dialogues and correspondence with the Thomistic scholar Victor White and published in Ann Conrad Lammers, *In God's Shadow: The Collaboration of Victor White and C.G. Jung* (New York: Paulist Press, 1994). The positions of the two protagonists seem irreconcilable.

45. Jung, *Psychology and Religion,* 99.

46. Fordham, *An Introduction to Jung's Psychology,* 79.

47. Jung is implicitly thinking of World War 11 where the German people followed or connived with Hitler's mass destruction of Jews and Gypsies. But he forgets that the invention of German policy and its implementation was not the work of the masses but of an elitist cabal who could tap popular prejudices in order to popularize their destructive ideology.

48. Jung's critique of Theosophy included much of the fads that we now associate with the Jungian-inspired dream movement. "People will do anything, no matter how absurd, in order to avoid facing their own souls. They will practice Indian yoga and all its exercises, observe a strict regimen of diet, learn theosophy by heart, or mechanically repeat mystic texts from the literature of the whole world—all because they cannot get on with themselves and have not the slightest faith that anything useful could ever come out of their own souls" (PA, 100–1). In *Modern Man in Search of a Soul,* 216. Jung criticizes Theosophy as a kind of "amateurish imitation of the East," which is true of his own appropriation of the "East." He also criticizes the Theosophical doctrine of the masters, even though his own beliefs incorporated strikingly similar notions.

49. See Leonard Fox and Donald L. Rose, eds., *Conversations with Angels: What Swedenborg Heard in Heaven,* trans. David Gladish and Jonathan Rose (West Chester, PA: Chrysalis, 1996). This volume is culled from several texts where Swedenborg talks with angels and spirits in his visions, but mostly from the popular work, *Conjugial Love.* In the spirit of that latter work, Swedenborg deals with sexual love on earth and its representatives in heaven. In heaven one experiences eternal love and eternal sexual potency, but transformed from the earthy to the spiritual. It is not altogether clear how sexual potency is spiritualized; and, if spiritualized, how can we call it sexual potency? The angelic spirits tell the inquirer: "Your sexual love, no, but an angelic sexual love, which is chaste and without any lewd enticements" (49). Also for Swedenborg, the oppositional dialectic that Jung and Blake endorsed cannot solve any problem. The angels say: "Now, this means that people who live by evil ways and the false concepts that come from this have formed a model of hell in themselves; and in heaven this model of hell is in torment under the surge and violent action of opposites against opposites. For hellish love is the opposite of heavenly love, and so the delights of the two loves clash with each other like enemies and kill each other" (78). Blake could not have disagreed more; and neither could Jung, I am sure.

50. Cited in Leonard Fox, "Introduction, ibid., 21–22. For an excellent discussion of this subject, see Benz, "The Doctrine of Correspondences," in Ernest Benz, *Emanuel Swedenborg:*

Visionary Savant in the Age of Reason, trans. Nicholas Goodrick-Clarke (West Chester, PA: Swedenborg Foundation, 2002), chapter 24, 351–62.

51. Jung mentions in many places his indebtedness to Heraclitus for this concept, for example in *Modern Man in Search of a Soul,* 204: "An intimation of the law that governs blind contingency, which Heraclitus called the rule of enantiodromia (conversion into the opposite)." Heraclitus might have had a similar idea, but my guess is that Jung was the inventor of the term.

52. Patricia Garfield, *The Universal Dream Key: The Twelve Most Common Dream Themes Around the World* (New York: Cliff Street Books, 2001).

53. Shafton, *Dream Reader,* 81.

54. Edward C. Whitmont and Sylvia Brinton Perera, *Dreams, a Portal to the Source* (London: Routledge, 1989), 97.

55. Edward C. Whitmont, "Jungian Approach," *Dream Interpretation: A Comparative Study,* ed. James L. Fosshage and Clemens A. Loew, rev. ed. (New York: PMA, 1987), 59–60.

56. For me this venture into history via the archetypal dream is bad ethnography and bad psychology. Jung himself used dubious sources, such as Bachofen on early matriarchy, Levy-Bruhl on primitive mentality, Frazer on initiation rites. But although Whitmont had access to modern sources he does not use them, fishing instead in the ethnography of the late nineteenth century.

57. Lindorff, *Pauli and Jung,* 26–27.

58. Shafton, *Dream Reader,* 124.

59. Jacobi, *Jung,* 60.

60. The proceedings of the seminar conducted in English for the most part have been published in a two-volume work that is somewhat tedious reading. I use the excellent abridgement by James L. Jarrett, ed., *Jung's Seminar on Nietzsche's Zarathustra* (Princeton: Princeton University Press, 1998).

61. Ibid., 24.

62. Ibid., 36.

63. In *Psychology and Religion* (and elsewhere) Jung speaks interestingly of Nietzsche. "Nietzsche was no atheist, but his God was dead. The result was that Nietzsche himself split and he felt himself forced to call the other self 'Zarathustra' or, at other times, 'Dionysos.' In his fatal illness he signed his letters as 'Zagreus,' the dismembered Dionysos of the Thracians. The tragedy of Zarathustra is that, because his God died, Nietzsche himself became a god; and this happened because he was no atheist. He was too positive a nature to content himself with a negative creed" (103). He adds, I think rightly, if one interprets the next statement metaphorically: "there are not many individuals as sensitive and religious as Nietzsche" (103–4). Then follows Jung's elitist conception of religion: "If dull people lose the idea of God nothing happens—not immediately and personally at least. But socially the masses begin to breed mental epidemics, of which we have now a fair number" (105). These are extremely insightful comments, but I think Jung in this work and in his seminar tries to reinvent Nietzsche in his own image, as most of us do anyway.

64. Jacobi, *Jung,* 47–48.

65. Ibid., 60.

66. For the impact of Jung on new age religion, see Frank McLynn, *Carl Gustav Jung* (New York: St. Martin's, 1996), chapter 25, "The New Age Guru," 487–509. For an account that

is critical of the new age appropriation of Jung as guru, see David Tacey, *Jung and the New Age* (Philadelphia: Brunner-Routledge, 2001). Tacey thinks that Jung "in some measure at least has helped to bring a popular spirituality movement into existence" (14). Unfortunately, while Tacey is hostile to new age religion, he sees Jung as a guru, albeit a guru of a higher Christianity, one of Tacey's own making. Tacey is right to point out, as I have done, that Jung expects human beings to confront the dark aspects of their inner lives, but at the same time there is another popular side to Jung represented in *Modern Man in Search of the Soul* (1933) and in *Man and His Symbols* (published in 1964, posthumously) and other works that attempt to reach a larger public. "He encouraged readers to believe that there was a wealth of spiritual life within them, and that in secular culture this wealth remained 'undiscovered' and hence untapped by both individual and society" (29). It is this latter position that is tapped by both Tacey's kind of Christianity and new age religion and, one might add, by agnostics and atheists seeking some kind of spiritual solace in a disenchanted world.

67. Max Zeller, *The Dream: The Vision of the Night* (Boston: Sigo, 1964), 1. Also cited in DR, 127.

68. Ibid., 2.

69. Ibid., 3.

70. The term itself was first used by Jung in 1930 in his memorial address for the pioneer Sinologist Richard Wilhelm, the translator of *I Ching*. However, the idea of synchronicity was in Jung's mind for a long time, from at least the time of his mental breakdown, which I describe later. "The science of the *I Ching* is based not on the causality principle but on one which—hitherto unnamed because unfamiliar to us—I have tentatively called the synchronistic principle," quoted in Lindorff, *Pauli and Jung*, 99. Jung's preoccupation with the *I Ching* as a hermetic text was anticipated in 1700 by a Jesuit, Joachim Bouvet, who corresponded with Leibniz about this work. Bouvet thought that the *I Ching* represents "as precious a remains from the debris of the most ancient and excellent Philosophy, taught by the first Patriarchs of the world" and resembled the work of Mercury Trismegistus "to represent visually the most abstract principles of science." Cited in Faivre, *The Eternal Hermes*, 101. Faivre adds that the author of the *I Ching* was considered by Bouvet to be "Zoroaster, Hermes, or most probably Enoch, and he lived before Moses" (102).

71. "On Synchronicity," Roderick Main, *Jung on Synchronicity and the Paranormal* (Princeton: Princeton University Press, 1997), 93 (93–102).

72. Victor Mansfield, *Synchronicity, Science, and Soul-Making* (Chicago: Open Court, 1995).

73. Soon afterward I mentioned Jung's idea of synchronicity to my research assistant. She then came out with several instances of her waking dreams, one in which she sensed that someone she loved was dying, a fact that was soon confirmed when the person actually died at approximately the same time that she had the experience. I have had friends and acquaintances recount similar dreams. People are reluctant to report these dreams for fear of being scoffed at but willing to mention them when they found I was writing a book on visions. I believe that one should not turn a blind eye on this phenomenon, which could be interpreted causally if neurologists and psychologists took them seriously, throwing aside their Enlightenment prejudices.

74. Jung refers to "innumerable" phenomena where meaningful coincidence exists. He says they can be grouped under three categories, which he lists, and I quote below from his 1951 article in Main, *Jung on Synchronicity*, 97–98:

1. The coincidence of a psychic state in the observer with a simultaneous, objective, external event that corresponds to the psychic state or content (e.g., [the dream of] the scarab) where there is no evidence of a causal connection between the psychic state and the external event, and where, considering the psychic relativity of space and time, such a connection is not even conceivable.

2. The coincidence of a psychic state with a corresponding (more or less simultaneous) external event taking place outside the observer's field of perception, i.e., at a distance, and only verifiable afterward (e.g., the Stockholm fire [of Swedenborg]).

3. The coincidence of a psychic state with a corresponding, not yet existent future event that is distant in time and can likewise only be verified afterward.

   In groups 2 and 3 the coinciding events are not yet present in the observer's field of perception, but have been anticipated in time insofar as they can only be verified afterward. For this reason I call such events synchronistic, which is not to be confused with synchronous.

75. Jung devised an experiment on astrology that he had hoped would provide evidence of a statistical sort for astrological synchronicity. The article, "An Astrological Experiment," is reprinted in Main, *Jung on Synchronicity*, 112–17. As Jung put it: "*How do the conjunctions and oppositions of the sun, moon, Mars, Venus, ascendant and descendant behave in the horoscopes of married people?*" He took 360 horoscopes of 180 married couples and gave them to a colleague to be analyzed. As a statistical study, the experiment was a failure, but Jung believed that statistics emphasizing chance could not grasp the reality of synchronicity where chance does not exist. Qualitatively speaking, he felt that the experiment did in fact give some validity to astrological synchronicity. I refer the reader to the article, which cannot be easily summarized.

76. Cited in Mansfield, *Synchronicity*, 23.

77. Ibid., 6. Mansfield is a physicist, a Jungian and one given to meditation. His examples of synchronicity, except one, come from fellow Jungians and meditators. In my opinion these are as flawed as Jung's. Mansfield's more recent book, *Tibetan Buddhism and Modern Physics*, is a much more challenging work and tries to effect a marriage between contemporary physics and Buddhism. I personally don't believe it works and I recommend the more insightful study by the Dalai Lama that not only points out the differences between science and religion but also the need for science to deal sympathetically with the idea of spirit, not denying it as many do. See Tenzin Gyatso, (The Fourteenth Dalai Lama), *The Universe in a Single Atom: The Convergence of Science and Spirituality* (New York: Broadway, 2005). The "convergence" that the Dalai Lama speaks of is something that he urges we should make happen, not something that has already occurred via quantum mechanics.

78. Sigmund Freud, "Dreams and Occultism," lecture 30 in *New Introductory Lectures*, SE, 36 (31–56).

79. See Main, *Jung on Synchronicity*, 96. Jung downplayed the idea of two minds in communion with each other for the more complex notion of synchronicity. He used the term *synchronous* for those coincidences where no connection between a psychic and a physical event exists. I use the term *coeval* (or *coevality*) to designate the psychic contact between two minds, the simplest example being what is popularly known as "thought reading."

80. In Jung, *The Practice of Psychotherapy*, 176.

81. Sigmund Freud, "Psychoanalysis and Telepathy," in *Beyond the Pleasure Principle,* SE, xviii, 184 (177–93).

82. Sigmund Freud, "Dreams and Telepathy," ibid., 208 (197–220).

83. Helene Deutch, "Occult Processes Occurring During Psychoanalysis," in George Devereux, ed., *Psychoanalysis and the Occult* (New York: International Universities Press, 1953), 134 (133–46). This is an important collection, but most of the articles are skeptical of the validity of telepathic phenomena. An exception is the sympathetic but sketchy account by Emilio Servado, "Psychoanalysis and Telepathy" (210–20). Most important, however, are the detailed accounts of patient-to-patient, doctor-to-patient dream transfer in Jule Eisenbud, "Telepathy and Problems of Psychoanalysis" (223–282); and another paper, "Analysis of a Presumptively Telepathic Dream" (339–62). Eisenbud and others employ case studies, but the genre does not permit easy verification, even though Eisenbud does recognize the problems involved (241). Hence the criticisms of their work by other analysts writing in this volume on "scientific" grounds, even though much of psychoanalysis is hardly scientific in any accepted sense of the term, especially in respect of verification or falsifiability.

84. Many post-Freudian analysts have dealt at length with the complicated nature of the transference, but I am not aware of more recent studies that deal with thought transference from analyst to analysand during the analytic situation. Ogden, however, comes very close to this idea in his discussion of the "frontier of dreaming" in Thomas H. Ogden, *Conversations at the Frontier of Dreaming* (New York: Karnac, 2001). "Our dreams can no longer be viewed as entirely our own. Instead (or, more accurately, in addition), the analyst's (and patient's) dreaming and reverie are dreams of the jointly but asymmetrically constructed analytic third. . . . The analyst's associations to the patient's dream are no less important than the patient's associations to 'his' dream. Conversations at the frontier of dreaming are not always private" (12). Ogden has extremely interesting discussions of the importance of "reverie" in the transference situation.

85. In Montague Ullman and Stanley Krippner, *Dream Therapy: Scientific Experiments in the Supernatural* (New York: Macmillan, 1973), but I am not persuaded by the experimental techniques employed in this and other studies by these two scholars. The dreams of the participants are "telepathic" only according to Ullman's interpretation of the symbolic meanings of the participants' dreams. They are too indirect to admit of genuine verification. The subtitle of the book, *Scientific Experiments in the Supernatural,* indicates the general bias of the "dream movement" in the West, namely, an attempt to open up the supernatural through dreams. My own prejudice is that, instead of such dubious "experiments," one should adopt the technique of reasonably detailed case studies as Freud did in his work on telepathy and the occult. My criticisms of Ullman and Krippner are also applicable to the detailed empirical study of altered states of consciousness in Imants Baruss, *Alterations of Consciousness: An Empirical Analysis for Social Scientists* (Washington, DC: American Psychological Association, 2004). The study provides valuable information, but Baruss's strength lies in his interpretations of detailed case histories rather than his experimental work using undergraduates and similar control and experimental groups. To parody Baruss, I would say that there is no way the visions and insights of the exceptional visionaries in my essay could be verified through experimental studies using Canadian undergraduates!

86. Jung, *The Practice of Psychotherapy,* 150–51. The account is from an earlier paper, "The Practical Use of Dream-Analysis" (1934), reprinted in the volume. Jung triumphs in the validity of his interpretation ("this was ecstasis with a vengeance") rather than mourning his friend's death.

87. We have only the guide's statement that this man deliberately jumped from the cliff to fulfill the dream prognostication. More likely he took chances and simply fell off the cliff. If so, an "accident" is translated by Jung into synchronicity.

88. Sabina was a patient of Jung's, and, by all accounts, they had a stormy and intermittent relationship beginning 1908 that was compounded by Sabina becoming Freud's patient. She confessed that Jung told her a not unfamiliar tale by errant husbands. "He preached polygamy, his wife was supposed to have no objection, etc., etc." (cited in BJ, 152). Apparently, some of his faculty colleagues were waiting to oust Jung from the Burghölzli owing to his reputation as a womanizer (BJ, 153). Another well-known affair was with patient and colleague Maria Moltzer in 1910, the very year, strange to say, that Jung began to analyze his wife Emma! It is hard to believe that Jung, who put emphasis on the shadow, did not feel guilty about these relationships, although he did later blame his anima for these affairs, which he apparently could not control. The relation with Toni Wolff was especially grating to his wife Emma, because she was a constant presence in the house, and it was Toni and not Emma who had access to the secret Red Book, and Toni was his close intellectual confidant. For details on these and other affairs, see Aldo Carotenuto, *Secret Symmetry: Sabina Spielrein Between Jung and Freud,* trans. Arno Pomerans, John Shepley, and Krishna Winston (New York: Pantheon, 1984); Maggy Anthony, *Valkyries: The Women Around Jung* (Shaftesbury: Element, 1990). For a good account of the relationship with Toni, see BJ, passim. Of Toni Wolff's presence in their house and the problems for Emma and the children, Jung's son Franz reminisced: "Can you imagine living with a man who left you with full responsibility for his house and his children while he passed the time playing their [children's] games and being in that same house with another woman?" Cited in BJ, 251. Jung's relationship with his children was aloof and especially so with his son. But all the children were aware of the father's relation with Toni Wolff. Bair records a frightening case of Jung's insensitivity toward his children, especially the following "game" with his daughter Gret: "Unfortunately, Gret was the butt of most of the jokes and 'nasty tricks' Jung liked to play on his children. Once he threw a lighted cracker between Gret's legs that went off and made her deaf in one ear. She [Gret] told her children that it was one of the two main reasons she grew up 'verbittern' (embittered)" (BJ, 317–18). That Jung couldn't see the significance of this horrendous act of violence, even a kind of displaced rape, is perhaps not surprising. What is surprising is that a discerning critic like Bair views it as a joke or an example of "nasty tricks."

89. Jung's mother died at age seventy-five, and, because his father died at the early age of forty-four, it is hard to believe that Jung hadn't been thinking of the possibility of her demise. We are not told the cause of her death, but she did suffer two days of illness. It is unlikely that Jung was not informed of her illness before the night of his dream.

90. I am indebted to Mrs. Surabhi Sheth for the retranslation of *sloka* 124 of *Kulārnava Tantra,* ed. and trans. Ram Kumar Rai (Varanasi: Panchya Prakashan, 1999), 221; and for correcting minor printer's errors in the Sanskrit text. *Kulārnava Tantra* is one of the texts of the Kaula tradition of Hindu Tantrism in which Siva engages in a dialogue with his wife Par-

vati, his "beloved." I have retained Rai's translation of *sloka* 123 with minor changes; the words in parentheses are mine. I have also adopted Rai's suggestion that *paśu* ("animals") refers to ignorant humans. For a detailed exposition of the Kaula tradtion, see David Gordon White, *Kiss of the Yoginī: Tantric Sex in Its South Asian Contexts* (Chicago: University of Chicago Press, 2003).

91. C. J. Jung, *The Red Book, Liber Novus*, ed. Sonu Shamdasani (New York: Norton, 2009), hereafter abbreviated as RB. The main part of *The Red Book* is entitled *Liber Novus* and is 190 folio pages with text and paintings.

92. *The Red Book* actually contains Jung's self-experiments during his long spiritual crisis, written down in several texts that were then bound together in red leather (hence *The Red Book*). The original interviews with Aniela Jaffé that went into MDR did contain excerpts from the earlier *Black Book*, but this, as well as other revealing episodes, was deleted from MDR or heavily edited by Jaffé. My essay was ready to go to the publishers when in September 2009 I heard that *The Red Book* would in fact be published. When I first heard this news, I had several options. If indeed *The Red Book* was crucial to understanding Jung's first dark night of the soul, as I once thought, then I might delete my own analysis of this episode or my whole discussion of Jung for a later book that fully dealt with the still unknown *Red Book*. Alternately, if *The Red Book* is fully congruent with my analysis, then I could include it without radically changing my own take on Jung. I managed to get a copy in early December and spent one month reading it. It struck me that my analysis of Jung's spiritual crisis could remain as it is because *The Red Book* did not make much of a difference to my analysis owing to the following reasons.

1. My main concern was with the unleashing of Jung's breakdown or spiritual crisis or psychosis as a consequence of his break with Freud. As I show in this essay, Jung clearly recognized the significance of this event in MDR, but not in *The Red Book*. It is as if Jung in the reminiscences of his old age imaginatively reedited *The Red Book* in MDR, putting down events that followed the 1913 break with Freud, whereas *The Red Book* gives one the impression that Freud was not involved in his self-avowed psychosis. For this reason my analysis of the Freud-Jung relationship and its psychological and oedipal significance remains. Freud is not even an "absent-presence" in *The Red Book*. Even the editor, a distinguished scholar of Jung, does not make much of the break with Freud in relation to the genesis of Jung's illness and its resolution.

2. *The Red Book* is not devoted entirely to Jung's spiritual crisis as I had thought. This crisis, with its ups and downs, periods of despair and creativity, lasted from 1913–1919. *The Red Book*, by Jung's own admission, was written during a much longer period and was terminated only in 1930. The crucial period of the illness episode is part of *The Red Book*, but *The Red Book* is not its documentation. Quite the contrary, it is a work that was subject to all sorts of visions and revisions during the long seventeen-year period and best read as a carefully constructed literary work, as Jung himself recognized. It is worth quoting the terribly important statement about the relationship between the *Black* and the *Red* in MDR 188 and Jung's own movement into scientific rather than aesthetic understanding: "I wrote these fantasies down first in the Black Book; later, I transferred them to the Red Book, which I also embellished with drawings. It contains most of my mandala drawings. In the Red Book I tried an esthetic elaboration of my

fantasies, but never finished it. I became aware that I had not yet found the right language, that I still had to translate it into something else. Therefore I gave up this estheticizing tendency in good time, in favor of a rigorous process of *understanding*. I saw that so much fantasy needed firm ground underfoot, and that I must first return wholly to reality (Jung's emphasis). *For me, reality meant scientific comprehension. I had to draw concrete conclusions from the insights the unconscious had given me—and that task was to become a life work*" (my emphasis).

3. Thus Jung had a continuing inner dialogue that his work should not be art but rational science. Jung is not Blake. About Jung's own revisions, the editor Sonu Shamdasani notes that Jung reedited his earlier drafts, "deleting and adding material on approximately 250 pages," modernizing language and terminology (RB, 214). As time progressed, Jung used Nietzsche's *Zarathustra* as his model, although it took Jung a lot more time than Nietzsche to complete his work. In my thinking, the fantasies especially of the period 1913–1916, the height of his spiritual crisis, were reworked much later in rational form in his prose and his highly crafted paintings of *The Red Book*. We noted that in Blake's case it was possible to relate his pit of melancholy to the images and words in *Urizen* and elsewhere, something I find impossible to do in *The Red Book*. Other analysts might, however, think otherwise. If indeed *The Red Book* is an attempt, whether successful or not, to construct a work of art, then one is not sure whether Jung's long dialogues with his soul, found in *The Red Book*, are an artistic strategy or something that occurred during his dark night or a combination of both. So with other episodes. What *The Red Book* reveals, as the editor rightly points out, is the vortex that eventually permitted Jung not only to overcome his crisis but helped him to discover through his self-experiments some of the basic ideas of his later thought. But then Jung decided to abandon *The Red Book*, which he stated in an incomplete, one-paragraph epilogue: "My acquaintance with alchemy in 1930 took me away from it. The beginning of the end came in 1928, when Wilhelm sent me the text of the 'Golden Flower' an alchemical treatise," a Chinese alchemy of course. Jung frankly admits that he might have indeed gone really mad, "had I not been able to absorb the overpowering force of the original experiences," but "with the help of alchemy, I could finally arrange them into a whole." I think the shift is easily explainable. In my own analysis I will show Jung's inner voice telling him that he must abandon his art, that is, the art of *The Red Book*, and replace it with the scientific approach that he had hitherto employed. But with a difference, and that is from now onward the science that he had developed is uniquely his own, without any borrowing from either Freud or Bleuler. Alchemy permitted that shift: for Jung alchemy is a proto-science that can be read as an earlier, somewhat disguised version of his own analytic psychology, as we have already shown.

4. This shift to science must surely have had the approval of his mistress, Toni Wolff, who we know did not quite appreciate Jung's occult and parapsychological leanings. Be that as it may, what *The Red Book* clearly shows is Jung's slow recovery and his realization of two issues that were both personal (related to his psychic condition) and also theoretical (related to his analytical psychology). This is the notion of individuation and the idea of the Self and the maṇḍala that symbolized the harmony of the unconscious with consciousness and the fullness of individuality, themes that I have already discussed. He had discovered an earlier form of the archetype in his

Transformations and Symbols of the Libido (1911–1912) in the idea of "primordial images" borrowed from Jacob Burckhardt (RB, 197). This idea is represented in visual form and scribal reflection in *The Red Book*, but it was his confrontation with alchemy that helped him to use the term *archetype* and give it full theoretical validation.

5. According to the editor, the *Black Book,* the key text that dealt with the period of his crisis, contains "dated entries" of his fantasies (RB, 200). There were other documents also that are related to the period 1913–1919. Unfortunately, all of the *Black Book* material is in the Jung family archives and remain unpublished. If these as well as the deleted parts of the interviews that went into MDR are published we might be able to make more of *The Red Book.* But then we are not sure whether the *Black Book* manuscripts are also an earlier version of *The Red Book,* that is, a preliminary attempt to construct a work of art out of Jung's self-experiments. These self-experiments, as I understand them, are not to be equated with the dark night of the soul but rather attempts by Jung to employ that experience to probe his psyche. That probing went on long after the end-time of his dark night in 1919 and it is that probing or self-experiments that eventually led to Jung's full individuation and the development of his Self, at least according to his thinking in *The Red Book.* It is no accident that the actual title of *The Red Book* is *Liber Novus,* "the new book" which is what it is.

I am not trying to belittle *The Red Book.* I am only suggesting that it does not help us understand the genesis of Jung's terrifying spiritual crisis after his break with Freud. In this regard MDR is a better resource. In fact the crucial dreams that occurred during the early period of his crisis are described in greater detail in MDR than in *The Red Book.* Perhaps these dreams are described in the *Black Book,* but its contents remain a black box. I will use some of the information in *The Red Book,* as well as information from the editor's own important "Introduction" wherever needed in the body of my essay or in endnotes.

93. William McGuire, ed., *The Freud-Jung Letters: The Correspondence Between Sigmund Freud and C. G. Jung,* abridged ed. (Princeton: Princeton University Press, 1994), 104.

94. I had missed this case in an early draft and I am indebted to Bair's excellent chapter on Schwyzer entitled "The Solar Phallus Man," in BJ, 174–90. The citations from Jung's *The Psychology of the Unconscious* are also from BJ, 177.

95. Jung's submission to the forces of the unconscious form the beginning of self-experiments described in *The Red Book.* These voices of the unconscious are metaphorically designated as the "spirits of the dead" at the very beginning of *The Red Book,* in contrast with "the spirit of the time," that is, normal everyday time (RB, 230). These are ideas worked out in *The Red Book* but I am not sure whether they are in the *Black Book.*

96. BJ, 612. Bair has a good account of some of the other deletions and substitutions that are worth citing. "In the original God sat on an enormous throne above the world, where he 'shit' on an 'enormous turd' upon the Basel Cathedral. . . . They changed Jung's boyhood dream from a 'gigantic phallus' to a 'fearful tree.' The Niehuses [daughter and son in law] deleted Jung's descriptions of his parents as highly 'neurotic.' . . . They eliminated everything about his mother, especially that she was 'grossly fat' and 'hysterical.' . . . They would not even let Jung describe some of his aunts as spinsters, or himself as a poor boy in tattered trousers whose feet were often wet in winter because his family was so poor that his shoes had holes and he had no socks. They also forbade his memories of inspect-

ing drowned corpses of pigs being slaughtered." One can only hope for a future unedited version of this key text.

97. Freud, *Beyond the Pleasure Principle*, 15. The reference is to Freud's observance of his eighteen-month-old grandson, who never used to cry when his mother had to leave him for a few hours, even though he loved her greatly. Instead, the child had a habit of taking small objects, throwing them away from him into a corner or under the bed, then uttering a long "o-o-o-o" followed by another expression of interest and satisfaction. Both the child's mother and Freud agreed that the interjection meant the German word *fort* (gone). Here is Freud's interpretation: "I eventually realized it was a game and that the only use he made of any of his toys was to play 'gone' with them. The child had a wooden reel with a piece of string tied around it. It never occurred to him to pull it along the floor behind him, for instance, and play at its being a carriage. What he did was to hold the reel by the string and very skillfully throw it over the edge of his curtained cot, so that it disappeared into it, at the same time uttering his expressive 'o-o-o-o.' He then pulled his reel out of the cot again by the string and hailed its reappearance with the joyful 'da' ('there'). This then, was the complete game—disappearance and return. As a rule one only witnessed its first act, which was repeated untiringly as a game in itself, though there is no doubt that the greater pleasure was attached to the second act."

98. These twelve fantasies are listed below:

1. 1–2 October 1913, two fantasies at least in October. "Repeated vision of flood and death of thousands and the voice that said that this will be real."
2. Autumn 1913. "Vision of the sea of blood covering the northern lands."
3. Visions 4 and 5 on December 12 and 15, 1913: "Image of a dead hero and the slaying of Siegfried in a dream."
4. Sixth vision: of December 25, 1913 "Image of a foot of a giant stepping on a city, and images of murder and bloody cruelty."
5. Seventh vision of Jan. 2, 1914. "Image of a sea of blood and a procession of dead multitudes."
6. Eighth vision of January 22, 1914. "His soul comes up from the depths and asks him if he will accept war and destruction. She shows him images of destruction, military weapons, human remains, sunken ships, destroyed states, etc."
7. Ninth vision of May 21, 1914. "A voice says of the sacrificed fall left and right."
8. Tenth through twelfth visions of June–July 1914. "Thrice repeated dream of being in a foreign land and having to return quickly by ship, and the descent of the icy cold."

99. This is a work on schizophrenia entitled *On the Psychology of Dementia Praecox*, trans. R. F. C. Hull (Princeton: Bollingen, 1974 [1908]).
100. Cited in Linda Donn, *Freud and Jung: Years of Friendship, Years of Loss* (New York: Scribner, 1988), 172.
101. Ibid.
102. Ibid., 174.
103. Several of Jung's maṇḍalas are reproduced in appendix 1, RB, 361–64. Jung did not understand the significance of his first maṇḍala; it was in August 16, 1917, that he recognized the maṇḍala as expressing the harmony of the Self.

104. The better known reference to Philemon is in the New Testament, the Epistle of St. Paul the Apostle to Philemon, the latter a Christian Roman landowner who probably has no link with Jung's pagan deity.

105. According to Sonu Shamdasani (RB, 203), Jung painted Philemon in the *Black Book* on January 21, 1914, but without the kingfisher wings. Very likely there were earlier and later representations of Philemon, because Philemon probably appeared to him in various guises. My guess is that Jung saw a dead kingfisher in his garden and then painted, or imagined he painted, Philemon with kingfisher wings. There are detailed accounts of Philemon in "Scrutinies," one of the additions to *The Red Book*.

106. According to MDR, Jung gave symbolic interpretations to these figures later on, particularly after his serious encounters with alchemy. The pair Salome and Elijah has its parallel in the Gnostic tradition where Simon Magus went around with a young girl he had picked up in a brothel. As for the black snake, it was for Jung "an indication of a hero-myth." The Salome of his dream is blind, because she does not see the meaning of things; she is also "the erotic element" perhaps associated with the anima figure. Jung is often given to wild symbolic analysis, here and elsewhere.

107. Shamdasani mentions a detailed dialogue that Jung had with himself regarding his work, whether it was art or science, in the second of the black books and reproduced in RB, 199.

108. Ronald Hayman, *A Life of Jung* (New York: Norton, 2001), 34–47, 57–61. Hayman says of this early period of Jung's life around 1895 and soon after: "Jung encouraged Helly to believe the dead were speaking through her. In some ways he was handicapped by conflict between his scientific interests and his interest in spiritualism, but in other ways he was helped. The tension sharpened his scientific curiosity about the psyche" (45–46).

109. BJ, 135. William James, who was president of the London-based Society for Psychical Research during 1894–95, was also one of the founding members of the American branch.

110. A detailed but highly edited and elaborate version of the Seven Sermons is found in "Scrutinies," the last section of *The Red Book* (RB, 346–54). In this version it is Philemon who speaks with the voice of Basilides, whereas in the original version in MDR it is Basilides who speaks directly, but with the voice of Jung or Philemon. But both Basilides and Philemon are Jung's own alter egos and hence they are in some sense the same. The elaborate version with Philemon as speaker goes on much longer in "Scrutinies" than the original text reproduced in MDR.

111. For a good account of Jung's indebtedness to Gnosticism, see C. J. Jung, *The Gnostic Jung: Selections from the Writing of C. J. Jung and his Critics*, ed. Robert A. Segal (Princeton: Princeton University Press, 1992). This useful collection of Jung's work on Gnosticism was selected by Segal and includes an excellent introduction. Segal does not think that Jung's *Seven Sermons* is an expression of Basilides's thought but rather Jung's own fantasies of this period. "Psychologically, it is not Basilides but Jung who is talking, and the dead are not other persons but Jung's unconscious. . . . Psychologically, then, Jung is channeling his own future self, which only in the course of the rest of his life does he come fully to develop" (37).

112. From the Protocol, which formed the basis for MDR and is cited in BJ, 290. In MDR he thinks it might be Philemon who spoke the voice of Basilides through the medium of Jung.

113. Jung-Basilides references to pairs of opposites that indicate the qualities of the "pleroma" are as follows:

> The Effective and the Ineffective.
> Fullness and Emptiness.
> Living and Dead.
> Difference and Sameness.
> Light and Darkness.
> The Hot and the Cold.
> Force and Matter.
> Time and Space.
> Good and Evil.
> Beauty and Ugliness.
> The One and the Many. (MDR, 380–81)

We have noted that Jung was preoccupied with opposites throughout his life and fully systematized them in his last work, *Mysterium Coniunctionis*. In the very first chapter of that work, Jung discusses the key alchemical opposites: *humidum* (moist) and *sicum* (dry); *frigidum* (cold) and *calidum* (warm); *superiora* (upper) and *inferiora* (lower); *spiritus-anima* (spirit-soul) and *corpus* (body); *coelum* (heaven) and *terra* (earth); *ignis* (fire) and *aqua* (water); bright and dark; *agens* (active) and *patients* (passive); *volatile* (volatile or gaseous) and *fixum* (solid); *pretiosum* (precious) and *vile* (cheap), *bonum* (good) and *malum* (evil), *manifestum* (open) and *occultum* (hidden); *oriens* (East) and *occidens* (West), *vivum* (living) and *mortuum* (dead, inert); *masculus* (masculine) and *foemina* (feminine), *Sol* (sun) and *Luna* (moon) (2).

Concern with opposites is found in European thought as early as Aristotle, who believed that "contrarieties are the principles of things," and he constructed his well-known table of opposites.

LIMITED	UNLIMITED
Odd	Even
One	Plurality
Right	Left
Male	Female
At rest	Moving
Straight	Crooked
Light	Darkness
Good	Bad
Square	Oblong

One can argue that the preoccupation with binary or contrasted opposites, whether they are separate or unified or opposed or articulated into the language of negative theology, is a major preoccupation in Western thought, at least from Aristotle and through to the medieval mystical thinkers, in Hegelian thought and into modern times in the work of Ferdinand de Saussure and Claude Lévi-Strauss and, of course, in the many European thinkers who appear in this essay. The meaning and significance attributed to such opposites would naturally vary with each author using them.

114. Bair tells us in BJ 497 that the protocol manuscripts make a great deal of the India visit, and Jung himself made a connection between his Indian visionary experience and the later one in 1944, both as enormously profound ones.

115. Jung's visit to India and Sri Lanka (Ceylon) is described in MDR 274–84, the Grail dream appearing in 280–83.

116. According to Bair (BJ, 499), on the day of the accident Jung had been reading a sixteenth-century alchemical text, *Pardes Rimmonim,* and "in his semi-delirium, he assumed a role within the text, of the Rabbi Simon ben Jochai, who officiates at the wedding of Malchuth and Tiferah."

117. For Jung, the fabulous cosmic visions and those that followed during the three weeks of his illness never repeated themselves. Yet soon afterward Jung had a dream that seemed to elucidate for him the meaning of the yogi or black Hindu within the stone temple. He was on a hiking trip and he came across a small chapel. He walked in, but to his surprise there was no Virgin on the altar and no crucifix either but instead a wonderful flower arrangement. "But then I saw that on the floor in front of the altar, facing me, sat a yogi—in lotus posture, in deep meditation. When I looked at him more closely, I realized that he had my face. I started in profound fright, and awoke with the thought: 'Aha, so he is the one who is meditating me. He has a dream, and I am it.' I knew that when he awakened, I would no longer be" (MDR, 323). Jung has a very complicated interpretation of this dream. He says that the "figure of the yogi, then, would more or less represent my unconscious prenatal wholeness, and the Far East [*sic*], as is often the case in dreams, a psychic state alien and opposed to our own" (MDR, 324). He says that the yogi's meditation projection is like a magic lantern reflecting his own empirical reality, that is, his wholeness that existed in his prenatal state. I take it that Jung means that in life this original wholeness is fractured and one must try to reconstruct it once again. But beyond that Jung uses the dream to emphasize his idea that while in the West ego-thinking is given primacy, not so in the "East," which recognizes that "our unconscious existence is the real one and our conscious world a kind of illusion. . . . It is clear that this state of affairs resembles very closely the Oriental conception of Maya" (MDR, 324).

118. I refer the reader to Jung's fascinating account of his giving mythological significance to the tower, aligning it with ancient archetypes, in the chapter entitled "The Tower" (223–27).

119. Apparently, Jung had from childhood a fantasy of being constituted of two beings, numbers one and two, as Hayman says in *A Life of Jung,* 22–23, 27–29. This is probably a manifestation of "imaginary playmates" that children sometimes fantasize.

120. Cited in Shafton, *Dream Reader,* 129, from Miguel Serrano, *Jung and Hesse: A Record of Two Friendships* (New York: Schocken, 1968), 104.

121. *Aion,* written in 1951, synthesizes Jung's work on the ego and its distinction from the self and theoretical constructs that take their bearing from the self, such as the shadow, anima, and animus, and ends with an examination of the structure and dynamics of the self. He also deals with Christ as the symbol of the self and has an interesting chapter on self notions in Gnosticism. The study is primarily historical, based on long forgot-

ten medieval texts and full of dense references. The historical research is impressive but "heavy" and not easy to read. Very little of his case studies appear in this work and consequently the work lacks contact with his interesting patients. It is as if Jung has given up the clinical studies on which his early reputation rested. This is also true of *Mysterium Coniunctionis.* Both studies deal with archetypal symbolism in alchemy and hermetic philosophy, but I miss the lightness of touch and humor that come with his engagement with patients.

122. Jung, as many of his time, often lumped together the various forms of Buddhism, Hinduism, and Taoism in what he labeled "Eastern" or "Oriental" religion. For example, he saw Buddhism as exemplifying his own doctrine of the self, whereas most forms of Buddhism did the very opposite, namely, undermined any notion of a stable self or for that matter any notion of wholeness. It seems that Jung appropriated the so-called Eastern religions into his own analytic psychology without actually telling us that this is what he was doing. Even though in his later life and work he affirmed his European heritage, he nevertheless admired what the Buddha image represented. For a discerning account of Jung's relation to Asian religions, see J. J. Clarke, *Jung and Eastern Thought: A Dialogue with the Orient* (London: Routledge, 1994).

123. I leave the reader to look up Jung's somewhat disorganized thoughts on the afterlife in MDR, 299–358. The reader might also wish to consult the collection of essays edited by Main, *Jung on Synchronicity;* and F. X. Charet, *Spiritualism and the Foundations of C. J. Jung's Psychology* (Albany: State University of New York Press, 1993).

124. Thrice-great Hermes is Hermes Trismegistus, the mythic founder of hermetic and alchemical thought. Fairve says in *The Eternal Hermes* (16) that around the beginning of the common era the Greeks had identified the Egyptian god Thoth with Hermes-Mercury, and Thoth-Mercury was credited with a large number of books listed under the title Hermetica. "The most famous ones, from the second and third centuries CE, are grouped under the general title of the Corpus Hermeticum, in which the Ascelpius and the Fragments collected by Stobaeus have been included. But a more fantastic tradition attributed thousands of other works to Hermes Trismegistus." It should be noted that it is this later figure that influenced Milton as well as European hermetic thinkers. Faivre's *The Eternal Hermes* is a readable account of the development of the Greek god Hermes to the fabulous Hermes Trismegistus.

125. Yeats "All Soul's Night," W. B. Yeats, *The Collected Poems of W. B. Yeats* (New York: Macmillan, 1956), 224–26. This poem is subtitled "Epilogue to 'A Vision,'" the Vision being a reference to the kind of automatic writing produced by Yeats's wife George, dealing with highly arcane material, much of it unintelligible and uninteresting, quite unlike the poetry inspired by the Ouija board for contacting spirits of dead persons by the poet James Merrill. See Alison Lurie, *Familiar Spirits: A Memoir of James Merrill and David Jackson* (New York: Penguin, 2002), 52–58.

126. The latter idea is spelled out in Jung, *Mysterium Coniunctionis,* 262.

127. Charles Webster, *From Paracelsus to Newton: Magic and the Making of Modern Science* (New York: Dover, 1982), 57.

128. C. G. Jung, *Flying Saucers: A Modern Myth of Things Seen in the Skies,* trans. R. F. C. Hull (Princeton: Princeton University Press, 1978 (1958), 26.

129. It was perhaps during the aftermath of his second trance illness that Jung could easily speak of the unspeakability of love. In MDR he seems to think, more radically than Freud, that Eros is kosmogonos, "the creator and father-mother of all higher consciousness." Hence Eros is transformed in manifold ways and might ultimately embrace what he calls "cosmogonic love," something beyond Christian caritas and but analogous to Buddhist compassion. See MDR, 354.

8. CONTEMPORARY DREAMING

1. Michel Jouvet, *The Paradox of Sleep: The Story of Dreaming*, trans. Laurence Garey (Cambridge: MIT Press, 1999), 76.

2. Stephen LaBerge, *Lucid Dreaming: The Power of Being Awake and Aware in Your Dreams* (New York: Ballantine, 1987); and Stephen LaBerge and Howard Rheingold, *Exploring the World of Lucid Dreaming*. LaBerge is the dominant figure and thinker in this book, and I shall often refer to him as the author. In *Lucid Dreaming*, LaBerge gives an excellent account of the history of lucid dreaming in two chapters, "The Origins and History of Lucid Dreaming" and "The New World of Lucid Dreaming," 21–77.

3. Hervey de Saint-Denys, the pioneer of lucid dreaming says, in *Dreams and How to Guide Them*, trans. Nicholas Fry (London: Duckworth, 1982 [1867]), 164–65, that one can develop lucidity by simply keeping a diary and with it a few other simple injunctions. But he admits this might not work for all.

4. The authors' use of Buddhist material is very eclectic. For example, they have a body chart with the sixty-one points of relaxation, and the prospective dreamer is given instructions as to how to use it. Unfortunately, this chart has little to do with the notion of the subtle body so central in Tibetan Buddhism, and, what is most interesting, the relaxation points bypass the entire genital area! (WLD, 56).

5. In *Lucid Dreaming*, 36, LaBerge refers to the Russian philosopher Piotr Ouspensky, who was one of the pioneers of lucid dreaming, even though he did not use that term. "*Was it not possible to preserve consciousness in dreams*, that is, to know while dreaming that one is asleep and *to think consciously* as we think when awake?"

6. Jouvet, *Paradox of Sleep*, 41.

7. Ibid., 45. Jouvet's experimental work was primarily with small animals, but he thinks that bodily insensibility is true of all REM or paradoxical dreaming. He adds: "Sometimes a few motor signals cross this inhibitory barrier, causing small movements of the fingers, or the ears and whiskers (in cats), but essentially only the eye and respiratory muscles escape this inhibitory activity" (47).

8. Ibid., 79.

9. Ibid., 66.

10. Cited in WLD, 136.

11. LaBerge, *Lucid Dreaming*, 123.

12. Ibid., 1.

13. This can, of course, occur, but in conditions of pathology. In a rare form of parasomnia known as "arousal disorder" a patient might get out of bed while in deep sleep and might

even engage in violent behavior, including murder. While in this condition a parasomniac might fight with an opponent and yet not awake; owing to the absence of muscle atonia, he cannot enter into the REM state at all. The pioneer work on this form of disorder has been done by Rosalind Cartwright, and there is a neat summary of her work in Andrea Rock, *The Mind at Night* (New York: Basic Books, 2004), 191–93. Rock cites Cartwright (183): "Parasomniacs with arousal disorder can navigate through space, but they have no visual recognition of faces, they can't hear screams, nor do they feel pain themselves." I am not qualified to deal with this issue, but surely in parasomnia there is neither ego nor dream ego at work.

14. LaBerge, *Lucid Dreaming*, 7.

15. Ibid.

16. Saint-Denys, *Dreams and How to Guide Them*, 163.

17. Ibid., 55.

18. Ibid., 35.

19. Apparently the term *lucid dreaming* was invented by a Dutch psychiatrist, Frederik Van Eeden, whose 1913 paper, "The Study of Dreams," is reprinted in Charles T. Tart, ed., *Altered States of Consciousness* (New York: Doubleday, 1972), 147–60. Van Eeden had kept a dream diary since 1896 and collected 500 dreams. Of these "in 352 cases I had a full recollection of my day-life, and could act voluntarily, although I was so fast asleep that no bodily sensations penetrated into my perception." He called these "lucid dreams" (149). See also, LaBerge, *Lucid Dreaming*, 32–33, for a further discussion of Van Eeden.

20. Saint-Denys, *Dreams and How to Guide Them*, 161–62.

21. Rock, *The Mind at Night*, 159.

22. Saint-Denys, *Dreams*, 150.

23. Shafton in *Dream Reader* (469–70) has a list of dream theorists who warn against the misuse of dream control by lucid dreamers and these include some lucid dream theorists.

24. The case of the black widow is but one example of the benefits of "healing" claimed by lucid dreamers. There are certainly cases of psychological conflicts and physical ones cured through lucid dreams; additionally interpersonal conflicts in the lives of lucid dreamers might be resolved through dream control. Yet, as far as healing is concerned, lucid dreamers are in a real disadvantage with most other contemporary dream theorists, some of whom are mentioned in Shafton's work, such as those either directly or indirectly influenced by existential analysis. The success of the latter is due to some version of a "talk-cure." In talk cure the dreamer is, often enough, a patient, and the coalition of therapist and patient (and sometimes a larger group seeking group therapy) articulates the dream with the life of the patient, irrespective of the theory underlying the therapy. By contrast, looking at the case studies in LaBerge and Rheingold, I notice only a few illustrative cases of healing of physical and existential conflicts; no serious neuroses and no psychosis of any sort can be cured through lucid dreaming. However, lucid dreamers are successful in giving enchantment to middle-class lives and sometimes providing glimpses for them of some other reality beyond the phenomenal world of everyday living.

25. This is chapter 12, titled, "Life Is a Dream: Intimations of a Wider World."

26. The poem is in *The Complete Poetry of Henry Vaughan*, ed. French Fogle (New York: Doubleday Anchor, 1964), 231. Plato employs the famous myth-vision of the chariot of the gods

as an allegory, but also as a vision of reality. See *Phaedrus and Letters VII and VIII,* trans. William Hamilton (London: Penguin, 1973), 50–52. The Pythagorean one pertains to the harmony of the spheres, a notion that has had great significance in the history of European thought, even though the Pythagorean harmony was that of sound, not of vision in its strict sense.

27. This lack of information on the dreamer inhibits our understanding of his dream. My own guess is that he is strongly influenced by new age religion, especially that branch of it which finds a bearing on the work of important scientific thinkers or on popular science, perhaps attempts to link up contemporary physics and holographic theory with Tibetan and other forms of Indic mysticism that we have already mentioned. For an attempt to use a holographic paradigm in the use of dreams, see Jeannette Mageo, "Toward a Holographic Theory of Dreaming," in *Dreaming* 14, nos. 2–3 (2004): 151–61.

28. For a discussion of the "higher self" in new age religion, see Shirley MacLaine, "Superconsciousness and the Higher Self," in *Going Within: A Guide for Inner Transformation* (New York: Bantam, 1989), 53–71.

29. What is fascinating about LaBerge's dream quoted earlier is that, in spite of his preoccupation with Tibetan thought, his dream ego meets with a cross on a steeple top and the Star of David, all part of his, not Tibet's, cultural heritage.

30. The discussion that follows is for the most part based on my article, "Thinking Globally About Buddhism," in Mark Jurgensmeyer, ed., *The Oxford Handbook of Global Religions* (Oxford: Oxford University Press, 2006), 60–82. Meditation retreats are in my view an important part of our modernity and not to be discounted as "inauthentic."

31. Richard Gombrich and Gananath Obeyesekere, *Buddhism Transformed: Religious Change in Sri Lanka* (Princeton: Princeton University Press, 1988), 238–39.

32. Gil Fronsdal, "Insight Meditation in the United States," in *The Faces of Buddhism in America,* ed. Charles Prebish and Kenneth K. Tanaka (Berkeley: University of California Press, 1998), 170 (164–80).

33. Ibid., 166–67. For the American adaptation of Buddhist meditation, read the important accounts in Mark Epstein, *Thoughts Without a Thinker: Psychotherapy from a Buddhist Perspective* (New York: Basic Books, 1995); and Anthony Molino, ed., *The Couch and the Tree: Dialogues in Psychoanalysis and Buddhism* (New York: North Point, 1998).

34. The whole issue of the adaptation of Vajrayāna by Europeans is exhaustively discussed in Donald S. Lopez, *Prisoners of Shangri-La: Tibetan Buddhism and the West* (Chicago: University of Chicago Press, 1999). Lopez, however, is unsympathetic to those who have adopted and adapted Tibetan Buddhism, whereas I see them ranging from the naive to the complex and many inventing new religious consciousnesses through the eclectic utilization of varieties of Indian and other religions. I believe that one can be as much a prisoner of Shangri-La as one could of postmodernism and other "isms."

35. Cited in LaBerge, *Lucid Dreams,* 17.

36. Another influential guru is Namkhai Norbu, a professor at the Oriental Institute of the University of Naples who presents a version of dream yoga that is practical and appealing to lucid dreamers. See Namkhai Norbu, *Dream Yoga and the Practice of Natural Light,* ed. Michael Katz (Ithaca: Snow Lion, 1992).

37. Hugh B. Urban, *Tantra: Sex, Secrecy, and Power in the Study of Religion* (Berkeley: University of California Press, 2003); see also White, *Kiss of the Yoginī.* My own criticism of these texts

and others like them is the view that South Asian Tantra or Vajrayāna is somehow or other "authentic," whereas the American and European adaptation is not. I doubt the discussion of "authenticity" is going to take us anywhere, especially because both authors, but especially White, shows the presence of multiple forms of Tantra, even in South Asia. Are all these forms authentic, and what are the underlying criteria for authenticity? I would also add that we can speak of American Tantra and even describe it as "authentically" or quintessentially American! And then I could ask: is there an authentic Christianity or Islam? I would favor one or more versions of Christianity or Islam, but not on the basis of authenticity.

38. This is neatly expressed in Patricia Garfield's book, which has a great title, *Creative Dreaming: Plan and Control Your Dreams to Develop Creativity, Overcome Fears, Solve Problems, and Create a Better Self* (New York: Simon and Schuster, 1995), especially "Learn from Yogi Dreamers" (181–200) where there is a marvelous account of an imaginary yogi named Ram practicing Garfield's kind of Tibetan Buddhism!

39. Although Garfield thinks that orgasms are *natural* to lucid dreams, she also believes that in normal life women only rarely experience orgasms, owing to cultural values and personal inhibitions. I assume she refers to conditions in the sixties and earlier. Another female subject had the opposite reaction from Garfield's and is cited in LaBerge, *Lucid Dreaming*, 114: "The nature of lucid dream experience may range up to the mystical, whilst *there seems to be an inherent resistance to anything erotic.*" As LaBerge rightly points out, there is nothing "natural" in erotic or any other form of lucid dreaming; rather they seem to be conditioned by cultural and personal values and predilections. However Garfield herself qualifies her views on erotic dreaming. In her early work, *Creative Dreaming*, she claims that orgasmic dreams are rare among women and "prior to exposure to Senoi concepts, orgasm was rare in my dreams" (127). Garfield employs what she considers to be "Senoi rules of dream control" to evoke orgasms and other pleasurable dream experiences (129). Senoi dreaming was made famous in a dubious study by an early ethnographer, Kilton Stewart, whose work "Dream Theory in Malaya" (1951) has been republished in Tart, *Altered States of Consciousness*, 161–70. For an account of the enormous influence of Stewart and a good critique of his work, see G. William Domhoff, *The Mystique of Dreams* (Berkeley: University of California Press, 1985), especially his chapter "The Magic of Kilton Stewart" (35–64).

40. Patricia Garfield, *Pathway to Ecstasy: The Way of the Dream Mandala* (New York: Prentice Hall, 1979), 135.

41. Ibid., 135–36.

42. Garfield says in *Pathway to Ecstasy*: "I placed in the Western Quarter [of Amitābha] of my Dream Mandala the strawberry, symbol of the Strawberry Lady, who is chief deity. In place of a peacock, I substituted my Ruby Bird, instead of a lotus, I set my pink rosebud" (138). She is substituting her own dream imagery for the conventional Tibetan ones and manages to give her dreams a deeper spiritual significance. "I move the current of my life throughout my whole self. I have become the Strawberry Lady, I have reached out to accept the Ruby Bird. And I am beginning to find out that these ecstasies are not confined to dreams" (140). For a systematic framing of her personal images in terms of Tibetan religion, see the chapter entitled "Through the Screened Porch to the Inner Circle of the Dream Mandala" (141–50) as well as the chapters that follow. Garfield incorporates

Tibet much more systematically and creatively than LaBerge. For an account of what we may learn from Tibet, see her chapter 7, "Learn from Yogi Dreamers," in Garfield, *Creative Dreaming*, 181–200. In my view the best examples of authentic American Tantra are from the virtuosos of Esalen, beautifully presented in Jeffrey Kripal, *Esalen: America and the Religion of No Religion* (Chicago: University of Chicago Press, 2008). Several key figures in the Esalen movement combined Tantra with a variety of other techniques and theories, including Freudian and gestalt psychologies and shamanism. Those employing eclectic and yet creative uses of Tantra are worth looking up in Kripal's work: Claudio Naranjo, Ida Rolf, Stanislav Grof, and the original thinker, Michael Murphy.

43. This is the subtitle of Garfield's *Pathway to Ecstasy*.

44. See Gananath Obeyesekere, *Medusa's Hair: An Essay on Personal Symbols and Religious Experience* (Chicago: University of Chicago Press, 1981), especially the subsection entitled "Tryst with the Black Prince: Incubus and Firewalker" (138–42), for a detailed account of a terrifying and yet pleasurable encounter with an incubus.

45. Melford E. Spiro, *Burmese Supernaturalism: A Study in the Explanation and Reduction of Suffering* (Englewood Cliffs, NJ: Prentice Hall, 1967).

46. Ibid. 210–11.

47. Ibid. 210.

48. Ibid., 217 and 214–15, for one model of a wedding chamber. From Spiro's account it seems that the term *nat kadaw* is used whether the shaman is male or female.

49. Ibid., 211.

50. Ibid., 212.

51. Edwin Muir, *An Autobiography* (Edinburgh: Canongate Classics, 1993); hereafter abbreviated as AA.

52. For example Revelation 7:13: "And one of the elders answered, saying unto me, What are these which are arrayed in white robes? And whence came they?" See also my discussion of white clothes worn by Margery Kempe in book 4, pp. 231–32, 254–55.

53. "Knots," in *Bhikkhu Bodhi, SN,* 1564.

54. AA., 159. The trance is described in an early poem entitled "The Ballad of the Soul" in Edwin Muir, *Collected Poems* (London: Faber and Faber, 1979), 26–31. Another poem describes a trance that reminds me of Wordsworth's vision in *The Prelude* and the many visions of Jung and A. E. (George Russell) that deal with episodes from the past. The poem is "The Labyrinth," and I quote the poet's recollection of his trance (165): "For once in a dream or trance I saw the gods / Each sitting on top of his mountain-isle, / While down below the little ships sailed by, / Toy multitudes swarmed in the harbors, shepherds drove / Their tiny flocks to the pastures, marriage feasts / Went on below, small birthdays and holidays, / Ploughing and harvesting and life and death, / And all permissible, all acceptable, / Clear and secure as in a limpid dream. / But they, the gods, as large and bright as clouds, / Conversed across the sounds in tranquil voices / High in the sky above the untroubled sea, / And their eternal dialogue was peace / Where all those things were woven, and this our life / Was as a chord deep in that dialogue, / As easy utterance of harmonious words, / Spontaneous syllables bodying forth a world."

55. In Plato *Phaedo*, 80e, for Socrates; for Buddhists everywhere in their religious traditions.

56. W. B. Yeats, *Autobiographies* (London: Macmillan, 1955), 517. The "skull beneath the skin" is not just T. S. Eliot's vision of Webster, but it is part of the medieval Christian visionary

tradition. Both Molly Allgood and Muir are unaware of the cultural structuralization of their visions.

57. The last line should read. "And Love in a golden bowl." For a discussion of this verse see book 7, n. 24.

9. ENVOI—INTIMATIONS OF MORTALITY

1. The poem is "Up-hill," and it reads thus: "Does the road wind up-hill all the way? / Yes, to the very end. / Will the day's journey take the whole long day? / From morn to night, my friend. But is there for the night a resting place? / A roof for when the slow dark hours begin. / May not the darkness hide it from my face? / You cannot miss that inn. Shall I meet other wayfarers at night? / Those who have gone before. / Then must I knock or call when just in sight? / They will not keep you standing at that door. Shall I find comfort, travel sore and weak? / Of labour you shall find the sum. / Will there be beds for me and all who seek? / Yea, beds for all who come." Christina Rossetti, *Complete Poems* (London: Penguin, 2005), 59–60.

GLOSSARY OF SELECTED BUDDHIST TERMS

s = Sanskrit, p = Pali, t = Tibetan

ABHIDHARMA (s), ABHIDHAMMA (p), the third "basket" of the Buddhist canon, dealing with epistemological and psychological issues.

ABHIŚEKA (s), anointing, such as a statue or a king; also meaning "empowerment" or initiation in Tibetan Buddhism

ADHIṢṬHĀNA (s), "resolve," also used in Tibet as sense of empowerment

ĀLAYAVIJÑĀNA (s), or "store-consciousness," that is, a repository of memory and ideation and karmic residues

AMALAVIJÑĀNA (s), "immaculate consciousness" or a pure state of consciousness

ANAGĀRIKA (s, p), "homeless one," a term used for monks, but nowadays for an intermediate role between lay person and monk

ANĀTMA (s), ANATTA (p), absence of soul or enduring self

ARHAT (s), ARAHANT (p), someone who has achieved nirvana while living in the world; sometimes even applied to the Buddha

ĀTMAN (s), ATTA (p), the individual self or soul in contrast with Brahman, the universal self or cosmic self

BARDO (t), ANTARĀBHAVA (s), intermediate stage between dying and rebirth; intermediate state being

BHIKṢU (s), BHIKKHU (p), mendicant or Buddhist monk

BODHI (s, p), Buddhist "awakening" or "enlightenment"

BODHI TREE or BO TREE, *Ficus religiosa,* the tree under which the Buddha realized his "awakening"

BODHICITTA (s, p), the awakening mind or the aspiration to be a Buddha

BODHISATTVA (s), BODHISATTA (p), a Buddha aspirant

BRAHMACARYA (s), BRAHMACARIYA (p) abstinence from sexuality, lit. "the way of Brahma" or "salvation quest"

BRAHMAN (s), the universal Self in Hinduism

CAKRA (s), "wheel"; in Tibetan religion *cakra*s are energy centers located in crucial places in the channels of the subtle or illusory body

ḌĀKINĪS (s, t), "skyfarers," female deities in Tibetan Buddhism

DEVA (s, p), god, or deity in Buddhism and Hinduism

DHARMA (s), DHAMMA (p), primary meaning, "the Buddhist doctrine"; also as *dharma*s or fundamental elements constituting our knowledge of reality

DHARMAKĀYA (s), "the body of the *dharma*" or the transcendent Buddha, the most perfect of the three bodies of the Buddha

DĪKṢĀ (s), initiation in Hinduism

DRAVYA, substance; inner-nature in the dharmas

DUKKHA, see Four Noble Truths

FOUR NOBLE TRUTHS, these are *dukkha* (p), suffering, the unsatisfactory nature of existence owing to the fact of impermanency; *samudaya* (p), how dukkha arises owing to *taṇhā* (p), thirst, attachment, greed, desire, or craving; *nirodha* (p), cessation of craving that will ultimately lead to nirvana; and *magga* (p), or *mārga* (s), or the path that might help us realize nirvana, also known as the "noble eightfold path": right understanding, right thought, right speech, right action, right livelihood, right effort, right mindfulness, and right concentration.

EKAYĀNA (s, p), "single vehicle or path," the idea that all forms of Buddhism are one overarching system

GAUTAMA (s), GOTAMA (p), the clan name of the Buddha

HĪNAYĀNA (s, p), or "lesser vehicle or path," a pejorative term for Theravāda Buddhism

IṢṬA DEVATĀ (s), YIDAM (t), guardian deity or deity.

JĀTAKA (s, p), birth story of the Buddha

JHĀNA (p), DHYĀNA (s), deep states of meditative trance; states of absorption

KALYĀNAMITRA (s), the "true friend," or guide that helps the meditating person to overcome psychic trouble spots

KARMAMUDRĀ (s), "action seal," the engagement with a consort in sexual union in Tibetan Buddhism

KARMAVIPĀKA (s), or KARMAPHALA (s), the consequences or fruits of karma

KṢATRIYA, see *varṇa*

LAMA (t), Tibetan for "guru"or teacher

MAHĀPURUṢA (s), "great man" possessing thirty-two bodily marks, signs of perfection

MAṆḌALA (s), "magic circle," generally referring to a circle of deities with a Buddha or a main deity or guru at the center

MANTRA (s), the magical formulaic utterance that is whispered into the right ear of the pupil; any magic formula

MĀRGA (s), or MAGGA (p), see Four Noble Truths

MĀYĀ (p, s), illusory nature of the phenomenal world; name of the Buddha's mother

NĀGA (p, s), "snake beings" with human characteristics, generally protectors of Buddhism; also means "cobra" or "elephant"

NAT (Burmese), "lord," Burmese term for *deva* or the gods of the pantheon

NIRMĀṆAKĀYA (s), the existent or historical form of the Buddha and exemplified in the Buddha Gautama and the previous "historical" Buddhas of the Theravāda tradition as well as the next Buddha, Maitreya

NIRODHA (s, p), see Four Noble Truths

PACCEKA BUDDHA (p), a minor Buddha who does not proclaim his salvific message to the world

PĀRAMITĀ (s, p), "perfections," those exemplary moral deeds, generally six or ten, performed by the Buddha in past births

PARAMĀRTHA (s), ultimate truth

PRATĪTYASAMUTPĀDA (s), PATICCASAMUPPĀDA (p), "conditioned genesis," or "dependent origination," the idea that every action is causally connected with another, such that there are no unconditioned truths

PRAJÑĀPĀRAMITĀ (s), *prajñā,* meaning "wisdom," and *pāramitā,* being the perfections; generally referring to a major early movement of Māhāyāna Buddhism and its texts

RŪPAKĀYA (s), another term for the actual body of the Buddha

SĀDHANA (s), Tantric practice

SAMATHA (p), ŚAMATHA (s), "tranquillity," generally refers to "calming meditation" in contrast to *vipassanā* (p), *vipaśyanā* (s), "insight meditation"

SAMBHOGAKĀYA (s), "body of bliss," the celestial body of the Buddha and manifest as the many Buddhas and Bodhisattvas

SAMSĀRA (s, p), the cycle of existence, endless series of births and rebirths

SAMĀDHI (s, p), deep concentration leading to meditative trance wherein truths can be apprehended or discovered

SAMVRTI (s), conventional truth, in contrast with absolute truth (*paramārtha*)

SIDDHI (s), or yogic powers; SIDDHAS, those possessing these powers

SKANDHAS (s) ("heaps"), broadly defined as the ever-changing aggregates of matter, sensations, perceptions, mental formations, and consciousness

STŪPA (s), relic chamber, originally a large dome-shaped burial mound

ŚŪNYATĀ (s), or ŚŪNYA (s), "emptiness," or the "void," the salvific ideal of Mahāyāna

SŪTRA (s), or SUTTA (p), "thread," but refers to Buddhist doctrinal texts, uttered by the Buddha

TAṆHĀ (p), TṚṢṆĀ (s), thirst, attachment, greed, desire, or craving; see Four Noble Truths

TATHĀGATA (p, s), Buddha, lit., "thus gone"

TATHĀGATAGARBHA (s), the Buddha womb, or matrix, or the Buddha nature within us

TERMA (t), a treasure, generally a text or sacred objects sequestered in earlier times by awakened ones and waiting to be recovered by legitimate treasure seekers

TERTON (t), treasure seeker; see also *terma*

THANGKA (t), a Tibetan wall-hanging painted with pictures of divinities.

THERAVĀDA, see Hīnayāna

TRIPIṬAKA (s), "three baskets" containing the *suttas* (p) or *sutras* (s), the discourses of the Buddha; the *vinaya* (p, s), or the book of monk discipline, and the *abhidhamma,* or *abhidharma,* the epistemological and psychological discourses written after the death of the Buddha

TULKU (t), reincarnations of previous masters or Buddhas

UPĀYA (s), "skill in means," a discursive strategy geared to the salvific receptivity of the audience

UPANIṢAD (s), the key doctrines of Hinduism, probably composed during or after 7 BCE

VARṆA (s), the four classes into which Hindu society is divided: Brahmin, royalty (*kṣatriya*), tradespeople and farmers (*vaiśya*), and commoners (*śūdra*)

VIMUKTI (s), VIMUTTI (p), freedom, generally freedom from existence, that is, nirvana

VIRĀGA (p, s), absence of desire

YATHĀBHŪTA (p, s), "things as they really are," "in truth," "in reality"

YIDAM (t), guardian deity, often a guru in Tibetan Buddhism; see also *iṣṭa devatā*

INDEX